For Reference

Not to be taken from this room

NOVELS
for Students

Advisors

NOVELS
for Students

**Presenting Analysis, Context, and Criticism
on Commonly Studied Novels**

VOLUME 34

Sara Constantakis, Project Editor

Foreword by Anne Devereaux Jordan

GALE
CENGAGE Learning·

Detroit • New York • San Francisco • New Haven, Conn • Waterville, Maine • London

GALE
CENGAGE Learning™

Novels for Students, Volume 34

Project Editor: Sara Constantakis

Rights Acquisition and Management: Beth Beaufore, Sara Crane, Leitha Etheridge-Sims, Barb McNeil

Composition: Evi Abou-El-Seoud

Manufacturing: Drew Kalasky

Imaging: John Watkins

Product Design: Pamela A. E. Galbreath, Jennifer Wahi

Content Conversion: Katrina Coach

Product Manager: Meggin Condino

For product information and technology assistance, contact us at **Gale Customer Support, 1-800-877-4253.**
For permission to use material from this text or product, submit all requests online at **www.cengage.com/permissions.**
Further permissions questions can be emailed to **permissionrequest@cengage.com**

Gale
27500 Drake Rd.
Farmington Hills, MI, 48331-3535

ISBN-13: 978-1-4144-4172-6
ISBN-10: 1-4144-4172-X

ISSN 1094-3552

This title is also available as an e-book.
ISBN-13: 978-1-4144-4950-0
ISBN-10: 1-4144-4950-X
Contact your Gale, a part of Cengage Learning sales representative for ordering information.

Printed in the United States of America
1 2 3 4 5 6 7 14 13 12 11 10

Table of Contents

The Informed Dialogue: Interacting with Literature

When we pick up a book, we usually do so with the anticipation of pleasure. We hope that by entering the time and place of the novel and sharing the thoughts and actions of the characters, we will find enjoyment. Unfortunately, this is often not the case; we are disappointed. But we should ask, has the author failed us, or have we failed the author?

We establish a dialogue with the author, the book, and with ourselves when we read. Consciously and unconsciously, we ask questions: "Why did the author write this book?" "Why did the author choose that time, place, or character?" "How did the author achieve that effect?" "Why did the character act that way?" "Would I act in the same way?" The answers we receive depend upon how much information about literature in general and about that book specifically we ourselves bring to our reading.

Young children have limited life and literary experiences. Being young, children frequently do not know how to go about exploring a book, nor sometimes, even know the questions to ask of a book. The books they read help them answer questions, the author often coming right out and *telling* young readers the things they are learning or are expected to learn. The perennial classic, *The Little Engine That Could, tells* its readers that, among other things, it is good to help others and brings happiness:

"Hurray, hurray," cried the funny little clown and all the dolls and toys. "The good little boys and girls in the city will be happy because you helped us, kind, Little Blue Engine."

In picture books, messages are often blatant and simple, the dialogue between the author and reader one-sided. Young children are concerned with the end result of a book—the enjoyment gained, the lesson learned—rather than with how that result was obtained. As we grow older and read further, however, we question more. We come to expect that the world within the book will closely mirror the concerns of our world, and that the author will *show* these through the events, descriptions, and conversations within the story, rather than *telling* of them. We are now expected to do the interpreting, carry on our share of the dialogue with the book and author, and glean not only the author's message, but comprehend how that message and the overall affect of the book were achieved. Sometimes, however, we need help to do these things. *Novels for Students* provides that help.

A novel is made up of many parts interacting to create a coherent whole. In reading a novel, the more obvious features can be easily spotted—theme, characters, plot—but we may overlook the more subtle elements that greatly influence how the novel is perceived by the reader: viewpoint, mood and tone, symbolism, or the use of humor. By focusing on both the obvious and more subtle literary elements within a novel, *Novels for Students* aids readers in both analyzing for message and in determining how and why that message is communicated. In the discussion on Harper Lee's *To Kill a Mockingbird* (Vol. 2), for example, the mockingbird as a symbol of innocence is dealt with, among other things, as is the importance of Lee's use of humor which "enlivens a serious plot, adds depth to the characterization, and creates a sense of familiarity and universality." The reader comes to understand the internal elements of each novel discussed—as well as the external influences that help shape it.

"The desire to write greatly," Harold Bloom of Yale University says, "is the desire to be elsewhere, in a time and place of one's own, in an originality that must compound with inheritance, with an anxiety of influence." A writer seeks to create a unique world within a story, but although it is unique, it is not disconnected from our own world. It speaks to us *because* of what the writer brings to the writing from our world: how he or she was raised and educated; his or her likes and dislikes; the events occurring in the real world at the time of the writing, and while the author was growing up. When we know what an author has brought to his or her work, we gain a greater insight into both the "originality" (the world of the book), and the things that "compound" it. This insight enables us to question that created world and find answers more readily. By informing ourselves, we are able to establish a more effective dialogue with both book and author.

Novels for Students, in addition to providing a plot summary and descriptive list of characters—to remind readers of what they have read—also explores the external influences that shaped each book. Each entry includes a discussion of the author's background, and the historical context in which the novel was written. It is vital to know, for instance, that when Ray Bradbury was writing *Fahrenheit 451* (Vol. 1), the threat of Nazi domination had recently ended in Europe, and the McCarthy hearings were taking place in Washington, D.C. This information goes far in answering the question, "Why did he write a story of oppressive government control and book burning?" Similarly, it is important to know that Harper Lee, author of *To Kill a Mockingbird,*was born and raised in Monroeville, Alabama, and

that her father was a lawyer. Readers can now see why she chose the south as a setting for her novel—it is the place with which she was most familiar—and start to comprehend her characters and their actions.

Novels for Students helps readers find the answers they seek when they establish a dialogue with a particular novel. It also aids in the posing of questions by providing the opinions and interpretations of various critics and reviewers, broadening that dialogue. Some reviewers of *To Kill A Mockingbird,* for example, "faulted the novel's climax as melodramatic." This statement leads readers to ask, "Is it, indeed, melodramatic?" "If not, why did some reviewers see it as such?" "If it is, why did Lee choose to make it melodramatic?" "Is melodrama ever justified?" By being spurred to ask these questions, readers not only learn more about the book and its writer, but about the nature of writing itself.

The literature included for discussion in *Novels for Students* has been chosen because it has something vital to say to us. *Of Mice and Men, Catch-22, The Joy Luck Club, My Antonia, A Separate Peace* and the other novels here speak of life and modern sensibility. In addition to their individual, specific messages of prejudice, power, love or hate, living and dying, however, they and all great literature also share a common intent. They force us to *think*—about life, literature, and about others, not just about ourselves. They pry us from the narrow confines of our minds and thrust us outward to confront the world of books and the larger, real world we all share. *Novels for Students* helps us in this confrontation by providing the means of enriching our conversation with literature and the world, by creating an *informed* dialogue, one that brings true pleasure to the personal act of reading.

Sources

Harold Bloom, *The Western Canon, The Books and School of the Ages,* Riverhead Books, 1994.

Watty Piper, *The Little Engine That Could,* Platt & Munk, 1930.

Anne Devereaux Jordan
Senior Editor, TALL (Teaching and Learning Literature)

Introduction

Purpose of the Book

The purpose of *Novels for Students* (*NfS*) is to provide readers with a guide to understanding, enjoying, and studying novels by giving them easy access to information about the work. Part of Gale's "For Students" Literature line, *NfS* is specifically designed to meet the curricular needs of high school and undergraduate college students and their teachers, as well as the interests of general readers and researchers considering specific novels. While each volume contains entries on "classic" novels frequently studied in classrooms, there are also entries containing hard-to-find information on contemporary novels, including works by multicultural, international, and women novelists. Entries profiling film versions of novels not only diversify the study of novels but support alternate learning styles, media literacy, and film studies curricula as well.

The information covered in each entry includes an introduction to the novel and the novel's author; a plot summary, to help readers unravel and understand the events in a novel; descriptions of important characters, including explanation of a given character's role in the novel as well as discussion about that character's relationship to other characters in the novel; analysis of important themes in the novel; and an explanation of important literary techniques and movements as they are demonstrated in the novel.

In addition to this material, which helps the readers analyze the novel itself, students are also provided with important information on the literary and historical background informing each work. This includes a historical context essay, a box comparing the time or place the novel was written to modern Western culture, a critical essay, and excerpts from critical essays on the novel. A unique feature of *NfS* is a specially commissioned critical essay on each novel, targeted toward the student reader.

The "literature to film" entries on novels vary slightly in form, providing background on film technique and comparison to the original, literary version of the work. These entries open with an introduction to the film, which leads directly into the plot summary. The summary highlights plot changes from the novel, key cinematic moments, and/or examples of key film techniques. As in standard entries, there are character profiles (noting omissions or additions, and identifying the actors), analysis of themes and how they are illustrated in the film, and an explanation of the cinematic style and structure of the film. A cultural context section notes any time period or setting differences from that of the original work, as well as cultural differences between the time in which the original work was written and the time in which the film adaptation was made. A film entry concludes with a critical overview and critical essays on the film.

To further help today's student in studying and enjoying each novel or film, information on media adaptations is provided (if available), as well as suggestions for works of fiction, nonfiction, or film on similar themes and topics. Classroom aids include ideas for research papers and lists of critical and reference sources that provide additional material on the novel. Film entries also highlight signature film techniques demonstrated, and suggest media literacy activities and prompts to use during or after viewing a film.

Selection Criteria

The titles for each volume of *NfS* are selected by surveying numerous sources on notable literary works and analyzing course curricula for various schools, school districts, and states. Some of the sources surveyed include: high school and undergraduate literature anthologies and textbooks; lists of award-winners, and recommended titles, including the Young Adult Library Services Association (YALSA) list of best books for young adults. Films are selected both for the literary importance of the original work and the merits of the adaptation (including official awards and widespread public recognition).

Input solicited from our expert advisory board—consisting of educators and librarians—guides us to maintain a mix of "classic" and contemporary literary works, a mix of challenging and engaging works (including genre titles that are commonly studied) appropriate for different age levels, and a mix of international, multicultural and women authors. These advisors also consult on each volume's entry list, advising on which titles are most studied, most appropriate, and meet the broadest interests across secondary (grades 7–12) curricula and undergraduate literature studies.

How Each Entry Is Organized

Each entry, or chapter, in *NfS* focuses on one novel. Each entry heading lists the full name of the novel, the author's name, and the date of the novel's publication. The following elements are contained in each entry:

Introduction: a brief overview of the novel which provides information about its first appearance, its literary standing, any controversies surrounding the work, and major conflicts or themes within the work. Film entries identify the original novel and provide

understanding of the film's reception and reputation, along with that of the director.

Author Biography: in novel entries, this section includes basic facts about the author's life, and focuses on events and times in the author's life that inspired the novel in question.

Plot Summary: a factual description of the major events in the novel. Lengthy summaries are broken down with subheads. Plot summaries of films are used to uncover plot differences from the original novel, and to note the use of certain film angles or other techniques.

Characters: an alphabetical listing of major characters in the novel. Each character name is followed by a brief to an extensive description of the character's role in the novel, as well as discussion of the character's actions, relationships, and possible motivation. In film entries, omissions or changes to the cast of characters of the film adaptation are mentioned here, and the actors' names—and any awards they may have received—are also included.

Characters are listed alphabetically by last name. If a character is unnamed—for instance, the narrator in *Invisible Man*—the character is listed as "The Narrator" and alphabetized as "Narrator." If a character's first name is the only one given, the name will appear alphabetically by that name.

Variant names are also included for each character. Thus, the full name "Jean Louise Finch" would head the listing for the narrator of *To Kill a Mockingbird*, but listed in a separate cross-reference would be the nickname "Scout Finch."

Themes: a thorough overview of how the major topics, themes, and issues are addressed within the novel. Each theme discussed appears in a separate subhead. While the key themes often remain the same or similar when a novel is adapted into a film, film entries demonstrate how the themes are conveyed cinematically, along with any changes in the portrayal of the themes.

Style: this section addresses important style elements of the novel, such as setting, point of view, and narration; important literary devices used, such as imagery, foreshadowing, symbolism; and, if applicable, genres to which the work might have belonged, such as Gothicism or Romanticism. Literary terms are explained within the entry but can also be found in the Glossary. Film entries cover how the director conveyed the meaning, message, and mood of the work using film in comparison to the author's use of language, literary device, etc., in the original work.

Historical Context: in novel entries, this section outlines the social, political, and cultural climate in which the author lived and the novel was created. This section may include descriptions of related historical events, pertinent aspects of daily life in the culture, and the artistic and literary sensibilities of the time in which the work was written. If the novel is a historical work, information regarding the time in which the novel is set is also included. Each section is broken down with helpful subheads. Film entries contain a similar Cultural Context section because the film adaptation might explore an entirely different time period or culture than the original work, and may also be influenced by the traditions and views of a time period much different than that of the original author.

Critical Overview: this section provides background on the critical reputation of the novel or film, including bannings or any other public controversies surrounding the work. For older works, this section includes a history of how the novel or film was first received and how perceptions of it may have changed over the years; for more recent novels, direct quotes from early reviews may also be included.

Criticism: an essay commissioned by *NfS* which specifically deals with the novel or film and is written specifically for the student audience, as well as excerpts from previously published criticism on the work (if available).

Sources: an alphabetical list of critical material used in compiling the entry, with full bibliographical information.

Further Reading: an alphabetical list of other critical sources which may prove useful for the student. It includes full bibliographical information and a brief annotation.

In addition, each novel entry contains the following highlighted sections, set apart from the main text as sidebars:

Media Adaptations: if available, a list of audiobooks and important film and television adaptations of the novel, including source information. The list also includes stage adaptations, musical adaptations, etc.

Topics for Further Study: a list of potential study questions or research topics dealing with the novel. This section includes questions related to other disciplines the student may be studying, such as American history, world history, science, math, government, business, geography, economics, psychology, etc.

Compare and Contrast: an "at-a-glance" comparison of the cultural and historical differences between the author's time and culture and late twentieth century or early twenty-first century Western culture. This box includes pertinent parallels between the major scientific, political, and cultural movements of the time or place the novel was written, the time or place the novel was set (if a historical work), and modern Western culture. Works written after the mid-1970s may not have this box.

What Do I Read Next?: a list of works that might give a reader points of entry into a classic work (e.g., YA or multicultural titles) and/or complement the featured novel or serve as a contrast to it. This includes works by the same author and others, works from various genres, YA works, and works from various cultures and eras.

The film entries provide sidebars more targeted to the study of film, including:

Film Technique: a listing and explanation of four to six key techniques used in the film, including shot styles, use of transitions, lighting, sound or music, etc.

Read, Watch, Write: media literacy prompts and/or suggestions for viewing log prompts.

What Do I See Next?: a list of films based on the same or similar works or of films similar in directing style, technique, etc.

Other Features

NfS includes "The Informed Dialogue: Interacting with Literature," a foreword by Anne Devereaux Jordan, Senior Editor for *Teaching and Learning Literature* (*TALL*), and a founder of the Children's Literature Association. This essay provides an enlightening look at how readers interact with literature and how *Novels for Students* can help teachers show students how to enrich their own reading experiences.

A Cumulative Author/Title Index lists the authors and titles covered in each volume of the *NfS* series.

A Cumulative Nationality/Ethnicity Index breaks down the authors and titles covered in each volume of the *NfS* series by nationality and ethnicity.

A Subject/Theme Index, specific to each volume, provides easy reference for users who may be studying a particular subject or theme rather than a single work. Significant subjects, from events to broad themes, are included.

Each entry may include illustrations, including photo of the author, stills from film adaptations, maps, and/or photos of key historical events, if available.

Citing Novels for Students

When writing papers, students who quote directly from any volume of *NfS* may use the following general forms. These examples are based on MLA style; teachers may request that students adhere to a different style, so the following examples may be adapted as needed.

When citing text from *NfS* that is not attributed to a particular author (i.e., the Themes, Style, Historical Context sections, etc.), the following format should be used in the bibliography section:

> "*Night.*" *Novels for Students.* Ed. Marie Rose Napierkowski. Vol. 4. Detroit: Gale, 1998. 234–35.

When quoting the specially commissioned essay from *NfS* (usually the first piece under the "Criticism" subhead), the following format should be used:

Miller, Tyrus. Critical Essay on "*Winesburg, Ohio.*" *Novels for Students.* Ed. Marie Rose Napierkowski. Vol. 4. Detroit: Gale, 1998. 335–39.

When quoting a journal or newspaper essay that is reprinted in a volume of *NfS,* the following form may be used:

> Malak, Amin. "Margaret Atwood's *The Handmaid's Tale* and the Dystopian Tradition." *Canadian Literature* 112 (Spring 1987): 9–16. Excerpted and reprinted in *Novels for Students.* Vol. 4. Ed. Marie Rose Napierkowski. Detroit: Gale, 1998. 133–36.

When quoting material reprinted from a book that appears in a volume of *NfS,* the following form may be used:

> Adams, Timothy Dow. "Richard Wright: 'Wearing the Mask.'" In *Telling Lies in Modern American Autobiography.* University of North Carolina Press, 1990. 69–83. Excerpted and reprinted in *Novels for Students.* Vol. 1. Ed. Diane Telgen. Detroit: Gale, 1997. 59–61.

We Welcome Your Suggestions

The editorial staff of *Novels for Students* welcomes your comments and ideas. Readers who wish to suggest novels to appear in future volumes, or who have other suggestions, are cordially invited to contact the editor. You may contact the editor via e-mail at: **ForStudentsEditors@cengage.com.** Or write to the editor at:

Editor, *Novels for Students*
Gale
27500 Drake Road
Farmington Hills, MI 48331-3535

Literary Chronology

1819: George Eliot is born Mary Ann Evans on November 22, in South Farm, Arbury, Warwickshire, England.

1828: Jules Verne is born on February 8, in Nantes, France.

1859: George Eliot's *Adam Bede* is published.

1864: Jules Verne's *Journey to the Center of the Earth* is published.

1869: Martin Andersen Nexø is born on June 26, in Copenhagen, Denmark.

1869: Booth Tarkington is born on July 29, in Indianapolis, Indiana.

1880: George Eliot dies of heart failure on December 22, in London, England.

1883: Franz Kafka is born on July 3, in Prague, Bohemia (now the Czech Republic).

1885: Sinclair Lewis is born on February 7, in Sauk Centre, Minnesota.

1902: John Steinbeck is born on February 27, in Salinas, California.

1903: Evelyn Waugh is born on October 28, in London, England.

1905: Jules Verne dies of diabetes on March 24, in Amiens, France.

1906–10: Martin Andersen Nexø's *Pelle the Conqueror* is published.

1914: Bernard Malamud is born on April 28, in Brooklyn, New York.

1918: Booth Tarkington's *The Magnificent Ambersons* is published.

1919: Booth Tarkington is awarded the Pulitzer Prize for Novel for *The Magnificent Ambersons*.

1924: Franz Kafka dies of tuberculosis of the larynx on June 3, in Kierling, Klosterneuberg, Austria.

1925: Sinclair Lewis's *Arrowsmith* is published.

1926: Evelyn Waugh's *A Handful of Dust* is published.

1929: Chaim Potok is born on February 17, in New York, New York.

1937: Avi is born Edward Irving Wortis on September 23, in New York, New York.

1942: Michael Crichton is born on October 23, in Chicago, Illinois.

1946: Booth Tarkington dies of a collapsed lung on May 19, in Indianapolis, Indiana.

1947: Octavia E. Butler is born on June 22, in Pasadena, California.

1951: Sinclair Lewis dies of a heart attack on January 10, in London, England.

1952: John Steinbeck's *East of Eden* is published.

1952: Bernard Malamud's *The Natural* is published.

1954: Martin Andersen Nexø dies on June 1, in Dresden, East Germany.

1955: The film *East of Eden*, directed by Elia Kazan, is released.

1955: The film *East of Eden* wins a Best Dramatic Film Award from the Cannes Film Festival for director Elia Kazan.

1956: Julia Glass is born March 23, in Boston, Massachusetts.

1956: Jo Van Fleet wins an Academy Award for Best Actress in a Supporting Role for her work in *East of Eden*.

1966: Evelyn Waugh dies on April 10, in Combe Florey, Somerset, England.

1968: John Steinbeck dies of heart disease on December 20, in New York, New York.

1975: Michael Crichton's *The Great Train Robbery* is published.

1976: Octavia E. Butler's *Patternmaster* is published.

1984: The film *The Natural*, directed by Barry Levinson, is released.

1985: Chaim Potok's *Davita's Harp* is published.

1986: Bernard Malamud dies of natural causes on March 18, in New York, New York.

1991: Avi's *Nothing But the Truth: A Documentary Novel* is published.

1992: Avi's *Nothing But the Truth: A Documentary Novel* is named a Newbery Honor Book by the American Library Association.

2002: Julia Glass's *Three Junes* is published.

2002: Julia Glass is awarded the National Book Award for *Three Junes*.

2002: Chaim Potok dies of brain cancer on July 23, in Merion, Pennsylvania.

2003: Elia Kazan dies on September 28, in New York, New York.

2006: Octavia E. Butler dies on February 24, in Seattle, Washington.

2008: Michael Crichton dies of cancer on November 4, in Los Angeles, California.

Acknowledgments

The editors wish to thank the copyright holders of the excerpted criticism included in this volume and the permissions managers of many book and magazine publishing companies for assisting us in securing reproduction rights. We are also grateful to the staffs of the Detroit Public Library, the Library of Congress, the University of Detroit Mercy Library, Wayne State University Purdy/ Kresge Library Complex, and the University of Michigan Libraries for making their resources available to us. Following is a list of the copyright holders who have granted us permission to reproduce material in this volume of *NfS*. Every effort has been made to trace copyright, but if omissions have been made, please let us know.

COPYRIGHTED EXCERPTS IN *NfS*, VOLUME 34, WERE REPRODUCED FROM THE FOLLOWING PERIODICALS:

Black American Literature Forum, v. 18, summer, 1984. Reproduced by permission.—*Children's Literature Association Quarterly*, v. 8, fall, 1983. © 1983 Children's Literature Association. Reproduced by permission.—*Contemporary Literature*, v. 27.3, fall, 1986. Copyright © 1986 by the Board of Regents of the University of Wisconsin System. Reproduced by permission of the University of Wisconsin Press.—*English Journal*, v. 81, November, 1992. Copyright © 1992 by the National Council of Teachers of English. Reproduced by permission of the publisher.—*The Explicator*, v. 42, spring, 1984. Copyright © 1984 by Helen Dwight Reid Educational Foundation. Reproduced with permission of the Helen Dwight Reid Educational Foundation, published by Heldref Publications, 1319 18th Street, NW, Washington, DC 20036-1802.—*John Steinbeck's Global Dimensions*, 2008. Edited by Kyoko Ariki, Luchen Li, and Scott Pugh. Copyright © 2008 by Kyoko Ariki, Luchen Li, and Scott Pugh. All rights reserved. All rights reserved. Reproduced by permission.—*Literary Review*, v. 38, spring, 1995 for "Genre to the Rear, Race and Gender to the Fore: The Novels of Octavia E. Butler" by Burton Raffel. Reproduced by permission of the author.—*MELUS*, v. 26, spring, 2001. Copyright *MELUS: The Society for the Study of Multi-Ethnic Literature of the United States*, 2001. Reproduced by permission.—*Midwest Quarterly*, v. 18, 1977. Copyright © 1977 by *The Midwest Quarterly*, Pittsburgh State University. Reproduced by permission.—*National Review*, v. 36, July 13, 1984. Copyright © 1984 by National Review, Inc., 215 Lexington Avenue, New York, NY 10016. Reproduced by permission.—*New Republic*, v. 172, June 7, 1975. Copyright © 1975 by The New Republic, Inc. Reproduced by permission of *The New Republic*.—*New York Times*, May 11, 1984. Copyright © 1984 by The New York Times Company, www.nytimes.com. Used by permission and protected by the copyright laws of the United States. The printing, copying, redistribution, or retransmission of the material without express written permission is prohibited.—*New York Times Book Review*, March 31, 1985. Copyright © 1985 by The New York Times Company. Reprinted with permission.—

Novel: A Forum on Fiction, v. 39, fall, 2005. Copyright, 2005, Novel, Inc. All rights reserved. Used by permission of the publisher, Duke University Press.—*Papers on Language and Literature: A Journal for Scholars and Critics of Language and Literature*, v. 44, spring, 2008. Copyright © 2008 by The Board of Trustees, Southern Illinois University at Edwardsville. Reproduced by permission.—*The Patriot Ledger*, April 26, 2003. Copyright © 2003 *The Patriot Ledger*, Quincy, MA. Reproduced by permission.—*Slant*, May 23, 2005. Copyright © 2005 *Slant* Magazine. Reproduced by permission.—*Steinbeck Quarterly*, v. XXV, winter-spring, 1992 for "'East of Eden' on Film" by Robert E. Morsberger. Copyright © 1992 Tetsumaro Hayashi. Reproduced by permission of the publisher and the author.—*Studies in the Novel*, v. 24, spring, 1992. Copyright © 1992 by the University of North Texas. Reproduced by permission.—*Washington Post*, November 6, 2008. Copyright © 2008 *The Washington Post*, www.washingtonpost.com. Used by permission and protected by the copyright laws of the United States. The printing, copying, redistribution, or retransmission of the material without express written permission is prohibited.—*The Writer*, v. 116, November, 2003. Reproduced by permission.

COPYRIGHTED EXCERPTS IN *NfS*, VOLUME 34, WERE REPRODUCED FROM THE FOLLOWING BOOKS:

Bloom, Susan P. and Cathryn M. Mercier. From *Presenting Avi*. Twayne, 1997. Copyright © 1997 by Twayne Publishers. All rights reserved. Reproduced by permission of Gale, a part of Cengage Learning.—Collins, Philip. From "Adam Bede: Overview," in *Reference Guide to English Literature*. Second Edition. Edited by D. L. Kirkpatrick. St. James Press, 1991. Reproduced by permission of Gale, a part of Cengage Learning.—Ermarth, Elizabeth Deeds. From *Twayne's English Authors Series Online*. G. K. Hall, 1999. Copyright © 2009 Gale. Reproduced by permission of Gale, a part of Cengage Learning.—Rietbergen, Peter. From "A Variety of Ambersons: Re-Reading Booth Tarkington's and Orson Welles' 'The Magnificent Ambersons'," in *Uneasy Alliance: Twentieth-Century American Literature, Culture and Biography*. Edited by Hans Bak. Rodopi, 2004. Copyright © Editions Rodopi B.V., Amsterdam 2004. Reproduced by permission.—Savater, Fernando. From *Childhood Regained: The Art of the Storyteller*. Translated by Frances M. Lopez-Morillas. Columbia University Press, 1982. Copyright © 1982 Columbia University Press. Reprinted with permission of the publisher.

COPYRIGHTED EXCERPTS IN *NfS*, VOLUME 34, WERE REPRODUCED FROM THE FOLLOWING WEBSITES AND OTHER SOURCES:

Julia Glass, "A Matter of Inspiration: When Characters From One Book Find Soul Mates in Another," *Powells.com*, accessed July 26, 2009. Copyright © 1994-2009 Powells.com. Reproduced by permission.

Contributors

Bay Anapol: Anapol teaches writing classes at the College of Santa Fe. She is an award-winning fiction writer and former Stegner Fellow in Fiction at Stanford University. Entry on *Adam Bede*. Original essay on *Adam Bede*.

Bryan Aubrey: Aubrey holds a Ph.D. in English and has published many articles on twentieth century literature. Entry on *Pelle the Conqueror*. Original essay on *Pelle the Conqueror*.

Melanie Bush: Bush holds a Master's degree in English. She is a teacher and writer in upstate New York. Entry on *Davita's Harp*. Original essay on *Davita's Harp*.

Scott Herring: Herring teaches both literature and writing at the University of California, Davis, specializing in writing for students of medicine. Entry on *Arrowsmith*. Original essay on *Arrowsmith*.

Laura Noll: Noll is a freelance editor and writer. Entry on *East of Eden*. Original essay on *East of Eden*.

A. Petruso: Petruso holds degrees from the University of Michigan and the University of Texas. Entries on *Nothing but the Truth* and *Patternmaster*. Original essays on *Nothing but the Truth* and *Patternmaster*.

Patrick Walsh: Walsh holds a Ph.D. in history from the University of Texas and has served as a professor of English, American Studies, and Multidisciplinary Studies. Walsh has published many articles on topics and figures in twentieth-century literature and history. Entry on *A Handful of Dust*. Original essay on *A Handful of Dust*.

Greg Wilson: Wilson is a freelance writer who has contributed material to dozens of books ranging in subject matter from statistics to mythology. Entries on *The Castle*, *The Great Train Robbery*, *Journey to the Center of the Earth*, and *The Natural*. Original essays on *The Castle*, *The Great Train Robbery*, *Journey to the Center of the Earth*, and *The Natural*.

Adam Bede

GEORGE ELIOT

1859

The first novel of renowned British Victorian writer George Eliot, *Adam Bede* (1859), is the tragic tale of a love triangle between a dairymaid, a carpenter, and a wealthy young squire. The name George Eliot is misleading; the novelist took this pen name to conceal her female identity, possibly from a culture less inclined to read women writers as seriously as male writers. George Eliot's real name was Mary Anne Evans.

Adam Bede is set in a rural English village, but the quiet country setting masks turbulent lives. A strong young carpenter named Adam Bede is in love with the beautiful dairymaid Hetty Sorrel and dreams of marrying her. Hetty, a vain and shallow girl, is soon seduced by the young village squire, Arthur Donnithorne. When he leaves her, she reluctantly accepts a proposal from Adam, only to find herself pregnant with Arthur's child. Unable to find a solution to her situation, she abandons her child. The child dies, and Hetty is forever exiled from her home. Adam ends up marrying the gentle and good Dinah, a Methodist preacher, while Arthur Donnithorne struggles to become a better man. The book sensitively depicts the inner lives of these villagers.

Eliot, raised an Evangelical Christian, based her 1859 novel on a story she had heard her Methodist Aunt Samuel tell about how she had preached and redeemed a fallen woman prisoner who was much like Hetty Sorrel. However, Eliot's charming portrait of rural English life comes

George Eliot *(The Library of Congress)*

directly from her own bucolic girlhood. This snapshot of everyday life in a serene country village was already fading when the book was published; the Industrial Revolution was rapidly changing the appearance and culture of British villages. *Adam Bede* was published to not only great critical acclaim but also great popularity among readers nostalgic for bygone days.

George Eliot went on to write classics such as *Silas Marner* and *Middlemarch*. But with her first novel, *Adam Bede*, she manages to create a masterpiece of realism. Each of the characters demonstrates a complexity of thought and action that became the standard for modern novels.

AUTHOR BIOGRAPHY

The provocative and unconventional Victorian novelist named George Eliot was born Mary Anne Evans on November 22, 1819. An avid reader, she was the youngest of five children in a family of Evangelical Protestants, and even as a child she taught Sunday school to local children. Her father, on whom her character Adam Bede was based, was a carpenter and land agent in a rural village in Warwickshire, England. It was from her aunt, a Methodist preacher, that Eliot

first heard the story that became the novel *Adam Bede*.

When Eliot was sent off to school at age nine, she met an influential teacher named Maria Lewis. Lewis became her spiritual and intellectual mentor for the next fifteen years. A woman of great religious convictions, she did her best to share her faith with her already-devout pupil. She felt Eliot's great intelligence should be nurtured. But Eliot was soon called back home when her mother fell gravely ill.

After her mother's death, Eliot never returned to school; she cared for her beloved father and continued her studies at home. As her education grew, so did her questions about God and faith. She began to break from her childhood religion, much to her father's chagrin.

Two years later she became acquainted with a nonconformist couple, the Brays, who would change the course of her life. Their circle of intellectuals and freethinkers expanded to include the shy but intelligent young woman. She continued to attend church and work on translations of religious work, but inwardly she began to think like her new rationalist friends. Rationalism was a new belief at that time. This philosophy argues that knowledge is acquired by reason, not religious faith.

Soon Eliot stopped attending church, and her distressed father threatened to disown her. They finally agreed that she would attend church, but he could not force her to believe in a faith she no longer held. Their close relationship never recovered. Neither did Eliot's relationship with her old teacher, Maria Lewis.

Following her father's death, Eliot traveled with her friends, the Brays. She then left her small village and moved to London. A married publisher named John Chapman had read and admired her translations and now offered her work. Eventually she became editor of the *Westminster Review*. However, Chapman's interest in her was more than professional. Though photos of Eliot reveal that she was a very plain woman, she was often described as compelling and charming. Her speaking voice was said to have a lovely musical quality. Her relationship with John Chapman was a society scandal.

Soon after, Eliot was introduced to the great love of her life, George Henry Lewes, a writer and critic. Although he too was married and could not divorce, they lived together until his death. It was from him that she took her pen name when she began writing fiction, claiming she wanted to be taken more seriously than women authors were at the time. In 1856 she began writing *Scenes From a Clerical Life*, a collection of stories. Her first novel, *Adam Bede*, was a great popular and critical success. Her realistic depiction of the poor won her many fans.

Over the following years she completed classics such as *The Mill on the Floss* (1860), *Silas Marner* (1861), and *Middlemarch* (1872). With each publication, Eliot's fame spread. She was one of the best-selling novelists of her time.

After Lewes's death in 1878, Eliot grew despondent. She refused to see her friends for a long period, causing concern. However, she agreed to marry her business advisor, John Cross, a man nearly twenty years her junior, in the spring of 1880. Their marriage lasted less than a year; Eliot died in December 1880, from a passing flu, at the age of sixty-one. She is buried next to George Lewes in Highgate Cemetery, England.

MEDIA ADAPTATIONS

- A filmed adaptation of the novel was released in 1918. The six-reeler was produced in England by International Exclusives, Inc. Bransby Williams plays the title role. The film is not available on DVD.

- A BBC television miniseries, starring the popular actress Patsy Kensit, was a great success. It was directed by Giles Foster. It first aired on the BBC in 1991, then aired as part of the PBS anthology *Masterpiece Theatre* in 1992. Iain Glen played the role of Adam Bede. The film is available on DVD in the United States.

PLOT SUMMARY

Book 1, Chapter 1: The Workshop
In the opening paragraph of *Adam Bede*, the reader is invited into a rural English woodshop, circa 1799. Adam Bede, a handsome young carpenter, and his kindhearted brother Seth work diligently among the other carpenters. Seth admits that a gentle young Methodist preacher named Dinah has captured his thoughts. He looks forward to hearing her preach that evening. The other workers are disdainful of a woman preacher, and Adam is somewhat disdainful of religion itself. He is also aghast at the way the other carpenters leave the shop the instant the workday is over. A visitor to the village admires his handsome form as he walks toward home.

Book 1, Chapter 2: The Preaching
That same evening, pretty Methodist Dinah preaches to a coolly receptive group of villagers. The villagers are not enthusiastic about Methodist teachings, or women preaching these teachings. However, Dinah is a gifted speaker, and her words about God's love are stirring and simple. She urges all her listeners to think about goodness and piety. Some of the villagers weep at Dinah's preaching, and embrace her despite their non-Methodist leanings.

Book 1, Chapter 3: After the Preaching
After her inspired sermon, Seth takes Dinah home. She is distant, and he feels little encouragement that his love for her is reciprocated. Instead, Dinah tells him she plans to return and preach to the mill town of Snowfield. She regrets leaving her aunt, Mrs. Poyser, and her cousin, Hetty Sorrel. Dinah prays for this young girl, and Seth bemoans his brother, Adam's, attachment to Hetty. Seth bumbles into a declaration of love for the godly Dinah. Dinah is gentle in her refusals, explaining that God will not allow her to marry or have children. She must continue to preach. Seth accepts Dinah's rejection with a heavy heart.

Book 1, Chapter 4: Home and Its Sorrows
Adam and Seth's pious mother, Lisbeth, waits for them at home. Their father is a drinker, and in a moment ripe with foreshadowing, Adam discovers that his father has left the house without completing a promised coffin. Adam is annoyed by his father's selfish actions. He angrily sits down to work. Seth attempts to calm his mother, who cries when she thinks of Adam marrying shallow Hetty Sorrel. After they go to sleep, Adam imagines he hears a

knock at the door. The villagers believe this means death is arriving. He manages to complete the coffin by the morning, and Seth assists him in bringing it to town. There they find their drowned, drunken father. The discovery fills Adam with bitter regret for his previous conduct.

Book 1, Chapter 5: The Rector

A shift of scenery takes the reader from the simple dwellings of the Bede family to the Broxton Parsonage. The parish clerk enters and tells Reverend Adolphus Irwine that Dinah and the other Methodists are stirring up the villagers. The parson is less upset than curious and resolves to talk to Dinah. He is pleased when his friend Arthur Donnithorne arrives. The dashing Donnithorne is recovering from a war injury. He is the favorite grandson of the town squire, due to inherit wealth and prestige. The parish clerk tells the men the upsetting news that Thias Bede died tragically the night before.

Book 1, Chapter 6: The Hall Farm

Dinah is staying at Hall Farm with her aunt's family. Her aunt, Mrs. Poyser, is plainspoken but sharp-tongued. She is clearly fond of her niece, but remonstrates with her for not marrying Seth Bede and raising a family. Mrs. Poyser uses the arrival of Mr. Irwine and Arthur Donnithorne to complain about the state of their land and property, as she is a tenant of Arthur Donnithorne's grandfather.

Book 1, Chapter 7: The Dairy

Mrs. Poyser shows the gentlemen her dairy, where they find the beautiful Hetty Sorrel working. Arthur Donnithorne is immediately taken with her. They gaze at each other flirtatiously, and the air is electric with their attraction.

Book 1, Chapter 8: A Vocation

Mr. Irwine talks with Dinah, admiring her sweet spirit and religious fervor. Dinah explains that God called to her, and so she answered. She works in a mill in Snowfield, and she yearns to heal those around her from spiritual pain. Mr. Irwine says nothing about Dinah's preaching on the village green. Later, Dinah and her aunt agree that Mr. Irwine is a gentleman. Dinah also tells Mrs. Poyser that Mr. Bede drowned the night before and she is going to go pray with the family. Although Hetty hears this, she is unmoved by Adam's tragic loss.

Book 1, Chapter 9: Hetty's World

Hetty indulges herself in romantic fantasies about Arthur Donnithorne. She knows that solid but unexciting Adam is taken with her, but she vastly prefers the rich Arthur Donnithorne's attentions. Meanwhile, Mr. Irwine advises Arthur Donnithorne not to lead the silly Hetty on, and Arthur Donnithorne protests that he has no intention of doing so.

Book 1, Chapter 10: Dinah Visits Lisbeth

Lisbeth Bede has spent the day in funeral preparations for her imperfect but now-mourned husband. No one can comfort her. When Dinah arrives, Lisbeth is not open to her ministry. However, Dinah's sincere and loving manner wins her over, as do her words of religious faith. Lisbeth finally embraces her as a daughter. Her grief ebbs with Dinah's care and prayers, and Seth is grateful for her attentions to his mother.

Book 1, Chapter 11: In the Cottage

Adam meets Dinah and thanks her for comforting his mother. He admires Dinah's serene beauty and appreciates his brother's infatuation. Lisbeth asks Adam to work on his father's coffin instead of at the shop in town. She insists that his father would have wanted Adam to do the work independently, and so he finally agrees. Seth arranges to walk Dinah back to Hall Farm. Adam urges his brother to hold on to hope that Dinah will someday accept his love.

Book 1, Chapter 12: In the Wood

Hetty Sorrel arrives at Arthur Donnithorne's estate to learn needlework from his servant, Mrs. Pomfret. He tries, but he cannot resist the urge to see her. He catches up with her as she crosses the woods. She tells him she would like to be a lady's maid, a rank far below his own. He is taken with Hetty's lovely face, and for a moment he holds her close. But he quickly recovers himself, and rides off with a quick good-bye. Hetty is sad and puzzled by his retreat. Later Arthur Donnithorne resolves to see Hetty once more to make sure she understands that, given their social classes, an attachment would be impossible.

Book 1, Chapter 13: Evening in the Wood

Hetty's girlish heart is still stirred by Arthur's attentions. Mrs. Pomfret, her needlepoint teacher, thinks to herself that Hetty's beauty is not a blessing. Men, she reasons, want a practical wife. Hetty anxiously waits to see if Arthur Donnithorne will cross her path again on her way home. He appears, but his original intention goes awry. Instead, he comforts the weeping girl with a kiss. When he says good-bye, he realizes anew that their connection is impossible. With fresh resolve, he decides to confess to his friend, Mr. Irwine.

Book 1, Chapter 14: The Return Home
Back at the Bedes' house, Lisbeth is very sad to say good-bye to Dinah. She remarks to Adam that he could marry her. Adam shrugs this off, as he is deeply in love with Hetty. Seth takes Dinah back to Hall Farm. Hetty says nothing about Adam's regard for her, or his family's recent loss. When Totty, the Poysers' little girl, becomes fussy, only Dinah can comfort her. Hetty seems to have no talent with children.

Book 1, Chapter 15: The Two Bed-Chambers
Hetty puts on a pair of earrings and admires her reflection. Just because a woman is beautiful, the narrative asserts, it does not follow that she is good. Hetty's silliness is in sharp contrast to Dinah's piety. Before Dinah goes to sleep, she takes a moment to assure Hetty that she will be there for her if trouble comes. Hetty fearfully rejects Dinah's words.

Book 1, Chapter 16: Links
Arthur Donnithorne is resolved to tell Mr. Irwine about Hetty, but on the way he runs across Adam Bede. The two remember their shared boyhood games, and Arthur Donnithorne urges Adam to accept money to start his own shop. Arthur Donnithorne loses his nerve and does not mention Hetty to Mr. Irwine. Instead, he remarks that a struggle with morals at least implies that the morals are within a man. Mr. Irwine suspects this is about Hetty, but he is too delicate to prompt any confession.

Book 2, Chapter 17: In Which the Story Pauses a Little
Here the narrator pauses to assure the reader that it is more important to be kind and well loved than to be a great preacher. The town regards Mr. Irwine with greater affection than the previous clergyman. Kindness is more important than intelligence and sophistication.

Book 2, Chapter 18: Church
The Poysers get ready to attend Adam's father's funeral. Hetty is hoping to see Arthur Donnithorne at the service. Adam is distressed by his unkindness to his father. He concentrates on Hetty's beautiful and grave face. She is not, however, thinking about the funeral. She is upset that Arthur Donnithorne has left town for a trip and will not be at the church. She worries that he is already tired of her.

Book 2, Chapter 19: Adam on a Working Day
The next morning the weather is fine. Adam ponders a future with Hetty. He is still unsure if she loves him, and he decides to press her when he goes to the Poyser farm that evening. He knows Mr. Poyser finds him the perfect suitor. The narrator assures the reader that Adam is an unusually good man of his station.

Book 2, Chapter 20: Adam Visits the Hall Farm
Adam spruces himself up to go to Hall Farm over his mother's objections. He finds the usual bustle at Hall Farm when he arrives. Hetty is flirtatious, and she leads Adam to believe she loves him. She puts a flower in her hair, and Adam expresses his disapproval of her desire to be ornamented. Hetty saucily goes up to her room and returns wearing a Dinah-style Methodist cap, implying that Adam has requested her to look this way. Adam leaves believing Hetty loves him, although she prefers her dreams of a life with Arthur Donnithorne.

Book 2, Chapter 21: The Night-School and the Schoolmaster
Adam meets his night-school teacher and friend Bartle Massey, a confirmed bachelor. He tells Adam about a job managing the squire's fields and offers to put a word in for Adam. Adam accepts, praising his wisdom. The two men part, Massey inviting Adam to a Friday outing.

Book 3, Chapter 22: Going to the Birthday Feast
Everyone is looking forward to Captain Arthur Donnithorne's coming-of-age party. Hetty tries on a pair of gold earrings he has given her, and a locket containing intertwining locks of hair. At the squire's house, the celebration is about to begin. Mr. Irwine tells Arthur that Adam has been offered the position taking care of the squire's lands, and the two men are pleased.

Book 3, Chapter 23: Dinner-Time

Adam Bede and Bartle Massey are invited to eat dinner with the more prosperous villagers. Everyone enjoys dinner, and Adam enjoys gazing at Hetty. He fails to notice that Hetty is impatient with Totty. This does not escape Mary Burge, who hopes Adam sees that she herself has a better temperament. However, when Hetty realizes her rival, Mary Burge, is watching them, she flirts with Adam.

Book 3, Chapter 24: The Health-Drinking

The tenant farmers salute Arthur Donnithorne with birthday speeches and praise. Arthur Donnithorne feels a secret shame about Hetty. However, he decides the flirtation has not been serious. He happily announces Adam's new position. Adam is slightly embarrassed to be the center of attention, but he gamely promises to do well. Arthur Donnithorne turns over a new leaf by ignoring Hetty.

Book 3, Chapter 25: The Games

The party continues with contests and games. Hetty's beauty is remarked upon, which excites Arthur Donnithorne's vanity. A winning girl cries when she is given an ugly dress as a prize. Arthur Donnithorne gives a shiny pocketknife to the boy who wins his race, and some money to the unhappy girl winner. One of the men from Jonathan Burge's carpentry shop dances a rustic dance to great acclaim.

Book 3, Chapter 26: The Dance

The formal dance begins. Hetty longs to dance with her captain. When she reluctantly accepts a dance from Adam, her small cousin Totty pulls the beads that hold her locket. Adam picks up the locket, noting the locks of hair inside. He decides to ignore the situation although Hetty is clearly embarrassed. Arthur Donnithorne makes one final date with Hetty, planning to finally end the relationship. Despite all evidence, Hetty still believes Arthur Donnithorne will marry her.

Book 4, Chapter 27: A Crisis

A few weeks later, Adam has added caring for the squire's fields to his work at the carpentry shop. He believes Hetty is finally falling in love with him. That afternoon, Adam goes to Hall Farm and discovers Hetty and Arthur Donnithorne kissing. He accosts the captain and demands an explanation. Arthur tries to convince Adam that the kiss was a mere thank-you. Adam rejects his words, telling Arthur that he has stolen Hetty's heart. He knocks him down angrily.

Book 4, Chapter 28: A Dilemma

Adam is afraid he has killed Arthur. He is relieved when Arthur finally awakens, and helps him to an empty cottage. He runs to find brandy. Arthur Donnithorne hides evidence of Hetty and lies about the extent of his relationship. He reluctantly promises to write a good-bye letter and tell her he is rejoining his regiment. He agrees to hand this letter to Adam the next day.

Book 4, Chapter 29: The Next Morning

Arthur Donnithorne is troubled by how Hetty will react to her abandonment. However, he comforts himself that it will lead to a better future for her. He can never marry her, so Adam should be encouraged to do so. He sends Adam the letter with a note admonishing him that Hetty will be devastated. Adam acknowledges that his feelings for Arthur Donnithorne will never recover. He plans to be gentle with Hetty when he speaks with her again.

Book 4, Chapter 30: The Delivery of the Letter

Adam meets the Poysers after church the next Sunday. While Hetty is relieved that Adam continues to be kind to her, she still fears he will tell her family about her deed. She decides to be secretive about her feelings. Adam tells her with great sensitivity that Arthur Donnithorne does not love her. Hetty blurts out that Adam is wrong. He gives her the letter as proof, but warns her to read it alone. She is shaken by Adam's words, but he hopes there is room in Hetty's heart for him. On the way home, Seth shows Adam a letter from Dinah in Snowfield. Adam urges Seth to see her, assuring him that sometimes women fall in love slowly.

Book 4, Chapter 31: In Hetty's Bed-Chamber

Arthur Donnithorne's letter is as painful to Hetty as Adam promised. The letter explains that while he loved their time together, they can never be man and wife; their class separation is too significant for them to find happiness. Hetty rails against her lover, weeps all night, and in the morning begs her uncle to allow her to leave Hall Farm to become a lady's maid. Her aunt is upset as she sees the desire to leave as disloyal. She calls Hetty a cherry with a stone at the center. Mr. Poyser refuses Hetty's request, suggesting it would be better for her to become Adam's wife. This idea sinks in slowly, but finally Hetty embraces the thought. The important thing is that her life will change.

Book 4, Chapter 32: Mrs. Poyser "Has Her Say Out"

Mrs. Poyser's talents in the dairy have become the talk of the village. This does not escape the old squire. He asks Mrs. Poyser to supply more from her dairy and give over some of the corn farming to another tenant. While Mr. Poyser reacts mildly to the request, his wife is angered and turns the squire out of the house. She is pleased with herself for being honest with their landlord.

Book 4, Chapter 33: More Links

Adam now reaps the rewards of being a fine worker. He has been made a partner in the carpentry shop. In other happy news, Hetty is seemingly more open to his attentions. Adam decides that perhaps Hetty never loved Arthur Donnithorne. The old squire has been thwarted in his plan to produce more dairy products. Mr. Irwine remarks that despite her sharp tongue he admires Mrs. Poyser. Everyone is amused that the old squire was put in his place by one of his tenants.

Book 4, Chapter 34: The Betrothal

When Adam tells Hetty he is to be the new partner at Jonathan Burge's shop, she leaps to the conclusion that he plans to marry Mary Burge. Noting how upset she is, Adam quickly asks her to marry him. Hetty calms and agrees. Her aunt and uncle are well pleased, and there is discussion of where they will live and when they will marry.

Book 4, Chapter 35: The Hidden Dread

Now that they are betrothed, Adam is completely happy. Seth is less happy as he has given up hope of marrying Dinah. Hetty is detached from her wedding plans. She is pregnant with Arthur's child. She contemplates suicide, but realizes she lacks the courage to kill herself. When she gets a letter from Dinah in Snowfield, she decides on a plan. She will tell everyone that she is visiting Dinah, while really she is going to find Arthur Donnithorne. When she weeps, Adam again mistakenly thinks she is attached to him and sad to say good-bye.

Book 5, Chapter 36: The Journey of Hope

After a long and treacherous journey, Hetty finally alights in the town of Windsor where she expects to find Arthur. When she inquires at a local inn, the innkeeper tells her Arthur Donnithorne is in Ireland. Hetty falls to the floor, believing her last hope is gone. The innkeeper quickly figures out her situation, but she is kind to her nonetheless.

Book 5, Chapter 37: The Journey in Despair

As she has little money, Hetty is forced to give up her earrings to pay for staying at an inn. She starts back toward Hall Farm, but she cannot face her aunt and uncle in her condition. Hetty resolves again to kill herself, but once again, she loses her nerve. After a sleepless night in a poor hut, Hetty remembers Dinah's letter and address. She heads pitifully toward Snowfield, thinking that Dinah might still be kind to her.

Book 5, Chapter 38: The Quest

Hetty has now been gone for nearly two weeks, and the Poysers are puzzled as to why she should stay so long. Adam sets off for Snowfield, certain he will return with his bride. But he soon discovers that Hetty never visited Dinah, who left to preach in Leeds before Hetty arrived. The news sends Adam into a tailspin. He secretly suspects she has left him for Arthur Donnithorne. He resolves to find Hetty in Ireland and bring her home, but before he does, he confesses his suspicions to wise Mr. Irwine.

Book 5, Chapter 39: The Tidings

Adam arrives at the parsonage to find Mr. Irwine uncharacteristically upset. He tells Adam he believes Hetty is in prison, accused of killing her own baby. He also tells him Arthur Donnithorne is not in Ireland but on his way back to Hayslope. His grandfather has sent for him. At first Adam rails against Arthur Donnithorne for his seduction. But he calms, remembering he loves Hetty. The two men agree to go speak to the girl in prison in the hope that it is not her.

Book 5, Chapter 40: The Bitter Waters Spread

The two men soon discover that the girl is Hetty, and worse, the evidence is strongly against her. Mr. Irwine returns home, but Adam stays behind, convinced she is innocent of the terrible charges. The next morning, Mr. Irwine awakens to the news that the old squire has died during the night, assuring Arthur Donnithorne's swift return to Hayslope. Meanwhile, Hall Farm is in mourning over the shame of Hetty's actions, and they send for Dinah to come back. Mr. Irwine is worried about Adam. His friend, Mr. Massey, hurries to the town where Hetty is held, in the hope of helping Adam.

Book 5, Chapter 41: The Eve of the Trial

Hetty's trouble seems to have aged Adam, and she refuses to see him or anyone else. Although his friend Mr. Massey urges him, Adam chooses not to attend her trial; he can't bear to see Hetty in the courtroom. When Mr. Irwine comes to visit, he is shocked at Adam's appearance. He tells him the Poysers are in town for the trial, but Dinah has still not been located. Adam talks about vengeance for Arthur Donnithorne's actions, but Mr. Irwine speaks to him gently and Adam finally drops the thought of violence. He ponders whether Dinah's loving ways could have swayed Hetty from her actions.

Book 5, Chapter 42: The Morning of the Trial

Mr. Massey returns from the courtroom with bad news. Hetty will surely be declared guilty of the charges. Mr. Massey tells Adam with some compassion that Hetty looked very alone and without anyone to support her in the courtroom. The prison chaplain is a sharp-faced man without Mr. Irwine's gentleness. Adam shakes off his fears and decides to go to the courtroom after all.

Book 5, Chapter 43: The Verdict

Hetty is the only one who doesn't turn to look at Adam when he enters the courtroom. Like a corpse, all her warmth and humanity seems to have been drained away. A widow testifies she helped Hetty give birth in her home, and a farmer found her dead child not far away. The police found her near her baby the next day. She listens, visibly trembling, to the testimony against her. When the verdict is read, no one is surprised that she is convicted of murder. She is hysterical as she learns she has been sentenced to hang.

Book 5, Chapter 44: Arthur's Return

Arthur Donnithorne happily nears Hayslope, after a very long journey. He knows his grandfather was unpopular, and he believes the villagers will now welcome him as the new squire. He thinks of Hetty, and wonders if he loves her. But while he relishes the memory of her kisses, he is pleased that she is about to marry Adam. However, his good mood is short-lived. When he opens a letter informing him of Hetty's misfortune, he immediately rides off to see her.

Book 5, Chapter 45: In the Prison

Dinah finally arrives at the prison to see Hetty. She meets a man who had been impressed by her preaching in Hayslope, and he turns out to be a magistrate. He permits Dinah to enter Hetty's cell and therefore unlock her heart. At first, Hetty is unresponsive. But after listening to Dinah's soft words about God's love, she finally tells her that she did abandon her child. She thought it the only way out of her dilemma. The two girls hold each other, and Hetty is comforted although she still fears her sentence. She tells Dinah she hears her dead child crying for her.

Book 5, Chapter 46: The Hours of Suspense

Adam agrees to go see Hetty on the day she will be executed. Ironically, it was to be their wedding day. Dinah is with her, and she tells Adam that God has not forsaken Hetty. She plans to be a source of strength for the condemned girl. Hetty begs Adam to forgive her for hurting him, and they say a mournful good-bye to each other. Dinah encourages Hetty to forgive her lover too. In this way, she tells her cousin, God will extend forgiveness to Hetty.

Book 5, Chapter 47: The Last Moment

At the gallows, it seems all hope is lost. Dinah and Hetty pray together in front of a quiet crowd awaiting Hetty's execution. Just then, Arthur Donnithorne gallops forward, waving a stay of execution. Hetty will not die that day after all.

Book 5, Chapter 48: Another Meeting in the Wood

The next night, Adam is back in Hayslope, as is Arthur Donnithorne. The two meet in the same cottage where Adam took Arthur Donnithorne after their fight. They are somber together, each having suffered. Arthur Donnithorne plans to rejoin the military, but he urges Adam to stay in the village. He allows that Dinah was wonderful to Hetty, and he gives Adam a fine watch in reward. Adam admits he is perhaps too hard on people. The two shake hands and part as friends. Hetty's death sentence has been commuted to exile.

Book 6, Chapter 49: At the Hall Farm

It is more than a year later. Mr. Poyser believes Adam will soon be the sole owner of the carpentry shop. Dinah is at last planning to return to Snowfield, as she feels the poor there have more need of her than the Poysers. She feels she must reject the ease of her lifestyle at the farm. Adam hears she plans to return to Snowfield and says he trusts she will always follow the right path. At this, Dinah mysteriously leaves Adam and the Poysers to their talk. When she returns, Adam asks her to come back with him and visit his mother.

Book 6, Chapter 50: In the Cottage

Dinah asks if Adam has heard anything of Arthur Donnithorne, and Adam tells her he is still upset about Hetty's disgrace. Dinah compares him to Esau from the Bible, and talks of him with sympathy. When they discuss Dinah's plan to go back to Snowfield, Adam urges her to stay and marry his brother. The words send Dinah into an unusually emotional state, and Adam is surprised. Lisbeth and Seth note that Dinah does not seem herself. Dinah tells Lisbeth that her emotions will pass. The next morning, Dinah meets Adam cleaning up his workshop, and feels a thrill at his deep voice. Adam asks her if she is upset with him, but she tells him she knows she is a sister to him. The narrator suggests Dinah is in love.

Book 6, Chapter 51: Sunday Morning

Lisbeth, who is very attached to Dinah, wails at the thought of her leaving town yet again. Lisbeth believes Dinah loves Adam, and that she might stay if Adam decided to marry her. Her words are hurtful to Seth, who still loves Dinah. He declares the two are like siblings, but he would still be happy if they found a match. Lisbeth decides to speak with Adam, and he quickly warms to the idea of the good and gentle Dinah as his wife. Seth reassures Adam that he would not object to the match; however, he believes she will never accept Adam's proposal.

Book 6, Chapter 52: Adam and Dinah

There is good news and bad news for Adam that Sunday. The good news is that Dinah returns his love for her. The bad news is that she has decided to return to Snowfield and remain single. She would no longer have the poor as her priority if she married and had children of her own. Adam attempts to argue, but she tells him she will go back to Snowfield and await God's word. Meanwhile, Mrs. Poyser claims she was not surprised by Adam and Dinah's love. Everyone enjoys the fine day, and the narrator calls attention to how important a day of leisure is in busy lives.

Book 6, Chapter 53: The Harvest Supper

The harvest is done, and to celebrate, the Poysers invite their field-workers and farmers to a special dinner. Adam is there, but Dinah has returned to Snowfield as she promised. However, the mood is still jubilant. Mr. Poyser is proud of his offerings, songs are sung, and a new spirit of renewal is in the air. Mr. Massey, Adam's schoolteacher friend, pokes fun at his love for women. They both agree that Mrs. Poyser's wit is admirable.

Book 6, Chapter 54: The Meeting on the Hill

Adam yearns to see Dinah. He decides to travel to Snowfield. On his journey, he remembers the beautiful Hetty, and he feels a pang at her memory. However, this experience may have paved the way to a deeper love for Dinah, and he can come to her with a full heart. When Dinah sees him waiting for her, she tells him their love is so true God must want them to be together. She agrees to marry him, and they share a tender first kiss.

Book 6, Chapter 55: Marriage Bells

Finally, it is Adam and Dinah's wedding day, a time of true joy for both. Their union pleases the entire village. Dinah wears a plain gray dress, but her pretty face glows with happiness. Although Mr. Irwine remembers the great sorrow Adam has suffered, he is especially happy that he can give this great news to Arthur Donnithorne, who has never returned to Hayslope.

Epilogue

The novel ends with a view of Adam and Dinah's happy marriage. It is nearly ten years later, and they are the parents of two children. Adam is also sole owner of the carpentry shop. Seth lives with Adam's family and the children are fond of him. Adam tells Dinah that Arthur Donnithorne is finally returning to Hayslope. He's been very ill, but is expected to recover. Hetty died just before she would have been allowed to return to her home. The three family members briefly discuss how women are no longer allowed to preach. Adam is in favor of this, but Dinah clearly is not. However, this is a small shadow over their great happiness.

CHARACTERS

Adam Bede

Adam Bede is a young and handsome carpenter, much admired in the village of Hayslope for his intelligence and industry. He is a good man to his friends and family, but he is also somewhat rigid and unable to see other perspectives. Eventually he becomes the steward of the lands, a very desirable position, through his boyhood camaraderie with the squire's grandson, Arthur Donnithorne.

Adam works at the Burges' carpentry shop with his brother, Seth, and he dreams of marrying the beautiful Hetty Sorrel. However, his love for Hetty is based primarily on her beauty, not her goodness. They become betrothed, but when Hetty is arrested for murdering her child and sent into exile, Adam turns to Dinah Morris. He becomes a much more compassionate man through his experience with Hetty, and eventually he and Dinah fall in love. When the novel ends, Adam is the owner of the carpentry shop. Dinah and Adam are parents of two children, and very happy.

Lisbeth Bede

Lisbeth is Adam and Seth Bede's mother. She is widowed when her husband, Thias Bede, drowns during a drunken spree. This causes Lisbeth much grief, although he was not always a good husband to her. Lisbeth appears to be very fragile, but actually she is quite astute. She realizes Dinah and Adam should marry before they do, and she guesses correctly that Dinah will not be interested in marrying her younger son, Seth. While she spends much of the novel in tears, she is often comforted by the preaching and soft words of Dinah, whom she loves like a daughter.

Seth Bede

Adam's younger brother, Seth, is good-natured but he lacks the steel of Adam's personality. The other men in the woodshop poke fun at him. While he is a gentle and caring man, he is also a bit of a daydreamer. Like Dinah Morris, he is a Methodist, and he loves hearing her preach. Although he declares his love for her early in the novel, Dinah rejects him. His sweet personality holds no grudges, and he continues to be her supporter and friend. When Adam marries her, he is happy for both of them. He is also in favor, unlike Adam, of woman preachers. At the end of the novel Seth has remained a single man. In fact, he is living happily with Dinah, Adam, and their children.

Thias Bede

The drunkard father of Adam and Seth dies tragically by drowning. While he was once an industrious carpenter, over time he has become a drinker. He represents a realistic portrait of an alcoholic in this time period. His sons discover his body while they are taking a coffin to town. His funeral is attended by much of Hayslope. Thias Bede is sincerely mourned by his wife and his sons, despite his drunkenness and his other faults.

Mr. Jonathan Burge

Mr. Burge owns the carpentry shop where Adam and Seth work in Hayslope. His daughter, Mary Burge, is in love with Adam. Although Adam marries Dinah and not his daughter, Mr. Burge decides to give his shop to Adam anyway. He tries to replace him but can never find another carpenter of Adam's ability.

Mary Burge

Mary is the daughter of the master carpenter in town, and her love for Adam Bede remains unrequited. She is a quiet and plain girl. She spurs Hetty Sorrel to flirt with Adam, an act that results in Adam and Hetty's eventual engagement.

Arthur Donnithorne

The weak-minded but handsome young captain is the rich heir to his grandfather's lands and estate. He is much admired in Hayslope, but his passion for Hetty Sorrel proves to be his undoing. Arthur wants everyone to like him, and so he often takes the easy way out of his troubles. He avoids telling Hetty Sorrel that he will never marry her until it is too late, and he neglects to confess to his friend and parson, Mr. Irwine, about his relationship with her.

However, by the end of the novel, Arthur has learned some important lessons. He saves Hetty from the gallows with a last-minute reprieve, and he never forgets he was the instrument of her sorrow. He also suffers through illness and despair, eventually returning to Hayslope a changed man. His kindnesses are also noted, not only to Adam Bede, but also to the other villagers. He awards the young winner of a race a pocketknife, and gives another a gift of money.

Squire Donnithorne

The aged squire is the grandfather of the dashing Arthur Donnithorne. He is extremely disliked in Hayslope, and a very bad landlord. When he asks Mrs. Poyser to give up rich farmlands and spend more time producing goods in the dairy, she publicly berates him to everyone's amusement. He dies a bitter old man.

Mr. Irwine

The lifelong bachelor Mr. Irwine is a shining example of a helpful clergyman. Eliot claims he is not brilliant but is, more importantly, well loved. Mr. Irwine is never judgmental about his flock, and he treats Hetty Sorrel with compassion. While he is a good friend with Arthur Donnithorne, he calls him to task for his actions toward Hetty. He also makes sure Adam finds Hetty in prison, and he encourages his friend Bartle Massey to take care of him during this difficult period.

A nonviolent man, he manages to talk Adam Bede out of further conflict with Arthur. He is also not upset that Dinah Morris preaches in the town square. Mr. Irwine brings his balanced wisdom to all situations in the novel that call for the voice of reason.

Bartle Massey

Bartle Massey is a disabled schoolmaster and a bachelor who pokes fun at Adam's love affairs. However, he stays beside him when Hetty is arrested, proving himself a very good friend. For Bartle, his female dog Vixen is a much better companion than any woman. Adam is one of the best students at his night school.

Dinah Morris

Dinah is a gentle and sweet-natured Methodist preacher. She is Mrs. Poyser's niece, and often visits the family at Hall Farm in Hayslope, where she preaches in the village square. When she is at home in Snowfield, she works at a mill. She is compassionate and helpful to those in need, and ministers to both Lisbeth Bede and Hetty Sorrel in their darkest hours. Seth Bede falls in love with her early in the novel, but she tells him she can never marry, as preaching is her calling. Later she belies those words by falling in love with his brother, Adam, and raising a family with him. Although her modest dress and demeanor are very different from those of her cousin, Hetty Sorrel, she is also described as very pretty. When Hetty is in prison, Dinah comes to her and begs her to confess so that she might feel God's forgiveness. She does, and faces her death bravely, although her sentence is commuted to exile. Dinah's modesty and goodness are apparent to everyone in the village, including Mr. Irwine, the village pastor.

Mr. Poyser

Martin Poyser is an easygoing, talented farmer and a happy man. He often worries about his flighty niece, Hetty, and encourages her to marry the admirable young carpenter, Adam. He is fond of his family, and is greatly upset at Hetty Sorrel's trial.

Mrs. Poyser

Witty and intelligent, Mrs. Poyser is a plain-speaking woman who expects a great deal from her family, although she spoils her youngest child, Totty. She is also compassionate when her niece Hetty gets into trouble. She is renowned in Hayslope for having the courage to speak up to the old squire when he crosses her, and she enjoys showing off her well-run dairy operation.

Hetty Sorrel

Hetty is a beautiful but shallow young peasant girl. She is very vain, and likes finery, although her social status is low. Her uncle is Mr. Poyser, and she works in Mrs. Poyser's dairy. She is also learning the skills of being a lady's maid, and she enjoys the attentions of Adam Bede and other young men. However, she has dreams of becoming the wife of Arthur Donnithorne, the grandson of the town squire. Although he falls in love and seduces her, he eventually tells her they can never marry. After Arthur leaves with his regiment, Hetty reluctantly accepts a proposal from Adam, feeling it will change her life for the better. However, before the marriage can take place, Hetty learns she is pregnant with Arthur's child. She runs off hoping to find him, and when she fails, she abandons her newborn child in a field. This leads to her exile, and eventually, her death. She dies before she can return to her home.

Colonel Towley

The magistrate at Hetty's prison remembers Dinah Morris from her sermon as he rode through Hayslope. Later he allows Dinah to enter Hetty's cell to pray with her.

THEMES

Appearance

The appearance of both the countryside and characters makes for a driving theme in *Adam Bede*. Although Hetty Sorrel is a peasant girl, she feels her beauty lends her higher aspirations. Rather

TOPICS FOR FURTHER STUDY

- The village of Hayslope is described as a beautiful place, full of fields and meadows. The village might be called a character in the book, down to the flapping of butterfly wings on a tree. Research what a small rural village at this time might have looked like, and then re-create it using cardboard and paint to make the houses and lands.

- George Eliot wrote, "Our deeds determine us, as much as we determine our deeds." How does this relate to Hetty Sorrel's actions? Research some historic examples of how people have been fairly or unfairly judged for their deeds. Then write a persuasive essay supporting either side of the issue, providing reasons and examples for your opinion.

- George Eliot was actually a woman named Mary Anne Evans. She took the pen name of George Eliot to hide her gender from the literary world. Does knowing the gender of a writer affect your reading of a novel? Research other writers who wrote under the name of a different gender, and discuss your findings in an essay.

- Hetty is exiled to another country after her sentence is commuted. Although it is never stated, the country is probably Australia, which served as a penal colony for many years. Read about the history of Australia and convicts. Write a story about what Hetty's life might have been like after she was exiled to this unfamiliar land.

- Nineteenth-century literature often features cautionary tales of young peasant women like Hetty who are seduced and betrayed by upper-class men. Thomas Hardy's *Tess of the d'Urbervilles* (1891) is a famous example. Director Roman Polanski adapted the book for a 1979 film called *Tess*. Watch the film, then write a paper in which you compared Tess to Hetty and address whether you think young women today face the same kinds of perils as Tess and Hetty.

---

than being satisfied with a life with a good man like Adam, she yearns to be a lady and the wife of Arthur Donnithorne. Her appearance, however, is deceptive. Both her suitors feel she is kind and sweet because they each believe that goodness is connected to a lovely face.

Hetty is clearly a silly and frivolous girl. Still, Adam supposes she will make a fine mother and good wife. Actually, Hetty actively dislikes children and is only truly interested in Adam when she is left without any recourse. Adam is not the only one fooled by Hetty's pretty face; Arthur Donnithorne believes Hetty is in love with him, instead of with the status he could bring her if he married her.

Dinah, on the other hand, dresses modestly and does not possess Hetty's lush beauty. However, her simple prettiness shines more brightly when her character is revealed as strong and honest. Appearances, Eliot implies, are not what they may seem; it is best for people to look within, and not without. This also holds true when Hetty trusts that Arthur Donnithorne will marry her because he looks upstanding to the community. Once again, looks are deceptive. Despite his stalwart appearance, Arthur is a coward who weasels out of confessing his time with Hetty to Mr. Irwine and writes a farewell letter to Hetty only after Adam beats him. Arthur is not what he appears to be either.

The beauty of the English countryside outside Hayslope is also deceptive. Although it is lovely and peaceful, with a noted quiet charm, the setting conceals the turbulent lives of the inhabitants. The countryside is also the scene of Hetty and Arthur's passionate embrace. When Hetty abandons her child, she does so in the midst of beautiful rural lands. Eliot seems to be urging readers to look deeper below the surface of the characters and their villages.

Family

Family ties play a key role in *Adam Bede*. "Family likeness," George Eliot writes, "has often a deep sadness in it. Nature, that great tragic dramatist, knits us together by bone and muscle, and divides us by the subtler web of our brains; blends yearning and repulsion; and ties us by our heart-strings to the beings that jar us at every movement." In these short sentences, she defines another strong theme: while the love and connection of family pulls the characters together, it also leads to despair.

When Thias Bede drowns early in the novel, his two sons are left to comfort their grieving mother. His father's passing also reminds Adam of his own less-than-wonderful qualities. It reveals he was often unkind and judgmental to his parents, and he struggles to be a better person when his father is gone. Lisbeth Bede can barely function without her husband, and she tries to draw her sons closer to her, even suggesting that Adam marry Dinah, Seth's longtime love.

Hetty's misdeeds also tear apart her family ties. She decides she cannot face her family in her condition, leading to her decision to abandon her child in a field. Her uncle, Mr. Poyser, is bereft at her trial and weeps at her sentence. Dinah returns from afar to hear her confession and accompany her to the gallows.

However, familial love can also be transformative. Seth embraces his brother's marriage to a woman whom he himself loved, and Mrs. Poyser does not judge Hetty for her actions. Although at the beginning of the novel Mrs. Poyser is hard on her family, she is surprisingly warm and accepting of Hetty's troubles. Family can be both blessing and curse for Eliot's characters.

STYLE

Realism

Realism refers to a type of fiction that depicts life as it is, without romanticizing or glossing over unappealing or unattractive elements. Authors who write in this style often focus on ordinary people, illuminating the characteristics that make everyone distinct and special.

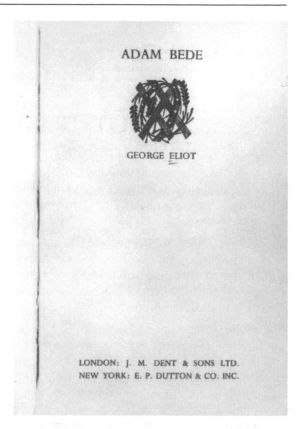

Title page of the novel (The Graduate Library, University of Michigan. Reproduced by permission.)

George Eliot is considered one of the first novelists who wrote realistic fiction. This was a distinct change in tone from that of earlier writers. By the early part of the eighteenth century, many writers wrote in the Romantic style. Novels written in the Romantic style tended to celebrate the world as beautiful and often used literature as an escape rather than an examination of everyday life. Characters in Romantic novels put imagination and feelings above measured thought.

Realism rejected these ideas, proposing that literature should be a conduit for observing the true inner framework of society. Most writers of this style also rejected overly dramatic or sensational events, preferring that characters make realistic decisions about situations. Realism emphasized humanism, a philosophy upholding reason above religious beliefs.

Hence, the decisions characters make are complex, often weighing an ethical or moral problem. While decisions have consequences, it is possible to argue both sides of the issue. Realistic novels are

COMPARE & CONTRAST

- **1800s:** Hetty Sorrel is disappointed in her hopes of marrying Arthur Donnithorne. In eighteenth-century England, a rich landowner and a dairymaid could not be married and accepted by society.

  Today: In 1986, Sarah Ferguson, a commoner, married Prince Andrew at Westminster Abbey. No longer is anyone in England barred from marrying whom they please because of divisions of wealth or property.

- **1800s:** Mrs. Poyser is incensed by the old squire's desire that she give up part of her land. In that time, farmers leased the land they worked. The owner of the land could decide to evict them if the crop failed or they felt the land could be better worked by another farmer.

  Today: Most modern-day farmers are owner-operators of their farms. They use computers and technical equipment to raise a large variety of crops.

- **1800s:** Dinah Morris is a Methodist preacher in *Adam Bede*. Female Methodist preachers were not uncommon in the middle and late 1700s. However, by the end of the novel, she has been forced to stop preaching. The Methodist church barred women from preaching in 1803.

  Today: Fifteen Protestant denominations regularly ordain women as ministers.

---

also objective and withhold judgment, despite depicting sordid lives or choices.

Many of these novels invoked the real language or dialect of the characters they portray. Middle-class readers were given insight into the struggles of the poor, and their own struggles as well.

Hetty Sorrel is a good example of a realistic character. Although she is beautiful, she is also described as shallow and materialistic. Yet her desire to have a wider life is understandable, and her family and friends are sympathetic to the desperation she feels before she abandons her child. Adam Bede is another example. He is both strong and enterprising, yet he is also unyielding and stubborn. Each of these characters behaves with the complexity of real people, struggling with the pain and problems of an ordinary life.

HISTORICAL CONTEXT

The Industrial Revolution

George Eliot wrote at a time when England's traditional agricultural economy was rapidly becoming replaced by industrialization. As the population grew and became richer, they wanted more available goods. Factories were established to fill this demand, and the population shifted from rural to city life. Growing towns meant larger labor pools were available to work in new factories.

Many young people left their farms to work in factories. These often were located where poverty was high. Poverty meant a high number of available workers. Their lives were hard, as they lived in shabby housing and worked long hours. Factory owners controlled many aspects of their workers' lives, often owning the poor housing. The conditions of the towns and factories were unsanitary and without laws to govern the conditions.

As a result of these conditions, many epidemics spread, including cholera. It was many years before an outcry over public health led to stronger laws and better conditions for the poor. The character of Dinah Morris in *Adam Bede* is not only a preacher, she is also a mill worker. George Eliot describes the town of Snowfield where the factory is located as a dismal place, where the poor needed her support and compassion. Dinah, in fact, must steel herself to go back to this work.

Realistic novels such as *Adam Bede* surged in popularity during this time period. Readers felt books describing the rise of factory towns and the squalid lives of factory workers accurately and movingly represented their own struggles. The nostalgic depiction of a vanishing rural life also may have led to the novel's immense popularity.

Women in Early Methodism

In *Adam Bede*, Dinah Morris is an inspirational and gifted Methodist preacher who goes to the village green to spread the word of God. She is also representative of the great evangelical revival movement that began in the early 1700s in both Great Britain and the United States.

Methodism was one of the primary new faiths of this movement. At a time when many churches preached about a wrathful God, Methodism took a gentler path. The church urged participants in services to understand God's love and guidance. From the beginning, women played an important role in this new church.

In the early years, Methodist leaders encouraged people of both genders to embrace their spiritual life. Famous women Methodist leaders included Jane Cooper and Ann Cutler, who were later revered for their work. Women also led Sunday school, visited the infirm and elderly, and often played a vital supporting role in their husband's ministries. These roles were encouraged within the church.

However, Methodism also encouraged the controversial practice of allowing females to preach publicly. In the mid-1700s, women went from enthusiastically welcoming new converts to gospel preaching and gathering. This was a shocking development for many, as the Church of England did not allow women to be ordained until the twentieth century.

But the situation soon changed. The Methodist church began discouraging the many women preachers who had sprung up in towns across the country. By the turn of the century, women were restricted from preaching to men. At the end of *Adam Bede*, an allusion is made to this when Dinah reveals she has been forced to stop preaching in the village. Some women, however, ignored the ban and continued to lead gospel readings. Many were responsible for converting thousands of parishioners.

In 1910, women Methodist ministers were finally welcomed back to the pulpit, and still later, they were granted equal status with male preachers.

Thatched-roof cottage (*Image copyright Chrislofoto, 2009. Used under license from Shutterstock.com*)

CRITICAL OVERVIEW

George Eliot was an unknown literary magazine editor when *Adam Bede* was published in 1859. With the publication of her first novel she quickly became revered with both critics and readers. Reviews of Eliot's debut were glowing.

An unnamed reviewer in the *Atlantic Monthly* lauded the work, saying, "*Adam Bede* is remarkable, not less for the unaffected Saxon style which upholds the graceful fabric of the narrative, and for the naturalness of its scenes and characters."

The influential Geraldine Jewsbury called *Adam Bede* "a novel of the highest class. Full of quiet power, without exaggeration and without any strain after effect, it produces a deep impression on the reader, which remains long after the book is closed."

Eliot's subsequent novels were also well received by critics, particularly her novel *Middlemarch*, considered by many to be her most accomplished work. However, some critics felt the books she wrote late in life were less successful and far more heavy-handed.

However, early feminists applauded the way Eliot addressed the fate of women, leading to a new vogue for Eliot's fiction in the early twentieth century. Later feminists also heralded her work, as it contemplated the role of women and questioned the nature of society and these roles.

It is undisputed that Eliot enjoyed great popularity during her lifetime. Her books were widely read and circulated. Eliot's prestige led her from poor literary editor to wealthy celebrity in a few short years. She is still considered one of the prominent writers of the Victorian age.

CRITICISM

Bay Anapol
In this essay, Anapol, an O. Henry Award–winning writer, muses on the narrow choices faced by eighteenth-century women like Hetty Sorrel and Dinah Morris.

Feminists theorize that the amount of freedom women have in society can be judged not on what choices they make with their lives, but on what choices are available to them. This becomes ever more clear when reading the Victorian classic *Adam Bede*. Author George Eliot, herself an independent and self-supporting writer and editor at a time when women rarely enjoyed any middle-class occupation, uses her female characters to illuminate their narrow choices. This is a probable consequence of Eliot's own struggle to live a fulfilling female life. Her struggle was so real, she did not identify herself as the author of her own books, fearful of revealing her unmarried relationship. As a result, the themes of choice and obstacles for women often arise in Eliot's work. The case can be made that Eliot shapes the characters of Dinah Morris, Hetty Sorrel, and to a lesser extent Mrs. Poyser, to fully illustrate how the society in which they lived—not their own desires—ultimately dictated their fates.

Noted women's history author Helena Wojtczak describes the early 1800s in England as a time when "women's sole purpose was to marry and reproduce.... Only if she had no brothers, came from a very wealthy family, and remained unmarried, could a woman become independent." Both Dinah and Hetty face additional constraints, as each is an orphan forced to rely on an extended family. Mrs. Poyser, a woman of some force and independent thought, gives shelter and advice to both women. All three exhibit an independence of thought and spirit that is hard-won and revealing.

Though Dinah is a poor orphan, she establishes her independence by working in a mill in Snowfield. This is hard and dirty work, but it does allow her to choose her own path, as she earns her own living. It is also historically accurate, as many women did resort to millwork at that

> FEMINISTS THEORIZE THAT THE AMOUNT OF FREEDOM WOMEN HAVE IN SOCIETY CAN BE JUDGED NOT ON WHAT CHOICES THEY MAKE WITH THEIR LIVES, BUT ON WHAT CHOICES ARE AVAILABLE TO THEM."

time. Dinah is unusual in some regards, however. While described as a pretty woman, she does not use her beauty for gain or position, but rather seems unaware of it. While she is soft-natured and quiet, her "feminine qualities" end there.

Dinah further establishes her independence by her preaching. Unlike traditional Church of England pastors such as Mr. Irwine, the Methodists embraced the idea of women in the pulpit. Women preachers in Methodist societies were not unheard of in 1799; in fact, many Methodist societies and bands were predominantly and sometimes exclusively organizations of women.

Yet the reaction of the Hayslope townspeople is one of curiosity and displeasure. Many want to run Dinah out of town, or at least out of the pulpit. As Mr. Casson remarks to a visitor, "She's own niece to Poyser's wife, an' they'll be fine an' vexed at her for making a fool of herself i' that way. But I've heard as there's no holding these Methodisses when the maggit's once got i' their head: many of 'em goes stark starin' mad wi' their religion." However, Dinah continues her preaching. She recognizes that not only has God called her, but that she is gifted at her calling.

Preaching is not a whim—Dinah has trained herself for the task. She is unusually literate. As Rebecca N. Mitchell points out in *Learning to Read: Interpersonal Literacy in Adam Bede,* the majority of people in Hayslope "do not hold books in church because 'not one of them could read,' but there is a palpable desire among the common workers to learn, despite very basic challenges.... Learning to read offers a means of achieving humanity for the characters within the novel." Indeed, in Bartle Massey's night school, Adam Bede struggles to approach Dinah's literacy. A modern-day reading would make Seth Bede somewhat patronizing when he remarks

WHAT DO I READ NEXT?

- *Middlemarch* (1872) is often considered to be George Eliot's masterpiece. Eliot tells the tale of social life in provincial England while recounting the unhappy and ill-fated marriage of a young doctor. Like her other novels, Eliot accurately and devastatingly depicts the social pitfalls and class system of her time.

- The Eliot novel *Silas Marner* (1861) also deals with the theme of status and family in Victorian England. When a miserly Silas Marner discovers an abandoned child and raises her, a community that had once rejected him embraces him. He also learns that love is more important than money.

- The classic *Tess of the d'Urbervilles* (1891) by Thomas Hardy also examines the life of a young woman who falls from grace. Tess, who gives birth to a child named Sorrow, is yet another victim of Victorian morality in this much-filmed novel. Often called a masterpiece of realistic fiction, Hardy's masterpiece is a worthy successor to George Eliot's work.

- Never the most popular of Jane Austen's domestic novels, *Mansfield Park* (1814) is the most complex study of mores and manners of Regency England. Fanny Price is sent away from her childhood home to live with her rich relatives at a large manor house. She falls in love with her cousin, but is considered unsuitable given her social status. However, Fanny's essential goodness prevails. Critics have decried the oddly happy ending that transpires.

- *Great Expectations* (1861) by Eliot's great fan and contemporary, Charles Dickens, truly defines the Victorian novel for some readers. Young Pip falls in love with the cold but beautiful Estella—a heartbreaker who resembles Hetty Sorrel in her desire to climb up the social ladder—but sees his love unrequited for many years. The novel was first published in the popular serial form in 1860 to great acclaim.

- Eric Hobsbawm's acclaimed *Industry and Empire: The Birth of the Industrial Revolution,* first published in 1968, provides a readable, engaging survey of the vast changes brought about in British society by the industrial revolution, which began just before the time in which *Adam Bede* is set.

---

that Dinah writes "wonderfully" for a woman, but in that era this is simply stating a fact.

However, though Dinah may have aspirations other than wife and mother, she also has characteristics that would suit her for a more conventional role. She is good with children and adept at comforting the bereaved Lisbeth Bede. Seth and Adam both want to marry her, and Mrs. Poyser also pressures Dinah to stay in Hayslope. But Dinah has made one of the only other choices available to her, forswearing marriage and children, saying, "I seem to have no room in my soul for wants and fears of my own, it has pleased God to fill my heart so full with the wants and sufferings of his poor people."

Dinah so fervently claims her wish to serve God and the afflicted, it comes as somewhat of a shock when, late in the book, she falls in love with Adam Bede. John B. Lamb argues that this was foreseen all along: "For all of the potential threat to the political and familial hierarchy Dinah's Methodism and her 'desire to live and die without husband or children' poses, she is a conservative influence on the inhabitants of Hayslope." Lamb further writes, "More importantly, she implies that such an arrangement, where one 'wait[s] to be guided' and is less bent on 'having his own will' is both natural and providential."

As Sarah Gates writes, "To her own eyes, Dinah is unequivocally a vessel of the Lord's

Word. Her calling is that of the Puritan saint, whose life is devoted to bringing religion to the 'flock.'" Yet she knew that by choosing to minister to that flock she must give up marriage and children. Ultimately, Eliot implies, this choice proves too difficult to make. When she finally gives in to her desire for Adam (and his desire for her), she seems to be at her happiest. Despite her devotion to her faith, she also appears to have saved herself from Snowfield and the mills where she must work to earn her keep. This classic choice of eighteenth-century women is the most efficient route out of a life of drudgery and poverty.

A life of poverty and drudgery also seems the likely fate for the lovely Hetty Sorrel, but Eliot is less kind in her descriptions. She is not a sweet speaker of God's word—she is a vain girl who wears shiny trinkets and dreams of living the life of the nobility. Though Hetty is even more physically beautiful than Dinah, she is shallow, silly, and vain. When Adam's father dies, she is completely disinterested in offering comfort or bringing funeral meats or sympathy. She seems almost oblivious to other people, and her treatment of those around her is rude and shabby. Even as she sits in her prison cell, she cannot bring herself to care deeply about the man who clearly loves her.

Unlike Dinah, Hetty attempts to put her beauty to use to buy herself a better life. Writes Rebecca Mitchell, "Her studied primping displays a vanity that is both controlling and controlled." But while sidelong glances and pretty blushes draw the attentions of Arthur Donnithorne, Hetty's beauty is ultimately useless in achieving her dream of a life of leisure. Her only possible choices in life are as a farmworker, a wife, or perhaps a lady's maid.

Instead of expanding her options, it can be argued that Hetty's beauty limits her choices even further. As Mrs. Pomfret observes, "She'll get neither a place nor a husband any sooner for it." And while Hetty's beauty may draw the interest of men, it also, as Mitchell writes, "eliminates the possibility of her being apprehended as an individual, a person distinct from that universal."

This opinion is borne out in Adam's perception of Hetty: he interprets her beauty to suggest an aptitude for children that she does not actually possess. "Nature has written out his bride's character for him in those exquisite lines

of cheek and lip and chin," Eliot writes. "How she will dote on her children!" But in fact, Hetty actively dislikes children, and describes her aunt's children as nothing but a nuisance, forcing Dinah to care for them. This clearly separates her from a traditional role.

In her most outrageous act, Hetty chooses a secret affair with Arthur Donnithorne. She embraces the notion that she will be able to flee her societal bondage through his love. When Arthur finally rejects her, Hetty becomes aware of her narrow choices. When her first choice to become a lady's maid is thwarted by her uncle, she agrees reluctantly to marry Adam Bede. This, she thinks, will at least be a change. Unlike her aunt, Hetty has no desire to make the most of her current situation in the dairy. She dreams of upward mobility, but her dreams, Eliot suggests, are on the scale allowed to her. Her dreams of a better life are based solely on her looks. There were, to be fair, few other avenues at that time to achieve what Hetty would call "change."

Of all three female characters, Mrs. Poyser appears to have taken the most conventional path with the least objection: not only is she a wife and mother, she encourages her nieces to be the same. Yet Mrs. Poyser serves in much more of a role than simply a matriach—she is a capable manager of the family's dairy farm, and she takes the lead in a matter that is expected to be handled by the men. Mrs. Poyser is the person who silences the landlord when he attempts to force the family to move away. Her outburst is also an assertion of her importance to her husband: he acknowledges he would be "loath to leave th' old place," yet he is reluctant to stand up to the landlord.

But even though Mrs. Poyser occupies a crucial place in her village and community, it has taken its toll on her. She is much admired, but "her health since the birth of Totty had not been equal to more positive labor than the superintendence of servants and children."

All three female characters show the effects of their choices in life. Hetty, of course, refuses to operate within the choices afforded her, and she pays a high price. Her fate is exile and disgrace. Dinah chooses to marry, but must sacrifice her ministry and her independence. By the end of the novel, the right to preach in public has been taken from her, with the approval of her husband. It can be argued that while each woman worked within the choices available to her, Eliot suggests that given the time period, they had tragically few choices from which to pick their path, if any.

Source: Bay Anapol, Critical Essay on *Adam Bede* in *Novels for Students,* Gale, Cengage Learning, 2010.

Rebecca N. Mitchell

In this excerpt, Mitchell discusses the ways Hetty Sorrel and Dinah Morris see themselves and others, essentially the ways in which they "read" themselves and others.

Adam Bede's rural setting is a particularly apt environment in which to document the wages of "reading" people because judgments are admittedly made based solely on appearance. This textual community and the assessments its members make offer a version of judgments that readers are likely to make, and when the characters' assumptions are proven incorrect, the critique applies to the meta-narrative as well. Mrs. Irwine, who insists that nature would not make "a ferret in the shape of a mastiff", is a typical voice within Hayslope. She explains that no one can ever "persuade me that I can't tell what men are by their outsides." Mrs. Irwine, as the novel shows, is wrong. Applying this paradigm to Hetty Sorrel—that charmingly pretty young woman whose looks overpower her true spirit—Eliot's intention seems clear. Nature may encode the body with messages about the soul, but they are neither explicit nor easily interpretable. (This explication is buttressed by Eliot's inclusion of the language of phrenology and physiognomy in the text.) These common critiques that Hetty is simply a soul-less ego nevertheless overlook what is achieved by reducing others' apprehension of her to pure surface: Hetty becomes a kind of text to be interpreted, allowing the novel to function as a critique of the ways her exterior is read.

While the contrast in appearance, style, and temperament between Dinah and Hetty is obvious, what is less immediately noticeable is the similarity in their psychical incompleteness. Both women demonstrate the drawbacks of an *incomplete* understanding of an individual possible both by others and by the individual herself. Hetty may be too invested in her physicality and Dinah not in touch enough with hers, but both negotiate their respective positions in the community—by attempting to regulate others' readings—through a renunciation of their bodies. The novel presents dual means of escape through growth, both consequences of slow and careful nuanced readings, not all of which are

focused on Hetty Sorrel. Hetty's problem—or the problem of Hetty—is not solved through a repudiation of her attractiveness, an overthrow of the sublimely beautiful and thoroughly shallow woman who has no place in Eliot's fiction. Instead, *Adam Bede* depicts the wages of personal and communal misreading.

To be certain, many Victorian novels depend upon the trope of reading and misreading to explore class relations and communality or, perhaps more commonly, to frame character growth. Eliot often employs a pair of characters whose progression through the plot is chronologically concurrent. Dorothea and Rosamond, Maggie and Lucy, Daniel and Gwendolen all progress, but their growth is measured not only by the protagonist's development from her younger days, but more often by her advancement over her counterpart. Rich readings ensue from those comparisons. But considering the stories of the two women as parallel rather than as constant contrasts highlights Hetty's (albeit relative) growth and Dinah's initial incompleteness.

Source: Rebecca N. Mitchell, "Learning to Read: Interpersonal Literacy in Adam Bede," in *Papers on Language and Literature: A Journal for Scholars and Critics of Language and Literature*, Vol. 44, No. 2, Spring 2008, pp. 145–167.

Debra Gettelman

In this excerpt, Gettelman examines how George Eliot comes to define realist fiction as relying on the author's discipline over the reader's unruly imagination.

Adam Bede is concerned at several levels with predicting, prescribing, and exploring how the mind of the reader might work. Eliot's addresses to the "lady reader" in chapter 17 are only the most contrived among several images the novel offers of the reading mind, and I want to suggest that these famous attempts at scripting her fictional reader's acts of imagining ultimately signal an acknowledgment that her real readers have minds of their own. For in contrast to other Victorian novelists, Eliot is remarkable for the extent to which she acknowledges that readers bring the private, affective content of their minds to bear on a text. Unlike Trollope, who in *Barchester Towers* repeatedly refers to the reader's mind as if it were stocked only with the reading of other novels, Eliot in *Adam Bede* makes use of the deepest stores of her readers' inner lives, in an effort to stir an imaginative response in its

> THROUGHOUT *ADAM BEDE*, ELIOT BRINGS
> TO THE SURFACE THE NOVELIST'S UNSPOKEN
> DEPENDENCE UPON THE READER'S CAPACITY TO
> ENVISION."

reader which will ultimately have an outward effect in the world.

Throughout *Adam Bede*, Eliot brings to the surface the novelist's unspoken dependence upon the reader's capacity to envision. The novel opens with the famous comparison of the novelist to a conjuror of images: "With a single drop of ink for a mirror, the Egyptian sorcerer undertakes to reveal to any chance comer far-reaching visions of the past. This is what I undertake to do for you, reader." At one level, such direct addresses to the reader are a component of the novel's realism: speaking directly to the reader appears as an acknowledgment of, and attempt to overcome, the underlying act of fabrication. Yet such unveilings also participate in a further invention, as the "reader" referred to at such moments turns out to be in many cases himself conjured—imagined to evince a great many prejudices, deficiencies, and objections in the process of envisioning. "'This rector of Broxton is little better than a pagan!' I hear one of my lady, readers exclaim," begins chapter 17. Bodenheimer suggests that such exaggerated, ironic attributing to the reader of thoughts unsympathetic to the author's aims is in fact meant to serve a rhetorical purpose, rather than to impute the real reader's response: as in Eliot's early letters, the author creates for herself an uninformed audience to whom she may explicate her views all the more earnestly.

But Adam Bede also at times addresses the real reader, and does so in order to invite him: to conjure his own, more realistic images. When Eliot first introduces the Poysers' farm, she prefaces her description of the house's interior with a command that the reader participate in the act of invention: "Put your face to one of the glass panes in the right-hand window: what do you see?...And what through the left-hand window?" While a description of the house follows, framing it in this way brings to the surface what Elaine Scarry shows, in *Dreaming by the Book*, are the usually embedded

instructions an author of a literary text gives the reader to perform a series of imaginative acts, in order to heighten the vivacity with which he envisions the fictional world. Here, however, Eliot highlights the act of solicitation. "I beseech you to imagine Mr Irwine...", she writes at another moment, laying bare the negotiation between author and reader on which her novel depends.

The more Eliot asks her reader to imagine on his own, the more she serves one of her stated aims: to develop the wishful reader's capacity to sustain continuities between the fictional and 'real' worlds. A particularly open–ended invitation, for instance, appears in an early passage in which Hetty's beauty is first described. Eliot claims that only the reader's own store of mental pictures can supply Hetty's likeness:

> It is of little use for me to tell you that Hetty's cheek was like a rose-petal, that dimples played about her pouting lips, that her large dark eyes hid a soft roguishness under their long lashes...; it is of little use for me to say how lovely was the contour of her pink and white neckerchief, tucked into her low plum–coloured stuff bodice, or how the linen butter-making apron, with its bib, seemed a thing to be imitated in silk by duchesses...—of little use, unless you have seen a woman who affected you as Hetty affected her beholders, for otherwise, though you might conjure up the image of a lovely woman, she would not in the least resemble that distracting, kitten-like maiden.

The iteration of authorial insufficiency here— "it is of little use for me to tell you"—is in one sense quite rhetorically conventional when Hetty's image is given in such purple, sensuous detail. Despite the sumptuous luxury of the passage which verges on irony, however, Eliot ends the catalogue with that sincere appeal to the reader's memory: "unless you have seen a woman who affected you as Hetty affected her beholders." Though an image might be conjured for the reader, and a sensation even stirred in him, neither carries the affect of real–life experience, which is seen to be beyond the novelist's representational ability, and yet is absolutely required to imbue the passage with deeper meaning in the reader's mind.

In inviting the reader to imagine his own past experience, Eliot not only recognizes but relies upon a second form of readerly mental activity: one which sends the reader's thoughts backwards, rather than forwards; out of the novel's pages, rather than further along in them; and is defined by its realist authenticity, rather than its wishful invention. What Eliot hoped to achieve in evoking such recollection is evident in a letter about the critical reception she sought for *Middlemarch*: "What one's soul thirsts for is the word which is the reflection of one's own aim and delight in writing—the word which shows that what one meant has been perfectly seized, that the emotion which stirred one in writing is repeated in the mind of the reader." This statement of Eliot's hoped-for response, however, comes as part of an expression of her ideal having not been reached; "the mind of the reader" had—from a variety of causes—a mind of its own. "In writing any careful presentation of human feelings, you must count on that infinite stupidity of readers who are always substituting their crammed notions of what ought to have been felt for any attempt to recall truly what they themselves have felt under like circumstances," she later writes of attempting to evoke recollection (52). Moreover, even as she expresses a desire for her meaning to be "perfectly seized" and "repeated" in the reader's mind, she also, in the opening of her essay "The Natural History of German Life," indicates an awareness that the very "picture-writing of the mind" is itself highly variable. The mental pictures called up even by the single word "railways," Eliot notes, differ widely in the railway engineer, traveler, or shareholder, from those of the man "who is not highly locomotive," and visualizes only "the image either of a 'Bradshaw,' or of the station with which he is most familiar, or of an indefinite length of tram-road."

The "picture-writing of the mind": such discussions point to the overlap between Eliot's understanding of how the mind conjures images and the work of her partner, G. H. Lewes. Lewes's range of writings in the fields of literary journalism, physiology, and natural history began to focus increasingly on the study of the mind from roughly 1857 until his death in 1878, the exact years of Eliot's novelistic career. The work of psychology in which Lewes was engaged serves as an important context for Eliot's representations of mental activity, particularly in *Adam Bede*, which was written, as mentioned earlier, in the same room as *The Physiology of Common Life*. In fact, with the two authors writing "at tables close to each other," Gordon Haight notes, "the scratch of pen and rustle of paper" were audible, and to Eliot at least, distracting. This literal proximity of Victorian psychology to Eliot's own writing is a powerful emblem of its influence on her representations of mind.

Source: Debra Gettelman, "Reading Ahead in George Eliot," in *Novel: A Forum on Fiction*, Vol. 39, No. 1, Fall 2005, pp. 25–47.

Elizabeth Deeds Ermarth

In this excerpt, Ermarth discusses Adam Bede *in the context of a larger thesis that explores how Eliot's work demonstrates an individual's influence and effect on an entire community.*

George Eliot originally planned a fourth "Scene," but her subject would "not come under the limitations of the title 'Clerical Life,'" as she wrote to her publisher, so she "inclined to take a large canvas for it, and write a novel" (Letters, 2:381). "It will be a country story—full of the breath of cows and the scent of hay" (2:387). *Adam Bede* (1859) traces in six books six phases in the community of Hayslope, a fictional rural community rooted in custom which change threatens and alters. Book 1 introduces the separate households and separate ways of the main characters. Adam Bede is a carpenter like his father and lives with his brother Seth in the cottage where they grew up, under the care of their querulous mother Lisbeth. The death of Adam's father early in the book makes way for changes in Adam's life, changes that in his mind include the blooming Hetty Sorrel, niece of the Poysers. The Poyser household at Hall farm, compared with the plain, even constricted ways of the Bede cottage, is full of vitality, with its dairy, orchards, meadows, and children. The Poysers, in turn, are tenants of Squire Donnithorne, grandfather of young Arthur, who will soon come of age and become master in Hayslope. Arthur lives with his grandfather at the Hall, a hereditary establishment for a hereditary landlord. The small but genteel household of the Reverend Irwine completes the group. He is one of George Eliot's sympathetic portraits of the honorable, effective clergyman, comfortable in his elegant habits but mindful of duties to a widowed mother and sickly sister, and far better for his parishioners than a more dogmatic and consistent man could ever be. The only main character not associated with a particular place in Hayslope is Hetty's cousin, Dinah Morris, a young Methodist minister who lives in Stoniton, a place that, as its name suggests, differs considerably from Hayslope.

These various households, linked by a common social order, differ in their particular habits but all rest complacently on the sense that their communal ways, confirmed over centuries, are the right, indeed the only, ways. They all belong to the same community, go to the same church on Sunday where they occupy the same places; they observe the same rituals of celebration and sorrow, during Sunday worship, or birthdays, or funerals,

> ONE OF THE STRIKING ACCOMPLISHMENTS OF THIS NOVEL IS THE WAY GEORGE ELIOT LINKS THE VISION OF NATURAL BEAUTY WITH THE SOCIAL HARMONY IN ITS MIDST."

or midsummer and harvest feasts. It is a concentric universe whose rhythmic harmonies, George Eliot makes us feel, have remained undisturbed for centuries. The problem in Hayslope is not absence of community, but absence of self–consciousness and responsibility about community, and consequently, a fatal lack of control over it. They mistakenly associate their customs with the natural events with which their livelihoods are so closely bound, and thus they do not recognize their cultural independence from nature and necessity.

The opening scene is a perfect example of this attitude. It opens in the carpenter's workshop where Adam works in the sunlight, his plane sending out pine-wood shaving to mingle their scent with the elder-bushes outside the open windows, and his voice intermittently singing a hymn. The whole scene—the carpenter's work, the sunshine, the song of religious celebration—has the serenity characteristic of Adam and his community, the serenity of people untroubled in their larger views. The sunshine itself seems to guarantee the human light of intention and reverence. But even as these circumstances are being introduced, we follow the flirtation between the young lord and the dairymaid that eventually will dissipate the sunshine and alter the basic conditions of life in Hayslope.

The only oblique notes in book 1 apart from this flirtation are introduced with Dinah Morris. It is she who comes to comfort the widowed Lisbeth Bede, to warn and comfort Hetty, and to bring the community her message as a preacher. Her ventures into Hayslope bring glimpses of another, darker world, as if even the beauty of Hayslope nature were partly a reflex of the human richness in its midst. When the people gather on the common to hear Dinah preach, they come together for something new and quite different from their customary ritual celebrations and observances, and they exercise in new ways their private consciences.

The second book, however, introduces various oblique perspectives and brings the viewpoints of various outsiders more to bear on the circumstances. These include the narrator, who discourses on the importance of common life, Mr. Irwine as seen from a perspective much later than the events of this story, and Bartle Massey, the night-school teacher, who is an outsider in Hayslope. Bartle lives on the edge of town and at night teaches the illiterate farmers and artisans of Hayslope how to read and write and do sums. In different ways both he and Dinah reflect the extensive power of the Evangelical revival in encouraging the rural population to learn: both how to work with their own heads rather than relying on the thinking of others, and how to gain the tools for self-governance, beginning with reading the Bible but, as in Bartle's school, extending far beyond. These two characters, however, remain marginal to the central events until those events blow apart the community's confidence in its "natural" ways.

Book 3 deals exclusively with the birthday feast for Arthur Donnithorne, a ritual celebration that is a long timeless moment in the novel. The dinner, the health-drinking, the games, and the dance all have their time-honored protocols and celebrate the renewal of a traditional, even feudal social organization. It is completely appropriate in such a vision that the point of view is handed to the older gentry, looking on this confirmation of an entire order. But even here, in the contacts between Arthur and Hetty, are clear hints of another agenda and another order of event. In book 4, time and the processes it unfolds threaten the timeless order with the consequences of secret life, consequences that become public knowledge in book 5 after Hetty has fled her engagement to Adam and fled Hayslope in search of Arthur.

The chief events of the plot are events that often are assumed to be natural—Arthur's seduction of Hetty, the birth of her baby, its death—and yet there is an almost complete suppression of natural explanation. None of the events just mentioned is represented in the novel. They are unmistakably foreshadowed, and their harsh, inexorable consequences are felt, but they remain invisible, as if outside the margins of consciousness in the text. George Eliot elides these events, not because she shrinks from the facts of life—a brief summary of *Adam Bede* disarms that speculation—but because she saw these events as the results of other, more powerful, less visible, events taking place in individual consciousness. The physical results of these private motives are concrete, indisputable, given, but they result from the operation of cultural processes of motivation and intention that are less visible but more complex and just as real. These are the more important focus of attention. As always in her fiction, moral life is a process, not a point. To consider events apart from these conditions is a potent kind of exclusiveness that is as vulgar and that distorts perception of the common ground just as much as doctrines and snobbery do. She deliberately minimizes the melodramatic, the heroic, the discrete event—what she calls the "vulgar coercion of conventional plot"—in order to concentrate on the links between events in those ideas people carry around with them, light as air but powerful as acid or sunlight. The event as incarnation is her constant object of focus. Ideas and acts are not separate; what we think, we do not necessarily do, but we rarely do something without precedents in consciousness and memory. In *Adam Bede* she follows most closely the development of such compelling precedents, especially in Arthur Donnithorne.

In Arthur's case, the precedents are simultaneously cultural and personal. The wicket gate that is "never opened" ch. 6, the one between the Hall and the farm, is the one Hetty and Arthur use for their secret meetings; it is also a symbol of the illicit connection, the classic privilege of lordship—a custom so barbarous that Arthur would be horrified to be associated with it, and yet it is a convention he revives by his actions as if it has wrought itself into his habitual thought in ways he is unconscious of and does not allow for. Despite his individual self-consciousness and good intentions, his story is an obvious traditional tale of the lord and the dairymaid, and he acts it out as if he had a script. What is at stake is not so much the compulsion of tradition as it is the way tradition itself and even legend arises from and is reconfirmed in the actions of individual men and women.

George Eliot remorselessly exposes the slow but certain process of Arthur's self-betrayal, and consequently betrayal of the community in which older depends upon his exertion of his proper function. His idea of himself as noble patron, on the brink of assuming his role as feudal master, and full of optimistic visions of himself in various acts of generosity, conflicts with his temptation to seduce the maid he knows he never will marry. Liking to believe in only one alternative, he does not hearken to the real presence of another. "He no

sooner fixed his mind on the probable consequence of giving way to the emotions which had stolen over him . . . than he refused to believe such a future for himself". Though he vacillates between two minds, his behavior is increasingly of a piece. Like "many men since his day" he rides a long way to avoid a meeting with Hetty, "and then galloped hastily back lest he should miss it". He loses himself wilfully, enjoying the oblivion, as does Hetty, with her "narcotic daydreams" of being married and a great lady. Whatever he may intend, what he does is what counts, and George Eliot brilliantly examines the process whereby thought and action go separate ways.

> This is not what he meant to say. His arms is stealing round the waist again, it is tightening its clasp; he is bending his face nearer and nearer to the round cheek, his lips are meeting those pouting child-lips, and for a long moment time has vanished. He may be a shepherd in Arcadia for aught he knows, he may be the first youth kissing the first maiden, he may be Eros himself, sipping the lips of Psyche—it is all one.

There was no speaking for minutes after. They walked along with beating hearts till they came within sight of the gate at the end of the wood. Then they looked at each other, not quite as they had looked before, for in their eyes there was the memory of a kiss.

In widening the scope to include mythic precedents George Eliot's narrator not only suggests a certain kind of sensation, but also suggests the way in which it momentarily obliterates the individual awareness. As personal memory disappears and with it the history that involves consequences, we momentarily lose the sense of choice and willed action. Arthur recovers himself after Hetty is gone, but he cannot resist losing himself again and again. Like Janet Dempster with her bottle of brandy, and like characters in all the novels who rely on gambling or moral superiority or daydreams, Arthur takes the opiate of delusion and absolves him of responsibility for his own actions, leaving them to the mercy of his changeable desires. He cannot govern his actions because he will not accept the fact that both of his conflicting desires cannot be satisfied. To be the rightful lord of the estate requires him to fulfill a trust to his friends. He betrays this trust when he seduces Hetty, good intentions notwithstanding. Good intentions, not acted upon, have no power compared with the intentions evident in his actual behavior, however he may wish it otherwise.

What Arthur does in particular can be determined only by him, but he could be hindered or influenced by others. As it happens, and because things are complex in human situations to begin with, and because each person is satisfied with his own picture of circumstances, Arthur's friends do not guess the problem in time. Adam believes that the flirtation is superficial and that Hetty's blushes are for him, "having woven for himself an ingenious web of probabilities, the surest screen a wise man can place between himself and the truth". Arthur determines to confess to Reverend Irwine but his determination is weakened by a series of deflections and he deflects again for fear of looking like a fool. "The idea of Hetty had just crossed Mr. Irwine's mind as he looked inquiringly at Arthur, but his disclaiming, indifferent answer confirmed the thought . . . that there could be nothing serious in that direction. There was no probability that Arthur ever saw her except at church". Even Dinah, possessed of some instinct to warn Hetty of trouble, only succeeds in annoying and frightening her. And so Arthur and Hetty maintain a life apart, and after Arthur's departure with his regiment, Hetty supports her secret alone. She disappears in search of Arthur, Adam follows in pursuit of false leads, Hetty seeks Dinah in Stoniton after failing to find Arthur, but Dinah has gone elsewhere. As she fades from our view she has become an alienated, scarcely human creature of "objectless wandering, apart from all love, caring for human beings only through her pride, clinging to life only as the hunted wounded brute clings to it". The terror of her solitude, the pathos of her dependence on the community she has contemptuously left behind make Hetty's value and the anguish of her helplessness exquisitely felt.

As customary usage begins to appear less "natural" and more problematic, and as the possibilities outside customary usage appear stronger, the marginal figures of Dinah and Bartle assume increasing importance. Unlike the other characters, each has a vocation that does not depend on the structure of custom in Hayslope, and so after custom has fallen away they still have a clear sense of purpose and have the freedom that attends it. As the pressures on customary ways intensify they become mediators, helping Adam and Hetty to imagine and accept alternatives. They are instruments of resignation that enable Adam and Hetty to gain control of their actions once again by beginning with their acceptance of the actual events in which they have been willing or unwilling participants.

Adam's case is not the most moving, but it is especially interesting because his strong sense of vocation and duty has none of the sympathy or fellow-feeling that might be expected to attend such commitment. He has little of the flexibility of the more artistic man of purpose painting his picture with an idea independent of specific results. His strengths have a "correlative hardness" that makes him humorless and short of patience. He shrinks from the suffering, imprisoned Hetty as if he were a cruel man, and his first response to the news of her arrest for child murder is, "It *can't* be!". But it not only can be, it is; what "ought" to be crumbles in the face of it. Bartle's ministrations are ungentle but effective in getting Adam his inability to accept the fact. And his acceptance given him a new consciousness beside which his old seems narrow and weak. The narrator describes the final result of this process in Adam in terms that evoke George Eliot's description of the artist in life, the one who follows an idea like the Evangelical conception of duty. "The growth of higher feeling within us is like the growth of faculty, bringing with it a sense of added strength: we can no more wish to return to a narrower sympathy, than a painter or a musician can wish to return to his cruder manner, or a philosopher to his less complete formula". "I used to be hard sometimes," Adam tells Bartle at Hetty's trial, but "I'll never be hard again".

Hetty's case is the most dramatic and painful because she is least prepared to cope with the violent changes she endures—abandonment in her pregnancy, the physical trauma of childbirth, the death of her baby, the prolonged psychological trauma of someone coping for the first time with anonymity and solitude, the humiliation of a public trial and of imprisonment, and the threat of execution. Here again the heaviest burden falls on the one least able to bear it. Mrs. Poyser complains early in the novel that "her heart's as hard as a pebble", but like Caterina, Hetty's anomalous position isolates her in a family where blood ties are everything; and her demonstrable incapacity for sympathy is not entirely surprising in a community based on hierarchical social bonds rather than on a sense of common ground. When she reappears at her trial, after disappearing from our view, she has the same remoteness and habits of concealment that undid her initially. Her "hard" heart gives up its secrets only on the eve of her execution after Dinah has come to her cell. There Hetty at first seems "like an animal that gazes, and gazes, and keeps aloof," but she clings to the "human contact" of Dinah's hand, a contact that finally invades her reserve. The brightness of the opening chapters has disappeared completely, along with the leisurely rhythms of the opening books. The pace has accumulated speed, contracting to a point "in that grey clear morning, when the fatal cart with the two young women in it was descried by the waiting watching multitude, cleaving its way towards the hideous symbol of a deliberately-inflicted sudden death". At this vertiginous moment, the last-minute reprieve that saves Hetty from the gallows for a more lingering death as a transported criminal, is brought through the crowd at a gallop by Arthur Donnithorne. By this point the entire style of the novel has unsettled the easy assumption made by the citizens of Hayslope that their ways belong somehow to the eternal nature of things.

While Adam and Hetty have painfully endured the loss of their dreams and the acceptance of harsh facts, Arthur has used his privilege in an attempt to prevent himself from losing any alternatives; his will and his way are one, or so he thinks. The degree of his self-absorption is stressed by the brilliant stroke of having Arthur shifted from one world to another abruptly. He leaves Hayslope complacently looking forward to returning as its master. As he steps off the coach after months of absence he positively savors his own "good nature." "Arthur had not an evil feeling in his mind towards any human being: he was happy, and would make every one else happy that came within his reach." Considering that Hetty is in jail awaiting execution, his friends are in disgrace and despair as a consequence of his actions, nothing could be more odious than this narcissistic fantasy, and nothing more false than his good intentions. His first thought is to refresh himself, his second to sit on his velvet cushion to open his letters, the first being a letter from Mr. Irwine marked urgent. With an agreeable anticipation of soon seeing the writer, Arthur breaks the seal and reality breaks in on him.

> "I send this letter to meet you...I will not attempt to add by one word of reproach to the retribution that is now falling on you: any other words that I could write at this moment must be weak and unmeaning by the side of those in which I must tell you the simple fact.

> "Hetty Sorrel is in prison, and will be tried on Friday for the crime of child murder..."

The recognition of what his actions mean, the recognition that he *is* what he has done regardless of intentions, the recognition that he has deliberately trod the path away from his own dreams, all dawn on Arthur too late to change more than Hetty's sentence. The "simple fact" is the incarnation of his will and his intention and no wishing can remove this unaccommodating actual fact. The private, invisible habits that permit him to overstep his own acknowledged bounds do not remain invisible forever. With the changes that he helps to bring into being, a whole public way of life is permanently altered.

Book 6 is more muted and restrained than the opening book. The glad, bright morning belonged to a confidence founded on unreliable illusions and visions of action out of touch with the facts of ambition, secret indulgence, and complacency about the commonplace things that bind together separate lives.

The novel demonstrates the truth of Mr. Irwine's observations to Adam and to Arthur that people cannot isolate themselves. "Men's lives are as thoroughly blended with each other as the air they breathe", and our actions have consequences that are "hardly ever confined to ourselves". Human influence extends to all perception, even perception of nature. One of the striking accomplishments of this novel is the way George Eliot links the vision of natural beauty with the social harmony in its midst. Hetty's example is the most extended. She blossoms in a security she takes for granted in Hayslope. In the supremely domestic context of the dairy farm, her beauty is the delicate, fragile beauty of "kittens, or very small downy ducks making gentle rippling noises with their soft bills, or babies just beginning to toddle." When she leaves the world of dairy sounds and sunshine she enters a cold, ugly, dark world where her beauty disappears, as if she passes from the world of light and speech to what might as well be a grave. In the darkness outside her society her beauty disappears immediately, as if at the snap of some magician's fingers an enchanted world had vanished. In "the horror of this cold, and darkness, and solitude—out of all human reach," where she can barely make out the rapid motion of some creature in the field, where she lies in a "hovel of furze" Hetty's beauty vanishes with her vitality. "It was almost as if she were dead already, and knew that she was dead, and longed to get back to life again". With Hetty's beauty as with Adam's sunny confidence, the tide of events completely changes the appearance of light, as if it and Hetty's beauty and Adam's confidence all are functions of their place in a changeable, even fragile human society.

Source: Elizabeth Deeds Ermarth, "Chapter 3: Common Ground: Scenes of Clerical Life, Adam Bede, The Mill on the Floss in 'George Eliot.,'" in *Twayne's English Authors Series Online*, G. K. Hall, 1999.

Philip Collins

In this article, Collins presents a brief overview of Adam Bede, *from the novel's reception and plot to characterization and the novel's ending.*

Appearing in 1859, an *annus mirabilis* of Victorian publication, alongside *A Tale of Two Cities*, *The Virginians*, Meredith's *The Ordeal of Richard Feverel*, Tennyson's *Idylls of the King*, Mill's *On Liberty*, Omar Khayyam, *The Origin of Species*, and other notable works, this first novel was a runaway success and established George Eliot "at once among the masters of the art" (the *Times*, 12 April 1859). It was the novel of the year, acclaimed by reviewers as "enlarging the scope of fiction" (Michael Wolff in *1859: Entering an Age of Crisis*, 1959). Eliot first intended it for her *Scenes of Clerical Life* but decided that its potentialities exceeded that series' short-story/nouvelle length. The public excitement about it led to renewed speculation about the identity of "George Eliot" and soon her incognito was destroyed.

The basic plot of the humbly-born pretty girl caught between a decent faithful lover from her own class and a more glamorous but unprincipled rich admirer (wicked baronet, squire, "gentleman," industrial magnate) was very familiar in contemporary drama and fiction (Mary/Jem/Carson in Gaskell's *Mary Barton*, Emily/Ham/Steerforth in *David Copperfield*) but Eliot's treatment of it was characteristically original. Not only does the girl fail to escape intact in time from this imbroglio but instead, tragically and realistically, becomes pregnant, lets her baby die and is sentenced to death for infanticide; but also the characters and motives of the girl and her seducer are explored with uncommon intelligence, inwardness, sagacity, and sympathy (which does not inhibit firm moral judgment). Henry James, in 1866, regarded the girl, Hetty Sorrel, as Eliot's most successful female figure. Adam Bede, her humble carpenter lover, has been less admired as a creation, though at a non-literary level his depiction was much praised by an old friend of the author's father: "That's Robert [Evans], that's Robert to the life!"

Adam, as George Eliot recorded, has some of her father's qualities (steady, proud craftsmanship, upright character): "Adam . . . by no means a marvellous man . . . was not an average man.

Yet such men are reared here and there in every generation of our peasant artisans with an inheritance of affections nurtured by a simple family life of common need and common industry, and an inheritance of faculties trained in skilful courageous labour."

The novel's climactic event the girl's conviction for infanticide came from family memory too. Eliot's Methodist preacher aunt Mrs. Samuel Evans had accompanied a lass during her final night in a condemned cell and on her way to the scaffold and had received her confession to killing her child. This incident implied a seducer and, given the fictional conventions of the day, another (socially humbler but morally superior) lover. To marry the latter off to the estimable Methodist lady, Dinah Morris, after a decent interval, was as predictable as the girl's last-minute reprieve at the scaffold ("a horseman cleaving the crowd at full gallop . . . it is Arthur Donnithorne [the seducer], carrying in his hand a hard-won release from death"). These later events and developments carry less conviction than the rest of the narrative where, as Eliot puts it in her famous chapter 17 manifesto, she is "dreading nothing, indeed, but falsity, which, in spite of one's best efforts, there is reason to dread. Falsehood is so easy, truth so difficult." Her later succumbing to temptation does not, however, negate the very substantial merits of the body of her "simple story," appropriately prefixed by an epigraph from Wordsworth, promising "Clear images . . . Of nature's unambitious undergrowth" and "something more than brotherly forgiveness" for those who went astray.

"Our supreme novel of pastoral life," V.S. Pritchett has called it, though he was irritated by what he regarded as failures in its presentation of sexuality. Eliot certainly fulfilled her promise to her publisher (17 October 1857) that it would be "a country story full of the breath of cows and the scent of hay." Memories of rural Warwickshire ("Loamshire") were backed by typically scholarly research into events before her lifetime (the action begins in 1799 and ends in 1807). This related especially to Methodist activities, here depicted with uncommon understanding and respect. The well-named village of Hayslope with its manor and parsonage, farms, workshops, and places of assembly, is presented in loving and convincing detail. Mrs. Poyser, the kindly but redoubtable farmer's wife who is Hetty's and Dinah's aunt, became a legendary figure overnight (quoted in Parliament soon after publication date) for her fluent forth-right folk-wisdom vigorously expressed in bucolic imagery: "I'm not one o' those as can see the cat i' the dairy, an' wonder what she's come after" (though, followed immediately by "I aren't like a bird-clapper, forced to make a rattle when the wind blows on me," this trick of speech can become mechanical).

The narrator, a more sophisticated and better informed Mrs. Poyser, is equally liberal with tough–minded generalizations: "Our deeds determine us, as much as we determine our deeds," "that fuller life which had come to him from his acquaintance with deep sorrow" and with sharp assessments of individuals ("Yes, the actions of a little trivial soul like Hetty's, struggling amidst the serious, sad destinies of a human being *are* strange"). Opinions differ on how fully and fairly Eliot "sympathises" trademark word with pretty but simple ("shallow") minded Hetty and high–minded greyclad Dinah. But Hetty's foolish dreams of marrying the heir to the manor and becoming a "lady" with a plentiful wardrobe, and her lone sufferings before and after childbirth, are splendidly rendered, as is the process whereby the fundamentally decent but wobbly-conscienced Arthur allows himself to continue seeing Hetty and eventually to seduce her and to lose the respect of Adam (whom he much values) and eventually of the whole village (Hetty's trial coincides with his coming into his inheritance).

As often in Eliot elements of the conventional happy ending the novel's penultimate chapter is entitled "Marriage Bells" are balanced by severer fates: death for Hetty as she was due for release, disappointment for Adam's brother Seth, who had unsuccessfully courted Dinah and is provided with no alternative mate, and disgrace for Arthur, though he is finally granted a purgatorial illness after which he may be largely forgiven (a frequent dénouement device in fiction of the period).

Source: Philip Collins, "Adam Bede: Overview," in *Reference Guide to English Literature*, edited by D. L. Kirkpatrick, St. James Press, 1991.

W. L. Collins

In this article, Collins provides a nineteenth-century review of Adam Bede, which focuses on characterization and theme.

[Precedence] may fairly be claimed by Dinah Morris, the Methodist preacher, both because . . . she is the true heroine of the story, and because she is a stranger . . . She believes herself called to preach. At twenty-one her call came.

The author of *Adam Bede* deserves our thanks for having selected a country rector of the old and much-abused type to play the ecclesiastical part in his story, and for having reproduced him with so much care and truth.

His character is drawn somewhat at length for Mr. Irwine is plainly a favourite with his author as well as his parishioners but there is not a word too much.

[Mrs. Poyser] will probably be the most popular individual in the book with the general reader, who takes it up chiefly in search of entertainment. A most delightful person is Mrs. Poyser; quite a character, but with a merit for which the comic characters of fiction are in general by no means remarkable, that she never conveys to the reader the least notion of exaggeration, or wearies him by the perpetual recurrence of the one note of facetiousness which is supposed to be characteristic, and at which he is expected to laugh long after the joke has become a melancholy nuisance. Not so Mrs. Poyser; she comes out with a fund of droll remarks in the most unexpected places, and possesses a vein of grotesque poetry, which embraces all objects from the highest to the most familiar. Yet she is as natural as a photograph.

We have only selected here some few of the most prominent characters, but these volumes are full of such individualities, either carefully finished, or sketched by as we hope our readers will by this time have satisfied themselves a master-hand.

[The] great merit of *Adam Bede* consists in the singular grace and skill with which [the] characteristic details of country life are rendered. To say of such a book that it does not depend for its main attraction on the development of a carefully-constructed plot, is little more than saying that it is a novel of character rather than action. With one great exception, the masters of fiction of our own day and among these Mr. Eliot has incontestably made good his place either fail in the constructive power, or will not condescend to write a story. They throw all their force into the delineation of character, and the enunciation of their own favourite philosophy by the actors whom they place upon the stage. This Mr. Eliot has done, and done it admirably. The story in itself is simple enough, and the interest of a very quiet order, until the commencement of the third volume, when it is worked up with great power of detail, and becomes even painfully absorbing. The whole account of Hetty Sorrel's night-wandering in the fields is as strong an instance of the author's power in vivid melodramatic description, as the lighter parts of the book are of genuine humour and truth...

It is quite possible that some of those who can devour with satisfaction the green trash of the railway stall, may lay by *Adam Bede* without much consciousness of having been in unusually good company. But the more thoughtful reader will feel at once that he has been sitting at the feet of a master; that he has been reading a book which, for original power and truth, has rarely been equalled. He will not lay it aside as is the fate of many a novel of perhaps higher dramatic interest content with having read and admired it; he will recur it again and again and each time, we can promise him, with increased delight to enjoy at leisure its quiet humour, its truthful feeling, its wise and large philosophy.

Mr. Eliot confesses that he is fond of Dutch painting; to which, indeed, in its most refined school, the construction of these volumes present a very apt parallel. It may be doubted whether in some cases he does not carry this fondness to excess. An instance of it may be found in the expressions put into the mouth of Adam the carpenter. He and others are too found of talking shop... This seems to us carrying out the Horatian rule rather too literally; *Sit Medea ferox* by all means; but do not let her always smell of drugs... It is very true that this kind of appropriate language is conventional on the stage; ... but Mr. Eliot paints character far too well to have any occasion to put scrolls into the mouths of his figures in order to distinguish them... But after all, this may be taken as a proof of the conscientious care and finish which, with the writer, has touched every point of the dialogue, which runs off so easily and naturally throughout, that the skill of the contriver is seldom apparent, and the uncritical reader is tempted to think such writing the simplest thing in the world.

One of the most real things in these volumes, which will at once strike all those who have had any experience of its truth, is the picture they give of the state of religious feeling in country villages as it was fifty years ago, and as it is now, for there has been little change.

Adam Bede is not a religious novel. It would hardly be recommended without reservation to that large class of readers who take Miss Yonge and Miss Sewell for their high-priestesses; and will run some risk of being placed in the *index expurgatorius* of Evangelicalism. The author has a presentiment that to some minds the Rector of Broxton will seem little better than a pagan. Yet for both parties it would be a very wholesome change to lay aside for an hour or two the publications of their own favourite school, and to read Mr. Eliot's story. For its religious principle is a large-hearted charity. And this, after all, is surely the right ground on which to treat religious questions in a work of fiction... [The] author of *Adam Bede* is not one of those who, in the eloquent words of a late preacher, have restricted God's love, and narrowed the path to heaven. No one handles Scripture more reverently; none with better effect; because it is not as a weapon against opponents, but as armour of proof.

It is very cheering too, setting the religious question apart, to read a book in which the writer has the courage to say that by living a great deal among people more or less commonplace and vulgar, he has come to the conclusion that human nature is lovable and has the ability to maintain his thesis. He does not conceal or palliate the weaknesses of humanity; there is no attempt to paint rural life as an Arcadia of innocence; we have Hetty's silly vanity, and young Donnithorne's weakness of principle, and Lisbeth's petulance, all truthfully set before us; and even Adam, the hero, has quite enough of his old namesake about him to be far from perfect; yet we part from all of them at last with an honest sympathy, or, at the worst, a mild and tearful pity. It is encouraging, as it is unfortunately rare, in fiction, to find ourselves watching the operations of a skilful anatomist, as he lays bare the secrets of our quivering frame, and to feel that the hand is not only sure and steady, but gentle as a woman's. It is pleasant to find, combined with all the power of the satirist, the kindly warmth of human charity, and to mark the light which it throws upon human failings; not concealing them, but softening the harsher outlines, mellowing the glaring tones, and bringing out beauties of which we were before unconscious. We have here no morbid dwelling upon evil, nor yet an unreal optimism which dresses out life in hues of rose-colour; but a hearty manly sympathy with weakness, not inconsistent with a hatred of vice. The common, coarse people shame us sometimes, as they do in actual life, by the delicacy of their moral organisation; the outwardly gentle and refined shame us no less by their coarse selfishness. It is no small praise to Mr. Eliot, that he has described to us the attractions of sense without allowing them to influence our judgment.

Source: W. L. Collins, "A Review of Adam Bede," in *Blackwood's Edinburgh Magazine*, Vol. 4, April, 1859, pp. 490–504.

SOURCES

"*Adam Bede* by George Eliot," in *The Atlantic Monthly*, Vol. 4, No. 24, October 1859, pp. 521–522.

Blaser, Kent, "John Wesley and the Women Preachers of Early Methodism," in *The Historian*, March 22, 1993, http://www.accessmylibrary.com/search?q = John + Wesley + and + the + Women + Preachers (accessed November 3, 2009.

Eliot, George, *Adam Bede*, Penguin, 2008.

Gates, Sarah, "The Sound of the Scythe Being Whetted: Gender, Genre, and Realism in *Adam Bede*," in *Studies in the Novel*, March 22, 1998, http://www.accessmylibrary.com/search/?q = The + Sound + of + the + Scythe (accessed November 3, 2009).

Jewsbury, Geraldine, "Adam Bede, George Eliot" (review date 1859), in Vol. 89 of *Nineteenth-Century Literary Criticism*, edited by Juliet Byington and Suzanne Dewsbury, The Gale Group, 2001, http://www.enotes.com/nineteenth-century-criticism/adam-bede-george-eliot/geraldine-jewsbury-review-date-1859 (accessed November 3, 2009).

Lamb, John B., "To Obey and Trust: Adam Bede and the Politics of Deference," in *Studies in the Novel*, September 22, 2002, http://www.accessmylibrary.com/search?q = To + Obey + and + Trust (accessed November 3, 2009).

Lampman, Jane, "Women Clergy Bring a New Sensibility to an Old Calling," in *Christian Science Monitor*, July 19, 2006.

Mitchell, Rebecca N., "Learning to Read: Interpersonal Literacy in *Adam Bede*," in *Papers on Language and Literature*, March 22, 2008, http://www.accessmylibrary.com/search?q = Learning + to + Read%3A + Interpersonal + Literacy (accessed November 3, 2009).

Uglow, Nathan, "George Eliot: *Adam Bede*," in *The Literary Encyclopedia*, March 21, 2002, http://www.litencyc.com/php/sworks.php?rec = true&UID = 6852 (accessed November 3, 2009).

Wojtczak, Helena, "Women's Status in Mid 19th-Century England: A Brief Overview," http://www.hastingspress.co.uk/history/19/overview.htm (accessed November 3, 2009).

FURTHER READING

Hellerstein, Erna O., Leslie P. Hume, and Karen M. Offen, eds., *Victorian Women: A Documentary Account of Women's Lives in Nineteenth-Century England, France and the United States*, Stanford University Press, 1981.

> This account of women's lives in the time of George Eliot offers a variety of examples of famous women and how they were raised.

Brontë, Emily, *Wuthering Heights*, Barnes and Noble Classics, 1985.

> A classic of Romantic writing, the story of Heathcliff and Cathy also offers insights into a class system and the need to marry wealth that often proved tragic for women of that time.

Vicinus, Martha, ed., *Suffer and Be Still: Women in the Victorian Age*, Indiana University Press, 1973.

> A collection of essays from both feminist scholars and historians.

Arrowsmith

SINCLAIR LEWIS

1925

Arrowsmith, published in 1925, is one of the classic novels produced by Sinclair Lewis during the period when he was writing his best work. This pioneering novelist had, in fact, just produced two other well-received American classics: *Main Street* in 1920 and *Babbitt* in 1922. By the time he wrote *Arrowsmith*, Lewis was well known for his attacks on what he saw as the mindless commercialism and "boosterism" of what we now call the Roaring Twenties, the long economic boom that set in after the First World War and ended a decade later with the stock market crash and the start of the Great Depression in 1929.

In *Arrowsmith*, Lewis gives us a more positive main character than we often find in his works: Martin Arrowsmith is an idealistic and talented young man who, as a medical student, a doctor, and finally a researcher, nurtures within himself an ideal of pure scientific research; he hopes some day to devote himself to the pursuit of scientific knowledge for its own sake. He manages to hold on to this ideal in spite of constant temptations to give in and use his talents solely to accumulate money and prestige. The novel, furthermore, gives us a remarkably thorough history of medical science between the late nineteenth century and the middle of the 1920s, the period when medicine was becoming a modern, scientific discipline. Many of the questions of professional and scientific ethics that appear throughout the novel remain topics of intense discussion today.

Sinclair Lewis (*The Library of Congress*)

Arrowsmith was another success for Lewis; although he turned down the award, he won the Pulitzer Prize for the novel. In 1931, it was made into a movie directed by John Ford and starring Ronald Colman, one of the major stars of the era.

AUTHOR BIOGRAPHY

Harry Sinclair Lewis was born in Sauk Centre, Minnesota, in 1885. Sauk Centre was then, and remains today, a small village, although it is proud of its association with Lewis, and the family home is now a museum. This situation is more than a little ironic, since Lewis spent much of his career making fun of places like Sauk Centre—small midwestern villages that, in his novels, he fills with small-minded, materialistic, nosy people. His father, Edwin Lewis, was a doctor; some aspects of Martin Arrowsmith's career in medicine would have been familiar to Lewis from his early life. His mother, Emma Kermott Lewis, died when Lewis was quite young, in 1891. The next year, his father married

Isabel Warner, so the young Lewis was not without a mother for long. Lewis attended Yale University and began his writing career while he was still a student.

After Yale, Lewis entered the period that critics and biographers usually think of as his apprenticeship as a major writer. Between 1908 and 1915 he traveled the country, gaining experience that would be vital later in his career when he created settings for his novels all over the United States. He built up some popular success writing for magazines, including the widely circulated *Saturday Evening Post*. His first novel, *Hike and the Aeroplane*, appeared under a pseudonym in 1912, and his next, *Our Mr. Wrenn*, appeared in 1914 under his own name. He was building a solid but unspectacular reputation, and continued to write novels. Also in 1914, he married Grace Livingston Hegger, and they soon had a son, Wells, named for the British science fiction writer H. G. Wells, whom Lewis admired. By 1916, Lewis was making notes toward a novel about a small Midwestern town that he eventually gave the unlovely name Gopher Prairie. The book he wrote about Gopher Prairie was *Main Street*, and it proved to be his breakthrough novel.

The start of Lewis's period of triumph thus nicely coincided with the start of the Roaring Twenties, a decade remembered today for its prosperity. Lewis saw the problems beneath that prosperity. *Main Street* punctures the myth of the happy rural small town, depicting Gopher Prairie as a tedious and oppressive place. In his next novel, *Babbitt*, he took on the Midwestern industrial city. The central character, Babbitt, is a successful businessman in the fictional city of Zenith, a city devoted solely to industry and the selling of consumer goods. Babbitt attempts to rebel against the conformity expected of him, but soon finds the lure of the good life too powerful. Having written two strongly negative novels, Lewis next turned to *Arrowsmith*, a book in which, as we will see, the main character has genuinely heroic qualities. Lewis was by now a literary star. He continued to produce classic work through the rest of the 1920s. His period of great success reached its peak in 1930 when he became the first American to win the Nobel Prize for Literature. This time, he accepted the prize.

He now entered a period that is widely considered one of decline. He divorced Grace Hegger Lewis in 1925, then married newspaper writer

Dorothy Thompson in 1928. This marriage, too, ended in divorce, in 1942. Lewis produced a great deal more work, but this latter period is remembered largely for his 1935 novel *It Can't Happen Here* about the election of a fascist American president (the middle of the 1930s, when Adolf Hitler ruled Germany, was the golden era of fascism, a form of right-wing government in which all power is given to a dictator). Lewis died of alcoholism in Rome in 1951, and his ashes were interred in Sauk Centre—his model for Gopher Prairie.

PLOT SUMMARY

Chapters 1–5

The novel opens by very briefly telling the story of Martin Arrowsmith's great-grandmother, a pioneer headed fearlessly westward in a wagon. The story immediately jumps ahead to Martin Arrowsmith himself. He is fourteen and is assistant to a doctor, Doc Vickerson, in the small town of Elk Mills, Winnemac, an imaginary upper-Midwestern state that Lewis frequently used as a setting. The doctor himself enters the scene, somewhat drunk, and we get a picture of old-fashioned small-town medicine: while the doctor is not a bad person, his medical knowledge is limited. The story then jumps ahead to the year 1904, when Arrowsmith is an undergraduate attending the University of Winnemac. Here Arrowsmith learns of the mysterious professor Max Gottlieb, a German Jew whose research into immunology is so advanced that few other people can understand it. After graduation, Arrowsmith enters medical school at the same university. He joins the medical fraternity, but discovers that he does not fit in perfectly; here, and throughout his life, he will be torn between a desire for conventional success and a tendency to constantly question how the medical profession works. In his second year at medical school, Arrowsmith begins working directly under Max Gottlieb. Gottlieb is impressed with Arrowsmith's zeal, and one night, when Gottlieb finds him working late in the lab, he invites Arrowsmith into his home for sandwiches and conversation; from this point, Gottlieb becomes a mentor to Arrowsmith. In the meantime, however, Arrowsmith has become engaged to Madeleine Fox, a classmate from his undergraduate years. To please Madeleine, Arrowsmith will

MEDIA ADAPTATIONS

- A film version of the novel appeared the day after Christmas in 1931. Samuel Goldwyn produced the film, which stars Ronald Colman as Martin Arrowsmith and Helen Hayes as Leora. It is widely available in both DVD and VHS formats. Film scholars and serious fans find the movie most interesting because the director was a young John Ford, who later became one of the most important directors in film history, especially for his development of the classic "Western" in movies like *Stagecoach* (1939) and *The Searchers* (1956).

have to become a successful doctor. This demand conflicts with his desire to pattern his life after Gottlieb's and become a researcher devoted purely to the discovery of scientific truth—a career which, unfortunately, does not pay well.

Chapters 6–10

While still working under Gottlieb, Arrowsmith is sent on an errand to the hospital in the nearby city of Zenith, another of Lewis's favorite fictional locales (*Babbitt*, for instance, is set here, and the character George Babbitt himself appears briefly in *Arrowsmith*). At the hospital, Arrowsmith meets Leora Tozer, a student nurse at the hospital. After initially quarreling, they become friends, and eventually Arrowsmith proposes to her, finding himself engaged to two women at once. Unable to decide between them, he invites both women to lunch and lets them choose; insulted, Madeleine leaves, but Leora stays. She is a better fit for Arrowsmith, since she is less demanding and does not care as much as Madeleine about material or social success. Leora is from the tiny town of Wheatsylvania, North Dakota. When she is called home to nurse her sick mother, Arrowsmith misses her so much that he takes to drink. His behavior becomes so erratic that he insults Gottlieb, and is temporarily expelled from school. The dean of the school, Dean Silva, tells him that he will only be readmitted if he apologizes for his behavior. He borrows money from a classmate, Clif Clawson, wanders pointlessly for a time, then visits Leora in Wheatsylvania. They elope, and her family, especially her brother Bert, is enraged. They will not allow the couple to live together until Arrowsmith finishes medical school. Arrowsmith returns to school, apologizes to the dean, and is readmitted. Leora has been expelled from nursing school. Against the wishes of her family, she moves to Zenith to study stenography, and the couple is reunited.

Chapters 11–15

During his senior year in medical school, Arrowsmith—under some pressure from Leora's family—agrees to move to Wheatsylvania after graduation and become a general practitioner there. First, however, he must fulfill a two-year internship at Zenith General Hospital, a position he finds at first exciting, then tedious. The narrative then shifts to Gottlieb, who has been having a difficult time. Frustrated with the science education at the University of Winnemac, he attempts to reform the school, and after a fight with the university authorities, he is forced to resign. His wife is ill. Desperate, he applies for a job at the Hunziker Company in Pittsburgh. Hunziker produces antitoxins commercially, and Gottlieb had previously thought their work shoddy, but he has no choice but to go to work there, where he is welcomed warmly because of his scientific reputation. He makes an important discovery there, refining a new form of antitoxin, but when he is pressured to patent it before he is certain his findings are valid, he takes a new job at the McGurk Institute, a privately funded research laboratory where he will be more free to pursue his research independently (the McGurk Institute is modeled on the real-life Rockefeller Institute of Medical Research, now Rockefeller University). In the meantime, Martin and Leora Arrowsmith have been trying to settle into life in Wheatsylvania. Leora's family is a constant nuisance, pushing Arrowsmith to adopt the path that will lead to the greatest social prestige and highest income; Arrowsmith is driven further and further away from his ideal of becoming a scientist. One of his patients dies of diphtheria, and the town loses faith in him, but a doctor in a neighboring town, Dr. Adam Winter, does him the kindness of speaking to a newspaper reporter, and a positive story restores Arrowsmith to respectability.

Chapters 16–20

Arrowsmith saves a baby with emergency surgery and cures the local hypochondriac, Agnes Ingleblad. His reputation soars. But the town notes that he likes to drink and gamble, and does not go to church often, and his reputation falls. Such is the fate of the small-town doctor. He attends a speech by Gustaf Sondelius, a Swedish crusader against epidemic disease who has fought plagues around the world, and is now on a cross-country speaking tour. Arrowsmith spends an evening with Sondelius, who has something of Gottlieb in him. Inspired by Sondelius, Arrowsmith decides to devote himself to public health. He correctly locates the cause of a local outbreak of typhoid, but incorrectly predicts a smallpox epidemic; after this failure, his reputation falls to its lowest point. He decides he must move, and Sondelius finds him a job in public health in the city of Nautilus, Iowa, where he will be working under Dr. Almus Pickerbaugh. Arrowsmith is optimistic, until he meets Pickerbaugh, whom Lewis makes a figure of fun. Pickerbaugh writes bad poetry, talks constantly, and never ceases leading crusades against public health "threats" that are often spurious. He has eight daughters who often join in the crusades, and Pickerbaugh has named them the "Healthette Octette." Arrowsmith flirts with the eldest daughter, Orchid, and Leora notices. She warns Arrowsmith that although she can tolerate high levels of misbehavior from him, she demands his love completely; she can tolerate no other women in their life. The flirtation with Orchid, nevertheless, is part of a pattern for Arrowsmith. Just as he cannot choose between clinical medicine and scientific research, he is also easily distracted by women to whom he is not married.

Chapters 21–25

Pickerbaugh, as Lewis portrays him, grows more absurd as the book progresses. He knows nothing of science, and he devotes all his time to propagandistic campaigns that, it becomes clear, are actually political campaigns for higher office. Arrowsmith continues to flirt with Orchid; during one meeting, they go so far as to kiss. His job, furthermore, has less and less to do with science or even medicine; just as he is betraying Leora, he is also betraying Gottlieb. As was inevitable, Pickerbaugh is nominated to run for Congress, and in his absence Arrowsmith must run the health department by himself. Since he is not a good administrator, he proves a terrible substitute and is denounced as a tyrant. Pickerbaugh wins his campaign, leaving for Washington and taking Orchid with him; this act removes at least one distraction from Arrowsmith's life. He is appointed acting director of public health, taking Pickerbaugh's place. There is, however, too much of Gottlieb's influence in Arrowsmith for him to be able to succeed at such a post. He ignores his duties and pursues a chance discovery he makes about streptococcus bacteria; for the first time in years, he is in the laboratory, and he likes it there as much as ever. He is attacked, however, for devoting too much time to research and too little to his public duties; when he does try to be a good acting director, he is again dogged by his failures as an administrator. He alienates the business community by denouncing unsanitary establishments, and he runs a free clinic that alienates doctors because it takes their patients away from them. He finishes his research on strep and reports it to the *Journal of Infectious Diseases* in Chicago, where he is invited to join the prestigious Rouncefield Clinic as pathologist; his friendly rival from medical school, Angus Duer, is now a successful doctor there. Returning to find the hostility against him in Nautilus unabated, he resigns, and he and Leora head for Chicago. Arrowsmith spends an unhappy year at the clinic, and is again pressured to do more practical work. Gottlieb, however, reenters the story at this point. He has heard of Arrowsmith's work on strep, and invites him to take a job at the McGurk Institute. Arrowsmith happily accepts.

Chapters 26–30

Arrowsmith arrives at the McGurk Institute, and is at first deeply impressed. He has his own laboratory space, with an assistant, and the freedom to work on whatever he chooses. He meets Gottlieb, and they are very quickly deep in conversation, as if no time has passed, Gottlieb again warning about the dangers of commercialism and its threat to the purity of science. Arrowsmith is shown around the institute by Dr. Rippleton Holabird, chief of the Department of Physiology. He meets the director, Dr. A. DeWitt Tubbs, a character who is at first impressive, but gradually reminds us more and more of Pickerbaugh. He also meets Terry Wickett, a man of his own age and rank who at first alienates him with his extreme cynicism. Both Gottlieb and Wickett, who have worked for some time at the institute, tell Arrowsmith that he needs to know more mathematics, chemistry, and physics before he can do any serious work; Arrowsmith is angry at first, but Wickett calms him and offers to help him with this task,

beginning a friendship between the two younger men. Their collaboration is interrupted when the United States enters World War I (we know, therefore, that the year is now 1917), and Wickett leaves to fight. Arrowsmith has been at the institute a year when he makes a tremendous discovery: something is killing the bacteria in his test tubes. He launches a series of experiments to determine just what is killing the bacteria, naming the unknown substance "The X Principle." He works so hard that his mental health is affected; he drives himself into a near mania in an effort to discover just what is happening. He tells only Gottlieb what he has found. Gottlieb is pleased, but tells Arrowsmith to keep his work a complete secret from the rest of the institute. When the management finally learns what he is up to, they are delighted and filled with plans that Arrowsmith finds premature. Gottlieb, however, breaks the news to Arrowsmith that he has been scooped: a French researcher has just published findings identical to Arrowsmith's, naming the unknown element "bacteriophage," a name Arrowsmith shortens to "phage." He vows to keep working on the substance; if it can be made to destroy disease organisms, it will result in a revolution in medicine. Sondelius returns to the story, going to work at the institute with Arrowsmith on the phage problem. They are excited to discover that phage may kill the bacteria that causes bubonic plague, the deadly disease that had killed one-third of all Europeans in outbreaks in the late Middle Ages, and in the era of the book still regularly flared up around the world.

Chapters 31–35

In careful detail, the author describes the beginning of an outbreak of bubonic plague on the island of St. Hubert, a British colony in the West Indies. Although the authorities deny they have a problem for as long as possible, a local physician, Dr. Stokes, eventually contacts Gottlieb with the news. Gottlieb formulates a plan: Arrowsmith will take a large supply of his phage to the island. He will divide the population in half: one half—the experimental group—will receive the phage, while the other half—the control group—will not. Sondelius will accompany Arrowsmith, although he disagrees with the plan; he thinks everyone should get the phage, and refuses a dose until all the other islanders have had theirs. Leora insists on accompanying Arrowsmith, who reluctantly agrees. The small mission sails for the now-quarantined St. Hubert; when they reach the island and go ashore, at night, among the first things Arrowsmith sees is a cart full of corpses. The plague is in fact raging here. The group is established in an estate thought to be free of disease-carrying rats, and well away from the plague areas. Sondelius, who has done this kind of work before, takes over from the ineffectual British surgeon general of the colony, Dr. Inchcape Jones, and begins to wage war on the rats (fleas on the rats spread the plague; medical science, by this date, understood this crucial fact, although doctors still did not have an effective treatment for the plague itself, which we today treat with antibiotics). Arrowsmith finds it nearly impossible to set up his experiment; nearly everyone wants him to use the phage throughout the island. He does find a small village where he can set up his experiment and, leaving Leora at the estate, he travels there. At the village, he meets Joyce Lanyon, a wealthy New Yorker who had been trapped by the quarantine, and Arrowsmith yet again begins to flirt. While he does so, back at the estate, Leora wanders into Arrowsmith's lab. She smokes one of his cigarettes, unaware that it has been soaked by plague germs, and soon dies in agony. When Arrowsmith finds Leora's body, he goes nearly insane with grief; only Joyce Lanyon is able to buck him up enough that he can at least partly finish his experiment. Among the victims of the plague is Sondelius himself, who dies and whose body is shoveled into the mass funeral pyre with all the other victims. The plague finally abates, the quarantine is lifted, and Arrowsmith leaves the island thinking that he has failed in his mission.

Chapters 36–40

Arrowsmith returns to New York to much acclaim, which he believes he does not deserve. The McGurk Institute declares his experiment a success, to Arrowsmith's disgust. Worse, Gottlieb is fading. His wife has long since died, and he suffers from what we would probably today call Alzheimer's disease. Arrowsmith visits Joyce Lanyon and discovers that she is vastly wealthy. They eventually marry and tour Europe together; Arrowsmith finds himself fully enmeshed in the social circuit of high society. He imagines that he is growing used to it, but it is clearly another in a long sequence of distractions from his real work, scientific research. Rippleton Holabird is now director of the McGurk Institute, and constantly interferes with Arrowsmith's work. Terry Wickett makes an exciting discovery about quinine, which, during the era of the novel, was the only effective treatment for malaria. Arrowsmith could become a famous man with his

work on phage, but he finds Wickett's discovery more interesting. Still, Holabird interferes, and in a rage, Wickett quits. He will continue his work independently in a cabin he owns deep in the woods of Vermont. Arrowsmith wants to follow him there, but Joyce insists that he stick with his steady job at the institute. She converts a part of their house into an expensively equipped laboratory, but even there, Arrowsmith cannot work in peace: Joyce's wealthy friends want to watch him at work, regarding him as a kind of entertainment. In the end, it is all too much for Arrowsmith. Holabird offers him the job of assistant director of the McGurk Institute, and Joyce has a baby boy. Still, Arrowsmith quits the institute, abandons Joyce, and joins Wickett in Vermont. When we last see him, Arrowsmith is happily living in the wilderness. He and Wickett are spending all their spare time on pure research.

CHARACTERS

Leora Arrowsmith

Leora is a nursing student when Martin Arrowsmith first meets her in Zenith. Raised in rural North Dakota, she is unpretentious and forgiving, which makes her the perfect match for Arrowsmith, since his work, during those periods when he is allowed to do scientific research, is so demanding. Leora supports his devotion to science entirely. She is so unconcerned about social status that her clothes and hair are usually unkempt, and some item of her clothing is usually missing a button. This shortcoming annoys Arrowsmith, who fails to see that it is precisely this carelessness that makes Leora someone capable of ignoring the temptations of wealth.

Martin Arrowsmith

The central character of the story, Arrowsmith is essentially a self-made man. He has started with nothing, works his way through both undergraduate training and medical school, climbs to an impressive height in his profession, and is a quite wealthy man by the end—yet he decides to throw it all away and work in the Vermont wilderness in the pursuit of pure scientific truth. Arrowsmith is constantly pulled two ways. He is offered temptations throughout the novel; in nearly every chapter, a situation arises in which he could profit by being a good social climber and stifling any qualms he has about the quality of the medicine or research he is practicing. Yet always, eventually, the devotion to pure science that he learns from Max Gottlieb pulls him back toward science of the highest caliber, no matter what the pay.

George Babbitt
The central character of Lewis's 1922 novel named for him, Babbitt is a salesman in the city of Zenith, Winnemac. Arrowsmith meets and interacts with him briefly there.

Clif Clawson
The class clown of Arrowsmith's medical school, Clawson is thrown out of school for a prank and goes to work as a car salesman, a job at which he excels. He reappears late in the novel after a fraudulent oil investment scheme he has cooked up falls apart. He wants Arrowsmith to market phage aggressively, whether it works or not. He is one of a number of characters in the novel who are natural salesmen and completely unscrupulous.

Angus Duer
Arrowsmith's rival at school, Duer is good at his studies and popular among his classmates. He is a natural aristocrat, in good and bad ways; in one scene, he nearly kills the night watchman of the Zenith hospital when the man touches him threateningly. He becomes a successful doctor at the Rouncefield Clinic in Chicago.

Madeleine Fox
Madeleine Fox is friendly with Arrowsmith when they are undergraduates. While Arrowsmith is in medical school, Madeleine is studying for a Ph.D. in English, and they become engaged. The problem, for Arrowsmith, is that she is what he thinks of as an "improver." She constantly tries to change Arrowsmith so that he is more respectable. When, for instance, he tells her that he wants to spend his summer vacation waiting tables in a Canadian hotel, she is aghast, thinking the work to be beneath his (and her) dignity.

Max Gottlieb
One of the most important characters in the novel, Gottlieb is a German Jew who has studied with some of the most important European scientists of his era; he has also suffered from anti-Semitism, however, and it has driven him from job to job. Lewis makes this character German in large part because German scientists, during this period, were widely considered the best in the world, and the most rigorous. Gottlieb believes in a pure science focused only on uncovering the truth about how nature works. In his view, whenever considerations of social prestige or monetary reward intrude on the scientist's work, then that work suffers. He becomes Arrowsmith's most important mentor.

Rippleton Holabird
Holabird is at first an impressive character. When the First World War had begun, before Arrowsmith meets him, he had rushed to volunteer as a doctor, and is only back in the United States because he has been wounded in combat. An important figure at the McGurk Institute, he is at first friendly to Arrowsmith, but later becomes an irritant, and finally an intolerable one, after he becomes Arrowsmith's boss. He is focused on just the sort of commercial success and social prestige that Gottlieb has always warned Arrowsmith against.

Agnes Ingleblad
Agnes Ingleblad is Wheatsylvania's resident hypochondriac. Arrowsmith cures her of her long-running problems. Since the problems are probably imaginary, her cure inspires a growing confidence in Arrowsmith among the people of Wheatsylvania.

Inchcape Jones
Dr. Inchcape Jones is the surgeon general of the British colony of St. Hubert. According to Lewis, Jones "had come out from Home only two years before, and he wanted to go back Home," to Great Britain, that is. When the plague breaks out, he is completely unequal to the crisis, dealing with it mainly by denial.

Joyce Lanyon
Arrowsmith first meets Joyce Lanyon on St. Hubert, during the plague. She is a wealthy New Yorker trapped on the island by the quarantine. After Leora dies and the plague ends, Arrowsmith looks her up in New York, and the two are eventually married. Joyce is, however, the opposite of Leora, and in fact seems to function in the novel as a reminder, at the end, of how perfect a match Leora was for Arrowsmith the scientist. Joyce is far more demanding, and will not allow Arrowsmith to put science ahead of her own comfort. She insists on all the conventional forms of respect a wife traditionally requires from a husband. She expects him, further, to accompany her on the social circuit. Arrowsmith finally

abandons her. She bears him a son, but by the end of the book, she and Arrowsmith are on the verge of divorce.

Almus Pickerbaugh

Surely the most ridiculous figure in the book, Almus Pickerbaugh is Lewis's parody of a 1920s go-getter. Even though he is a doctor in public office, he acts more like a salesman for a corporation, and in fact, he is driven mainly by ambition to run for higher office. Nearly every word out of his mouth—especially his poetry—is comical. To get mothers to sterilize their babies' bottles, he warns, "Boil the bottles or by gum / You better buy your ticket to Kingdom Come."

Orchid Pickerbaugh

Orchid is Almus Pickerbaugh's nineteen-year-old daughter, the eldest of eight. She and Arrowsmith strike up a flirtation, much to Leora's disgust. We do not learn much about Orchid; she seems an unexceptional young woman, and the attraction between her and Arrowsmith is mainly physical.

Dean Silva

Silva is the dean of the medical school at the University of Winnemac, an imposing but humane figure. It is Silva who temporarily throws Arrowsmith out of school for his drunken misbehavior when Leora is absent; he demands that Arrowsmith apologize to Gottlieb, whom he has insulted. It is also Silva who, in a forgiving and fatherly manner, accepts Arrowsmith back into school when he returns, repentant. Silva, in fact, becomes a father figure to Arrowsmith, and for a while competes with Gottlieb as his most important mentor. As the novel progresses, however, Silva fades out of the plot, while Gottlieb makes regular appearances until nearly the end.

Gustaf Sondelius

Sondelius is the Swedish crusader against epidemic disease whose speeches inspire Arrowsmith to go into public health. Later, Sondelius reappears and accompanies Arrowsmith to St. Hubert to fight the plague. He is garrulous and absentminded, but highly energetic; this quality especially comes out when he and the little party from the McGurk Institute arrive at St. Hubert. He immediately seizes control and wages war on the rats, killing them in a fury of hatred. In the end, however, he is himself killed by the plague.

Dr. Stokes

A doctor on St. Hubert, it is Stokes who first realizes the gravity of the plague outbreak and communicates with Gottlieb in New York. Although a mere country doctor in an obscure part of the colony, he essentially saves the situation when Dr. Inchcape Jones, the surgeon general, proves incapable of dealing with the crisis. He is both brave and intelligent, and his understanding of science is better than that of most of the doctors we meet in the book.

Andrew Jackson Tozer

Andrew Jackson Tozer is Leora's father. He rejects Arrowsmith at first, and interferes with the life of the young couple after they elope. There is a softer side to the father, however: he genuinely misses Leora's company, and that simple emotion motivates much of his behavior. He is a more old-fashioned figure, as his name suggests—Andrew Jackson was president of the United States during the early 1800s, long before the beginning of the novel.

Bert Tozer

Bert Tozer is Leora's brother. He is almost unbelievably opinionated and arrogant. He at first dislikes and rejects Arrowsmith angrily; when Leora and Martin elope, he is enraged. As the couple's life together evolves, he continues to interfere constantly. Intensely conscious of social standing and ambitious for worldly goods, he is, like Almus Pickerbaugh, a parody of the 1920s go-getter.

A. DeWitt Tubbs

Tubbs is the director of the McGurk Institute when Arrowsmith arrives there. Superficially impressive, he turns out to be one of the many figures in the novel who are less scientists than public relations men and politicians. He is closely aligned with Rippleton Holabird, and is in fact an older version of the younger man.

Doc Vickerson

Vickerson is the old-fashioned country doctor for whom Arrowsmith works as a youngster. He likes to drink, but is kind to Arrowsmith, and supportive of his ambition to be a doctor. Vickerson gives us a picture of what small-town medicine was like in 1897, the year during which the only scene where he appears takes place. His office is the opposite of sanitary, and his knowledge is almost purely practical, with little of it drawn from modern science. "[A] Physician's library [requires] just three books," he drunkenly declares: "'Gray's Anatomy' and Bible and Shakespeare."

Terry Wickett

Terry Wickett is a researcher at the McGurk Institute when Arrowsmith arrives there. He is cynical and often abusive; these qualities repulse Arrowsmith, until Wickett offers to help him brush up on his science knowledge, which Arrowsmith has neglected during the years since he left the University of Winnemac. The two become close friends, and the novel ends with the pair working alone at their own private scientific "institute," where they can operate in perfect independence. Wickett is, in fact, a younger version of Gottlieb.

Adam Winter

When Arrowsmith is working as a general practitioner in Wheatsylvania, Dr. Adam Winter is the physician in nearby Leopolis. He is "a man of nearly seventy," and wise in the ways of small-town prairie life. When Arrowsmith is first starting out, Winter gives him some crucial help in establishing his practice.

THEMES

Medicine at the Crossroads

Arrowsmith is not just the fictional biography of a young man. It also tells the story of American medicine as it moved through the scientific revolution of the late 1800s through Lewis's own time. We begin with Doc Vickerson, the classic country doctor. Lewis includes a detailed description of his office, and it is none too clean. Further, whatever Vickerson knows, he has learned by trial and error, not by following the developments coming out of the science of his era. We next move to Arrowsmith's education. While some students of the time were admitted to medical school without even having been to college, they were still required to study for four years and serve a two-year internship, a system not radically different from what we have today. Arrowsmith's work as a country doctor is somewhat better than Vickerson's by virtue of his education, but he fails as a public health official because the public does not value science as much as it wants the potential benefits brought by glad-handing politicians like Almus Pickerbaugh. Arrowsmith's experience ends at two sorts of institutions that are still very much with us: the expensive private clinic and the privately funded research institute. Here, modern medicine is taking shape, but characteristic problems are also appearing. The clinicians are constantly tempted to resort to expensive procedures that may not be needed but do pay well, and the scientist is always tempted to shout "Eureka!" prematurely.

The Temptations of the Scientist

Of course, any scientist, at the start of a career, is confronted with the question of whether to go to work in a field where employment at a private corporation will be easy to find, where the skills the scientist possesses will be in demand, and where salaries will be high (and there may even be stock options). *Arrowsmith* does a much more thorough job in collecting and presenting all the distractions that can ruin a scientist's ability to concentrate on his or her work. As scientists move up the ranks of whatever organization they have joined, they are more and more distracted by administrative tasks. Fund-raising and meetings with financial backers may consume enormous amounts of time. As the scientist grows older and more prominent, social functions begin to take their toll. And this list only scratches the surface. In a way, *Arrowsmith* is a catalog of all the possible distractions, which appear on nearly every page.

The Call of the Wilderness

It is an ancient motif in American literature and folklore: beyond the bounds of the city lies the wilderness, where the rules of civilization are relaxed or are simply absent. Here, a man can be a man—and, presumably, a woman can be a woman, and a scientist a scientist. A famous invocation of this theme is the book *Walden* (1854) by Henry David Thoreau. In it, he describes a situation similar to that which Arrowsmith and Terry Wickett arrange for themselves at the end of *Arrowsmith*. In fact, the conclusion of *Arrowsmith* seems to be a direct allusion to *Walden,* since in each case men retreat from society to a cabin beside a New England pond, where they try to think clearly without any interference from the demands of society. Arrowsmith and Wickett specifically hope to be spared all the temptations and distractions to which a scientist is subjected at a place like the McGurk Institute. Still, the principle is the same as that which motivated Thoreau.

TOPICS FOR FURTHER STUDY

- In small groups, discuss the role of women in the novel. When *Arrowsmith* first appeared, Lewis was praised for his portrait of Leora, whom some critics regarded as the first fully realistic female character he had created. Did he deserve the praise? Look closely at each of the women in the novel, even the minor ones like Ada Quist, Bert Tozer's fiancée. How does Lewis use women, and to what end?

- Write a paper in which you take a position on the novel's ending. At the end, we leave Arrowsmith and Terry Wickett in what many people would regard as absolutely ideal circumstances. They are free from intrusions from the modern world. Their biological expertise is of such high quality that they need only labor a few hours a day making serum from their small horse herd to sell. A certain amount of time is consumed by chores, but these are two independent bachelors (Arrowsmith, it appears, will be divorced soon) who do not care about impressing other members of their social group. They have no social group. What might go wrong? Keep in mind the severity of the Vermont winters, and the extreme isolation of the cabin, after snow has covered the roads. Keep in mind, also, that New Englanders had been coping with these conditions for over three centuries at the time the novel was written, and knew how to deal with snow and ice.

- Using the Internet and your library, research the early years of the AIDS epidemic. Follow your research through to the development of the first effective treatments for AIDS and the HIV virus, like the drugs AZT and, later, protease inhibitors. Notice how, in the early years, activists were angry with the government for releasing drugs too slowly—in effect, for being too careful and "scientific" in the same way Gottlieb always urges Arrowsmith to be. Keeping in mind what Gottlieb says, and what happens on St. Hubert, write a paper in which you argue for your position about what doctors should do when they have potentially life-saving drugs that have not yet been scientifically tested. Should they be tried out on humans, and how?

- Why are we so fascinated, as a culture, by the lives of doctors? Why are we so eager to watch TV shows and read books about them? Write a paper in which you develop a thesis that gives at least three explanations for this phenomenon. You must refer to the book *Arrowsmith* in your paper—but you also must discuss such recent hit TV shows as *House, Grey's Anatomy, Scrubs,* or others (you are not restricted to those shows, and are not required to cover every one).

STYLE

Characterization

"Characterization" is a catchall term that literary critics use to describe how an author makes a literary character seem like a real person. The author accomplishes this task in many ways. One technique that Lewis is known for is "Dickensian naming." This term refers to the practice of giving characters symbolic names that suggest some important quality of their personality (it is named for the English novelist Charles Dickens, who was a master of this practice). The novel *Arrowsmith* is filled with examples of this technique. If Lewis wants to make a character sound ridiculous, he gives the person a ridiculous name, like Almus Pickerbaugh, A. DeWitt Tubbs, or Inchcape Jones. The name may be a pun: Terry Wickett is more than a little wicked, in the context of the McGurk Institute. The name "Gottlieb" is German and can be translated in various ways, but *gott* means God, suggesting that

A doctor dressed for protection during a bubonic plague epidemic in 1912 *(Hulton Archive / Getty Images)*

Gottlieb is both Arrowsmith's god and that science itself is the god of the new, modern world of the 1920s.

Satire

Lewis became famous in part for his attacks on the commercial culture of the 1920s. On one level, he found it simply ridiculous; we see this in the fun he has at the expense of characters like Almus Pickerbaugh. On a more serious level, he found this commercial culture spiritually empty and often actually destructive of lives and ideals. The perfect example, in *Arrowsmith*, is the minor character Clif Clawson. Early in the book, Clif is a happy-go-lucky figure, popular for his sense of humor. After he is expelled from medical school, he becomes a car salesman, and is prospering when Arrowsmith loses track of him early in the novel. Late in the story, when he reappears as a forty-year-old, he is nearly a sinister figure. Lewis refers to him as "gross." He is on the run

from an apparently illegal investment scheme. He proposes to Arrowsmith a way of capitalizing on phage that is immoral and will likely cause real harm to anyone taken in by the scheme. Clif epitomizes the commercial culture of the 1920s that is destructive to the point of actually being deadly.

HISTORICAL CONTEXT

The Roaring Twenties

The 1920s remain a memorable period in American history, so much so that many people feel nostalgia for the time, even though few are left alive who can remember it. The qualities of the decade are contradictory. The 1920s (the Jazz Age, or the Roaring Twenties) were a time of genuine prosperity. They were also a period when the national literature thrived as it never had before. Novelists like Ernest Hemingway, William Faulkner, and F. Scott Fitzgerald joined Sinclair Lewis and others in producing some of the greatest classics of American literature. Furthermore, African Americans celebrated a cultural flowering that we today call the Harlem Renaissance. Zora Neale Hurston, Nella Larsen, Langston Hughes, Jean Toomer, and dozens of others took African American culture to new levels that we are still learning to appreciate. Technology and science flourished as well. Contrary to Gottlieb's criticisms in *Arrowsmith*, American scientists were pushing research institutes and universities to new heights. The nation had fought a world war for the first time and had won. The war, as President Woodrow Wilson had declared, had been fought to "make the world safe for democracy." Once the war was over, the nation seems to have decided that it had done its part. It turned away from Europe and other international responsibilities and set about enjoying itself.

The decade is often remembered today for its least appealing qualities. Ask a person to think of the 1920s, and that person may think first of a fad or a stunt. The 1920s saw fads for flagpole sitting, the Charleston dance, and raccoon-skin coats. When the aviator Charles Lindbergh flew non-stop from the United States to Paris in 1927, this stunt had little practical value, but it made him the most famous man in the world. In *Arrowsmith*, we get a taste for this side of popular culture in the 1920s in the various health fairs and events that Almus Pickerbaugh organizes,

COMPARE
&
CONTRAST

- **1920s:** Just before the start of the decade, a series of violent events reordered the international scene. These included the First World War (1914–1918), the communist revolution in Russia, and other disruptive events.

  Today: The terrorist attacks on New York and Washington on September 11, 2001, lead to a similar shake-up of the world order, including wars in Afghanistan and Iraq.

- **1920s:** Once the disruption calmed somewhat, the economy of the United States boomed, with consumers enjoying a level of prosperity unknown until that time.

  Today: A similar prosperity follows the disruptions at the start of the decade, fueled in part by borrowing and especially by a historic boom in real estate prices.

- **1920s:** As it turned out, much of the prosperity of the 1920s was based on unsustainable speculation, especially in the stock market. The market crashed in 1929, leading to the world economic crisis we now call the Great Depression.

  Today: The rise in real estate prices also proves unsustainable, and when the housing bubble pops, beginning in about 2006, it leads to an economic crisis that has proven to be the worst since the Great Depression.

complete with bad but propagandistic songs, embarrassing poetry, and stunts designed to draw the attention of crowds.

There is, furthermore, a dark underside to the decade. Americans had ratified the Eighteenth Amendment to the Constitution in 1919, prohibiting the transport, sale, or manufacture of alcohol. Subsequently, the illicit manufacture and sale of alcohol, known as "bootlegging," became a thriving underground business. Organized crime quickly moved into this business, and rival gangs battled each other for control of the trade, especially in Chicago, where the turf wars were exceptionally vicious, and the nation's most famous gangster, Al Capone, made his fortune. Gangsters killed each other from moving vehicles, essentially inventing the drive-by shooting; their favorite firearm was the Thompson submachine gun, and this weapon, with its characteristic round ammunition drum, became as much a symbol of the decade as the Charleston or the raccoon-skin coat. Note that in *Arrowsmith*, a number of characters enjoy drinking, but even when it is illegal, they never have much trouble finding illicit alcohol.

The prosperity of the decade was not as secure as people thought. Like Clif Clawson's oil investment scheme, the economy was in an increasingly perilous state as the decade advanced. As it did for Clawson, the bubble eventually burst, and the Great Depression began.

CRITICAL OVERVIEW

Arrowsmith was published in 1925 by Harcourt Brace to immediate success, both popular and critical. From the start, it was recognized as the work of a major writer at the apex of his talent. It was, in fact, awarded the Pulitzer Prize, although Lewis turned the prize down. He explained, in a statement quoted in *The Man from Main Street*, that "All prizes, like all titles, are dangerous. The seekers for prizes tend to labor not for inherent excellence but for alien rewards; they tend to write this, or timorously to avoid writing that, in order to tickle the prejudices of a haphazard committee." The explanation actually sounds like a statement Lewis might put in the mouth of Max Gottlieb.

One persistent question, among critics writing about it, is the role of religion in the novel. For

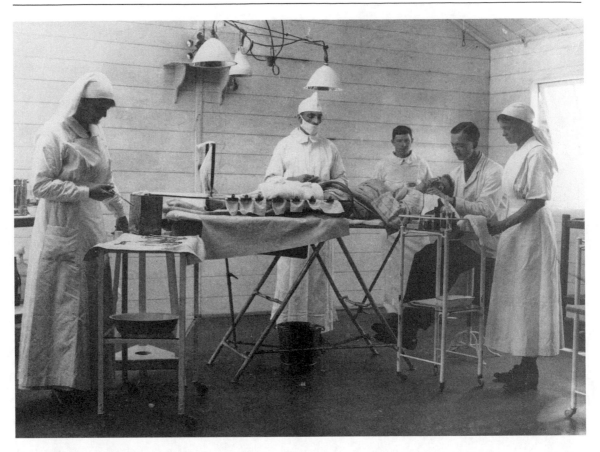

An operation during World War I *(Popperphoto / Getty Images)*

Arrowsmith, science itself seems to become a religion, as Everett Hamner explains: "Each of his successive masters is a 'god' seeking new apostles to spread an evermore technological gospel."

A central question in criticism about the novel is the nature of the ending. Is Arrowsmith merely fleeing? Can he and Wickett make a go of it in the Vermont wilderness, and is their primitive practice really science? Paul-Vincent McInnis argues that what the two are doing is actually not that radical:

> What Lewis appears to admire about scientific policy is the sharing and discussions of ideas. The proposal of solitude is in fact a guise for microcosmic teamwork and a simplified structure of decentralisation.... Their basic system of decentralisation will allow them to be detached but not totally withdrawn.

While *Arrowsmith* was widely regarded as Lewis's best work during his lifetime, he is best remembered for *Babbitt*, a novel that gave a name to middle-class conformity.

CRITICISM

Scott Herring

Herring teaches both literature and writing at the University of California, Davis, specializing in writing for students of medicine. In this essay, he considers whether the quest for scientific truth that Gottlieb demands of Arrowsmith is even possible, under the circumstances of the novel.

Sinclair Lewis's *Arrowsmith* present readers with a hero with whom they can readily identify. The ambitious and idealistic young doctor, Martin Arrowsmith, truly wants to do good in the world, but he is not perfect. He drinks. He gambles. He chases women to whom he is not married. In short, he is human. He strives to improve himself, but does not always succeed. When Arrowsmith joins the McGurk Institute, he meets Max Gottlieb, a medical expert he idealized, for the first time in a number of years. Gottlieb has not changed; he is still likeably eccentric, in a gruff way. And he gives Arrowsmith a short speech, in his German accent, on his view of the nature of science:

WHAT DO I READ NEXT?

- Any serious student of Lewis should read *Main Street,* first published in 1920. Its central character is trapped in a small town that is virtually identical to Wheatsylvania, and her experiences complement those of Arrowsmith.

- Next, look at *Babbitt,* which followed *Main Street* by two years. In *Babbitt* we get a detailed look at Zenith, Winnemac, where Arrowsmith and Leora spend a great deal of time.

- For a scholarly look at Lewis's best decade, see *The Rise of Sinclair Lewis, 1920–1930,* by James M. Hutchisson (1996).

- A good Web page about Sinclair Lewis can be found at http://english.illinoisstate.edu/separry/sinclairlewis and is provided by the English Department at Illinois State University.

- Another quality university Web site on Lewis is at http://lrts.stcloudstate.edu/showcase/sinclairlewis07.asp and is maintained by St. Cloud State University, in Sinclair's home state of Minnesota.

- *Arrowsmith* is unusual in its thorough focus on a single profession, medicine, and a number of readers may be more interested in the science of the novel than in its characters. For a readable introduction to a number of modern medical issues, check out *Better* (2007) by surgeon Atul Gawande, and other titles by the same author.

- Another similar doctor-author is Jerome Groopman. A good book to start with is *The Measure of Our Days* (1997), in which Groopman, whose specialty is fatal diseases like cancer and AIDS, frequently has to ask himself ethical questions about whether he should use an experimental treatment or not—the position Arrowsmith finds himself in at the end of the novel.

The normal man, he does not care much what he does except that he should eat and sleep and make love. But the scientist is intensely

> ON ST. HUBERT ISLAND, ARROWSMITH IS THRUST INTO A SITUATION IN WHICH IT IS FINALLY IMPOSSIBLE FOR HIM TO RISE ABOVE ALL TEMPTATION AND ACHIEVE PURE OBJECTIVITY. WHAT HAPPENS TO HIM THERE SUGGESTS THAT SUCH OBJECTIVITY, AS GOTTLIEB IMAGINES IT, MAY BE UNATTAINABLE."

---

religious—he is so religious that he will not accept quarter-truths...

As he is summing up, Gottlieb continues: "He [the scientist] must be heartless. He lives in a cold, clear light." As Gottlieb sees it, the scientist must rise above his entire society and make of himself an emotionless creature without entangling attachments. It is clear why Gottlieb makes this demand: it is only by rising above every other entanglement that the scientist can achieve objectivity. Arrowsmith wants to live up to Gottlieb's ideal. But in the climax of the novel, Lewis himself seems to call into question whether this objectivity is possible. On St. Hubert island, Arrowsmith is thrust into a situation in which it is finally impossible for him to rise above all temptation and achieve pure objectivity. What happens to him there suggests that such objectivity, as Gottlieb imagines it, may be unattainable.

It is important, first, to understand the symbolism of the island of St. Hubert, where Arrowsmith and Sondelius battle the plague. It is a British colony. The British Empire once stretched across the globe, include vast sections of Africa and Asia. In the years following World War II, most of the former British colonies and dominions became independent countries. In 1925, however, the British Empire was still extensive. St. Hubert was a typical island colony, with its British colonial overlords, small population of local poor whites, and large population of "natives." Note, however, that the word "colony" has multiple meanings. In the novel, it refers to a political entity, but in biology, it may refer to a mass of microorganisms, the creatures on which Arrowsmith normally performs experiments. The word "culture" also comes into play; scientists create cultures in the laboratory, and the island itself is a place of multiple human cultures. St. Hubert is like a giant petri dish, a huge scientific experiment.

Gottlieb expects Arrowsmith to treat St. Hubert as a set of laboratory cultures and perform a proper scientific experiment on them: he will have an experimental group that receives the possibly lifesaving phage, and a control group that does not. Today, Gottlieb's demand would be considered a gross violation of medical ethics, but he does not regard it as such. Medical ethics have changed since that time. More importantly, Gottlieb is saved by distance. Because he is in New York, under safe and easy circumstances, he does not have to confront the full horror of St. Hubert and have his objectivity tried by the distress of the people there.

Upon arriving on St. Hubert, Arrowsmith, Sondelius, and Leora in effect enter the petri dish themselves. Once they are inside the local cultures, objectivity eventually proves impossible. Arrowsmith is assaulted on all sides by demands for the lifesaving phage. He is subject to direct insults when he withholds it. The governor of the colony regards it as nearly insanity that Arrowsmith even considers withholding it, and only two of the local doctors support his plan. Arrowsmith is also presented by all the painful evidence of what the plague is doing. When the small party first arrives on the island, nearly the first thing Arrowsmith sees is a cart loaded with the corpses of plague victims, followed by mourners. It is like a scene from Europe in the fourteenth century, when more than one quarter of the population was killed by the bubonic plague. "'And I might have saved all of them, with phage,'" Arrowsmith whispers to himself, in distress. He has hardly set foot on the island, and it is already working powerfully on his emotions, as he discovers when checking into the hotel. He feels sweaty and disoriented, and is especially concerned about Leora's reaction to conditions on the island. The decision to bring her along on this mission now seems wildly reckless.

Arrowsmith finds himself trapped in a kind of emotional trap, the pressure building on him the longer he stays on the island and the more he sees. He quickly discovers that he "did not feel superior to humanity," even though he is expected to treat the people he meets as subjects of a research scheme in which he will be in charge of their lives. Instead, he empathizes, and sees himself in the faces of the plague victims.

His movement away from Gottlieb's ideal of objectivity reaches a climax when he visits the distant village of Carib, where, because of a particularly intense local infestation of ground squirrels that carry the plague fleas, the disease is at its worst, raging completely unchecked among the helpless population. Here, the descriptions of the plague become especially nightmarish: "He heard men shrieking in delirium; a dozen times he saw that face of terror—sunken bloody eyes, drawn face, open mouth—which marks the Black Death; and once he beheld an exquisite girl child in coma on the edge of death, her tongue black and round her the scent of the tomb." Arrowsmith now understands that Gottblieb had no practical experience trying to apply his scientific principles in the middle of the hysteria and suffering that characterize an actual epidemic.

It becomes especially clear that Arrowsmith cannot remain objective, of course, when Leora dies. As Lewis puts it, quite simply, "he went to pieces." He takes to drink, as he does throughout the novel when confronted by extreme stress. But most importantly, his experiment begins to fall apart. Although he maintains at least a trace of the experimental plan in St. Swithin's parish, where the experiment has just started, his resolve otherwise collapses. Because he has been touched by plague death in his own life, he can no longer be objective, and he gives the phage to anyone who asks for it.

Arrowsmith's situation on the island is the basic human condition: no one can ever rise completely above their circumstances to achieve perfect objectivity. Arrowsmith believes he has failed. By his own measure, he has. The only way Arrowsmith finds success, by his standards, in the end is by artificially separating himself from human society and important relations. Freed from caring and social interaction, he can pursue "pure" science. But readers are not likely to judge Arrowsmith's actions on St. Hubert's a failure. Through Arrowsmith, a battle between pure reason and human compassion is waged. Compassion wins. Few among us would want it any other way.

Source: Scott Herring, Critical Essay on *Arrowsmith* in *Novels for Students*, Gale, Cengage Learning, 2010.

James M. Hutchisson

In this essay, Hutchisson explains why Arrowsmith *is widely considered by critics to be a "breakthrough" novel for Sinclair Lewis.*

By the summer of 1922, Sinclair Lewis had established himself as a professional novelist and

"

ULTIMATELY, LEWIS MAY HAVE FOUND IN DE
KRUIF A SOULMATE WHO WAS ABLE TO BRING INTO
FOCUS THE IDEALISTIC VISION WHICH SEEMS
ALTERNATELY TO SHARPEN AND BLUR IN THE
UNEVEN SERIES OF NOVELS LEWIS PRODUCED."

had ample reason to believe that he was poised
on the brink of a brilliant literary career. He had
already secured a foothold in American literature by writing *Main Street*, which became both
a best seller and a paradigm for what would soon
be called "The Revolt from the Village." Awaiting the fall publication of his next novel, *Babbitt*,
which Lewis prophetically told his publisher
Alfred Harcourt would soon have America
"talking of Babbittry," he had finally, in the
words of H. L. Mencken, "come up from the
hulks" of writing magazine fiction. *Main Street*
had been nominated for the Pulitzer prize;
rumors were already circulating about Lewis as
a candidate for the Nobel.

As he thought about his next novel, however,
Lewis recognized that in order to win the unani-
mous critical acclaim that he most wanted he
would have to silence those carping voices whose
reviews of *Main Street* had said that Lewis was
"without spiritual gifts"; that his "exterior vision"
prohibited him from being sympathetic to his characters; and that he could not convey his notions of
the ideal in modern man. Similarly, reviewers of
Babbitt could not decide whether Lewis loved or
hated his creation and in effect asked Lewis to write
a novel in which his standards would be sufficiently
in evidence. That novel was *Arrowsmith*, a morality
tale about a young research scientist who seeks a
means of personal and professional fulfillment
without compromising his integrity. The book
answered Lewis's critics for it presented a hero of
whom Lewis approved—an idealistic truth-seeker
who is able to transcend the selfish, ugly environments that defeat the chief characters in *Main
Street* and *Babbitt*. *Arrowsmith* has remained
the most praised of Lewis's novels, in large
part because its satirical components—the one-
dimensional characters and the indictments of
twentieth-century culture that Lewis is known

for—are outweighed by its sobering, pervasive
idealism and its portrait of a character of some
complexity and depth. Indeed, *Arrowsmith* was
Lewis's "breakthrough" novel.

How Lewis was able to make such a giant
stride in his artistic development is an interesting
question that has never been studied. He did so
partly with the help of a young bacteriologist
named Paul H. de Kruif, whom Lewis employed
as a sort of research assistant for the novel.
Today, de Kruif's role in the making of *Arrowsmith* has been virtually forgotten, although de
Kruif went on to a distinguished literary career of
his own as a popularizer of science history. He
wrote thirteen best-sellers (some of which were
made into movies) that dramatized the scientific
detective work of such pioneers of microbiology
as Ehrlich, Leeuwenhoek, and Pasteur. Those
who know that de Kruif assisted Lewis believe
that his role was limited to providing the scientific
detail for the novel. I believe, by contrast, that de
Kruif's role was more involved than that, and
that his assistance accounts in large part for Lewis's ability to write a "heroic" novel. All the surviving notes and drafts for *Arrowsmith*, preserved
in the manuscript collections of Yale University
and the University of Texas at Austin, as well as
de Kruif's own testimony in his autobiography
and in two hitherto unpublished letters, affirm
that de Kruif was more than a mere technical
informant for Lewis; he served in a more imaginative and practical capacity. From his own various experiences de Kruif produced many of the
prototypes upon which Lewis based his characters; from de Kruif's own career Lewis drew
much of the plot about Arrowsmith's career;
and from de Kruif's personal philosophy Lewis
extracted the basis for Arrowsmith's idealism.

Even before he had finished *Babbitt*, Lewis
was "getting gleams" for his next novel, a work
Lewis told Harcourt would be "not satiric at all;
rebellious as ever, perhaps, but the central character heroic." What Lewis had in mind was a novel
about the American labor movement featuring a
Christ-like protagonist modeled on Eugene Debs,
the Socialist candidate for president who had been
imprisoned in 1918 for advocating pacifism. This
project would have fulfilled Lewis's ambitions to
write a "heroic" novel, but doubts clouded Lewis's
ability to work on it when he went to Chicago in
August 1922 to do research on labor unions.
(Throughout his career he made at least seven
recorded attempts to write this novel but never

progressed beyond the planning stages.) Unable to "work up a complete conformist sympathy" with the union men, Lewis told his wife Grace that he felt "melancholy and rather lost" and unsure whether he could write such a book.

At this point, then, Lewis was quite literally an author in search of a character. He found his hero through the help of Paul de Kruif. The two met by chance in the Chicago office of Dr. Morris Fishbein, at that time the spokesman for the American Medical Association and later editor of its *Journal*. The young de Kruif had been a rising star in the scientific world, studying microbiology under the most distinguished names in the field, and, after a brief service in the Army Sanitary Corps during the First World War, he was hired by the prestigious Rockefeller Institute in New York. There, he did research with Jacques Loeb, the high priest of the mechanist doctrine in science, which held that all living things are essentially chemical machines, and that behavior can therefore be determined genetically—a theory that anticipated the discovery of DNA. De Kruif soon became disenchanted with the Rockefeller, however, as he discovered the prevalence of commercialism in modern medicine and a disregard for the practical applications of experimental biology. For some time, de Kruif had had literary ambitions: in his autobiography, *The Sweeping Wind* (1962), he mentions working intermittently on an unfinished novel in 1920 and 1921: "What was trying to get written," he decided, "was *Arrowsmith* without Red Lewis's skill as a writer." He also discusses "getting a toehold in the literary world" through the help of Mencken, George Jean Nathan, Francis Hackett, and Harold Stearns, for whose omnibus of social criticism, *Civilization in the United States* (1922), de Kruif contributed the chapter on "Medicine," in which he mocked the lofty ambitions of the research scientists with whom he worked. When soon thereafter the *Century Illustrated Monthly* commissioned him to write a series of four anonymous articles "exposing" the medical establishment, he at once accepted, and again drew liberally on his experiences with the Rockefeller Institute. These were published from January through April 1922 under the running title, "Our Medicine Men By One Of Them." Three months later, de Kruif was unemployed.

Lewis and de Kruif ended up spending the rest of the day together, talking about how difficult it was in America for a young man to devote himself to science and repudiate ordinary "success." They became instant friends, and, just as

quickly, collaborators on a novel about medicine. Four months later, in December, they met again in New York at the Harcourt, Brace, offices to finalize their plans. A formal contract was drawn up: Lewis and de Kruif were to share top billing in a full collaboration, seventy-five percent of the royalties going to Lewis and twenty-five to de Kruif. However, Harcourt soon decided that de Kruif's name should not go on the title page with Lewis's, for fear that, as de Kruif recalled, "if the critics and the book buyers see Lewis and de Kruif on the cover, they'll say Lewis is finished. He's hiring an unknown to help write his book for him." De Kruif, however, knowing little about the vagaries of the publishing industry, acceded to Harcourt's wishes. After the novel was finished, his friendship with Lewis would cool because of a quarrel over how de Kruif's assistance would be acknowledged. De Kruif was more expansive about the incident thirty years later. Grace Hegger Lewis wrote him in 1952 and 1953 asking for information to use in her memoir of Lewis. In one reply, de Kruif confided that since he had accepted these terms, he would "try to make up for not being on the cover by being damn well between the covers in regard to what went in." On 6 January 1923, the two men left for an extended tour of the West Indies in order to gather material for the climax of the novel, the plague on St. Hubert which forces Arrowsmith to test his scientific scruples against his medical ethics and resist inoculating the whole population with his serum in order to maintain a control group.

On board the steamer *S. S. Guiana*, Lewis and de Kruif set to work. As was his habit, Lewis began a novel by recording factual or invented data in a looseleaf notebook. Then, drawing on these materials, Lewis would type out a "plan" or scene-by-scene outline of the entire novel as he then envisioned it. By the time the trip had ended and they had arrived in England, where Lewis then began the first draft, he had compiled a plan of over 60,000 words—the length of a short novel itself. The plan unfortunately does not survive, but the notebook is preserved among Lewis's papers at Yale. It is a fascinating literary artifact, yet its contents have never before been published or even commented upon in any detail. The notebook attests to Lewis's skills as a photographic realist. It is divided up by the six main settings in the novel: the University of Winnemac, where Arrowsmith is a medical student; Wheatsylvania, his wife Leora's hometown, where he briefly practices "country medicine"; Nautilus, where he works in the public health department under the zealous Almus Pickerbaugh; the Rouncefield Clinic in Chicago, where he is part of a "group" medical practice; the McGurk Institute in New York, where he joins his medical school mentor Max Gottlieb and makes his first important scientific discovery; and St. Hubert, the fictional Carribean island.

The notebook is a model of painstaking detail. Lewis drew intricately detailed maps of the interior and exterior settings, some of them with numbered keys to the exact locations of stores and houses. For each geographical area Lewis also invented an entire demographic profile, from its main industries to such minutiae as the political affiliations of its newspapers. For many of these details in the novel, Lewis simply drew from the notebook—he even checked off various items after he had used them. For example, in a section entitled "Nautilus—Main Outlines," Lewis listed the "'best' residence section—small & smart—" as "Ashford Grove," then, "next: Social Hill—here Mart & Leora in two-family house...About equal: The West Side—here Pickergill [Pickerbaugh]." There is also a page entitled "Nautilus data," which lists "Manufactures" as "Agricultural implements—especially the Daisy Manure Spreader," "Maize Mealies," the "Combelt Cooperative Ins[urance] Co," and the "Tredgold Steel Windmill Co—Clay Tredgold, pres." These particular details are found in chapters 19 and 20, but Lewis used this method on nearly every page of the novel. Eight pages of the notebook contain miscellaneous observations about the islands he and de Kruif visited. Here the notes are more random, but no less detailed: "in cocoa woods, piles of rotting red & yellow husks"; "Kids w[ith] nothing on but open cotton coat"; "Liquor wagon painted gaudy red w. 'His M. S. Hood'"; "pathetically pale white boys on bikes—always pale, thin hair, red-rimmed eyes, like albinos. 2 or 3 mile swarm of blacks."

Scattered throughout the notebook, too, are fragmentary thoughts which confirm Lewis's great expectations for the mythic proportions of the novel, such as this:

> Thru-out—how Mart falls & rises, again & again in his devotion to *religion of science*—w. Silva, Sond[elius], group med[ical practice] at the Rouncefield Clinic]—fable of the questing scientist...and how begins a new mind in man—yet not Utopian; real vision, at last clear & sure, of truth, and not just in genius like Voltaire or G'lieb.

And there are endless lists of names from which Lewis chose for the major and minor characters, some of which he developed full "biographies" for, others which merit only a line or two of identification. The most technical material in the notebook is five pages entitled "BACTERIO-LOGICAL NOTES." These were the result of de Kruif's tutoring Lewis in the methods of scientific research. This section contains meticulous descriptions of Arrowsmith's experiments, with step-by-step illustrations of laboratory equipment—and even drawings of various strains of bacilli.

Obviously Lewis would not have worked this material into the novel without de Kruif's help. Even though medicine was an important part of his family background (his brother was a respected surgeon and his father a general practitioner), Lewis was ignorant about experimental medical research. De Kruif provided technical aid, and all through their voyage, Lewis found that they could "work together perfectly. Each day I have greater respect for his totally unusual and fine though fiery brain." His letters during that period are virtually paeans—Lewis told Harcourt that de Kruif was "a damn clever man"; to H. G. Wells: "a man with a knife-edge mind and an iconoclasm that really means something"; to H. L. Mencken: "Paul was wonderful"; to his father, "it's extraordinary how well de Kruif and I work together...never a row, never a disagreement."

While it is clear that de Kruif provided the scientific ballast for *Arrowsmith*, it is not the "sober factuality" of the novel, to use Sheldon Grebstein's words, that distinguishes it. Indeed, most critics of Lewis commend *Arrowsmith* precisely because it is not overladen with the tedious detail that many feel mar the dramatic action of *Main Street* and *Babbitt*. No one, however, has asked how much de Kruif assisted with the non-scientific parts of the narrative. Much evidence shows that de Kruif helped Lewis extensively with the human story of the novel. At various ports of call along their route, Lewis and de Kruif would debark and explore the island, doing field research like anthropologists, scouting locations like film directors. While Lewis "kept peering from island to island for backgrounds against which to stage horrible epidemics," de Kruif's task was "to look for outlandish characters," some of whom came to life in the novel. The health officer in the Barbados village of Bridgetown, for example, one "little Doctor Hutson" who showed de Kruif "that horrible epidemics were improbable on his salubrious island," seems to have been the model for St. Hubert's Dr. R. E. Inchape Jones, who says much the same thing. The Ice House in Trinidad that de Kruif describes in his memoir with its "sinister" gloom and its "famous...planter's punches in cold tall glasses beaded with moisture," is echoed by the description of the Ice House in the fictional Blackwater. Many of Lewis's remarks about de Kruif during this period suggest that he assisted Lewis with some of the imaginative material. Lewis told Harcourt that in London he would "need to confer with [de Kruif] about not merely scientific points but the whole texture of the book for, even where I and not he have created a character, his understanding is perfect and always inspiring." At about the same time, Lewis wrote Mencken to say that "all through the trip, Paul was wonderful. His greatest pleasure was to be called on for some damn hard problem, involving not only sheer scientific knowledge but also an imagination, a perception of what was dramatic."

Lewis's creation of the central character also owes much to de Kruif. Much of the criticism of *Arrowsmith* has tended to emphasize the parallels between the character's career and Lewis's career. Just as Arrowsmith turns his back on marriage in favor of his work, so too did Lewis at the time shirk his responsibilities to Grace (though their marriage had been unstable from the beginning). It is also possible to read the narrative as an allegory of Lewis's own struggle as a writer. Just as Arrowsmith cannot decide whether he should use his talents to heal the sick or to devote himself to pure research (in loosely metaphorical terms, the conflict between craft and art), so too did Lewis move between writing slick magazine fiction and "serious" novels. This similarity, which Lewis himself had in mind when he later entitled a mock obituary of himself "The Death of Arrowsmith," was probably what led his biographer Mark Schorer to claim that "for all the importance of Paul de Kruif's contribution to the [scientific] material of *Arrowsmith*, it is interesting to note how much of Sinclair Lewis's own background went into the novel."

It is more important, I believe, to note how much of de Kruif's background went into the novel. In *The Sweeping Wind*, de Kruif says that his chief task was to write "'a treatment' of Arrowsmith's career." There are close parallels between the early career of de Kruif before he met Lewis and the fictional Arrowsmith to the point where he joins the McGurk Institute. A page in the notebook entitled "CHRONOLOGY OF MARTIN ARROWSMITH" divides the plot into fourteen phases of Arrowsmith's life from his birth to his resignation from the McGurk. The dates at which Lewis set these periods are each exactly seven years earlier than the dates of similar events in de Kruif's career. (The seven-year gap allowed for de Kruif's military service abroad in World War One; this event is treated only in a minor way in the novel.)

Like Arrowsmith, de Kruif was born in the Midwest, attended the state university (Michigan) and fell under the spell of a fatherly mentor, then entered medical school and became an assistant to a famous scientist. In de Kruif's case, this was the microbiologist Frederick G. Novy, who, with Loeb, afforded a composite model for the character of Gottlieb. Three years later, again like Arrowsmith, de Kruif married for the first time at age 25. Herein lies the most interesting parallel. De Kruif's first marriage ended in divorce seven years later, in December 1922; he then married one Rhea Barbarin, with whom he had been in love for some time, just before he and Lewis began work on the novel. De Kruif met Rhea while an intern at the university hospital, just as Arrowsmith meets Leora under the same circumstances. Like the fictional Arrowsmith, who must elope and keep his marriage a secret, de Kruif also married under tense circumstances. And as much as de Kruif's career resembles Arrowsmith's, Rhea seems to have been something of a model for the fictional Leora. De Kruif recalled that during the planning of the novel, Lewis's "portrait of Leora—lovely in her abnegation—was growing more and more to be the image of my Rhea." Elsewhere, de Kruif remarks that "Leora's death kept making me see Rhea dying." This similarity is significant because reviewers who had heretofore criticized Lewis for his inability to draw women characters realistically all praised the characterization of Leora. Indeed, Harcourt said that Leora was "just about the best woman character in American fiction," and suggested that Lewis end the book with her death and entitle it "Leora." Lewis himself publicly remarked that Leora contained most of his "capacity for loyalty to love and friendship." Yet Leora seems to have been more a part of de Kruif than of Lewis—indeed, Lewis's dream of the undemanding wife who requires only that her husband be left alone to work and achieve fame was hardly fulfilled by Grace.

Lewis seems to have deviated from the next phase of de Kruif's career as de Kruif entered the army in 1916. At this point in the novel come the Wheatsylvania, Nautilus, and Chicago sections. These scenes are almost completely satirical, and the characters in them are common Lewis "types"—the incompetents, the charlatans, the opportunists. I believe, in other words, that these sections are the only thoroughly satirical ones in the novel because here Lewis was not following de Kruif's experiences as a model (though here too, as I shall point out, Lewis probably owes something to de Kruif's view of public health officials in the Pickerbaugh scenes). According to the chronology, the last of these episodes ends in late 1917 or early 1918 as Arrowsmith joins the McGurk Institute—approximately the same time de Kruif returned to the United States and entered the employ of the Rockefeller Institute. And, of course, there is a clear parallel between Arrowsmith's repudiation of the McGurk and de Kruif's similar disenchantment with and resignation from the Rockefeller.

These surface connections may be simply the natural result of de Kruif's self-reflection as he thought about a hypothetical scientist. But there is a third level on which de Kruif entered the novel—the deepest and most important one: insofar as *Arrowsmith* is a commentary on medicine and biological research, it clearly reflects the values and attitudes of de Kruif. One can see his influence on *Arrowsmith* in the *Century* essays he wrote about medicine and science which predate his work with Lewis. In one article, "Are Commercialism and Science Ruining Medicine," de Kruif mourns the loss of the "old-fashioned general practitioner" who once fulfilled the role of the patient's "comforter and friend." The "old doc," as de Kruif calls him, is being replaced by "the new god of science." Here we see the two philosophies Arrowsmith struggles to reconcile—described in the very metaphor of gods and idols that Lewis weaves throughout the narrative. One is embodied in Arrowsmith's first "god," T. J. H. "Dad" Silva, Dean of the University of Winnemac Medical School, whose description in the novel is close to that of the anonymous "T. G. H." whom de Kruif cites as his own mentor (p. 417). The other is Max Gottlieb, who peers through de Kruif's portrait of the "cool, disinterested, and impartial" scientist in the essay. His insistence on maintaining "untreated cases" or "controls" (Gottlieb's watchword in the novel) in experimentation is at cross-purposes with the "good doctor," who believes that "*nothing should be left undone to cure the patient*." De Kruif's

essential argument, that "Humanity in general is certainly not ready . . . to take the place of the laboratory guinea-pig" clearly informs Arrowsmith's divided loyalties to his various "gods" and provides the basis for the dramatic climax on St. Hubert when Arrowsmith realizes that giving the serum under test conditions means condemning thousands to die. The commercialism Arrowsmith finds in his brief employment at the Rouncefield Clinic in Chicago probably also has its basis in some of de Kruif's observations in this essay. Throughout the article, de Kruif exposes the "hypocrisy, charlatanism, loud advertisement" and "meretricious efficiency" of the medical profession and specifically criticizes the "coalition of specialists known as 'the group'" for doing what Arrowsmith's Rouncefield colleagues do: advising rich patients to have operations "on the flimsiest evidence of their necessity," and to undergo a battery of "very expensive" tests at the direction of the "diagnostician," who in turn refers the "sufferer" to "the appropriate surgeon of the group."

The second *Century* essay, "What Is Preventive Medicine Preventing?" concerns public health movements and their relation to the study of disease. De Kruif's attack on these "shouters for public health," or "dubious Messiahs who combine the zealous fanaticism of the missionary with the Jesuitical cynicism of the politician" echoes through Lewis's descriptions of Pickerbaugh. In fact, when in 1953 Grace asked de Kruif if he "invented" Pickerbaugh, de Kruif replied, "Yes, largely. He came right out of the scrapbook of a health officer. But Red added some priceless touches. We invented him together." One public health doctrine de Kruif attacks is the refusal to endorse birth control, an issue that Lewis might have had in mind in chapter 21, where Arrowsmith fights Pickerbaugh's zealous publicizing of "More Babies Week." Arrowsmith's public health reforms in the next chapter were also probably inspired by a series of incidents de Kruif claimed could happen when the overanxious health official causes "serious embarrassment and needless economic losses" to a city. In one hypothetical scenario described in the essay, a group of plumbers are quarantined for diphtheria—over the protests of the city leaders, whose districts are being overrun by sewage problems; they eventually hound the health officer from his post. This situation is much like Arrowsmith's pyrrhic victory in quarantining an employee of Klopchuck's dairy and demolishing the unsanitary McCandless tenements in chapters 22 and 24, events which cause his resignation under fire.

These ideas surely guided Lewis as he drafted the novel. During the voyage, Lewis wrote to Harcourt that de Kruif had "not only an astonishing grasp of scientific detail" but "a philosophy behind it"; that he possessed "the imagination of the fiction writer"; and, Lewis confided, that de Kruif's role in the creation of the novel was at least as large as his own:

> He sees, synthesizes, characters. You've sometimes said that my books are meaty; this will be much the meatiest of all—characters, places, contrasting purposes and views of life; and in all of this there's a question as to whether he won't have contributed more than I shall have. Yet he takes it for granted that he is not to sign the book with me. And he loves work ... when I'm compiling notes into a coherent whole, de Kruif is preparing more data—clear, sound, and just the stuff for dramatic purposes.

At about the same time, he wrote to Mencken that de Kruif "proves to have as much synthetic fictional imagination as he has scientific knowledge, and that's one hell of a lot ... It's going to be my best book—though it isn't just *mine* by a long shot."

All this is not to say that de Kruif wrote *Arrowsmith*. Indeed, in his correspondence with Grace, de Kruif laid to rest the speculations of "the vast majority" of scientists who when the book was published thought that "de Kruif wrote ARROWSMITH and got gypped out of the credit." "This is nonsense," he stated. "Red wrote ARROWSMITH." However, de Kruif added, "I helped a substantial amount both with the science and the human story." Through all this, Lewis and de Kruif's arrangement seems to have been a marriage of true minds. Lewis needed de Kruif to help him understand the spirit of scientific research and show him the concept of the idealistic hero—even in some ways be a model for that figure. De Kruif needed Lewis to teach him how to write, for he was mired in the jargon-ridden, bloated prose of the laboratory researcher.

During the first week in March 1923, Lewis and de Kruif arrived in Plymouth, England, and by the end of April Lewis had finished the plan. By 3 May he had begun writing the first draft. Rhea joined de Kruif in London and they took an apartment in Chelsea, near Lewis's rooms in St. James, so that de Kruif would be available to Lewis when he needed his assistance. Among other things, de Kruif arranged for Lewis to meet "a number of scientists" and visit laboratories in order to watch some "actual work." In late June Lewis left England to meet Grace in Fontainebleau, where he pushed on with the typescript, finally completing it on 30 September. That week, the de Kruifs joined the Lewises in France and de Kruif read through the draft.

The typescript, preserved in the Lewis Collection at Austin, numbers over 850 leaves. Lewis revised it meticulously, interlining sentences, inserting pages of new material then revising them, changing a phrase or a single word sometimes as many as three or four times. (The final product was such a mess that when Lewis showed it to Arnold Bennett, the latter noted his journal, "All blue and red, with millions of alterations—a terrible sight!") Through the labyrinth of revisions, however, one can find a pattern: nearly all of Lewis's large-scale cuts deleted satirical material, material that to some degree undercut, digressed from, or obscured the theme of idealism. Based on de Kruif's role in the planning of the novel, one might assume that Lewis made these changes under his direction, but that was not the case. However, Lewis did solicit de Kruif's suggestions as he wrote and revised the typescript. Again, it was de Kruif's *presence* which seems to have guided Lewis's thinking. As Lewis typed the draft, he also typed into it notes to de Kruif, asking, as might be expected, for de Kruif to check or correct technical details. In Lewis's initial description of the McGurk Institute in chapter 26, to take just one of many examples, he asked de Kruif if any details were missing in the description of Arrowsmith's laboratory, to which de Kruif responded, "Yes—a microscope and logarithm tables and hydrogen-ion charts on the walls." Lewis then added these items in the revision.

But Lewis also solicited de Kruif's literary advice; some of the notes ask whether a scene should be deleted or retained. Most of de Kruif's pencilled answers are still legible on the typescript, though some of them are erased or marked through; presumably this means Lewis rejected them. However, several of them Lewis did not reject—and in these de Kruif urged Lewis to condense or cut altogether many of the satirical scenes in the book, especially in its midsection, where Lewis evidently did not follow de Kruif's career as a "model" for the narrative. For example, in chapter 16, which takes place one year after Arrowsmith has settled in Wheatsylvania and is beginning to adjust to that environment, Lewis had originally written four lengthy scenes that more fully developed Arrowsmith's experience there. These do not appear in the published text. In one passage,

Arrowsmith wins over the antagonistic pastor of the United Brethren Church and thereby becomes a "Good Citizen," an event which "almost" causes him "to be taken seriously by Bert and Mr. Tozer," Leora's brother and father. In this scene, Arrowsmith is seduced by the idea of being "prosperous and Settled for Life"—a phrase that might have been spoken by George F. Babbitt, or some similar character from Lewis's storehouse of stereotypes. In another scene, Lewis satirized small-town ethics and boosterism: at one point Bert Tozer bribes a minor-league baseball "star," Mike Shumway, to come to Wheatsylvania and organize a team there. The details of the town council's payoff to Shumway are clumsily covered up, and Arrowsmith refuses to sanction it. Lewis was probably trying to show Arrowsmith successfully escaping the claustrophobia of the environment, but the scene is related only tenuously to the idealism of the main character and is digressive. In the left-hand margin of two of these pages, de Kruif commented: "cut or condense?" and at the heading of the chapter he wrote, "Suggest the following scenes be condensed." Evidently reading over his comments, Lewis agreed, for he made a note in the top right hand corner of that same page, "Go over 294–313 and cut as a whole."

In the following chapter, there is a two-section interlude in the description of Arrowsmith's work in Wheatsylvania that describes a motoring trip taken by the buffoonish Dr. Coughlin of Leopolis. In typescript, the scene is twice its length in the published novel. The passages are humorous in their mockery of consumer culture and civic pride: Coughlin visits a physician in nearby St. Luke; they discuss collecting fees and the latest pharmaceutical products and office equipment. One again hears Babbitt-isms and sees a landscape like that of *Main Street*. Throughout these passages, de Kruif commented: "maybe condense a little"; "cut Coughlin's motoring trip a little", "is this scene *necessary*?" Lewis cut most of this material, reducing Wheatsylvania to a backdrop for the main focus of the novel, Arrowsmith's idealism and his work at the McGurk and then on St. Hubert.

Lewis might have been aiming to counterpoint this stage of Arrowsmith's career with the others, but the overdevelopment of this section would have amplified the contrast too much and become digressive. In these passages one can see Lewis's satirical tendencies and the typical objects of his scorn: the small-town yokel, the stupid American tourist, village hypocrisy. Whether Lewis himself saw this pattern or whether he saw it through de Kruif's comments one cannot tell. But given Lewis's admission of depending on de Kruif for assistance, one cannot help but think that de Kruif was responsible for curbing Lewis's instinctively satirical impulses here.

Of course, Lewis himself made many of the changes, though in some instances, he first asked de Kruif's opinion. Many of these revisions show him checking himself, being careful to keep the satirical elements of the novel subordinate to the theme. In chapter 22, for instance, Lewis had planned for Pickerbaugh to make a bogus scientific "discovery," according to a note addressed to de Kruif at the top of this typescript page:

> I have retained the notes . . . at the end of [your] special material. But I'm afraid of Nautilus running too long, with all of the crucial McGurk-St. Hubert-Terry-Joyce material coming; and also it now seems to me that this Pickergill-making-discovery matter gets too far from Martin-Leora-Gottlieb who *are* the book.

De Kruif responded "check!", presumably concurring with Lewis's judgment. What follows instead is a scene that more fully illustrates Arrowsmith's thorough dedication to his profession. For this chapter, Lewis seems to have used the example in de Kruif's *Century* article about a diphtheria "epidemic" and its effect on the young health officer's standing in the community. Two chapters later, Lewis considered extending Arrowsmith's battle with the city leaders, but noted to de Kruif that there was "no virtue to the scene—gets nowhere." De Kruif agreed, noting, "Vote against."

Later, Lewis made several similar changes in the McGurk chapters, again worrying aloud to de Kruif that they were too satirical. In chapter 26, Lewis wrote de Kruif a long note justifying his decision to discard a character, one Wallace Umstead, who was to be head of the "Dept of Psychometrics and Teleological Psych." Lewis thought this would sound "a false note." It would make "McGurk at least partly absurd that it should have such a dept. Umstead belongs in another novel with an atmosphere of cults and general idiocy, not in one of hard scientists who, with all their hardness, yet are often ineffective. Let's talk this over. What do you think?" De Kruif answered, "Yes!"

Finally, Lewis revised a scene that came before the satirical midpoint of the novel, again at de Kruif's suggestion. With the exception of the Pickerbaugh chapters, there are few scenes in the novel as satirical as the farewell address given by Roscoe Geake in chapter 8, on "The Art and Science of Furnishing the Doctor's Office." Geake has been called from the chair of otolaryngology at the medical school to assume the vice presidency of the New Idea Medical Instrument and Furniture Company. This scene, with its gentle satire of "the two warring schools" in office design, "the Tapestry School" and "the Aseptic School," recalls Babbitt's speech before the Zenith Real Estate Board about "Our Ideal Citizen" or Chum Frink's rhapsodic advertising jingle for the Zeeco Motor Car Company. As it reads in the published novel, the scene is Lewis at his best: a compact parody that is not heavy-handed. But the scene was approximately fifty percent longer in typescript. At this point, de Kruif noted, "foregoing undoubtedly a sermon—but it is a damned good one—keep as much as you can." Lewis's condensing of the scene may have resulted from de Kruif's prompting.

During the week that de Kruif worked through the draft, Lewis continued to praise his skills as an editor and as an advisor. On 28 September 1923, he told Harcourt, "if you could have seen how he went at *Martin* here—working night and day yet reading with such minute precision! My admiration for him is greater now than ever." During the late fall and winter of 1923, Lewis revised the typescript, then had a clean copy of the revised draft typed. The ribbon copy of this second typescript, which is in the Lewis Collection at Yale, served as setting copy for the book. He then probably cut from the carbon copy of this second typescript (it is not extant) for the serialization of *Arrowsmith* in the *Designer and Woman's Magazine*. This work was finished at the end of April 1924, and the serial ran from June of that year through April 1925. In March 1925, *Arrowsmith* was published in book form.

By the time the novel appeared, however, Lewis and de Kruif had angrily broken off their friendship because of a disagreement over how de Kruif's assistance should be credited in the published book. Separating truth from legend in this incident is difficult because the amount of surviving evidence about it is unusually sparse. As editor of Lewis's letters, Harrison Smith (then a junior partner at Harcourt, Brace), chose this point in the correspondence about *Arrowsmith* to summarize developments during late September and early October 1924, when the page proofs came through without any acknowledgment of de Kruif's work. Harcourt remained

conspicuously silent on the matter in his memoirs, which recounted most everything about the Lewis-de Kruif alliance except this point. However, de Kruif spoke of it at length in the information he supplied Grace for her book, information which, for whatever reason, she chose not to include: just before Lewis left London in July 1923 for Fontainebleau he showed de Kruif what he had written as an "acknowledgment of [his] collaboration that was going to run page after title page." De Kruif remembered it as "truly terrific in its eulogy and homage. I was by God no mere bacteriologist... but a creative writer et cetera et cetera for about 150 words— to the extent that I blushed with pride." Then, when the proofs were generated October 1924, "there was not this *eloge* but only thanking Paul H. de Kruif for his help in scientific and technical aspects of the work." De Kruif told Grace that he instructed the publishers simply to remove all mention of his "assistance"—"or at least have [Lewis] tell the truth about my part." Brace persuaded Lewis to write something else and finally this paragraph was run in the front matter of the first edition:

> To Dr. Paul H. De Kruif I am indebted not only for most of the bacteriological and medical material in this tale but equally for his help in the planning of the fable itself—for his realization of the characters as living people, for his philosophy as a scientist. With this acknowledgment I want to record our months of companionship while working on the book, in the United States, in the West Indies, in Panama, in London and Fontainebleau. I wish I could reproduce our talks along the way, and the laboratory afternoons, the restaurants at night, and the deck at dawn as we steamed into tropic ports.

Despite this controversy, however, de Kruif continued to think highly of Lewis: he remembered him as "a brilliantly imaginative man who dared to let his imagination go on paper," something de Kruif "had never dared to do" in his scientific writing. Most of all, de Kruif remained grateful to Lewis for the experience, because as he told Grace, "I could never have become a good writer without him."

The evidence for Paul de Kruif's influence on the conception, research, planning, and editing of *Arrowsmith* is strong. That he played such a significant role is important, for the heroic theme and the idealistic nature of the protagonist seem to owe a good deal to de Kruif's presence in the creative process that shaped the novel. While de Kruif clearly did not write *Arrowsmith,* he did in many instances tell and show Lewis what to write about. Trying to guess how *Arrowsmith* would have turned out had de Kruif not assisted Lewis is difficult to do, but I believe that *Arrowsmith* would have been a much different novel without de Kruif's influence: It would have been a novel mostly of caricature, not a novel of character—a novel that debunked and satirized but probably gave less of an affirmative view of the heroic in modern man.

Several facts support this theory. For one thing, Lewis's first impulses in planning *Arrowsmith* led him to think in comic terms. De Kruif recalled that when he first told Lewis of his experiences, Lewis "roared with laughter" and thought de Kruif's story was "an epic of medical debonkology, skeptical, yes, cynically satirical." Further, Lewis conceived of *Arrowsmith* in terms of his earlier novels: "Medicine and medical science... seemed... like *Main Street*, and many of its greatest names turned out to be oafs like Babbitt." De Kruif also said that Lewis's earliest "plots and characters" centered on "a flamboyant Swedish epidemiologist, a money-mad professor of otolaryngology, a buffoonish missionary of public health"—that is, foils to the stark hero. Even as the contract for *Arrowsmith* was about to be drawn up, Lewis changed his mind about the book. He pitched the idea to his publishers not as a novel about an idealistic truth-seeker, but rather as a magazine serial for *Hearst's*—"stories with a new type of hero, a character—bacteriologist, doctor, public health detective—all in one." De Kruif pejoratively characterized it as "a kind of scientific Clarence Budington Kelland production."

Moreover, Lewis was not able to draw a heroic character with complete success in any work except *Arrowsmith*. His novels contain a clear pattern: there is a representative American artist-figure (in various forms) who pursues an idealistic vision, is defeated by his environment, renounces his earlier idealism, then retreats back into reality and thereby metaphorically perishes. Only *Arrowsmith* deviates from this pattern. All of Lewis's characters before Arrowsmith have spiritual ambitions that go unfulfilled: Carol Kennicott and Babbitt come readily to mind, and the heroes of Lewis's apprentice fiction— the title character of *Our Mr. Wrenn* (1914), Hawk Ericson of *The Trail of the Hawk* (1915), and Una Golden of *The Job* (1917)—all possess idealistic notions which they cannot bring to fruition. Those novels following *Arrowsmith* portray either characters with false ideals or, again, submerged ideals that cannot be realized. In the next major novel after *Arrowsmith*, *Elmer Gantry* (1927), Lewis wrote his most vicious satire; there, he is openly contemptuous of his protagonist, who adopts the opportunistic compromises of his society as his "ideals." When in 1943 Lewis again took up the subject of the flim-flam man, he created in the title character of *Gideon Planish* simply another version of Elmer Gantry, someone who exploits the good in society, this time through a philanthropic organization instead of a church. In *Dodsworth* (1929), we see idealism in an expatriate, but European culture does not fill the emptiness in his heart after the breakup of his marriage. His remedy is to marry again, yet when Dodsworth reappears in Lewis's last completed novel, *World So Wide*, published posthumously in 1951, he warns Lewis's architect-hero, Hayden Chart, against the unreality of his European rootlessness. In *Work of Art* (1934), the artist-figure is an unabashed realist who gives up his ideal of transforming a second-rate hotel into a grand one in the European tradition and settles for owning an undistinguished motel, finding that in the end he can work hard and get along just as well. With the possible exception of *Ann Vickers* (1933)—in which a social activist reforms the System yet then renounces her work and marries, thereby achieving a partial sense of fulfillment—this strain of latent idealism found full expression only in *Arrowsmith*. Possibly de Kruif's presence enabled Lewis to release it.

Following the popular success but critical skepticism attending *Babbitt* Lewis knew that he had to create a hero with whom he was in sympathy. Harcourt emphasized the practical necessity for that in several letters to him, one of which argued for having the word "doctor" in the title of *Arrowsmith* because "The world pretty much knows now that your father was a small-town doctor, and it would readily connote to a good many thousands of people a more than glowing story with a hero of whom you approve as one of the bases of civilization." Lewis had tried hard to do that with Babbitt, to be at once critical of Babbitt's world view yet be sympathetic to him as well, and critical judgment of that novel has remained divided: it is not clear whether Lewis's attitude toward Babbitt is one of love or contempt. He in fact longed to write a "heroic" novel. He tried to do so at least twice before he met de Kruif and thought of medical research as a subject. The first of these, the labor novel, he could not write because he could find no heroism among union men, despite his admiration for Eugene Debs ("But there's so few Debses," he wrote Grace). Abandoning that idea, he next considered an "American abroad story" concerning "a business man, a Zenithite, but NOT a Babbitt," as he told Grace, "a university man" who is "a lover of books, music." This idea was the germ for *Dodsworth*. Lewis's first two impulses, then, for what would follow *Babbitt* led in the direction of a "heroic" novel, but he seems to have felt unconfident about acting on them. Yet with de Kruif's help, he successfully wrote *Arrowsmith*.

Ultimately, Lewis may have found in de Kruif a soulmate who was able to bring into focus the idealistic vision which seems alternately to sharpen and blur in the uneven series of novels Lewis produced. Both men were iconoclasts who exposed hypocrisy, but their temperaments were fundamentally different. De Kruif's whole career was characterized by what he once called "smoking out pseudo-scientific sonofabitches" yet at the same time crusading to recognize and reward legitimate medical discovery. The commonplace perception of Lewis is that he attacked fraud, but his satirical stereotypes were never counterbalanced by characters of integrity and his novels were based entirely on destructive criticism that offered no hope of improving human institutions. *Arrowsmith* rebuts that perception. But few admirers of the novel have seemed to know the extent of Paul de Kruif's influence on Lewis in this regard. Harold Bloom has recently called it "a fitting irony that the satirist Sinclair Lewis should be remembered now for this idealizing romance." Fitting irony, indeed.

Source: James M. Hutchisson, "Sinclair Lewis, Paul De Kruif, and the Composition of *Arrowsmith*," in *Studies in the Novel*, Vol. 24, No. 1, Spring 1992, pp. 48–66.

Leo Gurko

In this essay, Leo and Miriam Gurko argue that Arrowsmith, *while not Lewis's most famous novel, is his most mature and accomplished.*

In 1930 Sinclair Lewis became the first American writer to win the Nobel Prize. Yet, during the last twelve years, he has published only one novel, *Ann Vickers*, which by the remotest stretch of the imagination can be regarded as within the periphery of his great work; his last

> THE ONE TOWERING EXCEPTION TO THIS DUALITY, THE ONE NOVEL IN WHICH LEWIS SHAKES HIMSELF FREE FROM THE CONTRADICTIONS ENMESHING HIM, IS *ARROWSMITH*."

four books have been successively painful failures, representing in an ever downward arc the decay of a once flourishing and prolific talent.

An examination of his work, and more particularly the three principal divisions into which it falls, suggests that to the degree that Lewis practices the art of satire—and particularly satire against the Main Street which he made famous—to that degree his novels teem with an abundant life; conversely, his abandonment of satire drains his works of their élan and reduces them to pulpiness and routine. There are to be observed in him two distinct, fundamentally antithetical points of view with regard to his central theme. On the one hand, he satirizes the materialists of Zenith and Gopher Prairie for their ignorance, their standardized thinking, aggressive provincialism, and self-righteous tyranny over all those who do not rigidly subscribe to their ways. On the other, he finds in them much kindliness, honesty, a genuine idealism which on occasion assumes the guise of social reform, and even a certain poetic sensitivity. This antithesis, this alternation between attack and defense, permeates nearly all his novels and is to be found even in the great satirical classics of the 1920's.

Before the advent of these classics, however, Lewis wrote a number of little-known, small-scale novels, in which the roots of this antithesis are perhaps most clearly visible. He veers from whimsical apologias for the provincial, "folksy" people, later to be ridiculed in *Main Street*, to heated criticisms of them, their institutions, and their ways of life. If *Our Mr. Wrenn*, *The Innocents*, and *Free Air* represent the first attitude, then *The Trail of the Hawk* and *The Job* express the second. *The Job*—the most serious and perhaps the best of these early novels—straddles both sides. It begins with an exposure of what Lewis considers the uselessness and irrational mechanism of business life but concludes with roseate observations of this very life. The book—indeed, this whole early period—reveals the uncertainties within Lewis' mind. He has not succeeded, as, in a sense, he was destined never to succeed, wholly to resolve his central theme: whether to satirize or espouse Main Street. We have here a portrait of a novelist still grappling with his theme, testing it from various angles, giving free rein to his ambivalent feelings. This period of unfocused hesitation and doubt comes to an abrupt end with the spectacular appearance of *Main Street*, which opens the second large phase of Lewis' career—the phase of the great satires and the triumphant journey to the Nobel Prize.

Main Street lays the groundwork of Lewis' campaign against a crassly materialist society wherever it appears, in small towns like Gopher Prairie, as well as in sizable industrial communities like Zenith and metropolises like New York. As long as he maintains his satirical offensive, as long as Carol Kennicott rebels against the demoralizing philistinism of Gopher Prairie, the novel has enormous power. The point of the book is definitively clear, and the exposure of the soullessness of provincial life is deadly and all embracing. But Lewis is not content to let matters rest here. He blurs his focus by occasional confusing shifts in sympathy. At times he appears to side with Will Kennicott, who embodies and defends the solid qualities of Main Street; at such times it is Carol who appears ridiculous. More than once she and her cultured friends are accused of snobbishly pursuing a false and contentless spirituality. But perhaps the most formidable shift is Carol's inexplicable acceptance of Main Street at the end of the novel. She returns to Gopher Prairie, not resolved to make the best of a bad bargain, but suddenly and mystically enthusiastic:

> The prairie was no longer empty land in the sun-glare; it was the living tawny beast which she had fought and made beautiful by fighting; and in the village streets were shadows of her desire and the sound of her marching and the seeds of mystery and greatness.

To describe Gopher Prairie as beautiful and filled with mystery and greatness is to negate everything that was said before. These shifts reveal Lewis' uncertainty, his alternate acceptance and rejection of Main Street. Though the first of his great satirical novels of the post-war period, *Main Street* contains, in an almost Hegelian fashion, the seeds of its own antithesis.

Lewis' affection for Will Kennicott introduces a whole series of curiously sympathetic portraits, which expose still further the duality of his feelings. The bellicose materialism of George F. Babbitt and the Rev. Elmer Gantry seems no more abhorrent to Lewis than does Kennicott's. For all their faults, Babbitt and Gantry are presented as pretty decent fellows at bottom. Gantry is a cheat, rogue, bluff, coward; but he is also good company, and Lewis obviously revels in his gusto. As for Babbitt, though Lewis pillories his ideas and associates, he displays a warm affection for the man himself. Babbitt longs to revolt, has faint aesthetic stirrings, and labors under the weight of enough courage to take a few hesitant steps away from the fence by which he is generally bounded. Not an effectual person, certainly, but a very human and likable one. Even the pathetic Lowell Schmaltz, protagonist of *The Man Who Knew Coolidge*, awakens more pity than censure. Lewis may not have much use for the ideals of Main Street, but he has a very considerable use for a very considerable number of Main Streeters.

The one towering exception to this duality, the one novel in which Lewis shakes himself free from the contradictions enmeshing him, is *Arrowsmith*. The satirical issues are at their clearest: his hostility to materialism is undiluted by affection for any of its representatives. Here, for the first time, Lewis is ranged entirely on the side of the rebels, who in the persons of Martin Arrowsmith, Terry Wickett, and Professor Gottlieb variously epitomize the spirit of Carol Kennicott. The struggle between the individual seeking to live honestly and the world of the Babbitts driving him to live his life and practice his profession as it wills is joined most sharply. At medical school Arrowsmith collides with the bedside-manner charlatanism of the professors interested only in success. As a practitioner in the small town of Wheatsylvania, he is hamstrung by the crude superstitions of the residents of this Gopher Prairie. As a health officer in the larger city of Nautilus, he works under Dr. Amos Pickerbaugh, who is more interested in using medicine as a springboard for political advancement than as a means of implementing the Hippocratic Oath. As a research worker in a fashionable Chicago clinic, he encounters the suave worldliness of Angus Duer, the archetype of the society doctor. Finally, in the great McGurk Institute in New York he combats the disease of Administrative Success, which takes the form of publishing brilliant, half-finished experiments for their publicity value, with no concern for the true advancement of science.

The Angus Duers, Dr. Pickerbaughs, the crass instructors at medical school, the denizens of Wheatsylvania, the administrators of the McGurk Institute, are clearly enough the apostles of Main Street and Zenith. They represent the same standards of egotistical and aggressive materialism, but these standards are studied and satirized by Lewis without compromise, without the smallest trace of personal liking or sympathy for their exponents.

If *Arrowsmith* marks the apex of the synthesis of Lewis' satirical convictions, *Dodsworth* as clearly foreshadows the dissolution of that synthesis and therefore marks the beginning of the third period of his work. For the first time Lewis draws a completely friendly portrait of a successful businessman; for the first time the rebel is projected unsympathetically. Lewis' focus has shifted from a broad attack upon Main Street to a broad defense of it. Underneath the probing into the lives of the Dodsworths, Lewis' change of heart becomes increasingly apparent. In this change Fran is the key figure. Here is a kind of Carol Kennicott in her forties, chafing under the dulness of life in Zenith, passing a great many devastating observations upon her husband's Main Street friends and upon the empty materialism of Zenith society. These are, of course, Lewis' own observations, which he has been developing in earlier books; but Fran is not the heroine of her story, as Carol is of hers and Arrowsmith of his. Quite the reverse. She emerges as a disagreeable snob, vainly seeking to recapture her lost youth, utterly blind to the virtues of her faithful husband. The rebel here is more than a lost soul; she is an empty soul as well; and this emptiness signals what is to be Lewis' principal opinion of the rebel through much of his work in the 1930's.

In the struggle between Fran and Dodsworth, it is Dodsworth who comes out best. Like Babbitt, he is solid, dependable, dull, moved by a vague humanitarian desire to improve things, out of his depth in nearly all affairs outside the realm of business. But, whereas Lewis lampoons these qualities in Babbitt, he praises them in Dodsworth. In Dodsworth's triumph there lies foreshadowed, with an immutable finality, the new role of Lewis, no longer the satirist but the apostle of Main Street.

Before settling into his new role, Lewis takes one last fling at his old ideas in *Ann Vickers*. But, while it is true that this novel survives within Lewis' great tradition and that Ann, like Carol, fights for a better world, the satirical method has been significantly altered. In the earlier books the satire always coalesces around specific individuals. In *Arrowsmith*, for example, as differentiated symbols of medicine gone materialistically mad, we have Angus Duer, Amos Pickerbaugh, and the commercialists of the McGurk Institute; and the book is a very great one in part because it is so intensely human and cleaves so unfailingly to personalities. No such coalescence is evident in *Ann Vickers*. The attacks on settlement houses and prison administration remain generalized, detached from significant individual characters. Lewis' ideas filter through as much in the form of reportage as fiction, and because of this the satire is blunter and softer.

After *Ann Vickers*, Lewis' art comes apart at the seams. He appears to lose all interest in satire, now that he devotes himself more or less completely to defending Main Street and upholding its ways of life. Paradoxically, he defends Main Street against his own attacks and now views the Carols and the Arrowsmiths of the 1930's through the eyes of Sam Clark, Vergil Gunch, and their Main Street cronies. By a circular and devious route, he returns to the "hominess" and the small civic virtues of his first published work, *Our Mr. Wrenn*.

The evidences of this *volte-face* abound in the novels of his third and most recent period. *Work of Art*, for example, glorifies that very Service which Lewis ridiculed in *Babbitt*. Lewis has changed his conception of materialist pursuits: they no longer constrict, but release, the creative energies of those engaged in them. Myron Weagle, the hotelkeeper in *Work of Art*, and Fred Cornplow in *The Prodigal Parents* are more than successful and likable human beings: they are artists, poets, and idealistic dreamers as well. Conversely, the rebels and free souls come in for very rough treatment at Lewis' hands. They now fall into three categories: the dissipated bohemians like Ora Weagle, the Fascists of *It Can't Happen Here*, and the Communists of *The Prodigal Parents*. What a sad end to the struggles of Carol Kennicott and Martin Arrowsmith! And, to complete the transformation, Zenith and Gopher Prairie have been metamorphosed into the simple, charming towns of Lemuel, Kansas, and Fort Beulah, Vermont.

Lewis' critics have, on the whole, insufficiently noted the organic development of his ideas. V. F. Calverton, for example, bases his essays on Lewis largely on the thesis that Lewis really identified and associated himself with Main Street throughout his career, and he gravely underrates the hostility which frequently accompanied that process of identification. Professor Whipple dogmatizes in the opposite direction, stating that Lewis is profoundly antipathetic to Main Street and that this antipathy derives from Lewis' own "malignant hatred" of his environment. Stuart P. Sherman, in a brochure on Lewis written after the appearance of *Babbitt*, draws an instructive comparison between Carol Kennicott and Madame Bovary but fails to note the intellectual antagonisms present in *Main Street*. Mr. Robert Cantwell, who, together with Professor Whipple, has written perhaps the most generally useful criticism of Lewis, dismisses all the early novels as hackwork and consequently fails to note the sources of the later shifts in focus.

An inclusive examination of Lewis' novels from 1914 to 1940 makes a one-track view of his work impossible. It cannot be said that he hates or loves Main Street. He does both—and both simultaneously. This simultaneous coexistence of contradictory feelings is a source of much of the intellectual wavering present even in many of his great novels and is perhaps a major reason for his decline as a chronicler of the American scene. The hesitations and reversals of his first period, the satirical crystallization of the second, the apologetics of the third, are closely interwoven. During the 1920's the influence of H. L. Mencken upon Lewis (*Elmer Gantry* was dedicated to Mencken), added to the general disillusionment that set in after the First World War, had a catapulting influence upon his art and swept him out of both the coy whimsy of *Our Mr. Wrenn* and *The Innocents* and the intellectual floundering of *The Job*. These influences began waning with *Dodsworth* and were completely dead in *Work of Art*. Lewis was at his best as a satirist in a challenging frame of mind and as a writer who helped siphon the satirical tradition of Flaubert, Butler, and Galsworthy into the contemporary American novel and helped clear its air of the prettifications of the William Dean Howells school. As a satirist he was able to exploit his considerable talent for mimicry and caricature. When he abandoned satire, vitality drained away from his work, to which the succession of undistinguished novels of the 1930's bears witness.

This abandonment of satire, with its attendant perception of the remediable limitations of human life, has dimmed both his reputation and his talents in the last decade and has prevented him from keeping pace with Wolfe, Farrell, and Steinbeck—the major novelists of the American thirties.

Source: Leo Gurko and Miriam Gurko, "The Two Main Streets of Sinclair Lewis," in *College English*, Vol. 4, No. 5, February 1943, pp. 288–292.

SOURCES

Hamner, Everett, "Damning Fundamentalism: Sinclair Lewis and the Trials of Fiction," in *MFS: Modern Fiction Studies*, Vol. 55, No. 2, Summer 2009, p. 281.

Lewis, Sinclair, *Arrowsmith*, Harcourt Brace, 1925.

Maule, Henry E., and Melville Cane, *The Man from Main Street: A Sinclair Lewis Reader*, Random House, 1952, p. 19.

McInnes, Paul-Vincent, "Surviving Modernity: Sinclair Lewis and the 1920s," in *eSharp: Electronic Social Sciences, Humanities, and Arts Review for Postgraduates*, University of Glasgow, Vol. 4, Spring 2005, p. 7.

FURTHER READING

Bloom, Harold, *Sinclair Lewis*, Chelsea House, 1987.
 Bloom is a famous English professor who presents a wide range of views on Lewis in this collection of essays by experts.

Bucco, Martin, *Critical Essays on Sinclair Lewis*, G. K. Hall, 1986.
 Part of the "Critical Essays on American Literature" series, this book, like Bloom's, presents a range of views on Lewis by experts.

Hutchisson, James M., *The Rise of Sinclair Lewis: 1920–1930*, Pennsylvania State University Press, 1996.
 Hutchisson focuses on Lewis's miraculous decade, especially by examining the notes and sketches, stored today in various archives, that went into the making of his novels.

Hutchisson, James M., *Sinclair Lewis: New Essays in Criticism*, Whitston, 1997.
 This collection of essays is a more recent one, and is edited by one of the premier experts on Sinclair Lewis.

The Castle

FRANZ KAFKA

1930

If Franz Kafka, the author of *The Castle* (1930), had gotten his expressed wish, the unfinished novel would never have been read by anyone beyond his close friends. As tuberculosis brought him to a slow and painful death at the age of forty, Kafka famously requested that his close friend Max Brod destroy all of his unpublished writings, which included three novels that Kafka had never completed. Brod refused to honor the request, seeing in these writings the best of his friend's work. Instead, Brod actively sought publication for the works, starting with the novels. In 1926, *The Castle* was published in its original German, and an English translation was published in 1930. These early versions of the novel were somewhat different from what Kafka had left in his handwritten drafts. Since the novel was unfinished—literally ending in the middle of a sentence—Brod chose to omit some of the final chapters and end the book at a place that he thought made the most sense; Brod also cleaned up Kafka's text, which contained very little punctuation.

The novel concerns a man known only by the initial K.—though Kafka used his own name in his original drafts, and later changed it—who appears in a village that is under the rule of a Castle. K. claims to be a surveyor hired by the Castle authorities to work in the village, though the appointment appears to be no more than a glitch in the unwieldy Castle bureaucracy that governs the village. K. forms relationships with many

Franz Kafka (AP Images)

villagers as he attempts to access the Castle and straighten out the problem, but his efforts fail to provide the satisfaction he seeks.

Kafka's published works (a few stories and novellas) were mostly ignored in his lifetime. *The Castle* was also largely ignored until the late 1940s. In the 1960s, scholars at Oxford University, who had acquired Kafka's original manuscript and othe papers, led an effort to restore *The Castle* to its original form. This restored version was published in German in 1982. In 1998, translator Mark Harman created a new English translation of the novel based on this restored text, with the intent of preserving as much of Kafka's original writing style as possible.

AUTHOR BIOGRAPHY

Kafka was born on July 3, 1883, in Prague, the capital city of the region of Bohemia (then part of the Austro-Hungarian Empire), where his father owned a dry-goods store. His German-speaking family was Jewish, and Kafka was the oldest of six children. His parents were successful in their business and therefore financially comfortable, but Kafka had a difficult childhood and grew up to fear his father. In addition, anti-Jewish sentiment was flaring up in Prague at the time, which caused the family to downplay their religious heritage. Kafka finished his secondary schooling in 1901 and attended German University in Prague; although his initial plan was to study chemistry, he quickly switched to law. However, his true interest seemed to be in German literature and art, which he studied whenever possible. While at the university he met Max Brod, who would remain a close friend until the author's death. Kafka graduated with a law degree in 1906, and worked as a clerk in his uncle's law office.

Even as he pursued his law degree, Kafka wrote stories. In 1908, at the age of twenty-four, his first published works appeared in a magazine called *Hyperion*. Rather than embark on a career as a lawyer, Kafka instead chose to work in rather low-level positions in two different insurance companies. Kafka hoped these jobs would allow him enough free time to pursue his writing. His experiences with rigid bureaucratic organizations had a strong influence on his writing, especially *The Castle*. In 1912, Kafka wrote his most famous work, "The Metamorphosis," in which the main character awakens one morning to find that he has transformed into a giant insect. The story was published in 1915, and although Kafka wrote several other short stories, he devoted much of his time to working on novels, none of which was ever fully finished.

In 1917, Kafka was diagnosed with tuberculosis, an infectious illness that generally attacks the lungs (although it can attack virtually any part of the body). In this time before antibiotics were widely available, tuberculosis was extremely common and often fatal. The treatment doctors prescribed for the illness was the "rest cure," in which patients traveled to a location that had a reputation for "healthy" air (usually in the mountains, in the desert, or by the sea) and did as little as possible. In addition to tuberculosis, Kafka also suffered from depression and mental breakdowns. He spent much of his time convalescing in rural areas with clean air, which eased some of his physical and mental symptoms. In January 1922, he traveled to Spindlermühle, a mountain resort town near the Polish border, and began work on the novel *The Castle*. He continued working on the book even after returning to Prague, but by September, after another nervous breakdown, he abandoned the project. Over the next two years, Kafka wrote only a few stories, and his health worsened. By 1924, his tuberculosis became so advanced that he could no longer eat, and the author died of starvation on June 3, 1924.

Before dying, Kafka asked his close friend Max Brod to destroy all of his unfinished works and letters. However, Brod refused to follow through with Kafka's wish, convinced that the writings were the best work the author had done. Instead, Brod actively sought publication for the work, most importantly the three unfinished novels: *The Trial* (1937), *Amerika* (1946), and *The Castle*. Though it took several years before the books received critical attention, they are now considered classics of modern literature.

PLOT SUMMARY

Chapters I–II

The Castle begins with the arrival of the main character, known only as K., in an unnamed village late in the evening. He stops for lodging at the first inn he finds, the Bridge Inn. Though the landlord of the inn has no rooms available, he agrees to let K. sleep in the main barroom. K. falls asleep on a straw mattress but is soon awakened by a man claiming to be the son of the steward of the Castle; the castle he refers to is the Castle of Count Westwest, which overlooks the village. The village, as the son of the steward explains, belongs to the Castle. The man, named Schwarzer, tells K. that he must have permission to stay in the village. K. informs Schwarzer that he is a land surveyor, sent for by the Count himself, and therefore has permission to be in the village.

Schwarzer telephones someone at the Castle, and after receiving conflicting information, learns that K. is indeed a surveyor brought to the village by Castle request. He is allowed to sleep in peace and the next morning discovers that Schwarzer is the son not of the steward but of a low-ranking substeward. However, the landlord tells K. that even the lowest Castle substeward is very powerful. After breakfast, K. sets out on a journey to the Castle. He passes by a schoolhouse and engages the aloof teacher in friendly conversation. As he continues toward the Castle, he seems to make no progress at all. He finds the deep snow on the roads difficult to traverse and

MEDIA ADAPTATIONS

- A film adaptation of the novel was released in 1968 in West Germany. The film, directed by Rudolf Noelte and starring Maximilian Schell, is not currently available in the United States.

- A film adaptation of the novel was made for Austrian television by director Michael Haneke in 1997. The film, starring Ulrich Mühe, is available on DVD from Kino International.

- An audio adaptation of the novel based on Mark Harman's translation was released by Blackstone Audio in 1998. The audiobook, read by Geoffrey Howard, is available on tape, CD, and as an audio download through audible.com.

eventually must turn back. He stops in front of the cottage of a coachman named Gerstäcker, who offers to give him a ride back to the inn where he is staying. K. accepts, and by the time they make it back to the inn, the daylight has already disappeared—though it seems to K. that only a couple of hours have passed since he left.

At the inn, K. finds two assistants, Artur and Jeremias, waiting for him. They claim to be his old assistants from before he came to town—assistants K. told the landlord he was expecting to join him—though he has never seen them before and they clearly already know some of the villagers. The two do not have any surveying equipment or knowledge, but K. accepts them as his helpers. K. finds that he cannot tell them apart, even though other villagers can; he decides to call them both Artur and demands that they always act as a pair to avoid confusion.

K. states that their first order of business is to visit the Castle, but his assistants tell him that this is impossible without permission. Neither K. nor his assistants can find a way to obtain permission. Just then a messenger named Barnabas arrives with a letter to K. It comes from a Castle official named Klamm. The letter welcomes him into the service of the Count, and informs him that his direct superior is the village council chairman. K. gives Barnabas a simple and gracious reply to deliver to Klamm, and after Barnabas leaves the inn, K. chases after him, seizing the opportunity to travel with the messenger to the Castle. However, Barnabas travels not to the Castle but to his family's home in the village. K. meets the messenger's parents and his two sisters, Olga and Amalia. Disappointed that Barnabas does not live in the Castle as K. had assumed, K. leaves the house with Olga when she heads to the nearby Gentlemen's Inn to get beer. K. intends to stay the night there. Once there, he discovers that the inn, other than the barroom, is intended for exclusive use of gentlemen from the Castle, and he therefore cannot stay the night; he discovers, in fact, that the only gentleman from the Castle staying at the inn that night is Klamm.

Chapters III–VI

In the barroom of the Gentlemen's Inn, K. meets Frieda, a barmaid described as a "nondescript little blonde with sad features, thin cheeks, and a surprising gaze, a gaze of exceptional superiority." He asks Frieda if she knows Klamm, and she does. She even allows K. to see Klamm through a peephole that looks into an office area he uses. Klamm is a fat, middle-aged, unremarkable man who is sleeping rather than working. Frieda reveals that she is a former maid from the Bridge Inn and is currently Klamm's mistress; at this news, K.— who wants desperately to speak to Klamm about his position as surveyor—becomes quite interested in her. She clears the barroom at closing time, and K. remains behind, hiding behind the counter so the landlord cannot see him. K. spends the night with Frieda in the barroom, and she vows never again to be with Klamm. In the morning, the couple finds K.'s two assistants sitting in the bar, watching them; they claim to have been there all night, awaiting further instructions from K. Frieda gathers some clothes and the group returns to the Bridge Inn, where Frieda takes up residence in K.'s room.

K. sleeps for an entire day and night, and when he finally awakens, decides that he will visit the council chairman regarding his duties as surveyor. Before he can leave, however, he is approached by the landlady of the Bridge Inn, who feels a motherly responsibility for Frieda and demands to know if K. plans to marry her. He assures her that he will, though he must speak to Klamm first. The landlady argues with great

emotion that this is impossible, though K. cannot understand why.

K. and his assistants travel to the council chairman's home, where they find the chairman bedridden from gout. The chairman reveals some shocking news to K.: the village and the Castle have no need for a surveyor, and that K. was called to work as a surveyor through a complex chain of events that the chairman refuses to call an error, since the Castle officials are considered infallible. Central to the debacle are a Castle official named Sordini and a villager named Otto Brunswick, the former a stickler for procedure and the latter a loudmouth who seems to support the notion of hiring a surveyor. According to the chairman, the matter was eventually resolved in favor of not hiring a surveyor, and yet K. was apparently called to the village to serve as surveyor. Although the chairman tells K. he cannot work as a surveyor, he assures K. that he will be treated with great courtesy while staying in the village as the chairman works to resolve the matter.

K. returns to the inn, where he discovers the landlady is ill, seemingly due to K.'s previous conversation with her. He goes to speak to her again and learns that she was Klamm's mistress over twenty years ago. After being with him on three occasions, he never called for her again, which broke her heart. K. asks her to request that a conversation be arranged between himself and Klamm, and the landlady agrees to try.

Chapters VII–X

Back in his room at the inn, K. finds the village teacher waiting for him. He brings an offer from the chairman: K. can live and work at the schoolhouse as a janitor for the time being, until a final decision could be made as to K.'s status as a surveyor. K. rejects the offer immediately, but Frieda convinces him to take the job so they can move out of the inn.

That evening, K. returns to the Gentlemen's Inn in an attempt to speak with Klamm. He discovers that the bar has a new replacement for Frieda, a young woman named Pepi who used to work as a maid at the inn. From her K. learns that Klamm is about to leave the inn, and that his sleigh is waiting for him in the courtyard. K. rushes outside but finds only the sleigh coachman waiting patiently. K. also decides to wait, and the coachman asks K. to retrieve some cognac from inside the coach so they can share it. K. enters the coach and takes a bottle of cognac, but he spills it when someone turns on a light and approaches from the inn. K. hurries out of the sleigh and a young gentleman approaches, asking him to leave the courtyard. When K. refuses to leave, the gentleman has the coachman put up the sleigh, and they leave K. alone in the darkness.

When K. goes back inside the inn, he finds the gentleman waiting for him, along with the landlady of the Bridge Inn. The man reveals himself to be Momus, Klamm's village secretary. Momus explains that Klamm has already left, and that the coachman swept away K.'s footprints in the snow so that there would be no sign at all to Klamm that anyone had ever even been there. Momus then asks K. to complete a deposition recording the incident as part of an interrogation for Klamm's records—though Klamm will never read it. Even after the landlady advises him strongly to submit to the official interrogation, K. refuses and goes home.

On the way home, however, K. encounters Barnabas, who carries a letter for K. from Klamm. In the letter, Klamm compliments him on his surveying work so far—even though he has done no such work. Sensing more than ever the need to speak directly to Klamm, K. dictates a long response to Barnabas. He makes the messenger promise to deliver the message to Klamm and return with a response the next day.

Chapters XI–XIV

Back home at the schoolhouse, K. finds Frieda waiting for him with dinner in the large cold room that serves as their home and the gymnasium. The schoolteacher has locked up the supply of wood in a shed so that they cannot waste it during the night for heat, but K. chops down the shed door with an ax and brings in a pile of wood so they can sleep in warmth.

The next morning, K., Frieda, and the assistants all oversleep in the warm room, failing to clean up before the teacher and the schoolmistress, Miss Gisa, arrive for classes. The teacher discovers that the shed has been broken into, and he becomes even more furious. Frieda at first attempts to take responsibility for breaking down the shed door but eventually tells the truth. The teacher attempts to fire K., but K. points out that he was given the position by the council chairman, and therefore cannot be fired by the teacher. The teacher grudgingly accepts this, at least temporarily. K. decides to dismiss his assistants—who testified that K. was the one who broke into the shed—from his service. After

he forces them out, they stand outside the schoolhouse and plead for him to reconsider.

One of the schoolchildren, a fourth-grader named Hans Brunswick, visits K. and Frieda in their room of the schoolhouse. The boy, who witnessed the teacher abusing K., offers to help him somehow. K. discovers that the boy is actually the child of a woman he briefly met on his first day exploring the village; the woman claimed to be "from the Castle." K. asks if Hans might be able to arrange for him to speak to the boy's mother. Hans agrees, and they plan to meet in two days.

After Hans leaves, Frieda confronts K. over his scheming with the boy. She worries that K. was only interested in her because of her connection to Klamm, and that his obsession with the Castle drives all of his actions. K. attempts to allay her fears and seems to be at least partially successful.

Chapters XV–XX

When Barnabas fails to show up with news of K.'s message, he decides to go to Barnabas's home and inquire about the messenger. His sisters are home, and Amalia tells K. that Barnabas will likely be home soon. While waiting for Barnabas to arrive, Olga tells K. about her brother's experiences as a messenger for the Castle. It is all more ambiguous than K. supposes, according to Olga; for example, Barnabas suspects that the man he knows as Klamm might not actually be Klamm, and the letters he receives for delivery do not come from Klamm but from a copyist—even though he does not see Klamm dictate the letter to a copyist. On top of that, sometimes the letters appear to be very old.

Olga also reveals how Barnabas came to be employed as a messenger for the Castle. Three years before, a Castle official named Sortini—not to be confused with the official named Sordini who was involved in the surveyor debacle—spotted Amalia during a festival in the village. The next morning, Sortini sent a messenger to summon Amalia to meet with him immediately at the Gentlemen's Inn. Although the exact content of the letter is not revealed, Olga describes it as "most vulgar." Amalia, horrified and offended, tears up the letter and throws it in the messenger's face.

From that day forward, the family falls upon hard times. The father's successful shoe business fails, as does his health. The rest of the villagers shun the family, and Olga blames all this misfortune on the influence of the Castle. Her father tries to find a way to repair the family's reputation by bribing or somehow swaying a Castle official, but since the Castle has not directly condemned the family in any way, nothing can be done to reverse their fortunes. Olga comes up with a plan to offer up Barnabas as a servant of the Castle with the hope that this will restore their family name, and Barnabas agrees. However, even though Barnabas is able to get inside the Castle offices, he spends two years there before he is given a delivery. That delivery is the first letter he took to K., the day after K. arrived in the village.

After Olga finishes the story, someone knocks on the door. Upon hearing that it is one of his former assistants, K. leaves through the courtyard and encounters the assistant, Jeremias, in the road. K. learns that the other assistant, Artur, has gone to the Castle to file a complaint against K., and also that a Castle official named Galater—a substitute for Klamm—was the one who sent them to be his assistants, with the purpose of cheering K. up and keeping him from taking things too seriously. K. also learns that Frieda has left him and has gone back to being the barmaid at the Gentlemen's Inn.

Chapters XXI–XXIII

Barnabas finally returns with a message for K. The message is from Erlanger, one of Klamm's secretaries, and instructs K. to meet him at the Gentlemen's Inn as soon as possible to discuss matters. K. rushes to the inn, where he finds the coachman Gerstäcker waiting to speak to Erlanger as well, along with some other villagers. K. and Gerstäcker are led to Erlanger's room, but the official is asleep, so they must wait until he awakens. While waiting, K. sees Frieda and goes to her. She tells him that she left him because he insisted on seeing Barnabas's sisters and tried to hide the fact that he was seeing them. Frieda also states that she was abducted from the schoolhouse by Jeremias, but she blames K. for firing him. Even though Jeremias took her by force, the two were childhood friends and she has chosen to live with him in a servants' room at the Gentlemen's Inn.

After Frieda leaves, K. tries to locate Erlanger's room again, but he cannot. He instead enters the room of a secretary named Bürgel. Bürgel knows of K. and inquires about his surveying work. Upon learning that no surveying has yet been done, Bürgel is surprised and offers to help straighten out the matter. As Bürgel continues talking, he all but tells K. explicitly that he has been waiting for just such an opportunity. All that remains is for K. to open up and tell the secretary what he wants to be done. Unfortunately, due to the late hour and Bürgel's long-winded speech, K. falls asleep instead. K. is awakened only when Erlanger finally summons him in the early morning.

Chapters XXIV–XXV

When K. arrives at Erlanger's room, the secretary is already prepared to leave. Erlanger quickly gets to the point: in order to protect Klamm, who is apparently so sensitive that his surroundings cannot be altered for any reason, Frieda has been reinstated at the Gentlemen's Inn. After Erlanger leaves, K. remains in the hallway and witnesses the morning bustle of the Castle secretaries. They are all delivered documents through their doors, and it appears that these documents are more often than not handed to the wrong person and must be redelivered; the whole business appears to be a great deal of commotion with little productivity. K. is spotted by the landlord and his wife, and they remove him from the restricted area. K., overwhelmed with exhaustion, falls asleep in the barroom.

When he wakes, K. finds that he has slept through the entire day, and it is already evening again. Sitting in the bar, K. learns how Pepi became the barmaid after Frieda left. She had only been a chambermaid before, and she seized the opportunity to advance when it presented itself; however, Frieda has now returned, so Pepi will once again be a chambermaid, and she blames K. for this. Still, Pepi considers them both to be victims of Frieda. She asks K. to stay with her and the other chambermaids in their servants' room at the inn. K. agrees to meet Pepi later but goes home with the coachman Gerstäcker, who has waited for K. and offers to let him stay at his house. The novel ends mid-sentence with K. arriving at the Gerstäcker home and meeting the coachman's mother: "She held out her trembling hand to K., and had him sit down beside her, she spoke with great difficulty, it was difficult to understand her, but what she said"

CHARACTERS

Amalia

Amalia is the sister of Barnabas the messenger. When K. first meets her, she is described as a blonde with a "grave, fixed, imperturbable, and perhaps rather dull gaze." K. later notes that she always appears sad and tired. Olga tells him the reason for Amalia's state: three years before, she was spotted by a Castle official who became taken by her beauty. He sent a messenger to summon her to his room at the Gentlemen's Inn, presumably for sex; Amalia found his letter shockingly vulgar, so she tore it up and threw it in the messenger's face, thereby refusing the summons. Her action—offending a Castle official—had negative repercussions for the family, if not from the Castle itself then from their fellow villagers. When K. visits their house, Amalia is under the impression that he comes not to speak with Barnabas, but to visit with Olga, who Amalia believes is in love with him.

Artur

Artur is one of K.'s two assistants, assigned by a Castle official named Galater to help the surveyor. Artur and the other assistant, Jeremias, both insist that they are K.'s "old" assistants from outside the village, even though K. does not know them and everyone in the village does know them. They also know nothing about surveying. While living at the schoolhouse, Artur climbs in bed next to K. while K. is asleep; when he wakes, K. is so surprised that he hits Artur several times with his fist. After K. fires both Artur and Jeremias the next morning, Artur goes to the Castle to file a complaint against K.

Barnabas

Barnabas is a messenger for the Castle official known as Klamm. K. meets Barnabas on his second night in the village, when the messenger delivers a letter welcoming K. as the new surveyor. Barnabas lives with his mother, father, and two sisters, Olga and Amalia. Aside from being a messenger, he spends part of his time working for the shoemaker, Otto Brunswick. Although K. first admires Barnabas and wishes to spend time with him over the other peasants, his opinion changes when he realizes that Barnabas is also just a villager and not a resident of the Castle. K. later learns that Barnabas sought a position as a Castle messenger in order to clear the reputation of his disgraced family, and that the letter he delivered to K. was his first assignment after years of waiting.

Hans Brunswick

Hans Brunswick is Otto Brunswick's son; he is a fourth-grade student at the school where K. works as a janitor. After K. is reprimanded by the teacher and schoolmistress, Hans sneaks out of class and goes to K., offering to help him with his work. K. sees this as an opportunity to arrange a meeting with the boy's mother, who he believes is from the Castle and can gain him favor with Castle officials. Hans reluctantly agrees to allow K. to meet his mother and arranges for K. to visit his house two days later. However, the novel ends before this meeting occurs.

Otto Brunswick

Otto Brunswick is the shoemaker of the village. He once worked for Barnabas's father, but after that family became disgraced by Amalia's rejection of the Castle official Sortini, Brunswick left and started his own shoemaking business. Brunswick's wife is a sickly woman who tells K. that she is from the Castle; his son is Hans, a fourth-grader at the school where K. briefly works as a janitor. Brunswick is also the person that the council chairman blames for supporting the notion that the village needs a land surveyor, which ultimately leads to the confusion that brings K. to the village.

Bürgel

Bürgel is a Castle official who calls himself a "connecting secretary," meaning he acts as an intermediary between the Castle and the village secretaries for an official known as Friedrich. When K. goes to the Gentlemen's Inn to meet with Erlanger, he enters Bürgel's room by mistake. Bürgel knows of K., and upon hearing that K. is having difficulties with starting his surveying work, Bürgel offers in a roundabout way to help him. However, K. is too tired to pick up on this opportunity, and instead he falls asleep in the man's room.

Council Chairman

The council chairman is a bedridden village official who suffers from gout. He is named in Klamm's letter as K.'s direct superior when it comes to his surveying work. However, when K. visits the chairman, he discovers that the village has no need of a surveyor, and that no such request should have ever been sent through. The chairman is adamant about not letting K. work as a surveyor, since the issue seems to have become a battle of principles with some other villagers. The chairman does offer K. a job as janitor at the village school as a temporary solution until the matter of the surveyor position can be resolved.

Erlanger

Erlanger is one of Klamm's first secretaries, described as a "short, frail gentleman with a slight limp." Barnabas brings K. a message from Erlanger that he should meet the secretary at the

Gentlemen's Inn. When K. finally encounters Erlanger, the secretary does not even give him a chance to speak; he simply informs K. that Frieda is going to be reinstated as the barmaid at the Gentlemen's Inn for the sake of Klamm, who is too sensitive to face such drastic changes in personnel. By the time K. receives this message, Frieda has already returned to the inn and called off their wedding, so the message is pointless.

Frieda

Frieda is a barmaid at the Gentlemen's Inn and is also the mistress of the Castle official known as Klamm. Sometime in the past she worked as a maid at the Bridge Inn, and she still views Gardena, the landlady there, as a mother figure. When K. arrives at the Gentlemen's Inn and shows interest in her, Frieda decides to leave behind her job and her duty as Klamm's mistress, and she goes to live with K. at the Bridge Inn. The two become officially engaged to be married, though she worries that he is only interested in her because of her connection to Klamm. When K. is offered a job as the school janitor, she urges him to accept it, and the two move there. However, after K. sneaks away from the schoolhouse and spends an evening talking to Barnabas's sisters Olga and Amalia, Frieda decides to end their relationship. She also returns to her position as barmaid and shares a room with Jeremias, one of K.'s former assistants. Pepi, the replacement barmaid while Frieda is away, tells K. that she believes Frieda only took up with him as a way to create a scandal and make herself seem indispensable to the bar and to Klamm. Pepi describes Frieda as a spider, and states that she "has connections nobody knows anything about."

Gardena the Landlady

Gardena is the landlady at the Bridge Inn, where K. stays for much of the novel. She seems to dislike and distrust K. from the start, but her close relationship with Frieda—who becomes engaged to K.—causes her to tolerate his presence at the inn. Gardena eventually reveals to K. that she was once Klamm's mistress, just like Frieda. However, after being with him on three occasions, Klamm simply stopped sending for her. Though she is now married to another man, she has clearly never gotten over her love for Klamm and treats her husband poorly. Although Gardena warns Frieda to be wary of K.'s motives in marrying her, she also offers to assist K. in trying to secure a meeting with the elusive Klamm.

Gerstäcker

Gerstäcker is a coachman who lives near Lasemann in the village. When K. is sent out of Lasemann's house, Gerstäcker offers to give him a ride back to the Bridge Inn. Later, K. sees Gerstäcker again while waiting to meet Erlanger. Even though Gerstäcker does not appear to like K. at all, he offers to let K. stay at his house. The two arrive at Gerstäcker's house at the end of the novel.

Miss Gisa

Miss Gisa is the schoolmistress who works with the teacher. When K. fails to perform his janitorial duties on his first morning of work, she destroys Frieda's coffee pot and forces her cat's paw across K.'s hand, raising bloody welts. Miss Gisa is pursued by Schwarzer, a young man from the Castle who has chosen to live in the village so he can court her.

Hans the Landlord

Hans is the landlord of the Bridge Inn and husband of Gardena. After Gardena was rejected by Klamm twenty years before, Hans stood by her to provide emotional support, and the two married. When the owner of the Bridge Inn, who was Hans's uncle, became too old to operate it himself, the couple took over as proprietors. When K. first arrives in the village, the Bridge Inn is the first place he enters. Hans gives him permission to sleep in the barroom that first night and later prepares a room for him in the attic.

Jeremias

Jeremias is one of K.'s two assistants, assigned by a Castle official named Galater. After K. fires Jeremias and the other assistant, Artur, Jeremias abducts K.'s fiancée Frieda and takes her to the Gentlemen's Inn so they can live and work there together. Frieda does not appear to object to this, and chooses to stay with Jeremias when K. comes to speak to her. After the assistants have been fired, Jeremias reveals to K. that he and Artur were hired to both cheer K. up and keep him humble regarding his duties.

K.

K. is the main character of the novel, a surveyor who arrives in the village of the Castle because he has been summoned to work there. However, his efforts to work as a surveyor are complicated by bureaucracy and political feuds that leave his duties unclear. Throughout his stay in the village, K.'s main goal is to access the Castle that rules over it; at first he tries to reach the Castle itself, but discovers that this is a futile task, since he would never be allowed inside. Then he attempts to gain the attention of a Castle official through any of the villagers that might have such connections. The closest he comes to penetrating the bureaucracy of the Castle is when he meets with two different secretaries of Klamm, Momus and Erlanger. In the first case, K. stubbornly refuses to speak to the official, and in the second, the secretary merely passes on a message and does not wish to hear from K. at all. While he stays in the village, K. becomes engaged to Frieda, a barmaid and mistress of Klamm; his interest in her seems to center on her connection to Klamm. After several days, Frieda leaves him and returns to her job as a barmaid. Faced with opposition from the council chairman, K. gives up hope of working as a surveyor—at least temporarily—and takes a job as the janitor of the village school.

Klamm

Klamm is a mysterious official from the Castle who spends much of his time staying at the Gentlemen's Inn in the village. Like the other officials from the Castle, Klamm passes his time at the inn with a mistress; his current mistress is Frieda the barmaid, though he had three intimate encounters with Gardena, now the landlady at the Bridge Inn, twenty years before. K. spends much of the novel trying to speak directly to Klamm, with no success; Klamm sends him letters on two occasions, though the second letter clearly suggests that Klamm does not know anything about K.'s circumstances in the village. Klamm is described as being too sensitive to endure a direct encounter with K., and even K.'s footprints are removed from the snow before Klamm enters the courtyard of the inn so as not to disturb him. K. is able to see Klamm once, when Frieda allows K. to look through a peephole in the room where Klamm works. Based on this viewing, K. believes Klamm to be a fat man with a large black mustache. However, Barnabas and his sister Olga have suspicions about whether or not the man acting as Klamm really is Klamm.

Landlady of the Gentlemen's Inn

The landlady of the Gentlemen's Inn is described as wearing clothing that is "oddly threadbare, outmoded, and laden with pleats and frills, but city finery nonetheless." Because of her clothing—at once both fancy and ragged, and different from the other villagers—K. believes that she

is more than a mere landlady, yet he cannot guess what. The landlady in return doubts K.'s assertion that he is a surveyor.

Landlord of the Gentlemen's Inn

The landlord of the Gentlemen's Inn acts as a gatekeeper of sorts, keeping villagers like K. from interfering in the business of Castle officials who stay at the inn. The first time K. visits the inn, the landlord tells him that he cannot spend the night there, even though Klamm is the only Castle official staying at the inn. Later, the landlord looks for K. to make sure that he has left the inn, but K. hides from him behind the counter and stays there overnight with Frieda. After K. meets with Erlanger and remains in the hallway where the Castle officials stay, the landlord and landlady must physically remove him before the officials can exit their rooms. However, the landlord does not seem entirely unsympathetic and allows K. to sleep in the barroom until he regains his energy.

Lasemann

Lasemann is a village tanner related to Otto Brunswick. During K.'s initial exploration of the village, Lasemann allows the fatigued K. to rest inside his home for a while.

Mizzi

Mizzi is the wife of the village council chairman. She assists her husband in his duties, especially since he is bedridden from gout. Gardena, the landlady of the Bridge Inn, insists that Mizzi is actually the one who performs the important duties.

Olga

Olga is the oldest sister of Barnabas and Amalia. During K.'s second night in the village, Olga takes him to the Gentlemen's Inn to retrieve some beer. Although K. states that he will spend the night with Olga's family, he stays instead in the barroom with Frieda. Amalia later tells K. that she believes Olga is in love with him, and that he is also in love with her—which explains his frequent visits. After her family becomes disgraced, it is Olga's idea that Barnabas should become a Castle messenger as a way to improve the family name.

Pepi

Pepi is a chambermaid at the Gentlemen's Inn. After Frieda quits her job as barmaid, Pepi is called in as her replacement. However, after just four days, Frieda returns and Pepi must resume her position as a lowly chambermaid. Pepi believes that Frieda's departure from the inn—and her engagement to K.—was a calculated scandal intended to prove her own importance to Klamm and the inn. Although she partially blames K. for her misfortunes, she asks him to stay with her and two other chambermaids at the inn. K. eventually agrees, though his arranged meeting with Pepi does not take place before the novel ends.

Schwarzer

Schwarzer is the son of a substeward of the Castle; he lives in the village. When K. first arrives in town and falls asleep in the barroom at the Bridge Inn, Schwarzer informs him that he cannot stay in the village unless he has permission from the Count. After speaking with an official at the Castle, however, Schwarzer relents. Though he is from the Castle, Schwarzer chooses to live in the village because he is in love with Miss Gisa, the village schoolmistress, and he serves as her assistant.

Teacher

K. encounters the village schoolteacher on his first morning exploring the town. He attempts friendly conversation with the "small narrow-shouldered young man" and later learns that the teacher is also the assistant to the council chairman. After K. meets with the chairman, the teacher—who learns of the meeting through a detailed account by the chairman afterward—views K. as rude and disrespectful. Nonetheless, at the chairman's request, he offers K. a position at the school as janitor. The first morning on the job, K. neglects his responsibilities and the teacher tries to fire him; however, the teacher later admits that he does not have the authority to fire K.

THEMES

Bureaucracy

Central to *The Castle* is the theme of bureaucracy, or a needlessly complex system of government or business administration with many different divisions that has potentially confusing rules. The governing mechanism of the Castle seems to be a nightmare of bureaucracy; although mistakes seem to occur frequently, the official policy of the government is that no mistakes are ever made or acknowledged. One such mistake appears to have brought K. to the village in the first place, since the village does not appear to need a surveyor. The refusal of the Castle government to acknowledge the mistake places K. in the middle of a battle between a village official and higher authorities. Although the Castle officials are considered to be very powerful, hardworking men, at least some of them have enough free time to engage in affairs with women from the village. The only time K. is able to see a Castle official—Klamm—for himself, the man is not working but sleeping. The Castle officials and their many secretaries appear to spend a great deal of time traveling back and forth between the Castle and the village, though little work seems to get done.

Olga provides K. with a detailed description of her brother Barnabas's experiences as a messenger in the Castle offices. According to her, Barnabas is only allowed in a certain area and must wait hours or days for a Castle official to acknowledge his presence. Even then, he may not speak to the official directly; he must address a secretary or copyist. When he is finally given a letter to deliver, it sometimes appears to be old and outdated. Indeed, even when a letter seems current—such as the letter K. receives from Klamm, praising his surveying work—the facts contained within it are wrong.

After his meeting with Klamm's secretary Erlanger at the Gentlemen's Inn, K. remains behind in the hallway and witnesses firsthand the lowest-level workings of the Castle government. He watches as couriers deliver papers to each of the secretary's rooms along the hall and then spend much more time taking back and redistributing paperwork that was delivered to the wrong people the first time.

The Gap Between Social Classes

The clear division between Castle officials and villagers is an example of a common literary theme: the gap between social classes in a society. Although some Castle officials visit the village, they seldom interact with the villagers and only stay at an inn reserved especially for them and their assistants. The Castle officials are so rarely seen, in fact, that most would be recognized by villagers only through certain rumored physical traits. The villagers are told—and accept—that Castle officials like Klamm are too sensitive to interact with villagers. When K. waits in the courtyard hoping to speak to Klamm before he boards his coach back to the Castle, Klamm does not go to the courtyard until after K. has left—and even then, K.'s footprints are swept from the snow so that Klamm will never know he was

TOPICS FOR FURTHER STUDY

- The word "bureaucracy" technically means an organizational system designed to enact rules and policies. However, it has come to be associated with an obstructive, pointless adherence to rules and procedures by multiple levels of personnel at large businesses or government offices. Bureaucracy, to many people, means a confusing and inefficient business structure. The Castle bureaucracy is central to the novel. Can you think of any bureaucracies that you have firsthand experience with? It can be any organization, such as a club or a company, that you think operates inefficiently. Write an essay explaining the problems you see with this bureaucracy. Include your ideas for helping the organization run more smoothly.

- The novel famously ends in the middle of a sentence, with the coachman Gerstäcker's mother about to speak to K. What effect do you think the current ending has on a reader? Write your own conclusion to this scene between K. and Gerstäcker's mother. Can you bring closure to some of the unresolved elements of the plot?

- Kafka came from a Jewish family, but was raised in a region where Jews often had to hide their heritage in order to keep themselves safe. Kafka himself often denied the "Jewishness" of his works, but some critics disagree. Using your library, the Internet, or other available resources, research the challenges faced by Jews in Europe during the first three decades of the twentieth century. In your opinion, does *The Castle* reflect the experiences of Jews in Europe during this period in any way? How? Write an essay summarizing your argument. Be sure to provide specific examples from the text.

- There has been much scholarly debate over whether or not *The Castle* is meant as an allegory—a tale in which each element is meant to represent something beyond the literal meaning. Try writing your own short allegory, using people or places from your life as symbols for different ideas or feelings. For example, a family pet might represent loyalty, a locked diary might represent forbidden knowledge, or a popular brand of shoe might represent conformity. When you finish, have another student read your story, and see if he or she can identify the symbolism you used.

- The Terry Gilliam film *Brazil* (1985) was described by many critics as "Kafkaesque" in its portrayal of bureaucracy and its effects on individuals. Watch the film and write an essay comparing it to *The Castle*. How are the settings similar and different? How does the film's protagonist, Sam Lowry, remind you of K.? Do you think, if Kafka had finished it, that *The Castle* would have an ending similar to the one in *Brazil*?

---

there. The stark difference between the Castle officials and the villagers is also illustrated in this scene when K. steps into Klamm's carriage; the carriage itself is richly appointed, and inside he finds cognac that tastes unlike anything he has drunk before. When he returns to the barroom of the inn, he orders a cognac and judges it poor compared to what he tasted in Klamm's coach.

The main way in which Castle officials do interact with villagers is by summoning young village women for sexual favors. For the villagers, this is generally viewed as an honor. Gardena, for example, retains cherished mementos of her brief experience as Klamm's mistress, even though it took place twenty years before. To reject a Castle official when summoned is to invite disgrace and misfortune upon oneself and one's family. This is precisely what happens when Amalia rejects a vulgar summons from the Castle official Sortini.

There appears to be no possibility of moving up from the village to the Castle, which would represent a step up in social status. However,

Frydlant Castle in Bohemia, where Kafka worked for an insurance company. Some believe this to be the castle Kafka describes in the novel. (© Alexie Fateev / Alamy)

Schwarzer, the son of a Castle substeward, chooses to leave the Castle and live in the village because of his love for the schoolmistress, Miss Gisa. Even as a resident of the village, Schwarzer is considered very powerful. Hans Brunswick's mother also claims to be from the Castle, though K. is never able to substantiate this.

STYLE

Allegory

In the decades following its initial publication, *The Castle* was frequently viewed as an allegory. An allegory is a tale in which each literal element—such as character or setting—is meant to symbolize something else, usually something abstract. For example, a section of ancient Greek philosopher Plato's *The Republic* is commonly referred to as "the allegory of the cave." In this allegory, shadows on a cave wall are meant to represent the world that most people accept as reality—though it is in fact merely a

dim silhouette of reality. One of the best-known examples of allegory in English literature is *Pilgrim's Progress* (1678) by John Bunyan. In this allegory, the main character—named Christian— meets assorted characters such as Good Will and Civility on his journey from his hometown to the "Celestial City," passing places like the Slough of Despond and the Hill of Difficulty.

In *The Castle*, some scholars have argued that the Castle symbolizes the divine, while others have suggested it is meant to represent one of the many inefficient governments found across Europe after World War I. The various characters K. encounters may be meant to symbolize certain qualities or viewpoints relevant to the main character's quest, though the once-popular notion of *The Castle* as religious allegory has come under fire from some modern academics.

Surrealism

Surrealism is an artistic movement that became popular in the 1920s. Surrealists sought to startle or shock audiences by combining words or

COMPARE
&
CONTRAST

- **1920s:** In the wake of World War I and the dissolution of the Austro-Hungarian Empire, Bohemia is combined with several other central European regions to form Czechoslovakia.

  Today: Czechoslovakia, long under Communist rule, has split into two separate countries ruled by representative democracy, the Czech Republic and Slovakia. Bohemia is now a part of the Czech Republic.

- **1920s:** Researchers succeed in developing a vaccine for tuberculosis, a devastating infectious disease that kills half of those that contract it.

  Today: Massive vaccination efforts in many parts of the world have greatly reduced the number of tuberculosis cases worldwide. (In the United States, vaccination against tuberculosis is not generally recommended.) New vaccines are being developed that promise to be even more effective than the old vaccine.

images in ways that did not make logical sense but instead celebrated the irrational and the unconscious mind. In this regard, surrealism emphasized dreams as a path to the unconscious; many surrealist works, both in literature and the visual arts, evoke a dreamlike state in which real-world elements combine with fantastical elements in surprising or absurd ways. Surrealist authors include André Breton and Antonin Artaud.

Although Kafka was never formally a part of any literary movement, and he died the same year that Breton's *Surrealist Manifesto* laid out the aims of the movement, his work exhibits elements frequently associated with surrealism. For example, Kafka's depiction of the village itself is relatively realistic, yet the government that oversees it is nonsensical in its methods. Another trait often found in surrealist works is a dreamlike tone or mood. This tone is found throughout *The Castle*, as characters behave inconsistently from one moment to the next, and time and space seem to progress in ways that reflect the main character's state of mind more than they do an objective reality. Indeed, the main character spends much of the novel either sleeping or in a drowsy state, matching the style and mood of the tale. This is also reflected in the author's use of very long sentences separated by commas instead of periods, as well as paragraphs that last for several pages at a time.

HISTORICAL CONTEXT

Austro-Hungarian Empire During and After World War I

Kafka was born in Bohemia, a region of Austria-Hungary. The Empire of Austria and the Kingdom of Hungary became united as one domain under the Austro-Hungarian Compromise of 1867. Austria-Hungary was a vast, multinational empire that encompassed many different cultures and religions. It was ruled by Franz Joseph I of the Habsburg Dynasty, who was recognized as both an emperor (of Austria) and a king (of Bohemia and Hungary). Since Franz Joseph's only son died at a fairly young age, the ruler's nephew, Archduke Franz Ferdinand, was the next in line to become the ruler of Austria-Hungary. At the turn of the twentieth century, rising nationalism among many of the ethnic groups within the empire led to widespread unrest. In 1914, Franz Ferdinand was assassinated by political enemies who objected to Austro-Hungarian control of the Serb population of Bosnia—an event that led to armed conflicts between Austria-Hungary and Serbia, which set off the larger conflict that became World War I. During World War I, Austria-Hungary and its allies Germany and Italy—known as the Triple Alliance—fought against Russia, France, and Great Britain, and later the United States as well.

Spindlermuhle in the Czech Republic. Kafka began writing The Castle *upon his arrival here in 1922.*
(© imagebroker / Alamy)

When the Triple Alliance was defeated in 1918, one of the terms of surrender was the dismantling of Austria-Hungary into several different states, which included Austria, Hungary, Yugoslavia, and Czechoslovakia—the last of which contained the region known as Bohemia. A democratic system of government was established soon after, and despite the cultural differences between the regions that comprised Czechoslovakia, the new country operated with relative stability until the rise of the Nazi Party in Germany, which occupied the country in 1938 and retained control until the end of World War II in 1945.

Feudal Society in Europe

Although *The Castle* is not set during a historical time period, the relationship between the villagers and the Castle officials is somewhat similar to the relationship between peasants and nobles under the feudal system found across Europe during the Middle Ages. In a feudal society, the members of the lowest social class worked lands owned by a noble, who generally passed these lands down through the family line. The lowest workers, or peasants, paid a tax or tribute to the noble in exchange for using his land as well as other services, such as providing fresh water or defense from nearby rivals. All laws and policies were established by the lord of the region, who sometimes lived in a fortified structure such as a castle that overlooked the lands he controlled. By the 1600s, feudal society in Europe had largely given way to the first forms of capitalism, in which private individuals controlled the goods produced through their own labor.

CRITICAL OVERVIEW

Kafka is perhaps the twentieth century's best example of a literary giant virtually unknown during his lifetime. Although he published several short stories in German, his novel-length works were all published—against his expressed wishes—after his death. Even these did not necessarily reflect the author's intended output;

none of his novels were finished, so Max Brod, his executor and literary advocate, found it necessary to edit the fragmentary works so that they appeared to be complete and whole. Brod also had his own ideas about the themes Kafka's work addressed, and occasionally adjusted the text to fit this view. In addition, translators who brought Kafka's work to English readers worked not from the author's original texts but from Brod's versions. For these reasons, the earliest editions of Kafka's work—both in his native German and in English—were not necessarily true to the author's original vision.

Willa and Edwin Muir translated the first English-language edition of *The Castle* in 1930, based on Max Brod's reconstruction. This version omitted the final three chapters and imposed upon the work themes the author may or may not have intended. Edwin Muir, writing for *The Bookman* in 1930, refers to Kafka's three long works—*The Trial*, *Amerika*, and *The Castle*—as "a trilogy corresponding with grotesque differences to the *Divine Comedy*," with *The Castle* being equivalent to Dante's *Paradise*—though he notes that such a paradise is never actually attained. Muir refers to the works as allegories, much as Brod seems to have viewed them, and writes that "his allegory is not a mere re-creation of conceptions already settled; and the entities he describes seem therefore newly discovered, and as if they had never existed before."

Erich Heller, in his *Franz Kafka*, disputes the notion that *The Castle* is meant by the author as a symbolic tale of religion. "*The Castle* is as much a religious allegory," writes Heller, "as a photographic likeness of the devil in person could be said to be an allegory of Evil." Unlike an allegory, in which a story's meaning can be unlocked through simple explanation of what each element represents, Heller notes that "there is no key to *The Castle*." Albert Camus, in his collection *The Myth of Sisyphus and Other Essays* (1955), calls *The Castle* "the individual adventure of a soul in quest of its grace, of a man who asks of this world's objects their royal secret and of women the signs of the god that sleeps in them." Camus also asserts, "The whole art of Kafka consists in forcing the reader to reread."

Some critics see in Kafka's work a reflection of the artist's troubled mind. Philip Rahv, writing for *The Kenyon Review*, sees both *The Castle* and *The Trial* as "enormous projections of self-punishment, of imagined wrong-doing and atonement. No measure of suffering, however, can atone for the unnamed guilt continually welling up from the unconscious." Thomas Mann, writing in 1940, states, "*The Castle* is through and through an autobiographical novel. The hero, who should originally speak in the first person, is called K.; he is the author, who has only too literally suffered all these pains and these grotesque disappointments." Mann also writes of the novel, "It is the most patient, obstinate, desperate 'wrestling with the angel' that ever happened; and the strangest, boldest, most novel thing about it is it is done with *humor*."

While some critics praise Kafka's novel even though its form is far from definitive, others still view his work as the half-done musings that the ever-critical Kafka himself seemed to consider them. Edmund Wilson, writing in 1947, refers to *The Castle* and *The Trial* as "rather ragged performances—never finished and never really worked out." Wilson states of the author, "What he has left us is the half-expressed gasp of a self-doubting soul trampled under. I do not see how one can possibly take him for either a great artist or a moral guide." However, this opinion is not shared by most readers; although it took ten years for Kafka's translated works to make an impact outside the realm of literary scholars, they have remained popular ever since. In recent decades, great efforts have been made to publish complete translations of the author's work that remain as true as possible to the original German texts.

CRITICISM

Greg Wilson

Wilson is an author, literary critic, and mythologist. In this essay, he examines the contradictory nature of the text and judges it to be essential to the book's true meaning.

It is impossible to know precisely what Kafka intended with *The Castle*. He never finished the work, and even though he mentioned to Max Brod a vision of the book's ending—in which K. learned on his death-bed that his approval to live in the village still had not gone through—Kafka himself may have decided that the project was a literary dead-end. This uncertainty of the author's true intent has perhaps

WHAT DO I READ NEXT?

- *Metamorphosis and Other Stories* (1961) is a collection of Kafka tales translated by Willa and Edwin Muir. Included in the collection is the title tale, in which a salesman awakens one morning to find himself transformed into a giant insect.

- *Amerika* (1946) is the first of Kafka's three unfinished novels, begun by the author in 1912. Originally titled *The Man Who Disappeared* by the author (and changed by Brod for publication), the tale concerns a young European man named Karl Rossmann who flees scandal by moving to New York. In the United States, Rossmann has bizarre and comic adventures with a peculiar assortment of characters.

- *The Trial* (1937) is perhaps the most widely praised of Kafka's unfinished novels. In it, the protagonist—Josef K.—is arrested for a crime, though he is never told what the crime is, and he is not immediately taken into custody. He spends a year trying to determine how to acquit himself of the unspecified charges, only to grow increasingly suspicious that his situation is hopeless.

- *The Unbearable Lightness of Being* (1984) is a novel by famed Czech novelist Milan Kundera. Like Kafka, Kundera is intimately familiar with Prague, and this novel takes place during the region's time under Communist rule, including the brief relaxation of artistic and political restrictions that took place in 1968, known as the Prague Spring.

- *The Magic Mountain* (1927) by Thomas Mann is a tale from one of Kafka's contemporaries in German literature. The novel tells the tale of a young man who visits a cousin suffering from tuberculosis—much like Kafka—in a sanatorium in the Swiss Alps. The young man himself falls ill with tuberculosis. and must stay at the resort until his symptoms subside. During his stay he learns much about both life and death from the other residents.

- *One Hundred Years of Solitude* (1970) is the first novel of Colombian author Gabriel García Márquez. García Márquez was influenced by Kafka's writing, and he is recognized as one of the foremost practitioners of magical realism—a combination of the commonplace and the absurd that in some ways resembles Kafka. In this novel, García Márquez relates the sweeping history of a family and the Colombian town in which they live.

- *Day of the Assassins* (2009) by Johnny O'Brien, is a time travel novel in which a fifteen-year-old named Jack Christie finds himself transported back to Austria-Hungary in the period leading up to the beginning of World War I. His adventures land him in Sarajevo on the very day of the assassination of Archduke Franz Ferdinand.

---

fueled more critical analysis of the work than it would have received if it were actually finished. Most of this attention is focused on the symbolic meaning of various elements in the book; however, such examination generally ignores the most pervasive element Kafka included in the work: almost every part of the book is deliberately and cleverly contradicted by another part. The characters themselves seem to represent not just a duality, but completely contradictory realities that converge in space at the village.

One of the biggest contradictions is K. himself. When he first arrives at the village, he acts toward Schwarzer as if he has no knowledge of the Castle or its Count. Yet he almost immediately claims that he was sent for by the Count to work as a surveyor for the village. Since this claim is substantiated by an unknown Castle official, it is accepted by Schwarzer and the villagers. However, other evidence suggests that K. was never called to the village as a surveyor in the first place, and that this was simply a fortuitous lie. First, K. brings no surveying equipment with him; he claims that it is being brought by his assistants, who never show up throughout the entire course of the tale. Later in the novel, K. imagines what might have happened if Schwarzer had never confronted him on his first night in the village. K. suggests that he would have found himself

> knocking on the door at the council chairman's during office hours the following day and registering as a foreign journeyman who had already found a place to sleep at a local citizen's and would probably continue his journey next day, unless, and this was most unlikely, he found work here, but then only for a few days, since he hadn't the slightest intention of staying longer.

He also notes that he probably would have "found a place somewhere as a farmhand." In other words, K. all but admits that he was never called as a surveyor by Castle officials and merely capitalized upon a glitch—doubtless one of many—in the official workings of the Castle. The only person who doubts him—after Schwarzer calls the Castle on his first night—is the landlady of the Gentlemen's Inn, who accuses him of lying when he tells her. At the same time, K. believes that she is also deceiving everyone, since she does not dress like a landlady. Aside from lying about being a surveyor, K. also appears to lie about his family status. On his first morning there, K. says to the landlord, "Anybody traveling as far from his wife and child as I am wants to have something to take home with him." However, this is the only mention he ever makes of having a family, and he soon gets engaged to the barmaid Frieda.

So K. could be an experienced surveyor with a wife and child who is summoned to work in the village by Castle officials, or he could be a drifter who lies to keep himself from being thrown out of town and then seizes an opportunity to secure himself a job. Or he could be some combination of the above. Similarly, Frieda is a mysterious character who abandons her affair with Klamm and immediately becomes engaged to K., a virtual stranger; then, almost as quickly, she leaves K. and takes up with a man who abducts her—and who is nonetheless regarded as a childhood friend. And her words are as deliberately contradictory as her actions. In her farewell to K., she tells him, "Don't object, you can certainly contradict everything, but in the end nothing would be contradicted."

The workings of the Castle are even more confusing than Frieda. The council chairman declares with great conviction that the government of the Castle does not make mistakes, and yet the more he describes the process, the more it seems that mistakes happen almost constantly. This is witnessed firsthand by K. when he watches the deliveries made to the assistants in the Gentlemen's Inn. Most of the deliveries are misdirected and have to be redistributed. At one point, Olga tells K. that the slow response of the Castle officials "can mean that the official procedure has begun, but it can also mean that the official procedure has not yet even begun . . . it can even mean that the official procedure is already over . . ."

Barnabas and his job as a Castle messenger, at least as it is explained by his sister Olga, is also full of contradictions. While Olga states that Barnabas is often kept waiting in a room at the Castle for days before receiving an assignment, Barnabas himself states that he always comes home at night. Olga also reports that the letters Barnabas receives to deliver to K. are not freshly typewritten but are instead pulled from old files and have the appearance of age. Later, however, Olga states that the delivery of letters to K. represent the first messenger job that Barnabas received from the Castle, after years of waiting. In order for the letters to be old, they must have been prepared prior to K.'s arrival, and indeed they do not mention K. by name, nor do they conform to any real-world happenings. However, the first letter does mention Barnabas by name as K's messenger, though Barnabas has not worked as a messenger prior to this delivery—which indicates the message is actually not old. Such strange contradictions lead Olga to doubt everything about Barnabas's job:

> He can enter an office, though it doesn't even seem to be an office but rather an anteroom to the offices, and perhaps not even that, perhaps it's a room intended for all those who aren't allowed into the real offices. He speaks to Klamm, but is it Klamm? Isn't it rather someone who merely resembles Klamm?

The differences between the Castle and the village are denied by many, yet seem glaringly obvious to others. Villagers such as the teacher state that there is no difference between the people of the Castle and the people of the village, yet the treatment shown to the Castle officials differs greatly from that shown to villagers. They have their own inn, where they carry on affairs with young village women summoned to submit to them, and even drink cognac of a substantially higher quality than what is served at village inns. As Olga observes:

> True, they say that all of us belong to the Castle and that there's no distance between them and us, and that there's nothing to bridge, and in general this may indeed be so, but unfortunately we had a chance to see that when everything is at stake it isn't that way at all.

Even the Castle official Klamm is described by his assistant as "quite overcome by weariness here in the village because the way of life is so different." This is odd, since Klamm appears to spend most of his time in the village by choice. It is worth noting that *klam* in Czech—a language Kafka spoke—means "deception" or "sham," which reinforces Olga's doubts about whether Klamm is really Klamm at all.

Even though the novel was compiled from fragmentary, handwritten drafts that Kafka requested to be destroyed, there is no doubt that these contradictions were intentionally woven into the fabric of the tale by the author himself. They occur so pervasively and at every level—even one of Barnabas's sisters mysteriously changes from being a blonde to later having black hair. With so many deliberately contradictory versions of reality all competing against each other, what is the reader supposed to believe? This is, in my opinion, the entire point of the book. The reader is given no firm grasp on what is real—or rather, is given contradictory versions of what is real—not with the idea of having the reader determine what is true, but with the idea that objective truth is irrelevant. For example,

even though K. is not really a surveyor, he might as well be, since the villagers all believe it to be true, and the Castle even appoints him assistants to help with the surveying work that will never come—and yet he is officially praised for this nonexistent work anyway.

Many analyses of *The Castle* search for the symbolic meaning of the Castle and its various inhabitants, in an effort to somehow find the key that unlocks the puzzle-box and reveals the work to be a grand, sensible allegory of some-such-thing or that-other-thing. I would argue that the whole message found in the work—screaming through in every line on every page—is that such a search is completely futile. However, I cannot help but think that with all the scholarly expeditions deep into the Escher-like bowels of the book, and with so many imaginary artifacts unearthed and brought back to be praised as significant to the book's meaning, Kafka himself would be greatly amused.

Source: Greg Wilson, Critical Essay on Franz Kakfa's *The Castle*, *Novels for Students 34*, Gale, Cengage Learning, 2010.

Alan Klein

In this review, Klein contends that the novel's true meaning is a religious one.

Franz Kafka's novel *The Castle* has become one of the most enigmatic masterpieces of our time. From its earliest appearance, *The Castle* has been received as a parable about an individual's search for salvation. In an "Homage" written in 1940, Thomas Mann saw K., the protagonist, as an alienated member of the faith, who wishes "to get into the community and attain to the state of grace." This somehow does not ring true upon a reading of the text. We find K. not to be Everyman struggling for salvation, but rather extraordinary in his vision and persistence.

However, Kafka wrote and spoke of a "secret cabbala" behind *The Castle,* a frame of reference which would provided the key to his thinking. One discussion of the novel has to some extent provide that key. [In "The Law of Ignominy: Authority, Messianism and Exile in *The Castle*," an essay collected in *On Kafka,* edited by Franz Kuna] W. B. Sebald has pointed out, in passing, the similarity between the Hebrew word for Land-Surveyor, K.'s title in the novel, *meshgeach,* or in the diminutive *mesheoach,* and the Hebrew word for Messiah, *meshiach.* [In his *Franz Kafka: A Biography*]

Max Brod, Kafka's executor and earliest biographer and editor, has noted Kafka's extensive knowledge of Hebrew. Confident therefore that Kafka had sufficient knowledge of Hebrew to be conscious of any double-meaning in the Hebrew equivalent of titles he had assigned his characters, we should examine any further double-meanings in order to reassess the text that Kafka has presented for our unraveling.

We find that the modern Hebrew word for "castle" is *Tzreach*. However, in Biblical Hebrew *Tzreach* refers to "cave" or "cellar." In addition, the ruler of the Castle is named Count Westwest. The Hebrew for "west" is *ma'arov*. Its closely related noun is *ma'aroh,* meaning again "cave" or "cavern."

The nature of K.'s central struggle with the Castle now becomes clear. The Castle is not a symbol of Heaven, of what is above, of grace, but rather of hell. It is an outpost of what is below. It is the fortress of evil that has subdued the villagers and even blocked any knowledge of the path to redemption. Count Westwest, given our new understanding of the Hebrew double-meaning of his name, becomes the leader of the cave, the leader of the fortress of evil blocking our connection with God. Count Westwest might even be Satan, the representatives of the Castle his legions of demons.

Thus, the novel is no longer about a Job-like figure trying to retain his faith in the face of an incomprehensible God. The Messiah has no need to attain salvation; he grants it. Instead, if we are to see K. as the Messiah in the tradition of the Hasidic folk tales upon which Kafka was obviously drawing, but filtered through his unique sense of the ironic and the comical, a whole, new, fresher, and wittier understanding of the novel comes alive for us.

The moment and the atmosphere of K.'s introduction of himself, for example, take on a whole new meaning. The passage could be read, "Let me tell you that I am the Messiah whom the Count is expecting. 'Messiah?' he heard the hesitating question behind his back and then there was a general silence." There is something amiss in the townspeople's reaction to the introduction of K., if we are to assume he is the Messiah. They do not regard this event as a miracle, as their redemptions—"Oh, I know all about you, you're the Messiah, and then adding: 'But now I must go back to my work,' she returned to her place behind the bar..." The townspeople do not realize that they are in need of any sort of redemption; the Castle and its ethic have come totally to dominate their lives.

It is part of the paradoxical irony of the book that K. cannot enter into the struggle with the Castle unless the Castle fights back. The second paradox weaving its way through the novel is the utter blindness of the villagers to their state. The Castle has come to control the minds and acts of the villagers so completely that they have lost even their desire for redemption. It is the mark of the power of the Castle that in the course of K.'s struggle he is subsumed by the very forces against which he is working. He begins to lose even his power of self-determination.

Perhaps *The Castle* is a statement of the condition of mankind in a war-torn, secular world, where not only have all individuals become oblivious to the need for redemption, but even the Messiah, were he to come to earth, would also be forced to succumb to the forces of evil which block our faith in God.

Source: Alan Klein, "Review of 'The Castle,'" in *The Explicator*, Vol. 42, No. 3, Spring 1984, pp. 43–45.

Ronald Gray

In this excerp, Gray views the plot of the novel from an objective perspective rather than through the eyes of K.

It is time now to stop seeing [*The Castle*] through K.'s eyes and to look for those inter-relationships and significances which he, being part of the story, is unable to perceive. K. is never in a position to reflect, for example, on the sequence of events in the final chapters, where he is first abandoned by his assistants, their work being apparently done, then summoned to Erlanger and, having withstood temptation, feels in harmony with the officials. A document has been torn up, a victory seemingly celebrated, and K. is content to imagine Klamm in the most loving relationship with Frieda. It is not K.'s business to inquire into the meaning of all this. Yet it is not unreasonable for an outsider to assume a pattern unifying these apparently unconnected events. With good will towards the castle, the pattern is clear—K. has been persuaded of his insignificance, his humility has been subjected to an exacting test, and his endurance is rewarded. It may at least be so, and while it would be presumptuous for K. to claim it, it is less presumptuous in a reader. Adopting, then, a more well-disposed point of view towards the castle and to K.'s environment in general, what picture emerges?

To take a point at random, there is Klamm's second letter to K., which he regarded at the time with such suspicion:

> To the Land-surveyor at the Bridge Inn. The land-surveying you have carried out so far meets with my approval. The work of your assistants is also praiseworthy, you manage to keep them hard at it. Do not slacken in your zeal. Continue your work to a good conclusion. Any interruption would make me embittered. For the rest, be of good cheer, the question of wages will be decided shortly. I am keeping you in mind.

In the light of the reward K. does receive at the end, this makes much better sense. Casuistry is needed to interpret K.'s spying out the land as surveying, and this must be accounted a fault, from the present point of view. Apart from that, the letter is straightforward. As with the first letter from Klamm, it is in the main K.'s unquiet conscience ('an unquiet, not a bad one') that hinders him from trusting Klamm's word. He rejects the assurance because the castle merely insists that he knows enough already. The fact that in the first letter the words 'as you know' are added to the statement destroys its value in his eyes. Given a quiet conscience he need have troubled no further.

Almost from the outset, K. is encouraged to see events and people in a friendlier guise. It is not a simple matter, however, to ascribe good motives, and may need passionate determination as well as trust. Frieda indicates this to K. when she says 'If only you knew, with what passion I search for a grain of goodness for myself in everything you do and say, even if it hurts me.' His fashion of interpretation is a matter of his disposition, as hers is; things are to him as he is disposed to see them. He can at least recognize this, though he cannot himself change his disposition. That, at least, is how both villagers and castle present the situation to him from the first day of his stay.

The choice between sympathy and hostility, trust and suspicion, is first presented to K. by the carrier Gerstäcker, who offers to drive him back to the Bridge Inn after his brief visit to the laundry in Lasemann's house. K. is puzzled by this act of kindness, which he imagines to be in conflict with the strict ordinances of the castle, and calls out after a while to ask whether Gerstäcker has permission to drive him around on his own responsibility. Receiving no answer he throws a snowball full in the man's ear. This brings Gerstäcker to a halt, but although he makes no reply, the sight of his wretched face compels K. to put his question in a different tone of voice. 'What he had said before out of spite he now had to repeat out of sympathy.' This time he asks whether Gerstäcker will not be punished for giving him a lift. Gerstäcker's answer ends the first chapter on a note of choice: '"What do you want?" ['Was willst du?'] asked Gerstäcker uncomprehendingly, but awaited no further explanation, called to his horses, and they drove on.'

From K.'s point of view, Gerstäcker simply does not understand what K.'s question means. The phrase 'Was willst du?' implies, like the French 'Que veux-tu?', some weary resignation. At the same time it can be read as asking 'What do you want? Do you choose that I shall be punished or not? Will you put the question in spite or in sympathy?' The fact is that Gerstäcker has already suffered for his action, not as the result of any intervention by the castle but at K.'s own hands. The question asked in spite carries its own punishment. A good deal of the real or imagined hostility towards K. arises similarly from the assertiveness or presumptuousness of the villagers; when he suffers, as he does at the hands of Gisa, the castle has no hand in it. Indeed the castle bell has just rung out in its ambiguous fashion (as it seems to K.), 'with rhythmic gaiety' and 'painfully too': it can be heard in both ways, and there is a second bell for those who will make no choice at all, a 'weak and monotonous chime' that seems to K. at this stage to suit the weary journey through the village. There is nothing pure, certain or unchangeable about it as yet.

Shortly afterwards Gerstäcker's question is repeated to K. by an official at the castle. When K. has explained (though falsely) his situation and desires over the telephone, the answer comes 'Was willst du?' There is no possibility of weary resignation in the words this time, it is a direct question. But K. scarcely hears it; convinced that nothing can come of this conversation he makes an insincere inquiry and hangs up. A little later, he sees the fact of choice quite consciously. Looking at Klamm's letter, 'he saw in it … an open choice presented to him; it was left to him to make what he wanted of the orders in the letter.' But the recognition of the fact cannot alter the choice he does make. He is disposed towards suspicion and acts accordingly.

For a great part of the novel K. realizes the good intentions of others almost against his will.

The schoolmaster strikes him at once as 'a really domineering little man', and K. fancies he is flattered by his position of authority and the attentiveness of his pupils. Yet the schoolmaster's first words are 'more mild' (or 'more meek'—'sanftmütiger') 'than K. had expected.' A little later, when Gerstäcker offers to take K. home, K. feels that 'the whole scene did not give an impression of particular friendliness,' although he has been treated in a 'not unfriendly' fashion for the last hour or so. Similarly, in his conversation with the hostess at the Bridge Inn, the woman's laughter sounds 'mocking, but much more gentle than K. had expected.' K.'s expectation is disappointed in this way on other occasions. He is unwilling to be persuaded that he has 'a host of good friends at the castle', and treats the suggestion with mockery. Not until after the horrifying experience of freedom and isolation in the Herrenhof courtyard is it said of K. himself that he had 'grown more mild.'

All this is a matter of K.'s mood. In saying that the villagers and the castle are hostile, dictatorial, well-disposed or acting in K.'s best interests, one is saying that they appear so to him. Yet the mere fact that he has an inkling of their good will, even when on the whole he expects only hostility from them, is an indication that in his transformed mood at the end he might be prepared to reflect on his past experiences differently. And since we are now taking a bird's-eye view denied to K. it may become possible to observe significances of which K. is oblivious.

An episode where, if K.'s limited viewpoint is adopted, there is a sense of frustration and meaninglessness, whereas from the general viewpoint there is possible meaning, is that in Lasemann's house. This follows immediately on K.'s first and only attempt to reach the castle on foot; utterly exhausted, he leaves the 'straitening street' ('die festhaltende Strasse') for a narrow alleyway. Seeing a house, he enters and finds himself in a room filled with smoke and steam, surrounded by people who seem not particularly pleased to see him. He is told to sit down, water is splashed in his face, and since nobody takes any further notice of him he falls asleep. Nevertheless, on waking, he offers thanks for hospitality, only to be more or less dragged to the door and sent out into the snow again. From K.'s point of view the whole affair looks rude, inconsequential and inhospitable. There is, however, another aspect of which even he seems partially aware. He cannot be wholly aware of it since he cannot know the pattern of events later in the book. K. arrives at the house, as he arrives for the Bürgel interview, at a moment when he has at least temporarily given up hope of entering the castle. The sight of the house he interprets as a sign that he is 'not abandoned'. And there *are* suggestions, at least to begin with, that the inhabitants are well disposed towards him: a 'friendly' peasant welcomes him in, and a woman's hand reaches out to save him from stumbling. Thus far there is normality. Inside, the scene has more of a dream-like quality. In the rolling smoke and steam K. stands 'as though in clouds'. Not, it should be noted, in 'clouds of steam', not the usual metaphor, but as though he were actually standing in clouds, as if he were taken out of his earthbound existence. A voice then calls to K. asking who he is, and the narrator's comment on his reply again has overtones of meaning. '"I am the Count's land-surveyor", said K., and sought thus to justify himself before the still invisible ones' ('und suchte sich so vor den noch immer Unsichtbaren zu verantworten'). Why should these villagers be described as 'invisible ones', instead of by the more normal phrase, 'these invisible people?' A vague sense of mystery is conjured up by these words. The mystery increases when K.'s attention is suddenly caught by the sight of a woman suckling a child in the corner. This is the woman whose appearance has already been described, and which suggests indistinctly the figure of the Virgin in some Nativity scene. K. himself finds her surprising, though he is unable to say wherein the surprising element consists. For the reader, there comes a feeling that the scene is of some importance for K., though he too is unable to say why. The girl seems to preside over the scene—K.'s attention is repeatedly drawn to her, and before he leaves he actually jumps round so as to face her. As soon as he does so, however, he is dragged away by a man at each elbow, much as he is dragged away later from the officials' corridor by the landlord and his wife. Has all this any recognizable significance?

Scarcely—it remains for the most part a mystery. But as K. leaves there is a small incident, for which no explanation is given, but which seems more readily placeable.

'All this had lasted only a minute, and at once K. had one of the men to right and left of him and was being dragged by them, as though there were no other means of making themselves understood, silently but with all their strength towards the door. The old man was delighted over something in all this, and clapped his hands. The washerwoman too started laughing, and the children suddenly shouted like mad.'

Is this applause for K., or are they delighted to see the last of him? K. in his present mood would be more likely to assume the latter, though once again he is too weary to speculate about it. Yet the same question of dual interpretation arose after the Bürgel interview, when the bells seemed to proclaim a joyous victory, while the landlord heard them expressing exasperated anger. It may well be applause here; the peasants have been by no means unfriendly towards K., and there is a sense in which he seems to have benefited by his stay in the house. He is refreshed, he moves 'more freely' than before, and when he arrives outside the scene seems 'a little brighter'. He has also become 'rather more sharp of hearing', as though he were better able to interpret what he hears than formerly. It is conceivable that K. has been present at some strange ceremony of whose meaning he has been only dimly aware through the impressive figure of the girl, and that the clapping of the old man, the laughter of the woman, the shouting of the children was a rejoicing at its happy conclusion. The fact that K. is not allowed to remain does not contradict this—he is, as one of the villagers observes, an exceptional case, whereas they are content to remain where they are. The mystery that still envelops the scene is of the kind that must accompany any supposed contact with spiritual forces.

Kafka's style always compels the reader to adopt first the standpoint of the character whose story is related, since only the reflections of this character are actually recorded. The rest is related without causal or logical connection. Friedrich Beissner has observed this effect in Kafka's story *Die Verwandlung*, in which Gregor Samsa is transformed into a repulsive insect. Since only Samsa's account is given, the reader is gradually forced into accepting it. Beissner recalls however that in an early edition Samsa was portrayed in a text-illustration as a man, suggesting that to all outward appearance he remained one. Similarly, K.'s subjective experience here is not solely valid. From the villagers' point of view, this episode in Lasemann's house may have represented K.'s first acceptance by the castle, to be confirmed almost at once by the arrival of the two assistants.

The actions of the castle are often perceived thus dimly in the background, being related to the events in the narrative much as the text-illustration is related to the story of *Die Verwandlung*. They are not openly asserted because of the limitation of the narrator to K.'s position. The task of a reader at his second reading is to inquire what other interpretation may be placed on the events other than that presented to him through the eyes of K. Thereupon the contours of the castle are perceived surrounding the story like the air round an open hand. The difficulty lies in forcing one's gaze away from the hand and concentrating it on the enveloping insubstantiality. This is of course the difficulty with all religious or metaphysical thought, but to imagine the hand without the air about it is even more difficult. (pp. 83–92)

Source: Ronald Gray, "Excerpt from *Kafka's Castle*," in *Kafka's Castle*, Cambridge University Press, 1956, pp. 83–92.

SOURCES

Camus, Albert, "Appendix: Hope and the Absurd in the Work of Franz Kafka," in *The Myth of Sisyphus and Other Essays*, translated by Justin O'Brien, Knopf, 1955, pp. 124–138.

Heller, Erich, *Franz Kafka*, edited by Frank Kermode, Viking Penguin, 1974, pp. 102–103.

Kafka, Franz, *The Trial*, translated by Mark Harman, Schocken Books, 1998.

Mann, Thomas, "Homage," translated by H. T. Lowe-Porter, in *The Castle* by Franz Kafka, translated by Willa Muir and Edwin Muir, Knopf, 1954, pp. ix–xvii.

Muir, Edwin, "A Note on Franz Kafka," in the *Bookman*, Vol. LXXII, No. 3, November 1930, p. 237.

Rahv, Philip, "Franz Kafka: The Hero as Lonely Man," in the *Kenyon Review*, Winter 1939, p. 66.

Wilson, Edmund, "A Dissenting Opinion on Kafka," *Classics and Commercials: A Literary Chronicle of the Forties*, Farrar, Straus, 1950, pp. 383–392.

FURTHER READING

Brod, Max, *Franz Kafka: A Biography*, translated by G. Humphreys Roberts and Richard Winston, Da Capo Press, 1995.
    This account of Kafka's life and work is written by the author's close friend and literary executor, one of the few people who recognized and nurtured Kafka's literary talents during his lifetime.

Calasso, Roberto, *K.*, translated by Geoffrey Brock, Knopf, 2005.

> Calasso, an Italian novelist and literary scholar, here offers an extended essay analyzing Kafka and his work, with a particular emphasis on *The Castle*.

Kafka, Franz, *The Diaries of Franz Kafka*, edited by Max Brod, translated by Joseph Kresh and Martin Greenberg with the cooperation of Hannah Arendt, Schocken Books, 1976.

> This compilation of the author's diaries—which cover his most creative years, from 1910 until 1923—offer an invaluable portrait of Kafka as a man tormented by both his real-life anxieties and tribulations, and by his doubts about his own abilities as a writer.

Teich, Mikulas, ed., *Bohemia in History*, Cambridge University Press, 1998.

> This collection of eighteen essays spans over one thousand years of significant events in the history of the region of Bohemia, including the dark era of Communist rule and the subsequent formation of the Czech Republic.

Davita's Harp

CHAIM POTOK
1985

Davita's Harp is the haunting and painful story of a girl growing up in the first half of the twentieth century. Although she lives in New York, she is thrust into the middle of that brutal period's European wars through her parents and their friends, all activists, writers, and communists. Her mother, Anne, or "Channah," as she is known to her friends from Poland, survived pogroms (massacres) that killed her family; she was a Hasidic Jew in Poland and an atheist and intellectual in Vienna before immigrating to America. Davita's father, Michael Chandal, is the son of Christian lumber tycoons who has rejected his parents' wealth and their religion to work as a journalist documenting the struggle of the working class in America. As Spain succumbs to fascism during the Spanish civil war, Davita's parents dedicate their lives to fighting for justice through their work in the Communist Party. Her father pays the ultimate price for his beliefs, dying in the bombing of Guernica while, with terrible irony, trying to save a nun.

The events of the novel are related through the eyes of a child. Davita is around eight at the book's opening; at its conclusion she is thirteen. This rhetorical device gives the book its tremendous power and pathos. The child tells about the things in her life in the order in which they are important to her, and this order changes as, with age, her reflections develop more sophistication and subtlety. Throughout the book, a reader is aware of the vast difference between knowing

Chaim Potok (*AP Images*)

things and understanding them; Davita describes what she experiences without judgment, and this innocence defines the novel just as the novel defines the twentieth century itself, in a voice that grows less innocent with each new horror that history manifests.

AUTHOR BIOGRAPHY

Herman Harold Potok was born on February 17, 1929, and raised in New York City in an Orthodox Jewish home, the oldest son of Polish immigrants. Following Jewish tradition, his parents also gave the boy a Hebrew name, "Chaim," which means "life." Potok went to Jewish schools as a child, where he studied regular academic subjects along with the Talmud, the book of Jewish law and tradition. He developed an early interest in more secular forms of Judaism and at the age of twenty-five was ordained a Conservative rabbi at the Jewish Theological Seminary in New York. Beginning in 1955 Potok served as an army chaplain on the front lines for sixteen months during the Korean War, an experience that exposed him to deeply religious cultures in a world where there were few Jews.

Potok started writing fiction at age sixteen, after being profoundly moved by Evelyn Waugh's *Brideshead Revisited* (1945), and received a B.A. in English Literature from Yeshiva University in 1950. He went on to write ten novels, the most famous being *The Chosen* (1967), which tells the story of two friends growing up in Jewish Brooklyn, one the son of a secular Jewish family, the other the son of a *tzaddik,* or Hasidic holy man.

This book and its sequel, *The Promise* (1969), follow these two friends as they make hard choices about their lives and their Jewish faiths. *The Chosen* remained on the best-seller list for more than six months and was made into a feature film in 1981 and a Broadway musical in 1985. Other well-known novels include *My Name Is Asher Lev* (1972), *The Gift of Asher Lev* (1990), and *I Am the Clay* (1992). Potok also wrote the nonfiction *Wanderings: Chaim Potok's History of the Jews* (1978). His first novel, *The Chosen*, was nominated for a National Book Award; *The Gift of Asher Lev* won the National Jewish Book Award.

Beginning in 1964 Potok served as managing editor of the magazine *Conservative Judaism*. He became editor in chief of the Jewish Publication Society in Philadelphia in 1965. Also in 1965, Potok received his Ph.D. in philosophy from the University of Pennsylvania. After 1983 Potok served as a visiting professor at institutions of higher education including the University of Pennsylvania, Bryn Mawr, and Johns Hopkins. Potok lived in Pennsylvania for most of his adult life, except for short stints in Israel, along with his wife, psychiatric social worker Adena Sarah Mosevitzsky, whom he married in 1958, and their three children. Chaim Potok died of brain cancer on July 23, 2002, at the age of 73.

PLOT SUMMARY

Book One
The first section of *Davita's Harp* introduces the main characters in the novel: Ilana Davita Chandal, the narrator; her mother, Anne, an intellectual and activist in the Communist Party, who is known as Channah to her European relatives; and her father, Michael Chandal, a journalist for a left-wing newspaper. The Chandal family is poor, living in a series of run-down apartments in New York City. Ilana's earliest memories are of the family's frequent moves—a result of being evicted because of the many noisy political meetings her parents held on the premises.

Davita describes what she knows of her parents' pasts; this is important to her as she tries to construct her identity. Her mother, Anne, came from a devout Hasidic family in Poland. After a terrible pogrom in which her grandfather and sister were murdered and she herself was raped, Anne went first to Vienna to study, then to America, where she lived with relatives and finished college with a degree as a social worker.

Davita's father, Michael Chandal, was the son of a wealthy Episcopalian family of timber barons in New England who owned forests and mills—in Marxist terms, both the raw materials and the means of production. After witnessing horrific events that occurred in Centralia, Washington, in 1919, in which a logger named Wesley Everest was castrated, then murdered, for protesting for basic workers' rights, Michael left his family and their fortune behind to fight for the rights of working people.

Davita recounts her memories of the places in which the family lived: dirty, cold buildings with bad smells, gray snow piled in front, cruel children who threaten her because she is half-Jewish or half-Gentile, or just because her family is different. She describes the harp of the title, a small instrument made of wood strung with fishing wire, on which four wooden balls play a sweet "ting tang tong" each time the front door opens or shuts. This is the "door harp" whose sound pervades her childhood and gives Davita a sense of continuity through all the painful and bewildering events of her young life.

Anne becomes pregnant and gives birth to a boy, who is sickly and soon dies. Michael's sister, Sarah, a Christian missionary and nurse, comes to care for Anne, who is paralyzed with grief. Sarah tells Davita stories unlike any she has heard, of the brave pioneer women of America who helped tame the harsh American West, women who survived for years on their own while their men were off hunting and trading with only their imaginations for company. Davita is deeply impressed by Aunt Sarah's abilities and convictions and is sad when she leaves as abruptly as she arrived.

Her mother recovers her strength and continues her political organizing; her father is often away covering strikes by workers all over the country. He comes home tired, covered with cuts and bruises. Davita often lies in her bed at night listening to the words flying around in the living room, where the political meetings are held. Her room is often very cold at night, her bed "a frozen lake." She drifts off to sleep hearing words such as "proletariat," "capitalist," "fascism," and "idea." In the morning she asks what these words mean and her mother explains each one very precisely, first giving the origin of the word, then explaining all of its various meanings. Davita is surrounded by words and is very aware of their power to shape the world. "Everything has a name, Ilana," her mother explains. "And names are very important. Nothing exists unless it has a name."

Davita never seems to notice that her own name is up for grabs: her mother calls her "Ilana," but her father calls her "Davita." Her Uncle Jakob calls her "Ilana Davita," after first asking her permission to do so. He tells her, "It is very important to call people by their correct names." The name "Ilana" was her mother's dead mother's name; "Davita" is the feminine form of David, one of her father's brothers, who is also dead. Each of her parents calls her by the name that refers back to his or her own family history, thus underscoring that she is made up of two completely different pasts; she is half Old World European Jew, and half blue-blooded New England Episcopalian.

Davita's mother is haunted by her past, and her past never seems very far away. Anne is visited from time to time by "a tall courtly man" named Ezra Dinn. He is Anne's only relative in America, the son of the woman Anne had lived with when she first arrived. He will be the family's quiet but steady helper throughout the book.

Another emissary from her past is Jakob Daw, Anne's friend and possibly ex-lover from her school days in Vienna. Daw is a famous writer now; his character may have been modeled on Franz Kafka. Like Kafka, Daw writes fairy tale–like stories about real life, which he tells to Davita when he visits, staying with the Chandals in New York for months at a time. Like them, Daw is fighting against the forces of injustice, and he is in demand as a speaker at rallies and demonstrations against the fascism rising in Spain as that country moves closer to civil war. Like Anne, Jakob lived through World War I, during which his lungs were damaged by poison gas and he was incarcerated in an insane asylum for many years.

The Chandals spend idyllic summers in Sea Gate, a beach-cottage community near Coney Island in Brooklyn. Davita loves the ocean and is comfortable swimming in its wild water. She also loves the wildness of the nature around her: the noises of birds, and the enormous insects that batter themselves against the windows at night. Her father commutes by trolley to his newspaper office in Manhattan. Jakob Daw comes to stay with them. Davita spends the long days of a heat wave building sand castles modeled on the ones she has read about in books about Spain.

A boy her age and his family come to stay in the beach house next door. He is David Dinn, son of her mother's one cousin in America, Ezra Dinn. David's mother has just died and the boy has been sent to live with his aunt and uncle at Sea Gate to get out of the terrible heat in the city. He is brokenhearted by his mother's death. One day Ilana follows behind David and his uncle as they journey to the local synagogue to say *kaddish,* the prayer for the dead, for David's mother. Ilana likes the songs David's family sing together on Friday nights, songs her mother tells her are called *zemiros.* Her mother tells her that she too once sang zemiros with her family when she was a child in Europe, but cautions her about the family, who are Orthodox Jews: "There is a lot more to them than their songs. The ideas they live by are false." Anne tells Davita, "We will build the new world in our own way. The old way is false." Michael tells her that he, Jakob Daw, and Ezra Dinn were once all in love with Anne, but that she had chosen him.

Davita's parents and Jakob Daw talk all day and into the nights about the impending war in Spain. Davita builds her sand castles stronger and bigger. At night the wind and the waves tear them down, but in the morning Davita rebuilds them. "It's our protection against the fascists on the other side of the ocean," she tells Jakob Daw. "I have to rebuild it."

Soon Uncle Jakob leaves for Europe, to help in the fight against fascism. Aunt Sarah also leaves for Spain, to work as a nurse to those wounded in the war. Davita's beloved father is also sent to Spain as a war correspondent for his newspaper. "Europe was devouring the people I loved," recounts Davita. David Dinn's family returns to the city, followed several days later by Davita and Anne. Davita's early childhood and Book One have ended.

Book Two

As Book Two opens, Ilana and her mother see Michael off on a huge ship called the *Lisbon,* which will carry him across the ocean to the war in Spain. They return to their new apartment in Brooklyn, which is owned by Mr. and Mrs. Helfman, cousins of Ezra Dinn. They have a daughter, Ruthie, who is Davita's age. On their

first night in the new apartment without Michael, Davita hears the Helfmans downstairs singing their Sabbath songs, zemiros. The singing sounds warm and happy to Davita upstairs in the silent apartment she now shares with Anne, who tries to drown her loneliness and fear for Michael's safety by constant work for the communist cause.

Davita is alone many evenings as her mother goes to meetings. "You can spend the time doing your homework or reading your father's articles on the war," Anne tells Davita. "There's a lot of work that has to be done now for the people of Spain. And I can't do it from here." Sometimes Ruthie comes up to play with Davita in the evenings, although she won't accept any snacks, as the Chandals are not kosher, meaning they are not concerned with preparing food according to Jewish law. Ruthie's explanation of words like "kosher" and "Torah" are Davita's first exposure to the many baffling rituals of Judaism.

Davita begins to unpack boxes, something her mother has no time to do. One evening she and Ruthie come across a box of old photographs of people Davita vaguely recognizes but cannot identify, adults who may have been her grandparents, children who may have been her parents. She leaves the pictures on her father's desk. The next morning they are gone and her mother says nothing to her about them. She knows so little about her past; seeking a world into which she can fit, she has little knowledge to build upon.

One day Davita follows Ruthie and her mother on their weekly Saturday morning walk. They come to a synagogue named after David Dinn's great-grandfather, who had been a famous rabbi in Europe. Davita follows them in. She realizes she must sit on the side with the women, which is screened off from the main part of the temple so that the women cannot see what is going on. Davita finds a hole in the curtain and peers through at the singing and rejoicing, all done in a mysterious language. Afterward she sees David Dinn and his father; David's friends laugh at Davita for her questions about the synagogue, but his father, Ezra, described as "tall and courtly," asks after her parents in a kindly way.

Michael comes home from covering the war for his newspaper. He is pale and thin, yellow with jaundice and with a wound in his right hip that makes walking difficult. Davita almost does not recognize him. Aunt Sarah has brought him back and stays with the Chandals to nurse him back to health. Mrs. Helfman brings them chicken soup and agrees to lend Davita books from which she can learn Hebrew. Aunt Sarah gives her books of Christian stories. In her apartment the adults talk endlessly about the war. Davita strains to hear the singing of zemiros coming up through the floor from the Helfmans' apartment over her parents' visitors' angry, frightened voices.

Michael tells her the story of what happened to him in Centralia, Washington, when he was a young man, how he witnessed an event that changed his life forever and made him a fighter for justice. Michael had seen the murder of a logger named Wesley Everest, who tried to create a better life for himself and his fellow workers, and was murdered by timber barons not unlike Michael's own family. "Davita, listen. There are two kinds of America. That's what I realized that day. And I knew which kind I belonged to." The next day Michael sails back to Spain. He waves his cane as the ship pulls away and is lost to Davita's view.

Anne again throws herself into her work as a social worker to diminish her fear about Michael. In the evenings she teaches English to new immigrants or attends Communist Party meetings. Davita, often alone, begins to go downstairs to the Helfmans' for the Friday night *shabbos* (Sabbath) dinners. Ezra Dinn, Mrs. Helfman's nephew, is often there too, with David. Davita sits in their warm, crowded kitchen, hearing the songs and prayers. Speaking about politics or worldly issues is forbidden on the Sabbath, and the men discuss religious questions, Jewish history, and the yeshiva (school) where both David and Ruthie are students and where Mr. Helfman teaches Hebrew. It is clear to Davita that their rituals and their religion are central to their lives, and the synagogue and yeshiva are the center of their community.

One night Davita dreams someone is standing beside her bed. She feels a warm, moist kiss on her cheek—her father's kiss—and a "dark sadness." On the way to school she spends the money her mother gave her for candy on a newspaper and reads about a terrible bombing that has destroyed an ancient town called Guernica, where her father is stationed. Stories in his newspaper begin to appear that day written by another writer. No one at his paper seems to know where Michael is. Several weeks pass until a British journalist, who had also been at

Guernica, visits to relate to them a report he received from a Spanish priest. The priest had seen a tall, brown-haired man emerge from a car just as the bombs started falling on Guernica. The man ran toward a nun who had been knocked down and lifted her in his arms. Running for shelter under a bridge, the man's right leg suddenly appeared to give way and he collapsed. Then a bomb fell and there was nothing. The man tells them no one can really be sure if the man was Michael, but Davita and her mother know it was him because of his wounded right hip.

Davita goes to the public library and reads *Nineteen Nineteen* (1932) by John Dos Passos, which recounts the events her father had witnessed in Centralia in much more detail. Davita learns the logger Wesley Everest was not simply murdered, but was first castrated by a Centralia businessman. The line "Wesley Everest gave a great scream of pain," repeats itself over and over in Davita's mind.

She continues to go to the synagogue on Saturday mornings, where she has begun to understand both written and spoken Hebrew. She is increasingly drawn to the synagogue's life and warmth, as she explains to David: "It feels good and everything feels like it's being changed into something very beautiful like when I was building castles on the beach." It is a world outside of the reality of Davita's life, outside of any reality at all. Davita decides to say kaddish for her father, even though, as David explains, it is not considered correct or even necessary for women to do that, nor is it necessary for women to come to the synagogue at all. Davita does it anyway, for eleven months. Several women on her side of the curtain repeat the responses to Davita's recitation, but none speak to her about it directly.

Jakob Daw returns to Brooklyn to help Anne in her grief. One evening Mr. Dinn and David come to the door, and Daw requests they make *Havdoloh* together in the apartment; although he does not believe in God, he explains that his late grandfather loved this ritual, which marks the separation of the work week from the Sabbath. It is the first time Davita has seen a Jewish ritual performed in her own home.

Unknown people in the United States government want Daw deported, although his experiences in Spain have caused him to renounce Stalinism. Dinn, an immigration lawyer, tries to save him. One night two men come to the apartment and take Daw away in handcuffs. Davita and her mother and Mr. Dinn watch Uncle Jakob's ship pull away from the pier. Another of Davita's loved ones has sailed away, never to be seen again except in memory and dreams.

After Daw's deportation Davita gets very sick. In this part of the book she refers to herself in the third person, Ilana Davita Chandal. She walks off a rowboat into the lake in Prospect Park, and seems to no longer inhabit her own body. Again Aunt Sarah arrives, as she does each time one of the family is sick, and brings Davita with her to the beach house in Maine that Davita's great-grandfather had bequeathed to Sarah and Michael. There, in the silence and the hugeness of the ocean and sky, Davita slowly gets better. She joins her aunt in her daily prayers to "our Lord Jesus Christ."

When she returns to Brooklyn she is still in a dreamlike haze, and she wanders away from her public school a few times without a word. After many long talks with her mother, Mr. Dinn, Mr. Helfman, and other grownups she does not know, Davita enters David's school, the yeshiva attached to the synagogue. The young male teacher asks if anyone knows what is going on in Spain. Davita raises her hand and talks, and for the first time in all her school years, both the students and the teacher listen intently to her words.

Book Three

In Book Three Davita enters puberty, and the direction her life will take moves into sharper focus. She continues to say the kaddish for her father at prayer time in her new school, although she is again warned that this is against the rules for girls. All around her other students recite the proper responses to her prayer. She is respected for her excellent mind and brilliant scholarship and feels more and more at ease in the serious atmosphere of the school.

Her mother continues to work at a feverish pace, editing unfinished manuscripts of Michael's writing and translating stories by Jakob Daw. She begins to date a chain-smoking professor in the Communist Party, Charles Carter, and asks Davita if she would like to have him as a stepfather. Davita says no, and asks if she can live with the Helfmans if Anne marries Carter and moves with him to Chicago, where he has received a professorship. Ezra Dinn also begs Anne to consider what she would be doing

to Davita's life were she to move Davita to Chicago, away from everyone and everything she knows.

Davita is saved from this fate by the surprising development of Stalin's nonaggression pact with Adolf Hitler. This pact assures that Hitler will not be opposed by Russia in his quest to dominate Western Europe and eliminate world Jewry. Her mother, having survived anti-Jewish pogroms and lost her family to them, cannot understand how Stalin, upon whom the Communist Party had pinned all of its hopes, could make such an alignment. Anne is broken-hearted and bewildered, and although she is a high-ranking official, she abandons the party and is in turn abandoned by Charles Carter. Now it is as if she has nothing left to live for, and she grows old before Davita's eyes: "Her face sagged and became strangely dull, her eyes took on a pinkish inflamed look.... An odor began to rise from her, sour, fecal. Her skin became dry and flaky, her long hair scraggly. She seemed to be growing smaller and smaller." One day Anne collapses at work and Mr. Dinn drives her to the farmhouse in Maine to be cared for by Aunt Sarah.

When she returns Anne is healthy and rested, and soon she marries Mr. Dinn. He and David move into Davita's apartment, bringing new furniture, rugs, books, and all the accoutrements of an Orthodox Jewish home. Anne cries the first time she lights the Shabbos candles. Mr. Dinn takes the family to Sea Gate for the summer, to the same community where Davita's parents used to go. The new family is happy there, and Davita likes and respects her new father, who is well read, fair-minded, and intelligent. She studies the Torah with David, who is considered a genius by his classmates and hopes to someday lead his own yeshiva. In answer to her question, David tells her that a girl could not lead a yeshiva, and that in fact no girls ever study at the higher levels.

Davita's depiction of her life reaches a new level of maturity in Book Three. Her mother and Mr. Dinn create a secure environment and she has no bad dreams. The family observes all the proper Jewish laws and rituals and attends the synagogue every Saturday. Davita is now in what seems to be a healthy community she can really belong to, unlike the violent and unstable world of politics to which her parents belonged.

When Jakob Daw dies of pneumonia in France, Anne follows her daughter's example and says kaddish for him every morning for a year at their synagogue. Ezra suggests this will cause a fuss, but he does not object since this is what she wants. One day Davita accompanies her mother to the synagogue and is surprised to see that she sits in a tiny prisonlike space behind a wall. Davita asks in her classroom why women are not allowed to sit with the men and pray as equals. Her teacher counsels her to stop asking questions and obey the laws that pertain in the school and the synagogue. He says she is his best student and tells her that at the end of the year, which will mark her graduation from middle school, "there are awards and prizes. Keep up your good work and we will all be proud of you."

Davita describes her life in 1941 as "a dream time for me, an idyll, the loveliest time of my young life." Her body is maturing into that of a woman, she has a loving family, friends, and is in a school where she is well respected. The award she hopes to win at the end of the school year is not the Talmud prize for excellence in Jewish study that David wins at his graduation, a year ahead of hers, but the Akiva Award, which is given to the pupil who has the highest grades, the best student overall.

It is clear to everyone in the school that Davita should win this award. Her only competition is Reuven Malter, a handsome, athletic boy who has been in the school since first grade and whose father is a renowned Talmud teacher. One day Mr. Helfman calls her into his office. He tells Davita that although she has the highest grades in the class, that even though she should win the award, she will not because the school cannot give the highest award to a girl. How would it make the boys of the school look, he asks? How could any academy of higher Torah learning accept a boy who came from a class in which the best student was a girl? Davita cannot believe what she is hearing. Her mother and Ezra Dinn don't believe it either, but all of their efforts to reverse the decision come to nothing. Word has come down from the highest school authorities that Davita cannot receive the Akiva Award. The world of Judaism that Davita has adopted has rejected her, betraying her just as painfully as her mother was failed by communism.

She graduates from the school with the two next-highest academic prizes. Reuven Malter turns down the Akiva Award because, as he tells her privately, he does not want something he didn't earn. Another male student receives the prize and makes the valedictory speech. Davita realizes she has come to a major turning point in her life—this one moment will change her life forever, just as her mother's life was changed by a pogrom and her father's life by what he saw in Centralia.

After the graduation ceremony, lying on her bed in her white dress, Davita hears the wooden balls of the door harp playing although no one has entered the room. Dreamily, she finds herself entering the door harp and riding through the sky to Aunt Sarah's beach house, where her father and Jakob Daw are waiting. They have come to hear the speech Davita would have made if she had received the Akiva Award. She tells them that this century will not defeat her. Clearly she is well prepared to fight her own fights in this world in order to make a good life for herself. Her father and Jakob Daw ride off into the ocean. Davita will be going to a public high school, "a very good one," in the fall. Aunt Sarah tells her, "Be discontented with this world. But be respectful at the same time."

The novel ends with Davita's mother giving birth to a baby girl, Rachel. As Davita holds her tiny sister, she begins to tell her a story, a story like the ones Uncle Jakob had once told her. "It doesn't have an ending.... Are you listening, little... It's about a door harp." Undeniably, Davita will become someone who will not only survive the twentieth century but will reshape it in a nobler and more just image.

CHARACTERS

Anne/Channah Chandal (later Dinn)

Anne Chandal, called Channah by Ezra Dinn, Jakob Daw, and others she knows from her several pasts, is Davita's mother. She is the central person in Davita's life and a source of continual fascination to the girl. Her mother's pasts include a girlhood as an observant Hasidic Jew in Poland, a period brought violently to an end by a pogrom that left her family dead, and later as a student in post–World War I Vienna, where the writer Jakob Daw was her lover. Still later, Anne/Channah came to New York, where she met Ezra Dinn, and later Michael Chandal, her first husband and Davita's father. A complicated woman, she has dedicated all of the passion of her early immersion in Jewish scholarship to fighting against the ravages of capitalism on the working class in America and fascism rising in Europe. She is a strong person who believes that people can create a fair and peaceful world, and reconciling her ideals to reality is a struggle that almost kills her several times throughout the book.

Ilana Davita Chandal (later Dinn)

Davita is the narrator and central figure in *Davita's Harp*. At the start of the book she is a child of about seven or eight and by the end she is fourteen. All of the events and the other characters in the book are described through her eyes, becoming clearer and more detailed as her level of comprehension of the world around her becomes more sophisticated and subtle. An only child, she is almost always in the company of adults, and thus has a vocabulary well beyond the average for her age, and an awareness of the events that preoccupy her parents and the few other people who populate her world, such as the condition of the working class in America and abroad, the rise of fascism in Europe, and the terrible events of the Spanish civil war. All of the events in the novel are seen through the eyes of a child, giving *Davita's Harp* both a terrible pathos and tremendous power. Davita seems at times to represent the world's people as they enter the twentieth century as innocent children, are beaten by unending waves of brutal wars, and emerge scarred and older, determined to survive and fight for a better day.

Michael Chandal

Michael Chandal is Davita's father. Son of a wealthy lumber family in Maine, Michael has rejected a life of privilege to fight for the rights of working people. He is a journalist and writer and in the course of the book he travels frequently to scenes of strikes throughout America, and eventually goes to cover the bloody events of the civil war in Spain, where he is killed by a bomb. He is a relaxed and good-natured man whose affable demeanor lends warmth and stability to the otherwise black-and-white extremes of Davita's life. Michael's dedication to his cause was shaped by events he witnessed in 1919 in Centralia, Washington, during which timber barons murdered a logger named Wesley Everest, who was fighting for workers' rights, by castrating him.

Sarah Chandal

Sarah Chandal is Michael's sister and Davita's aunt. Sarah is a nurse and a Christian missionary, and as the story opens she is just back from Ethiopia. Later she goes to Spain to help the wounded and preach Christianity. She is also a stabilizing presence in Davita's life, visiting the family whenever one of them is sick or injured to nurse them back to health. After Michael is killed, Davita attempts suicide, and Sarah takes her to a farmhouse in Maine to recuperate. Although Davita tries Aunt Sarah's religion, praying on her knees to Jesus Christ, she prefers the Judaism of her mother and the families who surround them in Brooklyn.

Jakob Daw

Jakob Daw is a Polish writer who was Anne's lover in Vienna when both were college students. Possibly modeled on Franz Kafka, he is a writer of fantastical fairy tale–like stories that give Davita much to ponder. Often she does not like Uncle Jakob's stories because they don't have happy endings, or sometimes any endings. Daw is also a committed communist and is active in the fight against fascism in Europe. Targeted by authorities as a dissident, eventually Daw is deported despite the best efforts of Ezra Dinn, an immigration lawyer. Davita's beloved "Uncle Jakob" dies of pneumonia in France at the dawn of World War II.

David Dinn

David Dinn is Ezra's son, and he becomes Davita's half-brother after their parents marry. David has also recently lost a parent, his mother, and Davita is affected strongly by seeing him recite the *kaddish* for her three times a day for one year. He is a devoted student of the Talmud and hopes to lead his own yeshiva (Jewish school). He is at first shy around Davita, but it is clear he respects her even though her parents are different from anyone he knows. At the book's end they live together in what had been Davita's apartment and experience the first stirrings of adult sexual feelings for each other. They are able to talk about it, and the reader is left with the feeling that they will work it out as each goes on his or her path toward the adulthood they desire.

Ezra Dinn

Ezra Dinn is a devoutly Jewish cousin of Anne's who helps the Chandal family throughout the book. He becomes Anne's second husband after Michael's death. An honorable immigration lawyer, he is the third man, after Michael Chandal and Jakob Daw, to be in love with Anne, whom he met during their years as students at Brooklyn College. Ezra becomes a stable and kindly second "Papa" to Davita, drawing her and her mother into the security of his beliefs, although it is clear Davita will never forget her real father.

The Harp

The harp of the title is as important a player in Davita's life as any character in the novel. It is a small harplike instrument that her parents hang on the front door of each of the many apartments in which the family lives. It plays a tune each time the door opens and shuts and gives Davita a sense of continuity and safety. It comes to mean home to her almost as much as her parents do. The harp is said to have come from her father's side of the family, and is thus even more precious as her parents seem to have no keepsakes of their families, and almost no relatives.

Mr. Helfman

Mr. Helfman is the Chandals' neighbor and landlord in Brooklyn. Ezra Dinn finds the apartment for the family after they have been evicted from numerous apartments for having communist meetings on the premises. Mr. Helfman is also a teacher at the Jewish yeshiva Davita attends after her mother's marriage to Ezra Dinn. It is he who tells Davita she will not receive the school's highest honor, the Akiva Award, which goes to the pupil with the highest grade average, because she is a girl. How would the world look upon the boys of the school, asks Mr. Helfman, if a girl was known to be the smartest student? Nothing Anne or Ezra do can change the school's decision, and this event sets Davita on a course she will follow for the rest of her life—a struggle for equal rights for women that will define her generation just as the fight for workers' rights defined her parents' lives.

Reuven Malther

Reuven Malther, one of the lead characters in Potok's most famous novel, *The Chosen*, appears in *Davita's Harp* briefly toward the end only to turn down their school's highest honor, the Akiva Award. Reuven undertakes this honorable act because the prize belongs to Davita as the yeshiva's best student; the school's

authorities want to give it to him, the second-most highly ranked student, only because he is a boy.

THEMES

Belief

Davita's Harp concerns itself very seriously throughout with notions of belief. Davita's parents are fervent believers in the political system of communism. This is what they believe will end the tremendous inequalities in wealth throughout the world that lead to hunger, homelessness, and many other miseries. The intensity of her parents' belief shapes Davita's life. When her mother loses her belief in the communist cause after Stalin signs a nonaggression pact with Hitler, it almost kills her.

The second belief system that Davita is saturated by, especially after her father's death and her mother's loss of conviction in communism, is Orthodox Judaism. In her new father and brother, and through the influence of the synagogue and the yeshiva, the Jewish grade school she begins to attend weekly, Davita discovers a world in which people believe as deeply as her parents in a completely different kind of creed. She finds that Jewish belief is not based on tactics that can be put into action nor does it have measurable results in the social or economic world. Instead it is based in the repetition of certain ritual acts and in the study of ancient texts.

Davita is initially amazed that her classmates in the yeshiva know nothing about current events, including the Spanish civil war, in which her father was killed, and the run-up to World War II, which will ultimately result in the deaths of six million European Jews. Instead they celebrate ancient events reported as truths in the Torah, such as the freeing of Jews from slavery in Egypt. They rage against indignities supposedly perpetrated against Jews many thousands of years earlier.

These two sets of contradictory belief systems are a profound learning tool for Davita as she grows up questioning both systems in her quest to find her own way.

Inequality

Davita's Harp opens and closes with its characters fighting against inequality in various guises. Davita's parents have committed their lives to

TOPICS FOR FURTHER STUDY

- Create a timeline of the Communist Party in America, starting before and ending after the time period covered in *Davita's Harp*. Note reasons for the rise and fall of party membership caused by world events and U.S. events, such as the pact signed by Stalin and Hitler discussed in the novel.

- List topics Potok was able to explore in *Davita's Harp* because he uses a female narrator (the only time in any of his novels he does so), subjects he may have been unable to touch on had he used a male narrator. Consider topics both religious and secular in nature.

- Pablo Picasso's great painting, *Guernica,* is discussed toward the end of *Davita's Harp,* both in terms of the narrator's strong reaction to it and in the context of a story she writes using its imagery. Study the painting and identify some of the elements Davita mentions. Write a short paper describing your reaction to the painting.

- Imagine Davita's future. What kinds of social and political struggles might she take part in? The character will become an adult in the 1950s. List five areas of social and political activism to which a character like Davita might be drawn.

- Dave Boling's novel *Guernica* (2008) has been praised for its accurate portrayal of the context of the Spanish Civil War. Read the novel, then have a group discussion about how a fuller understanding of the war and the deadly attack on Guernica affect your understanding of *Davita's Harp*.

bringing communism to America as a means of equalizing wealth among the rich and the poor, or in communist terms, the owners and the workers. Each of her parents has had terrible personal experiences with the consequences of inequality. Her mother watched her family murdered as she herself was raped by Christians in a pogrom against Jews in Poland. Her father witnessed the castration and murder of a logger who was working for workers' rights in the lumber industry, the industry in which his own family were tycoons. Communism, they believe, is the only political system that can bring about equality, safety, and dignity for the working class. "Capitalism," Davita's mother tells her, "is incompatible with compassion."

As Davita witnesses world events through her parents' eyes, through letters from friends and relatives in Europe, and through radio and newspaper reports she sees this inequality at play. Fascists take over and destroy Spain, killing thousands, and they mass against the Jews of Europe. Davita sees inequality perpetrated by the government of the United States as well, when her beloved Uncle Jakob is deported to die in Europe. Daw's supporters and lawyers can do nothing to change the minds of those in the government who have made this decision, even though Daw has renounced his communist sympathies, because they are never allowed to speak to the people who are deporting him. "In our time," Daw says, "a man whose enemies are faceless bureaucrats almost never wins."

Davita begins her own fight against inequality when she encounters the discrimination against women implicit in Orthodox Judaism. After the death of her father she decides she wants to say kaddish, or the prayer for the dead, for the eleven-month period specified by Jewish law. She is informed that this is against the law, and even worse, that it is "not necessary." It is not even necessary, she learns, for women to go to a synagogue at all. She encounters this sexist discrimination even more brutally at her graduation from the yeshiva when she is denied the school's highest academic award because she is a girl. Mr. Helfman, her teacher, explains that this coveted prize can only be given to a boy. "We would be the only yeshiva with a girl as head of the graduating class," he tells her. "What would the world think about our boys? It would not be nice." The community in which Davita has invested all her hopes and dreams for the future has betrayed her, and the blow is as devastating as the loss of communism had been to her mother. The reader senses she will carry this fight for equal rights for women into her adult life, perhaps becoming one of the leaders of modern feminism.

Ruins of Guernica, Spain, destroyed during the Spanish Civil War (*Bettmann | Corbis*)

STYLE

Conflict

In *Davita's Harp* many of the characters are in conflict with the world itself, specifically with the ways in which people have set up their cultures and governments. These characters question the deepest premises of societal norms, such as the inequality of women and the poor under the capitalist system of government in America, and the ways in which religion works to distract people from these inequities. Characters also come into conflict with each other over these issues, such as when Ezra Dinn begs Channah to consider her family before doing what is best for the Communist Party, or when Davita defies both her mother and the members of the synagogue by saying kaddish for her father although it is forbidden for women to say the prayer for the dead.

Hero/Heroine

Davita's Harp is filled with heroes and heroines, beginning with the title character's parents, who live and die for their beliefs, and extending to her Aunt Sarah, a missionary and nurse who travels to war-torn countries, and her Uncle Jakob, a writer who risks his life traveling the world giving speeches for the communist cause. Davita herself, however, is the book's central heroine as she navigates her baffling and often terrifying world. Her heroism is a child's heroism, and she meets each new challenge with honesty and strength. Because she is a child and the adults around her are very busy, she has no choice other than to be brave, but she has role models who define bravery through their every word and deed, true heroes of the twentieth century.

Narration

Potok chose an unusual form of narration in *Davita's Harp* in using a child narrator, Davita, who ages from approximately eight to fourteen during the course of the novel. In Book One her narrative voice is entirely without reflection or evaluation; she simply reports what she knows about her life and what she sees around her. Books Two and Three relate the other characters' actions and motivations in a more subtle way as Davita herself becomes aware of more. Her own feelings and views are revealed as she experiences them, and so, in a way, the reader is allowed to grow up along with her. It's a powerful device, and one which Potok perhaps chose knowingly, as Davita's journey to maturity reflects the world's journey through the twentieth century. Her dawning consciousness, reflected in her narration of the book, mirrors the century's growing awareness of itself and of the struggles that must be fought to create a less violent, more equitable future.

HISTORICAL CONTEXT

Communism in America

Davita's Harp is steeped in the political realities of the era in which it is set. Although actual years or dates are rarely mentioned, it is clear from world events what years Davita moves through during the book. When the novel opens she is around eight years old and her parents are members of the Communist Party in New York. Her father, Michael, a journalist, travels all around the country covering workers' strikes for his newspaper. This is the dawn of communism in America, and Davita's parents, especially her Jewish Polish-born mother, Anne, want desperately to show American workers that the capitalist system must be overthrown before they will be able to reach their goals for better lives.

During the first decades of the twentieth century, the communist philosophy attracted many people, including prominent intellectuals and artists, around the world. This attraction to communism was frequently inspired by a desire to improve the lives of the working class, who, at the turn of the century, toiled under dangerous and difficult conditions in the factories of major world cities. The Communist Party was active in the United States as well, and many writers and activists watched with interest the changes that were happening in Russia. American journalist John Reed, a communist himself, was an eyewitness to the Russian revolution of 1917 that ushered in the country's communist government. His book *Ten Days that Shook the World* details his experience. The success of the Russian Revolution profoundly disturbed many American

leaders, as well as ordinary citizens, who sensed in communism a direct threat to American capitalism. The "Red Scare" of 1917 to 1920 was a response to that unease. Several incidents of violence and agitation targeting politicians and major business, presumably by communists hoping to spark an American communist revolution, sparked a crackdown by law enforcement officials. American communist groups saw their membership dwindle during this time.

Fascism in Europe

During the 1930s, an intense nationalism seized several European nations, including Germany, Italy, and Spain. That intense nationalism, coupled with a repressive and dictatorial government, is generally described as "fascism." During weekly political meetings in their ever-changing apartments (they are evicted repeatedly for hosting such meetings), Davita hears her parents and their friends use the words "Hitler," "Mussolini," and "brown shirts." Clearly, her parents are staying abreast of the advances of such leaders as Germany's Adolf Hitler and Italy's Benito Mussolini. As the book progresses her parents become consumed with the fight against fascism taking shape during the Spanish Civil War as the military dictator, Francisco Franco, wrests control of the country away from the government by use of some of the most brutal tactics known yet in war. Davita's father goes to Spain to report on the atrocities and is blown up by a bomb in the ancient Basque city of Guernica. The bombing of Guernica on April 26, 1937, by the German air force (the Germans backed Franco) killed hundreds of civilians. Another important character in the book, Uncle Jakob, a famous writer and political activist, also goes repeatedly to Spain and dies in Europe after he is barred from returning to the United States.

Molotov–Ribbentrop Pact

Davita's mother had great hopes for the communist regime in the Soviet Union. These hopes are dashed by the Molotov-Ribbentrop Pact, an 1939 agreement between Soviet leader Josef Stalin and German leader Adolf Hitler in which the two countries promised mutual non-aggression for ten years. Davita's mother cannot reconcile her vision of communism with the fact that Stalin has align himself with the virulently anti-Semitic Nazi regime. Historically the Communist Party worldwide lost many adherents during this period. When Germany breaks the

COMPARE & CONTRAST

- **1930s:** Newsreels, shown in movie houses before the feature film, are an influential news source for millions of Americans, as a supplement to daily newspapers.

  1980s: The majority of Americans turn to television, and the three dominant TV networks, for their news.

  Today: With the rise of the Internet, daily newspapers are in danger of folding nationwide; twenty-four-hour cable news channels have greatly reduced the mass audience for the major U.S. broadcast networks.

- **1930s:** The turmoil of the Great Depression fosters the growth of communist parties in the United States and countries around the world; Soviet Russia, despite Joseph Stalin's dictatorial rule, seems to offer a model for radicals and revolutionaries.

  1980s: The fall of the Berlin Wall in 1989 marks the defeat of communism in Eastern Europe; the Soviet Union itself disintegrates two years later, bringing an end to the cold war.

  Today: Communist ideology is in worldwide decline, despite a resurgence of the political left in Latin America.

- **1930s:** Women face limited educational and career opportunities and discrimination in many professions; marriage and motherhood represent the most socially acceptable occupational path for women.

  1980s: Following the women's liberation movement that began in the late 1960s, American women make major gains in higher education and the workplace, although discrimination and the "glass ceiling" continue to hinder their advancement.

  Today: Women in twenty-first-century America enjoy an unprecedented level of freedom and opportunity; while they are still greatly outnumbered by men in the top ranks of government and business, it is no longer unusual for women to hold positions such as secretary of state, speaker of the House, and Supreme Court justice.

---

pact and invades the Soviet Union (which happened in 1941) Anne is glad. "I hope they destroy each other." But in fact it was Germany that was destroyed. The decision to invade the Soviet Union proved disastrous.

CRITICAL OVERVIEW

The critical and commercial success of Potok's four prior novels as well as his nonfiction effort, *Wanderings,* assured *Davita's Harp* its share of critical attention. Nevertheless, the reviews were mixed. Like Potok's previous novels, *Davita's Harp* earned praise for the complexity of its thematic issues along with some disparagement over the execution of the narrative. Cynthia

Greiner, in the *Wall Street Journal,* lamented the novel's "stiff dialogue and stilted characters." A *Kirkus* reviewer found the pacing too slow and the first-person narration heavy-handed. On the other hand, Paul Cowan, in the *New York Times Book Review,* praised Potok's prose style and characterizations. "The people he depicts live in a community held together by ancient laws," Cowan wrote. "Those people nourish each other in the worst of times. In doing so, they nourish Mr. Potok's readers too."

Most reviewers noted that the novel, with its female protagonist and concern with the status of women in Judaism, represented a new direction in Potok's work. A lengthy summary by Sanford Sternlicht in his book *Chaim Potok: A Critical Companion* (2000) went so far as to call *Davita's Harp* a feminist novel. Because the narrative unfolds from the point of view of its young heroine, some critics have placed it in the young-adult genre.

Davita's Harp appears to have been mostly neglected even by scholars of Potok's work. An issue of the journal *Studies in American Jewish Literature* devoted entirely to Potok appeared in early 1985, just before the novel's publication, but failed to mention the new book. Similarly, Edward Abramson's book-length biography of Potok, published in 1986, contained only a nominal postscript on *Davita's Harp*.

CRITICISM

Melanie Bush

Bush is a writer and journalist. In this essay, she explores the development of the main character in Davita's Harp as she searches for an identity and a community in a way that mirrors the development of the twentieth century itself.

Davita's Harp is a coming-of-age story in the classic sense as the title character, Davita, struggles to create an identity for herself and to do so in a context of conflicting signals from those around her. Her mother, Anne, is a Polish Jew who was raised in the Hasidic tradition, the strictest form of Judaism. Her father, Michael, is an American Episcopalian from a family of lumber barons. Davita is by birth half Old World European Jew and half New World blue-blood. Her identity is influenced by two very different worlds.

The character's very name embodies this dichotomy. Throughout the novel, each of Davita's parents—along with each set of their relations and friends—calls the child by the name that refers to his or her side of the family. She is named "Ilana" after her mother's mother, who died in Poland. Her own mother calls her by that name, as do her mother's Jewish friends and relations. Her middle name is "Davita" after her father's uncle David, who died in a boating mishap in Maine, and the child is called by that name by her father and his sister. (This name has the additional twist of being a feminized version of a male name, giving Davita, as she is called throughout the book, a certain androgyny, or blending of sexes. Davita is the only female narrator of any of Potok's novels, so this androgyny may not be unintentional.)

> DAVITA CLEARLY UNDERSTANDS THAT HER MOTHER HAS RETURNED TO JUDAISM BECAUSE HER SPIRIT HAS BEEN BROKEN, AND THAT EZRA IS HER ONLY LIFELINE."

This discrepancy in her given name is one of many facts about her life that Davita, with a child's lack of critical judgment, mentions only once in passing. Interestingly there is one character, her mother's oldest friend, Davita's "Uncle Jakob," who calls her by both names. A famous European writer and political dissident, he asks if that is the name he should call her. "Is it all right to call you Ilana Davita? Good. It is very important to call people by their correct names." Uncle Jakob is the only one to do so.

Davita comes to understand the power of names in shaping a person's identity in another manner. Late in the novel, Davita's mother informs her that her last name will change from that of her birth father, Chandal, to that of her adoptive father, Dinn. To Davita this makes no sense. "I found I could not reconcile myself to no longer carrying my father's name," she says. "I told myself I would do something about that one day." (Interestingly, none of the adults around her knows the actual meanings of their surnames. Mr. Dinn does not know the meaning of Dinn, nor can Davita's mother, a meticulous linguist, find any meaning for the name Chandal.)

It does not help Davita's search to form a cohesive identity that each of her parents has completely rejected his or her roots, so that the child has no access to either of her parents' pasts. Her mother has left the restrictive world of Judaism for the Communist Party, which is more welcoming to women as intellectuals and leaders, and which she also believes will pave the way to a just world for people of all genders, races, and classes. Davita's mother's family all died in Poland during or before the First World War; she has no connection to them except through her one cousin in America, Ezra Dinn. Davita's father has had an equally stark break with his own family: he was disowned by them after marrying Davita's mother or after becoming a political

WHAT DO I READ NEXT?

- James Baldwin's *Go Tell It on the Mountain* (1953) is a novel about an African American preacher's son growing up in Harlem in New York City in the 1950s. The boy at first follows the religion of his father, becoming a sort of preacher child prodigy, but must drop out when he experiences hypocrisy in the practice of Christianity.

- In Judy Blume's *Are You There, God? It's Me, Margaret* (1970), Margaret's mother is Christian, her father is Jewish, and the book explores her need for a single religion. Margaret is twelve and the book also details her early feelings for boys as she matures through her preteen years.

- *The Diary of a Young Girl* by Anne Frank (1947) is a world-famous account of the day-to-day life of a young girl in hiding from the Nazis in Amsterdam. In this book published after her death, Anne Frank depicts her budding sexual feelings for a boy her own age whose family is hiding in the same building.

- Franz Kafka wrote *The Trial,* which was published in 1925. In this novel Kafka, who may have been the model for the great dissident writer Jakob Daw in *Davita's Harp,* describes the labyrinthine nightmare of modern bureaucracy, the same anonymous machine that deports Daw to his death in Potok's novel.

- In Chaim Potok's novel *My Name Is Asher Lev* (1972), a Hasidic Jewish boy from Brooklyn must choose between his family and his calling as an artist. His struggle between community and identity is parallel to Davita's, although the content of the struggle is different.

- *Yentl* (1983) is a film based on Isaac Bashevis Singer's story titled "Yentl the Yeshiva Boy," about a rabbi's daughter with "the soul of a man and the body of a woman." The young woman, Yentl, is so hungry for learning that she defies Talmudic law by disguising herself as a man in order to attend a yeshiva, or religious school. The story, set in nineteenth-century Poland, was adapted for the stage in 1974 and later became the basis of the multimillion-dollar Hollywood musical produced and directed by Barbra Streisand, who also plays the title role.

radical—the novel does not explain how it happened, as this is of little concern to Davita, and all of the events are told through her point of view.

Davita is exposed to several models of community throughout the book, as her parents, especially her mother, explore them in search of their own fullest personhood. Davita is therefore thrust into their various communities or investigates them herself by choice. Community, a reader senses, will be very important to Davita in her adult life, as she has seen how vitally important it is to adults. The novel celebrates the idea of community as the basis for a healthy adult life. The adults in Davita's world are either building new communities or fleeing old communities—or they are enmeshed in stable communities. The first example of a community Davita sees is under construction: the American Communist Party, a community for her mother until Anne rejects it after becoming disillusioned with Josef Stalin, leader of the Soviet Union (the world's only communist country at that point). Anne is then expelled from that community, and none of her old friends and coworkers will continue to socialize with Anne. Davita then watches with horror the effects that this loss of community has on her mother. She she stops sleeping, eating, or bathing and eventually has a complete physical and emotional breakdown.

The second community Davita experiences in depth is the world of Orthodox Judaism. This is the community her mother was raised in and the community to which she returns after she has been betrayed by the Communist Party. This world seems more forgiving than the communists. Anne is escorted back to this old, familiar community on the arm of Ezra Dinn, who has been in love with her for the twenty years since they met as college students. Despite the facts that Anne does not believe in God and has not observed Jewish rituals for years, that she married a Gentile and had his child, and that she was a high official in the Communist Party, the Jewish community welcomes her back in her identity as Ezra's wife and mother to his teenage son.

Anne begins to observe Jewish rituals in her home after her marriage, such as keeping kosher and lighting Sabbath candles. She dutifully goes to the synagogue with the family, although, as Davita observes, she does not pray but rather reads the prayer book. Again this seems acceptable to those around her, and when Anne, now known as Channah, becomes pregnant with Ezra's baby, she is fully accepted by the group.

Davita clearly understands that her mother has returned to Judaism because her spirit has been broken, and that Ezra is her only lifeline. But she does not conclude that it is fear that draws people to religion. Davita has already been trying out Judaism herself by going to a temple on Saturdays (without her mother) and having Sabbath dinners with their downstairs neighbors, the Helfmans, on nights her mother is out at Communist Party meetings.

Davita is attracted to the Jewish community for several reasons. She sees families all around her in their Jewish neighborhood in Brooklyn singing songs and celebrating rituals that seem to have a happy meaning. The Jewish rituals have a place for all family members, unlike the endless political meetings held in Davita's apartment during which she is sent to her room and told to go to sleep, hearing angry words flying around the living room night after night, words that she cannot understand. The party is a community that has no place for children, or even much use for family units. Davita must conclude, however, that Orthodox Judaism is not a community she can embrace either, because she, as a woman, will be asked to sacrifice too much. She would need to jettison her intellectual capabilities, as women are valued in this community for their role as wives and mothers, as vessels for the next generation rather than models of wisdom and leadership.

The few individuals shown to be without a community around them in the novel are Davita's Aunt Sarah and her Uncle Jakob Daw. They are loners, both without family, who have devoted their lives to helping others in the best ways they know—Sarah through her nursing and work as a Christian missionary, and Jakob through his writing, both fictional and political. These two travel to the many war-torn places in the world, seemingly sustained by their causes themselves. They are both deeply sad and haunted people, but they both will serve as role models for Davita's own search for her identity, and they each have a powerful effect on her childhood. Writers, especially, are shown to be outsiders, and Daw's sense of humor and his tenderness toward Davita—the way he always treats the child as someone whose wisdom he values—make a lasting impression on her.

Davita will need to create a new community for herself, one built on a different model, not of subsuming personal achievement in deference to a larger community, but built around the identity of the individual. Whatever community Davita chooses to build for herself will have to fulfill certain requirements. It will have to be based on precepts that are not dependent on external events, she realizes, after seeing the disastrous dissolution of her parents' community. But neither can it be entirely insular, revolving around events that happened thousands of years ago, upon which the Jewish community of her new father is premised. Davita's world will have to be built on scholarship and deep understanding of the past, as is the Jewish world she inhabits, but will also need to have tangible effects on today's world, as did the community of her parents. Davita, in her role as a modern twentieth-century woman, wants to create the most fully realized version of herself.

The reader has every reason to believe she will succeed. As the book concludes, we learn Davita will enter a "very good public school" in New York, a secular school where, the reader assumes, she will be recognized as a brilliant and original thinker. Potok himself described Davita as "feminist writer," and planned a sequel that would describe her journey into adulthood. Unfortunately, a sequel to *Davita's Harp* did not appear before the author's death in 2003, so readers are left to imagine the brilliant future that Davita will build for herself as she strives to become the fullest person she can.

Source: Melanie Bush, Critical Essay on *Davita's Harp* in *Novels for Students,* Gale, Cengage Learning, 2010.

Elaine Kouvar

In this interview, Kouvar and Potok discuss the significance of both history and fine arts on Davita's Harp.

The interview took place over brunch at the St. Regis Hotel in Manhattan, which, as Chaim Potok remarked, was the "New York thing to do." That sense of the fashionable in contemporary urban life is characteristic of the complexity of Potok's personal stance. Philosopher, rabbi, historian, and novelist—Potok has chosen his imaginative materials from the generation immediately preceding our own, and his novels provide access to a past that enables us to deepen our understanding of the present. It was an especially propitious time to have this interview, for Potok's most recent novel, *Davita's Harp,* has established a new direction for the writer. The conflicts and rewards inherent in religious belief are central to all of his novels from *The Chosen* to *The Book of Lights,* yet none of those novels has a woman as its central character. In Davita, Potok has created a sensitive young girl who is drawn to Orthodox Judaism despite the fact that her mother has turned away from it. Through Davita's eyes, the reader witnesses the dilemmas now facing contemporary Judaism and indeed all religions within which women are struggling in their desires to play active and meaningful roles. Beginning in the thirties, *Davita's Harp* brings together the religious and artistic themes in Potok's earlier novels. The first of a planned trilogy, it examines issues at the core of American Jewish life, and through Potok's creation of a central female sensibility, his concerns are given wider significance and an entirely new dimension.

The moment in his career when an artist changes his direction is always exciting. As he moves toward the realization of his plans, the critical reader follows, questioning and discovering. Chaim Potok's discussion of these matters produces a literary as well as a philosophical event.

Q. Which modern novelists have been significant to your development as a writer?

A. Joyce was seminal because *A Portrait of the Artist as a Young Man* is a core encounter.

> *DAVITA'S HARP* IS ABOUT THE UTILIZATION OF THE HUMAN IMAGINATION AS A WAY OF COMING TO TERMS WITH UNBEARABLE REALITY. EVERY TIME DAVITA CONFRONTS SOMETHING UNBEARABLE, SHE RESTRUCTURES IT THROUGH THE POWER OF HER IMAGINATION."

When I read *Portrait,* I was about nineteen, and I would suspect that I absorbed whole components of that novel into the deepest recesses of my being; they simply remain there. Joyce has a storyteller's way of structuring a certain kind of confrontation that makes a lot of sense to me. In *Portrait* he deals with an individual at the heart of his Catholicism encountering elements from the very heart of Western civilization.

Q. And that encounter is the reason for your attraction to that book?

A. That's precisely my attraction to *Portrait.* Joyce was very close to what I'm trying to do. Interestingly enough, when I was young, the book that really started me writing was *Brideshead Revisited,* because Waugh utilizes this form also. He shows somebody at the heart of one culture encountering elements from the heart of another culture, and we find out what happens when parts of the cultures come into confrontation. When I read Mann's *The Magic Mountain,* it was a transforming experience because, for the first time, I realized that you could handle ideas inside the novelistic framework and not have the framework collapse.

Q. Have those novelists contributed in any way to your choice of historical time, the time in which you set your novels?

A. You mean the time in which we live. Well, I think that for the most part, serious novelists, and I can think of very few exceptions, really use their own lives and/or what they know best as raw material for their creativity. My work is set in the time that I experienced, the time I know best, the time that's problematic to me. I'm trying to record a certain aspect of what I experienced. First of all, I'm trying to record it because I want to straighten it out inside my own mind:

I'm trying to understand what it is that happened to me. Originally, I thought that just a few people might be interested in this setting. No one could have anticipated the reaction to the novels.

The central problem of our time, I think, is how people confront ideas different from their own. We tend to forget that two hundred and more years ago, most people grew up, lived, and died within a twenty-five-mile radius of where they were born. Most people never encountered a new idea or, indeed, never encountered a stranger in an entire lifetime. We encounter new ideas and strangers all the time today. We think it's a normal way to live, and we automatically set up a mechanism to deal with this encounter. We still don't like to meet a stranger: we're on our guard, but we anticipate that, sooner or later, there is going to be a stranger with whom we're going to have to cope. That's new in the history of the species. We meet new ideas and new people in a variety of ways, and what I'm trying to explore is one such way.

Q. I see. But none of your novels is set in the late twentieth century, and I'm curious about why you've made that choice.

A. What I'm doing is setting the groundwork, and I'm finished with that now. I have in my cast of characters a psychologist, Danny Saunders; a talmudist, Reuven Malter; I also have a Bible scholar, David Lurie; an artist, Asher Lev; a mystic, Gershon Loran. Now I have a feminist writer; that's what Davita's going to be.

Q. Oh, so there will be a sequel to Davita's Harp? *Does Reuven Malter's appearance at the end of* Davita's Harp *mean that he will play a part in the sequel?*

A. Absolutely! All of these people are going to be brought into the contemporary period, and the first one who will be brought into this part of the century will be Davita. As a matter of fact, she is going to be brought right into the eighties on a journey that she makes to the Soviet Union. That's the point to the whole Communist background in the first of the Davita novels.

Q. One structural similarity in your novels is the scenes with which you open your novels—the baseball game in The Chosen, *the birth of the pups on the roof in* The Book of Lights, *and the harp and the picture of the three stallions in* Davita's Harp, *for example. How are these seminal scenes related to the way you begin writing a novel?*

A. I use the openings to make the statement concerning the central metaphor of the novels. The central metaphor of *The Chosen* is combat of various kinds, combat on the baseball field, combat in Europe, and then what happens when the combat in Europe is actually brought home to Brooklyn because of the Holocaust and the subsequent hunger to create the State of Israel. The central metaphor in *The Promise* is people gambling and winning or losing. The central metaphor in *The Book of Lights* is the mystery and the awe that some of us sense in the grittiness of reality. Sooner or later, somewhere at the beginning of the novels, you're going to find the central metaphor treated in one way or another.

Q. Those central metaphors are visual. I understand that you paint; and I'm interested in whether you visualize these scenes, whether they appear in your mind like paintings.

A. Yes, and the imagery may very well come from the fact that I do see the world the way a painter does. I started painting when I was about nine years old, but it became a big problem in my family. I come from a very fundamentalist Jewish background, and my father would have nothing to do with painting. Painting to him was the preoccupation of the gentile world.

Q. He thought painting was idolatrous?

A. Absolutely. It was all right as long as I was a child, But once I became a *bar mitzvah*, my painting turned into a very difficult problem in the house. There were quarrels, and I think what happened was that sometime around the age of fifteen, I simply shifted the hunger to create from images on canvas to words on paper.

Q. Was writing acceptable to your family?

A. It was more acceptable than painting because you didn't smell up the house with turpentine and you weren't so visible. It was certainly more acceptable ideologically because the Jewish tradition has always been far more comfortable with words than with iconography. Words and texts, after all, are the stock-in-trade of the Jewish tradition. Images are, for the traditional Jew, the stock-in-trade of the gentile world. The Jewish tradition simply has not participated in Western art: there hasn't been a single instance in the history of Western art of a Jew participating in art in a seminal way. Not one instance! I'm talking about a religious Jew. Even in the modern period, no religious

Jews participated in Western art. Chagall was not a religious Jew.

Q. What does Picasso's work mean to you? And why is Guernica *so important?*

A. Well, Picasso's *Guernica* is a central element in my life. I don't remember the first time I saw it. All I know is that every time I came into New York, I used to go to see *Guernica* as one goes on a pilgrimage. I've read about *Guernica,* and I almost know its creation step by step as well as what came out of it, the work that Picasso did after he finished *Guernica. Guernica* is just one vast element in a whole series of things that Picasso did by way of reacting to that bombardment. I also have studied that event, and I've written about it in *Davita's Harp* exactly the way the event happened, so far as historians have been able to record it. It's inconceivable to me that anybody who's serious about art can ignore Picasso. That's like being serious about Renaissance art and ignoring Michelangelo. I think it'll take two or three hundred years before the Western world absorbs what Picasso did with art, but certainly he changed the way we look at the world.

Q. Did Picasso change the way you look at the world?

A. Oh, yes. The ability to restructure reality in terms of a single individual's vision of it and have that change people's eyes is what the artist's power is all about.

Q. And that power is what makes art such a problem for Jews?

A. Exactly. That's why people are afraid of artists, because artists possess the power to create metaphoric visions of reality. Reality is, for our species, the sum total of all the ways that we see reality, and even that doesn't begin to tap into what reality is. But for an artist like Asher Lev, Picasso is the beginning and the end because Picasso is the possibility of creating truth.

Q. Why is Picasso important for Davita Chandal, the writer?

A. Davita's Harp is about the human imagination. The aboutness of the novels is one of the things that I always think of as I structure a novel in terms of its central metaphor. I would say that *The Chosen* is about two components in the core of Judaism or the core of any tradition, one component looking inward and one component looking outward to solve its problems. Both of those elements are in confrontation with an

element from the core of Western civilization. *The Promise* is about the confrontation with text criticism. *My Name Is Asher Lev* is about a confrontation with Western art. *Davita's Harp* is about the utilization of the human imagination as a way of coming to terms with unbearable reality. Every time Davita confronts something unbearable, she restructures it through the power of her imagination. Finally at the end of the novel when she suffers this terrible indignity, she restructures the graduation ceremony by having her uncle, her father, and her aunt there along with everything that she has imagined. All the metaphors of her imagination are present in that last scene—the birds, the horses, the sea, the cabin. So you have this seesawing back-and-forth between reality that's unbearable and the imagination that tries to rethink reality. One of the people who has powerfully restructured reality in our time is Picasso, and the metaphor par excellence for that restructuring is *Guernica.* Guernica is the prime example, the first example in modern Western civilization of the destruction of an entire civilian area solely for psychological purposes. It's a horror, isn't it? Would you visit a Guernica during its bombardment?

Q. No.

A. Would you go and see Picasso's *Guernica*?

Q. Yes, of course, I would.

A. Why?

Q. There is truth in it even if it's about a horror.

A. That's the point. That's the redemptive power of art. The artist, in strange fashion, redeems the horror of reality through the power of his or her art. For me, Picasso's *Guernica* has become the most significant achievement in this century of the redemptive power of the artist.

Source: Elaine Kouvar, "An Interview with Chaim Potok," in *Contemporary Literature*, Vol. 27, No. 3, Fall 1986.

Paul Cowan

Reviewer Cowan argues here that, despite some flaws, Davita's Harp *is a success because of the strength of its title character.*

Chaim Potok is a writer who defies easy categorization. Though he does not have the instinct for the fast-paced plots and sleek characters that usually make novels popular and though he has not attracted the intellectual following of a Saul Bellow, still, four of his five novels and his one nonfiction book have been best sellers. By exploring the themes that fascinate him, Mr. Potok has opened a new clearing in the forest of American literature.

Davita's Harp is Mr. Potok's bravest book, though it is not his best. It will almost certainly be one of his most popular. Set in New York during the 1930's, it portrays the lives of Communist Party members and religious Jews. Until Mr. Potok's novel *The Chosen*, almost all popular American Jewish fiction—like most ethnic American fiction—focused on protagonists intent on escaping their childhood environments. The characters who were born in Saul Bellow's Chicago and Philip Roth's Newark may remember the neighborhoods they grew up in with affection or rage; their adult speech may retain traces of immigrant English; they may feel tangled emotions toward a parent they have left behind. But they set out to create themselves anew.

Most of Mr. Potok's characters leave their childhood environments too, at considerable pain to the people who love them. In *The Chosen*, Danny Saunders, who was expected to inherit his father's role as a Hasidic rabbi in Brooklyn, decided to study psychiatry. Conversely, in *The Book of Lights*, Arthur Leiden, primed to follow in his father's footsteps and become one of the great physicists of his age, left the genteel scientific community his parents inhabited—pardoxically, the community that created the atomic bomb—to become a rabbi. But the worlds in which Mr. Potok's characters grew up retain a tight hold on their loyalties. Danny Saunders, Arthur Leiden and now Davita Chandal in *Davita's Harp* are all haunted by memories of the past that echo in their present.

Davita is the daughter of Michael Chandal, a gentile from Maine, a left-wing journalist whose father, a lumber magnate, has disinherited him, and Channah Chandal, a Jewish woman from Poland, a Marxist intellectual whose dreadful memories of her stern Hasidic father have left her disillusioned with religion. For the first quarter of the novel, the Chandals' political work sustains them emotionally as they live like urban gypsies, evicted by one landlord after another. They are protected materially by Ezra Dinn, an Orthodox Jew and Channah's friend since childhood.

These are some of Mr. Potok's most disappointing pages. Though Michael is a robust, loving father, Channah—like so many mothers in Mr. Potok's novels—is a somewhat sickly, withdrawn woman. The Chandals talk about the political horrors of the 30's—the Spanish Civil War, Italy's invasion of Ethiopia, lynchings in the South—without ever explaining them to their baffled, terrified daughter. Since Davita, a child when the novel begins, is the novel's sole voice—and since she is so often bewildered—she (and Mr. Potok) fails to furnish much insight into her troubled parents. But Mr. Potok's prose style is so rich that even these pages have an enchanting quality. Soon Channah Chandal's Orthodox landsmen find the family an apartment in the Crown Heights section of Brooklyn. That is the urban soil Mr. Potok always describes with a master's certainty. While living in Crown Heights and in the summertime community of Sea Gate, Davita meets a young girl who is a refugee from the Spanish Civil War. She also comes to love a surrogate uncle, a left-wing writer her mother knew as a young woman. Presently the United States Government sends her uncle back to Hitler's Europe. History begins to shape the child's consciousness.

At the same time, Davita ricochets between the religions her parents have rejected. Michael's sister Sarah, a Christian missionary, often stays with the family. One summer she invites Davita to spend time with her in Maine. She teaches the child to pray on her knees and encourages her to believe in Jesus. Davita loves Aunt Sarah but not her creed. Though Davita's parents don't observe any religious ceremonies, the girl is delighted by the way her Orthodox neighbors greet the Sabbath. Their Judaism appeals to her more than Aunt Sarah's Christianity.

As Davita comes to life, so does the book. She can't bear her beloved father's compulsive need to cover the civil war in Spain. He seems to be choosing politics over her. The Sabbaths she experiences intrigue her so much she begins to attend the neighborhood synagogue despite the fact that her mother rejects religion, despite the fact that almost all the yeshiva boys make derisive remarks to the ignorant girl whose father is a gentile. When her father is killed in Spain, Davita insists on saying the mourner's kaddish in the woman's section of the synagogue. In the 1930's this was so rare as to seem almost heretical. But as Davita becomes an increasingly observant

Jew—and soon a brilliant student in a Brooklyn yeshiva—she continues to insist on her rights as a woman within the limits of Orthodox law.

At the very end of the novel, after Davita, now in her early teens, has been denied a prize in the study of the Talmud because she is a girl, she imagines the speech she would have delivered if she had won the award. It reflects the faiths of her childhood—Judaism and radicalism:

> I wanted to say that my mother was once badly hurt in Poland because she was a Jewish woman, and my father was killed while trying to save a nun in Guernica, and my uncle died in part because of his politics and in part because he wrote strange stories. I wanted to say that I'm very frightened to be living in this world and I don't understand most of the things I see and hear and I don't know what will happen to me and to the family I love. I wanted to say that I would try to find and join with the side of America that wouldn't hurt people who (fight for justice), and that I would also try not to let this century defeat me.

As the imagined speech suggests, *Davita's Harp* is full of the horrors of the 20th century. As in all of Chaim Potok's novels, those horrors don't simply exist in the minds of intellectuals. They are not symbols. Hitler's death camps, Franco's troops, the atomic bomb kill people the reader has come to love and alter the survivors' lives completely.

Yet they don't defeat Mr. Potok's characters. For there is a sweet, loving bond that links their lives, a bond symbolized by the gentle tones of the small harp that has been fixed to a door wherever Davita has lived. A frail glory infuses the world these people see when they open their doors and windows each morning. Those qualities are unusual in modern fiction. They draw the reader into Chaim Potok's world. The people he depicts live in a community held together by ancient laws. Those people nourish each other in the worst of times. In doing so, they nourish Mr. Potok's readers too.

Source: Paul Cowan, "The Faiths of Her Childhood," in *New York Times Book Review*, March 31, 1985.

SOURCES

Abramson, Edward, *Chaim Potok,* Twayne Publishers, 1986.

Cowan, Paul, "The Faiths of Her Childhood," in *New York Times Book Review,* March 31, 1985.

Greiner, Cynthia, "In Search of a Spiritual Pacifier," in *Wall Street Journal,* April 29, 1985.

Kauvar, Elaine M., "An Interview with Chaim Potok," in *Contemporary Literature,* Vol. 27, No. 3, Fall 1986, pp. 291–317.

Kirkus Reviews, Vol. 53, January 1, 1985.

Potok, Chaim, *Davita's Harp,* Ballantine, 1985.

Sternlicht, Sanford, *Chaim Potok: A Critical Companion.* Greenwood Press, 2000.

Walden, Daniel, ed., *Studies in American Jewish Literature,* No. 4: *The World of Chaim Potok,* State University of New York Press, 1985.

FURTHER READING

Marx, Karl, *The Communist Manifesto,* Broadview Press, 2004.

> This is the classic work of theory by communist forefathers Karl Marx and Friedrich Engels. The book analyzes class-based societies and the problems of capitalism.

Potok, Chaim, *Wanderings: Chaim Potok's History of the Jews,* Fawcett, 1978.

> In this epic nonfiction work, Potok, a scholar and rabbi, details the 4,000-year history of the Jewish people.

Preston, Paul, *A Concise History of the Spanish Civil War,* Fontana, 1996.

> This is an introduction to the events and conflicts leading up to one of the bloodiest civil wars in history, a major milestone in the spread of fascism across Europe.

Walden, Daniel, ed., *Conversations with Chaim Potok,* University Press of Mississippi, 2001.

> A collection of interviews spanning nearly a quarter of a century that discuss the literary and religious roots of Potok's work.

East of Eden

1955

Based on John Steinbeck's 1952 novel of the same title, *East of Eden* was released on April 10, 1955. The film achieved immense commercial success and critical acclaim, including the nod of approval from Steinbeck himself, who declared it was the best film he had seen. Directed by Elia Kazan, *East of Eden* is a modern retelling of the biblical story of Cain and Abel set in the Salinas Valley of California during the early twentieth century, just as the United States enters World War I. Taken from the final section of Steinbeck's original work, the film adaptation, written by playwright Paul Osborn, begins in Part Four of the novel. It focuses almost exclusively on the conflict between two teenage brothers, Aron and Cal Trask, over the love of their father Adam and a girl, Abra. *East of Eden* won the award for Best Dramatic Film at the Cannes Film Festival in 1955. The following year, the film received four Academy Award nominations with Jo Van Fleet winning the Academy Award for Best Actress in a Supporting Role. *East of Eden* was awarded the Golden Globe award for Best Motion Picture Drama and received three nominations at the BAFTA (British Academy of Film and Television Arts) awards that same year.

Although it is not as popular as his most famous novel, *Grapes of Wrath* (1939), many critics consider *East of Eden* to be Steinbeck's most ambitious novel. In contrast to Kazan's film, the novel spans several generations—playing out the biblical story of Cain and Abel not once but

twice. According to Steinbeck, the epic contained all of his knowledge about the human struggle between good and evil. Set in the Salinas Valley of California where Steinbeck grew up, the book contains many people and events based on Steinbeck's experiences during his childhood, although the main conflicts in the story are somewhat removed from the author's history. Despite its ambition and best-selling commercial success, *East of Eden* received mixed critical reviews due to what some perceived to be a diffuse treatment of the novel's key themes and inadequate character development. After Oprah Winfrey, an American celebrity and television icon, selected *East of Eden* for her book club in 2002, the novel experienced a resurgence in popularity, which peaked in the summer of 2003. A new film adaptation of the work is scheduled for release by Universal Pictures in 2010.

PLOT SUMMARY

Due to the length and complexity of Steinbeck's novel, director Elia Kazan and playwright Paul Osborn chose to begin the film at approximately Chapter 37, in Part Four of the book. The film opens in 1917 in northern California, just before the United States enters World War I. As the opening credits roll, the setting of the picturesque Salinas Valley is established with a long panning shot of Monterey, a city on the Pacific coast. The Trask family lives in a small agricultural town named Salinas, roughly fifteen miles from Monterey. The two cities are separated by the "dark and brooding" Santa Lucia Mountains.

James Dean Makes His Debut as A Troubled Boy in Search of His Mother

The action begins as Cal Trask (played by the soon-to-be-famous James Dean) a teenage boy, quietly follows an older woman through the streets of Monterey as she runs errands. While she is dressed like an upstanding lady, the reactions of the townspeople indicate that she is not very respected by the community: the bank teller giggles as she makes a large deposit, indicating to viewers that the source of her income is questionable. Cal suspects that this woman is his mother and he is correct. He has never met her because when he was young, she left the family and moved to a brothel in Salinas, although this only becomes clear to Cal much later in the film.

In Steinbeck's novel, Cal is led to the brothel by a local rancher who he meets one night at a bar. Kate's character is complex and her disturbing history (including murdering her parents and later shooting Adam Trask in the shoulder as she leaves the family) comprise a substantial portion of the story, whereas in the film she appears only in her interactions with the two Trask boys. Despite the considerable focus on Kate in Steinbeck's novel, her characterization is often criticized for being unrealistic and disruptive of the plot's narrative coherence. By contrast, Kate in the film is generally regarded as a believable character, so much so that Jo Van Fleet won the Academy Award for Best Actress in a Supporting Role for her performance as Kate. While the novel candidly discusses the nature of Kate's involvement with prostitution, the film treats the matter with discretion, as would be expected for films released by Hollywood in the 1950s, implying but not explicitly stating that it is a brothel Kate runs.

Kate observes Cal following her and asks Anne, a girl working at Kate's brothel, if she has seen him before. After Kate disappears into the house, Cal throws a stone at one of the house's windows. He is then questioned by Joe, Kate's assistant. Cal expresses a desire to speak to Kate but then tells Joe to tell her that he hates her. Joe's full story is not portrayed in the film; in the novel he is an escaped convict who tries to gain access to the power and money Kate has acquired during years of running the brothel. Late in the novel Kate again demonstrates her keen intellect and unparalleled ability to use people while protecting herself when she anticipates Joe's actions and informs the police of his previous jailbreak, prompting them to gun him down as he tries to leave town.

Due to the length and multigenerational nature of Steinbeck's novel, many characters are omitted in the film adaptation. Of these, perhaps the most significant is the character Lee. In Steinbeck's novel Lee is a Chinese immigrant who lives with the Trasks and raises Aron and Cal after they are abandoned by their mother, while Adam mopes about and wants nothing to do with the children. A philosophical man, Lee is mostly content with his role as a housekeeper and caters to the expectations of the people around him by faking a Pidgin accent and speaking in broken English, despite his ability to speak fluently.

FILM TECHNIQUE

Kazan was one of the first film directors to successfully experiment with CinemaScope, lens series used to shoot widescreen movies; this technique almost doubled the aspect ratio (the width of an image divided by its height) of the previous formats used by the Academy of Motion Picture Arts and Sciences and was perfectly suited for the panoramic views of the Salinas Valley, which establish the film's setting. Kazan took full advantage of this new technique, adding to his already growing reputation as one of the most innovative and adventurous directors of his time.

In adapting Steinbeck's novel for film, Kazan faced the challenge of depicting the inner lives of the characters, as much of the story' action centers around their emotional experience. In order to convey the emotional vibrancy of his characters and their relationship to one another, Kazan combined the use of WarnerColor and unusual lighting with showy camera work, much of which might seem obvious and forced to the modern viewer. The innovative use of camera angles also conveys the destabilization of the Trask family due to the emotional distance between father and sons. The director uses physical distance, for example, when Cal approaches one of his parents from a physical distance, such as a hallway, to symbolize this emotional disconnection within the family. In one of the film's most famous scenes, Cal tries desperately to win his father's love by presenting him with a hard-earned birthday gift of money to replace what Adam lost with the spoiled lettuce shipment. To depict the emotional distance that exists between the father-son pair, Kazan physically separates them after Aron announces his engagement to Abra, placing Cal at one side of the dining room and Adam with Aron and Abra at the other. When Adam finally returns to open Cal's gift, instead of seeing him for who he

is, Adam harshly rejects Cal's hard-earned money because he wrongly assumes Cal must have stolen it. Here, Kazan depicts Adam's painfully skewed view of Cal as the bad son by distorting the camera angle, as he does in many instances where the characters misunderstand one another.

Similarly, to convey a sense of the power gradients that exist between characters, particularly between the adults and children in the film, Kazan uses canting (tilting) to produce extreme camera angles, thereby depicting one character as literally above the other. By contrast, in scenes where Cal is in conversation with his brother Aron or Aron's fiancé Abra, the camera remains at eye-level, conveying a sense of neutrality or non-judgment between these characters.

Kazan maintains a sense of the story's momentum and epic scope with swinging pans and unusual settings. As Cal travels back and forth on the rooftop of the train, sitting curled up in a ball looking deeply unhappy, viewers are given a sense of his racing thoughts and brooding emotions. Similarly, the internal motion and emotional ambivalence of the characters is conveyed using similar techniques in the Ferris wheel and swing scenes, which are two of the film's most famous. Complementing this camera work, Kazan adjusts the lighting in many scenes to reflect the mood of the characters; in scenes where the characters are brooding or psychologically confined, the lighting is unusually dark (such as when Abra tries to comfort the rejected Cal who hangs from the willow tree, brooding in the dark), whereas in scenes where the characters are feeling a sense of openness and possibility (the scene with Abra and Cal in the field of flowers, for example), the lighting is enhanced accordingly.

A Brooding, Violent but Tragically Misunderstood Loner

After hitching a ride on the top of a train back to Salinas, Cal follows his brother Aron and his brother's girlfriend, Abra, as they walk, eavesdropping on their conversation. The boys' father, Adam Trask, has just purchased an ice factory because he is in the process of inventing a novel system for shipping lettuce by train to cities on the East coast. In Steinbeck's novel, the father of the boys is known by Cathy (who changed her name after moving to Salinas, in part to hide her dark past) to be Adam's brother, Charles, reflecting the first instantiation of the Cain and Abel story. They were conceived after Cathy drugged Adam on their wedding night and slept with Charles. Adam moved out to California with Cathy, in part to get away from his brother who nearly beat him to death when they were children after being rejected by their father, Cyrus Trask. Cathy did not want to go, a fact that is alluded to at various points in the film, and eventually left Adam and her children to live a life of financial independence. In the film, Cal, who has been out wandering the streets all night, arrives at the ice factory but offers no explanation or apology to his father. Adam is angry and confused by Cal's behavior. In contrast to his cold interaction with Cal, Adam is warm toward Aron who supports his purchase of the ice factory. While spying on Abra and Aron in the factory, Cal overhears Abra saying that she is afraid of him because he reminds her of an animal. Aron, by contrast, sees Cal as harmless and laughs at Abra's concern. Cal becomes violently angry and sends huge blocks of ice down the ice shoot, again displeasing his father.

The Truth about Kate: A Confrontation

Later, after Cal is made to atone for his sin by reading from the Bible, he confronts Adam about the lie he and Aron were told as children about their mother. Not wanting them to know the truth, Adam told the boys that Kate was dead and in heaven. Cal reveals to Adam that he knows the truth, that she is alive. Adam and Cal talk briefly before Cal leaves abruptly to wander the streets of Monterey, as he does frequently.

Cal learns from Anne the whereabouts of his mother, Kate, and begs her to talk to him as he is being thrown out by Joe. Cal wants to know if there is anything good in his mother because he wants to understand why he is all bad. At the Monterey jail, Sam, the sheriff, shows Cal a photo of Kate and Adam on their wedding day. Cal cannot understand why Kate would hurt Adam and abandon the family.

The Lettuce Disaster

The entire town of Salinas helps prepare lettuce to be shipped on the train in ice-cooled cars. Cal designs a method to prepare the lettuce more efficiently and oversees the operation, earning his father's praise. When Aron is nowhere to be found, Abra and Cal have an intimate conversation about Abra's family life, in which she forgave her father for not understanding her. During their interaction, Abra flirts with Cal and teases him about a girl who has been following him, and it becomes increasingly clear that Abra is romantically interested in the older of the two brothers. Finally, Aron arrives. Adam becomes unhappy with Cal when he finds out that, in an effort to carry out the lettuce operation, Cal has taken equipment from some coal miners without asking. The whole town celebrates as the train, full of lettuce as well as Cal's hopes to earn his father's love, pulls away headed east. Unfortunately, the train gets stuck, the ice melts, and the lettuce rots before it arrives at its destination. In the novel, both Cal and Aron are made fun of by their peers for their father's foolishness, an incident which is omitted in the film.

Cal decides that he wants to recoup for his father the money that was lost with the lettuce. He knows that the price of beans will increase as World War I progresses and the United States becomes involved, and he decides to invest in beans. He consults with Will Hamilton who is excited by the idea and tells Cal he will need to borrow five thousand dollars. In the film, Cal borrows this money from his mother, whereas in the novel, it is Lee who offers to lend him the money. Will Hamilton is the son of Sam Hamilton, a family friend of Adam Trask who figures quite prominently in the novel but not in the film. In the novel, Will mentors Cal after seeing in him a keen intuition for business. He feels like Cal is in some ways like a son to him. Will and Cal profit from the scarcity of food and their foresight.

Kate and Cal Connect

Cal approaches Kate as she is walking on a dirt road and Kate asks him questions about himself and Aron. When she asks about Adam, Cal responds that he does not want to talk about him. Cal asks to borrow the money for the beans. Kate takes Cal back to her place, where they talk about the business venture and why Kate left the family, explaining many of the details that Lee explains to Cal in the novel. Kate explains that she shot Adam because he wanted to keep her on the ranch where she was not happy. He was too consumed with the Bible and his purity to really understand or appreciate what Kate wanted. Cal identifies with much of what Kate describes. Kate lends Cal the money and Kate tells him he is "a likable kid." In the novel, Kate's preference for Cal over his brother is made explicit when she leaves her entire fortune to Cal before committing suicide, an event that does not take place in the film.

The United States Enters World War I
Monterey comes alive with patriotic celebration as the United States enters World War I against Germany. During a parade (an event that does not take place in the novel), the town officials speculate that the war will be over in a couple weeks. Aron hangs back behind a tree and tells Abra that he thinks the war is not right and that nothing will ever make him go. The town officials turn out to be wrong, and word trickles in that soldiers from the area are being killed in battle. Some townsfolk lash out in anger by throwing a rock through the window of Gustav Albrecht's business because he has a foreign accent. Adam grows tired from working at the draft board office and Aron becomes depressed by the war.

Abra and Cal enjoy each other's company at a carnival, exchanging flirtatious glances, while Abra simultaneously worries about Aron's absence. On the Ferris wheel, Abra wonders if Aron really loves her. She feels like she lost him because she cannot tell if he loves her. Abra and Cal kiss and Abra pulls away crying, saying, "I love Aron, I do, I do!" An altercation arises below the Ferris wheel between Gustav Albrecht and the townspeople who are angry that their sons are being killed in the war. Cal sees his brother among the people defending Albrecht and runs to help. A fistfight breaks out in front of Albrecht's house and is broken up by Sam, the sheriff. Aron sees that Abra is carrying Cal's coat and becomes angry and jealous. He yells at Cal for throwing the first punch in the fight. Cal and Aron exchange blows. Afterward, Abra begs Cal to admit that the kiss on the Ferris wheel meant nothing.

Cal Tries to Win His Father's Love
Cal sneaks out in the middle of the night to visit Abra. He tells her his secret about making money with beans. He has made a profit and plans to give the money to his father the next day at a birthday party he is planning. He invites Abra to come over for the party. Cal is drunk

and feels remorse for hitting Aron. The next day, Abra helps Cal decorate the Trask's home and Cal is both nervous and excited about giving his father the money. Adam comes home tired from his job at the draft board.

Just as Adam is about to open Cal's gift, Aron announces that he and Abra are engaged. Adam says that no gift could be better. Abra, feeling Cal's pain, looks distressed and reminds Adam about Cal's gift. When Adam opens the gift containing Cal's money, Adam is unhappy, explaining that the money was made from the suffering of others. Crushed, Cal leaves the dining room wailing. Abra follows to comfort him, while Aron watches. Dean's extremely emotional portrayal of Cal won him critical praise at the time, but many viewers today find it melodramatic.

The Truth Is Revealed with Devastating Consequences
Aron tells Cal never to touch Abra again and speaks cruel words to him about his badness. Cal invites Aron to look at the truth just once and takes him to see their mother at her brothel. Cal introduces Aron to Kate as "everything that is good." Aron tries to leave but Cal forces him to stay in the room, slamming the door behind them. Back at home, Cal tells Adam what he knows and what he has done. He admits to trying to buy Adam's love and declares that he no longer wants it. Sam the sheriff comes to the house and informs the family that Aron has gone crazy and plans to leave town and enlist in the morning. The sight of Aron crying on the train overwhelms Adam and causes him to suffer a stroke. In the novel, Adam suffers a stroke after learning from Lee that Aron has been killed in battle. It is left unclear in the film what will become of Aron, although many of the young men who enlisted were killed in World War I. The doctor informs Cal and Abra that Adam might only live a week and may not recognize Cal anymore. Sam suggests that Cal go away someplace like Cain did in the Bible story. Cal visits his father's bedside where Adam is attended to by an obnoxious nurse. Cal apologizes for his actions and, feeling guilty, leaves the bedroom. Abra explains to Adam how Cal has felt unloved his whole life. She begs him to release Cal from his suffering by giving him some sign that he loves him, like asking Cal to help him in some way. Abra begs Cal to talk to his father before it is too late and ushers him into the bedroom. Cal goes to talk with his father and Adam does as Abra has

asked by requesting that Cal get him a new nurse. He also asks Cal to take care of him. Cal gets up to kiss Abra and then returns to his father's bedside where the movie ends.

CHARACTERS

Gustav Albrecht
Played by Harold Gordon, Gustav Albrecht is a man of German descent who is harassed by the townspeople after the United States enters World War I. He is a friend of the Trask boys who defend him when he is attacked.

Cathy "Kate" Ames
Played by Jo Van Fleet, Kate is the estranged mother of Aron and Cal Trask. While the boys were told that Kate had died, Cal discovers that Kate actually runs a brothel in Salinas. While Adam believes that she lacks kindness and is inherently bad in some way, Cal understands that Adam never loved her because he was blinded by his need to see her as completely pure, a mistake that also blinds him to seeing and understanding Cal. In Steinbeck's novel, readers are given access to Kate's perspective as she grows up feeling unloved by her parents. While the narrator initially describes her as a monster (and, indeed she commits many heinous crimes worthy of the description) he also hints that her actions stem from a life of pain and fear. Compared to the novel, Kate's character in the film lacks a complex past but makes up for it with added warmth toward Cal. In the novel, Kate commits suicide and leaves all the money she made from prostitution to Cal.

Anne
Played by Lois Smith, Anne works in the whorehouse run by Kate Ames. A nervous girl, Anne is afraid of angering Kate who has the power to throw her out. Anne shows Cal the door to Kate's room at his request.

Abra Bacon
Played by Julie Harris, Abra Bacon is the daughter of the county supervisor in Salinas and the love interest of both Aron and Cal Trask. Abra's mother died when she was thirteen and her father remarried shortly afterward. Abra became enraged, prompting her to throw a three-thousand-dollar ring in the river. Early in the film, Abra is in love with Aron;

however, she turns away from Aron after she feels he does not love her for herself but rather has an idealized, pure image of her. In contrast to the character in Steinbeck's novel, who is noble and serious, Abra in the film is flirtatious and passionate. She loves Adam Trask as though he were her own father and shows affection to him and both his sons. She is compassionate and understanding, often empathizing with Cal's feelings of rejection. After it becomes clear that Cal's capacity for loving her is greater than that of Aron's, Abra turns her ardor toward Cal. After Adam suffers a stroke, Abra pleads with him to show love toward Cal, knowing that he needs to feel loved by his father in order to become a man.

Will Hamilton
Played by Albert Dekker, Will Hamilton is a friend of the Trask family who goes into the bean business with Cal. Steinbeck's novel explores the history of the Hamilton family. Samuel Hamilton, the family patriarch, shares a long-standing friendship with Adam Trask and helps pull Adam out of the foggy depression he suffers after his wife shoots him in the shoulder and then abandons him and his sons. Samuel is an Irish immigrant who shares a connection with Lee, a Chinese character completely omitted from the film.

Rantani
Played by Nick Dennis, Rantani is a Swiss-Italian man renting the Trasks' place.

Sam the Sheriff
Played by Burl Ives, Sam the Sheriff is a stout man who keeps tabs on Cal as he discovers the truth about Kate. He is an old friend of Adam. He knows all the town secrets and maintains order when an angry crowd follows Gustav Albrecht home, harassing him about being sympathetic to the Germans. After Sam learns that Cal is responsible for informing his father and Aron of the truth about Kate, he tells Cal that he should go away just like Cain did in the Bible.

Adam Trask
Played by Raymond Massey, Adam Trask is the deeply religious father of Aron and Cal Trask. In contrast to Steinbeck's novel, where Adam appears as the protagonist for the first half of the story, he is a secondary character in the film. Adam favors Aron over Cal, seeing Aron's actions as good and Cal's as bad. Adam is cold

toward Cal, saying that he has never understood him, just as he never understood his wife, Kate. Adam has a scar on his shoulder from the bullet wound inflicted when Kate shot him before leaving the family. Early in the film, Adam buys an ice factory so that he can ship lettuce to cities on the East coast. Cal tells Adam that if he wants to make money, he should invest in beans that will increase in price as World War I progresses, but Adam dismisses his idea, saying he is not interested in making money. According to Kate, Adam is "living in the Bible," the implication being that he is not grounded in the reality of everyday life. Indeed, he is unable to bear the truth about Cal's actions toward his brother and suffers a stroke when he learns that Aron plans to enlist in the army. Omitted from the film is the complex relationship Adam shares with his own unloved brother, Charles, who lives on a ranch they inherited from their father. Like Aron, Adam was his father's favorite—causing Charles much pain and suffering.

Aron Trask

Played by Richard Davalos, Aron is the favored son of Adam Trask. He is romantically involved with Abra and loves his brother, in spite of Cal's brooding nature. He is in love with Abra but his disposition changes when the United States enters World War I. He becomes depressed by the news of what the Germans are doing and of the casualties from the fighting. He withdraws increasingly from Abra, becoming more and more religious like his father. Abra believes that he no longer loves her, preferring instead an idea of her that is his vision of purity. In the end, Aron's worldview is shattered when Cal takes him to visit Kate at the brothel and he learns the truth. Aron gets drunk and leaves on a train to enlist in the army, causing his father to suffer a stroke at the train station.

Caleb "Cal" Trask

Played by James Dean, Cal Trask is the son of Kate Ames and Adam Trask. He resents his brother Aron because his father, Adam, favors him. After his brother withdraws into a puritanical commitment to religion, Cal becomes romantically involved with Aron's girlfriend, Abra Bacon. In contrast to Cal in Steinbeck's novel, Cal in the film is more intensely violent and brooding but also more likeable with increased vulnerability. He believes that he is

"bad," an idea supported by his father who calls him that in anger. After Cal learns that his mother runs a brothel, he thinks that he is all bad because Kate is all bad—and that his brother, Aron, is all good because he inherited all of Adam's goodness.

THEMES

The Struggle between Good and Evil

For his novel, Steinbeck drew heavily from the stories contained in the book of Genesis in the Bible, particularly the tale of Cain and Abel. These stories would have been familiar to both Steinbeck and Kazan's audiences and resonated deeply with their struggle to understand how the horrors of the Great Depression and World War II were possible. In most Jewish and Christian religious traditions, Cain and Abel are the sons of Adam and Eve. The story is also present in the Qur'an, although the two accounts differ slightly. In the Jewish and Christian versions, Cain, the older of the two brothers, was a farmer, and Abel, the younger brother, a shepherd. The tension in the story begins when God rejects an offering of produce made by Cain but accepts an animal sacrifice made by Abel. Unable to bear the rejection, Cain sinfully murders his brother, an event that is sometimes interpreted as the first instance of evil in the world. Why God rejected Cain's offering remains open to interpretation and is explored in both Steinbeck's novel and Kazan's film. Emphasizing the importance of this story for both the novel and film, both versions of *East of Eden* begin with powerful portrayals of the Salinas Valley—an area enclosed between the sunshine of the east and the dark mountains of the west. In the film, this description takes the form of sweeping views of the California coastline and picturesque Monterey. Everything looks Eden-like and it is hard to imagine the presence of evil in this idyllic setting. However, the Salinas Valley serves as a symbol of the place Adam and Eve lived after they were exiled from the Garden of Eden. It is here that the characters of the story struggle to be good in the face of human drama and their own imperfections.

In contrast to Steinbeck's novel, which retells the biblical story of Cain and Abel twice—first with Adam and his brother Charles and then with Adam's sons Cal and Aron—the

READ. WATCH. WRITE.

- Some critics of Steinbeck's novel have argued that Cathy "Kate" Ames is a weak and two-dimensional character, with whom readers cannot sympathize. By contrast, Kate in Kazan's film adaptation is very human and realistic. Using examples from both the novel and film, write an essay in which you explain to what extent you agree with this assessment of Kate's character. If you were to remake Kazan's film, is there anything that you would change about her character? What, and why?

- In small groups, discuss the major problem each brother faces in *East of Eden*. How are their problems similar? How are they different? Do teenagers today face similar problems? Make a list of problems faced by teens today, and compare them to the problems faced by Aron and Cal.

- Watch one or two more films by director Elia Kazan. Examples are: *A Streetcar Named Desire* (1951), *On the Waterfront* (1954), and *Splendor in the Grass* (1961). As you are watching, make note of any stylistic choices that remind you of *East of Eden*. Does Kazan have a consistent, recognizable style as a director? Write a paper in which you identify Kazan's cinematic style, giving examples from the films you watch to support your argument.

- Using your library and Internet, research the geography, culture, economy, and history of the Salinas Valley in California. Write a travel brochure in which you describe the region's history, major industries, and most significant or interesting features. Make your brochure colorful, creative, and detailed.

film explores this theme through the latter pair of brothers only. In the film, when Cal acts out in anger as a teenager, Adam explains to him that what separates man from the animals is his freedom to choose to be good. In the novel, this concept is introduced first by the narrator and then later as *timshel* by the character Lee, who is notably omitted in the film. In both versions, Cal struggles with his feelings that he is inherently bad, presumably because he inherited all of his mother's badness whereas his brother inherited all of their father's goodness.

In addition to the central conflict of the film, the struggle between good and evil in humanity also plays out in the backdrop of the story, in the plight of immigrants trying to make a living in California, and in World War I.

Rejection, Sin, and Redemption

Adam Trask shows only one of his sons, Aron, understanding and love. Deprived of paternal understanding and connection, Cal grows up feeling unloved and comes to believe that unlike his brother who is all good, he is all bad. When he learns that his mother is alive and running a brothel in Monterey, Cal begins to think that he inherited his badness from his mother. Cal tries throughout the film to earn his father's love, only to be misunderstood and rejected. However, after Kate explains to Cal why she left Adam, Cal questions his assumptions about himself and realizes that things are not so black and white. Cal's struggle about his relative goodness and badness composes the key conflict in the film.

Like Cal, Abra grew up feeling the pain of her father's rejection, and she plays a key role in facilitating a healing moment between father and son. Abra loves Cal but believes that he will never be a man unless he feels loved by his father. After Adam suffers a stroke and lies dying in bed, Abra begs him to give Cal a sign that he loves him. Clearly moved by her request, Adam complies, thereby relieving Cal of his suffering.

STYLE

A Realist Drama of Epic Proportions

Kazan's effective use of CinemaScope and WarnerColor combine with the work of cinematographer Ted D. McCord to convey the epic scope of *East of Eden*. In film, the term epic is reserved for works that depict human dramas that are played out on a large scale. Often, these are among the most popular and highest-grossing productions. Kazan's realist drama may not seem like an epic when compared to the high-budget films that are

(© *Pictorial Press Ltd | Alamy*)

produced now; however, in its day *East of Eden* was regarded by many as belonging to this genre. Even today, scholars discuss the epic nature of its style and content.

Steinbeck's home in the Salinas Valley is beautifully shot, particularly in scenes that depict the vast California landscape, much of which was shot on location in Mendocino, California. From the beginning, viewers are given a sense that what is at stake in the story that is about to be told extends far beyond the fields of California and deep into the human experience. During the opening credits, downtown Monterey, the mountains in the distance, and the rocky shores of California are presented with slow panning shots set to music, which plays an equally important role in establishing the film's mood. Kazan's techniques and McCord's cinematography are enhanced by the film's score, which was written by Leonard Rosenman, an artist who had once taught James Dean to play the piano. This was Rosenman's first movie score, and he received abundant praise for his role in establishing the mood of the film.

1950s Melodrama and Method Acting

In the 1950s, directors such as Nicholas Ray, Elia Kazan, and most notably Douglas Sirk, created a body of films that were later labeled by film critics as family melodramas, owing to their use of intense emotionality and focus on family conflict. In particular, the action of these films concerned the anxieties of bourgeois families and their engagement with the contradictory ideologies of the postwar era. These films were marked by an exaggerated and excessive style,

which some argue served to subvert repressive notions of suburban life in America. Kazan's other films belonging to this genre include *A Streetcar Named Desire* (1951; starring method actor Marlon Brando), *On the Waterfront* (1954; again with Brando), and *Splendor in the Grass* (1961). As a film genre, it is important to remember that melodrama has taken on many meanings, of which the family melodramas of the 1950s represent one of many.

Today, *East of Eden* is remembered by many as the film that made James Dean famous. Modern viewers are often bemused by Dean's over-the-top performance and violent emotionality. This style, called Method acting, first became popular in New York during the 1930s. James Dean, along with Brando, Marilyn Monroe, Al Pacino, Robert De Niro, and James Fonda, is among the most famous American actors to use this technique. Method acting is different from other forms of acting, in that the actors try to create lifelike emotional performances by drawing on their own emotional memories; in other words, they are trying not to simulate the emotions but to actually feel them during their performance.

CULTURAL CONTEXT

U.S. Entry into World War I

The U.S. entry into World War I forms the backdrop for both Kazan's film and the final portion of Steinbeck's novel used for the film adaptation. Since the novel spans several generations, with earlier portions of the book stretching back as far as the American Civil War, World War I is de-emphasized in its overall significance. The portions that do concern the war are diluted by complex secondary plots that take place outside of the Trask family—like the action at Kate's brothel—that are completely omitted from the film. By contrast, Kazan's adaptation contains several central scenes—the Salinas parade scene and the Ferris wheel scene, for example—portraying in vivid detail the nationalistic, prowar and anti-German sentiments that swept through the country as the United States prepared to enter the war. The U.S. entry into World War I is discussed by the novel's narrator, briefly in Chapter 42, as he discusses the town's growing realization that the Salinas Valley is being effected by the events abroad.

(© INTERFOTO | Alamy)

While Adam Trask works for the government as an enlistment officer in both works, the immense difficulty he faces daily in sending the young men of the Salinas area off to fight (often only to hear later of their deaths) is emphasized in greater detail in Steinbeck's novel. However, when he learns that his son Aron has enlisted, the impact is equally devastating in both works.

Racism and Gender Inequality in the Salinas Valley

Whereas Kazan's portrayal of racism in the Salinas Valley is limited to the Ferris wheel scene, where Cal and Abra witness Aron trying to stop a mob of angry townspeople from lashing out at a local, Gustav Albrecht, Steinbeck's treatment of race relations in the area is much more complex. Unlike Kazan, Steinbeck uses Lee, the Asian servant and philosopher, to suggest that racism is not merely a reaction to the losses of World War I, but rather deeply imbedded into the cultural fabric of the Salinas Valley. In the

novel, it is easier for Lee to fake a Pidgin accent than use fluent English when dealing with most characters because their racist expectations limit the possibilities for relating.

In both the film and novel, Kate leaves Adam Trask because he completely disregards her feelings about settling in the Salinas Valley, expecting her instead to eventually come around to settling into motherhood and being content as a housewife. In both stories she shoots him in the shoulder, unequivocally refusing to submit to this fate. In the novel, Steinbeck gives us greater insight to the numerous barriers faced by women who wanted to survive on their own without the support of a man—although in both novel and film, Kate chose to run a brothel rather than be a housewife, a rather grim option for female independence. Because Kate meticulously documents the sexual exploits of men in the Salinas Valley, readers can see the pervasive nature of gender inequality in the social make-up of America in the twentieth century.

CRITICAL OVERVIEW

By many measures, *East of Eden* was a huge success. In the year of its release it won the award for Best Dramatic Film at the Cannes Film Festival. In 1956, the film received four Academy Award nominations with Jo Van Fleet winning the Academy Award for Best Actress in a Supporting Role for her performance as Kate. Also in 1956, *East of Eden* was awarded the Golden Globe award for Best Motion Picture Drama and received three nominations at the BAFTA awards. Despite its huge commercial success, the film was not without its critics, many of whom found it melodramatic and overly simplistic, hardly doing justice to Steinbeck's original. Today, the film is remembered by many as James Dean's first (and for some best) major performance. Scholars continue to compare and contrast the film with Steinbeck's novel, although many within film studies often treat it as a stand-alone work, often praising Kazan for his innovative use of CinemaScope.

CRITICISM

Laura K. Noll

Noll is an independent scholar of English literature and composition. In this essay, she considers Kazan's film East of Eden *in the historical context of postwar America, arguing that the film's enormous commercial success speaks to a widespread need to repress the traumas of World War II.*

In the wake of the Great Depression and the near-global devastation of World War II, Americans struggled to move forward in the face of traumatic loss and rebuild their lives. During the first half of the twentieth century, the stock market crash of 1929, the atrocities committed by Hitler in the Holocaust, and America's atomic bombing of the Japanese cities Hiroshima and Nagasaki, among other horrors, challenged people's sense of security and safety. What it meant to be human in the modern world and, most relevant to a discussion of Elia Kazan's blockbuster *East of Eden* (1955), what it meant to be an American in the postwar era were open questions that many struggled to answer during the 1950s. When one considers the overwhelming magnitude of these traumas, it is perhaps not surprising that the need to make sense of them

WHAT DO I SEE NEXT?

- *A Streetcar Named Desire* (1951), directed by Elia Kazan and starring Marlon Brando, Vivien Leigh, Kim Hunter, and Karl Malden, is based on the Pulitzer Prize–winning play of the same name by Tennessee Williams. This film was among Kazan's most successful and controversial, due to its thematic content.

- *America, America* (1963) is a black-and-white film written, produced, and directed by Elia Kazan. In this epic drama, the young Greek Stavros Topouzoglou chases his dream of immigrating to America from Turkey.

- *Of Mice and Men* (1939), directed by Lewis Milestone, is an adaptation of Steinbeck's novel of the same name. Lennie and George struggle to fulfill their dream of owning a ranch and being their own bosses. The film was nominated for four Oscars.

- *Member of the Wedding* (1952), directed by Fred Zinnemann, earned a nomination for the Academy Award for Best Actress, Julie Harris. The film tells the story of twelve-year-old tomboy Frankie Addams, her family's maid Berenice Sadie Brown, and her six-year-old cousin John Henry West.

- *From Here to Eternity* (1953) is a dramatic film directed by Fred Zinnemann based on the novel of the same name by James Jones. It concerns the lives of several soldiers stationed in Hawaii during the months leading up to the Japanese attack on Pearl Harbor that led to U.S. entry into World War II. The film received thirteen Academy Award nominations, winning eight.

- *Picnic* (1955) is a film adaptation of William Inge's Pulitzer Prize–winning play of the same title. It was written by Daniel Taradash and directed by Joshua Logan. This CinemaScope film in Technicolor paints a vivid portrait of life in the American Midwest during the 1950s.

was often superseded by a desire to forget, regain a sense of security, and get on with life. Tired of so much senseless suffering, many Americans were eager to enjoy life and find evidence that things were going to be okay. Moreover, while most people did not feel personally responsible for the losses of the war, it is likely that many suffered from feelings of guilt, as is so common with survivors of tragedy. Moving forward under these conditions was not an easy task, but it was made considerably easier, for some, by the relative prosperity brought by the postwar economy and reassurances from Hollywood that resonated deeply with audiences afraid of the world and of themselves. As a director, Kazan deftly negotiated the public need for cautiousness and lighthearted relief from trauma with Steinbeck's anti-establishment themes to create a film that continues to resonate with audiences today. A close examination of several key omissions made during the process of adaptation reveals that the film's immense commercial success is due, at least in part, to a widespread desire to repress the cultural traumas of World War II and quietly maintain the subjugation of racial minorities and women, while simultaneously reassuring viewers that their sins were part of the universal human experience and, hence, forgivable.

While it is certainly true, as Hyang Mann Lee notes in his article "The Disappearance of the Oriental Philosopher in the Film Adaptation of *East of Eden*," that a need for increased structural coherence and plausible characters motivated many of the changes made during the process of adaptation, such explanations lack the specificity necessary to account for the deletion of both Lee and specific mention of *timshel*, a Hebrew word used frequently in Steinbeck's novel. Lee is not, as he is frequently considered by literary critics, a secondary character in Steinbeck's novel. On the contrary, he embodies the totality of Steinbeck's moral philosophy, so much so that the author considered him to be a necessity. "I need Lee," he writes in *Journal of a Novel*, "not only as an interpreter but as an active figure." Without Lee, the Trask boys might never have survived boyhood, as their father was utterly indifferent to their existence after being abandoned by the boy's mother, Kate. It is simply not enough to say, as Steinbeck scholar Lee does, that "the deletion of Lee *may* [emphasis added] have been influenced by the cultural background of the 1950s." More accurately, it *was* the cultural background itself that

KAZAN'S RETELLING BECAME WILDLY POPULAR, IN PART, BECAUSE IT WAS A NARRATIVE THAT HELPED PRESERVE AN UNTARNISHED AND SELF-CONGRATULATORY NATIONAL IDENTITY, WITHIN WHICH ANTI-SEMITIC AND ANTI-ASIAN PREJUDICES COULD BE QUIETLY MAINTAINED."

accounts for what counted as structural coherence in the mid-1950s and therefore forced Lee out of the story. Lee and the Hebrew concept of *timshel* were unwanted reminders of the trauma endured by Asian Americans, the Japanese, and Jews during World War II. To include them would have meant also introducing traces of history that would have made audiences uncomfortable. For Kazan's film to appeal to the tastes of middle-class white America these reminders needed to be eliminated completely.

In other words Lee, a character who bore the racist ignorance of the Salinas Valley without complaint, had to be deleted if Kazan's film was to aid the repression of trauma. Just as American-born citizens of Asian descent were forced out of their homes and into internment camps during World War II, the racial prejudice successfully silenced Lee's expression of Americanness in Steinbeck's novel. Despite his fluency in English, Lee speaks in a fake pidgin accent to suit the expectations of his white peers. By making him the mouthpiece of his moral philosophy, Steinbeck gave voice to Asian experiences of racial inequality. Kazan's retelling became wildly popular, in part, because it was a narrative that helped preserve an untarnished and self-congratulatory national identity, within which anti-Semitic and anti-Asian prejudices could be quietly maintained. It is no coincidence that the locus of Steinbeck's moral philosophy was relocated from Lee and diffused unnamed into the exclusively white cast of Kazan's film, some of whom actively confront racism as they fight the anti-German sentiment in Salinas. For example, in the film, the townspeople grow increasingly frustrated as it becomes clear that they are not immune from the losses of the war, which drags on much longer than they were anticipating earlier in the story. As the town loses more and more of its sons to battles beyond their control, they turn their anger and frustration on poor Gustav Albrecht, an innocent immigrant with an accent. Following the famous Ferris wheel scene, Aron heroically struggles to defend Gustav from the angry town mob until the sheriff steps in and puts an end to the brawl. By identifying with the heroic actions of Aron, the 1950s viewers would have been quietly relieved of their powerlessness to prevent loss and suffering during World War II, including racially motivated incidents at home. Any guilt that they were feeling would have been suppressed by this identification, thus allowing them to move forward feeling better about themselves and more able to enjoy their prosperity that was largely a product of the war.

Before turning to Kazan's treatment of the women in *East of Eden*, it is worth mentioning that while many women had been employed during World War II, there was a cultural expectation that they return to their domestic activities to help stabilize the country in the postwar era. This was not an expectation that all women readily accepted, and the resulting tension can be seen in both Kazan's film and Steinbeck's novel, although in drastically different ways. In addition to removing much of Kate's monstrous history, Kazan omits the character of Liza Hamilton and portrays Abra as much more meek and submissive than Steinbeck's Abra. By contrast to Lee, Liza is firmly a secondary character, so one could argue that her omission was primarily due to pragmatic considerations, although other secondary characters of arguably equal importance are included. In the novel, Liza is a cold, asexual, and unfeeling religious woman who can be seen as an icon of domesticity. Though the Hamiltons are extremely poor, she makes do with what they have and provides for her many children. In contrast to Kate, who rejects the life Adam plans for her despite her desires and emotional needs, Liza embraces her domestic duties with religious vigor, so much so that her husband both respects and fears her. The contrast between the two women is striking, and when juxtaposed against one another, they make a strong statement about the cost of domesticity, namely that to embrace the role of housewife requires rejecting one's emotional needs completely, something only possible by turning away toward God. Including a character like Liza alongside Kate in the film would have challenged the cultural ideal of the 1950s

> PEOPLE SHOULD WATCH THE MOVIE AND READ THE NOVEL, *EAST OF EDEN*, WITHOUT REGARDING EITHER THE MOVIE OR THE NOVEL AS FAILED WORKS OF ART."

housewife and her omission is perhaps a reflection of a cultural need to maintain the subjugation of women as well as racial minorities. In the novel, Abra and Cal establish an egalitarian relationship, carving out a new place for domesticity in the feminine experience, one which is only part of a woman's identity. This progressive ideal is largely absent from the film.

By examining key omissions made by Kazan during the process of adapting Steinbeck's epic for film, it becomes clear that the instant popularity of Kazan's work speaks to a widespread desire to forget the horrors of the first half of the twentieth century and return to previous notions of the status quo, norms that included the subjugated social status of minorities and women.

Source: Laura K. Noll, Critical Essay on *East of Eden*, in *Novels for Students*, Gale, Cengage Learning, 2010.

Hyang Mann Lee

In the following essay, Lee discusses the omission of the character "Lee" in the film adaptation of East of Eden.

East of Eden has a special significance for the understanding of Steinbeck's literary thought and his attitudes toward life, although it has been criticized as a weak novel on account of its diffuse structure, implausible characters, and excessively moralistic themes. Despite its critical failure, *East of Eden* was regarded as his most endearing novel by Steinbeck himself, and also has been enjoyed as a bestseller by the public since the time of its publication. This success must certainly be due to Steinbeck's important themes concerning ethics and human nature. As for Elia Kazan's movie, which greatly contributed to spreading the book's fame all over the world, critical evaluations have been divided into two camps, some finding it an outdated morality play on the one hand, or a superb film of auteurism on the other hand.

(© INTERFOTO / Alamy)

The most prominent aspects of the transformation from novel to film are that the role of the Chinese servant Lee and the earlier part of the story have both been deleted. By carefully observing this process of elision, we can gain new perspectives on the author's main themes, especially by focusing on the traces of the deleted oriental philosopher. What is immediately striking is the author's changed attitude toward suggestions to cut and rework the novel and the film. When *East of Eden* was ready to be published, Pat Covici at Viking had suggested that Steinbeck not only cut but also rewrite the bulk of the book, but he refused, probably thinking that *East of Eden* was to be his great work (Millichap 138). But a year later, when Warner Brothers bought the screen rights in 1953, Steinbeck willingly agreed to Kazan's suggestion that some other playwright might do the screenplay, drastically deleting events from the original. When he attended the movie premiere in 1955, he acknowledged the changes from the novel and said that "he was glad that his book had contributed, among all other contributions, to what is probably the best motion picture he had ever seen" (Millichap 138).

What is it that made Steinbeck praise Elia Kazan's movie, *East of Eden*, so highly? Even if we admit that it is inevitable to omit three-fourths of the story for the dramatic unity of the movie, it surely would not have been pleasant for Steinbeck to watch the precious stories about his mother's family and the Chinese philosopher disappear or transform. Steinbeck always took a firm stand to retain the spirit of a novel to be adapted for the cinema. In 1939 when *The Grapes of Wrath* was supposed to be adapted for John Ford's movie, Steinbeck told the producer, Darryl Zanuck, that he was going to put the $75,000 paid for the rights to the novel into escrow, and that if the movie was watered down or its perspective changed, he would use the money to sue him (Benson 409). Watching the film version of *East of Eden* and comparing it to the cases of *An American Tragedy* or *The Grapes of Wrath*, Steinbeck might well have been dissatisfied with the transformed plot of the movie. Joseph R. Millichap asserts that Steinbeck's attitude toward this movie demonstrates his perception of failure about *East of Eden* as novel and film (145). However, judging from Steinbeck's statement that his book had contributed to what was probably one of the best motion pictures he had ever seen (Millichap 145), he seemed to acknowledge that the movie had sufficiently retained the spirit of the novel.

The fact that Steinbeck welcomed Paul Osborn's adaptation of *East of Eden* raises a couple of important questions about the author's attitude toward the movie. Steinbeck may have found the movie appealed to a great many people, even though his novel had been attacked for its diffuse structure. The author admitted that "he liked the movie version because of its tightness, its unity, because it grabs an audience and shakes it, like a terrier shaking a squirrel" (Fields 59). Unfortunately, it is not easy for audiences to perceive how Steinbeck's main theme permeates the movie, as Lee, an advocate of *timshel*, the idea of free choice, was completely omitted. It is important that Steinbeck constructed his fiction around the concept of *timshel*, which Lee introduces in the middle of the story. Therefore the thematic function of Lee's speculations and his relationships with the other characters is indispensable to understanding John Steinbeck's concept of man's destiny and his cosmogony. The importance of Lee's role in the plot is well expressed by the author in *Journal of a Novel: The* East of Eden *Letters*.

> And the opening of Book 4 is not light and airy. The balance of everything has to be maintained. And so I am going to begin with Lee ... I need Lee, not only as an interpreter but as an active figure. I have a feeling of goodness about the book now but there is so much to come, I don't for the life of me know how I got in what I have already. (148–49)

Like the black woman Dilsey in William Faulkner's *The Sound and the Fury*, or other minor characters who develop an author's ideas, Lee plays a crucial role. If Steinbeck could not find the concept of *timshel* adequately presented in the movie, it is improbable that Steinbeck would have felt Kazan had effectively transferred the story of the novel from one medium to another.

Why did Paul Osborn eliminate the part of the oriental philosopher? The deletion of Lee in the movie may have been influenced by the cultural background of 1950s America. It seems that Kazan, at the time of directing *East of Eden*, had in mind the intellectual atmosphere of the times, that is, the absolute approval-or-disapproval, which may be interpreted as the absolute Puritanism of "this is right and this is wrong" (Morsberger 30). Lee's disappearance may have much to do with the fact that his role as an observer of the events has a structural limit: he appears only as a minor character whose function of observing may be identified with the narrator as another alter-ego of Steinbeck, unlike other observers who remain from beginning to end. And the prominent representation of Lee's moral philosophy may injure the dramatic coherence of the story as well as the taste of the audience. However, did Kazan let such an important character disappear just for the effect of dramatic unity? Transformation of a plot, or elimination of some events (especially of an ending) in the movies based on Steinbeck's major novels, such as *Of Mice and Men* and *The Grapes of Wrath*, constitutes significant change in a novel's structure. The different endings for *Of Mice and Men* as a book, film, and play result from considerations of the sense of values of the middle-class viewing audience. In John Ford's *The Grapes of Wrath*, the elimination of the final episode of the breast-feeding has been accepted without much complaint, because the scene in the novel had caused controversy for being too sentimental or too shocking. But it would be a fatal distortion of *East of Eden* to omit the part of Lee, whom the author needed "not only as an interpreter but as an active figure" in the story (*Journal of a Novel* 149), without considering the resulting effects. The transformation of the final section in the film adaptation, especially the elimination of Lee, generates significant differences in meaning.

It is not an overstatement to say that the spiritual leader of the novel is Lee, who, like Slim in *Of Mice and Men* or Jim Casy in *The Grapes of Wrath*, integrates all the conflicting worlds of the novel. He represents Steinbeck's ideal character as well as philosophical mouthpiece throughout the novel, like Casy and Crooks. By removing the philosophical Chinese servant, Paul Osborn risked omitting discussion of the novel's main theme, *timshel*. Lee may be regarded at times as a secondary character, as an onlooker, but he also represents the voice of wisdom and reason in the crucial events of the story, and he often articulates some of the novel's most important themes. Therefore, even if he is merely a servant in the Trask family, he serves as a sort of moral lens through which the deeds of the other characters in the novel are revealed.

In a sense, Lee's past and present life itself is a living example of the theme of *timshel*, which may be interpreted as a vision of free will. He is an educated man whose parents immigrated to America from China. As he talks about his own childhood in chapter twenty-eight, his humorous introduction of his life shows his status as a marginal man often exposed to racial prejudice. His father had worked on the railroads with his pregnant wife, who disguised herself as a man so that she could join her husband on the voyage to the United States. His mother, after giving birth to Lee, was raped and killed by a mob of American railroad workers. But he was raised as an adopted son of a railroad worker who had repented of the repulsive deed. Lee is of American birth, and his English is fluent, but he often pretends to speak with a Chinese pidgin accent to meet Americans' expectations of him. In spite of this, Lee serves as a stabilizing force in the Trask household throughout the novel. He is content to be a servant, saying that "being a servant is the refuge of the philosopher, and can offer him a position of power, even of love". Lee, as events unfold, illustrates repeatedly the power and the love that his intelligence can wrest from his unflinching servitude. Lee's dignity and power beyond that of other characters in the story comes from the invisible quality of his status in the story. He always locates himself as a silent observer behind the scenes, willing to heal old wounds in the Trask family. By lowering himself, he brings out the true value of a balance between hard reality and humane idealism to the Trask family, just as Casy in *The Grapes of Wrath* contributes to the awakening of the Joad family by sacrificing himself.

According to Steinbeck's own confession in the journal entries of August 21–23, 1951, the author had great affection for his character Lee, as well as great agony about the future development of the story beyond book four. In the entry for August 22, Steinbeck explains the reason for Lee's departure and return.

> I hope you [Pat Covici] liked the work yesterday, Lee's departure and return. Elaine liked it because it made her laugh and cry at the same time. I thought I might go to San Franscisco with Lee. But there would be no point in it. This book doesn't need richness now. It needs tightness, story, character and to a certain extent, speed. (*Journal of a Novel* 148)

In fact, the structure of the three chapters from thirty-four to thirty-six may appear unnatural to readers, as Lee leaves the Trask family suddenly and comes back home abruptly on the night of the same day. Judging from the author's diary, we can surmise two things. First, Steinbeck may have planned to send his character Lee out of the story. Or his nostalgia for his boyhood California and the concern with his family was too great to keep the balance in creating the novel. After overcoming such conflicts, the author began to develop the characters Aron and Abra, who Steinbeck says are also terribly important to this complicated book, *East of Eden* (*Journal of a Novel* 149). Taken all together, these factors foreshadow the possible deletion of Lee from the movie to be directed by Elia Kazan a few years later.

The oriental philosopher may have disappeared in the process of moving from one medium to another, but the traces of his philosophy and moral views can be found in the transformed images of the characters. Lee's altered part in the story reveals the paradox of absence and presence in oriental philosophy, for it can be said that Lee's concept of *timshel* is revealed in the movie not through his direct speeches but in the transformed actions of characters, especially through the changed images of Abra and Kate. Also, some part of his role in explaining about Cathy's past has been filtered into the film's dialogue, especially that of Adam and the county sheriff. Therefore, Lee's influence, though not easily visible in the movie, overshadows that of all the characters and events, as did Jim Casy's in *The Grapes of Wrath*.

Particularly prominent is the transformed image of Abra. The true mutual affection shared by Abra and Lee is best expressed when Lee says to Abra, "I wish you were my own daughter" and Abra answers, "I wish you were my father". It is evident that Lee's philosophy of life has greatly transformed Abra's view of life in the movie when she tells Cal about her past in the harvesting scene. In an idyllic field of Adam's lettuce, Abra explains to Cal how she overcame jealousy toward her father when he remarried a woman as soon as her mother died. She confesses that she had thrown her stepmother's $3,000 wedding ring into the river because she was disgusted with her father and hated everything. However, she says that she felt much more mature for having forgiven her father.

The value of growing up is one of the key measures by which Lee judges all the members of the Trask family, regardless of whether they are morally good or bad. Let us contrast the above scene from the movie with an episode in the novel. In the novel, Lee advises Cal with a message of sense and optimism, saying that Cal should remember that he is simply a flawed human being, not a monster of evil like his mother. Lee's advice helps Cal to realize that *timshel*, the freedom to choose between good and evil, really exists, just as Abra helped Cal in the movie. Abra Bacon in the novel is the daughter of the corrupt county supervisor in Salinas. Like Cal, she worries that her father's corruption and theft will taint her. But despite her worries and family problems, Abra herself grows more mature and, like Lee in the novel, helps Cal grow up as well.

Another example of Lee's philosophical influence can be found in the transformed image of Kate. In the novel, Steinbeck portrays Kate as a near-inhuman creature of seemingly inherent evil. For this reason, Kate has been dismissed as an implausible character and a seriously weak link in Steinbeck's novel. But Kate as modified for the movie shows a more human and sympathetic side. When she meets Cal, who wants to borrow 5,000 dollars from his mother rather than from Lee, as in the novel, she explains to Cal the reason she cannot help him run away from Adam. What she says to Cal about her past life is quite different from the original's picture of her life. Her attitude toward life, surprisingly, is rather similar to the narrator's. In chapter thirteen, the narrator shows his belief that "the free, exploring mind of the individual human is the most valuable in the world." And he declares that he would fight for the "freedom of the mind to take any direction it wishes, undirected".

In a similar way, Kate in the film asserts that Adam, her former husband, was the embodiment of ideological and religious forces that threatened to constrain this freedom of the individual. So Kate criticizes Adam's self-righteous possessiveness. In a dramatic scene, Cal speaks to his mother in Monterey, telling her he is more like her. He asks her why she abandoned Adam and the family. She responds,

> He wanted to tie me down. He wanted to keep me on a stinking little ranch away from everybody. Keep me all to himself. Well, nobody

holds me ... He wanted to own me. He wanted to bring me up like a snot-nosed kid and tell me what to do ... Always so right himself, knowing everything. Reading the Bible at me!

Eventually, Kate decides that Cal is a likeable boy and gives him the check. This action suggests that Kate acknowledges her own wish to make amends, to give up her status as a conventional villain. Such an action also foreshadows the development of the idea of *timshel*, or freedom to choose between good and evil, which becomes the main theme of *East of Eden*. The action also implies that she has the power to choose her own path. In consequence, Cal struggles to understand her and revises his opinion of her.

So, in the process of film adaptation, Lee's disappearance actually helps to recreate more plausible characters. It also allows his sometimes overbearing message to permeate naturally throughout the stream of the story. In the novel, Lee is not only a character; he is also a kind of central spirit from which all the conflicts of the Trask family may gain resolution and harmony. In the movie, with the help of Abra's mediation, things come together, overcoming "the thematic dichotomy of good vs. evil, naivete vs. experience, illusion vs. reality" (Rathgeb 38), as one critic put it. Lee, as an intellectual observer, and an estranged and solitary man, has clear insight into the essence of the tragic relationships of the Trask family. Lee can be usefully compared to Ishmael on the masthead, who embodies, for the reader, a man as a thinker, and whose reveries transcend space and time as he stands watch high above the seas.

In the movie, Paul Osborn placed Abra and Cal on the ferris wheel high above the carnival, rather than having the oriental philosopher Lee preach the theory of free will. The message from the carnival scene newly added to the movie nevertheless corresponds to some degree with the essentials of Lee's philosophy of life. This carnival episode offers a chance for Abra and Cal to have a broad view of the society around them, and as a result, they can contemplate the inner state of their own minds. Douglas Rathgeb, in his essay on the film, asserts that "this carnival sequence becomes a metaphor for the real world, free of the illusions that blind both Aron and his father" (38). However, it would be more accurate to say that the carnival episode reflects the world full of prejudices. The ferris wheel on which Abra and Caleb sit together high above the earth allows them to watch the confused world of narrow-minded, blindly patriotic people below. And the ugly images of their faces reflected in the mirror imply that people in the real world tend to fall into distorted judgments of others.

Warren French says that "Steinbeck should be called to task for his creation of the implausible witch-like Cathy." He complains that Steinbeck tries to disappear from *East of Eden*, possibly in order to create a kind of "open-ended" parable (147). French's argument might better be applied to the case of Lee, however. Kazan found ways to have Lee disappear and yet had Abra take his place. In the final scene of the film, it is Abra rather than Lee who is the intermediary between Cal and Adam, and the old man asks Cal to take care of him instead of a talkative nurse, before dying.

It has been suggested that, when one considers that Kazan's film encompasses only the last third of Steinbeck's novel, it should be thought of as an independent and original work (Rathgeb 36). Whenever a novel is adapted into a movie, people are likely to want the stories in the two media to be somehow the "same." Steinbeck himself had worries on this point.

> There is one thing that has occurred to me— Films and Books—a man reads a book and he makes his own picture. If he reads the book first he resents the picture because it's not the picture he's made in his mind. Maybe it would be better if books and pictures didn't cross, and the person reading the book didn't see the picture and the person seeing the picture didn't read the book. Maybe that would be better. (Rathgeb 36)

Despite such concerns, people should watch the movie and read the novel, *East of Eden*, without regarding either the movie or the novel as failed works of art. There are, of course, plot changes, but considering the long friendship and collaboration of Steinbeck and Kazan, Kazan would never have forgotten the precious message the author represented through the creation of the Chinese philosopher, Lee. It cannot be denied that Kazan consistently kept in mind Lee's philosophy, even though Paul Osborn deleted Lee in the course of adaptation. As Lewis Nichols says, "Steinbeck was deeply fascinated by everything about the dramatic arts, including film" (52), and *East of Eden*, though significantly transformed for the screen, shows how adaptable his fiction truly is. Whether or not the oriental philosopher remains visible in the novel or the screen adaptation, Lee will always remain a representative voice of Steinbeck's enduring significance.

Source: Hyang Mann Lee, "The Disappearance of the Oriental Philosopher in the Film Adaptation of *East of Eden*," in *John Steinbeck's Global Dimensions*, edited by Kyoto Ariki, Luchen Li, and Scott Pugh, Scarecrow Press, 2008, pp. 183–190.

Dan Callahan

In the following review of the DVD release of East of Eden, *Callahan argues that Elia Kazan's direction is stagey and James Dean's acting is dated and melodramatic.*

Elia "Sledgehammer" Kazan's wildly uneven *East of Eden* inaugurated the 50-year-old James Dean cult. It hasn't been on video in at least 10 years, and it has never been available in its full widescreen format, so its appearance on DVD is something of an event. Kazan took the last 80 pages or so of John Steinbeck's novel and fashioned his own distinctly overheated variant on the Biblical tale of Cain and Abel. Subtle it ain't. It's all about a son who wants his father's love; in simplistic '50s fashion, we have "Daddy loves me, so I'm good" and "Daddy doesn't love me, so I'm bad." This unfortunate naïveté, founded in psychoanalysis and based on blaming parents for everything, persists to this day.

Kazan's rap as a McCarthy stool pigeon has not dimmed his reputation as a filmmaker. He was one of the most popular and sought-after film and theater directors of the '50s, but his big movies of the time (*A Streetcar Named Desire*, *On the Waterfront*, *Splendor in the Grass*) haven't held up. He didn't have much of a visual sense, and the careful off-kilter framing in *East of Eden*, at last seen in its original aspect ratio, is more decorative than expressive. The camerawork is just as flashy and unfelt as some of the performances (and that goes double for Leonard Rosenman's pseudo-Stravinsky score). Even viewers who acknowledge Kazan's lack of visual imagination usually concede that nobody got better performances out of actors, but this last vestige of his reputation is in real need of examination.

Actors often ignorantly speak of unsuccessful pre-1950 performances as "so pre-Brando." This misses two important points: first, great acting is great acting regardless of its time period. Lillian Gish's performances from the 1910s still have startling immediacy, and in the '30s James Cagney and Barbara Stanwyck were both natural and more than natural. The second thing, almost never acknowledged, is that the early work of Marlon Brando, Kazan's protegee, has dated. Watching him in *Streetcar* now is akin to taking part in an archeological dig: his fabled naturalism is utterly technical and tricksy.

Which brings us to James Dean in *East of Eden*. Dean has outstripped even Brando in iconographical status, and there's a reason for that: he was a crazed exhibitionist who, in the last few years of his life, was almost always in front of a camera. It is in still photos that the Dean legend is most potent and most understandable (he has this in common with Marilyn Monroe and Elvis Presley). His cool vibe still works in photo books and on T-shirts, on mugs and mousepads. But in *East of Eden* he's doing a Brando imitation deepened by his own aggressive need to charm every man, woman, child, and dog around him. Dean even tries to charm plants: Hoping to raise a bean crop to help his financially insolvent father (Raymond Massey), Dean does a dance around the crops and talks to them as if they were a lover. His miming of vulnerability is hair-raisingly calculated.

If you turn the sound down on *East of Eden* (and, by all means, do), you'll see why Dean is a legend. Physically he's a very original actor. He crouches, slouches, throws himself to the ground, throws his head back in agony or ecstasy. Radioactively sexy, Dean is also a grotesque—a weird mixture of Frankenstein's monster and the prettiest of pouting pretty boys. But whenever he talks, he's doing his extravagantly mannered idea of Brando: taking pauses for no reason, hesitating over words, repeating words, scratching himself, pulling his ear, mumbling. Meant to be naturalistic, his performance here seems incredibly self-conscious, even in the famous moment when he tries to give his father money and explodes in frightening, far-out grief.

Dean is so lost in his own acted-out neuroses that he forces Julie Harris, his gifted, lyrical leading lady, to mop up his excess in scene after scene, which she does successfully, especially in their lengthy jaunt through an amusement park. But even her sensitive appreciation of Dean cannot make us interested in him or his monstrously immature character past a certain point. Finally, even she has had enough; in the last scene, she asks him, "Are you going to cry for the rest of your life?" with a touch of exasperation.

Dean's scenes with Massey play out like a much less inspired version of Kazan's Vivien Leigh/Brando dichotomy in *Streetcar*. Kazan sets up the older performer (Massey and Leigh) as the hollow, fussy standard bearer, while his young Turks (Brando and Dean) wear tight clothes and deploy an arsenal of Method mannerisms in order to sexily sneer at the establishment. It all finally seems to have more to do with acting than with anything else the movies are supposed to be about. A whole subplot in *East of Eden* about World War I and prejudice against Germans is especially tin-eared and crude.

Kazan's direction of Jo Van Fleet, who won a supporting actress Oscar as Dean's long-gone madam mother, points up the director's schizophrenic mix of styles. Van Fleet is compelling in her scenes with Dean, rough-edged, sentimental, filled with bitter humor. Dean has come to ask her for money for his bean venture. When she realizes that her money is meant to help Dean's father, Van Fleet is memorable when she points out how funny it is that her ill-gotten gains are going to help her self-righteous ex-husband. "If you don't think that's funny, you better not go to college," she says (a resonant non sequitur). But Van Fleet, good as she is, is stagy, too. Her performance shows that Kazan was a theater director above all. He did change American acting, but his achievement is more a historical footnote than a still-viable artistic statement.

Source: Dan Callahan, "*East of Eden* on Film," in *Slant*, March 23, 2005.

Robert E. Morsberger

In the following excerpt, Morsberger compares the film adaptation of East of Eden *to Steinbeck's novel.*

Part I Movie: *East of Eden*

In the late 1940s, John Steinbeck began a collaboration with his friend and sometime neighbor Elia Kazan to make a film about Emilio Zapata and the Mexican Revolution. The 1952 film, *Viva Zapata!*, was sufficiently successful to earn Academy Award nominations for Steinbeck as best screenwriter, Marlon Brando as best actor, and Anthony Quinn (who won) as best supporting actor. Kazan's next film, *Man on a Tightrope*, was not so popular with critics and bombed with audiences, but in 1954 Kazan had his greatest success with *On the Waterfront*, which won the Oscar for best picture, best director, best actor (Marlon Brando), and best supporting actress (Eva Marie Saint). After it, recalls Kazan, he could have everything: "any story, any power, any money". At that point, he chose to collaborate again with Steinbeck on a film based upon *East of Eden*. Jack Warner,

> THERE IS NOTHING NEW IN *EAST OF EDEN*'S
> ANALYSIS OF REJECTION, BUT THE FILM DOES NOT
> FUNCTION ON AN INTELLECTUAL LEVEL; THROUGH
> ACTING AND IMAGERY, IT COMES ACROSS ON AN
> EMOTIONAL LEVEL, GIVING THE CATHARSIS OF
> IDENTIFICATION, AND ON THIS LEVEL, PRACTICALLY
> ALL FILM BOOKS FIND IT OVERWHELMINGLY
> POWERFUL."

who had not read the book and did not intend to, gave Kazan *carte blanche* on the screenplay and casting. Claiming that he found a "diffuseness" about *Viva Zapata!*, Kazan wanted more unity in his next work and asked Steinbeck if it was all right to get someone else to do the screenplay. When Steinbeck, who felt he had already given himself as much as he could to the novel and did not feel up to the problem of adapting it to the screen, responded, "Sure, fine," Kazan recruited playwright Paul Osborn, whom he considered excellent at construction. Besides his own plays, *On Borrowed Time* and *Morning's at Seven*, Osborn had done celebrated adaptations for the stage of John Hersey's *A Bell for Adano* and J. P. Marquand's *Point of No Return*.

Steinbeck's sprawling novel, with its two loosely connected story lines of the Trasks and the Hamiltons, was far too long for a movie unless cut drastically or made with the scope of the Russian *War and Peace*. Accordingly, Osborn cut everything except the final section, the conflict between teenage Cal and Aron Trask for the affection of their father, Adam, and of Aron's girl, Abra. Omitted were the Hamilton family as a counterpoint to the Trasks, except for a few brief appearances by Will, and all of Adam's background—his childhood, his rivalry with his evil brother Charles, his service in the army, his marriage to the innately and totally evil Cathy or Kate Ames, the birth and early years of his sons. The film opens at approximately Chapter 37 in Part Four of the novel. Even so, Osborn eliminated many details from Steinbeck's remaining 170 pages. Lee, the

philosophical Chinese servant, is missing, and with him the discussion of *timshel*, and the plotting at Kate's brothel is deleted. Instead, Osborn added a good many episodes involving the three young people—such as a scene at Adam Trask's newly purchased ice house, a carnival sequence, a fight between the brothers, Aron's drunken mockery of his father as he departs on the troop train, moments of compassionate communication between Cal and Abra. By intensifying the conflict between the two brothers, rearranging some scenes, inventing new ones, and sharpening others, Osborn improved on Steinbeck's handling of the material. The section of the novel covered by the film is too diffuse, shifting focus among Cal, Kate, Lee, Adam, Abra, and Aron. The film gains intensity by keeping the focus on Cal and relating everything to him.

Kazan says that what attracted him to *East of Eden* was partly "the story of a son trying to please his father who disapproved of him" and partly "an opportunity for me to attack puritanism; the absolute puritanism of 'this is right and this is wrong.' I was trying to show that right and wrong get mixed up, and that there are values that have to be looked at more deeply than in that absolute approval-or-disapproval syndrome of my Left friends." Here, Kazan is referring to his testifying before the House Committee on Un-American Activities and naming names of people he had known to be Communists, an action for which Lillian Hellman and other liberals denounced him. But in the film version of *East of Eden*, the mixture of right and wrong shows up in the character relationships. The sheriff calls Adam Trask the kindest man he has ever known, but in his high-minded righteousness, Adam is too quick to condemn Cal for what are basically minor flaws, such as defiantly reading aloud the numbers of Bible verses when his father repeatedly asks him not to during a family Bible reading. Though rejected and feeling outcast, Cal loves his father more deeply than the favored brother Aron does, but to demonstrate this love, he steals a coal chute to speed up the processing of lettuce and later takes advantage of the war to profiteer in bean futures in order to pay back the money his father lost in a debacle over refrigerated lettuce. Aron, the supposedly good son, lacks Cal's sensitivity to the feelings of others. When their father seems to shrug off the loss of all his money in the refrigeration fiasco, Aron says he thought Adam would be more disturbed, but Cal, who sees the depth of the hurt, replies, "You don't understand him." Aron is too smugly pure, so that Abra tells Cal that she fears it is not herself but some abstract ideal of herself that Aron loves. She confesses that she sometimes feels herself to be bad, to have a wildness that makes her feel closer to Cal. When Cal interferes to rescue Aron and a German neighbor from an anti-German mob, Aron turns on him instead of thanking him, and Cal, hurt by the rejection, saying, "I only wanted to help you," strikes out at Aron in retaliation.

In numerous ways, Osborn strengthened the final section of the story. Steinbeck's Cal, though a Cain figure, is not really very diabolical; we are told of his vaguely wicked ways, but he basically comes through as a well-meaning and clean-cut lad. Though he is said to suffer from a sense of rejection, he generally has his father's affection as well as the loyalty of Lee and the friendship of Abra. Abra, he insists, is his brother's girl, and Cal makes no attempt to take her from Aron, though he does end up with her, more because of Aron's puritanism than by any intense effort on Cal's part. In the film, Cal is much more moody and violent, an embittered young man whose actions are often self-destructive and who attempts from the first to steal Abra from his insipid brother. Osborn makes the relationship of Cal to Abra and Aron a bit like that of Heathcliff to Cathy and Linton in *Wuthering Heights*. Abra, though played by the delicate Julie Harris, whom Kazan cast because "her face is the most compassionate face of any girl I've ever seen," is sometimes a tantalizing flirt in the film rather than the invariably noble, vibrant young girl in the novel. As played by James Dean, the film's Cal is an intense if somewhat inarticulate romantic who has a number of passionate scenes with Abra. Aron, played by Richard Davalos, is comparatively colorless, but he is not planning, as in the novel, to become a celibate priest. In the novel, Abra finally turns from Aron because of his proclaimed program of celibacy and his impossibly high-minded standards of goodness. In the film, she is swept away by the more sympathetic character of Cal. Behind his aggressiveness she can see his vulnerability and the fact that his capacity for love is greater than his brother's.

Osborn's script never explains the degenerate background of Kate, the boys' murderously evil mother, nor does she commit suicide after encountering Aron; she merely appears as the black-shrouded madam of a brothel. On the other hand, Osborn and Kazan make the father (Raymond Massey) into a coldly aloof patriarch, much less kindly and sympathetic than Steinbeck's Adam Trask. Kazan calls Massey's face "a piece of wood" by contrast to that of Julie Harris, with its feelings "of compassion and understanding of pain."

By a brilliant stroke, Osborn moves Adam's financial ruin with refrigerated lettuce from the beginning to nearer the end of the final sequence, so that it is more climactic and makes Cal's efforts to salvage his father's fortune more dramatic. In the novel, Cal borrows from Lee the $5,000 that he invests in beans; the film adds a layer of irony by having him borrow it from his mother, who hates Adam Trask but finds herself reluctantly drawn to Cal. Osborn adds a compelling scene not in the novel in which Cal and his mother get to know each other and grudgingly find that they have some temperamental affinities. This is Kate's major appearance in the film, and on the strength of it, Jo Van Fleet, in her first film role, won the Oscar as best supporting actress. In the book, the growing of Cal's beans is not shown, but the film evokes a lot of lyric and emotional intensity from Cal's eager husbandry, showing him at one point running through the vast fields "looking like a little child," so that when his father rejects as tainted the gift of money earned from the beans, the hurt is much harsher and more acute. Film audiences, sharing vicariously Cal's intense hope finally to please his father, identified with the rejection and its trauma. In the novel, the occasion of Cal's gift is his brother's homecoming from college, but in the movie, Aron does not go away, and the gift is a birthday present. Aron gives no present in the novel, but in the film he offers as a gift the announcement of his engagement to Abra (without her consultation or consent), which for Cal is turning the knife in the wound, as the girl he loves is claimed, and his father says this is the finest gift anyone could give him. Nothing Cal could give would match it. In this, the most intense scene in the film, Osborn follows Steinbeck's dialogue rather closely, but Kazan's direction and the tortured eloquence of Dean's performance make the scene immeasurably more moving. Steinbeck presents Cal's dialogue in cut and dry fashion and does not attempt to give it an emotional resonance or get into his feelings until the end, when he writes merely that "Cal felt that he was choking. His forehead streamed with perspiration and he tasted salt on his tongue. He stood up suddenly and his chair fell over. He ran from the room, holding his breath." Then he goes to his room, talks to Lee, and apologizes to his father. In the film, Dean offers his gift with an eager, shy smile, his words coming out hesitantly, as if he is trying to overcome an emotional handicap. When his father not only rejects the gift but denounces it as immoral, Dean registers at first disbelief, then intense pain, as he tries stammeringly to justify what he has done. Weeping incoherently, he embraces his father, who stands woodenly unresponsive; then Cal doubles over in pain, makes tortured, incoherent animal sounds, and runs choking out of the house. In defiance of Aron's protests, Abra follows him into the night, and the two of them are hidden beneath the branches of a weeping willow as Cal sobs that his father wants nothing from him, while Abra tries to comfort him. This scene becomes a climax far more shattering than Steinbeck's and made the movie into a cult film for young people, particularly because of the performance of James Dean as Cal.

Following them, Aron snarls that Cal must never touch Abra again, that Cal is no good, has never been any good, that Aron and their father have repeatedly forgiven him, but that this time, he is beyond forgiveness. This heartless speech motivates Cal, immediately thereafter, instead of later, as in the novel, to take his brother to meet their mother, and the film adds the actual confrontation, missing in the book. The book then cuts to a vignette at the enlistment office, but the film has the sheriff announce the enlistment and then adds a scene in which Adam and Cal go to the railroad station to try to stop Aron from going off on the troop train. When the drunken Aron smashes his head through the train window and laughs in lunatic fashion at his father, Adam has his stroke. The novel postpones the stroke by months, until news comes that Aron has been killed in the war, but the film not only leaves him alive but gains power by concentrating the sequence of events.

Elia Kazan had wanted Marlon Brando as Cal; but when the star was unavailable, Paul Osborn advised him to see a young man cast in the small role of an Arab at a play off Broadway. Kazan recalls that, at first, he was not impressed with Dean, but for Osborn's sake, he called him into Warner's New York offices, where he found him "slouched" in the waiting room, "a heap of twisted legs and denim rags, looking resentful for no particular reason." After a frustrating

interview, Kazan called Osborn and said that "this kid actually *was* Cal." For further reassurance, Kazan sent Dean to see Steinbeck, who reported that he thought the actor "a snotty kid" but conceded that he "sure as hell" was Cal. Despite his twitchiness, Dean took to the camera, and Kazan found his face "very poetic, ... wonderful and very painful" and that "his body was more expressive, actually, in free movement, than Brando's—it had so much tension in it." But Dean did not take to Raymond Massey, whom he considered an old fogey authority figure; Massey, in turn, had only contempt for Dean, according to Kazan, though Massey himself, looking back, says Dean "was a good choice. In every respect he was the Cal of Steinbeck's novel." Massey did, however, object to Dean's "truculent spirit," his lack of preparation, his arrogance in considering "simple technicalities, such as moving on cue and finding his marks" to be "beneath his consideration." Massey claims that he would not have put up with such conduct but that Kazan not only endured it all but even encouraged it. Kazan admits that he played up the tension between Dean and Massey, to bring it out on the screen. All too often, recalls Kazan, Dean was either narcissistic or sullen and inarticulate, and Kazan doubts that Dean would have gotten through the film except for the patient sympathy and kindness of Julie Harris.

Dean's nervous, mumbling, Actors Studio method irritated many reviewers, who called him a shambling imitation of Brando, but he projected his own sympathetic image as an intensely vulnerable, sensitive, suffering youth. Adolescents identified with him; his inarticulateness and smoldering sullenness spoke for those who, like Cal, felt unappreciated by their parents, unable to communicate with them. Killed at twenty-four in a sports car accident in September 1955, after completing only three films, Dean became a tragic legend for the young, to whom he was the rebel, not without a cause, for the cause was being misunderstood, rejected, unloved by the adult world, personified in *East of Eden* by Adam Trask. One fan wrote, "To us teenagers, Dean was a symbol of the fight to make a niche for yourselves in the world of adults." Boys admired his rebelliousness, and girls wanted to comfort him like a stray pet. Many of Dean's bereaved fans refused to believe that he was dead; others developed a morbid necrophilia over him that surpassed the hysteria over the death of Valentino. A year after Dean's death, the studios still received more than seven thousand fan letters a month addressed to him. Exploiters vended model heads of Dean in stone, bronze, and plastic Miracleflesh, and spiritualists put heartbroken fans in touch with Dean's spirit. The adulation of Dean became so emblematic that John Dos Passos included a capsule biography of him in his novel *Midcentury*, entitling it "The Sinister Adolescents," describing Dean's

> . . . resentful hair,
> the deep eyes floating in lonesomeness,
> the bitter beat look,
> the scorn on the lip,

and making him into a symbol of the disillusioned, resentful, alienated young in the latter half of our century. Thirty-six years after his death, Dean is still a cult figure; despite having made only three films, he is still more newsworthy than such superstars as Chaplin, Gable, Cooper, and Coleman. Dean would now be sixty, but he has become a mythic figure of the eternal adolescent, largely on the strength of his role in *East of Eden*, the first and best of his films.

On its own terms, the film records the Steinbeck country around Salinas in splendid color photography by the cameraman Ted McCord, who had photographed *The Treasure of the Sierra Madre*. Standing in for Monterey in 1917 was Mendocino, and Salinas was recreated on the Warners lot. *East of Eden* was both the first film that Kazan made in color and his first in Cinemascope. The shape of the Cinemascope screen prevented his cutting as often as he had before, and since the faces did not fill the screen, he blocked his players in a more relaxed fashion, "More like a stage—more 'across,' more at ease." At the same time, he tried to fight the shape, by getting inner frames, putting something big in the foreground on one side and putting the action on the other side. He also had a color plot, using lots of green to stress the verdure of the Salinas Valley.

A critical and commercial success, *East of Eden* received Academy Award nominations for best director, actor, supporting actress (for which Jo Van Fleet won), and screenplay. Gerald D. McDonald called it "one of the best films of this or any other year; a film which gives deeply disturbing insight into what psychologists call the feeling of rejection." Steinbeck himself once called it the best film he had ever seen. In *Steinbeck and Film*, Joseph Millichap disagrees; he places little value in the novel, and though he considers the film an improvement, he belittles it

for its pop psychology. But Millichap misses the point. There is nothing new in *East of Eden*'s analysis of rejection, but the film does not function on an intellectual level; through acting and imagery, it comes across on an emotional level, giving the catharsis of identification, and on this level, practically all film books find it overwhelmingly powerful.

Source: Robert E. Morsberger, "*East of Eden* on Film," in *Steinbeck and Film*, edited by J. R. Millichap, 1983, pp. 28–42.

SOURCES

Byars, Jackie, *All that Hollywood Allows: Re-reading Gender in 1950s Melodrama*, University of North Carolina Press, 1991.

Gladstein, Mimi, "Steinbeck's Dysfunctional Family: A Coast-to-Coast Dilemma," in *John Steinbeck's Global Dimensions,* edited by Kyoko Ariki, Luchen Li, and Scott Pugh, Scarecrow Press, 2008, pp. 57–69.

Kazan, Elia, director, *East of Eden*, Warners, 1955.

Lee, Hyang Mann, "The Disappearance of the Oriental Philosopher in the Film Adaptation of *East of Eden*," in *John Steinbeck's Global Dimensions*, edited by Kyoko Ariki, Luchen Li, and Scott Pugh, Scarecrow Press, 2008, pp. 183–90.

Millichap, Joseph R., ed., *Steinbeck and Film*, Ungar, 1983.

Morsberger, Robert E., "*East of Eden* on Film," in *Steinbeck and Film*, edited by J. R. Millichap, Ungar, 1983, pp. 28–42.

Pugh, Scott, "Horrifying Conclusions: Making Sense of Endings in Steinbeck's Fiction," in *John Steinbeck's Global Dimensions*, edited by Kyoko Ariki, Luchen Li, and Scott Pugh, Scarecrow Press, 2008, pp. 105–14.

Shillinglaw, Susan, "The Book Club that Brought Oprah's Book Club Back: *East of Eden*," in *Steinbeck Studies*, Martha Heasley Cox Center for Steinbeck Studies, Vol. 15, No. 1, Spring 2004, pp. 136–140.

Steinbeck, John, *East of Eden*, Penguin, 2002.

———, *Journal of a Novel: The East of Eden Letters*, Penguin, 1990.

FURTHER READING

Cahir, Linda Costanzo, *Literature into Film: Theory and Practical Approaches*, McFarland & Company, 2006.
    Cahir presents a detailed discussion, with an emphasis on film theory, of the relationship between original works of literature and their film adaptations.

Internet Movie Database (IMDb), entry on James Dean. http://www.imdb.com/name/nm0000015.

IMDb provides comprehensive information on the projects of people involved in the film industry. Dean's entry contains a complete list of films and television programs in which he acted, along with links to further information on each film.

Kazan, Elia, *Kazan on Directing*, Vintage, 2010.

This book includes notes and journal entries by Kazan relating to almost all his films, from the most significan to the nearly forgotten. The book includes Kazan's essay "The Pleasure of Directing," which outlines his ideas on the craft of directing films.

Lynch, Audry L., *The Rebel Figure in American Literature and Film: The Interconnectedness of John Steinbeck and James Dean*, Mellen Press, 2009.

This study examines the intriguing similarities between John Steinbeck and James Dean, and explores Steinbeck's feelings about Dean's portrayal of Cal Trask.

The Great Train Robbery

MICHAEL CRICHTON

1975

The Great Train Robbery (1975) is a historical novel by Michael Crichton about a group of criminals who steal several hundred pounds of gold bullion from a moving train in England in 1855. The novel is based very loosely on a real event that Crichton became familiar with while reading about the criminal underclass in Victorian London. *The Great Train Robbery* was Crichton's third novel published under his own name, though he had already achieved great success as a mystery and suspense writer working under various pseudonyms, and it was his first venture into writing about a bygone era. The novel was a success, and Crichton continued his interest in historical fiction with his next novel, *Eaters of the Dead* (1976).

Though *The Great Train Robbery* focuses mainly on an elaborate plot to steal gold, Crichton provides many fascinating glimpses into Victorian life, particularly into the harsh conditions endured by London's poor and destitute in the slum area known as "the Holy Land." The characters in the book also use a great deal of Victorian slang; some readers may find these words confusing in the early chapters, but most of the terms are either explained or easily understood when taken in context.

The Great Train Robbery was successful enough as a novel to attract interest in a film adaptation, which was written and directed by Crichton in 1979. The film, starring Sean Connery,

Michael Crichton (Getty Images)

Donald Sutherland, and Lesley-Anne Down, was well received, and Crichton won an Edgar Award from the Mystery Writers of America for Best Screenplay in 1980. Although *The Great Train Robbery* has become overshadowed by some of the author's later novels, such as *Jurassic Park* (1990) and *State of Fear* (2004), it remains a beloved tale of a most unusual heist set in a fascinating historical era.

AUTHOR BIOGRAPHY

Crichton was born on October 23, 1942, in Chicago, Illinois. His father was a journalist who was drafted to fight in World War II soon after his son was born. By the time he was thirteen years old, Crichton was six feet, seven inches tall; the shyness he experienced from being so different from other children led him to concentrate largely on reading and studying. Crichton grew up on Long Island, New York, and being around his journalist father led him to view writing as a

natural career choice. He even sold a travel article to the *New York Times*—about Sunset Crater National Monument in Arizona, which he visited with his family—when he was only fourteen. While attending college at Harvard, however, he feared that writing was not a realistic career choice, so he chose instead to become a doctor.

Yet Crichton continued to write and even helped to pay for medical school by writing paperback thrillers under the pseudonym John Lange. The same year Crichton graduated from Harvard Medical School, he also won the Edgar Award from the Mystery Writers of America for his medical mystery novel *A Case of Need* (1968), originally published under the pseudonym Jeffery Hudson.

His earliest successes under his own name were *The Andromeda Strain* (1969) and *The Terminal Man* (1972), both thrillers with science-fiction premises and heavily influenced by his knowledge of medicine. After 1972, Crichton wrote novels only under his own name, and he also began working as a screenwriter and director. He was inspired to write *The Great Train Robbery* (1975) after reading about the criminal underworld of Victorian London, and in particular the crime on which the novel is loosely based. He later wrote and directed a film adaptation of the novel, which won an Edgar Award for Best Screenplay in 1980.

After continuing through the 1980s as a popular novelist and somewhat less popular screenwriter/director, Crichton wrote the novel that would become the defining work of his career: *Jurassic Park* (1990). The book, which tells of a wealthy businessman's attempt to recreate dinosaurs from preserved genetic material and exhibit them in an amusement park, was adapted into a film by Steven Spielberg in 1993. The film became the top-grossing film of all time (though it has since been surpassed). By the end of the 1990s, *Jurassic Park* had sold over twelve million copies in the United States alone, and Crichton was finally considered a heavyweight in commercial fiction.

Crichton continued writing at a pace of about one novel every two years, occasionally working in film and television as well. He was the co-creator of the long-running hit medical television series *ER*, which as of 2009 had earned more Emmy Award nominations than any other television show in history. His later novels include the controversial *State of Fear* (2004), in which the author argues against the idea of global climate change as a result of human activity.

Crichton died from throat cancer on November 4, 2008, at the age of sixty-six. His final two novels, *Pirate Latitudes* and an unnamed technological thriller, are due to be released in late 2009 and 2010, respectively.

PLOT SUMMARY

Part I: Preparations (May–October, 1854)

The Great Train Robbery begins with a South Eastern Railway train speeding away from London, across the surrounding countryside, at its top speed of fifty-four miles per hour. The door on the luggage van at the end of the train opens, and a young man is thrown from the train by a railway guard and dies. Soon after, a gentleman in a carriage drives by and spots the dead young man near the tracks; after confirming the man is dead, he rides away.

The gentleman is Edward Pierce, described as "a tall, handsome man in his early thirties who wore a full red beard." Shortly after, in May 1854, he meets with a man named Robert Agar, known for his ability to break into safes. As they talk, it becomes clear that the young man who was thrown from the train was known as Spring Heel Jack, and was working for Pierce at the time. Pierce is planning a large criminal endeavor and wants Agar to help him obtain "waxes," or wax impressions of keys, that will be needed to carry out the crime. Agar agrees to take part in the plan.

Pierce then meets with an acquaintance named Henry Fowler, who happens to be the general manager of Huddleston & Bradford, a banking firm responsible for providing payment to British troops fighting in the Crimean War against Russia. This involves overseeing the transport of large amounts of gold by train to the English coast at Folkestone, where it is then ferried to France. Pierce asks Fowler about a recent attempt to rob the train, referring to the incident involving Spring Heel Jack. Fowler dismisses the attempt as amateurish and lists in detail the many security measures instituted by the bank to protect the gold. He also reveals the locations for the four keys necessary to unlock the impenetrable Chubb safes in which the gold is stored aboard the train. Two of the keys are

MEDIA ADAPTATIONS

- A film adaptation of the novel, written and directed by Crichton, was released in 1979. The film stars Sean Connery as Pierce and Donald Sutherland as Agar, and was released on DVD by MGM in 1998.

- An abridged audio recording of the book, read by Michael Cumpsty, was released in 1996 by Random House Audio. It is currently available on audio cassette. The same recording was released as an audio download in 2001 and can be purchased from audible.com.

kept in the railway station, one is kept by a senior partner at the bank named Mr. Trent, and one is kept by Fowler himself. When pressed, Fowler reveals that he keeps his key around his neck at all times.

Pierce and Agar travel to the London Bridge station, where two of the safe keys are kept in the South Eastern Railway offices. Using stopwatches, they try to determine the best time for Agar to enter the offices and make wax impressions of the keys, which will allow him to create his own copies of the keys later. They conclude that entering the office by day is too risky, since there are always agents present. Even at night the area is patrolled, and Agar suggests that they employ a snakesman—a small young man or boy able to enter tight spaces—to somehow enter the office and unlock the door for Agar ahead of time. Agar notes that Clean Willy is the best snakesman, but he is currently serving a sentence in Newgate Prison, a place considered impossible to escape from. Pierce visits Clean Willy's girlfriend, Little Maggie, and tells her to get a message to him: if he can make a break from Newgate during the next public hanging, he will have a big job waiting for him.

Another of Pierce's major obstacles is Mr. Edgar Trent, the holder of one of the keys. After studying Trent's habits, Pierce cannot tell where the man keeps his key. Pierce hires a pickpocket named Teddy Burke to bump into Trent one particular morning before the man enters work at the bank; Burke is not to actually take anything from Trent but to make him suspect he might have had his pockets picked. Burke does as instructed, and Trent immediately feels for the key in his side pocket—indicating that he stores the key at home and brings it with him only on the days he needs to access the safes for the gold shipment. Pierce spends additional weeks looking for some indication of Trent's recreational habits, hoping for a way to insinuate himself into the man's household. Finally, he discovers that Trent is involved in a sport known as "ratting," in which an owner places his dog in a small space with a large number of rats and bets on the number of rats the dog can kill within a set time limit.

Pierce makes contact with Trent at a ratting event, where Trent's bulldog is unsuccessful at killing the required number of rats. Pierce compliments Trent on his dog nonetheless, and offers to broker the acquisition of another fighting dog for him. During their conversation, Trent discovers that Pierce is unmarried; with an eligible daughter, Elizabeth, at home growing older by the day, Trent strikes upon the idea of introducing Pierce to Elizabeth, hoping to make a match. Trent invites Pierce to his house, where he meets the less-than-pretty Elizabeth. Pierce feigns interest in the woman, hoping it will help him gain insight into where her father keeps his safe key hidden.

In August 1854, Pierce reserves a room for a group in a rooming house overlooking Newgate Square, ostensibly to watch the public hanging of a murderess named Emma Barnes. In truth, Pierce awaits Clean Willy's escape, and this is their designated meeting place. As everyone focuses their attention on the impending execution outside the prison walls, Willy scales the inside wall and grabs the spike-covered iron bar that lines the top. Bleeding profusely, he manages to climb over the spikes and jump to the roof of a nearby building. He makes his way to the building where Pierce and the others wait for him. When he enters the room, he is still bleeding badly and barely conscious. He is bandaged and given some pain medicine, then he is dressed in a woman's gown and carried out of the building as if faint from the sight of the hanging.

Willy is kept at Pierce's house, both for his own recovery and to keep him in hiding until the authorities give up looking for the escaped convict. He spends a great deal of time with Miss Miriam, Pierce's female companion and a key member of the robbery team. After the newspapers declare that he has been found dead—an obvious lie meant to conveniently close the case—Willy is able to leave the house and await instructions for the job Pierce has in mind for him.

Meanwhile, Pierce continues to woo Elizabeth Trent. While riding on horseback one afternoon in October, Elizabeth confides in Pierce, saying that she believes her father might be drinking before work on the days he handles the monthly gold delivery. She suspects this because he goes down into the wine cellar alone on the morning of each delivery, something he never does at any other time. This bit of information confirms to Pierce that Trent keeps his safe key somewhere in the wine cellar of his home.

Part II: The Keys (November, 1854–February, 1855)

In November 1854, Pierce is approached by his acquaintance Fowler, who asks a favor. Fowler has apparently contracted a venereal disease, and believes—as some did during that era—that the only way to cure it is by having sexual intercourse with a virgin. Fowler asks for Pierce's help in finding a "fresh" girl to help him alleviate his condition. Seeing the perfect opportunity to copy Fowler's key—otherwise permanently kept around the man's neck—Pierce makes the arrangements.

Meanwhile, Pierce and his team come up with a way to infiltrate the Trent household. Miriam pulls up to the front door of the house in her carriage, thereby distracting the doorman and luring him away from the entrance as Pierce and Agar sneak inside. They quickly make their way to the cellar and begin searching for the safe key. After almost an hour of searching, they find it and make a wax impression of it. Then another of Pierce's accomplices, a coachman named Barlow, creates a diversion by releasing rats into the dog pen near the servants' quarters. This allows Pierce and Agar to slip undetected out the front door.

Pierce then focuses on Fowler's key. He sets up a meeting between Fowler and a young girl named Sarah; alone in their room—or so Fowler believes—Sarah undresses him and removes the key from around his neck, placing it near a red velvet curtain. While Fowler and Sarah are occupied, a hand reaches around the curtain and takes the key to make a copy, then returns it unnoticed.

With the first two keys copied, Pierce and Agar return their attention to the two keys in the office of the railway station. They are dismayed to discover that the railway has hired a security guard to stand directly outside the office at night; the only chance to access the office is during his nightly trip to the restroom, which lasts scarcely more than a minute.

Meanwhile, Pierce continues to advance other elements of the plan. He has his coachman Barlow steal a policeman's uniform, and he arranges for a man to obtain a leopard for him. Then, back at the railway station, he hires a boy to pretend to steal something from Miriam while Barlow, dressed as a policeman, fakes a pursuit. As instructed, the boy runs into the railway office—where the keys are kept—and breaks out one of the windows, in what appears to be an attempt to escape. Barlow grabs the boy, making it appear that he is being arrested. In truth, it was all part of the plan: with the window broken out, Clean Willy will be able to enter the office at night undetected and unlock both the front door and the key cabinet in order to give Agar enough time to make impressions of the final two keys.

On the night of January 9, 1855, Clean Willy climbs onto the roof of the railway station and quietly enters the office through the broken window. He unlocks the key cabinet and front door, with Pierce acting as a drunk to distract the guard in case Willy makes noise. As soon as the security guard in front of the office leaves for the restroom, Agar runs out from his hiding place and enters the office. One of the wax blanks cracks as he removes the key, but he has a spare blank with him and manages to make the impressions and clear out of the office just before the security guard returns.

With all the keys copied, Pierce then works on the last, and perhaps most critical, part of the plan. He meets with a railway guard named Burgess, a man at the bottom of the company pay scale who has a sick child at home. Pierce offers the man two hundred pounds to "look away" while on duty in the luggage van. Pierce assures Burgess that he will not be a suspect in whatever transpires. Desperate for money, Burgess accepts. Pierce also orders two hundred and fifty pounds of lead shot, an amount so great that it vexes his supplier.

On February 17, Agar boards the luggage van of the gold delivery train along with a caged leopard. Agar pretends to be the animal's keeper and insists on riding in the luggage van in case anything should happen with the exotic and dangerous animal. The guard of the luggage van, Burgess, soon realizes that Agar is there not to watch the leopard but to try out his home-made copies of the safe keys. After making adjustments to each one, Agar finally ends up with a full set of working keys. However, he does not touch the gold . . . yet.

Part III: Delays and Difficulties (March–May, 1855)

Pierce and his crew plan to rob the gold shipment on March 14, in much the same way that Agar had already done: by having Agar ride in the luggage van along with Burgess, open the safes, toss the gold off the train to a waiting Barlow somewhere along an isolated stretch of track, and replace the gold with lead shot of comparable weight to conceal the crime for as long as possible. However, the death of Czar Nicholas I of Russia at the beginning of March causes changes in the delivery schedule. The following month, their informant gives them the incorrect date for the delivery, causing them to be at the station a day too late. They decide to rob the train on May 22, the next delivery date.

However, complications continue to arise. First, the two Chubb safes are removed from the luggage van and returned to the manufacturer for an unknown reason. Fearful that the locks might be changed, Pierce enlists Miriam to meet with the head of the safe company, pretending to be a very wealthy woman in need of a safe for her valuables. While at the safe factory, she discovers that the railway safes are not being altered in any way that will affect the robbery. The plan moves forward.

Several days before the robbery, however, Pierce receives a letter from Clean Willy, asking for a meeting. Willy asks Pierce for more money, even though he has already been paid for his part. Pierce gives him ten pounds, but suspects—correctly—that the meeting was set up so that Willy could point out Pierce to the police, who are watching. Pierce and Agar assume that Willy was arrested for some other crime, and in order to reduce his sentence, offered to lead the police to the mastermind of a much bigger criminal endeavor. Though the police try to keep an eye on Pierce, he is able to elude them and offers no hint of the crime he is planning—nor can they get Willy to provide specifics, since information is the only leverage he has with the police. As payback for Willy's betrayal, Barlow tracks him down and strangles him.

In order to further throw the police off their true plans, Pierce visits a pawnshop owner that he suspects is a police informant. He leads the pawnshop owner—and therefore the police—to believe he is going to rob the payroll of a company in Greenwich, two days after the actual planned train robbery.

The night before the robbery, Burgess brings terrible news. Security measures for the luggage van have been stepped up considerably; in addition to a padlock being placed on the outside of the car, a new security agent at the station ensures that no unauthorized personnel be allowed inside the car at any time. This calls for a drastic change in plans, though Pierce refuses to postpone the robbery.

The next morning, Miriam—wearing the plain black dress of a servant girl—accompanies a casket, which is to be loaded into the luggage car of the South Eastern Railway train to Folkestone. Inside the casket is Agar, covered in greenish makeup and in the smell of a dead animal in an attempt to pass for a corpse. The ruse is successful, and Agar is loaded into the luggage car. Meanwhile, Pierce accompanies Miriam to a compartment at the rear of the first-class section of the train. His plan—to climb from the compartment window and move backward across the tops of the train cars until he reaches the luggage car—is almost ruined when his acquaintance Fowler appears and insists on riding with him. However, Miriam gets Fowler to take her back to his own compartment, leaving Pierce free to follow his plan.

Part IV: The Great Train Robbery (May, 1855)

Inside the luggage car, the guard Burgess helps Agar out of the coffin. Agar unlocks the safes and removes the gold, then waits for Pierce to come and unlock the car from the outside. Pierce climbs out the window of his compartment and makes his way carefully back to the luggage car. He drops ropes down two ventilation windows in the top of the car, and Agar grabs hold. Pierce then ties the rope to himself and, with Agar holding tight, lowers himself down to the outside padlock. He manages to unlock it and hide inside the car just before the train passes the station at Godstone.

Once inside the car, Pierce and Agar prepare to drop the gold at an isolated point along the

track where Barlow waits to retrieve it. It is then that Pierce discovers another unforeseen problem: the soot from the train's smoke has blackened both his face and clothes, which would undoubtedly raise suspicions regarding his actions. Pierce takes Agar's clothes, since he will be hidden in the casket anyway. After dropping the gold, Pierce begins his slow and dangerous return trip across the tops of the train cars. When he re-enters his compartment, he changes clothes and attempts to remove the soot from his skin.

As Pierce disembarks from the train, Fowler spots him and comments on his ghostly pallor. Luckily, Fowler concludes that Pierce is ill from the train ride, and no suspicion is raised. Barlow arrives in a coach, and collects Miriam, Agar's "coffin," and Pierce. The robbery has been pulled off without detection.

The following day, after the gold shipment arrives in France, it is discovered that the gold bars have been replaced with lead shot. This prompts an investigation that lasts several months, with English officials blaming the French, and French officials pointing fingers at the English. Even after it is determined that the robbery must have taken place during the train journey from London to Folkestone, no legitimate suspects are uncovered.

Part V: Arrest and Trial (November, 1856–August, 1857)

Eighteen months later, the police pick up a woman suspected of robbing a drunkard. In an effort to avoid arrest, the woman claims to have information about the crime that has come to be known as the Great Train Robbery. The woman is Alice Nelson, mistress of Robert Agar. Agar, already in Newgate prison on a forgery charge unrelated to the robbery, tells the police everything after they threaten to ship him off to Australia, which was then still functioning as a penal colony for British criminals.

The police arrest Pierce and the railway guard Burgess and put all three men on trial. Agar is sent to Australia, despite his cooperation with police; he later becomes a successful businessman there. When Pierce is asked by the prosecutor why he committed such a diabolical crime, his answer is simple: "I wanted the money." After his testimony, Pierce is taken from the court to a police van. He passes by a crowd of admirers; one old woman grabs him and kisses him on the mouth. The old woman is actually Miriam in disguise, and she passes a key for his handcuffs from her mouth to his. Pierce boards the police van, which is actually driven by his coachman Barlow, and makes his escape. Pierce, Miriam, and Barlow are never seen again, nor is the money that was stolen in the Great Train Robbery.

CHARACTERS

Robert Agar

Robert Agar is an expert "screwsman," a criminal who specializes in the opening of locks and safes. Prior to becoming a criminal, Agar worked in a matchstick factory; the phosphorous that permeated the air in the factory gave him a chronic lung problem. Pierce recruits Agar to participate in the Great Train Robbery because the safes that contain the gold are locked with four different keys. Agar is instrumental in making copies of the four keys and even poses as a corpse to gain access to the luggage car on the day of the robbery. Long after the robbery, Agar is arrested for an unrelated crime—forgery—and he does not say anything that will link him to the robbery. However, when his mistress, Alice Nelson, is arrested for stealing from drunks, she immediately reveals what she knows about the robbery in an attempt to stay out of jail. After being threatened with transportation to Australia, Agar reluctantly admits to his part in the robbery. In the end, he is still sent to Australia, where he becomes a wealthy and respected man.

Barlow

Barlow is Pierce's loyal coachman and henchman, described as a tough brute with a white scar across his forehead. Though Barlow rarely speaks, he carries out many important tasks in Pierce's robbery scheme. In addition to killing Clean Willy before he can provide more information to Scotland Yard, Barlow is the man responsible for picking up the gold bars that Pierce and Agar toss from the moving train during the robbery. Although Pierce and Agar are both arrested and tried for their part in the crime, Barlow is never apprehended and even plays a crucial role in Pierce's escape outside the courthouse.

Richard Burgess

Richard Burgess is a "Mary Blaine scrob," or a security guard who works for the railway company. He is the man scheduled to ride inside the luggage car during the monthly gold shipments from London to Folkestone. Pierce offers Burgess two hundred pounds to participate minimally and keep quiet about the robbery, and Burgess accepts. Burgess takes the money because his oldest child is chronically ill and requires frequent, expensive trips to the doctor. He assists in the robbery by letting Agar out of his coffin and is arrested with Pierce many months after the robbery.

Teddy Burke

Teddy Burke is a pickpocket hired by Pierce to carry out a deliberately unsuccessful attempt at picking Edgar Trent's pockets. The goal is to worry Trent and see if he reaches for his safe key to ensure it is still there. He does, and this confirms to Pierce that Trent brings the key with him from home rather than leaving it somewhere inside the bank.

Chokee Bill

Chokee Bill is a pawnshop owner in Battersea described as "a red-faced Irishman whose complexion gave the appearance of perpetual near strangulation." Pierce and his team believe that in addition to being a pawnshop owner, Bill is a police informant. In the days prior to the robbery, Pierce visits Chokee Bill and leads him to believe that Pierce and his crew are going to commit an entirely different crime than the one they are actually planning.

Laurence Chubb

Laurence Chubb is the head of Chubb's, the premier safe manufacturer in England. The safes located in the South Eastern Railway luggage car are Chubb safes. When the safes are removed from the car, Miss Miriam visits Laurence Chubb at the company's factory and pretends to be interested in buying a safe. While there, she questions Chubb about the luggage car safes to find out why they were removed.

Clean Willy

Clean Willy is a "snakesman," a specialist among criminal types who can get through small passages. Agar contends that the only way to access the safe keys in the railway office is by making use of a good snakesman. Clean Willy has a reputation as the best snakesman around, but he is imprisoned at Newgate—a fortress that everyone believes is impossible to escape from. Pierce sends word to Clean Willy, telling him to attempt an escape during the next public execution. Willy successfully scales the prison wall and climbs over the razor-sharp spike wheels lining the top. After successfully infiltrating the railway office, Willy later gets arrested for an unrelated matter and "turns nose," becoming an informant for the police. However, he does not provide details regarding the robbery. Under orders from Pierce, Barlow strangles Clean Willy for betraying the group.

Dalby

Dalby is the station sergeant on duty when Alice Nelson is arrested. He is also the person to whom she offers information about the perpetrators of the Great Train Robbery. Dalby, sensing that Nelson is telling the truth, contacts Scotland Yard, which leads to the arrest of Pierce and Burgess.

Henry Fowler

Henry Fowler is the general manager of Huddleston & Bradford, the banking firm tasked with supplying the gold that is used to pay British soldiers fighting in the Crimean War. Fowler is responsible for one of the four keys to the safes used to store the gold aboard the South Eastern Railway luggage car. He keeps the key around his neck at all times, including while sleeping and showering. Pierce and Agar manage to copy the key by furnishing Fowler with a young prostitute who removes the key as she undresses Fowler; the key is taken, copied, and returned before Fowler notices.

Harkins

Harkins is an "eel-skinner," a maker of weapons and bullets for criminals, who works in Manchester. Pierce orders fifty pounds of lead shot from Harkins; this is just one of five orders Pierce places, in order to obtain enough lead shot to equal the weight of the gold he and his gang plan to steal.

Edward Harranby

Harranby is the Scotland Yard officer in charge of undercover agents and informers. When Clean Willy turns informant against Pierce—or John Simms, as he is known—it is Harranby who leads the investigation. Harranby is also the official who pressures Agar into confessing the crime by threatening him with transportation to Australia.

Henson

Henson is a "skipper," a homeless person who takes refuge in a confined space such as an outhouse in order to sleep undisturbed. Agar hires Henson to hide in a crate in the railway station overnight for three nights; Henson keeps track of the station security guard's movements so Pierce and Agar can figure out when they might have an opportunity to break into the office and copy the safe keys.

Constable Johnson

Constable Johnson is the officer who arrests Alice Nelson, Robert Agar's mistress, for robbing a drunk on Guy Fawkes Day (November 5) in 1856. This is what ultimately leads to the arrest and trial of three of the main participants in the Great Train Robbery.

Jeremy Johnson

Jeremy Johnson runs a livery stable that includes a side business training and selling fighting dogs. Pierce visits Johnson and purchases his fiercest dog as a way to establish a relationship with Edgar Trent.

Brigid Lawson

See Miss Miriam

McPherson

McPherson is the Scottish nephew of the London Bridge Station dispatcher, hired as a security guard just before the robbery. McPherson is an eagle-eyed rule enforcer, ensuring that no one other than the guard on duty be allowed to ride in the luggage car of the train. However, his quick and inadequate inspection of a coffin containing Agar's "corpse" allows the robbery to be carried off as planned.

Miss Miriam

Miss Miriam is the mysterious partner of Edward Pierce, the mastermind of the Great Train Robbery. Although she remains largely behind the scenes, she plays key roles in the successful execution of the plot. For example, when Pierce needs to find out why the Chubb safes have been removed from the South Eastern Railway train, Miriam visits the owner of Chubb's and pretends to be an aristocrat looking to make a purchase; this allows her to find out why the safes were moved without arousing suspicion. Miriam also plays the role of a servant girl whose brother has died, which is instrumental in getting Agar access to the luggage car—by way of a coffin. Miss Miriam is never apprehended by authorities, and it appears that she helps Pierce escape after his trial.

Edna Molloy

Edna Molloy is a woman who runs a boarding-house overlooking Newgate Square, adjacent to Newgate Prison. It is here that public hangings of criminals are carried out in London. Pierce rents a room from Molloy during the hanging of Emma Barnes, not for the purpose of watching the execution but to provide Clean Willy a safe haven after he escapes from Newgate.

Alice Nelson

Alice Nelson is Robert Agar's mistress, left alone after the robbery when Agar is jailed for an unrelated crime. Nelson, desperate for money and unable to get access to Agar's proceeds from the robbery, resorts to "bug-hunting," stealing from drunks. She is apprehended by Constable Johnson on Guy Fawkes Day in 1856. Because of her fear of going to prison, Nelson offers to tell the police about the robbery with the hope that it will secure her freedom.

Edward Pierce

Edward Pierce is the mastermind behind the Great Train Robbery. He is a "putter-up," a criminal with enough money to devise and fund large-scale criminal endeavors. He is described as tall, handsome, always refined in dress and manner, and sporting a red beard. The true facts of his early life are unknown, though he claims to be descended from a distinguished family in the Midlands. He has two very loyal partners: the chameleon-like Miss Miriam, who appears to be his mistress; and Barlow, a coachman who also performs any tasks that might require brute violence.

Although Pierce presents the image of a proper gentleman, he has no problem using violence to further his own ends or to punish those who cross him. For example, he hires Spring Heel Jack to infiltrate the luggage car of the South Eastern Railway train he plans to rob, which results in Jack being thrown from the train and killed. He also orders the killing of Clean Willy after Willy tells the police of Pierce's plan. Although he is eventually arrested and tried for the robbery, his partners Miss Miriam and Barlow help him escape, and Pierce—like the stolen gold—is never seen again.

Sarah

Sarah is a young prostitute whose company Pierce arranges for Henry Fowler, at Fowler's request. Working under Pierce's direction, Sarah removes Fowler's safe key when she undresses him, which allows Pierce and Agar to make a wax impression of the key.

Jonathan Sharp

Sharp is Edward Harranby's assistant at Scotland Yard. He routinely gets blamed when the investigation of Pierce does not go as planned—for example, when Clean Willy is killed or when tailing agents are not able to keep track of Pierce.

Jimmy Shaw

Jimmy Shaw is a former boxer and the owner of a pub named Queen's Head. He runs a ratting pit in the upstairs room of the pub, where gentlemen bring their fighting dogs to take on large numbers of rats as others bet on the spectacle. Pierce introduces himself to Edgar Trent at one of these ratting events, gaining the man's trust in an effort to discover where he hides his safe key.

Charlotte Simms

See Miss Miriam

John Simms

See Edward Pierce

Spring Heel Jack

Spring Heel Jack is a pickpocket hired by Pierce to infiltrate the luggage car of the South Eastern Railway train from London to Folkestone—the one that carries monthly gold shipments bound for British soldiers in the Crimea. At the beginning of the novel, Spring Heel Jack is thrown from the speeding luggage car by a security guard, and he dies from his injuries.

Andrew Taggert

Andrew Taggert is a former convict known to operate as a horse thief and a "christener," a person who can take in stolen goods and make them appear to have been legitimately obtained. Pierce meets with Taggert in December 1854 and asks Taggert to acquire a leopard for him as part of the robbery plan.

Edgar Trent

Edgar Trent is the senior partner at the banking firm of Huddleston & Bradford. He is responsible for one of the four keys required to open the safes aboard the luggage car of the South Eastern Railway train that Pierce intends to rob. Trent is a stiff, routine-oriented man who partakes in few social activities. Pierce discovers, however, that Trent is involved in ratting, an illegal sport that involves placing a dog in a pit with live rats to see how many rats the dog can kill in a set period of time. This allows Pierce to become acquainted with Trent, who views Pierce as a prospective suitor for his daughter Elizabeth. It is through Elizabeth that Pierce discovers the location of Trent's key. Trent dies not long after Pierce and his crew are arrested and tried for the robbery.

Elizabeth Trent

Elizabeth Trent is Edgar Trent's daughter. Still single at twenty-nine, she is in danger of becoming a lasting burden on her parents' household, as well as a source of family shame among the higher social circles. When Edgar Trent meets the confessed bachelor Pierce, he sees Pierce as a potential suitor for his daughter. Pierce pretends to be interested in Elizabeth—whose lack of beauty is notable—in an attempt to find out where her father keeps his safe key. After discovering this, he breaks off communication with Elizabeth. When he runs into her one day several months later, he pretends that he has become engaged to a French woman. At the end of the book, the author notes that Elizabeth goes on to marry Sir Percival Harlow in 1858.

THEMES

The Nature of Criminal Behavior

One theme that appears throughout the novel is the definition and cause of criminal behavior. Although fraud, embezzlement, and forgeries were often committed by members of the upper classes, the author notes that still there remained the notion that "criminal behavior sprang from poverty, injustice, oppression, and lack of education. It was almost a matter of definition: a person who was not from the criminal class could not be committing a crime." In the novel, Crichton offers many examples of individuals who appear little more than victims of awful circumstances; Little Maggie, for example, is a prostitute with a boyfriend in prison, yet she is only twelve years old. At the same time, he offers examples of acts committed by the wealthy and powerful that might objectively be viewed as far worse crimes—for example, the incompetent military leadership of Lord Cardigan that leads to the unnecessary deaths of five hundred British soldiers. Still, Pierce's ultimate reason for committing the robbery is not described as a

forgivable product of his wretched upbringing; as he puts it quite simply, "I wanted the money."

The Gap between the Social Classes

Mid-Victorian England was marked by rigid class distinctions that were more or less determined by birth. At the top of the social ladder was the landed aristocracy. This class held noble titles and land, from which they derived their income (in the form of rent and profits from agricultural or other pursuits conducted on their land). These wealthy landowners managed their estates, but they did not "work" for a living. Indeed, working was seen as something distinctly beneath the stature of a nobleman. Women of the upper-classes did not work either, and lived upon the incomes of their fathers or husbands, or, if they failed to find a suitably rich husband, on the largesse of one of their male relatives. Beneath the aristocracy was the merchant class—business owners who did work, quite hard, for their livings and often became very wealthy in the process. In fact, many members of the merchant class became far wealthier than many aristocrats. This led to some tension between these classes, as the rich merchants strove to find their way into the aristocracy (a difficult, but not impossible, process), and the aristocrats strove to differentiate themselves in any way possible from the ambitious merchants. The largest class, however, was the working poor. The poor lived without benefit of education, often in dangerous and unsanitary conditions, and they had little hope of moving up the social ranks.

In his depiction of Victorian London, Crichton offers a stark portrayal of the differences between the upper classes and the lower classes of the time period. The wealthy, like Edgar Trent, live in estates staffed by various specialized servants and are very concerned—at least on the surface—with maintaining decorum and propriety through their words, behavior, and dress. Their biggest concerns center on how they and their family appear to others in their social class; for example, Elizabeth Trent, at age twenty-nine, is considered to be a "problem" for her family because she has not yet found a prospective suitor. By contrast, the lower classes are concerned only with surviving from day to day on meager earnings or on what they can steal. They live in crowded conditions, with some homeless people—known as skippers—specially skilled in finding small spaces like outhouses in which to sleep undisturbed. While upper-class women like Elizabeth

TOPICS FOR FURTHER STUDY

- One of the key questions in *The Great Train Robbery* is whether or not crimes are committed because of desperate circumstances or because of greed. Based on the text, which position do you think the author supports? In your opinion, which of the two factors is more likely to influence someone to commit a crime? Why? Write a short essay in which you provide specific examples from the book to support your position.

- Many different groups of professionals utilize jargon, a special collection of words or phrases specific to a single occupation or activity. In *The Great Train Robbery*, a great deal of jargon is used by professional criminals. Sometimes, this involves completely made-up words, such as "snakesman." Often, however, it involves the use of common words in a new context, such as "dipper," which is used to describe a pickpocket. Choose a single occupation or group that utilizes jargon and create a glossary defining at least ten terms specific to that group or occupation. Why do you think these terms needed to be created for the people who use them?

- In modern times, there is much debate over the depiction of violence on television, in films, and in video games. Many people believe that such depictions are harmful, and that the media is causing people to become increasingly tolerant of grisly violence. In *The Great Train Robbery*, Crichton describes brutal activities such as "ratting" and public hangings, which are attended by large, enthusiastic audiences. How do these displays differ from violence in modern media? In your opinion, has the public developed a taste for more and more violent entertainment since the 1850s? Has the tolerance for violence remained about the same? Or has society become less tolerant of violence? Write a short essay explaining your answer. Be sure to provide reasons and examples to support your position.

- *The Great Train Robbery* takes place mainly in 1855. Make a list of common items you interact with on a typical day—for example, a toothbrush, a telephone, or a computer—and determine whether or not each of these items existed in 1855. If you had to live in 1855, which items do you think you would miss the most? Why?

- *The Great Train Robbery* is a work of fiction based on a real crime. Read another piece of fiction that features a famous crime, such as *Kidnapped* by Robert Louis Stevenson, or Truman Capote's *In Cold Blood*. Using the library and the Internet, research the facts of the actual crime. Does the author of the fictional version change any important facts of the crimes? In what other ways does the fictional version differ from the factual version of events? Why do you think the author made the changes he or she made? What effect do they have? Write your analysis in essay form.

Trent feel socially disgraced for being without suitors in their twenties, lower-class girls like Little Maggie and Sarah are forced to work as prostitutes while still in their early teens just so they can survive.

One passage in particular emphasizes the stark contrast between the classes. Not far from the decaying structures jammed with the poor, the upper-class Trents are having a brand-new "ruin" installed on their vast rear lawn. The ruin is a water mill carefully constructed—at great expense—to appear old and dilapidated. "But of course," Mrs. Trent notes, "we must wait for the weeds to grow up around the site before it takes on the proper appearance." The rich treat "ruin" as an amusement, while the poor live in ruin every day.

Sean Connery as Pierce and Lesley-Anne Down as Miriam in the 1979 film version of The Great Train Robbery *(© Sunset Boulevard / Corbis)*

STYLE

The Historical Novel

Historical novels are set in a past time period and often focus on recreating the "feel" of that period for modern readers. This is typically done through detailed descriptions of dress, customs, and daily activities, as well as referencing important historical events or historical figures from that period. Often the main characters in a historical novel are fictional, though some historical novels focus on a well-known historical figure in an attempt to dramatize the known facts of his or her life. Although some examples of historical fiction—or at least fictionalized historical chronicles—are arguably found in medieval Chinese and English literature, the works of Sir Walter Scott in the early 1800s are generally acknowledged as the first significant and fully-formed examples of the historical novel.

The Great Train Robbery is set over a century before it was written and contains a mix of fact and fiction. Like many historical novels, it contains a great deal of information intended to provide context for the reader. For example, Crichton explains how trains at the time allowed people to travel faster than ever before in human history, which led to some confusion regarding the consequences and risks of moving at such high rates of speed. Crichton also explains the enormous difficulties involved in stealing objects contained within a safe, at a time when dynamite had not yet been invented.

Victorian Slang

In *The Great Train Robbery*, Crichton makes ample use of Victorian slang, particularly the special jargon employed by the British criminal underclass of the era. For example, every different type of criminal has a specialized job

COMPARE
&
CONTRAST

- **1850s:** Dog fighting sports such as ratting are illegal in places like London, yet remain popular.

  1970s: Philosopher Peter Singer publishes the book *Animal Liberation* (1975), which was instrumental in launching the animal rights movement.

  Today: A resurgence in the popularity of dog fighting becomes a widespread problem in the United States. In 2007, Atlanta Falcons quarterback Michael Vick is convicted of participating in a major dog-fighting ring.

- **1850s:** The population of London is about three million, and rapidly growing. A large portion of its inhabitants live in dirty, dangerous, overcrowded slums.

  1970s: The population of London is about 7.5 million. It is a difficult decade in London, marked by high unemployment, social

unrest, and terrorist attacks by the Irish Republican Army.

  Today: The population of London is just over seven million. A global economic downturn that starts in 2008 drives up unemployment rates throughout Great Britain.

- **1850s:** The British public is shocked by the theft of twelve thousand pounds' worth of gold from on board a moving train.

  1970s: A robbery at Lloyds Bank on Baker Street in London nets its perpetrators approximately three million pounds in cash and gold. It also spawns urban legends and conspiracy theories about possible cover-ups of the crime.

  Today: In 2006, the largest amount of cash ever stolen in a single robbery in Great Britain—over fifty-three million pounds—occurs at a Securitas Cash Management Ltd. Depot in Kent.

description; a pickpocket is known as a "dipper," a thug is a "cosher," a lookout is a "crow," and someone who robs drunks is a "bug-hunter." To "snaffle" is to steal, a "pogue" is the item or items being stolen, and a "lay" is a planned criminal endeavor that could land its participants "in the stir," or in prison. This special language conveys to the reader the notion that the criminal subculture is both extensive and impenetrable by mainstream society. It also lends an authentic flavor of the time period in which the tale is set.

HISTORICAL CONTEXT

The Height of the Victorian Era
The Victorian era is defined by the reign of Queen Victoria of the United Kingdom. She took the throne in 1837 at the age of eighteen and ruled until her death in 1901. This era is known for the rapid expansion of industry and urban centers in England and other countries, as

well as the growth of a relatively wealthy middle class. As Crichton notes in the novel, the population of London tripled in the first half of the nineteenth century and nearly doubled again by the end of Victoria's reign. Though the era is generally regarded as a peaceful and prosperous one, conflicts such as the Crimean War—in which the United Kingdom, France, and others battled the Russian Empire—and the Indian Rebellion of 1857 were indications that Britain's military might was not a guarantee of order and unquestioned rule.

Another characteristic of the Victorian era notable to modern readers is the deep concern with social manners and rules of decorum, coupled with a sensationalistic curiosity about criminals and other "dreadful" topics. This split between strict morality and baser instincts is illustrated in the novel by many characters, but especially Edgar Trent; though he is known to friends and acquaintances as being punctual and extremely rigid in his observance of rules and law, he also partakes in the illegal sport of ratting in a seedy pub late at night.

The Great Train Robberies of 1855 and 1963

The Great Train Robbery is inspired by an actual crime, though Crichton retained only some of the facts of the case for his novel. On May 15, 1855, two hundred pounds of gold were stolen from the rear car of a South Eastern Railway train traveling from London to Folkestone. The main culprits were William Pierce, a former employee of South Eastern Railway, and Edward Agar, a noted criminal. They obtained impressions of the keys necessary to unlock the safes containing the gold beforehand, though no elaborate schemes were necessary; one key was pulled from the railway office while the clerks had stepped out, and the others were obtained from another bribed clerk who had access to them. Pierce and Agar, working with the guard James Burgess, sneaked into the car containing the safes and replaced the gold with bags of lead shot. However, they did not evenly distribute the shot, resulting in a discrepancy in weight measurements taken once the cargo reached France. This and other details led police to determine that the gold was stolen while it was on the train. However, it was over a year before police—with the help of Agar's testimony—managed to arrest and convict Pierce, Burgess, and the other railway employee who assisted in the crime. Agar, who was already in prison at the time, did not receive an additional sentence.

Over a century after this crime, another robbery took place that became popularly known as the "Great Train Robbery." On August 7, 1963, a postal train traveling from Glasgow to London was stopped in Buckinghamshire by what appeared to be a red signal on the track. When the train stopped, it was boarded by a crew of fifteen unarmed robbers who took control and emptied the train of its valuable parcels, estimated at the time to be worth over two million pounds (or nearly fifty million U.S. dollars when measured in 2009 values and exchange rates). In the years that followed, all the participants were ultimately arrested and jailed, though one—Ronnie Biggs—escaped from prison and lived abroad as a fugitive from British justice for about thirty-five years. In 2001, Biggs finally returned to England to finish his sentence. He was finally freed for health reasons in August 2009. At the time Crichton wrote *The Great*

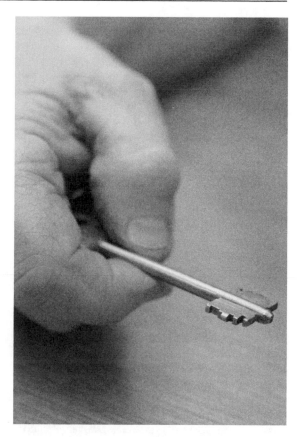

A key similar to the ones Pierce and his accomplices must copy in order to unlock the safes containing the gold bullion (Glow Images)

Train Robbery, the 1963 crime was regarded as the largest or second largest theft in British history. It was so well known that the British release of the 1979 film adaptation of Crichton's novel was titled *The First Great Train Robbery*.

CRITICAL OVERVIEW

Though Crichton was a commercially popular novelist beginning in 1969 with *The Andromeda Strain* and continuing even after his death in 2008, critics have been generally unenthusiastic about his work. When his novels receive praise, it is often coupled with lowered critical expectations regarding the quality of "commercial" fiction. Considering this, contemporary reviews of *The Great Train Robbery* were relatively positive. Many reviewers applauded Crichton's uncharacteristic subject matter; the two previous novels that had been published under his real name were both science-fiction thrillers.

Much of the praise regarding the novel concerns the detailed research that apparently went into its creation. Edward Weeks, in his review for the *Atlantic Monthly*, states that the author "tells this suspenseful story with the cool calculation of a mastermind" and calls the book "an exciting and very clever piece of fiction." Doris Grumbach, writing for the *New Republic*, states that the novel is "a cannot-put-it-down narrative" and that the author is "talented and canny." In a review for *Time*, Michael Demarest calls the author "a skillful researcher and popularizer" who "wittily lances the pomposities of 19th century England."

Other reviewers are generally complimentary, though they seem to draw a clear distinction between entertainment and literature. Peter S. Prescott, reviewing the novel for *Newsweek*, states, "This is a charming, diverting summer tale that will surely be translated into yet another medium." Allen J. Hubin, writing for the *Armchair Detective*, suggests that the author's frequent digressions to explain various aspects of Victorian life do not help to keep the book's pacing appropriately tight. However, he concludes, "Unbearable suspense the book may not have, but I found the whole affair completely fascinating." Peter Andrews, in the *New York Times Book Review*, characterizes the typical Crichton novel as "always entertaining enough to pass a pleasantly idle hour, and if you lose it or someone swipes it, you're not out that much."

L. E. Sissman's review for the *New Yorker*, on the other hand, is harsh, calling it "a nonbook by an unskilled writer." Sissman finds fault not only with the story but also with Crichton's attempts to recreate the speech and customs of the Victorian era. Sissman ultimately asserts, "To read 'The Great Train Robbery' with enjoyment through [the] cataclysm of gaffes, one must be wholly unaware of the real world."

CRITICISM

Greg Wilson

Wilson is an author, literary critic, and mythologist. In this essay, he analyzes Crichton's mixing of fact and fiction and concludes that the resulting work fails both as literature and as historical document.

> NOVELISTS WHO WRITE ABOUT HISTORICAL EVENTS AND PERIODS OWE A DUTY TO THE KNOWN TRUTH—OR AT LEAST THE SPIRIT OF THE KNOWN TRUTH. CHANGING FACTS WITHOUT A GREATER PURPOSE—JUST BECAUSE THE AUTHOR FEELS LIKE IT—IS NOT AN ACCEPTABLE COURSE OF ACTION."

In *The Great Train Robbery*, Crichton makes use of clever techniques to convince the reader that the tale is a true one. These include the use of false documents, an extensive vocabulary of period slang, and the incorporation of a nonfiction-style narratorial voice to provide historical information as asides to the main story. But the author's strangely composite creation is ultimately one that cannot satisfy on either level: it is too fictional to work as a tale of true events, and it is too factual to be classified as simply a work of imagination. So what is the point in combining fact and fiction in such a seemingly arbitrary way?

First, Crichton does an exceptional job at offering the tale as a factual account, so much so that one might ask, "But that's because it is true, is it not?" Unfortunately, the answer is an equivocal "sort of." The basics of the case are true enough; three men named Pierce, Agar, and Burgess were responsible for stealing around twelve thousand pounds' worth of gold bullion from a train traveling from London to Folkestone in 1855. The gold was locked inside two safes, for which the men had obtained copies of the keys, and they replaced the gold with lead shot in an attempt to disguise their crime for as long as possible. The men were caught over a year later after Agar's mistress revealed the truth to police, and Agar himself, already in prison for a different crime, confirmed it.

To cement the novel's veracity, Crichton deftly weaves transcripts from the trials of the men into the narrative, along with other documents such as a list of rules for office staff working in a bank and a passage from a biography of Sir John Alderston. He offers excerpts of articles from the *Illustrated London News* and the *Times*.

WHAT
DO I READ
NEXT?

- *Eaters of the Dead* (1976) is another historical novel by Crichton, this time set in the tenth century. The main character is a Muslim ambassador who ends up in the company of a group of Vikings. The bulk of the story is largely a retelling of the Anglo-Saxon epic *Beowulf*.

- *Jurassic Park* (1990) is the work that made Crichton a household name. In the book, a billionaire secretly funds a project to clone dinosaurs from preserved remnants of their DNA. His goal is to open an amusement park in which the dinosaurs are exhibited to the public; however, before his masterwork is unveiled, human error and animal ingenuity lead to deadly dinosaurs on the loose.

- *Timeline* (1999) is another of Crichton's recreations of a bygone period—in this case, fourteenth-century France. In the novel, a group of modern archeologists is sent back in time in an attempt to locate a colleague who has become trapped in the Middle Ages and bring him home.

- *Monster* (1999) by Walter Dean Myers offers a decidedly unglamorous view of robbery, in this case of a drugstore holdup gone bad. Told from the perspective of sixteen-year-old Steve Harmon, one of the accused in the murder of the shop owner, this award-winning novel offers a sobering view of juvenile justice in America.

- *State of Fear* (2004) is Crichton's most controversial work, though it employs the same familiar style—informational asides intercut with a tale of suspense—as many of his other novels. In the book, a group of radical environmentalists attempts to scare humanity into taking action against global warming; they do this by orchestrating massive natural disasters, such as a tsunami that will devastate much of the California coast. The book's controversy stems from the suggestion—both in the novel and in an afterword by Crichton—that the notion of global warming is not sufficiently supported by available data and is a product of scientists succumbing to political influence.

- *Nobody Runs Forever* (2004) by Richard Stark is a darker and more modern heist tale than *The Great Train Robbery*. Stark, the pseudonym for master mystery author Donald Westlake, continues his long line of novels about Parker, a thief whose perfect plans are inevitably proven to be fallible thanks to human nature. In *Nobody Runs Forever*, Parker joins the robbery of an armored car that, despite its appeal, has the potential to go painfully awry.

- *King of Heists: The Sensational Bank Robbery of 1878 That Shocked America* (2009) by J. North Conway is the true account of an American crime similar to the one depicted in *The Great Train Robbery*. George Leslie, an architecture student from Ohio, moved to New York in 1869 and quickly became the head of a notoriously successful bank robbery ring. His greatest success, and the subject of this work, was the theft of around three million dollars from the Manhattan Savings Institution in 1878.

He also provides quotations from contemporaries such as Miss Emily Downing and A. H. White regarding the state of women in Victorian England. All of these are completely fictional but are offered in such a way that the reader might never guess. This is, in itself, no small feat.

Crichton also utilizes a stunning amount of Victorian slang, much of it taken from the criminal class of the time. Every bit of it appears to be genuine, though some may question the author's overzealous use of these words at some points—almost as if he were challenging himself to use as many bits of slang in a single sentence as he could. Still, it successfully flavors the text with the air of legitimacy one would expect in historical fiction.

In addition to the fictional sources noted above, Crichton also provides a great deal of accurate historical information taken from real sources. He references a work by the noted Victorian chronicler Henry Mayhew, though he does not quote him directly. He does, however, quote the likes of novelists Henry James and Fyodor Dostoyevsky, and offers detailed and informative asides related to the Crimean War, the Indian Uprising, and even the construction of the Crystal Palace. Unfortunately, the source from which Crichton pulls much of his material goes strangely unmentioned: *Pickpockets, Beggars and Ratcatchers: Life in the Victorian Underworld* (1970), by Kellow Chesney. In fact, one can read through Chesney's book and find passages that inspired virtually every element in Crichton's novel. Notable examples include the section on ratting, where Crichton's version reads like a summary of Chesney's work and happens to match pretty exactly an 1850 painting used as an illustration in the Chesney book. Another notable example is in Chesney's description of the actual train robbery, in which an offhand remark about how passengers were sometimes allowed in the luggage car "for instance, if a valuable animal had to be looked after" becomes a key plot point in the Crichton novel. One wonders if the novelist ever thought of offering a share of his royalties to his contemporary, the historian he relied upon so heavily for his ideas.

A reader might be compelled to ask at this point, "What's the problem with all of this? Other historical novels combine fact and fiction, too." This is true; however, Crichton has chosen to mix fact and fiction in a way that does not benefit either. In a typical historical novel, the setting is depicted in as genuine a manner as possible, since one of the most important elements in a historical novel is the recreation of a bygone era. Typically, the main characters or small-scale events in a historical novel are made up by the author, and constitute the story the author chooses to tell in this realistic setting. Such authors, once they have established trust with the reader that the setting is genuine, are largely free to let their imaginations run wild with regard to the plot and characters. For example: a story about three men who plan and

execute an audacious robbery aboard a train in 1855? Sounds great.

But wait a moment. This is not just a tale about three men who plan and execute a robbery. This happens to be a story about three men who really existed in 1855, planning and performing a robbery that they actually did execute. If nothing were known of these men or how they did it, a novelist would be limited only by his imagination and the credulity of the reader. Unfortunately, that is not the case here. The facts are fairly well established through court testimony and several contemporary sources. So what is an author of historical fiction to do in such a case?

One option is to create an entirely fictional version of the tale, changing the details significantly enough that it will not be confused for the real thing. Knowledgeable readers might still recognize that the story was inspired by a true event, but that is more a benefit than a hindrance—a wink and a nod from the author to those in the know. In such a case, the realistic setting serves as a backdrop for an invented tale, so neither seems compromised for the sake of the other. Another option for an author is to build a story in which all the known facts are included and to fill in any gaps with the creative sparkle of the author's imagination. A fanciful example of this style of work would be *Kidnapped* (1886) by Robert Louis Stevenson, in which the details of famous, politically motivated murder are preserved and woven into an adventure tale of a young man stolen from his home to be sold as a slave. Several characters the young man meets along the way are based on actual historical figures, and though their personalities are largely pulled from the author's imagination, the story maintains the integrity of the facts known at the time. Another example is *Schindler's Ark* (1982; later published as *Schindler's List*) by Thomas Kenneally; the book was so accurate in its historical details, in fact, that there was some controversy over whether or not it should be classified as fiction. However, there are clearly many scenes in the book—unverifiable conversations and interactions—that were the product of the author's mind, working within the known constraints of fact.

Novelists who write about historical events and periods owe a duty to the known truth—or at least the spirit of the known truth. Changing facts without a greater purpose—just because the author feels like it—is not an acceptable course of action. Crichton's violations in this regard, unfortunately, are numerous and egregious. He even alters the first names of the two main characters; William Pierce becomes Edward Pierce, and Edward Agar becomes Robert Agar. Why? Only the author knows. The details of the case are altered in ways that make the whole affair more elaborate and daring, presumably for increased entertainment value, and Pierce is made into a figure with charm and bravado far exceeding what is documented by observers at the time. In fact, some sources indicate that it was Agar who led the team of robbers, a detail supported by his rather extensive life of crime compared to Pierce's true past as a lowly ticket agent for the railway. In addition, Agar—who is transported to Australia in the novel—was in reality spared a sentence for his part in the crime, since he came forward and testified against Pierce and Burgess (as well as Tester, another accomplice who has disappeared completely in the novel). Every example of court testimony included in the novel is made up, rather than being based on the actual court testimony from the trials. Most significantly, though, Pierce never escaped his sentence and disappeared with the money as he did in the novel; the last of the gold—two thousand pounds's worth—was easily discovered where Pierce buried it, inside his house. Aside from these details, the dates of both the robbery and subsequent trials are also inexplicably changed.

The fictional elements are not limited to the main events or characters in the novel, however, and this is where Crichton truly begins to destroy the verisimilitude he worked so hard to create. Rather than relying on known historical details to flesh out his world, Crichton too often invents his own even though they run contrary to reality. For example, the group of robbers view the public hanging of "notorious axe murderess" Emma Barnes, during which Clean Willy escapes from Newgate. The execution date is listed as August 28, 1854. In truth, Emma Barnes is a completely fictional creation; in fact, no women were executed by hanging in all of England in 1854 or 1855. To find a woman being hanged at Newgate, as in the novel, one would have to go back to 1848 or forward to 1862. In the context of the novel, this is such an insignificant detail that the question arises: why did Crichton feel the need to make it up at all? There were other hangings at Newgate in 1854—three, in fact, that all took place in April—

but the author preferred to toss accuracy out the window rather than make his story fit within existing historical details. One might suppose that Crichton was just tickled with the idea of an axe murderess and decided to indulge himself.

Crichton even goes so far as to use fictional sources to support his purportedly factual observations. Most of his quoted "contemporary observers" are made up, and these are the voices he relies upon to confirm assertions as varied as the importance of keys to a robber and the pressures of being the unmarried daughter of a wealthy businessman. These are such minor pieces of the work that this might seem like nitpicking. But here is the problem: there is simply no way for the average reader to discern which bits are true and which are not. This leaves readers in an "all or nothing" position, where they can accept the work as a reasonably accurate account or they can dismiss it as fiction—neither of which is respectful of the truth. Most readers, I would venture, believe that the work tells a true tale, if slightly embellished; this means that Crichton has carelessly (or intentionally) misinformed millions of readers. If that were the point of the novel—to pull a con on the reader, in a sense—then this might be seen as clever. But there is no indication that this is the author's intent at all. In addition, omniscient narrators—as in this work—are not allowed to be unreliable; it simply violates the implicit trust with which the reader approaches the work. (Rules are made to be broken, of course, but only by those who do so deliberately and with purpose—not by those who do it out of sloppiness or ignorance.) It is important to remember that Crichton specifically chose a true event to write about and then proceeded to eliminate much of the truth in favor of crude spectacle. He could have easily come up with some entirely fictional robbery, using all of the extravagant bits he created for this novel but changing the key players and circumstances, and the work would have been functionally identical to many readers. However, he did not.

The greatest disappointment in all this is that the true story, as far as it is known and documented, is interesting in ways that never make it into the novel. For example, at Pierce's sentencing, the judge actually said to him, "A greater villain than you are, I believe, does not exist" not because of his part in the infamous robbery, but because he afterward kept for himself thousands of pounds meant for Agar's

Folkestone, England, where the real-life train robbery took place. Folkestone is now a terminal point for the Channel Tunnel, which connects England to France. (Scott Barbour / Getty Images)

impoverished mistress and child while Agar was in jail. The judge's statement drew raucous applause from the court spectators; this detail alone reveals more about the Victorian age than any hijinks involving leopards and fake corpses. But since Crichton has already written what many believe to be a comprehensive account of the robbery, it is not likely the true facts will ever penetrate into the popular culture. What an odd legacy for a writer who, in the years between *The Great Train Robbery* and his death, became renowned as a champion of scientific truth; it is unfortunate that the respect with which he wrote of science was not also afforded to history.

Source: Greg Wilson, Critical Essay on Michael Crichton's *The Great Train Robbery*, *Novels for Students 34*, Gale, Cengage Learning, 2010.

Alan Cooperman

In this survey of the author's style and selected works, which appeared shortly after his death in 2008, Cooperman attempts to explain why Crichton was popular despite the negative reviews of many critics.

Michael Crichton once compared writing a novel to being deep in the bowels of a ship. "All you can see are the pipes and the grease and the fittings of the boiler room, and you have to assume the ship's exterior," he said, adding that the role of an editor is to stand on the dock and say, "Hi, I'm looking at your ship, and it's missing a bow, the front mast is crooked, and it looks to me as if your propellers are going to have to be fixed."

Despite that admission, Crichton, a physician turned author who died of cancer this week at age 66, was a master of narrative structure. Fans loved the way he mixed fact (especially science) into his fiction. Hollywood loved his action-packed, potboiler plots. But structure and pacing are paramount in Crichton's novels, and everything else—plausibility, characterization—is subservient.

Here's a small example: In *Jurassic Park* (the book, not the movie) the mathematician Ian ("I hate being right") Malcolm dies. But when *Jurassic Park* became a colossal success and Crichton sat down to write a sequel, *The Lost World*, he knew he needed Malcolm back, if only to explain the science. So Crichton simply revived him. As our review noted at the time, the ludicruously shallow explanation—"but as it turned out I was only slightly dead," Malcolm says—showed "splendid panache on the author's part."

A second key to Crichton's success was that he eschewed literary pretensions. Back in 1970, he wrote a review for *Book World* of *The Body Has a Head*, a long reflection on biology and philosophy by Gustav Eckstein. Crichton's review is a short masterpiece of savage criticism.

"Anyone floating to the surface after 800 pages of this book feels a compulsion to speak plainly," he began. "For plainly, this book represents monumental self-indulgence." He went on to mock Eckstein's pretentious statement that "a literary tone fell of itself over the writing" of the book. "One yearns to reprimand the author, and shoot his editor," Crichton wrote. "We remember Galileo, among other things, for his crisp writing style. He set the tone for all scientific writing of the last 350 years. He got to the point, said what was on his mind, and shut up."

That's a pretty good summation of what Crichton tried to do in his books and why they sold millions of copies even though critics, as you will see, have generally found his characters to be cardboard. I wish I could give you electronic links to the full texts of all these reviews, but I can't; some of them appeared so long ago that I had to retrieve them from the ProQuest Historical Newspapers database.

The Andromeda Strain (1969). Thanks partly to the hit movie, everyone knows the plot of Crichton's first novel published under his own name (he had previously written a handful under the pen name John Lange). A military satellite returns to Earth bearing a deadly microbe, and government scientists race to prevent a nuclear-cum-biological doomsday. It feels pretty dated now, but this techno-thriller was a stunning genre-bender four decades ago—as I realized this week when I dug up *Book World*'s original review. The splicing of fact and fantasy was just too much for our reviewer, British author Alex Comfort, who lamented that "science fiction has undergone an unwelcome change. It used to minister to our need for prophecy; now it ministers to our need for fear." "Worse still," he added, "we are now using real science as if it were fiction, for the physical acting out of the brainsick matter of such tales."

The Great Train Robbery (1975). The story of an 1855 gold heist aboard a steam-powered passenger train through Victorian England, this novel demonstrated Crichton's evolving talent for description and scene-setting. Many die-hard Crichton fans think it's his best. What's more, the multi-talented brainiac author himself directed the 1979 film starring Sean Connery and Donald Sutherland. But *Book World*'s reviewer, Bruce Cook, thought the book was "written directly with the requirements of the screen in mind" and said Crichton "never really gets inside his characters."

Sphere (1987). This time, the extraterrestrial threat is underwater, in a spacecraft discovered by the U.S. Navy more than 300 years after it landed on the sea floor. Real-life astronaut Michael Collins, who reviewed *Sphere* for *Book World*, waxed enthusiastic about Crichton's ability to explain how oxygen under pressure becomes toxic to humans. "These details, rather than the characters, make this book seem more believable," he wrote.

Jurassic Park (1990). Once again making full, frightening use of the biotech background Crichton gained at Harvard Medical School, Jurassic Park played on legitimate fears as we entered the era of genetic engineering, even if scientists rejected the exact mechanism he propounded for generating dinosaurs from amber-encased DNA. *Book World*'s reviewer said the novel produced "excitement in large quantities" and predicted that it would "make a terrific movie." But he didn't much care for Ian Malcolm's "extended philosophizing" about chaos theory. "Long before Malcolm has his say, this reader, at least, was hoping for some more dinosaurs to put him out of his misery," wrote science fiction author Greg Bear.

State of Fear (2004). Crichton annoyed environmentalists but made a fan of George W. Bush with this book, which sought to debunk warnings about man-made global warming and included a 20-page annotated bibliography. *Book World*'s reviewer, Dennis Drabelle, wasn't bothered by its politics but found its "flatline prose" rather dull and added, "it is my unpleasant duty to tell you that Crichton's characters are strictly from Woodville."

What do you think was Crichton's best? And what did the public see that the critics missed?

Source: Alan Cooperman, "Why Readers Loved Michael Crichton and Critics Didn't," in *Washington Post*, November 6, 2008.

Doris Grumbach

In this review, Grumbach asserts that Crichton's novel is both authentic and entertaining.

Educated readers always have a problem of conscience with crime and suspense stories. They feel guilt at enjoying them so much, and seek intellectual explanation of their appeal to them. Well, they need seek no longer, for Michael Crichton's wonderful crime-suspense-Victorian-cultural history, *The Great Train Robbery* combines the pleasures, guilt and delight of a novel of gripping entertainment with healthy slices of instruction and information interlarded...

[What Crichton] has done in this new book is extraordinary because it is authentic. Anyone who wanted to write a novel based upon England's 1855 train robbery that stunned the Victorians (contemporary accounts called it "The Crime of the Century" and "The Most Sensational Exploit of the Modern Era") could have done so from the court trial records and from a careful perusal of the classic *London Labour and the London Poor* written by Henry Mayhew in 1861–1862. Indeed I suspect Crichton may have resorted to Mayhew to find some of the criminal class jargon he uses so convincingly...

Having done his research so well, and using it in a way that convinces the reader he knows the culture of Victorian England, he has produced a cannot-put-it-down narrative about all the events that led up to the daring and successful robbery. It is a fascinating crime story during which you are involved in step-by-step strategies of a master criminal, in this case Edward Pierce, upper-class, well-to-do thief, a man of high intelligence, great patience, an infinite capacity for detail. When asked at his trial why he did the robbery, he responded with the simplicity of which only a complex mind is capable: "I wanted the money."

Crichton is talented and canny. He makes no attempt to "analyze" or "understand" his characters. He gives us his thieves, his "skippers" (people who sleep in outhouses and barns at night), his "canaries" and "dolls" straight, letting us listen to them talk in authentic street slang of the time, and educating us, incidentally, in the ways they live and make a living. We do not so much understand them—there is no fakery about the criminal mind or sociological overlay about the terrible effects of poverty on the criminal mind—as we watch them, delighting in their ingenuity, and yes, wickedly urging them on to success.

While we see how it was done, and stand by while it is being done, we learn about such matters as a "carriage fleecement," a trick of using an attractive woman to engage the butler of a wealthy house at the curb with a question about direction while two "lurkers" get into the house, make impressions of keys in wax and slip out again...

The object of the great robbery was the money that was on its way to the Crimea, the army payroll to be exact, during that war. It is "grifted," no, "gafted," no, "tooled." Whatever it is, the "pogue," that is the object of the whole scheme, is a seemingly impossible "lay" (job). But it works; and we are delighted that it does.

You learn more, you find out something about the sporting events of the day, including "ratting sports" in which a "fancy dog" or a most excellent "made dog" is sent into a ring to kill a rat against wagers as to how long it will take... You will be right there, running with the "miltonians" (police), or the "kinchin lay" (robbing children), listening to "beefers" (complainers) who may be "glocky" (crazy) or "lushington" (drunk) with "reeb" (beer), or dressed in "crusher's dunnage" (a policeman's uniform to help along the gaff).

You may have noticed that I have no beef with any aspect of *The Great Train Robbery*, neither the writing nor the research nor the choice of subject. Sure, there is some fiction mixed in with the facts. No one could have known for sure all that Crichton tells us; he has said in an interview that he added to the number of keys required to pull off the pogue, among other inventions... The book will be widely read, much enjoyed, and without doubt make a first-rate adventure movie...

Source: Doris Grumbach, "Fine Print (Review of *The Great Train Robbery*)," in *New Republic*, Vol. 172, No. 23, June 7, 1975, pp. 30–31.

SOURCES

Andrews, Peter, Review of *The Great Train Robbery*, in the *New York Times Book Review*, June 22, 1975. p. 4.

Chesney, Kellow, *Pickpockets, Beggars and Ratcatchers: Life in the Victorian Underworld*, Konecky and Konecky, 1970.

Crichton, Michael, *The Great Train Robbery*, Harper, 2008.

Demarest, Michael, Review of *The Great Train Robbery*, in *Time*, July 14, 1975, p. K4.

Gelder, Ken, *Popular Fiction: The Logics and Practices of a Literary Field*, Routledge, p. 111.

Grumbach, Doris, "Fine Print," in the *New Republic*, Vol. 172, No. 23, June 7, 1975, pp. 30–31.

Hubin, Allen J., Review of *The Great Train Robbery*, in the *Armchair Detective*, Vol. 8, No. 4, August 1975, p. 309.

MichaelCrichton.com, "For Younger Readers: Q & A," at http://www.michaelcrichton.com/foryoungerreaders-qa.html (accessed August 21, 2009).

Prescott, Peter S., Review of *The Great Train Robbery*, *Newsweek*. June 23, 1975, p. 88.

Robbins, Michael, "The Great South-Eastern Bullion Robbery," in the *Railway Magazine*, May 1955), pp. 315–17.

Sissman, L. E., Review of *The Great Train Robbery*, in the *New Yorker*, August 4, 1975, pp. 89–90.

Weeks, Edward, Review of *The Great Train Robbery*, in the *Atlantic Monthly*, Vol. 236, No. 1, July 1975, p.80.

FURTHER READING

Evans, D. Morier, *Facts, Failures, and Frauds: Revelations, Financial, Mercantile, Criminal*, Groombridge & Sons, 1859.
This volume offers a fascinating glimpse of the most sophisticated crimes of the nineteenth century, written while the incidents were still fresh in the minds of the Victorian public. The book contains a chapter devoted to the South Eastern Railway bullion robbery.

Mayhew, Henry, *The London Underworld in the Victorian Period: Authentic First-Person Accounts by Beggars, Thieves and Prostitutes*, Dover Publications, 2005.
This comprehensive document of the Victorian criminal class has proven invaluable for understanding the era from an often ignored perspective.

Reynolds, Bruce, *The Autobiography of a Thief*, Bantam Press, 1995.
This work chronicles the life of Bruce Reynolds, the mastermind behind the 1963 heist that earned the popular name, the Great Train Robbery. After the robbery, Reynolds lived as a fugitive for five years before being caught.

Trembley, Elizabeth A, *Michael Crichton: A Critical Companion*, Greenwood Press, 1996.
This detailed survey of Crichton's first ten major novels also contains biographical information and an analysis of the author's literary influences.

A Handful of Dust

EVELYN WAUGH

1934

Although it is not Evelyn Waugh's most famous work, many critics consider *A Handful of Dust*, published in 1934, to be his finest novel. Written in a scathing if understated style, *A Handful of Dust* skewers the English high society of the years between the world wars. Waugh, who himself was a product of elite schools and the London social scene, had poked fun at modern society in earlier novels as well. But in *A Handful of Dust* Waugh employs satire and irony as a way of dealing with issues both more personal and more meaningful than mere social criticism. In his telling of the break-up of the marriage of Tony and Brenda Last, Waugh deals with his feelings of shame and humiliation after the collapse of his first marriage a few years before. At the same time, Waugh uses the story of Tony Last to ask broader questions about the role of tradition in English society as well as the value of the more modern and materialistic culture of the 1920s and 1930s. Waugh had converted to Catholicism shortly before he began the novel and, although there is little explicit mention of religion in the book, it is a highly moral story, exhibiting what Waugh believed to be the utter emptiness of secular, modern life.

AUTHOR BIOGRAPHY

Evelyn Arthur St. John Waugh was born in 1903, in London, England. His father was Arthur Waugh, a publisher and biographer, and his brother was Alec

Evelyn Waugh (The Library of Congress)

Waugh, also a novelist. Waugh attended the elite secondary school, Lancing College, where he edited the school's literary magazine, before enrolling in Hertford College at Oxford University. Not an outstanding student, Waugh tended to focus on art and his social life rather than on his studies. While still at the university, Waugh published short stories in student periodicals. After graduation, Waugh co-produced the 1924 film *The Scarlet Woman, An Ecclesiastical Melodrama*. In the years that followed Waugh struggled to settle into a career, studying art and teaching at a number of secondary schools. In his early twenties, Waugh was heavily depressed, drank far too much alcohol, and considered (and perhaps even attempted) suicide. All the while he continued an active social life in London's fashionable circles of young people, and he would mine both this world as well as that of elite schools for much of the material in his early novels.

In 1927, Waugh's life took a new turn as he fell in love with the aristocratic Evelyn Gardner, the daughter of Lord Burghclere. The family of Ms. Gardner, who became known by many friends as "she-Evelyn," was strongly opposed to Waugh's romantic interests as the two Evelyns became increasingly intimate. Waugh received a contract to write a biography of the poet and painter Dante Gabriel Rossetti that same year. Although Waugh wrote the book hurriedly, it received largely positive reviews. While finishing the Rossetti biography, Waugh began writing the manuscript for his first novel, *Decline and Fall*. The following year the Evelyns were secretly married, though the relationship would soon sour.

In 1928, *Decline and Fall*m a wickedly sharp satire of the life of the upper class, appeared to rave reviews, and Waugh's career as a novelist was promisingly launched. He also wrote numerous articles for newspapers and magazines and managed a growing public reputation. His personal life suffered, however, as he learned of his wife's infidelity. Much like the marriage of Tony and Brenda Last in *A Handful of Dust*, the Waughs' marriage crumbled when Evelyn secluded himself (in his case, to finish a novel) and his wife enjoyed the London party scene. There she fell in love with another man and told Evelyn so in a letter. Their marriage ended soon after.

In part as a reaction to his rejection by his wife, and in part fulfilling a long-held dissatisfaction with modern English life, Waugh converted to Catholicism and was received officially into the Church in 1930. From this point on, his novels would be deeply affected by his religious faith. They would also reflect his worldwide travel, often done as a journalist, which resulted in popular works of travel writing. His novels continued to be comic and satirical, often at the expense of the English elite. *A Handful of Dust*, which appeared in 1934, was no exception and also contained a scathing though disguised portrait of his marriage. When the Catholic Church annulled Waugh's first marriage in 1936, he quickly married again, this time to Laura Herbert, also a member of the English gentry. Herbert's family had converted to Catholicism and the match was ideal for the ambitious and religious Waugh. With the earnings from his novels, Waugh purchased a country estate, where he and Laura raised six children.

As the clouds of war gathered over Europe in the late 1930s, Waugh took the unpopular stand of supporting the Italian invasion of Ethiopia as well as the fascist side in the Spanish Civil War. No fascist himself, Waugh saw it as preferable to Marxism and the lesser of two evils. When England went to war against fascism in 1939, Waugh joined the Royal Marines. His experiences in battle became the basis for his highly regarded wartime novels, including *Put Out More Flags*m published in 1942, and *Brideshead Revisited*, published in 1945. It was this latter novel that would solidify Waugh's reputation in the United States, and it remains his most popular work.

After the war, Waugh settled into the life of a famous and respected novelist. He toured the United States, giving lectures. Yet the postwar American world order and the Labour government in England sickened the traditional Waugh, and he felt increasingly estranged from modern society. These feelings were reflected in his novels of the 1950s and 1960s. Seen by many as increasingly cranky and out of step, Waugh became disheartened with the democratization of England and even of the Catholic Church itself. Waugh died on April 10, 1966, after attending a Latin mass in Somerset. As biographer Calvin Lane wrote, "To the end, he remained a complex, often difficult, idiosyncratic person who could not and would not accommodate himself to the temper of contemporary British life."

PLOT SUMMARY

Chapter 1: Du Côté de Chez Beaver

A Handful of Dust opens with Mrs. Beaver and her son John discussing a house fire. At first it appears they are concerned with the victims of the fire. It quickly becomes clear, however, that Mrs. Beaver's interest in the fire is financial: she wants to sell the victims' home furnishings. John, who lives with his mother, is waiting for a phone call, not from anyone in particular but rather for an invitation to lunch. Since the beginning of the "slump," what Americans call the Great Depression, he has been idle as "no one had been able to find anything for him to do." John and Mrs. Beaver discuss various members of high society and their contacts with them. Clearly, Beaver (as Waugh calls him), is peripheral to this world but labors for acceptance. He mentions that he has been invited to visit Tony Last and his wife for the weekend at their country estate, Hetton, and Mrs. Beaver advises that he reply with a telegram because it will give them no chance to back out of the invitation. The two discuss the Lasts in a somewhat critical way, though Beaver clearly intends to take advantage of their hospitality.

MEDIA ADAPTATIONS

- *A Handful of Dust,* adapted as a film by Charles Sturridge and starring James Wilby, Kristin Scott Thomas, and Anjelica Huston, was released by New Line Cinema in 1988. It was nominated for an Oscar that year.

- *A Handful of Dust* was also adapted for the London stage by Mike Alfreds in 1982. The play was revived to mostly positive reviews in 2005.

After Beaver receives a phone call from a lady who wants to know the name of someone Beaver knows so she can invite this other man to lunch, the scene shifts to Beaver's club, Brat's, a place at which he is not very popular. He runs into the handsome and wealthy Jock Grant-Menzies, who is a member of Parliament. They chat about the Lasts, and Jock assures Beaver that he will like Brenda Last. "I often think Tony Last's one of the happiest men I know," he continues. "He's got just enough money, loves the place, one son he's crazy about, devoted wife, not a worry in the world." Beaver checks his messages and discovers he has received a last-minute invitation to lunch. He hurriedly leaves Brat's.

Chapter 2: English Gothic-I

The chapter begins with a guidebook description of the Lasts' house, Hetton Abbey. Hetton was renovated in the 1860s in a faux-medieval style and is therefore "devoid of interest." Tony, however, loves the house and is sure it will be considered stylish again someday. It matches his boyish enthusiasm for the England of King Arthur. In fact, he names the bedrooms after characters in the Arthurian legends—Guinevere, Lancelot, and so on.

Tony and Brenda seem very happy together, eating breakfast as she reads him the papers. Although Brenda seems less enthusiastic about staying in the country, their life together seems almost perfect. Outside, their son, John Andrew, rides his horse under the tutelage of Ben Hacket, who looks after the horses at Hetton. John falls from the horse but is not hurt and after more effort clears a jump. John's nanny, who is also present, is insulted by John, and she sends him to the nursery. Brenda speaks to John about this but he is disrespectful, telling her he likes Ben more than anyone else. Brenda reminds John he is a gentleman, though she later admits her scolding is a failure.

Later, Tony and Brenda receive Beaver's telegram and struggle to remember much about him. They decide to put him in the Sir Galahad bedroom because it is uncomfortable. When Beaver arrives, Tony slips off on business and Brenda entertains him. On Sunday, Tony again slips away from Beaver and enjoys his ritual visit to church. While he has little or no religious feeling, Tony enjoys listening to the reverend's sermons, although they were written and first delivered when he was overseas and bear no relation to English life. Tony also enjoys chatting after church, walking home, pausing in the hothouses for a flower for his buttonhole, and then having dinner before retiring for sherry in his library. It is a routine that pleases Tony very much.

On his return from church, Tony finds Beaver telling Brenda's fortune. Tony takes Beaver on a two-hour tour of the house, which Beaver appears to enjoy greatly. Back with his mother, Beaver admits he would like to see more of Brenda. He tells his mother that Brenda is thinking of finding a flat in London. Mrs. Beaver is sure she could find Brenda something to her liking.

Brenda impulsively visits her sister Marjorie in London. Brenda tells of Beaver's visit. When Marjorie asks if she "fancies" Beaver, Brenda says, "Heavens, no." Later she admits she is attracted to him. They see Mrs. Beaver in a restaurant and briefly discuss a flat for Brenda. Beaver accompanies Brenda to the train station but the potentially romantic moment falls flat. The next day he telegrams her at Hetton, asking her to a party. She replies that she is "delighted." Tony notices her high spirits.

Beaver arrives at Marjorie's home to pick up Brenda for Lady Cockpurse's party. They bicker about who will pay for dinner as Beaver wonders if he should try to kiss Brenda. Both seem to have accepted the fact that they are beginning an affair. They chat excitedly at a restaurant and kiss in the taxi. As she had earlier with Tony, Brenda rubs Beaver's cheek "in the way she had." They enjoy the party. Beaver takes Brenda back to Marjorie's home. She calls him a little later but again he seems incapable of romantic talk.

The next morning Brenda tells Marjorie that the evening before was quite innocent and that she fears Beaver found her boring. She admits she finds him "as cold as a fish." When Beaver does not call her she believes their affair is over. But they run into each other at a restaurant at lunchtime and decide to see a movie. Afterward, Brenda telegrams Tony, saying she is staying with Marjorie for a few more days.

Brenda returns to Hetton and tells Tony she has been "behaving badly" and "carrying on madly with young men" while spending "heaps of money." She also tells him she has found a flat she wants in London. Tony is against it, feeling they cannot afford it and do not need it. Three days later she is back in London, where the social scene was abuzz with news of her affair with Beaver. Brenda takes the flat against her sister's advice and, once there, calls Tony. He is disappointed but sends her flowers. Beaver goes to Ireland for Christmas and Brenda is bored at Hetton. When Tony asks her if her New Year's resolution is to spend more time at home she tells him that, quite the opposite, she intends to spend more time away, perhaps enrolling in a course in economics.

Chapter 3: Hard Cheese on Tony

Jock Grant-Menzies finds Tony eating and drinking alone at Brat's. Together they get drunk while Tony unhappily talks mostly of Brenda. Brenda has Beaver call Tony, pretending to be a servant, saying she has gone to bed early. Tony calls back and tells Brenda he is coming to her flat. Brenda calls Brat's and tells Jock to keep Tony away. Jock tries to convince Tony to go to Brenda's but they end up at a seedy nightclub called 64. There Tony and Jock meet two young women named Milly and Babs who may or may not be prostitutes. Tony and Jock continue to argue about going to Brenda's, ending up at Jock's. The next day, Tony calls Brenda and apologizes for his drunken calls. She tells Beaver that all this is fortunate because Tony will now leave her alone. Tony returns to Hetton, feeling guilty. Alone, he sleeps in Brenda's room.

Brenda returns from London with Polly Cockpurse, her friend Veronica, and Mrs. Beaver. They essentially ignore Tony, insulting Hetton and talking of renovating it. Brenda talks about her flat as if she has moved there permanently. On Saturday night Brenda tells Tony she has drunk too much and cannot speak with him. The next morning she sleeps in and he goes to church alone. The next day, the women try to plan an affair for Tony. Brenda sends a woman called Jenny Abdul Akbar to Hetton, hoping she and Tony will become involved. Tony, who has no idea of the plan, greets her as a guest of Brenda, whom he expects to follow shortly. He does not like Jenny, who inexplicably calls him "Teddy." She is uncouth and pretentious and Tony is relieved when John enters. The boy speaks frankly with Jenny and later tells his nanny he thinks she is the most beautiful woman he has ever seen. Brenda arrives and encourages Jenny despite her poor start. The next morning, John finds Jenny in Galahad; he is clearly smitten with her. Jenny goes to church with Tony and he almost warms to her. Still, the scheme for romance is a complete failure. Tony is worried that their marriage is not going well but Brenda tells him not to brood. Clearly lonely, he begs Jock to extend a weekend visit. Jock cheers up Tony, which makes Brenda feel better about her treatment of him.

Jock's lover, an American named Mrs. Rattery, arrives at Hetton as the house is in preparation for an annual hunt. John begs to be as involved with the hunt as possible though the adults only want him there at the beginning. A young local woman, Miss Ripon, is also at the hunt, though she struggles with her horse. The hunt is called off and John is sent home. As they ride back to Hetton, Miss Ripon, Ben, and John are involved in an accident and John is struck by a horse's hoof. He is killed instantly. Tony sends Jock to tell Brenda and tries to make funeral arrangements. Mrs. Rattery waits behind to comfort Tony, who in turn worries about Brenda.

Tony struggles with the fact that he knows of John's death so long before Brenda. He wants to tell the extended family but also wants to wait until he knows Brenda has heard. Mrs. Rattery tries to help him forget his trouble by having Tony play silly children's games. Tony is embarrassed and the servants are scandalized. Jock arrives at Brenda's and meets Jenny Abdul Akbar. She inexplicably blames herself for John's death, claiming that wherever she goes bad things happen. Jenny then begins to feel sorry for herself. Jock and Jenny find Brenda at a party where a number of women are having their fortunes told. Alone, Jock tells Brenda that John is dead. Brenda thinks he means John Beaver and when Jock clears up the misunderstanding, Brenda says, "Oh thank God." She weeps but it is unclear that it is not from relief. Returning to Hetton, Brenda keeps to herself. She tells Tony that their life at Hetton is "over," though he does not see why. Tony talks to Jock about Brenda's puzzling behavior: she has gone off to Veronica's. There she tells Beaver that she now realizes she loves him though he seems unmoved. The following Monday, Tony receives a letter from Brenda announcing that she is not coming back to Hetton, that she loves John Beaver, and that she wants a divorce. Tony does not fully understand the letter for several days.

Chapter 4: English Gothic-II

Tony is bombarded by friends and relatives who try to make peace between the married couple. A phone call with Brenda makes Tony realize the relationship is over. In order to give Brenda a divorce, Tony decides that he will allow her to portray herself as the wronged party. His lawyer, who does not share Tony's faith in Brenda, advises him to get all agreements in writing. It is decided that Tony will pretend to have an affair and that private detectives will collect evidence against him. At first he struggles to come up with a woman to help him. Jock suggests they return to 64 and there they meet up again with Milly and Babs. The women have taken part in such arrangements before and Milly agrees to accompany Tony to Brighton, a beachside resort, if her young daughter can also come along. Tony is aghast at the idea and says no.

Tony, Milly, and the private detectives meet later at a train station. Tony is angered to see Milly's daughter, Winnie, with her, but he is unable to prevent her from coming. At the hotel, the detectives look on disapprovingly on this new twist and they tell Tony of their feelings when he joins them for a drink in the hotel bar. For his part, Tony feels that his world has suddenly become "bereft of order," so farcical are the events in his life now. Dan, a friend of Milly, arrives with his girlfriend Baby, and Tony joins them for a party.

Early the next morning, Winnie wakes Tony and demands they go to the beach. Back at the hotel, Tony eats breakfast in the dining room, only to be told by one of the detectives that they need more evidence. So Tony goes back upstairs and pretends to eat breakfast in bed with Milly.

Returning from the trip, Tony meets with Reggie St. Cloud, Brenda's brother. A stout man who seems much older than he truly is, Reggie is an archaeologist and a member of the House of Lords. Reggie, who had been in Tunisia until he heard about the affair, accuses Tony of being vindictive and of pushing Brenda and Beaver together. Reggie lectures Tony about drinking too much and seeing other women. For Tony, this talk seems a continuation of his surreal life of late. Finally, Reggie demands Tony quadruple his proposed annual payment to Brenda. Tony protests that this would mean giving up Hetton and that Brenda would never want him to do that. Tony defends Brenda to Reggie but when he calls her she confirms that this is her wish. The conversation is a turning point for Tony. "A whole Gothic world had come to grief...." His vision of his life at Hetton now shattered, Tony asserts that there will be no divorce and that he is going away.

Chapter 5: In Search of a City

The scene shifts to the deck of a ship bound for Trinidad. Tony meets a man who asks him why he is traveling. When Tony tells him he is "looking for a city," the man is a bit put off. Soon, however, Tony gains a reputation with the other passengers as an explorer. He has left England because he believes that is what a person in his circumstances should do. Tony had met Dr. Messinger, a young bearded man who tells him he is on his way to Brazil to search for a fabled city in the heart of the South American continent. Tony, who had planned to go on a simple cruise, had torn up his pamphlets and joined Dr. Messinger on his quest. In Tony's mind the city is "Gothic in character, all vanes and pinnacles, ... a transfigured Hetton...."

Also on the ship is a young woman named Thérèe de Vitré, returning to Trinidad after years of studying in Paris in order to marry. She asks Tony about his exploring and they become friends, playing shuffleboard and other games. Nearing Barbados their relationship becomes romantic. They kiss and she asks him to visit her in Trinidad. This changes suddenly when he tells her he is married. Thérèe, a strict Catholic, is horrified and does not introduce him to her father when he greets her in Trinidad. In town, Tony sees her. She waves but does not stop to speak to him. Another passenger assures him this is typical of the local elites.

For some time during the chapter, the scene shifts back and forth between Tony's journey and events back in London. Tony and Dr. Messinger chug upstream toward "the City." Tony is tortured by the many biting insects and small animals of the jungle. Meanwhile Brenda, out dancing with Jock, says she is still fond of Tony despite his behavior. Tony camps in an Indian village, waiting for the men to return. Jock worries about the dumping of low-price pork pies on the English market. Tony hunts with the Indians and thinks of his old history teacher. Beaver admits to his mother that he does not know where his relationship with Brenda is going. Tony and Dr. Messinger walk for two weeks, speaking rarely because of their exhaustion. Mrs. Beaver suggests John should have a holiday.

Tony and Dr. Messinger's supplies run low and their Indian guides refuse to hunt because of fears of evil spirits. Dr. Messinger repeatedly asks their interpreter, Rosa, when their canoes will be ready. He cannot get a straight answer from her. Finally, she declares that the men will go no farther, though the canoes are now ready. Dr. Messinger tries to entice them with mechanical toy mice. When he demonstrates them, the Indians run away into the bush. Brenda and Beaver bicker about his intention to travel to America with his mother. The Indians desert Tony and Dr. Messinger. "The situation is grave," says Tony's companion.

Tony and Dr. Messinger travel on together, down the treacherous river. Tony develops a fever, which comes and goes, making him delirious. One afternoon he has a vision of Brenda. Dr. Messinger nurses him. He leaves in his canoe to look for a sign of a village nearby. Approaching rapids, he tries to get to the bank, but tips over, falls over a waterfall, and dies of his injuries. Brenda sees the family lawyer in the hopes of receiving more money. Instead she learns that Tony has made a new will, leaving Hetton to his cousins. Alone in the jungle and feeling unwell, Tony begins to cry. His fever returns. Brenda realizes that her affair with Beaver is over. She breaks down. Tony dreams surreal dreams, in which Rosa, Milly, Lady Cockpurse, and others discuss the widening of a road. Brenda declares her love for Beaver. Voices come and go. Finally, Tony sees a vision of "the City." It is like a gothic castle with ramparts and battlements. Tony stumbles through the jungle toward his hallucination of a shining version of the Hetton of his imagination.

Chapter 6: Du Côté de Chez Todd

Tony is rescued by a Mr. Todd, a man of European descent who has lived in the Amazon for almost sixty years. Mr. Todd humors the hallucinating Tony and gives him medicine that makes him sleep. After several days he feels much better. Tony asks Mr. Todd about his background. Todd claims to be the father of most of the people in the area. He is the most powerful man in the region but is ashamed that he cannot read. He asks Tony to read to him. Tony learns that Mr. Todd has a great fondness for the novelist Charles Dickens and has many of his books. At first Tony enjoys reading Dickens's novels to Mr. Todd, but he begins to find his host somewhat threatening. When he asks about a canoe to return downriver, Mr. Todd is evasive. Tony finds a note from an earlier visitor who seems to have shared his predicament. As Tony presses for a boat, Mr. Todd begins to hold his shotgun on his lap when they are reading. After they are visited by a prospector, Tony is cheered because he feels he may be rescued soon. Mr. Todd gives Tony a local drink that causes him to sleep for two days. When he wakes he discovers a rescue party has come and gone. Mr. Todd has let on that Tony had died. He is stuck with Mr. Todd forever.

Chapter 7: English Gothic-III

Tony's cousin, Richard Last, now runs Hetton. The staff has been reduced and life there is simpler. Over an informal breakfast with his family, he reads a letter from "Cousin Brenda." She writes to say that she cannot attend the dedication of a memorial to Tony. She is stuck in London where her new husband, Jock Grant-Menzies, has business before Parliament. Later that morning, Reverend Tendril unveils a memorial to "Anthony Last of Hetton, Explorer." The novel closes with one of the Last children, twenty-two-year-old Teddy, dreaming that someday he can restore Hetton to its former glory under his cousin Tony.

CHARACTERS

Jenny Abdul Akbar

Jenny is a shallow and emotional woman in Brenda's circle of friends. Brenda sends her to Hetton to try to have an affair with Tony, but she fails. Jenny irrationally and selfishly thinks John's death is her fault because of her very presence. Despite her declarations of deep fondness for Brenda, she drifts away from her after Tony's departure leaves Brenda with little money.

Allan

Allan is Marjorie's husband, Brenda's brother-in-law. He takes a dim view of Brenda's affair with Beaver. Like Marjorie, he is "hard up and smart."

Babs

Babs is one of two young women Tony and Jock meet when they spend an evening drinking at the nightclub 64. She is surprised when the men do not go home with them.

Baby

Baby is the girlfriend of Milly's friend Dan. She meets Tony at the hotel in Brighton. She is distressed because she sees people she believes to be Jewish at the hotel.

John Beaver

Usually referred to as "Beaver" in the novel, John Beaver is a somewhat handsome but rather dull young man on the outskirts of British high society. With little money, he is compelled to live with his ambitious mother. Beaver drifts in and out of his relationship with Brenda Last with seemingly little emotion. His speech is clipped and repetitive. He seems incapable of emotion, even when he writes his lover, Brenda, a note of thanks for a lovely ring she has given him for Christmas. When it is clear that Brenda will not make him rich, Beaver goes with his mother to America, though it is fairly clear that even this was not originally his idea.

Mrs. Beaver

Mrs. Beaver is an ambitious businesswoman who uses her social contacts to further her interior design business. She appears to be without any interest besides furthering her own career and the amorous adventures of her son. It is she who pushes Beaver into the affair with Brenda Last and suggests the trip to America as a way of bringing it to an end.

Lady Polly Cockpurse

Despite her aristocratic title, Polly Cockpurse is shallow and boorish. She convinces Brenda that

Tony needs to have an affair and disastrously chooses Jenny Abdul Akbar for the job.

Dan

Dan is a friend of Milly whom she and Tony chance upon at the hotel in Brighton.

Jock Grant-Menzies

Jock is Tony's best friend and a member of Parliament. Jock is a highly eligible bachelor and had been considered a likely match for Brenda before she married Tony. Tony turns to Jock when he is confused over Brenda's decision to get a flat in London. It is also Jock who travels from Hetton to London to tell Brenda of John Andrew's death.

Ben Hacket

Ben is a worldly man who looks after the stables at Hetton. He is John Andrew Last's hero and described by Waugh as "a man of varied experience in other parts of the country."

James and Blenkinsop

Detectives hired to record Tony's pretended infidelity. They travel to Brighton where they befriend Tony despite company rules.

Brenda Last

Brenda is Tony Last's wife, a pale beauty who had been considered one of the most eligible young women on the London social scene before her marriage. She is not happy living at Hetton, finding life there secluded and boring, though at the beginning of the novel she appears to have a perfectly happy marriage. The events of the story show her to be self-centered and self-deluding as she somehow comes to see herself as the victim of Tony's poor behavior.

John Andrew Last

The only child of Brenda and Tony Last, John is a precocious and painfully honest young boy. He speaks his mind openly to guests at Hetton, often embarrassing his parents. He is interested only in horses and idolizes Ben Hacket, who looks after the Lasts' stable. John begs his parents to take part in the annual hunt. They allow him to watch and stay out of the action, but he is killed in an accident nevertheless.

Richard Last

Richard is Tony's poorer cousin who inherits Hetton after Tony alters his will. At the end of the novel, Richard is raising silver foxes at Hetton and living there with his less aristocratic family.

Teddy Last

Teddy is Richard Last's twenty-two-year-old son who lives with his parents at Hetton at novel's end. Like Tony before him, he dreams of restoring Hetton to its previous glory, though in his mind it is Tony who is the model to be imitated.

Tony Last

Tony is the somewhat pathetic hero of the novel. He is the lord of a manor house, Hetton, and wants nothing except to live there comfortably. He has never really grown up and fantasizes about the romantic past of his family and his house. He is devoted to his wife, Brenda, but is clueless about her unhappiness at Hetton. Tony is the character readers sympathize with, but his romantic nature and his blindness to the reality around him make him less than heroic.

Marjorie

Marjorie is Brenda's younger sister. She is against Brenda's affair with Beaver. She lives in a small flat in Partman Square with her husband, Allan.

Dr. Messinger

Dr. Messinger is a young, bearded explorer who leads Tony on his adventure in search of "the City." He believes he understands the Indians' minds and this overconfidence leads to his death.

Milly

Milly is one of the young women Tony and Jock meet at the club 64. When Tony struggles to think of someone to have his supposed infidelity with, he settles on Milly. They travel to Brighton but Milly insists on bringing her young daughter along for the trip.

Mrs. Rattery

The American Mrs. Rattery is Jock Grant-Menzies's lover. She is an able card player and an occasional morphine user. She makes a splash by arriving at Hetton in a plane, but she fails to console Tony after John Andrew's accident.

Miss Ripon

Miss Ripon, a pretty local girl, rides a nervous horse her father hopes to sell at the hunt. She is involved in John's accident.

Rosa

Rosa is the Indian guide and interpreter hired by Tony and Dr. Messinger. She continuously demands cigarettes and often confuses and confounds the Englishmen with her statements.

Lady St. Cloud

Brenda's mother, who, although she had not initially been keen on Brenda's choice of Tony for a husband, feels her daughter's extramarital affair is foolish.

Reggie St. Cloud

Reggie St. Cloud is Brenda's heavy-set brother who returns from Tunisia to convince Tony to accept her demand that Tony give up Hetton. Reggie only succeeds in angering Tony and scuttling the divorce settlement.

Reverend Tendril

Reverend Tendril is the vicar at Tony's church. He seemed to believe he was preaching to Britons in India. The parishioners seem not to notice his references to exile from home and to Queen Victoria, who had died thirty years before.

Mr. Todd

Mr. Todd lives with the Pie-Wie Indians and saves Tony's life after the death of Dr. Messinger. He has lived in the jungle about sixty years and, unlike Dr. Messinger, is familiar with the environment and people. He claims to be the father of most of the Indians in the vicinity. Mr. Todd nurses Tony back to health but then imprisons him, demanding Tony read him the novels of Charles Dickens.

Veronica

Veronica is a friend of Lady Cockpurse who visits Hetton and criticizes its furnishings.

Thérèe de Vitré

Tony meets this slight young woman aboard ship. She is returning to Trinidad from two years studying in Paris and is intending to find a husband. They strike up a shipboard romance but she abruptly drops Tony when she discovers he is married.

Winnie

Winnie is Milly's eight-year-old daughter who tags along on Tony's trip to Brighton. She torments Tony on the trip and creates public scenes by making him look like a monster.

THEMES

The Emptiness of Modern Life

A Handful of Dust is at heart a scathing indictment of modern, consumer-oriented life. Waugh is savage in his treatment of characters, including Polly Cockpurse and Brenda Last, who seek only pleasure in life without recognizing the role of morality, discipline, and sacrifice. With the expansion of industry in the early twentieth century, the prices of many consumer goods fell sharply. At the same time, new venues of entertainment, including the radio and the cinema, opened up a world of fun for those who had the resources. And it is fun that Brenda and her group of friends seek. Waugh portrays them as shallow and lacking any true interest in each other. When Brenda's relationship with Beaver falters and Tony leaves her without much money, her group moves on in search of the new "it girl" of the season. Waugh pointedly shows that none of these characters seems to truly enjoy themselves or gain anything lasting out of their modern, urban, materialistic lifestyles.

The Folly of Self-determination

Between 1900 and the outbreak of World War II, new forms of popular culture began to promise Britons that life was what you made it. Despite this growing power of optimistic imagery from advertising, film, and other forms of rhetoric seeking to convince people they could control the outcome of their lives, Evelyn Waugh had no faith in the power of self-determination. In his mind, human beings were largely corrupt and separated from God while the modern belief that most people were mostly good was delusional. Since only God could determine the outcome of a life, people should not strive to "recreate" themselves. In fact, doing so was a form of rejection of God's design. This is clearly mirrored in *A Handful of Dust* through the plot as a whole as well in the experiences of most of the central characters. Any attempt at liberation from social bonds, such as Brenda's affair and her flat in London, or Tony's dream of re-creating a gothic fantasy world, end in failure. This is also true of John Beaver's wish to be socially popular, Jenny's desire to be exotic and interesting, and Dr. Messinger's hope of becoming a scientist who understands Indians. In the end, Waugh seems to argue, people's identities are determined, and those who try to radically alter their public personas are bound to be disappointed.

TOPICS FOR FURTHER STUDY

- Research the ways in which Evelyn Waugh used his own experiences, especially the collapse of his first marriage, as inspiration for *A Handful of Dust*. What did he change? How did he elaborate on his experiences and what did he do to disguise or reveal the characters of the people involved? Write a paper looking at the choices Waugh made as an author in order to use his personal suffering as a way of investigating larger ideas.

- The novels of Charles Dickens play a large role in *A Handful of Dust*. Using guides such as this one, look at the story lines of the novels Tony read to Mr. Todd. Lead a class discussion on Waugh's ambitions as a writer in the English tradition, focusing on the differences and similarities between *A Handful of Dust* and the novels of Dickens.

- Watch the 1988 film version of *A Handful of Dust* and prepare a video report for your class. Showing key scenes, discuss the ways in which the director, Charles Sturridge, adapted and perhaps condensed the novel. What did he leave out or add? Why do you suppose he made these choices? Were they successful?

- Waugh spends no effort in developing the characters in *A Handful of Dust* who are either servants or people of color. John's nanny, for example, is not even given a name. She is simply called "Nanny." Likewise, with the exception of Rosa, the people who guide Tony and Dr. Messinger are never named and hardly described, as if they were not important. Using your library and the Internet, research relations between classes and races in 1930s England and write a three-page paper showing how these prejudices are portrayed in the book.

Anjelica Huston as Mrs. Rattery in the 1988 film version of A Handful of Dust *(© Murray Close/Sygma/Corbis)*

The Uselessness of Nostalgia

History plays a central role in *A Handful of Dust*, in large part because of the rapidly changing nature of English society. Between the year of

Waugh's birth and the publication of *A Handful of Dust* in 1934, England fought a devastating warm which decimated a generation of young men and crippled the nation's ability to hold on to its sprawling and expensive global empire. Thus, while the United States emerged from World War I with a booming economy and a new sense of global power, many in England came to believe that their nation's glory days were past. Many Britons took a reactionary stance against modern, socialistic England and had a nostalgic fondness for the bygone Victorian age of clear-cut social roles and expanding global power. Tony Last embodies this view, and from his introduction in the second chapter until his final hallucination in the jungle, he looks longingly back at a romanticized past, hoping somehow to be touched by its glory. Thus the names of the bedrooms at Hetton are from Arthurian legend. This is also why he prizes Hetton itself, remade in 1864, and why he enjoys the literally Victorian sermons of Reverend Tendril. Even his escape from Brenda into the jungles of South America is a search for a lost city of the past, a passageway out of the present. It is not by chance that Tony's view of "the City" is not South American but rather resembles a medieval castle. In effect, this nostalgia paralyzes Tony, making him unable to either participate in the contemporary world or to find a viable alternative to it. Waugh did not share his hero's nostalgia, however, at least not for the solidity of the Victorian age. As Tony's experience shows, for Waugh, nostalgia was another force separating people from the true nature of their lives.

STYLE

Irony

Waugh uses irony to create the collapsing world of the Lasts in *A Handful of Dust*. Irony as a literary style is a way authors can use words to bring out a meaning separate from the ones the actual words convey. Often, the intended meaning is the opposite of the meaning of the words, such as when Brenda writes Tony a note to tell him she loves John Beaver and signs it, "Best love from Brenda." Clearly, Waugh's intended meaning is not that Brenda is giving Tony her best love. Another example is when Waugh notes that Tony "had got into the habit of loving and trusting Brenda," the actual meaning of the sentence is that Tony is blind to the fact that his wife has been openly cheating on him. Or, to cite another example, when Brenda complains to Tony that "Everything has been so difficult," Waugh's intention is to show how selfish Brenda is, not how hard a time she has had after leaving Tony. Thus, by using irony, Waugh allows his characters to speak for themselves, to reveal their true selves through their unguarded words and feelings. This style is pleasing because it releases Waugh from having to comment on the action of the novel and keeps the narrator from hovering over every conversation. It also highlights the farcical nature of both Tony's failing marriage and the broader culture of narcissism.

The Hero's Journey

As identified by the scholar of mythology Joseph Campbell, Western literature is filled with heroes who leave home as young men, face a challenge or a danger, and return home transformed by the experience. Tony Last is clearly the hero of *A Handful of Dust*, but he

far from overcomes his challenges. Like the classical hero he leaves home, though he is not altogether blameless for his situation. His journey is one into delusion rather than one of revelation. However, he is searching for the very myth that he had sustained at Hetton. Only late in his journey does he realize that "the City" does not exist. *A Handful of Dust* is in some ways a classical tragedy: Tony's fatal flaw is his inability to see the world as it is and his delusion is ultimately fatal.

HISTORICAL CONTEXT

The Great Depression

In Great Britain, the Great Depression, also known as the Great Slump, caused economic and social unrest throughout the early 1930s. Waugh makes reference to the Slump early in the novel. In the introduction of the character John Beaver, Waugh notes that since the Slump began "no one had been able to find anything for him to do." Unlike in the United States, where the economy in the 1920s boomed on a spree of speculation and credit, the British economy had struggled to recover from World War I. Throughout the 1920s exports suffered and unemployment was high. In 1926, a general strike spread from the coal mines through British industry, resulting in widespread clashes between strikers and the police. As a result of these factors as well as the crash of the American stock market in 1929, a national government was formed in 1930, comprised of representatives from the three major parties, the Liberals, Labour, and the Conservatives. Still, the economy struggled to regain its status as the world's most powerful. At the same time, England's hold on many of its colonies slipped, even as the ultra-nationalist Hitler took power in Germany (in 1933, the year before *A Handful of Dust* was published) and as Italy, led by the Italian fascist Benito Mussolini, invaded Ethiopia in 1935. At first, the government responded with measures that arguably made the Slump worse, including lowering benefits paid to unemployed workers and raising the income tax. By the mid-1930s, however, stimulating measures, such as the government-sponsored construction of millions of homes, helped the economy rebound. For those less affected by the economic downturn, the 1930s proved to be an exciting decade with the introduction of sound cinema, radios, vacuum cleaners, and

COMPARE & CONTRAST

- **1930s**: In England and the United States, a married person who seeks a divorce is compelled to prove unreasonable behavior on the part of their spouse and then wait a lengthy period for the government to finalize the divorce. When couples share a desire to end an unhappy marriage in which there has been no abuse or infidelity, they are often compelled to fabricate an affair, such as Tony Last does in *A Handful of Dust*.

  Today: Although the United States began adopting so-called "no fault" divorce laws in the 1960s, the United Kingdom continues to offer only "fault divorce." Briefly, in the 1990s, reform advocates managed to pass legislation introducing a law under which couples could quickly end marriages, but it was rejected by the government. Today, it continues to take between two and five years to obtain a divorce in Great Britain.

- **1930s**: With no national system of roads and highways, travel by automobile between cities and towns was time-consuming and often frustrating. Most travel of more than a few miles was conducted by rail or, often in the case of freight, canals. In the late 1930s, a few years after the publication of *A Handful of Dust* the Ministry of Transport began a centrally planned Motorway system. This plan was shelved, however, because of World War II.

  Today: Great Britain is crisscrossed by a national Motorway system. Beginning with the opening of the Preston Bypass in the late 1950s, the Motorways were a response to the increasing popularity of automobile travel. Today, 2,200 miles of motorway serve some 28 million British cars. Train travel remains popular as well. Although travel by rail lost popularity between World War II and the 1980s, it has almost regained its highest historical levels of ridership.

- **1930s**: Great Britain continues to hold on to a number of Central and South American colonies, including British Honduras, British Guiana, the Faulkland Islands, Jamaica, the Bahamas, and Trinidad and Tobago. British control of the Caribbean is especially extensive. It is through many of these colonies that Tony travels on his quest for "the City."

  Today: Except for the Faulkland Islands, over which the United Kingdom fought a war with Argentina in the 1980s, all British colonies in South America have been granted independence or, in the case of the Mosquito Coast, have become divided up among neighboring countries. A handful of Caribbean islands remain under British control, including Turks and Caicos, Montserrat, and the British Virgin Islands.

washing machines. This is the world of expanded opportunities for consumerism in which Brenda and her circle move, mostly untouched by the economic downturn. By the late 1930s, preparations for war with Nazi Germany invigorated the British economy as industry retooled along military lines. Thus, the coming war, one which would again ultimately hurt the British economy, ironically helped Britain emerge from the Great Depression.

English Fascism

As capitalism suffered during the Great Slump, a new political movement appeared in England, one which attracted many among the aristocracy. Founded by Sir Oswald Mosley in the early 1930s, the British Union of Fascists (BUF) was an authoritarian party on the political far right. Mosley, who had formerly represented first the Conservative Party and then the Labour Party as a member of Parliament, formed the group after a visit to fascist-ruled Italy in 1932. The BUF was completely top-down in structure, with Mosley himself the unquestioned leader of the movement. It is difficult to know how many members the BUF actually had, but the success of fascism in Italy and, after 1933, in Germany, caused many to take it more seriously than its actual size might have deserved. Still, the BUF staged several impressive mass rallies that resembled Nazi rallies in their use of spectacle. After Hitler's rise to power, Mosley also became more openly anti-Semitic, claiming Jews in Britain were all essentially foreigners and should be viewed with suspicion. He also called for increased royal power and a concentration of industry in a high commission, run by a prime minister to be appointed by the king. Eventually, Mosley would be incarcerated for the duration of World War II, and the fascist movement in Britain would collapse.

However, in the 1930s, many aristocrats and conservative intellectuals, including Evelyn Waugh and some notable heads of British corporations, were sympathetic to Franco in Spain, Mussolini in Italy, or, as in the case of King Edward VIII himself, Hitler in Germany. In fact, some historians have argued that Edward's wife, the American Wallace Simpson, in fact passed important secrets to the Nazis. Evelyn Waugh was friendly with Mosley and his wife, Diana Mitford Guinness Mosley. In fact, in 1930 Waugh dedicated his novel, *Vile Bodies*, to her. Waugh's feelings about fascism were complex. His approval of the Mussolini regime in Italy was colored in large part by his desire to support the policy of the Catholic Church. Initially, many English Catholics perceived Mussolini as a protector against Hitler's threat to Catholics, especially in Austria. Waugh's fondness changed in the late 1930s when Mussolini aligned himself with Hitler and began his own racist policies. For most Britons sympathetic to fascism, any positive feeling was snuffed out when war broke out in 1939.

CRITICAL OVERVIEW

When *A Handful of Dust* appeared in 1934, Evelyn Waugh was already a writer well known for his satirical novels about the upper classes. Some reviewers saw *A Handful of Dust* as a continuation of this trend, though others perceived it to be more openly religious in tone. According to biographer Christopher Sykes, "When the

book came out in 1934 the general opinion of Evelyn's public and critics was that he had written his best book to date." The Catholic periodical *The Tablet,* however, published a highly critical review, arguing that the book failed to represent Catholic ideals. Over time, however, it has come to be regarded as Waugh's finest work. Writing in the 1950s, the renowned critic Northrup Frye elevates Tony Last's plight to classical terms, calling it "close to a parody of tragic irony." In recent decades, critics have almost unanimously favored *A Handful of Dust* over Waugh's most famous work, *Brideshead Revisited*. Writing in the early 1990s, Frederick L. Beaty applauds Waugh's ability to simultaneously parody both the materialistic characters like Mrs. Beaver and Brenda Last as well as the powerless romantic Tony Last. "Indeed Waugh's outstanding success as an ironist in *A Handful of Dust* owes much to his ability to challenge the assumptions of both commercial and chivalric codes." Beaty points out that the novel does not preach. Rather, it argues through negative examples. "By showing the disorder wrought through living according to either instinct or hollow tradition, the novel demonstrates...the need for something higher than man-made ideals." David Wykes, in his 1999 book, *Evelyn Waugh: A literary Life,* summarizes the enthusiasm of most current critics of Waugh's work when he calls *A Handful of Dust* "Waugh's greatest single achievement."

CRITICISM

Patrick J. Walsh
Walsh is a former Fulbright Lecturer at the University of Passau in Germany and is currently a teacher at the Catlin Gabel School in Portland, Oregon. In this essay, he considers the pessimism about modern life that lies at the center of A Handful of Dust as well as how Waugh's Catholicism is reflected in a story that seemingly spends little time on questions of faith.

By the mid-1930s, Evelyn Waugh was something of a celebrity novelist. Though still in his early thirties, his books, which included novels, a biography of a Catholic saint, and a travel narrative about his time in Ethiopia, made him a literary figure of much renown in Great Britain. His work in journalism and close friendship with some of London's best-read newspaper writers on the

WHAT DO I READ NEXT?

- D. J. Taylor's *Bright Young People: The Lost Generation of London's Jazz Age,* published in 2009, is a history of the social circle Evelyn Waugh cavorted with in 1920s London. Full of anecdotes and gossip about the "Bright Young Things," this book offers ample historical background to the action of *A Handful of Dust.*

- *Vile Bodies,* published in 1930, is Evelyn Waugh's second novel and, like *A Handful of Dust,* it parodies upper-class customs. In this case, the setting is the 1910s, on the eve of World War I. Like *A Handful of Dust,Vile Bodies* has a dramatic change of setting and tone in the second half of the novel as the hero, Adam Fenwick-Symes, is thrust into the war.

- *Brideshead Revisited,* which was published in 1945, is Waugh's most famous novel. It is much more overtly religious than *A Handful of Dust* and focuses much more squarely on the attraction of Catholicism to Britons in the years between the wars. It is also much more nostalgic, in large part because of the disruptions of life in Britain caused by World War II. It is *Brideshead Revisited,* and not the earlier, comedic novels, which made Waugh a literary figure in the United States.

- Novelist Graham Greene was a good friend of Evelyn Waugh's in large part because both men were converts to Catholicism. In 1951, Greene published his own novel on infidelity and religion, *The End of the Affair.*

- Zora Neale Hurston's novel, *Their Eyes Were Watching God,* published in 1937, is the story of a poor African-American's three marriages in the U.S. South of the early twentieth century. The main character, Janie Crawford, is a fascinating contrast to Brenda Last and provides insight into how race and class affect people's ideas about marriage and love.

---

social scene, added an air of fame and celebrity to his intellectual standing as well. He was well on his way to becoming a famous man. Yet at the same time, Waugh was in retreat from the very world of publicity and prestige he had courted over the previous decade. His writing displays a deep discomfort with the modernization of Britain and the widespread adoption of a secular culture based on the pursuit of worldly pleasures. In fact, in 1930, he had become a member of the Roman Catholic Church, an act which distanced him from England's established Anglican Church and signaled his dissatisfaction with what he believed to be the mainstream society's drift away from a culture built around the love of God. The ongoing economic crisis in England led many of his countrymen to question the validity of capitalism and to turn to socialist solutions to social and economic problems. Others, especially those in the aristocracy, began to express sympathy with the fascism taking hold in Italy and Germany. Waugh

appears to have recoiled from a turn toward both materialism and nostalgia, instead using the novel to point toward a third way, though without much hope that his fellow Britons would choose to look down his preferred path.

It is at this personal and historical moment that Waugh produced *A Handful of Dust,* a novel which is one of the main achievements of his forty years of work as a professional writer. Like much of his other early fiction, it is something of a satire on modern British high society, lampooning the emptiness of lives circumscribed by trips to parties, private clubs, and expensive restaurants. It is easy to see Waugh's criticism of the shallow lives of London's wealthy class and its imitators such as the interior decorator Mrs. Beaver. But the second pole of his social criticism, and one that may have been more personal to him, is his rejection of a return to the old order of rule by the aristocracy.

Waugh is not heavy-handed in his ironic critique of London's "Bright Young Things." It

> WAUGH'S GOAL IS TO ALLOW HIS READER TO
> WITNESS THE DESTRUCTION OF HAPPINESS BY TWO
> PURPOSELESS PEOPLE BENT ON RATIONALIZING
> THEIR OWN MISERABLE AND SELFISH BEHAVIOR."

is with a skilled and light touch that he allows the self-serving words of his characters to speak for themselves, showing how lives spent frivolously spending money in pursuit of fun have very little substance. In the early section of the novel, Brenda's chit-chat with her family and friends reveals the level at which she encounters the world. Reading the newspaper to Tony, for example:"

> Reggie's been making another speech.... There's such an extraordinary picture of Babe and Jock.... a woman in America has had twins by two different husbands.... Would have thought that possible? ... Two more chaps in gas ovens.... a little girl has been strangled in a cemetery with a bootlace. ... that play we went to about a farm is coming off." Then she read him the serial.

Later, after she has cheated on Tony, left him, and then demanded most of his money, Brenda proudly states, "I'm very fond of Tony, you know, in spite of the monstrous way he behaved." In such a fashion Waugh permits the narrator to stand back, without passing judgment on the characters. The reader listens in as Brenda and Lady Polly Cockpurse brainstorm about a woman to have an affair with Tony. When Brenda worries that a bored Tony might become an alcoholic, Polly declares, "We must get him interested in a girl." Of course, Tony loves his life the way it is with Brenda and Hetton. Waugh's goal is to allow his reader to witness the destruction of happiness by two purposeless people bent on rationalizing their own miserable and selfish behavior. As the scene closes, the narrator simply notes that "They discussed this problem in all its aspects," ironically commenting without doing more than noting that the conversation continued."

The woman Polly and Brenda select for Tony is the self-absorbed Jenny Abdul Akbar, who gets Tony's name wrong and brags of her awful marriage to a man from Morocco. She calls herself "Princess," admitting her husband never called himself "Prince," and then casts aside her self-appointed title because it is too formal. When Tony offers her muffins with her tea, and, desperately trying to make conversation, tells her that "I think muffins one of the few things that make the English winter endurable," Jenny soberly informs him, "Muffins stand for so much," before eating so greedily that crumbs and butter coat her face. Here, then, is a princess without grace who will eventually respond to John Andrew's death by crying out, "I am hunted down ... without remorse. Oh God, ... What have I done to deserve it?"

Jenny, then, is presented as something of a buffoon, a parody of someone actually royal in bearing or rank in an era when the aristocracy was losing its grip on power. Throughout the novel, the desire for a return to the past is treated as destructive, even delusional. The three chapters that bear the title "English Gothic" point to this. The title does not refer to the actual gothic era but rather to the Gothic Revival of the nineteenth century when, as Frederick L. Beaty argues in his study on Waugh, the revival "enabled the Victorians to invest a crumbling religion, threatened by scientific skepticism, with visual charm designed to conjure up an age of genuine belief." Tony's house, Hetton, had once been an abbey before passing to the Last family. In the 1860s, it had been "entirely rebuilt" and was now a shadow of its old self. And it was this replica, every "glazed brick and encaustic tile," that Tony loves. Douglas Lane Patey argues that faux-gothic Hetton is a Victorian imitation of its Catholic self, just as, to Waugh, modern, liberal Anglicanism is a pale imitation of the faith it has replaced. "Modern Anglicanism," writes Patey, "with its picturesque churches, vaguely ethical outlook and fuzziness over doctrine represents in this view the final phase of the Victorians' substitution of sentiment for faith." Keeping this idea in mind, Mr. Todd's enthusiasm for the Victorian and secular Charles Dickens must be read as a rejection of that author's outlook as well. With Mr. Todd, Tony is trapped in a fantasy similar to his own, although it is liberal rather than romantic.

The aged Reverend Tendril is one of the most comic figures in *A Handful of Dust,* and embodies what Waugh sees as the demise of a meaningful established religion in England. Tendril is "reckoned one of the best preachers for many miles around" despite the fact that little that he says in his sermons has anything to do with the lives of his parishioners. Written "in his more active days," the sermons are unedited versions of those given when Tendril served in India some thirty or forty years before. He asks his flock to "remember our Gracious Queen Empress in whose services we are here," and the people know that "when he began about their distant homes, it was time to be dusting their knees and feeling for their umbrellas." This is a parody of a living faith, and in such scenes Waugh belittles a religion reliant upon the weight of history and habit rather than an active faith. Tendril is kind, well spoken and well meaning, but his words are essentially meaningless.

Even so, besides Hetton, Tony derives much of his pleasure and satisfaction from his Sunday activities. Tony's Sundays are more ceremonial than religious, having "evolved, more or less spontaneously, from the more severe practices of his parents." While in church he thinks about his renovations to Hetton. Performing "the familiar motions of sitting, standing, and leaning forward, his thoughts drifted from subject to subject, among the events of the past week and his plans for the future." The day is completed by a stop in the greenhouse, dinner, and a glass of sherry in the study. Clearly, Tony is not a man of faith, but rather one who seeks comfort in routine and a sentimental attachment to tradition.

So what is Waugh's solution to this double bind? With his very public conversion to Roman Catholicism in 1930, it can be expected that his prescription would include a return to the Church. But in *A Handful of Dust* religion operates on the edges of the narrative, primarily in the persons of Reverend Tendril and Thérèe de Vitré. Later in life, Waugh noted that the novel "was humanist and contained all I had to say about humanism." Thus, it is in essence a negative argument, an attack on what he felt to be wrong with contemporary life. Had Waugh included an upstanding, moral character in the midst of the romantics and materialists, it is more than likely the novel would have become hopelessly didactic. It also would have lost its savage comic punch, more likely resembling the preachy Victorian melodramas that Waugh held in low esteem. Therefore Waugh offers no answer to the question, no clear-cut preferred option.

The question that arises from this then is whether or not *A Handful of Dust* is a Catholic novel. The random accidents that befall John Andrew Last and Dr. Messinger do not suggest a transparent moral order. Neither does the fact that

goodness is not rewarded nor evil punished. According to biographer David Wykes, Evelyn Waugh, by temperament, enjoyed it when things went awry because he believed that "human life can never be anything but exile, and the fantasy of an earthly paradise of El Dorado [and here Tony's 'City' comes to mind]... is the product of a grave misunderstanding of human nature." For Waugh, the Catholic Church fit his pre-existing beliefs about human nature and "provided a sustaining framework for ideas about human life and society that had been forming in him for some time." The Catholicity of the novel, then, in part rests on the critiques of humanism and modern Anglicanism, paired with the recent and public conversion of the author.

And what of the single Catholic character, Thérèe de Vitré? Her appearance in the novel is relatively brief, her true feelings are never displayed, and her exit is sudden and rendered with understatement. Tellingly, many scholars on Waugh and his novels all but omit Thérèe from their discussions of the novel. She and Tony have a shipboard romance, kiss, and talk about marriage. When Thérèe (whose surname may be roughly translated as "a sheet of glass") discovers Tony is married, her interest ends abruptly. She decides to return to the ship and thanks Tony in a way that suggests to him she is saying good-bye forever. This is because she lives by a code, one beyond serving her own pleasures. She is returning from France in search of a husband, but unlike the modern pleasure-seekers of London, her choices are circumscribed by her faith. She leaves Tony to his delusion and returns to her father's house and, it can be assumed, to a Catholic wedding in the near future. Cut loose by Thérèe, Tony returns to his errant quest after his imagined lost gothic city. In Waugh's understated and negative way, he offers Tony a final impossible chance to avoid the suffering his fantasies will ultimately bring. Tony misses his chance and moves on to the jungle and Mr. Todd's copies of Dickens.

Source: Patrick John Walsh, Critical Essay on Evelyn Waugh's *A Handful of Dust* in *Novels for Students,* Gale, Cengage Learning, 2010.

Jane Nardin

In the following review, Nardin argues that A Handful of Dust *is not rooted in a nostalgic desire for the past but rather employs the "myth of decline" to show the reluctance of many characters to deal with the realities of their modern lives.*

Evelyn Waugh's early novels are often thought to express the view that a traditional,

> BOTH TONY AND TODD'S EMOTIONAL LIVES TAKE PLACE IN A PAST WORLD WHICH NEVER REALLY EXISTED AS THEY IMAGINE IT—BOTH NEGLECT THE PRESENT."

stable, and dignified social order in England is quickly being replaced by a state of near chaos in which dishonesty and ruthless hedonism reign supreme.

But *A Handful of Dust* does not really support the view that Waugh believes the modern era to be marked by a decline in the quality of life. The Myth of Decline, the belief that beauty, order, and significance existed at some point in the past, but exist no longer, is certainly present in the novel, but it seems to be certain of the novel's characters, rather than its author, who cling to this belief. For Waugh undercuts these characters in a variety of subtle and not so subtle ways. If Waugh's earlier novels, *Decline and Fall* and *Vile Bodies*, did indeed embody a simple version of this Myth of Decline, then in *A Handful of Dust* Waugh is carrying his satire a step further by attacking one of his earlier positives. But probably it would be more accurate to say that although Waugh's early novels of English life all play with the idea of decline, it is only in much later novels, like the notorious *Brideshead Revisited*, that Waugh uses the Myth of Decline uncritically, as an organizing principle which gives meaning to his book.

The main technique that Waugh uses in *A Handful of Dust* to undercut those characters who believe in one or another version of the Myth of Decline is that of playing off their beliefs against each other through ironic juxtaposition. Various characters choose to locate the lost "golden age" at various periods of the past, but no character is able to give very compelling reasons for his choice. Tony's vision of the golden age is at once the most interesting and the most confused in the novel. For Tony, the golden era is that of the immediate Edwardian and late-Victorian past—the age when owners of country houses like Hetton had the resources with which to maintain them, when the country

house and the county family were still important elements in English society. Tony's dream is to restore Hetton in all its details to its late-Victorian state... Of course, it isn't really possible for Tony to restore prelapsarian purity to Hetton. As Tony himself tacitly admits..., there is a contradiction at the heart of a dream that tries to preserve a social institution that was once vital but now has no significant function to perform. The country house, once a center of English social and economic life, is so no longer. People will not even come to such a house for the weekend unless they are offered all the amenities of modern city living.

The antique Hetton Abbey was entirely rebuilt in 1864 in the Gothic style, and this extravagant gesture suggests that Tony's Victorian forbears, like Tony himself, found beauty and significance in the past rather than in the present. Yet, ... the Middle Ages was hardly the era of beauty, order, spirituality, and elevated ideals that certain Victorians, in full retreat from materialism and modernity, imagined it to be. Apparently the Victorian era was not so satisfying to Tony's forbears as Tony feels it would be to himself, so they in their turn idealized the Middle Ages in a manner notorious for its disregard of historical fact. And ... their confused Gothicism has become an element in Tony's essentially Victorian dream world.

Tony's unsatisfactory, obsolete life style is ... idealized by his impoverished successors, just as Tony himself idealized the lives of his Victorian forbears, who in turn idealized ... and so on. The golden era exists not in the past but in the mind.

Reggie's absorption in a supposedly significant past distracts him from truly significant present responsibilities... It's no accident that Reggie is going to search for meaning in a desert. His rejection of the present in favor of the past makes him a worse man, just as the well-meaning Tony's sterile preoccupation with the restoration of Hetton blinds him to such important present problems as his wife's unhappiness.

Tony and Reggie are not the only characters in *A Handful of Dust* who satisfy their longings for order and significance by retreating into dream worlds located in the past, while remaining selfish and insensitive to others' sufferings in their handling of everyday life. The syndrome takes its most extreme form in the case of Mr. Todd. Todd's golden era is located in the fictionalized Victorian world of Dickens' novels—where kindness and charity have the power to alter reality, where human suffering has meaning and arouses pity and indignation. Superficially, Todd is Dickens' ideal reader: "at the description of the sufferings of the outcasts in 'Tom-all-alone's' tears ran down his cheeks into his beard"... But Dickens intended his readers to be moved to moral action by his novels, and for Mr. Todd, the retreat into the imaginary, significant past which Dickens' work provides is an end in itself, giving his altruistic emotions a good workout which apparently incapacitates them for further action... Todd has located all moral significance in an imaginary past totally severed from the ugly and hedonistic present which he accepts quite matter-of-factly. This is the danger inherent in using a Myth of Decline to satisfy one's longings for a more beautiful life. Both Tony and Todd's emotional lives take place in a past world which never really existed as they imagine it—both neglect the present.

Tony actually encounters two people—Thérèse de Vitré, daughter of an old, Catholic family in Trinidad, and Mr. Todd—who unmistakably suggest or represent the two past periods that are blended in Tony's English Gothic dream, the Victorian era and the Middle Ages.

Given Waugh's Catholicism, we might expect him to idealize the conservative Catholic society of Trinidad. Here, if anywhere, Waugh would be likely to employ a straightforward version of the Myth of Decline by portraying traditional Trinidadian life as more satisfying than English modernity. But in fact what is most striking about Thérèse's response to the stable, ordered life of Trinidad is her unavowed, yet obviously violent, desire to escape from it.

In addition, Waugh's description of Thérèse's father as "the complete slave owner" reminds the reader that Trinidad's aristocrats did not gain their social pre-eminence in a morally irreproachable manner. So the encounter with Thérèse vaguely and suggestively, yet unmistakably, undercuts Tony's belief that the orderly Victorian past was a satisfying and edifying time to live.

The Gothic element in Tony's English Gothic Myth of Decline is at least as deeply undercut by his dealings with Mr. Todd as its Victorian element is by Thérèse.

Critics of *A Handful of Dust* often describe Todd as crazy, but Todd's sanity isn't really at issue here. Whether he is sane or not, it is clear that Todd's behavior closely resembles the behavior of all the aristocratic English characters in the novel. Like them he uses the social power circumstances have placed in his hands ruthlessly and selfishly (Tony...is at best a partial exception to this generalization); like them, he demonstrates a schism between moral ideals and practical conduct. If Todd is extreme, he is also typical, and the ruthlessness with which he uses his power demonstrates something about the nature of power which undermines the Gothic element in Tony's Myth of Decline. Those whose society gives them great and unquestioned authority over other human beings (the sort of authority Todd has inherited, with the gun, from his missionary father; the sort of authority feudal aristocrats inherited from their fathers) are likely to accept that authority as their right and to use it with little human sensitivity. The extremely powerful feudal aristocrats who use their monoply of physical force chivalrically, in the interests of the whole community, are a figment of Tennyson's and Tony's imaginations. The real aristocrats are Reggie, Brenda, Mr. Todd, and, alas, Tony himself, who all unquestioningly accept the social arrangements which give them rank and power and use their power in a basically selfish manner. And Todd's cruelty is the greatest at least in part because his powers are the most absolute. Thus Tony's "journey into the past," like so much else in this novel, suggests, not decline, but rather the essential similarity between past and present.

Source: Jane Nardin, "The Myth of Decline in 'A Handful of Dust,'" in *Midwest Quarterly*, Vol. 18, 1977, pp. 119–130.

James Nichols

In the following essay, Nichols discusses Waugh's use of satire in his early novels, focusing on what he considers Waugh's often contradictory ideals of romanticism and realism.

Evelyn Waugh has been asked, "Are your books meant to be satirical?" He replied, "No. Satire is a matter of period. It flourishes in a stable society and presupposes homogeneous moral standards—the early Roman Empire and 18th Century Europe. It is aimed at inconsistency and hypocrisy. It exposes polite cruelty and folly by exaggerating them. It seeks to produce shame. All this has no place in the Century of the Common Man where vice no longer pays lip service to virtue."

WAUGH COMES TO THE CONCLUSION THAT A MAN ARMED ONLY WITH A TRADITIONAL CODE OF VALUES IS HELPLESS IN THE MODERN WORLD. HE IS NO PHILOSOPHER; HE HAS NO ALTERNATIVE TO PROPOSE."

The article from which the quotation is taken appeared in *Life* in 1946, not long after the publication of *Brideshead Revisited*, the first of Waugh's novels to win him a wide transatlantic public. The tone of the article suggests that he was not entirely serious. A "satire," as far as the novel is concerned, is a novel so constructed and so written as to embody a point of view which adversely criticizes the manners and morals of its characters—and often the society to which they belong, as well. Even a casual reading will make plain that most of Waugh's early novels are intended to be satiric, as well as comic.

But he raises an issue which concerns all contemporary writers of satire. Most great satire has been written at times when there was general agreement about what constituted right moral standards. The modern satirist cannot count upon homogeneous moral standards in his audience. Therefore he has to establish *within* the satire a moral norm which his audience will accept. One way of doing this is to let the reader know that a character is intended to represent the author's point of view. His actions or comments, then, can embody or focus the satiric attack. Waugh seldom did this in the early novels. Instead, he chose to let the tone—his implied attitude toward characters, events, social scene—bear the burden of, first, establishing a standard by which his characters, and the incidents in which they figure, may be measured, and, second, of embodying the adverse judgment upon these characters and incidents which is essential to satire.

An understanding of how satiric tone is created and employed, then, is crucial to an understanding of the satire in Waugh's early novels. Seven had been published when the quotation above was printed: *Decline and Fall* (1928), *Vile Bodies* (1930), *Black Mischief* (1932), *A Handful of Dust* (1934), *Scoop* (1938), *Put Out More Flags* (1942), and *Brideshead Revisited* (1945). *Decline and Fall*, *Vile Bodies*, and *A Handful of Dust* form a relatively homogeneous group. All three have similar backgrounds; all satirize the English upper classes during a crucial period in their history and that of their country, the late 1920's and early 1930's. All are informed with a tone which is distinctively Waugh's. It sharpens the edge of the comedy and provides the moral standard which is essential to satire.

A Handful of Dust (1934) is Waugh's masterpiece. In it his wonderfully fertile comic imagination, his ability to set, and to modulate, satiric tone, and his feeling for the macabre fuse; the result is an unforgettable picture of a brilliant, but sick, society whose decadence he emphasizes not only by choosing both his title and his motto from *The Waste Land* but also by echoing Proust in two of his chapter titles.

Each of his chief characters, Tony Last and his wife Brenda, epitomizes one of the things that is wrong with their society. Brenda can find no real satisfaction in being a wife and mother. Bored by her marriage to Tony, who is decent and honourable, but dull, she begins an affair with John Beaver, a half–man who lives beside his telephone on the fringes of the fashionable world. Though she is well aware of Beaver's worthlessness, Brenda insists upon a divorce and, to support her Mr. Beaver, makes such demands for a settlement upon Tony that he breaks off divorce proceedings and goes abroad. Beaver leaves her, too, but things end happily for Brenda. Tony is reported dead in the Amazon jungle and she promptly marries an old friend of his.

A good deal of the satire in the novel is aimed at Brenda and her friends, a group of aging Bright Young Things. All of the satire is indirect; Waugh doesn't tell us what kind of people his characters are, their own actions and conversation do. Thus when Tony Last, who has acted decently towards Brenda, refuses to sacrifice Hetton, his beloved home, to buy John Beaver for Brenda:

> "Who on earth would have expected the old boy to turn up like that?" asked Polly Cockpurse.
>
> "Now I understand why they keep going on in the papers about divorce law reform," said Veronica. "It's too monstrous that he should be allowed to get away with it."

"The mistake they made was in telling him first," said Souki.

"It's so like Brenda to trust everyone," said Jenny Abdul Akbar.

Although Brenda epitomizes certain qualities which Waugh detests, she is not merely a caricature—or perhaps it would be more accurate to say that she is more subtly drawn than most caricatures. Despite her general bitchiness, she has an oddly appealing quality even in the depths of her affair with Beaver, and Waugh so nicely tempers Tony Last's decency with dullness that the reader is not entirely out of patience with Brenda when she wants a freer life in London. What does kill the reader's sympathy for her is her reception of the news of the death of her son, John Andrew. She is in London, visiting friends, while John Beaver flies over to France with his mother. Jock Menzies, Tony's best friend, brings the news to her:

> "What is it, Jock? Tell me quickly, I'm scared. It's nothing awful is it?"
>
> "I'm afraid it is. There's been a very serious accident."
>
> "John?"
>
> "Yes."
>
> "Dead?"
>
> He nodded.
>
> She sat down on a hard little Empire chair against the wall, perfectly still with her hands folded in her lap, like a small well-brought-up child introduced into a room full of grown-ups. She said, "Tell me what happened. What do you know about it first?"
>
> "I've been down at Hetton since the week-end."
>
> "Hetton?"
>
> "Don't you remember? John was going hunting today."
>
> She frowned, not at once taking in what he was saying. "John...John Andrew...I ...oh, thank God..." Then she burst into tears.

At first it seems that Tony, who is dull, but a decent sort, is to embody the standards by which the Bright Young Things are judged. He is an innocent who lives amid dreams of Victorian Gothic stability and morality at Hetton Abbey, the family seat, which, slowly, he is trying to modernize and restore to its former glory. He has gotten into the habit of loving and trusting Brenda and does not suspect her affair with Beaver until she announces she wants a divorce.

Even then he wants to do the traditional gentlemanly thing—to give her a generous settlement and to take all the blame for the divorce action. It is only when she demands so much that he will have to give up Hetton to satisfy her that he balks, refuses to go through with the divorce action, and leaves England.

But it is evident throughout that Tony is not only an innocent, but an adolescent as well. His room at Hetton, called Morgan le Fay, is a "gallery representative of every phase of his adolescence," and his conduct bears out the impression his room gives of his character. When Brenda takes to staying in London to be near her Mr. Beaver, Tony comes up for the night and when he can't see her gets drunk and pesters her by telephone. The whole sequence is one of the funniest things Waugh has ever done, but it is basically the record of an extended series of undergraduate pranks. Tony acts like a Victorian romantic hero during the divorce proceedings, and his leaving England when the divorce falls through is the action of a romantic juvenile.

Tony's fate in the Amazon jungle, although grotesquely out of proportion to whatever his just deserts may be, has a certain macabre appropriateness. He is seeking the city of his romantic dreams, "a transfigured Hetton, pennons and banners floating on the sweet breeze." What he finds is the distorted, but still recognizable, underside of the Victorian world. Mr. Todd is a Victorian father, monstrously selfish, despotically strict, but he provides sustenance and protection. The reading aloud from Dickens to which Tony is condemned is not only an ironic repayment for the agony he had caused Brenda by reading aloud at Hetton, but a grimly amusing suggestion of the boredom which must have made many a Victorian family evening a horror. The cream of the jest is that he should be condemned to read novels about the Victorian commercial classes, whose world and whose values overwhelmed the Victorian Gothic world Tony had dreamed of.

To put the whole matter succinctly, Tony as well as Brenda is being satirized. I make the point at some length because it is a crucial one and because Waugh has been criticized on the ground that he approves of, and sympathizes with, Tony. Quite the contrary. Neither Tony nor Brenda and her group represent values which he admires. Brenda and her circle are heartless; Tony is incapable of coping with the modern world.

A distinctive point of view is embodied in the tone of Waugh's early novels... Something is wrong—the traditional standards of value no longer seem to apply. Not morality, but immorality pays. In *Vile Bodies* he extends his portrait of English society. The values he prizes most are those of order, of selfless devotion to the service of God and country. But he is well aware that these values no longer receive even lip service. The First World War, he implies, caused or accelerated the decay of moral values, and another war, one which will destroy all civilization, is in progress as the novel ends.

A Handful of Dust complements the two earlier novels, but the main focus is upon marriage, the family, the individual. It contains some of Waugh's finest tonal effects. In the scenes at Brighton, for example, the farcical tone of the incidents in which "evidence" for the divorce action is gathered is tempered by Waugh's compassion for Tony Last's very real anguish. Thus he is able to imply a point of view—that modern marriage is hollow and farcical, although capable of causing deep distress to one who takes it seriously—which is never stated directly. Presumably, he had scenes like this in mind when he said that the novel "contained all I had to say about humanism."

Earlier I suggested that in Waugh's early novels the tone establishes the standard of values which is necessary to the satiric attack. Tone is essentially the projection of an attitude toward, a point of view about, the characters of his novels and the world they inhabit. The basis of this attitude is a conflict between what I should call "realistic" and "romantic" ideas and feelings. Waugh understands that the modern world is one in which the traditional standards—ones which he cherishes—no longer apply: "vice no longer pays lip service to virtue." But he recognizes that the *rewards* of vice—the world's esteem and the world's goods—are not despised, and recognizes, too, that the way in which goods and esteem are gained may not spoil the enjoyment of them.

Thus far his point of view is a good deal like that of the satirists of the past. But these satirists tempered attacks upon their times by at least implying that there was an alternative set of values, or an alternate course of action, which *could* rectify the evils they portrayed. Waugh too

has an alternative, one which he examines in his early novels. The alternative is a romantic one—a hope that a return to the traditions and values of the past offers a way of ameliorating the beastliness of the modern world. But when this idea is put to test, it is found wanting.

Waugh's attitude toward Tony Last is a good example of this. Tony belongs to, and to some extent represents, a tradition to which Waugh is strongly attached. D. S. Savage calls Tony's outlook "adolescent romanticism" and infers that this represents Waugh's *own* way of looking at the world. This is only part of the truth, I think. Waugh comes to the conclusion that a man armed only with a traditional code of values is helpless in the modern world. He is no philosopher; he has no alternative to propose. But he *wishes* that Tony's values were not so completely outdated. The tension between Waugh's realistic appraisal of what the modern world is like and his romantic yearning for a system of values that he *knows* no longer works informs the tone and provides the satiric standard in his early novels.

Source: James Nichols, "Romantic and Realistic: The Tone of Evelyn Waugh's Early Novels," in *College English*, Vol. 24, No. 1, October 1962, pp. 45–56.

SOURCES

Beaty, Frederick L., "A Handful of Dust," in *The Ironic World of Evelyn Waugh: A Study of Eight Novels,* Northern Illinois University Press, 1992, pp. 86, 90, 110.

Frye, Northrup, "Historical Criticism: History of Modes," in *The Ironic World of Evelyn Waugh: A Study of Eight Novels,* edited by Frederick L. Beaty, Northern Illinois University Press, 1992, pp. 86–87; originally published in *Anatomy of Criticism,* Princeton University Press, 1957, p. 48.

Lane, Calvin W., "Chapter 1: The Artist and His World," in *Evelyn Waugh,* Twayne's English Author Series, No. 301, Twayne Publishers, 1981, p. 42.

Oldmeadow, Ernest, Review of *A Handful of Dust,* in *Evelyn Waugh: A Biography,* by Christopher Sykes, Little Brown and Co., 1975, pp. 140–41; originally published in *The Tablet,* September 8, 1934.

Patey, Douglas Lane, "Political Decade I (1930–1935)," in *The Life of Evelyn Waugh: A Critical Biography,* Blackwell Publishers, 1998, pp. 119, 123.

Sykes, Christopher, "1932–1934," in *Evelyn Waugh: A Biography,* Little, Brown, and Co., 1975, p. 140.

Waugh, Evelyn, *A Handful of Dust,* Back Bay Books, 1999 (1934).

Wykes, David, "Introduction," and "1930–1939," in *Evelyn Waugh: A Literary Life,* St. Martin's Press, 1999, pp. 8, 9, 103.

FURTHER READING

Kennedy, Dane, *Britain and Empire: 1880–1945,* Longman, 2002.

> This survey of British imperial history is a great introduction to the ways in which the empire affected people in the colonies as well as in Britain itself.

Lovell, Mary S., *The Sisters: The Saga of the Mitford Family,* W.W. Norton and Co., 2003.

> This history of the glamorous and scandalous Mitford sisters sheds light on the world in which Evelyn Waugh lived. Nancy was a friend of Waugh and a novelist; Unity was a close friend of Hitler; Diana was the wife of the leader of the British fascists.

Orwell, George, *The Road to Wigan Pier,* Mariner Books, 1972.

> Originally appearing in 1937, this book is one-half a report on the miserable conditions of the English working class during the Great Depression, and one-half an essay on the role of socialism in making conditions better.

Waugh, Alexander, *Fathers and Sons: The Biography of a Family,* Anchor, 2008.

> The grandson of Evelyn Waugh traces four generations of tension between fathers and sons in his famous family. Beginning with his great-grandfather, the publisher and critic Arthur Waugh, this book looks at the lives of the often unhappy, yet undeniably brilliant men of the Waugh family.

Journey to the Center of the Earth

JULES VERNE

1871

Journey to the Center of the Earth (1871) was Jules Verne's second published novel, and despite the dozens of works he went on to create afterward, it remains one of his most enduring tales. The story revolves around esteemed mineralogist Professor Otto Lidenbrock and his nephew Axel, who discover a coded message hidden in an ancient Icelandic manuscript. The message suggests that it is possible to travel to the center of the Earth through a passage in a dormant volcano in Iceland. The two men, accompanied by an Icelandic guide, travel to the volcano and successfully make their way to the Earth's interior, where they discover a fascinating subterranean world.

Originally published in French in 1864, the novel has been translated numerous times with varying levels of quality and fidelity. The most popular English translation, for example, changes the names of several main characters, removes some of Verne's original content, and adds material not written by Verne. In addition, the basic premise of the book has so embedded itself into popular culture that it has been borrowed, altered, and re-used perhaps more than any other modern literary works. For decades this kept Verne well known but largely unappreciated in literary circles, where his works are viewed as little more than adventures for young readers. Still, *Journey to the Center of the Earth* is a perfect representation of Verne's work—heavily reliant upon scientific data, aimed at

Jules Verne

educating the reader while at the same time offering adventuresome entertainment in exotic and unfamiliar places. In 1894, in an interview with *McClure's Magazine,* Verne describes himself in the following way: "I am a man of letters and an artist, living in the pursuit of the ideal, running wild over an idea, and glowing with enthusiasm over my work."

AUTHOR BIOGRAPHY

Verne was born on February 8, 1828, in the port city of Nantes, France. His father, Pierre Verne, was a lawyer, and Jules was the oldest of five children. Although his childhood is generally regarded as happy, one incident related by an early biographer may have helped shape the young Verne into the writer he would become. Eager to taste the adventure of the seas, at the age of eleven or twelve he arranged to stow away on a ship called the *Coralie,* which was headed for the West Indies. His parents discovered his

plan and intercepted him before he left port; after returning home, the contrite Verne told his parents that all his future travels would take place only in his imagination.

In 1847, Verne moved to Paris to study law, feeling pressure from his father to assume a role in the family business. However, Verne was drawn to the worlds of theater and literature, and his focus on writing instead of studying law led his father to cut off his living allowance. Though he ultimately completed law school, his passion for writing led him to work at more modest jobs that allowed him time to continue working on plays and novels. In 1857, he married a widow and mother of two named Honorine de Viane Morel, and took a job as a stockbroker to support his new family. Their only child was born in 1861.

Verne's career as a novelist was launched when he met Pierre-Jules Hetzel, one of the most famous French editors and publishers of the time. After Verne made requested rewrites, Hetzel accepted his African adventure novel *Five Weeks in a Balloon* (1863) for publication. The novel was a success, and led to a contract between Hetzel and Verne that guaranteed a steady income for the author as long as he continued to produce new books as part of a series, which were known collectively as *The Extraordinary Voyages.* The second book in the series, inspired by a meeting with a geographer who had studied volcanic craters, was *Journey to the Center of the Earth.*

Verne continued writing his successful series of adventure novels and nonfiction works for over forty years, including classic works such as *Twenty Thousand Leagues Under the Sea* (1872) and *Around the World in Eighty Days* (1873). A common thread throughout Verne's works is exploration and travel to unfamiliar lands—the same impulse that led him as a boy to board the *Coralie,* channeled through his imagination and into his novels. Verne died on March 24, 1905, in Amiens, France, at the age of seventy-seven.

PLOT SUMMARY

Chapters I–V

Journey to the Center of the Earth begins on May 24, 1863, in Hamburg, Germany, in the home of Professor Otto Lidenbrock. Lidenbrock's nephew Axel, his servant Martha, and his seventeen-year-old goddaughter Gräuben also live there, though

MEDIA ADAPTATIONS

Note: There have been countless adaptations of *Journey to the Center of the Earth* in various forms of media. Many of these have strayed far from the original tale, often being adaptations in name only. The list of media adaptations below consists of works that are the most faithful and/or significant adaptations available at this time.

- A film adaptation of the novel, directed by Henry Levin, was released in 1959. The film stars Pat Boone and James Mason in the lead roles, and is currently available on DVD from Twentieth Century Fox Home Entertainment.

- A 3-D film adaptation of the novel was released in 2008 starring Brendan Fraser and Josh Hutcherson. The film, directed by Eric Brevig, is available on DVD and Blu-Ray from New Line Home Video.

- An audio dramatization of the novel was released under the Alien Voices imprint of Simon & Schuster Audio in 1997. Originally available on CD in both abridged and unabridged versions, this currently out-of-print adaptation features performances by actors such as Leonard Nimoy and John de Lancie.

- An unabridged audio adaptation of the novel was released by Blackstone Audiobooks in 2008. This adaptation, read by Simon Prebble, is available on CD and audiocassette; it is also available as an audio download through audible.com.

- An unabridged audio adaptation of the book was released by Brilliance Audio in 2006. The adaptation is read by David Colacci, and is currently available on audio CD and as an audio download through audible.com.

- A musical adaptation of the novel was created and composed by Rick Wakeman in 1974. Recorded live at the Royal Festival Hall, this adaptation is available on audio CD from Fontana A&M.

- A graphic novel adaptation of the book, aimed at younger readers, was released by Stone Arch Books in 2008. Verne's tale is retold by Davis Worth Miller and Katherine McLean Brevard, and illustrated by Greg Rebis.

Gräuben—whom Axel has fallen in love with—is away visiting relatives. Lidenbrock arrives home early from the school where he teaches mineralogy, and excitedly calls Axel into his study. Lidenbrock shows Axel a 700-year-old book he has just purchased from a local shop; it is a handwritten copy of Snorre Turleson's *Heims Kringla,* a collection of sagas about former rulers of Iceland, written in a Runic alphabet.

As they examine it, a page of parchment that had been tucked between the pages of the manuscript falls out. It is also covered in Runic letters, though Lidenbrock cannot make sense of it. He deduces that it is a cryptogram, or puzzle in which the letters must be rearranged, and that it was written at least two hundred years after the book. He also discovers the name of the book's former owner: Arne Saknussemm, a sixteenth-century Icelandic scholar. Convinced that the secret message must be of some significance, Lidenbrock vows to neither eat nor sleep until the mystery is solved. Unfortunately for his housemates, they are not allowed to eat either.

After converting the Runic characters to English letters, Lidenbrock guesses that the language of the message is Latin. He also has Axel rearrange the letters of the message by taking the first letter from each word in succession, then going back and writing the second letter from each word, and so on. Lidenbrock is disappointed when this method does not yield a comprehensible message, and hurriedly exits the house, presumably in search of another answer for the puzzle. Axel, unable to concentrate on other matters, finds himself drawn back to the puzzle. Frustrated, he begins fanning himself with the paper on which he had written the letters as instructed by his uncle. Catching a glimpse of the message from the back side, with the letters showing through, Axel realizes that the original solution is correct—but the message is written backwards.

When he reads the message, however, he vows to destroy it for everyone's well-being; he feels certain that it will send his uncle on a journey that will lead to his death. Before he can destroy it, Lidenbrock returns, still unable to crack the mysterious message. Axel holds his tongue, fearing what will happen if the message is revealed. However, after more than twenty-four hours without food, Axel finally cracks and tells his uncle the secret of the message. After being translated from Latin, the message reads:

> Descend the crater of the Jokull of Snäfell, that the shadow of Scartaris softly touches before the Kalends of July, and thou wilt reach the center of the earth. Which I have done. Arne Saknussemm.

Just as Axel fears, Lidenbrock immediately begins to make plans for the dangerous—if not impossible—journey to the center of the Earth. Worse, Lidenbrock insists that Axel join him.

Chapters VI–X

The members of the house are finally allowed to eat, and afterward, Axel tries to convince his uncle that the trip is ill-advised. First he unsuccessfully argues that the note may not be authentic; then he proclaims, based on accepted scientific theories, that traveling to the center of the Earth is impossible, because the farther one travels toward the Earth's center, the hotter and more pressurized it becomes. Lidenbrock argues that humans have knowledge of only a small fraction of the outer crust of the Earth, and cites the renowned scholar Sir Humphry Davy as someone who discounts the "accepted" theories. Lidenbrock also reveals that the location referred to in the message is a volcanic mountain along the western coast of Iceland, and that the purpose of their trip must be kept secret, so that no other scientists try to reach the destination first. Since the message indicates they must be there before July, they must set out immediately if they wish to complete the trip in time.

Gräuben returns to Hamburg, and Axel meets her on the way to tell her of the secret trip. Axel is stunned when, instead of begging him not to go for fear of his safety, she endorses the trip, and even packs his suitcase for him. She kisses him on his cheek as he departs, and suggests that they will be married upon his return.

Lidenbrock and Axel travel by train and steamer to Copenhagen, Denmark, where they make plans to travel to Reykjavik aboard a schooner named the *Valkyria* that leaves on June 2. To accustom themselves to heights, Lidenbrock and Axel climb to the top of a Copenhagen church spire every day until their departure. The boat leaves on schedule, and they sail north around the tip of Denmark, past northernmost Scotland and the Faroe Islands, and on to the western coast of Iceland, into the capital city of Reykjavik. Lidenbrock and Axel are welcomed by no less than the governor of Iceland and the mayor of the capital; a local science professor named Fridrikson offers them boarding in his home, and they accept with gratitude. Without revealing the true purpose of their trip, they make plans to visit Snäfell, and Fridrikson recommends a guide who can take them there.

Chapters XI–XVI

The next morning, Lidenbrock and Axel meet Hans, their guide to the crater. Hans is tall, strong, and cool-headed, and agrees to serve not just as their guide to the mountain, but also to remain in their service throughout their time studying the region—in other words, unbeknownst to him, he would be accompanying the pair on their trip into the Earth. Before departing, Lidenbrock and Axel take inventory of their equipment, which includes: a special thermometer for measuring high levels of heat; a manometer, which measures high atmospheric pressure; a chronometer to keep time; two compasses; and two of a device known as Ruhmkorff's apparatus, an early example of an electric lamp. They also bring a great deal of basic climbing equipment, both for ascending the mountain and for descending once inside the crater.

On June 16, the trio leaves Reykjavik and heads northwest. On June 21, they reach Stapi, a village at the base of Snäfell. They spend the night in the home of the unpleasant village rector and his even more unpleasant wife, who present the men with an inflated bill for the services they received while staying there. After settling up, the team heads for the mountain along with a handful of local guides.

The team climbs to one of the two peaks, nearly a mile above sea level, then descends into the crater. They find three different chimneys that lead downward, as well as a large granite rock engraved with the name "Arne Saknussemm." Lidenbrock sends the local guides home, leaving just the trio behind. To determine which chimney to enter, they must figure out which one is touched by the shadow of the peak they just descended from. However, clouds and rain keep them waiting for several days. Finally, on June 28, the sun breaks through and reveals the middle chimney as the correct passage.

Chapters XVII–XXV

With the help of a long rope, the team descends cautiously into the abyss. After traveling for a few days into the depths of the passage, they find themselves running low on water. This problem is exacerbated when they travel down a dead-end path for several days and must backtrack, with no water in sight along the way. Axel grows weak, but Lidenbrock urges him to continue for one more day in search of water. If they do not find it, they will return to the surface. Axel agrees.

They descend farther beneath the Earth's crust, until Axel's legs will no longer carry him. They stop to rest, and Lidenbrock seems prepared to admit defeat. Hans, hearing a sound, heads off on his own while the other two rest. He returns with news that he has discovered water. The group travels down to a spot where they can hear the rush of a subterranean river, but they can find no water. Hans pulls out a pickaxe and begins chipping away at the rock wall; after digging a hole two feet deep, he finally breaks through, and a jet of boiling hot water shoots out of the hole. The group is relieved to finally be able to quench their thirst, and Lidenbrock decides to name the subterranean river Hansbach, after its discoverer.

The jet of water soon forms a stream that not only leads them along the quickest path downward, but also allows them access to a continuous supply of water as they travel. The path they follow descends at a slow grade, so that they travel a great distance southeast for every mile they travel downward. By July 15, they calculate that they have traveled far enough southeast to be no longer under Iceland, but underneath the ocean instead.

Chapters XXVI–XXXI

By August 7, they estimate that they are about ninety miles below sea level, though the heat and pressure have both proven to be quite bearable—which seems to support the arguments of Lidenbrock and his colleague Davy. On that same day, Axel becomes separated from the other two when he inadvertently walks off the trail made by the stream. He tries to retrace his steps, but cannot locate the stream; his cries for help go unanswered in the silent darkness. He continues to backtrack with the hope of finding the stream, but soon his electric lamp goes dead, and he is left unable to see. He descends in a panic, feeling his way along the walls, until he passes out from exhaustion and fear.

When he wakes, he hears the sound of his uncle's voice somewhere in the distance. He calls out to him, and discovers that although they can hear each other, they are nearly four miles apart; a strange acoustic effect allows their voices to be heard clearly across the distance. Lidenbrock tells Axel to follow the passageway down, and he is sure to meet up with them. Axel descends, but the path becomes steep and he slips on loose rocks. He strikes his head and is knocked unconscious.

When he wakes, Axel finds that he has been reunited with his uncle and Hans. He also discovers that they have reached a vast open space under the ground, complete with a sea and an atmosphere of sorts, which gives off a blue light similar to the aurora borealis, but much brighter. Lidenbrock estimates the sea to be about one hundred miles across, and names it after himself. The group also discovers vegetation such as giant mushrooms forty feet tall, and primitive tree-like mosses growing up to one hundred feet tall and blanketing the land like a forest. They also discover fossils of prehistoric animals scattered everywhere in the soil, as well as partially fossilized wood. Hans uses this wood to build a raft to sail across the sea, where they hope to continue their descent toward the center of the Earth.

Chapters XXXII–XXXVII

On August 13, the trio departs from the shore to sail across the Sea of Lidenbrock. As they leave, Axel suggests that they name the harbor from which they depart Port Gräuben, and Lidenbrock agrees. As they sail, they pass giant ribbons of algae nearly a mile long. The group also tries fishing, and manages to land several prehistoric fishes, all blind—the product of evolution in a subterranean environment. After traveling several hundred miles, the group still finds no sign of land. However, they witness a violent encounter between an ichthyosaurus and a plesiosaurus, both prehistoric sea creatures long thought extinct. Then they spy what appears to be a mammoth whale-like creature, over a mile long, breaking the surface and spewing plumes of water through its blowhole. As they draw close, they realize that it is an island, and the blowhole merely a geyser. They briefly explore the island, which Lidenbrock names in honor of Axel, and Axel notes that they have traveled about eight hundred miles across the sea—which puts them approximately beneath England.

After they leave Axel Island, they note a change in the weather. The wind picks up, and they are quickly carried into a terrible storm that lasts several days. During the storm, lightning strikes the raft, magnetizing everything on board that contains iron. The raft is eventually smashed into the shore; thanks to Hans, they survive the crash, and most of their supplies are saved as well. When they attempt to determine their location, they are shocked to find that, according to the compass, they have been brought back to the same shore they left almost two weeks before.

Chapters XXXVIII–XLII

Although Lidenbrock is upset at the setback his exploration party has encountered, he decides that they will cross the sea again and continue their journey. Before they do, however, he explores the new section of shore upon which they have landed. They find a giant graveyard of ancient bones, and among them, they discover human bones older than anyone at the time believes possible. As they continue, they discover something even more amazing—a herd of living mastodons, being herded by a prehistoric-looking man over twelve feet tall.

They return to shore, and as they contemplate departing across the sea once again, Axel discovers a dagger on the sand. Knowing it did not come from their party, they realize that this must be a sign left by Arne Saknussemm during his journey centuries before. They search along the shore, and find a tunnel; at the entrance, carved into a block of granite, they find the initials "A. S." Lidenbrock decides to name the area Cape Saknussemm.

They return up the coast to retrieve Hans, and the three sail back with their supplies to Cape Saknussemm. They enter the marked tunnel, but almost immediately find their progress cut off by a giant boulder. Since it is too large to break through with a pickaxe, they resort to explosives. They place fifty pounds of guncotton in a hole chopped into the boulder's surface and set a long fuse. The next morning, August 27, as Lidenbrock and Hans wait on the raft a safe distance away, Axel lights the fuse and runs to join them on the raft. Instead of just blowing up the boulder, the explosion opens a fissure that draws the sea down into the abyss beyond the rock. The men on the raft, powerless, are pulled along with the water at terrifying speed. As Axel states: "Beyond a doubt this was the passage of Saknussemm; but instead of traveling along it by ourselves, we had, by our imprudence, brought a sea along with us."

Chapters XLIII–XLVI

After several hours holding on aboard the rushing raft, Axel comes to the realization that they are no longer traveling down, but up. Lidenbrock concludes that the force of the water is pushing them up another volcanic channel similar to the one that they followed down Snäfell. It may lead to an outlet that provides escape, or it may lead to a dead end that leaves them crushed or drowned. They eat the last of their remaining provisions as a final meal, and consult the compass to discern their direction of travel. The compass is useless, fitfully pointing by turns in any and every direction.

As they continue, Axel notices that the rock walls and the water beneath them are getting hotter, and the passage is filled with thunderous booms. He fears that they will soon be crushed by the shifting masses of an earthquake. Lidenbrock tells him that what they are experiencing is not an earthquake, but an eruption. Indeed, the clear water beneath them has given way to a boiling volcanic mud. Just as the heat grows unbearable, the raft and its passengers are ejected from the passage.

When Axel regains his senses, he finds Hans securely holding both himself and his uncle. Safe on the surface, they look around and try to determine where they have ended up. Their guesses are all wrong, however; they happen upon a local boy who informs them that they are on the volcanic island of Stromboli, off the coast of Sicily. They are taken in by Stromboli fishermen as shipwrecked seamen, keeping the true details of their journey to themselves for now. They begin the long journey home, and arrive in Hamburg on September 9.

Gräuben and Martha welcome them warmly, and soon the whole town is abuzz regarding their impossible trip. Lidenbrock publishes an account of the expedition that brings him great fame, if also some controversy from skeptics. Hans returns home to Iceland, and Axel marries his beloved Gräuben. The final mystery of their malfunctioning compass, which nagged at Lidenbrock ever since their return, is solved by Axel: during the electrical storm on the Sea of Lidenbrock, when the raft and its metal contents became magnetized, the polarity of the compass had been reversed, causing it to point south instead of north.

CHARACTERS

Axel

Axel is the nineteen-year-old nephew of Otto Lidenbrock, and the narrator of the novel. He lives with the professor in Hamburg and also functions as his assistant in numerous scientific endeavors. Axel is in love with another resident of the household, Lidenbrock's seventeen-year-old goddaughter Gräuben. When Lidenbrock brings home an old book containing a coded message, it is Axel who decodes the message, though he at first hides the solution from his uncle because he fears it will lead to a dangerous journey. A hungry Axel ultimately reveals the message so that everyone in the household can finally eat. Although Axel attempts to talk his uncle out of going to Iceland, he eventually agrees to accompany the professor on the risky journey. Over the course of their adventure beneath the surface of the Earth, Axel becomes braver and more willing to consider unusual scientific ideas. When they return home, Axel marries Gräuben and they continue to live with Lidenbrock. At the end of the tale—just as in the beginning—Axel proves his cleverness by solving the final mystery of their trip: the mystery of the malfunctioning compass. In the most popular English translation of the novel, Axel's name has been changed to Harry.

Hans Bjilke

Hans Bjilke is the Icelandic hunter who serves as a guide for Lidenbrock and Axel on their journey to Snäfell. After arriving at the crater, Hans agrees to continue with the men on their journey into the deepest reaches of the Earth. Hans is described as a tall, strong man with pale blue eyes and long red hair. As Axel states, "Everything about him revealed a temperament of the most perfect calmness, not indolent, but placid." Though described as a hunter, Hans actually collects eider-down from the nests of eider-ducks along the rocky coast, and does not actually hunt or kill any animal. Hans seldom speaks, and when he does, it is in Danish and usually consists of a single word. Though he is quiet and a late addition to the exploration team, Hans proves invaluable during their journey. It is he who discovers water when they run out, and he also saves their provisions after their raft is damaged during a huge storm. After the three are expelled from the volcano at the end of their journey, Hans saves Axel by keeping him from falling back into the crater. While Lidenbrock and Axel become famous for their adventure upon arriving back in Hamburg, Hans wants nothing more than to return to his family in Iceland, which he does.

M. Fridrikson

M. Fridrikson is an Icelandic professor of natural science that Axel and Lidenbrock meet when they arrive in Reykjavik. Because he speaks Latin as well as Icelandic, Axel notes that Fridrikson is the only person he is able to have a conversation with among all those he meets in Iceland. Fridrikson offers the men a place to stay, and they accept. Over dinner, Fridrikson provides information to the travelers about Icelandic scholar Arne Saknussemm—the one who wrote the coded note that launched their journey. Unaware of their true plans, Fridrikson recommends that Lidenbrock and Axel visit the summit of Snäfell, which has seldom been studied. Fridrikson even arranges for them to be guided to the mountain by a trustworthy local, Hans Bjilke.

Gräuben

Gräuben is Otto Lidenbrock's seventeen-year-old goddaughter. She hails from Virland, a region in Estonia, though she lives with Lidenbrock in Hamburg, Germany. Living under the same roof, Axel and Gräuben fall in love;

although Axel thinks she will try to dissuade him from traveling to Iceland with his uncle, she surprises him by fully supporting the trip. She even helps him pack his suitcase. Gräuben implies that when Axel returns, he will have proven himself worthy of marriage. Indeed, after he returns, the two get married. In the most popular English translation of the novel, Gräuben's name has been changed to Gretchen.

Otto Lidenbrock

Professor Otto Lidenbrock is a mineralogist and professor at the Johanneum, a prestigious school in Hamburg, Germany. He is described as "a tall, spare man, with an iron constitution, and a juvenile fairness of complexion, which took off full ten years of his fifty." He is also described as having large eyes that "rolled about incessantly behind his great goggles," and a long nose that "resembled a knife blade." He is considered an expert in his field, though also impetuous and occasionally obsessive when focusing on certain scientific quandaries. He also has difficulty pronouncing the many long names of specimens encountered in mineralogy and geology. At the beginning of the novel, Lidenbrock brings home a very old copy of an Icelandic manuscript that contains a coded note. Lidenbrock vows to crack the code, and proclaims that no one in the house may eat until he does so. During the subsequent underground journey spurred by the note, Lidenbrock becomes obsessed with the idea of progressing downward, farther into the Earth, and is frustrated when the group must sail across an underground sea before continuing their descent. After they return from their adventure, Lidenbrock—despite his newfound fame and prestige—is still bothered by one event of the journey that he cannot explain: the malfunctioning of their compass. In the most popular English translation of the novel, Lidenbrock's name has been changed to Professor Hardwigg.

Martha

Martha is Otto Lidenbrock's live-in servant at his home in Hamburg, Germany. She is occasionally put-upon by the professor's strange habits; for example, while trying to solve the coded message found in the ancient Icelandic manuscript, Lidenbrock leaves the house with the key, locking Martha and Axel inside. This prevents Martha from being able to buy food to fix the household meals. When Lidenbrock arranges a trip to Iceland on short notice,

Martha asks Axel if the professor is suffering from madness. When Axel and Lidenbrock return from their adventure, they discover that Martha has already revealed the purpose of their trip to many skeptical townspeople. In the most popular English translation of the novel, Martha is referred to throughout most of the book as simply "the old cook."

THEMES

The Value of Scientific Knowledge

One of the most obvious messages to be found in *Journey to the Center of the Earth* is the importance of science and the pursuit of scientific knowledge. The entire tale springs from Lidenbrock's desire, as a man of science, to discover the true nature of the Earth's interior. Axel, doubtful though he may be, also appreciates the potential value to mankind that such a discovery would make. Even Gräuben states: "Ah! Axel, it is a grand thing to devote one's self to science. What glory awaits Mr. Lidenbrock, and will be reflected on his companion!" Indeed, when Axel and Lidenbrock return from their voyage, they receive fame and prestige for their contributions to science. In addition, knowledge of science becomes an important survival tool for Axel and Lidenbrock during their adventure. For example, their knowledge of sound and its speed help them figure out how to reconnect after Axel is separated from the rest of the party.

After their adventure, even though Lidenbrock becomes famous for his accomplishments, he is still distracted by the one occurrence he cannot explain scientifically: the failure of their compass, which led them to believe they were headed in an entirely different direction than they were actually traveling. It is telling that even after his spectacular journey, Lidenbrock is still driven by a need for science to explain this relatively unimportant occurrence, because his whole way of viewing the world is based on the belief that everything—even the malfunction of a compass—can be explained scientifically.

Exploration and the Wonders of the Natural World

The entire novel is structured as a journey across geographic space, which makes the theme of exploration a persistent and recurring element. Even before reaching the path that leads to the

TOPICS FOR FURTHER STUDY

- In the decades following the publication of *Journey to the Center of the Earth,* advances in geology rendered much of Verne's plot implausible, if not scientifically impossible. In a short paper, identify at least two scientific details in the novel that no longer fit with currently available data, and explain why these details are inaccurate. Do these inaccuracies affect your enjoyment of the book? Why or why not?

- Exploration and mapping is an important part of the characters' journey in the novel. Create a map that shows your own personal "journey" on a given day, starting and ending at your home. Try to make your map as accurate and properly scaled as you can. You can even come up with descriptive names for the various landmarks along your route.

- Verne has been criticized for creating characters that seem one-dimensional and not realistic. Some science fiction writers, such as Isaac Asimov, have argued that characterization is not of critical importance when the purpose of the writing is to explore new scientific ideas. Which viewpoint do you support? Write a short essay expressing your views; remember to include examples and reasons to support your opinions.

- The entire adventure experienced by Axel and Lidenbrock is set into motion by a type of coded message called a cryptogram. Try creating your own cryptogram similar to the one found in the book. Exchange messages with another classmate and see if you can break each other's codes.

- Like the science fiction writers who followed him, Verne used cutting-edge science as the basis for his fiction. Pick a scientific area in which rapid strides are being made today, and read a science fiction novel based on that area. Some examples include Patrick Cave's *Sharp North* (2004) or Nancy Farmer's *House of the Scorpion* (2002), which both deal with cloning; or M. T. Anderson's *Feed* (2004) or William Gibson's *Neuromancer* (1984), which both deal with computer technology. As you read the novel, make note of details that seem to be based on real science. After you finish the novel, use your library and the Internet to research the "fact" behind the fiction presented. Does the author's vision seem plausible based on current scientific knowledge? Write a paper in which you explain why or why not. Make sure to use specific examples from the novel you read to back up your argument.

---

center of the Earth, the author spends a great deal of time describing the trip from Hamburg to Iceland, as well as the environments the main characters encounter. In this way, the novel also focuses on the wonders of the natural world. At a time when few in the world would have the opportunity to make such a trip, Verne describes remote areas of the real world with the same wonder as the deep caves of his imagined subterranean world. It is also worth noting that his imagined underground world features only plants and animals that once existed or currently exist in smaller forms; for example, the group finds forests of tall mushrooms that seem identical to typical garden mushrooms, except in size. Rather than create this environment purely from fantasy, Verne chooses instead to illustrate the wonder and beauty to be found in actual specimens of the natural world by showing these specimens in a new context.

The Quest and Coming of Age

Journey to the Center of the Earth can also be viewed as an example of the quest tale, in which a young man goes on a voyage as a symbolic path to adulthood. The young man is Axel, and Verne makes it clear from the start that the story is as much about Axel becoming a man as it is about

Josh Hutcherson, Anita Briem, and Brendan Fraser in the 2008 film adaptation of the novel (© *Photos 12 / Alamy*)

what lies in the center of the planet. Before Axel leaves on his trip, his beloved Gräuben states, "When you come back, Axel, you will be a man, an equal, free to speak, free to act. . . . " His immaturity early in the story is reflected in his fear of going on the trip, as well as his unquestioning acceptance of prevailing scientific theories. His timidity later disappears, most notably after discovering the cave on the beach marked with Arne Saknussemm's dagger. Before they enter the marked tunnel, Axel suggests that they burn the raft so that they cannot change their minds about plunging forward. In the end, Axel gains his own perspective on the debate about the Earth's interior based on his own experience; although the question is not fully resolved, he no longer follows blindly the popular scientific opinions of his day. He also marries Gräuben, and proves himself to be a clever thinker in his own right, solving the mystery from their journey of the malfunctioning compass.

STYLE

Science Fiction

The genre of science fiction includes literature that is focused on the application of scientific principles to an imaginary premise. Verne was one of the first practitioners of this type of literature, though there were notable precursors. Thomas More's *Utopia* (1516) imagines an island society in great detail, including commerce, health care, and criminal justice. Jonathan Swift's *Gulliver's Travels* (1726) is an examination of society from both a scientific and comedic viewpoint. Mary Shelley's *Frankenstein* (1818) is often considered one of the first true science fiction novels, for it treats with scientific rigor the idea of reanimating human tissue after death. Another important, though often neglected, pioneer of science fiction is Edgar Allan Poe. Though generally considered a writer of horror tales, Poe also wrote tales such as "A Descent into the Maelstrom" (1841), in which the main character relies on scientific thinking to save himself from a tragic fate, and "The Balloon-Hoax" (1844), which resembles Verne's own later hot-air balloon tale *Five Weeks in a Balloon* (1863). These early examples notwithstanding, Verne's work applies science and scientific thinking to an extent that no previous author had undertaken. Aside from crafting his imaginary scenarios in ways that seem believable based on known science, Verne often has characters utilize scientific principles in order to solve problems they encounter.

The Serial Novel

Most of Verne's novels were written first as serials, published chapter by chapter in a periodical and later collected in book form. Serial fiction dates back to the collection of Middle Eastern folk tales called *One Thousand and One Nights* (1706; first published in English as *The Arabian Nights' Entertainment*). In the book, the clever young woman Scheherazade tells tales to the brutal King Shahryar in such a way that each tale must be told in installments over the course of several nights, thereby holding the king's interest and sparing herself execution. Serial fiction was common in Victorian England, when magazines were easier to produce and cheaper to buy than books. One common feature of serial fiction, clearly evident in Verne's work, is the use of cliffhangers. A cliffhanger is a suspenseful, shocking, or unexpected moment that occurs at the end of a chapter, which encourages the reader to seek out the next chapter and find out how the complication is resolved. Cliffhangers enticed readers to continue purchasing new issues of the magazine until the tale was complete.

HISTORICAL CONTEXT

The Victorian Era and the Second Industrial Revolution

The Victorian Era is a period of time defined by the rule of Queen Victoria of the United Kingdom, which lasted from 1837 until 1901. During this time, Britain—like much of Europe—experienced a general prosperity and relative peace that fueled the formation of a stable middle class and improvement of education among all classes. This helped to cultivate a general appreciation for the sciences among average citizens, which in turn helped to popularize writers like Verne and H. G. Wells, who wrote stories in which science played a key role.

During the latter half of the Victorian Era, the modern world also experienced the Second Industrial Revolution. This rapid increase in the development of the sciences and technology brought about sweeping and fundamental changes to modern society, including electric lights, the internal combustion engine, and the telephone. Much of this scientific progress was made in Germany, the home of Professor Lidenbrock and his nephew Axel in *Journey to the Center of the Earth*. The high level of industrialization also led to more people moving from rural areas to urban areas, as well as the exploitation of workers by industrial companies. This in turn led to increased labor laws and the development of strong labor unions to empower lower-class workers.

The Debate over Human Evolution and Geological Theory

Prior to the 1800s, most scientists and laypersons viewed the natural world around them as relatively young—several thousand years old, a figured based largely on guesswork tailored to fit the Bible's account—and static, or unchanging. Many believed that mountains and lakes existed because God created them in more or less the form they still held. Some argued that natural formations such as canyons were caused by accepted Biblical events like the Great Flood. However, as scientists began to uncover data from rock layers, which included fossilized remains of animals no longer living, new theories were formed that better fit the evidence at hand. These theories generally acknowledged that the planet was much older than previously believed, and suggested that geological processes such as volcanism and erosion served to constantly shape and reshape the environment. This scientific movement was known as uniformitarianism, and suggested that the natural laws of the universe operated consistently in the past as they do in the present. Charles Lyell, in his *Principles of Geology* (1830), outlined the basic evidence and arguments in support of this idea, which quickly became established as the best fit for the physical data available at the time.

Lyell's book about geological formation also played an important role in the development of ideas about biological evolution. In 1831, Charles Darwin was a young naturalist hired to work aboard the sailing ship HMS *Beagle,* collecting geological data and biological specimens during a survey of the coasts of South America. During the trip, the captain gave Darwin a copy of Lyell's *Principles of Geology,* which had a lasting impact on Darwin. Although Lyell himself did not subscribe to the notion of biological evolution, in which organisms could change over time to adapt to their environments, Darwin thought the ideas were a good match with Lyell's views on geological evolution. In Darwin's day, the idea that living things could change or evolve was considered contradictory to the teachings of the Bible, in which God

COMPARE
&
CONTRAST

- **1860s:** Geologist Charles Lyell releases *Geological Evidences of the Antiquities of Man* (1863), which controversially suggests that both the Earth and the human race are much older than previously believed.

  Today: Modern geologists estimate the age of the Earth to be about 4.5 billion years.

- **1860s:** The scientific adventure stories of Jules Verne mark the modern beginnings of the genre later known as science fiction.

- **Today:** Science fiction is one of the most popular genres of storytelling in books, film, television, and video games.

- **1860s:** The invention of the induction coil allows the creation of the first portable electric lamps.

  Today: Researchers test induction coil technology as a way to provide power wirelessly to electric vehicles.

---

created all things in their ideal form. For similar reasons, in the early 1800s, many people still did not believe that any species of animal had ever gone extinct; instead, they believed that fossils of species no longer present in one habitat—such as the mammoth—were likely to be examples of animals still living somewhere else on the planet.

By the 1860s, the ideas that form the basis for modern geology had been established, though specific details—such as what the core of the Earth was composed of—were still debated. Also by this time, Charles Darwin's ideas about biological evolution—in particular, the idea that evolution occurs as the best-adapted members of a population survive and reproduce, passing on their beneficial traits—had been published in his *On the Origin of Species* (1859). Darwin's ideas about this natural selection process as a mechanism for evolution, which were seriously debated in his own time, did not become widely accepted until well into the twentieth century.

CRITICAL OVERVIEW

When *Journey to the Center of the Earth* was first published in its original French in 1864, Verne was still new to the literary world. His only previous novel was *Five Weeks in a Balloon*, published the year before; this book proved popular, and Verne added to that popularity with *Journey*, continuing what would become a long string of novels aimed at both educating readers about science and entertaining them with tales of adventure. Despite the author's success in his native France, however, his second novel was not published in English until 1871. The book proved successful with younger audiences, though it was not viewed as serious literature by most scholars. George Orwell, in a 1941 essay, states of the novel and its author, "He set out to combine instruction with entertainment, and he succeeded, but only so long as his scientific theories were more or less up to date." Kingsley Amis said of the author in 1960, "With Verne, we reach the first great progenitor of science fiction. In its literary aspect his work is, of course, of poor quality, a feature certainly reproduced with great fidelity by most of his successors."

Journey to the Center of the Earth was also the source of some controversy for Verne. He was sued by another writer, Léon Delmas, who argued that Verne's tale was taken from a short story he had written the previous year. Despite some similarities between the works—such as the inclusion of an important message coded in Runic characters and an underground journey—the case was finally settled in Verne's favor in 1877, thirteen years after the publication of *Journey to the Center of the Earth.*

Snaefellsjokull Glacier in Iceland. In the novel, it is here that Lidenbrock discovers the passage into the earth. (© Bart Pro | Alamy)

The main problem with evaluating the reputation of Verne's work in English is that many of the first and best-known translations have been judged unsatisfactory by later scholars. The earliest English editions of *Journey to the Center of the Earth* contain revisions, abridgements, and changes to the original text; these even include name changes for several of the main characters. The first and most popular edition of the book, published by Griffith and Farran, is less a translation and more like a rewrite of Verne's original. Even more accurate translations, such as the one by clergyman Frederick Amadeus Malleson in 1877, had certain religious remarks removed or added by the translator.

Aside from translation issues, it has also become clear in recent years that editor and publisher Pierre-Jules Hetzel had substantial input regarding the final content of Verne's works. This includes the removal of passages that might be deemed too mature for younger readers, as well as themes considered overly dark or pessimistic by the editor. It has also been suggested that Hetzel, an author himself, rewrote or added passages to some of the author's novels. As William Butcher notes in *Jules Verne: The Definitive Biography* (2006), "Because Verne's novels were twice mangled, by the French and the English publishers, the translated texts were, more often than not, travesties of what Verne had actually written."

Still, Verne remains one of the most translated authors in the history of literature, and academics in recent decades have begun to treat his work as a serious part of the literary canon. Scholars such as Andrew Martin and Arthur B. Evans have written comprehensive analyses of Verne's works that aim to elevate the reputation of the author beyond simply being a science fiction writer or an author of children's adventure tales. Herbert Lottman, in *Jules Verne: An Exploratory Biography* (1996), states, "Verne seems to have been the sole inventor of what would become identified as Vernian—the combining of contemporary and future scientific knowledge with an imaginary exploration of little-known but attainable worlds."

CRITICISM

Greg Wilson

Wilson is an author, literary critic, and mythologist. In this essay, he asserts that Jules Verne was "the Michael Crichton of his day."

For modern readers, the works of Jules Verne may be difficult to place in any sort of literary context. This is inevitable, since these works have been absorbed into popular culture and have been repurposed countless times by others, with Verne's ideas often appearing in "new" forms that fail to acknowledge the original source. This means that much of what people associate with Verne is absorbed secondhand, rather than from his original work. There is also a tendency to group anything older than a century as "classic" literature, which can cause a reader to view such a work differently from a modern book with similar characteristics. It might perhaps be beneficial, then, to explain Verne's place in literature in the following way: he was the Michael Crichton of his day, and *Journey to the Center of the Earth* (1871) is a perfect example to illustrate this comparison.

Some might view this comparison as backward—and perhaps offensive to Verne—and suggest that it would be more correct to say, "Michael Crichton is the literary descendant of Jules Verne." The problem is that this comparison does not enlighten modern readers to the characteristics of Verne's work. Viewing Verne as a Victorian-era Michael Crichton is an easy way for modern audiences to make the connection between the writer and the world in which he lived. It also serves to illustrate how Verne was the originator of a style of popular literature that, in the hands of writers like Crichton, continues to this day.

One of the most obvious characteristics of just about any Crichton novel is its emphasis on scientific theory as the launch pad for the story. In particular, Crichton uses cutting-edge science and scientific theories as a key part of the premise in many of his works. For example, *Jurassic Park* (1990) was inspired by research in which paleontologists sought to extract dinosaur DNA from prehistoric mosquitoes trapped in amber. It was also heavily influenced by modern ideas about dinosaurs being warm-blooded. In much the same way, Verne's work was based on the most up-to-date science of the era. For example, in *Journey to the Center of the Earth*, there is

> ASIDE FROM THE OBVIOUS SIMILARITIES IN DEALING WITH SCIENTIFIC AND TECHNICAL INFORMATION, CRICHTON AND VERNE ARE ALIKE IN ANOTHER WAY: THEY BOTH WRITE OF EXOTIC LOCATIONS GENERALLY UNFAMILIAR TO THEIR READERS."

much debate between Axel and Lidenbrock regarding what exists at the center of the planet; one believes the center to be too hot and pressurized for humans to withstand, while the other expresses doubts about this theory. At the time Verne wrote the novel, there was little evidence to confirm what lay at the center of the planet—and it is this debate that lies at the core of Verne's adventure tale.

Rather than just being inspired by contemporary science, though, Crichton has developed a habit of including many references to real-world research as a way of imbuing his novels with a certain level of authenticity. Verne himself was an expert at this technique, which can be seen in his many references to actual scientists and their work in *Journey to the Center of the Earth*. Although many of these scientists are unknown to modern readers, they were familiar enough in Verne's time to lend legitimacy to his work.

Along these same lines, Crichton is known for including numerous scientific or historical digressions in each of his works, in which the narrator essentially imparts knowledge directly to the reader in much the same manner as a textbook. For example, in *The Great Train Robbery* (1975), Crichton pauses his story to explain Bernoulli's principle to the reader. Similarly, in *Journey*, Verne provides a lovely but unnecessary description of how eider-down is collected in Iceland. He later provides background information on the state of paleontology in the years before the novel takes place.

Another key ingredient in Crichton's novels is the use of science to overcome obstacles the main characters face. This too is a common

WHAT DO I READ NEXT?

- *Twenty Thousand Leagues Under the Sea* (1872) is one of Verne's most famous adventure tales, and deals with an environment as alien as the interior of a volcano: the undersea world. A French marine biologist, his assistant, and a Canadian harpoonist are called to assist in an attempt to locate a mysterious sea monster that is terrorizing ships on the open ocean. Instead of a monster, they find a brilliant scientist named Captain Nemo and his ultra-advanced submarine, the *Nautilus*.

- *The Mysterious Island* (1874) is a sequel to *Twenty Thousand Leagues Under the Sea,* though the story it tells stands alone. In it, five Americans imprisoned in the South during the Civil War make a daring escape by balloon, but end up on an island in the South Pacific. While there, they experience strange providences that lead them to believe they are not alone on the island.

- *Around the World in Eighty Days* (1873) is a Verne tale small on science but big on adventure. Phileas Fogg, a wealthy Englishman, bets some of his colleagues that he can travel around the world—in an era long before airplanes—in just eighty days. He takes his new valet, a Frenchman named Passepartout, along for the adventure across land and sea.

- *From the Earth to the Moon* (1867) is another Verne tale of wagers and daring trips, but with a more fantastical twist. Impey Barbicane, the president of a gun club in Baltimore, hits upon the idea that a long cannon would be capable of launching a capsule at high enough speed to reach the moon. With the support of benefactors around the world, Barbicane and his fellow club members build the cannon at a launch site in Florida, all the while facing opposition from Barbicane's enemy, a man named Nicholl.

- *The Lost World* (1912) by Arthur Conan Doyle is an adventure that carries in it the spirit of Verne's best work. In the novel, a scientist, a reporter, and a heroic explorer lead a team to a plateau in South America where dinosaurs have been found to still exist. This book is the first in a series of tales concerning the brilliant but difficult Professor Challenger and his associates.

- *At the Earth's Core* (1914) by Edgar Rice Burroughs is an adventure clearly inspired by *Journey to the Center of the Earth*. In it, the wealthy heir to a mining empire tests an experimental digger that burrows five hundred miles straight into the Earth and uncovers a secret subterranean world called Pellucidar. As in Verne's tale, this interior world is populated by primitive creatures such as dinosaurs, though Burroughs does not limit himself to known prehistoric animals. The world of Pellucidar appeared as the setting for six more Burroughs novels over the years.

- *The Calcutta Chromosome* (1996) by Indian author Amitav Ghosh won the Arthur C. Clarke award in 1997. Though set in the future at an unspecified time, it is inspired by the life of malaria researcher Sir Ronald Ross (1857–1932). Ross won a Nobel Prize in Medicine for his breakthroughs in malaria research. The main character's interest in researching Ross leads to the discovery of a chromosome that can change people's personalities.

theme in Verne's work, perhaps even more so. For example, in *Journey*, when the trio of explorers release a stream of water from a subterranean lake, they realize that the water—at the mercy of gravity—will automatically guide them along the most direct path downward. Later, when Axel becomes lost and stumbles upon a sound corridor in which he can hear his uncle, they use their knowledge of the speed of sound to determine how far apart they are.

With so much scientific information to present to the reader, Crichton makes use of "reader surrogate" characters. These are characters whose main purpose is to function as being equivalent in knowledge and viewpoint to the average reader; this allows the author to present otherwise dry scientific information in a way that makes sense within the story. In other words, technical or scientific explanations meant to educate the reader are directed at the surrogate character in the story, so that the reader and reader surrogate learn the information simultaneously. For example, in *State of Fear* (2004), Crichton uses the main character of Peter Evans as a reader surrogate; Evans believes global warming exists, but does not know any information about the actual studies undertaken by scientists. When he is presented with (arguably) persuasive evidence that global warming does not exist, Evans—like the reader—is meant to question what he believes to be true. Verne also uses reader surrogates, though with perhaps less finesse than Crichton. In *Journey*, Lidenbrock is often required to explain technical matters to his nephew Axel; however, Axel is occasionally the one doing the explaining to Lidenbrock.

Another literary device common in Crichton's works is the false document. This is a fictional piece of writing contained within the novel that purports to be an authentic creation. For example, *The Great Train Robbery* contains several fictional news articles that appear to be taken from Victorian-era newspapers. False documents such as these provide a feeling of authenticity to the work, and serve to make other events in the novel seem more believable. Verne also uses false documents in *Journey*, most notably with his inclusion of the journal Axel wrote while aboard the raft sailing across the Sea of Lidenbrock. Verne also reproduces the coded Runic document found by Lidenbrock and Axel at the beginning of the novel, which launches them on their journey. This document also meets another characteristic common to the works of both authors: the inclusion of puzzles or riddles that a character must solve, which simultaneously gives the reader a chance to solve them before the solution is revealed. This is also seen in the alien code in Crichton's *Sphere* (1987), among others.

Aside from the obvious similarities in dealing with scientific and technical information, Crichton and Verne are alike in another way: they both write of exotic locations generally unfamiliar to their readers. Crichton's *Jurassic Park*, for example, takes place on a remote tropical island near Costa Rica. *State of Fear* takes place in numerous locations around the world, including France, Malaysia, Japan, and Iceland—all in the first fifty pages. Verne, however, succeeds in providing more detailed descriptions of these exotic environments than Crichton does. His descriptions of real places in *Journey*, such as Iceland, are as vivid as his fantastical descriptions of the planet's interior.

The two authors also share similar stylistic shortcomings. Inspired by science, both create works that center on a high-concept premise, which is easy to understand and is immediately compelling. The high concept of *Journey*, for example, would be: "A mineralogist and his nephew discover a secret path that leads to the center of the Earth." The emphasis on high concepts also explains why both writers's works are so frequently adapted for film and television—a medium that craves high concepts for their ability to quickly capture the interest of an audience. Unfortunately, in these idea-driven stories, characterization frequently falls by the wayside, and neither Verne nor Crichton has a reputation for developing realistic characters. This is most obvious in the dialogue; in *Journey*, for example, one can easily lose track of whether Lidenbrock or Axel is speaking in any given conversation, since both speak in a formal, stilted style; both "sound" alike on the page. Even worse—and this is especially common in Crichton's work—the characters are simply mouthpieces used to provide whatever information the author must give to the reader in order to keep the story moving.

Another stylistic weakness leveled at Crichton's work is the frequent use of coincidence or happenstance to help move the story forward. This is common in many adventure stories, and Verne is a master of it, judging by the unbelievably lucky breaks he grants to his characters. In *Journey*, these coincidences are so numerous that Verne even has the characters discuss how unbelievably lucky they have been. Here are just a few examples: Axel gets lost and happens to fall right where a sound corridor allows him to hear his uncle's voice; the storm the explorers experience happens to deposit them on shore almost right where Arne Saknussemm had traveled, even though the subterranean cavern is hundreds upon hundreds of miles across; and at the end, the passageway through which their raft is thrust upward by rushing water happens to be just wide enough for the raft to pass unharmed, and happens to extend all the way to the surface, though it also conveniently places them away from the deadly main crater of the volcano they ascend.

Another fault of both authors might be surprising to some readers: they sometimes get their facts just plain wrong. This is different from using scientific theories that are later disproven or fall out of fashion, such as the notion that the center of the Earth is actually cold. We are talking about established, objective facts that are incorrectly conveyed in the author's work. One notable instance of this occurs in Crichton's *Jurassic Park*. The Velociraptors he describes in the book are nothing at all like those that exist in the fossil record, the main problem being that real Velociraptors were about the size of chickens and were likely covered in feathers. Crichton's raptors much more closely resemble the real-world Deinonychus. This seems less like a blunder than a deliberate distortion of scientific truth, for reasons known only to Crichton (though I would guess he just liked the name "Velociraptor" better). Verne, on the other hand, makes mistakes on such common facts as the distance between Iceland and Greenland, and provides two different dates for the volcano Snäfell's last eruption (both of which are off by almost a thousand years).

Despite these weaknesses, there is one other trait Crichton and Verne share: they were both wildly popular among readers during their own lifetimes. Though their lives and works were separated by a century of scientific and technological progress, Crichton and Verne hold remarkably similar niches in the world of literature. If any readers should still, after the previous comparisons, take offense at the suggestion that Verne was essentially the Michael Crichton of his era— laurels, warts, and all—they can always find solace in one important difference between the two men: Verne did it first.

Source: Greg Wilson, Critical Essay on Jules Verne's *Journey to the Center of the Earth,Novels for Students 34,* Gale, Cengage Learning, 2010.

Janis Svilpis

In the following excerpt, Svilpis analyzes how Verne combines the ancient story template of self-discovery with the more modern theme of scientific discovery.

[*Journey to the Center of the Earth*], published in 1864, is an early and influential embodiment of many recurrent patterns, not least its blend of adventure and didacticism. The youthful protagonist, Axel, accompanies his uncle, Professor Lidenbrock, on a subterranean scientific expedition prompted by a sixteenth-century Icelandic manuscript that alludes to an earlier descent. Axel undergoes a rite of passage into manhood on the way. Lidenbrock's ward, Gräuben, his sweetheart, urges him to go, saying he will find a wife when he returns, and she welcomes him back with the promise, "Now that you are a hero, Axel ..., you will never have to leave me again." He becomes a hero not only by braving dangers but also by absorbing a scientific perspective, and this process of absorption poses dangers of its own.

The book's slow opening detracts from the adventure by delaying the descent until Chapter 17, two fifths of the way through, but it serves a number of purposes, including the establishment of a pattern of testing associated with visionary experiences. Axel's perceptions of the world around him are modified and he becomes hardened to the resulting disorientation. He deciphers the manuscript "in the grip of a sort of hallucination," saving the household from a farcical threat of starvation caused by Lidenbrock's refusal to allow a meal until the problem is solved. Despite his fears, he finds himself maneuvered into going on the expedition. Lidenbrock browbeats him into climbing to the top of the Vor-Frelsers-Kirk in Copenhagen to give him "lessons in abysses," and five such lessons inure him to the vertiginous "optical illusion" that the world is spinning. From Sneffels Yokul, on Iceland, Axel sees the landscape "as if one of Helbesmer's relief-maps were spread out at my feet," and he becomes pleasantly intoxicated by this scientific mode of perception. To be sure, this *is* intoxicating, for it detaches him from his immediate surroundings and even from his personal identity, in an abstract and impersonal vision, a view from a height: "I forgot who I was and where I was, living the life of the elves and sylphs of Scandinavian mythology." This is vertigo in a more insidious form, and only a short while later, Axel must be restrained from throwing himself down the volcano's central chimney.

The testing pattern changes once the group moves underground. In two incidents, nearly miraculous rescues stress the importance of faith and courage. Lidenbrock takes a wrong turn, they run out of water, and Axel despairs, though his uncle counsels fortitude. Axel awakens from delirium to hear Hans, the Icelandic guide, announce in Danish his discovery of a subterranean river, and though he does not know Danish, he understands. A bit after this, like Moses in the wilderness, Hans smites the rock with his pickaxe and brings forth water. Subsequently, Axel strays from the others and becomes lost in the dark. By chance, he happens upon an acoustical phenomenon that enables him to speak with Lidenbrock, though they are almost four miles apart, and in this he sees God's providence, "for He had led me through those huge dark spaces to what was perhaps the only spot where my companions' voices could have reached me."

But his faith is not yet sufficient to let him stand his most severe visionary trial alone. When they enter the huge subterranean cavern and go rafting on the Lidenbrock Sea, he has a "prehistoric daydream," in which he looks back over the development of life on Earth, and farther back to the condensation of the planet out of a gaseous nebula. As before, he loses his sense of identity and his consciousness of his surroundings, overcome by a vision of the paleontological, geological, and cosmological past, and Hans has to stop him from throwing himself overboard. When this vision seems to come true, and especially when he glimpses the gigantic shepherd of mastodons, he flees in panic, as he did when lost, but this time Lidenbrock shares his fear. This sequence culminates in the discovery that Arne Saknussemm, Icelandic alchemist, heretic, explorer, and author of the manuscript that Axel has deciphered, had reached this place before them. Seeing this sign that faith and courage may be more successful than he has believed possible, Axel exchanges places with his uncle, temporarily becoming fearless and insisting that they press on: "the Professor's soul had passed straight into me, and the spirit of discovery inspired me." His enthusiasm leads to the blasting of a rock that bars the way, which plunges them into an abyss, and results ultimately in their return to the surface by being shot out of a volcano.

Axel still has fears, but he learns to control them, and he passes his final test of vision by emerging from this last abyss. That he has become a mature scientist is proven by his explanation of the puzzling malfunction of their compass, which baffles even Lidenbrock. Unlike his decipherment of the manuscript, this is an application of scientific reasoning, not a chance perception. From the first, he has been a knowledgeable commentator on geological matters—his identifications and classifications form much of the book's didactic content—but he becomes much more than a spouter of facts, and the progress of the story reflects this development. The opening is primarily travelogue, loaded with encyclopedic detail; after the subterranean descent the emphasis shifts to data-gathering, observation, and measurement, and then, as their instruments are lost or grow unreliable, it shifts again, this time to an imaginative grasp of the larger picture to which the isolated data belong. Axel proceeds from book-learning to active observation and finally to a vision of the order of the world which complements and helps create his new faith and courage.

Something akin to this vision, the presupposition that the world has an order, has been present from the beginning. Lidenbrock's reasons for undertaking the expedition include a desire to determine which of two competing hypotheses about the Earth's core is true. One, commonly accepted and supported by Axel, says that it is molten; the other, attributed to Humphry Davy and supported by Lidenbrock, holds that it is cold and that vulcanism is a surface phenomenon. Their disputes on this subject appear frequently, giving substance to Lidenbrock's otherwise unconvincing assertion that "I no longer regard you as my nephew, but as my colleague." In this debate, as in their other debates, Lidenbrock dominates until Axel supersedes him. The question about the Earth's core is answered inconclusively, but Axel's new intrepidity and force of personality show that he has emerged as his uncle's equal in authority.

Voyages of discovery are often voyages of self-discovery, and the archetype of Verne's story is very old. He applied it, however, to some specifically science-fictional themes, broadening the idea of discovery to include all past time, and the idea of self-discovery to include the individual's relationship to the cosmos. He explored the developing scientific mind's relationship to authority, both scientific and parental; he displayed that mind in the act of solving problems; and he analyzed the qualities required by both science and adulthood. Verne's primary concern in this book is with the intellectual, rather than the moral or social being, and in this he anticipates a major emphasis in twentieth-century science fiction.

Source: Janis Svilpis, "Authority, Autonomy, and Adventure in Juvenile Science Fiction," in *Children's Literature Association Quarterly*, Vol. 8, No. 3, Fall 1983, pp. 22–26.

Fernando Savater

In this excerpt, Savater examines Verne's use of initiation or pilgrimage in his novel.

The initiatory nature of adventure novels whose plot consists of a journey is widely recognized even by critics who most obstinately resist the mythologization of storytelling. In fact, eighty percent of adventures either explicitly or implicitly take the form of a journey, always easily interpretable as a series of steps toward initiation. The pattern is obvious: the adolescent, still within the placental confines of the natural, receives the summons to adventure in the form of a map, a riddle, a fabulous tale, a magic object. Accompanied by an initiator, a figure of demoniacal energy whom he simultaneously fears and venerates, he undertakes a journey rich in sudden reversals, difficulties, and temptations. He must overcome successive trials and finally defeat a monster, or, more generally, confront death itself. In the end he is reborn into a new life which is no longer natural but artificial, a mature life and one of a delicately vulnerable kind.

This plot is so well known that I recall it to the reader's mind only as a clarification of the use I ordinarily make of the word *initiation*, employed in its least pretentious and most habitual sense ... [The] pattern of initiation itself can serve vastly different aims and that the result of the ritual can as well be the attainment of man's estate as resignation, the enrichment of possibilities, or acceptance of their finiteness. Both the journey of Gilgamesh and the quest for the Grail are initiatory tales: the denouement of the first is the inexorability of death, that of the second is immortality. Epic wisdom always sees the journey as something significant; for the storyteller, no one ever travels with impunity. But the initiate's experiences vary from the most unmistakable triumph of strength to the no less complete realization of weakness, solitude, or annihilation. Initiation does not offer a lesson with a single meaning; at its highest level, neither wisdom nor ignorance is alien to it. All these perspectives have already been minutely studied by modern critics.

I would like to emphasize here some aspects of the actual experience of the journey in one of its possible variants—the descent.

To descend is to plunge into that which sustains us, to plumb the foundations that lie beneath us. It is a dangerous mission, perhaps one leading to madness, for everything seems to indicate that the earth sustains us precisely insofar as it preserves its opacity, its stubborn resistance to our investigative gaze. To open it in any way is to put it out of action as a support; the investigation which uncovers it to our eyes takes it out from under our feet by that very act. Not only our physical stability but also our mental equilibrium, our reason itself, can falter in the course of this attempt. When we descend radically—that is, not when we descend a staircase, which is something raised, but when we descend to what is really below—we lose our firmest coordinates and have to invert our points of reference very oddly. What formerly upheld us now becomes something that covers us; what is closed surrounds us and opens before us, while what was formerly open acquires a faraway, opaque indeterminateness; to leap upward takes us closer to the rocks while falling brings us closer to the air. Our head no less than our feet needs solid foundations, and this exercise in geographical perversion can make it spin. Nonetheless, throughout the ages what lies beneath us has always been particularly tempting. The kingdom of the dead is there but also hidden treasures. The secret places of all things are there, which will permit us to control them better when we return to the surface. Whatever is deepest and most profound is there, which verbal intuition tells us is the most desirable. Everything decayed lies there but also everything that is forgotten, feared, all that must be concealed, that is, *buried*. There the deepest darkness awaits us—dead or alive, we will go there in the end, and to descend while we are still alive predisposes and prepares us for the last descent of all—and everything denied to the light of day. And there, lastly, down there, must be the center, for we cannot forget that we crawl about upon a sphere—and that center is not so much a geometrical equidistance as a point of spiritual power, the terrible divine umbilicus that contains the whole meaning of the world. One day we emerge from the nether, the dark, the enclosed places, from the earth; and on any night we will return to it. We descend in order to rise again, that is, to be reborn. This second birth endows us with renewed strength, an impeccable desire to live tempered by contact with hell, and a familiarity with fundamental things which causes the unavoidable to lose its horrible prestige.

We shall take our examples of the essential pilgrimage from Jules Verne. Curiously, though some descry in Verne the very paradigm of the initiatory novelist, a critic as shrewd as Michel Foucault denies the initiatory nature of his tales, arguing that at the end of their heroes' journeys "nothing has changed, either on earth or in the depths of themselves." Perhaps here we would have to distinguish between the story of an initiation and an initiatory story: *Treasure Island* obviously belongs to the first category and Verne's novels to the second (with relative shades of difference which we will discuss). The story that narrates an initiation is the chronicle of the things that happen to a character in his progress toward initiatory enlightenment and maturity; in the initiatory story the reader is the initiate. Indeed, Verne's characters are usually purely external, eyes that see and hands that grasp, thermometers of temperature changes or bellows registering the absence of oxygen; their minimal inner selves are noted only in such primary phenomena as resistance to adventure (Axel in *Journey to the Center of the Earth*) or mystery: Captain Nemo has a secret, not a psychology. Following the initiation that undeniably takes place in Verne's novels, the characters display about as much change as the odometer of an automobile after the twenty-four-hour race at Le Mans: they register the distance covered, but otherwise are exactly the same as when they started out. But they have done their job of being the reader's eyes and ears during the initiatory process. Hence the documentary nature of so many of Verne's novels, his obsession with giving the reader reliable data about the circumstances of an adventure which concerns him more closely than the characters who are supposedly experiencing it, and who are really no more than the *sensorium dei* of the reader-god.

Reading Verne is like going up in an unballasted balloon, like riding astride a kite, like being pulled down into the abyss on a bottomless waterfall: and all this within the strictest and even the most prosaic matter-of-factness. It means dreaming, of course, but without having to give up calculation, reflection, and even plans. It means joining hands with delirium and placing myth at our service, only to reach the fullest and most irrefutable realism, to install ourselves

irrevocably in the soberest ordinariness which surrounds us, accepted as imagination brought to life.

Let us say, in order to make ourselves a little clearer, that there are "hard" fantasies and "soft" fantasies. These last are rambling, cumulative, and unstructured, like their prototype, Lucian's *True History*; things that are portentous, unlikely, or conceivable only in the last resort by a generous stretch of the imagination succeed each other with the suspicious arbitrariness of a world where everything is possible except order. It is the realm not so much of the chaotic, which at least postulates an absent cosmos with which it contrasts, but of the amorphous. Since it is the only kind of fantasy conceivable by persons who lack imagination, and since it permits a certain harmful proclivity toward the allegorical, it has produced unreadable and pretentious jumbles like certain subproducts of German romanticism or a few French "rêveries". Let us, rather, remember the masterworks it has given us: *Alice in Wonderland*, Lord Dunsany's *A Dreamer's Tales*, H. P. Lovecraft's *The Dream-Quest of Unknown Kadath*.

"Hard" fantasy, on the other hand, prefers what Borges calls "the secret adventures of order" and abhors the gratuitous reversal of fortune as much as the juggling of inverisimilitude or the absurd. In this kind of fantasy surprise arises from careful plotting, not from incongruousness, and its most prodigious element is precisely the familiar gradations by which we approach the improbable. Certain rules of the game are laid down and respected, certainly broader rules than the usual ones but profoundly indebted to them, of which they are both extrapolation and counterpoint. In hard fantasy the most strictly regulated realities, such as ethics or science, can become the nucleus of the novel's plot. Let us recall with a thrill of gratitude *The Strange Case of Dr. Jekyll and Mr. Hyde*, the works of H. G. Wells and Olaf Stapledon, Arthur C. Clarke's *Rendezvous with Rama*, and others. Need we say that the works of Jules Verne are paradigms of the hard fantasy, that they not only aspire to attain the ephemeral triumph of perplexity but also the deepest and most permanent spells of prophecy, the initiatory ritual, and utopian freedom?

Apparently, Verne is anything but an *écrivain maudit*. His work enjoyed tremendous popularity almost from the beginning of his career, and his fame has remained intact, or even increased, to the present day, when his books have been published dozens of times in all civilized languages. But it has not only been the common reader who has supported him in this spontaneous and permanent vote of confidence; some of his most illustrious contemporaries had no hesitation in proclaiming his genius, with unaccustomed agreement: Tolstoy as well as Alfred Jarry, Kipling and Gorki as well as Paul Claudel, Raymond Roussel, and the surrealists.

Present-day French critics like Butor, Michel Foucault, Roland Barthes, and Claude Roy have "rediscovered"—the fashionable phrase—Jules Verne, burying the simple flow of his writing under mountains of Freudian interpretations, structural diagrams, or sociological digressions. It is an effort in which one is astonished as much by the writers' ingenuity as by their repetitiveness and superfluity; but I will not belabor the point, for maybe I am making the same mistakes on this page—in this book—and maybe I lack the gift of simplicity more than other writers do.

Verne was an unknown writer, they tell us, and the prestige he gained arose from a misunderstanding: he was confused with a "minor" author of the same name, taken for a simple writer of adventure novels or scientific prophecy, and his symbolic value, the mythical and political levels made possible by more "adult" readings of his work, was ignored. Miguel Salabert, his translator into Spanish, sharply accuses Verne's own readers of concealing these levels: "Readers of 'adventure books' are bad readers. Carried away by interest in the sudden change of circumstance, the story line, they unabashedly skip everything that they do not think essential. Descriptions and digressions bore youngsters."

Well, well, so readers of adventure books are bad readers because they like good stories well told, without any false padding; good readers, on the other hand, enjoy putting up with the superfluous. So much for them, then, but where did Salabert get the idea that youngsters don't like descriptions and digressions? The youngster who is writing this read Salgari with other youngsters like himself, and it was not uncommon for us to rush off to verify in the pages of the encyclopedia one of the technical references to animals or trees that are scattered through his stories. No one is more meticulous than a child reader, my friend Salabert. In cases like Verne's, literary critics especially are made victims of

their intrinsic limitations: *they* are the ones who have decided that writers of adventure or scientific prophecy are "minor," they are the ones who decree that adolescents enjoy only the picturesque or the unimportant, they are the ones who, in the nineteenth century, limited Verne's interest to his ability to foresee scientific advances and string together curious turns of plot. They are the ones who have always been mistaken about Verne; children, however, were right about him from the start. Now we must rescue Verne not only from his enthusiasts but from "serious" criticism's prejudices against "minor" literature. But even in the middle of this rescue operation, critics seize the opportunity to blame their own compulsions on those who have maintained a little freshness with respect to the stories' value, a freshness they have in large measure lost. Naturally mental retardation and childishness are not indispensable to make an adult interested in Verne: it is enough that he has not lost his capacity to enjoy reading. But this does not deny the fact that Jules Verne is indeed a writer of fantastic adventures and hence the possessor of a magnificent poetic and mythical spirit, like many other "minor" writers: Stevenson, Kipling, Wells, Salgari, Conan Doyle. Whether in the depths of the sea, in the clouds, in the impossible jungles of our nighttime terrors or on the moon, the voice of Jules Verne repeats his secret hymn, which sings persuasively of the many faces of courage, the miracles of reasoning power, and also—why not?—the paradoxical joys of resignation.

The first of the two Verne novels I have chosen to illustrate the downward journey is *A Journey to the Center of the Earth*, one of the most marvelous and unforgettable of the whole cycle. All of Verne is in it: the unusual scene, the tremendous enterprise, the timid and shrinking but resourceful adolescent, the energetic adult who performs the initiation, the untamable forces of the occult, the implicitly metaphysical meaning of risk and discovery. Professor Lidenbrock decides to give lessons in abysses to his nephew Axel; his plan is nothing less than to take him down to the very center of the earth. The adventure begins when they find an ancient manuscript written in unintelligible runic letters: it is the word of the Traveler, the Alchemist, which comes from far away, clothed in a ritual of concealment worthy of Poe. Axel does not want to answer this summons; his objections repeat those of a common sense that we might well call "superficial," since his chief argument is that everything that interests him in the world is on its surface and that he hasn't lost anything in that remote center. Lidenbrock, however, convinces him that to reach the center would best help him to possess the pleasures of the surface. What Paul Valéry said was true: "The deepest part of all is the skin"; the truth of this maxim lies in the fact that to regain the skin, one must first pass through the depths. Axel will take some time to learn this: he will take the whole novel, to be exact, for even when at the end of the journey he seems to be just as interested as Lidenbrock in reaching the center of the earth, this interest appears to be a sort of "rapture of the deep," more suicidal than regenerative. The center, after all, marks only half the journey: it is certain that the travelers have descended in order to come up, this time in a profound sense, to the surface.

We have spoken of *Treasure Island* as a reflection on audacity; we can undoubtedly think of *A Journey to the Center of the Earth* as an epic of effort. Few stories are so palpably toilsome, so humbly approving of effort and perseverance. It is made very clear that to descend is first of all a question of effort. Axel must undergo all the tests that effort has to face: hunger and thirst, exhaustion, vertigo, being alone in the dark, injuries, burns, disorientation, starting over, panic in the face of the unknown, monsters of the lower regions, storms, the power of lightning, rough waters, hurricane—and also obstructed paths and blind alleys. Only his persistence in what he has undertaken allows him to extract from weakness, in every case, the necessary strength to pass the test successfully. In the chronicle of other exploits, what shines brightest is the heroes' skill or courage; in this story the chief trait is obstinacy. Except for the proofs of his passage which the long-dead Arne Saknussemm tried to make in order to mark the downward path, and the positive indications in his manuscript, no special intelligent initiative guides the descent of the travelers, who are fundamentally carried along by stubborn inertia. Rather than descending they seem to fall. And their ascent through the volcano will be no less unplanned and will display the pneumatic automatism of the cork popping out of a champagne bottle. All that is left for the travelers to do is put up with the confusion of the different accidents of their journey, while they feel pressing above their heads those thousands of kilometers of rock which, miraculously, do not decide to crush them. Perseverance is second nature to Professor Lidenbrock, while the keenness of his scientific knowledge is considerably less obvious. But in this stressful descent wisdom is superfluous. All they need to do is want, not to know or even be able to act.

As he descends, Axel finds more and more open space where everything ought to be opaque, as we would think. Just as modern atomic physics has shattered the solidity of matter, making it identical to the near-emptiness of stellar space, so the ever larger caverns encountered by Verne's explorers reproduce the open expanse of the surface they had left behind. As Hermes Trismegistus said, "What is above is equal to that which is below." After descending many kilometers Axel reencounters breeze and ocean, clouds and vegetation. Everything is the same, but everything could not be more different. The lower world is the past of the surface world, its ocean is what our oceans have forgotten, its vegetation takes us back to the Jurassic period or even earlier, its formidable beasts no longer harass the earth's outer surface. A gigantic antediluvian shepherd drives a flock of mastodons among giant ferns; the dust that covers the ground comes from the calcareous remains of prehistoric mollusks. Just as memories of mute infancy pile up in our unconscious, which is our lower depths, so the earth's past is stratified and joined in its interior. The Herculean keeper of mastodons is Utnapishtim, the Eternal Ancestor, whom Gilgamesh approached in his search for immortality. What seemed hopelessly lost—the past—is only buried, has sunk, in order to offer a solid foundation for our present. To descend is to go backward. What sustains us is what precedes us. Axel will not succeed in carrying the flower of immortality to the surface, as Gilgamesh also was unable to do; the frozen, fundamental shadow of Utnapishtim awakens his horror and postulates an even more radical descent, of which he will no longer be capable. Really, only the young man has fulfilled the purpose of the journey, for Professor Lidenbrock belongs to the abstract scientific sphere of the dispute of forms, and the descent has chiefly affected him as a verification or rejection of existing theories. As for Hans, he fully belongs to the ferocious silence of the primitive, as is revealed in the raft crossing under the magical light of St. Elmo's fire. "Hans did not budge. His long hair, blown forward by the hurricane over his motionless features, gave him an odd appearance, for the end of every hair was tipped with little luminous plumes. This frightening mask reminded me of the face of antediluvian man, the contemporary of the ichthyosaurus and the megatherium."

Only Axel has truly descended, following the footsteps of the alchemist Arne Saknussemm, but he does not succeed in completing the journey of the perfect initiate. The center of the world, which is perhaps ultimately made of fire, is closed to him; the hasty violence of explosives he sets off will arouse the bowels of the earth against him and result in his expulsion. In fact this is the only initiative he takes during the whole trip, and it causes the end of his initiation before he has completed it. To descend is indeed a task for the tenacious man, not for the merely resourceful.

Source: Fernando Savater, "The Journey Downward," in *Childhood Regained: The Art of the Storyteller*, translated by Frances M. Lopez-Morillas, Columbia University Press, 1982, pp. 39–52.

SOURCES

Amis, Kingsley, "Starting Points," in his *New Maps of Hell: A Survey of Science Fiction*, Harcourt Brace Jovanovich, Inc., 1960, pp. 15–41.

Butcher, William, *Jules Verne: The Definitive Biography*, Da Capo Press, 2006, p. 228.

Lottman, Herbert, *Jules Verne: An Exploratory Biography*, St. Martin's Press, 1997. Excerpt reprinted in "Critical Excerpts" section of *Journey to the Center of the Earth*, Enriched Classics edition, Simon & Schuster, 2008, p. 321.

Orwell, George, "Two Glimpses of the Moon." *The New Statesman & Nation*, Vol. XXI, No. 517, January 18, 1941, p. 64.

Verne, Jules, *Journey to the Center of the Earth*, Enriched Classics edition, Simon & Schuster, 2009.

———, "Jules Verne at Home: His Own Account of His Life and Work." Interview with R. H. Sherard, in *McClure's Magazine*, Vol. II, No. 2, January 1894, p. 124.

FURTHER READING

Allègre, Claude, *From Stone to Star: A View of Modern Geology*. Translated by Deborah Kurmes Van Dam, Harvard University Press, 1994.
    This book is a comprehensive survey of modern views on geology. Since so much has been learned about the Earth over the past century, these ideas are often quite different from those believed in Verne's own time.

Costello, Peter, *Jules Verne: Inventor of Science Fiction*. Hodder and Stoughton, 1978.
    Costello builds on several earlier biographies of Verne, and looks at the author's life in chronological order according to his work. Costello offers insight into the scientific research that inspired Verne's novels.

Roberts, David, *Iceland: Land of the Sagas*, Villard, 1998.
    Combining history and narrative with photographs by acclaimed journalist Jon Krakauer, this book aims to capture the essence of a country forged from ice and fire in equal parts.

Singh, Simon, *The Code Book: The Science of Secrecy from Ancient Egypt to Quantum Cryptography*, Anchor, 2000.
    This sweeping look at codes used throughout history covers topics ranging from the Rosetta Stone to the use of the Navajo language as a secret Allied code in World War II.

The Magnificent Ambersons

BOOTH TARKINGTON

1918

The Magnificent Ambersons (1918) by Booth Tarkington is something of a literary oddity: a Pulitzer Prize–winning novel widely panned by critics; a once well-known novel now virtually forgotten by modern readers; and a book eclipsed in the popular culture by its own trouble-plagued 1942 film adaptation. At the time of its publication, Tarkington was already a best-selling author; with *The Magnificent Ambersons*, however, he became a literary superstar. He was even chosen in a 1922 *Literary Digest* contest as the "greatest living writer."

The Magnificent Ambersons is the chronicle of a wealthy family's declining fortunes in a growing Midwestern city at the turn of the twentieth century. The tale focuses mainly on George Minafer, a child born into prosperity who has been spoiled by his mother and grandfather. He derides work as something for the lower classes, and runs roughshod over the town citizenry as if it were his inherited right. When the family's wealth begins to run dry, George sees the world he knows slip away.

Although the novel has fallen out of favor with many critics and scholars, it remains a significant depiction of Midwestern city life in the early 1900s, as urbanization spread outward and radically shifted both the psychology and habits of all those it touched. Indeed, many critics—even while faulting the work on a literary level—have acknowledged its value as a detailed document of a bygone facet of American life.

Booth Tarkington (The Library of Congress)

AUTHOR BIOGRAPHY

Newton Booth Tarkington was born on July 29, 1869, in Indianapolis, Indiana. The upper-middle-class family in which he was raised was a prestigious one; his father was a lawyer, and the uncle for whom he was named served as both governor and a senator of California. He attended both Purdue and Princeton universities, though he failed to earn a degree at either college. However, he served as editor of the *Nassau Literary Magazine* while at Princeton, and decided to focus his efforts on a career as a writer.

After he spent several years honing his craft, Tarkington's first novel, *The Gentleman from,*, was published in 1899. This was followed by a quick succession of other works, interrupted only by a brief career as a congressman for the state of Indiana, with the author averaging about one novel per year. Among these works were *Penrod* (1914), a popular collection of comical adventures about a Midwestern boy, and *The Turmoil* (1915), the first of what would become the author's *Growth* trilogy.

The second novel of the trilogy, *The Magnificent Ambersons*, proved to be one of the author's greatest successes, winning the Pulitzer Prize in 1919. Like many of his works, it relied heavily upon the author's own experiences growing up in Indianapolis, with the unnamed "Midland city" serving as a fiction representation of his hometown. This success was followed by another Pulitzer Prize winner, *Alice Adams*, in 1921. In 1922, Tarkington was voted "the greatest living writer" in a contest held by the *Literary Digest*.

These books would prove to be the height of Tarkington's career. Although he continued to write at a prolific pace, his eyesight began failing, and neither readers nor critics responded enthusiastically to his later works. Still, the author continued producing books up until his death in 1947, at the age of seventy-seven. Unlike that of many other authors from the same era, Tarkington's work has largely failed to capture the attention of modern audiences, though it does provide a valuable glimpse of American Midwestern life at the turn of the twentieth century.

PLOT SUMMARY

Chapters I–V

The Magnificent Ambersons tells the story of a wealthy family in an unnamed Midlands town at the turn of the twentieth century. The novel begins with a brief history of the Amberson family, beginning with "Major" Amberson becoming wealthy in 1873. The Major then bought two hundred acres of property at what was then the edge of town, and developed it into a neighborhood complete with streets that have classically inspired statues or fountains at each intersection. He sold plots in the neighborhood for others to build houses, which proved popular and extended the Amberson fortune. The Major kept four acres at the entrance to the neighborhood for his own family's estate, and built a mansion described as "the pride of the town." In this environment is raised Isabel Amberson, the Major's daughter, as well as his sons George and Sydney Amberson. Isabel is the target of many suitors, but the two she considers most seriously are Eugene Morgan and Wilbur Minafer. Morgan is a poor but passionate soul, always eager to serenade Isabel at her window, or write her a poem. However, after an incident in which a drunken Morgan steps on a bass viol and destroys it during a serenade, presumably embarrassing Isabel and her family, she decides to accept a proposal from Minafer.

MEDIA ADAPTATIONS

- A film adaptation of the novel, written and directed by Orson Welles, was released in 1942. The film stars Joseph Cotten, Anne Baxter, Tim Holt, and Agnes Moorehead, among others. Though the film is highly regarded by critics and film historians, it is not currently available on DVD.

- Another film adaptation of the work was released in 2002. The film, directed by Alfonso Arau and starring Jonathan Rhys Meyers and Gretchen Mol, is based largely on Orson Welles's original shooting script. It is available on DVD from A & E Home Video.

- An unabridged audio recording of the novel was released by Blackstone Audio in 2007. The audiobook, read by Geoffrey Blaisdell, is available in both CD format and as an audio download through audible.com.

Wilbur Minafer is practical, not particularly handsome, but a good businessman. Some speculate that Isabel chooses Wilbur for sensible reasons rather than for love, while others suggest that her actions are intended to punish Eugene Morgan for his poor behavior. Isabel and Wilbur marry, and soon after they have a child, George Minafer. Isabel seemingly pours all her love into this child, and soon it becomes evident to all but Isabel that he is spoiled rotten. Neighbors are terrified of him, not only because of his bullying and insults but because they are afraid to say anything negative about the youngest member of the powerful Amberson clan. As the author states, "There were people—grown people they were—who expressed themselves longingly: they did hope to see the day, they said, when that boy would get his come-uppance!"

At sixteen years of age, George is sent away to prep school; however, he is soon sent back, expelled for his insolent behavior. When he returns home, he discovers that a club he founded with his friends—and of which he was elected president—has decided to elect a new president in his absence: Fred Kinney, a red-headed boy whom George sees as his chief rival. George refuses to acknowledge the new leadership, and Kinney quits the club.

Chapters VI–IX

George is again sent off to school, and when he returns home for Christmas during his sophomore year of college, his parents host a ball in his honor. At the party he meets a "dark-eyed little beauty of nineteen" named Lucy Morgan, who is not a local; her father is visiting friends in the area. George takes an immediate liking to her, and demands as much of her time as he can. Lucy does not appear at all intimidated by George or his powerful family, though she does seem to like him nonetheless. Lucy asks George what he plans on being when he gets out of college, and he dismisses the idea of being a lawyer or doctor in favor of doing something he sees as far more suitable: being a yachtsman.

George sees a "queer-looking duck" at the ball who waves at Lucy and then later dances with her. He then discovers that this is Lucy's father, Eugene Morgan. George feels an almost instant dislike for the man. This is exacerbated by his family's fondness for Eugene, which seems to stem from old friendships forged with George's mother and uncle before Eugene moved away and became a successful inventor. When George discovers that Eugene has invented a new kind of horseless carriage, he scoffs at the idea as a waste of time and effort.

The day after the ball, George insists on taking Lucy out for a ride in his sleigh. On the way, they pass Eugene in his horseless carriage, giving a ride to George's mother Isabel, uncle George, and aunt Fanny Minafer. The horseless carriage breaks down, and as young George is busy ridiculing the contraption, he drives his sleigh off the road and crashes, losing his horse. The young couple end up having to squeeze into the horseless carriage, repaired by Eugene, in order to get home.

That night, George, his mother, and his aunt Fanny—who lives with the family in the slightly more modest second house on the expansive Amberson lot—attend another dance in the company of Eugene and his daughter Lucy. George is at first upset that Lucy has already committed herself to spending time with Fred Kinney, George's enemy; however, after fulfilling her previous obligations, Lucy spends much of her time with George, and the two continue to remain in each other's company throughout the holidays.

Chapters X–XV

The following summer, George again returns home from college, eager to spend time with Lucy. Lucy and her father, meanwhile, have relocated to the town, where Eugene has decided to set up a factory for his horseless carriages. It becomes clear to George that his aunt Fanny, an unmarried woman, is interested in the widowed Eugene, and the families spend a great deal of time together. George and Lucy continue to grow close, though occasional spats sometimes get in the way. By the following summer, Eugene is successfully fabricating and selling his automobiles, and he and Lucy have had a house built on the edge of town. When George returns home from college, Fanny shocks him by repeating a rumor that Lucy has become engaged to Fred Kinney. George confronts her and discovers that the rumor is untrue; seizing the opportunity, he asks Lucy if she will become engaged to him. She refuses, but does not provide a substantive reason. He tells her that he will ask again on his last night before returning to school.

Meanwhile, the rest of George's family is occupied with distressing financial matters. Both George's father and his uncle have lost a great deal of money in a bad investment, and his father appears to be in failing health because of it. George's other uncle, Sydney, is pressuring the Major for his share of the family inheritance early, rather than waiting for the Major to die. During this family quarrel, George overhears Sydney's wife Amelia say something about his mother Isabel: that she has been using Fanny as an excuse to spend time in the company of Eugene Morgan herself, and that her behavior borders on the scandalous since she is still married. George asks both his uncle George and his aunt Fanny about this, but both deny the possibility that Isabel is still interested in Eugene.

At the end of summer, Lucy tells George that they are "almost" engaged. While George is back at school, his father Wilbur dies and he must return home. At the funeral, George notes that his aunt Fanny is especially distraught over the loss of her brother. He assumes that Fanny is worried she will not be allowed to continue to live with them, since she has no other connection to the Amberson family. George and Isabel assure Fanny that she can remain living with

them, and they even give Fanny the sole asset that remains from Wilbur Minafer's estate: his life insurance payout.

In June, Isabel, uncle George, Lucy, and Eugene all travel back East to attend George's graduation from college. When Lucy meets George's school friends, she is reminded that he is not interested in a career, but instead just wants to spend his time "being a gentleman."

Chapters XVI–XIX

When George and Isabel return home after his graduation, Fanny is surprised to learn that Eugene was also there, even though his stated reason for going back East was to attend to business in New York. George, on the other hand, is surprised by something else: the four-acre Amberson plot, once home to only the main mansion and his mother's house, is being parceled out for the building of additional homes. The Major sees it as a financial necessity, hoping that the modest homes will offer steady income as rentals.

Soon after, George tells the Major that he would like to expand his skills as a coachman by getting a second horse to add on to his carriage. The Major asks if the young man would not rather attend law school, so he can make a career for himself. George makes it clear that law school interests him as much as the new automobiles Eugene Morgan is successfully manufacturing: not at all. When George once again presses the issue of marriage with Lucy, she cites his lack of a career choice—or rather his decision not to have one—as a main obstacle in her agreeing to marry him. George sees this as her father's influence, and grows to loathe the man for standing in their way.

The next time Eugene comes over for dinner with the family, Lucy is not with him; George discovers that she has gone away to visit a friend without informing him. George takes the opportunity to say that automobiles are a nuisance that should never have been invented. While the rest of the family is shocked at George's rudeness to their guest—who makes his living inventing and building automobiles—Eugene himself simply laughs and concedes that the vehicles are sure to change the city, and probably not for the better. After Eugene leaves, Fanny tells George that he has done a good thing by saying what he said to Eugene, though he cannot understand why she thinks so.

Chapters XX–XXVI

Lucy returns in the autumn, but George is too flustered to speak to her. However, he finally discovers why Fanny has encouraged his dislike of Eugene: Fanny believes, just as Aunt Amelia once suggested, that George's mother Isabel is romantically interested in Eugene, and has been since before her husband Wilbur died. According to Fanny, this is resulting in scandalous talk around the town. When George demands to know who has been spreading such talk, Fanny vaguely implicates a neighbor, Mrs. Johnson. George visits Mrs. Johnson and confronts her about it, but she kicks him out for being rude. When George tells his uncle what he has done, his uncle warns that while such idle talk may have occurred, it would have dissipated on its own. Now that George has made such a scene, however, the talk is sure to spread.

The next day, Eugene stops by to visit Isabel. George meets him at the door before his mother even knows he has arrived, and tells Eugene that he is not welcome in their house. Eugene leaves, and sends a letter to Isabel by way of her brother. In the note, Eugene reveals that he had asked Isabel to marry him the day before, and that she seemed to think it could happen in the future. Eugene also asks Isabel to live her life for herself, and not for her son George. Isabel shows the note to George, hoping he will understand how much she cares for Eugene. Instead George reacts to the letter as a personal insult, and tells his mother that she should never see Eugene again. Wanting to please her son, she reluctantly agrees, and mails a farewell letter to Eugene the next morning.

Chapters XXVII–XXX

The following day, George encounters Lucy on the street. She does not seem to know anything of the events that have transpired between their parents, and greets him cheerfully. George tells her that he is leaving town with his mother on an extended trip, ostensibly to keep his mother free of the scandalous talk about her. George tries to tell Lucy that the trip will last indefinitely, and that their relationship is over, but she shrugs the matter off with a carefree attitude that stuns him. After he says good-bye and walks away, Lucy steps into the drugstore nearby and collapses.

When Lucy recovers and returns home, she finds Fanny waiting for her. Fanny tells her everything about the incident between George and Eugene, and how he has forced his mother

to break off her relationship with Eugene. Lucy destroys all her letters and pictures from George, though she cannot completely extinguish her love for him.

Time moves on even in the absence of George and Isabel, and the town spreads out farther, leaving the Amberson property falling in value. The new houses built by the Major as rentals descend quickly into disrepair, with two of them never even seeing tenants. As the Amberson fortune dwindles, uncle George Amberson and Fanny Minafer put together much of their money to invest in a new electric automobile headlight. Meanwhile, the increasingly successful Eugene and Lucy move into their newly completed house on the outskirts of town: a mansion on four acres, just as the old Amberson estate once was.

There are occasional reports from George and Isabel overseas, all of which indicate that Isabel's health is declining rapidly. Finally, George agrees to return home with her, knowing that she does not have long to live. Hoping George has gotten over his hatred, Eugene shows up and asks to see Isabel. But George refuses, stating that the doctor has demanded peace and quiet for her. Just before her death, Isabel tells George that it would have been nice to see Eugene just once more.

After Isabel's death, George discovers that there never was much talk around town about his mother, despite George's behavior. George is wracked with guilt over not letting his mother see Eugene one final time, and lashes out at the older adults in his family for allowing him to get away with behaving so immaturely.

The headlight venture backed by Fanny and Uncle George fails, and both lose virtually all of their money, though Fanny hides the true extent of her losses out of shame. Not long after Isabel's death, her father, the Major, also passes away.

Chapters XXXI–XXXV

The Amberson estate, long in decline, proves to be worth as much as the family owes to various creditors, and almost every bit—including the houses—is sold off to creditors. George accepts a job as a law clerk with Frank Bronson, the family's lawyer, that pays eight dollars a week. Uncle George manages to secure a low-paying position as a foreign diplomat, and while he promises to send money whenever he can, he suggests that he will probably never see George or Fanny again. Meanwhile, Fanny makes arrangements for her and George to live in a small apartment; however, George discovers that Fanny has no money, and was relying on him to be able to cover the rent. Since his job as a law clerk is not sufficient, George visits Frank Bronson and asks for his help in securing a better-paying job; the only positions he knows that pay well are high-risk jobs transporting and handling chemicals and explosives. Impressed by George's dedication to providing a suitable place for his aunt, Bronson helps George get a job at a chemical plant outside of town.

One Sunday, while out on a walk in the increasingly dismal sprawl of the city, George discovers that the mansions of the Amberson estate—the Major's and his mother's—have been demolished to make room for new construction. He also finds that the main road that once ran through the neighborhood, Amberson Boulevard, has been renamed Tenth Street. He returns home to the apartment, and in the lobby finds a book about the history of the city. In the book are listed the five hundred most prominent families from the city's history. George scans the list, but finds no mention of the Ambersons. With that, "Georgie Minafer had gotten his comeuppance, but the people who had so longed for it were not there to see it, and they never knew it."

Lucy occasionally visits Fanny at their apartment, though she only comes when George is gone and never speaks of George to Fanny. Lucy's father Eugene becomes concerned that she has not been interested in another man since George; Lucy explains in a roundabout way that although she could no longer tolerate George the way he was, the love she felt for him had nonetheless ruined her for other men. The next day, Eugene happens to meet an old friend who informs him of George's dramatic change, both in station and in attitude. George has become the man in charge of the chemical company's nitroglycerin plant, and has proven himself a hard worker. The acquaintance asks Eugene if he might be able to offer George a safer job in one of his automobile plants, if only to ensure that George stays alive to take care of Fanny. Eugene says that he has no job to offer.

Rather than death in an explosion, however, a much more mundane accident sends George to the hospital: he is run over by an automobile. Although he lives, both his legs are broken. Eugene reads about the accident in the newspaper on his way to New York, and the next day he receives a letter from Lucy with a copy of the same article. Sensing more than just coincidence, Eugene visits a "trance-medium," a woman who claims the ability to communicate with the dead. Though skeptical at first, Eugene is surprised when a spirit whose description matches Isabel offers him a simple message: "Be kind." Eugene knows that, whether or not the medium was genuine, Isabel would want nothing more than for him to be kind to her beloved son George, who had finally grown up enough to become a man deserving of kindness. When Eugene returns home, he heads to the hospital, where Fanny and Lucy are already waiting. When George sees Eugene, he asks for forgiveness for the way he treated Eugene in the past. Eugene feels the presence of Isabel in the room with them: "He knew that he had been true at last to his true love, and that through him she had brought her boy under shelter again."

CHARACTERS

Amelia Amberson

Amelia Amberson is the wife of Sydney Amberson, one of the heirs to Major Amberson's estate. Interested more in spending money than making it, Amelia and Sydney manage to obtain their share of the family fortune without having to wait for the Major to die. One day, while going to visit his grandfather, George overhears Amelia talking about his mother Isabel. She states that Isabel is behaving scandalously, spending time with her old love Eugene Morgan while her husband Wilbur is at home, ill. By doing this, she sets into motion many of the tragic events that befall the family—just as their extraction of part of the family fortune cripples the Major's business enterprises, and plays a key role in their failure.

George Amberson

George Amberson is the son of Major Amberson, leader of the wealthy Amberson clan. Although he serves as a congressman for a time, George seldom works and has no real career, preferring instead to invest his father's money in various business schemes—all of which fail. He once was good friends with Eugene Morgan, and their friendship resumes when Eugene returns to town many years later. George often functions as the intermediary between bickering family members. After his father dies and the estate is sold off to pay creditors, George secures a modest position for himself as a foreign consul. He borrows money from his nephew George Minafer in order to travel to his new job, but promises to send money back whenever he can.

Isabel Amberson

Isabel Amberson is the only daughter of Major Amberson. She is described as a notable beauty, and while a young woman she is pursued by two potential suitors. One, Eugene Morgan, is poor but passionate; the other, Wilbur Minafer, is dull and business-minded, but sincere and persistent. After being embarrassed by Eugene's drunken serenade one night, Isabel decides to marry Wilbur, and Eugene leaves town. Many years later, with her son George a young man, Isabel encounters Eugene once again. The two families begin spending a great deal of time together, with George interested in Eugene's daughter Lucy, and Isabel's sister-in-law, Fanny, interested in the widower Eugene. After Isabel's husband Wilbur dies, however, it becomes clear that she still has feelings for Eugene herself, and vice versa. Fearful of the scandal that such a relationship might cause, George demands that Isabel no longer see Eugene. Wanting to please her son, Isabel agrees, and she and George leave town on an extended tour of the world. During the trip, Isabel becomes increasingly ill; George brings her back home not long before she dies. Her final wish is that she be able to see Eugene one last time—not knowing that Eugene has already tried to visit her, but George turned him away. Later, the ghost of Isabel Amberson appears to send a message to Eugene through a medium. She asks him "to be kind," and Eugene assumes that she wants him to take care of her son George despite his monstrous actions.

Major Amberson

Major Amberson is the patriarch of the Amberson clan, who became wealthy in the years following the Civil War. Although he is rich, he does not spend his money wisely; for example, he builds a very expensive mansion, including a single walnut staircase that cost sixty thousand dollars (equivalent in 2009 to more than one million dollars). The Major also provides for every whim of his children and eventually his only grandchild, George Minafer. The Major's sons Sydney and George Amberson squander much of the family wealth through conspicuous spending and bad investments, and the Major's own business acumen fails to pay off in his later years. He decides to build five new houses on the Amberson estate lot with the hope of renting them out, but he does not anticipate the spread and popularity of apartment buildings in the city, which leaves his new houses unable to generate revenue. After his daughter Isabel dies, the Major retreats into a pensive state that some mistake for senility. By the time he dies, the Amberson family fortune, after all debts are paid, is roughly zero.

Sydney Amberson

Sydney Amberson is the son of Major Amberson and brother of Isabel and George. He is married to his second cousin Amelia, also an Amberson. Like many in the Amberson family, Sydney chooses not to work, but instead to spend his father's money. When the couple runs short of funds, they pressure the Major into giving them their share of the family inheritance long before he actually dies. They use this to buy a villa in Italy. By the time the Major dies, the family fortune is gone, with no inheritance left for anyone else—but Sydney and Amelia refuse to share the wealth they extracted earlier from the estate.

Frank Bronson

Frank Bronson is the Amberson family's lawyer. When George overhears his Aunt Amelia speaking scandalously about his mother Isabel, Bronson tries to convince him that she is speaking nonsense, and tells George not to worry about it. Later, after Major Amberson dies and George is left virtually penniless, Bronson offers George a job as a law clerk; the job pays modestly, but would allow George to eventually become a lawyer. George instead asks for Bronson's help in obtaining a more dangerous, higher-paying job so that he can afford to support his Aunt Fanny. This causes Bronson to say of the suddenly changed George: "You certainly are the most practical young man I ever met!"

Charlie Johnson

Charlie Johnson is a childhood friend of George Minafer who lives across the street from the Amberson estate. Charlie is also a member of the social club Friends of the Ace. When George returns from college to find that the club has elected a new president in his absence, Charlie tries in vain to resolve the matter without conflict. George views Charlie as his "chief supporter" and "henchman," but after George rudely confronts Charlie's mother concerning rumors being spread about his own mother Isabel, Charlie abandons the mostly one-sided friendship.

Mrs. Johnson

Mrs. Johnson is Charlie Johnson's mother and friend of Fanny Minafer. She lives across the street from the Amberson estate, and is described as a stout woman with a round head and large bosom. Isabel notices that she spies through her front window on the neighbors—mostly the Ambersons—with a pair of opera glasses. When George discovers from his Aunt Fanny that rumors are circulating about his mother and Eugene Morgan, George demands to know who is spreading such rumors. Fanny implicates Mrs. Johnson at George's suggestion, and George confronts the woman about it in her own home. Mrs. Johnson denies any wrong-doing, and demands that George leave her house. She dies several weeks later, while George and Isabel are away on their extended trip.

Fred Kinney

Fred Kinney is a red-headed childhood friend of George Minafer. Along with a few other boys, they form a social club known as Friends of the Ace. George serves as president of the club, but when he goes away to college, the other members decide to elect Fred as president in George's absence. When George returns, he is furious, and refuses to acknowledge the new club leader. Fred decides to quit the club rather than deal with George's harassment, and the two become rivals. Later, while casually courting Lucy Morgan, George gets angry when he hears a rumor that Lucy has become engaged to Fred.

Fanny Minafer

Fanny Minafer is Wilbur Minafer's sister and George Minafer's aunt. A single woman, she lives in the same house as Wilbur, Isabel, and George. Fanny and George have a somewhat antagonistic relationship, often bickering or slyly insulting each other. When family friend and widower Eugene Morgan returns to town after a long absence, Fanny sees Eugene as suitable material for a husband. Her sister-in-law Isabel agrees to invite Eugene over frequently to spend time with the family, hoping that Eugene will notice her and become smitten. When Fanny realizes that Eugene is really in love with Isabel, she becomes bitter and vengeful, encouraging George's poor treatment of Eugene. After Isabel dies, Fanny has no family left but George, and he vows to take care of her to make amends for ruining his own mother's chance at happiness. After losing their home and money, Fanny and George share a small apartment in town, paid for by George's job at a chemical plant.

George Amberson Minafer

George Amberson Minafer is the child of Isabel Amberson and Wilbur Minafer, and as the only grandchild of Major Amberson, he is the heir apparent to the Amberson family fortune. He is raised in an environment not only of wealth and privilege, but of unconditional love, with very little discipline. This causes him to be a spoiled little monster in the eyes of nearly everyone except his own family, particularly his mother, who sees no fault at all in her beautiful boy. As a result, George grows up to be a selfish, immature young man who bullies others to get his own way, and is generally feared by his peers—both because of his personality and because he carries with him the power of the Amberson family name. The first person to challenge George on his immaturity and sense of entitlement is Lucy Morgan, the daughter of Isabel's old love Eugene. Though she loves him despite his flaws, Lucy holds off on committing to marry him until he matures enough to decide on a career. Unfortunately, George does not mature until long after their relationship has ended; it takes the death of his mother, and the loss of the family fortune, for George to finally commit to a career—working with explosive chemicals, which pays more than safer, more reputable careers. George does indeed begin to mature, and comes to regret that he never allowed his mother to see her true love Eugene again, not even on her death-bed. As misfortune piles upon misfortune, George is run over by an automobile after absently stepping into the street without looking. Still, this event proves to be a blessing, for it draws both Lucy and Eugene to George's bedside in the hospital, where he finally asks forgiveness for the pain he has brought them.

Wilbur Minafer

Wilbur Minafer is the sensible, rather dull suitor Isabel Amberson chooses over Eugene Morgan after Eugene embarrasses her during a drunken serenade. Wilbur is described as "no breaker of bass viols or hearts, no serenader at all." The two have a child, George Minafer, whom Isabel spoils—presumably as an outlet for her love, since she does not really love Wilbur. Still, Wilbur is a hardworking, dependable business-man, and does not squander money the way Isabel and George do. Wilbur also takes in his unmarried sister Fanny, who has no one else to look after her. Despite his normally solid business sense, he puts a great deal of money into an investment with Isabel's brother, and the money is lost. After this financial failure, Wilbur's health begins to deteriorate. Isabel takes him on a vacation to improve his condition, but he dies during the trip. In the end, he leaves his family only the proceeds from a life insurance policy, which they give to Fanny.

Eugene Morgan

Eugene Morgan is the one-time love of Isabel Amberson and father of Lucy Morgan. As a poor but lively youth, Eugene courted Isabel, showering her with poetry and serenades expressing his feelings for her. However, after a drunken serenade in which he stepped through a viol and created an embarrassing scene, Isabel decided to marry another suitor instead. Eugene became a lawyer and left town. When he returns many years later, Eugene is a widower with a daughter. He is also a successful inventor working on creating horseless carriages. Eugene's own business grows as the Amberson empire crumbles, so that the two families have essentially switched places by the end. Eugene spends a great deal of time with Isabel and her sister-in-law Fanny; although Fanny hopes he is interested in her, it eventually becomes clear that he still loves Isabel, and even asks her to marry him. Isabel's son George, however, dislikes Eugene almost instinctively, and ruins their chance at happiness by keeping his mother from seeing Eugene again—even on her deathbed. Although Eugene has a difficult time forgiving George's actions, he becomes convinced that Isabel's spirit wants him to make amends with her son. At the end of the novel, Eugene visits the injured George in the hospital, and George asks him for his forgiveness.

Lucy Morgan

Lucy Morgan is Eugene Morgan's daughter and George Minafer's love interest. Raised by her father after her mother died, Lucy has a critical and inquisitive mind, which is perhaps unusual for a young woman of the time. Although she falls in love with George from the first time she meets him, she is not afraid to challenge him on his snobbish attitudes or his immature behavior. She repeatedly puts off an official engagement to George, eventually telling him that she is worried by his lack of desire to engage in a career. Although she presents a nonchalant façade to

George when he reveals that he is leaving on an extended trip, and therefore ending their courtship, she faints in the drugstore after George has walked away. Even after Lucy learns of George's awful behavior toward her father, she still cannot help having feelings for him, and never allows herself to become attached to other potential suitors. When Lucy reads that George has been run over by a car, she sends the news clipping to her father and visits George in the hospital, repairing the rift that George had caused between the families.

THEMES

The Transitory Nature of the Modern World

A major theme in *The Magnificent Ambersons* is how impermanent so many elements of the modern world can be. In the beginning of the tale, the Ambersons have risen as one of the wealthiest and most prominent families in the city. The Major builds a hotel, an opera house, and even an entire neighborhood that all carry the Amberson name. Over the course of less than twenty years, the Ambersons lose all their wealth and prestige; even the family name is destined to die, with the only member of the youngest generation being a Minafer. The decline of the Ambersons is reflected in the swift decay of all that the Major created, such as the hotel rooms that quickly become embarrassingly out of fashion or the houses that fall into disrepair and are destroyed. The decline is also reflected in Neptune's Fountain, one of the cast-iron statues that stand at the center of each intersection within the neighborhood Amberson built. At first, it is one of the most impressive sights in town. Then, the plumbing that powers the fountain malfunctions, resulting in a dry fountain that the Major is not willing to pay to fix. The statue becomes streaked with dirt, since no one is employed to keep it clean, and begins to erode. Ultimately, the statue and fountain are torn out completely.

The transitory nature of the city is also reflected in its rapid urbanization. The houses that once stood on the outskirts, like the Amberson mansion, quickly become engulfed as the city continues to grow. The process is accelerated by the rise of the automobile, which allows people to live further from the city center, which is crowded, decaying, and dirty. At the beginning of the

TOPICS FOR FURTHER STUDY

- With his depiction of "the Midland city," Tarkington seems to suggest that progress marches onward for better or worse, and it will run undeterred over those who try to resist it. Find at least two examples in the novel that demonstrate this message. Do you agree that it is futile to resist progress, whether it is good or bad? Might progress be good for some but bad for others? Write a short essay explaining your views.

- In the novel, George Minafer is frequently critical of the styles of clothing worn by others, particularly older members of his family. George also insists on dressing up for dinner each night. Find at least three examples in the text where a character's clothing is described in detail. Based on what you have read in *The Magnificent Ambersons,* do you think people are more fashion-conscious now than they were back then? Why or why not? Be sure to include examples and reasons to support your view.

- Ever since the novel was first published, critics have pointed to the ending of the book as a failure, considering it weak and disrespectful both of the reader and the characters. Do you agree? If so, try writing your own Chapter XXXV to replace Tarkington's and end the tale as you feel it should. If you disagree with the critics, write a short essay explaining why you think the ending is appropriate.

- In the novel, Tarkington depicts the fledgling auto industry in the United States just after the turn of the century, before and during what is known as the Brass Era of automobile manufacturing. Using your library, the Internet, or other available resources for research, write a short report about one aspect of this early era in the history of the automobile. You may focus on the technological developments of these early cars, provide a portrait of someone influential in their development, or even offer a survey of public opinion toward these vehicles during this time.

- The 1942 film version of *The Magnificent Ambersons,* directed by Orson Welles, is better known today than Tarkington's novel. Watch the film (available in VHS format only) and read some critical articles on it, both recent and from the time of the film's release. Write an essay in which you compare the novel and film, explaining why you think the film has remained more popular than the novel.

---

novel, horseless carriages are a novelty ridiculed by children as they pass. By the end, they have virtually replaced horse-drawn carriages entirely. The Morgans, whose wealth is owed to the popularity of the automobile, build a mansion on the new outskirts of the city, much like the one Major Amberson built years before—but already the city is spreading, catching up to these new areas, ready to engulf them just as it did the Amberson neighborhood.

Family Prestige

The nature of family prestige is another theme that runs throughout the novel. When Georgie is young, the Amberson family name inspires enough fear and respect among the townspeople that the boy is often allowed to behave awfully and get away with it. Eventually, it becomes clear that the family's prestige is derived exclusively from their wealth; once the wealth disappears, so does the family's status. When George is a young man, he forbids his mother from seeing Eugene Morgan, and even leaves town with her in an effort to protect her good name and the reputation of the family. George fails to see that his efforts are pointless, and have done nothing except destroy his mother's one chance at happiness.

Joseph Cotten as Eugene and Dolores Costello as Isabel in Orson Welles's 1942 film adaptation of the novel (© Photos 12 / Alamy)

The Benefits of Adversity and Work

One clear message in the novel is that adversity and work help to strengthen a person's character. This is most obviously reflected in George, a young man raised with every desire fulfilled and every hardship held at bay. Because he gets everything he ever wants, George becomes a spoiled, temperamental monster. He subscribes to the notion that only people of a lower class should be bothered with work, and that those with prestige should concern themselves only with being prestigious. He does not begin to mature and grow until he faces obstacles such as the death of his mother and the loss of his family's wealth. These help to forge and strengthen his character.

By contrast, Eugene Morgan is at first poor but ambitious, and starts his professional life with nothing but debts; he works hard to pay them off, and then builds a business for himself through hard work and dedication. The adversity Eugene faces from a young age helps to drive his success. It is only after he has become comfortably successful that he reveals—briefly—a vengeful and bitter side to his personality, when

he refuses to help George obtain a safer position at the chemical company.

STYLE

Regionalism

In literature, regionalism refers to writing that focuses on capturing the look and feel of a specific location. In Tarkington's case, the location is Indianapolis, where he grew up and lived most of his life. Tarkington concentrated on this location in many of his works, including *The Magnificent Ambersons*—though he never specifies the location as Indianapolis, instead referring to it vaguely as "the Midland city." The author spends a great deal of time describing the city as it grows over the course of the novel, so much so that some have suggested that the city itself is one of the most important characters. Unlike many regionalist writers, who are concerned with documenting natural elements such as types of trees or wildlife in an area, Tarkington focuses on urban landmarks, the styles of

COMPARE & CONTRAST

- **1900s:** Horseless carriages appear alongside their horse-powered counterparts; they are viewed largely as a novelty.

  Today: Approximately 600 million cars can be found across the globe.

- **1900s:** Woodruff Place, the first suburb of Indianapolis, serves as the inspiration for Tarkington's *The Magnificent Ambersons*.

- **Today:** After falling into disrepair for decades, the neighborhood is restored and designated as a historic preservation district.

- **1900s:** Young adults meet and interact socially at dances and formal balls such as cotillions.

  Today: Young adults prefer to meet and interact at informal dance clubs, though one important formal dance event remains: the high school prom.

---

houses, and the state of the roadways. Regionalism is often associated with a romantic tone, in which the author celebrates a way of life specific to a certain area. However, beginning around the turn of the twentieth century, regionalist writers such as Kate Chopin sometimes offered scathing snapshots of towns and communities that ran counter to this romantic ideal. In *The Magnificent Ambersons*, Tarkington presents a fairly objective view of the changing city, lamenting its loss of charm and elegance while also criticizing those who wish to keep things as they once were.

HISTORICAL CONTEXT

The Rise of the Automobile and the Suburbs

The modern automobile is largely the invention of European engineers working in the latter half of the nineteenth century. The most important of these was Karl Benz, who came up with a practical design for an internal combustion engine and was the first to popularize the idea of motor cars as a replacement for horse-drawn carriages. Of equal importance was Benz's wife and business partner Bertha, who in 1888—reportedly without her husband's knowledge—undertook a sixty-mile drive in one of her husband's creations. This was the longest trip ever made at the time; with that single trip, Bertha earned a great deal of publicity and proved the potential of the automobile. Aside from the basic engine design, Benz was also the first to perfect many other components now considered essential, such as the spark plug, radiator, and clutch.

Although the arrival of the automobile in the United States was somewhat delayed when compared to Europe, its adoption was far more pervasive, and it became a critical element in shaping the American landscape. West of the Mississippi River, the United States was expansive and sparsely populated; the automobile made it possible for people to travel over greater distances in less time than before. The value of automobiles was proven when a man named Horatio Nelson Jackson completed the first cross-country journey of the United States by car in 1903. Still, the automobile industry in the United States was composed of hundreds of different manufacturers of varying quality and consistency, with designs that borrowed from each other yet failed to reach a uniform standard. All that changed in 1908 when Henry Ford created the Model T, the first automobile whose price and reliability—thanks to its assembly-line production—made the vehicles desirable to the average American.

With citizens no longer reliant upon horses, which required land and upkeep, or public transportation, which only served the most populated areas, neighborhoods expanded outward from city centers. With a car, living in semirural

Lithograph by Braden and Burford, ca. 1888, depicting the entrance to Woodruff Place in Indianapolis. This neighborhood inspired Tarkington to write the novel. (The Library of Congress)

settings outside the established city limits did not mean being cut off from the city factories where jobs were most likely to be found. These semi-rural areas close to the city, consisting mostly of spacious houses on large lots, became known as "suburbs." The spread of suburban areas exploded after World War II, when millions of young men and women—just married and ready to start families—fueled the need for new homes. Ever since, the automobile and the suburbs have been an integral part of the American lifestyle.

CRITICAL OVERVIEW

Although Booth Tarkington was a popular author in his time—with over twenty books published by 1918—he was not without many vocal critics. Even *The Magnificent Ambersons*, which went on to win the Pulitzer Prize for the Novel in 1919, met with mixed reviews from critics upon its initial publication; subsequent critical opinion has proven sparse, with the work overshadowed by both the author's other novels and by a well-known film adaptation.

The majority of criticism is leveled at the very end of the novel, where George redeems himself for his previous selfish actions. Carl Van Doren, in an essay for *The Nation,* notes that while the novel contains a "wealth of admirable satire," the author mistakenly "rounds out its narrative with a hasty regeneration." Van Doren also refers to the opening chapters of the book as "splendid," though he considers the remainder of the book less so. "According to all the codes of the more serious kinds of fiction," Van Doren writes, "the unwillingness—or the inability—to conduct a plot to its legitimate ending implies some weakness in the artistic character; and this weakness has been Mr. Tarkington's principal defect." Joseph Collins, writing in *The Bookman,* states that the novel "remains powerful until the closing episode wrecks it irretrievably." Charles C. Baldwin, in an essay about Tarkington's work, condemns not only the ending of the novel but also the author's inability to produce thoughtful art, stating that "it is folly to criticize Mr. Tarkington or to expect great things of him." Van Wyck Brooks, in his literary survey *The Confident Years: 1885–1915,* sums up the prevailing critical feeling about the novel: "*The Magnificent Ambersons* might have been a great symbolical American story if the family had been irrevocably engulfed and lost in the town, but the arrogant George Amberson, suddenly poor, becomes a considerate, hard-working young man, already on the way to retrieve the family fortunes."

Despite the ending, many critics did compliment the author's ability to portray the urbanization that had taken place in America at the turn of the century, particularly in the Midwest. In *Booth Tarkington: Gentleman from Indiana,* James Woodress states that the author "not only told a good story against the social and economic background of Indianapolis, but he also worked out appropriate themes to give the novel significance." A critic for the British magazine *Punch* makes it clear that the main character of the work "is a spoilt and egotistical cad," and that in the hands of an English family his comeuppance "would have commenced at an early age." The critic also notes that the sudden turnaround and happy ending "leaves us cold." However, the author's ability to chart the decline of an American family at the turn of the century is, according to the critic, "almost a contribution to American social history."

Modern evaluations of the novel have proven few and far between, and not much more positive. In fact, the majority of critical attention is reserved for Tarkington's 1922 novel *Alice Adams,* which also won the Pulitzer Prize and received glowing reviews even from Tarkington's contemporaries. Aside from that, a great deal of material has been written about Orson Welles's 1942 film adaptation of *The Magnificent Ambersons*. The film was the subject of a battle for creative control between Welles and film studio RKO, with one central issue being the ending: Welles, agreeing with Tarkington's many critics, wanted to change it to remove the author's original, hopeful coda. Still, even in its "studio-approved" form, the film was nominated for four Academy Awards, and is recognized by the American Movie Classics Web site filmsite.org as one of the one hundred greatest films of all time. Thus Tarkington's legacy is assured, thanks to a medium in which he never directly worked.

CRITICISM

Greg Wilson

Wilson is an author, literary critic, and mythologist. In this essay, he attempts to refute the criticisms made by Tarkington's contemporaries, and to explain why these critics responded the way they did.

Less than a century after its initial publication, *The Magnificent Ambersons* is a novel in danger of becoming nothing more than a literary footnote—one more unknown title in a long list of award winners that had no lasting impact on the world of literature. To be sure, the book started off at a disadvantage; even in its own time, it was maligned by many professional critics and academics. Two decades after its release, Orson Welles thought enough of the novel to adapt it for film as his follow-up to *Citizen Kane*—and yet, at the same time, he thought so little of the book's original ending that he was intent on writing a new one. (He was overridden by the studio on that matter when he lost control of the film during the editing phase.) Its reputation has not grown much in the intervening decades, with far more academic attention paid to Welles's adaptation than to the original work itself. This disheartening history leads to one important question: why has the book been so set upon by critics and scholars? The answer could simply be that the book is not very good, and deserves to take its lumps. I would argue, however, that there is another explanation.

First, however, let us address the main complaints leveled at the book. Most critics seem to agree that the final chapter is the problem, and

> WHILE CRITICS OF THE TIME WERE PLEASED TO SEE AN ANTIHERO LIKE GEORGE IN THE SPOTLIGHT, THEY WOULD HAVE PREFERRED IT IF THE JERK REMAINED A JERK, AS IS USUALLY THE CASE IN LIFE, AND CONTINUED TO GET HIS COMEUPPANCE UNTIL HE DIED."

that it is problematic enough to undo whatever good was done by the preceding thirty-four chapters. In particular, it is the idea that awful Georgie Minafer—the terror of the Midland city—could so quickly become a decent person and enjoy a happy ending. There are several reasons, however, why this is not a fair criticism.

First, as any reader can attest, one of the criteria for judging the success of a literary work is whether or not the main character undergoes a significant change as a result of the events in the story. This is an admittedly simplistic litmus test, yet it holds up remarkably well, suggesting that it is perhaps part of an underlying "deep narrative structure" that writers consciously or unconsciously aim for. In any case, to say that George's change in character is a flaw is to miss the entire point of the book. The climax of the novel is George's realization that, by being selfish and shallow, he ruined his mother's chance at happiness. This is what makes him finally grow up and be a man. Without this realization, he is a flat, unsatisfying character.

Some might suggest that the main problem critics found was not with the fact that George changes, but with the fact that it happens so quickly at the very end, as if tacked on as an afterthought. However, this is simply not true. As mentioned above, George begins his transformation in earnest after his mother dies, which means he takes six chapters to reach a modest but encouraging level of maturity and humility at the very end. To get mathematical for a moment, this is just a tad shy of one-fifth of the entire length of the novel. This hardly qualifies as "last-minute" or "tacked-on."

With those two possibilities dismissed for the time being, one might say that the real problem

WHAT DO I READ NEXT?

- *The Turmoil* (1917) is the first of Tarkington's *Growth* trilogy, and concerns a frail, artistic son of an industrialist who discovers strength and purpose when forced to work in the family business. Tarkington would continue to explore the theme of work as a vital part of a man's development in the second volume of the trilogy, *The Magnificent Ambersons*.

- *Alice Adams* (1921) is in a sense Tarkington's counterpoint to *The Magnificent Ambersons*, and like its predecessor, earned the author a Pulitzer Prize. In it, a young woman of modest means but endless ambition tries to hide her lower-class roots from a wealthy potential suitor, whom she sees as her best chance to improve her station in life.

- *Babbitt* (1922), by Sinclair Lewis, is a satirical depiction that, in a sense, picks up where *The Magnificent Ambersons* leaves off: in a large, quickly expanding Midwestern city overrun with hustling business types all eager to make their fortunes. George Babbitt, one of these upwardly mobile civic boosters, soon begins to feel oppressed by the conformity required to fit into his role as a successful businessman. However, his quest for happiness shows him that things are not so different in other social circles, either.

- *His Family* (1917), by Ernest Poole, won the first Pulitzer Prize for the Novel in 1918. The book offers a snapshot of life in New York in the early twentieth century, focusing on the Gale family, consisting of a widower and his three daughters, and their failing fortunes before and during World War I.

- *My Life and Work* (1922) is the autobiography of Henry Ford, the founder of Ford Motor Company, who is recognized as one of the great pioneers of the auto industry. In the work, Ford discusses not only his life and work on the development of the automobile but also his strategies for creating and maintaining a successful business.

- *How the García Girls Lost Their Accents* (1991), by Julia Alvarez, tells the story of a wealthy family who must leave behind their comfortable lifestyle in the Dominican Republic due to political upheaval, and start over in the United States. The story is told in reverse chronological order, and focuses on the four very different daughters of the García family.

---

critics had with the novel is the ease with which all the characters enjoy a happy ending. This argument is a puzzling one. A young man is rendered penniless, must work as an explosives handler just to be able to afford a small apartment which he shares with his aunt, and ends up having both his legs broken when he is run over by a car. So just because he is finally able to ask forgiveness of the two living people he has hurt the most, his ending is considered happy and overly convenient? I would hate to see what such a critic has in mind for a tragedy.

Finally, there is one other plausible criticism of the novel's final chapter, and it is one with which I agree completely. The introduction of a supernatural element into the story is not only pointless, but detracts from the power of the scenes that surround it. It is not at all necessary to confirm Eugene's feelings about what Isabel would want by having him visit a trance-medium, especially since it requires the reader to accept that the trance-medium is indeed a legitimate channel through which the dead may speak. However, it is worth noting that this sensible criticism of a singularly silly scene is not mentioned in any contemporary review that I could find.

Even if one does not feel particularly comfortable with the pace or tone of the ending, there are many other elements of the book that make it worthwhile. As some reviewers were willing to concede, its depiction of a Midwestern city on the cusp of urbanization and the rapid changes that accompany it is both unique and valuable as a historical snapshot. Aside from that, though, the book is chock full of fantastic dialogue—mostly from the mouth of Lucy Morgan, ever the foil for Georgie's pomposity and snobbishness. The narrator's observations to the reader about the Amberson family and the changing city are equally witty.

The quality of the writing is attested to by the fact that when Orson Welles—an Academy Award–winning screenwriter for his *Citizen Kane*—wrote the script for his film adaptation of *The Magnificent Ambersons,* he used a great deal of the original dialogue and text from the book, verbatim. It is in fact somewhat humorous that the Orson Welles adaptation of the book is viewed by cinema purists as creatively compromised due to the studio's forcing a "tacked-on" happy ending; many have wondered aloud and in print how much greater the film would have been if only Welles had been allowed to bring his vision to the screen without studio interference. How many of these film experts realize that this "tacked-on" ending was part of the original tale they otherwise praise so highly (since Welles's film is, by and large, very faithful to the book)? What about the original author's creative vision? Is it worth less than Welles's? Apparently, they seem to think it is.

Interestingly, the plight of *The Magnificent Ambersons* is remarkably reminiscent in many ways of a novel that, on the surface, could not seem more dissimilar: Anthony Burgess's violent and dystopic science fiction novel *A Clockwork Orange* (1962). In both novels, the main character is a young man who is perceived by both other characters and by the reader as a monster. In both novels, the main character ultimately matures enough to realize his past actions were foolish. In the Burgess novel, this transformation really does take place solely in the final chapter—a criticism unfairly leveled at the Tarkington novel. For the American edition of the Burgess novel, American publishers were so put off by the fact that Alex, the main character, shows maturity at the end of the book that they successfully pressured the author to leave out that final chapter, resulting in an incomplete story featuring an apparently static character. For both novels, a film adaptation was made;

in each case, the auteur filmmaker wanted to end the story on a bleak note rather than use the original ending. Where Welles was unsuccessful due to studio intervention, Stanley Kubrick—with his film adaptation of *A Clockwork Orange*—was able to get his way. Both movies are considered classics, with *A Clockwork Orange* even being listed by the American Film Institute as one of the one hundred greatest American films ever made. Let us hope that Burgess's novel and its superior ending, already eclipsed by Kubrick's film, are not swallowed by history.

Back to the point: if the criticisms of *The Magnificent Ambersons* are, when viewed from a modern and more objective viewpoint, not entirely fair, one must ask: why did Tarkington's contemporaries in the literary realm respond so negatively to the book? To answer that requires a small bit of historical context.

The biggest problem with *The Magnificent Ambersons* and its relatively hopeful ending was simply its timing. It was published after the genie of Modernism was already out of the bottle, yet had not fully exhausted itself. Many new writers were questioning all the established rules of literature, most especially those involving happy endings. These were people who looked at the world around them—which included cities choking on the by-products of industrialism and an entire generation of young men utterly erased by war—and saw no happy endings forthcoming. Many works had already been created that focused on the darker side of human nature, including Wilfred Owen's horrific war poem "Dulce et Decorum Est" (1917) and Joseph Conrad's *Heart of Darkness* (1899). Small-town life had already been exposed for its secrets and hypocrisies in Edgar Lee Masters's *Spoon River Anthology* (1915). Sigmund Freud's theories of psychoanalysis—and in particular his ideas about how sons relate to their mothers—had already been explored by D. H. Lawrence in *Sons and Lovers* (1913). The artistic aesthetic just before, during, and after World War I was composed primarily of cynicism: bad things were likely to stay bad, no matter how hard one tried to change them.

The net effect of all this was that *The Magnificent Ambersons* must have seemed, even in 1918, somewhat old-fashioned in its ultimate redemption of George Minafer. While critics of the time were pleased to see an antihero like

George in the spotlight, they would have preferred it if the jerk remained a jerk, as is usually the case in life, and continued to get his come-uppance until he died. And this is where the critics are simply wrong, blinded by the admittedly dire world in which they were immersed. Their desire for satisfaction at George's downfall is a base desire, like bloodlust; it is simple, and it is dumb. Tarkington aims for something higher: he wants to show the reader that even a selfish, immature monster can be forged by the fires of adversity into a reasonably decent person.

In the end, none of this may matter to modern readers. Tarkington's overly intricate descriptions of clothing styles, name-dropping of unfamiliar songs from the era, and use of nearly inscrutable catchphrases of the day like "Boost! Don't Knock!" might be enough to turn potential readers away. However, understanding the context of critical opinion about the work is, in the end, perhaps as important as understanding the work itself. All criticism—even this essay—reflects the biases of the author and the culture in which it is created. The most important message here is not that *The Magnificent Ambersons* is a great novel. Instead, it is this simple piece of advice: do not judge a book by its critics.

Source: Greg Wilson, Critical Essay on *The Magnificent Ambersons* in *Novels for Students,* Gale, Cengage Learning, 2010.

Peter Rietbergen

In this excerpt, Rietbergen argues that the novel is meant to reflect not only the maturation of George but also a coming of age for America.

Throughout the novel, Tarkington seems to hint at a psychological problem that is never really made explicit. Even before he becomes aware of who Eugene Morgan is, at the big ball at the Amberson Mansion described in Chapter IV, we find George, who is unconsciously experiencing his own sexual awakening, ruminating on the femininity and the sexual allure of his mother, however, he rejects both when he realizes that they imply that she might ever belong to a man—excluding, of course, his father from this picture, for we do not consciously think of our parents as sexual beings. It seems as if the author shrinks from this almost Freudian element, and yet cannot withstand its possibilities, even finds them essential to the development of his plot: indeed, after George has told his mother that

she cannot marry Eugene and has to stop seeing him altogether, Tarkington observes: "not less like Hamlet did he feel and look" (249).

I find this interpretation, which has been advanced before, convincing since Tarkington was too good a novelist to convince either himself or his reader that a credible plot could be built on George's wounded sense of social status and family pride alone: notwithstanding the fact that such feelings played a not unimportant role in the life of small communities like the one the author knew and wanted to sketch. Nevertheless, it is also evident that Tarkington, even if he may subconsciously have been casting George into a Freudian, oedipal relationship with his mother, did not intend this to be the novel's main theme. Admittedly, there are powerful traces of such a relationship, like the recurring hysteria with which George rejects any idea of Isabel ever loving another man and like her own letter, in which, after she has called him the sacred gift God gave her, she remarks:

> Good night, my darling, my beloved, my beloved! You mustn't be troubled. I think I shouldn't mind anything very much as long as I have you "all to myself"—as people say—to make up for your long years away from me at college. (251)

Their departure on a trip that forces them to live together for a number of years—a honeymoon, a marriage?—might be interpreted as hinting at a more than normally strong bond as well. But then, so might Eugene's happiness in the face of his daughter's decision not to marry after she has broken with George (referred to in Chapter 34) and, indeed, Lucy's own admission: "I don't want anything but you." If one decides to hold to the oedipal interpretation of Tarkington's novel, one must accept that the two situations mirror one another.

Yet, to find out what the novel really is about, it is necessary to have a closer look at its structure, in particular at the way in which the novel intertwines two major themes and develops them through a number of metaphors.

In Chapter 18, significantly half-way through the text, the town is serenely sketched as evening falls, with moonlight shining on the trees, the patter of carriage horses plodding along the roads, and the almost silent sounds of bicycles swishing by, carrying singing, guitar-playing youngsters to their parties. The atmosphere is idyllic. But it is the eventide of a vanishing society, for the quiet is broken by the "horrid sounds" of a "frantic devil," the car: "there are a great many more than there used to be," someone says. Tarkington follows this up with a few, cleverly ambiguous words: "there, in the highway, the evening life of the Midland city had begun" (178–79).

Equally significantly, in Chapter 15 George and Lucy quarrel: a man grounded in tradition, *his* supreme wish is to be "a gentleman"—"don't you think that being things is rather better than doing things?" a friend of his had once asked Lucy (154–55)—while *she*, the daughter of a modern automobile maker, finds that his ideas do not seem like ideas to her at all; after all, she was, as Tarkington remarks elsewhere, "an independent, masterful, self-reliant little American" (253). Once more, two cultures clash. Once more, an idyll ends.

In the next chapter, George, to his entire family's dismay, brusquely attacks Eugene as the maker of a monster, the automobile. From then on, his dislike of his mother's suitor grows to ever greater intensity. When, in Chapter 25, George, unknown to Isabel, has told Eugene not see her again, and awaits his mother's reaction on the big staircase, Tarkington describes the large stained-glass panels that light the landing: they show the figures of "Love and Purity and Beauty", but "the colours were growing dull; evening was coming on" (238). People, through their own actions—but also through the process of time?—are losing the things that seem most valuable.

While, through his decision regarding his mother's future, George consciously also gives up his chance of happiness with Lucy, denying, in a way, his love for her, the larger scene of the town must lose its happy innocence as well. In Chapter 28, Tarkington concisely and visually describes the fundamental change from a rural to an industrial society, will all its social and cultural implications. By now, the town "befouled itself and darkened its sky … Gasoline and electricity were performing the miracles Eugene had predicted" (263–64).

But the novel is not an exposition of simple and simplified opposites. Tarkington has made clear already that Eugene is far from being a crass modernist. Responding to George's vehement rejection of automobiles at the dinner party given by old Major Amberson, he said:

I'm not sure he's wrong about automobiles … With all their speed forward they may be a step backward in civilization—that is, in spiritual civilization. It may be that they will not add to the beauty of the world, nor to the life of men's souls. (Chapter 19, 188–89)

Unlike George, who is still young, Eugene accepts the inevitability of change while at the same time deploring its consequences. So does Tarkington, who in that same Chapter, goes on to describe the new society, for "the great change was in the citizenry itself." The town was increasingly populated by people who had not been born there:

There was a German quarter; there was a Jewish quarter; there was a negro quarter— square miles of it—called "Bucktown"; there were many Irish neighbourhoods; and there were large settlements of Italians, and of Hungarians, and of Rumanians, and of Serbians and other Balkan peoples. But not the emigrants, themselves, were the almost dominant type on the streets downtown. That type was the emigrant's prosperous offspring … A new Midlander—in fact, a new American—was beginning dimly to emerge. (264–65)

Clearly, Tarkington is not entirely happy with this new 'type.' It is idealistic, and optimistic, yes, but it believes "in hustling and honesty because both paid." It sees "the perfect beauty and happiness of cities and of human life" in the building of ever more factories, as these bring "Prosperity." But his prosperity amounts to nothing more than credit at the bank that, in its essence, brings them "nothing that was not dirty, and, therefore, to a sane mind, valueness" (265–66). To introduce the metaphor dear to him, Tarkington has Lucy, who on first coming to the town had decorated her drawing room in white, decide to "put everything into dull grey and brown," knowing that it could not drive away the encroaching soot. We realize that she is willfully deceiving herself because in doing so "it no longer looked so dirty as it was" (267). She is losing some of her innocence; we feel she is growing up.

A definite clue to Tarkington's intentions comes in Chapter 35, when the tale nears its end. To me it seems that Tarkington wants his readers to see George's decision—the cruelty of which he admits to himself only after his mother had died, feeling "sorrow for what sacrifices his pride and youth had demanded of others" (Chapter 32, 307)—as part of a process. It is the process of personal growth that by the very loss of youth entails the awareness of the inadvertent cruelty of youth that thinks its own values and interpretations of life and the world absolute. Yet I feel that, at the same time, this very process is the novel's emotional, personal counterpoint to a far more encompassing socio-cultural one, viz. that of the coming of age of America itself, which was losing its innocence as well:

> ... the new great people who had taken their places—the Morgans and Akerses and Sheridans—they would go, too. George saw that. They would pass, as the Ambersons had passed ... Nothing stays or holds or keeps where there is growth, he somehow perceived vaguely but truly. (Chapter 35, 338)

This hints at acceptance, both on George's and on Tarkington's part; elsewhere George realizes "he had to emphatically support the ideal of being rather than doing"—which, surely, is another of youth's characteristics. Yet we are also made to realize that becoming an adult, losing one's innocence, is painful, and that something irretrievable has been lost in the process: purity. That, indeed, seems one of the novel's main themes, metaphorically and at the same time realistically rendered by the recurring reference to the soot that comes to cover everything: the town, the houses, the people living there, and even their souls "all people were soiled," it is said in Chapter 31.

Though, on a first reading, George may not appear to be the most appealing of characters, his personal development is indeed the necessary counterpoint to the larger process. He articulates his rejection of the "new age" represented by the motor car—though it is partly inspired by his very personal, emotional rejection of his mother's suitor, who every way looked the part of the man of "the new era"—and yet in the end he has to become part of that process, working in a gunpowder plant, with the machines he loathes. For not only has he grown up, he has also personally grown, and logically so, Tarkington implies, for, as George's uncle had told him at their final parting in Chapter 31: "the stuff of the old stock is in you. It'll come out and do something" (294). And when, in Chapter 32, George applies for his job, his new boss tells him: "You certainly are the most practical young man I ever met" (317).

Like his town, then, George, too, becomes part of the new era, and inevitably grows up, as part of a historical process. The ending might thus be seen to reflect the essentially optimistic view that Tarkington had of his country and its people, however much he might deplore the passing of certain of its old ways. After all, as Eugene had remarked in Chapter 6: "There aren't any times but new times" (69).

In the end, Booth Tarkington's *The Magnificent Ambersons* seems to be about youth and adulthood, about safety and growing up, about the loss of old, unquestioned ideals and certainties, and the painful acceptance of change, of uncertainties, of new responsibilities.

Source: Peter Rietbergen, "A Variety of Ambersons: Re-Reading Booth Tarkington's and Orson Welles' *The Magnificent Ambersons*," in *Uneasy Alliance: Twentieth-Century American Literature, Culture and Biography*, edited by Hans Bak, Rodopi, 2004, pp. 38–42.

Carl Van Doren

In this survey of the author's work, Van Doren finds that Tarkington's plots are "sophomoric" and that he shortchanges the setting—Indiana—which he has sought to capture.

Booth Tarkington is the glass of adolescence and the mold of Indiana. The hero of his earliest novel, Harkless in *The Gentleman from Indiana*, drifts through that narrative with a melancholy stride because he has been seven long years out of college and has not yet set the prairie on fire. But Mr. Tarkington, at the time of writing distant from Princeton by about the same number of years and also not yet famous, could not put up with failure in a hero. So Harkless appears as a mine of latent splendors. Carlow County idolizes him, evil-doers hate him, grateful old men worship him, devoted young men shadow his unsuspecting steps at night in order to protect him from the villains of Six-Cross-Roads, sweet girls adore him, fortune saves him from dire adventures, and in the end his fellow-voters choose him to represent their innumerable virtues in the Congress of their country without his even dreaming what affectionate game they are at. This from the creator of Penrod, who at the comical age of twelve so often lays large plans for proving to the heedless world that he, too, has been a hero all along! In somewhat happier hours Mr. Tarkington wrote *Monsieur Beaucaire*, that dainty romantic episode in the life of Prince Louis-Philippe de Valois, who masquerades as a barber and then as a gambler at Bath, is misjudged on the evidence of his own disguises, just escapes catastrophe, and in the end gracefully forgives the gentlemen and ladies who have been wrong, parting with an exquisite gesture from Lady Mary Carlisle, the beauty of Bath, who loves him but who for a few fatal days had doubted. This from the creator of William Sylvanus Baxter, who at the preposterous age of seventeen imagines himself another Sydney Carton and after a silent, agonizing, condescending farewell goes out to the imaginary tumbril!

Just such postures and phantasms of adolescence lie behind all Mr. Tarkington's more serious plots—and not merely those earlier ones which he constructed a score of years ago when the mode in fiction was historical and rococo. Van Revel in *The Two Van Revels*, convinced and passionate abolitionist, nevertheless becomes as hungry as any fire-eater of them all the moment Polk moves for war on Mexico, though to Van Revel the war is an evil madness. In *The Conquest of Canaan* Louden plays Prince Hal among the lowest his town affords, only to mount with a rush to the mayoralty when he is ready. *The Guest of Quesnay* takes a hero who is soiled with every vileness, smashes his head in an automobile accident, and thus transforms him into that glorious kind of creature known as a "Greek god"—beautiful and innocent beyond belief or endurance. *The Turmoil* is really not much more veracious, with its ugly duckling, Bibbs Sheridan, who has ideas, loves beauty, and writes verse, but who after years of futile dreaming becomes a master of capital almost overnight. Even *The Magnificent Ambersons*, with its wealth of admirable satire, does not satirize its own conclusion but rounds out its narrative with a hasty regeneration. And what can a critic say of such blatant nonsense as arises from the frenzy of propaganda in *Ramsey Milholland*?

Perhaps it is truer to call Mr. Tarkington's plots sophomoric than to call them adolescent. Indeed, the mark of the undergraduate almost covers them, especially of the undergraduate as he fondly imagines himself in his callow days and as he is foolishly instructed to regard himself by the more vinous and more hilarious of the old graduates who annually come back to a college to offer themselves—though this is not their conscious purpose—as an object lesson in the loud triviality peculiar and traditional to such hours of reunion. Adolescence, however, when left to itself, has other and very different hours which Mr. Tarkington shows almost no signs of comprehending.

The author of *Penrod*, of *Penrod and Sam*, and of *Seventeen* passes for an expert in youth; rarely has so persistent a reputation been so insecurely founded. What all these books primarily recall is the winks that adults exchange over the heads of children who are minding their own business, as the adults are not; the winks, moreover, of adults who have forgotten the inner concerns of adolescence and now observe only its surface awkwardnesses. Real adolescence, like any other age of man, has its own passions, its own poetry, its own tragedies and felicities; the adolescence of Mr. Tarkington's tales is almost nothing but farce—staged for outsiders. Not one of the characters is an individual; they are all little monsters—amusing monsters, it is true—dressed up to display the stock ambitions and the stock resentments and the stock affectations and the stock perturbations of the heart which attend the middle teens. The pranks of Penrod Schofield are merely those of Tom Sawyer repeated in another town, without the touches of poetry or of the informing imagination lent by Mark Twain. The sighs of "Silly Bill" Baxter—at first diverting, it is also true—are exorbitantly multiplied till reality drops out of the semblance. Calf-love does not always remain a joke merely because there are mature spectators to stand by nudging one another and roaring at the discomfort which love causes its least experienced victims. Those knowing asides which accompany these juvenile records have been mistaken too often for shrewd, even for profound, analyses of human nature. Actually they are only knowing, as sophomores are knowing with respect to their juniors by a few years. In contemporary American fiction Mr. Tarkington is the perennial sophomore.

If he may be said never to have outgrown Purdue and Princeton, so also may he be said never to have outgrown Indiana. In any larger sense, of course, he has not needed to. A novelist does not require a universe in which to find the universe, which lies folded, for the sufficiently perceptive eye, in any village. Thoreau and Emerson found it in Concord; Thomas Hardy in Wessex has watched the world move by without himself moving. But Mr. Tarkington has toward his native state the conscious attitude of the booster. Smile as he may at the too emphatic patriotism of this or that of her sons, he himself nevertheless expands under a similar stimulus. The impulse of Harkless to clasp all Carlow County to his broad breast obviously sprang from a mood which Mr. Tarkington himself had felt. And that impulse of that first novel has been repeated again and again in the later characters. *In the Arena*, fruit of Mr. Tarkington's term in the Indiana legislature, is a study in complacency. Setting out to take the world of politics as he finds it, he comes perilously near to ending on the note of approval for it as it stands—as good, on the whole, as any possible world. His satire, at least, is on the side of the established order. A certain soundness and rightness of feeling, a natural hearty democratic instinct, which appears in the novels, must not be allowed to mislead the analyst of his art. More than once, to his credit, he satirically recurs to the spectacle of those young Indianians who come back from their travels with a secret condescension, as did George Amberson Minafer.

> His politeness was of a kind which democratic people found hard to bear. In a word, M. le Duc had returned from the gay life of the capital to show himself for a week among the loyal peasants belonging to the old chateau, and their quaint habits and costumes afforded him a mild amusement.

Such passages, however, may be matched with irritating dozens in which Mr. Tarkington swallows Indiana whole.

To practise an art which is genuinely characteristic of some section of the folk anywhere is to do what may be important and is sure to be interesting. But Mr. Tarkington no more displays the naïveté of a true folk-novelist than he displays the serene vision that can lift a novelist above the accidents of his particular time and place. This Indianian constantly appears, by his allusions, to be a citizen of the world. He knows Europe; he knows New York. Again and again, particularly in the superb opening chapters of *The Magnificent Ambersons*, he rises above the local prejudices of his special parish and observes with a finely critical eye. But whenever he comes to a crisis in the building of a plot or in the truthful representation of a character he sags down to the level of Indiana sentimentality. George Minafer departs from the Hoosier average by being a snob; time—and Mr. Tarkington's plot—drags the cub back to normality. Bibbs Sheridan departs from the Hoosier average by being a poet; time—and Mr. Tarkington's plot—drags the cub back to normality. Both processes are the same. Perhaps Mr. Tarkington would not deliberately say that snobbery and poetry are equivalent offenses, but he does not

particularly distinguish. Sympathize as he may with these two aberrant youths, he knows no other solution than in the end to reduce them to the ranks. He accepts, that is, the casual Hoosier valuation, not with pity because so many of the creative hopes of youth come to naught or with regret that the flock in the end so frequently prevails over individual talent, but with a sort of exultant hurrah at seeing all the wandering sheep brought back in the last chapter and tucked safely away in the good old Hoosier fold.

Viewed critically this attitude of Mr. Tarkington's is of course not even a compliment to Indiana, any more than it is a compliment to women to take always the high chivalrous tone toward them, as if they were flawless creatures; any more than it is a compliment to the poor to assume that they are all virtuous or to the rich to assume that they are all malefactors of a tyrannical disposition. If Indiana plays microcosm to Mr. Tarkington's art, he owes it to his state to find more there than he has found—or has cared to set down; he owes it to his state now and then to quarrel with the dominant majority, for majorities occasionally go wrong, as well as men; he owes it to his state to give up his method of starting his narrative himself and then calling in popular sentimentalism to advise him how to bring it to an end.

According to all the codes of the more serious kinds of fiction, the unwillingness—or the inability—to conduct a plot to its legitimate ending implies some weakness in the artistic character; and this weakness has been Mr. Tarkington's principal defect. Nor does it in any way appear that he excuses himself by citing the immemorial license of the romancer. Mr. Tarkington apparently believes in his own conclusions. Now this causes the more regret for the reason that he has what is next best to character in a novelist—that is, knack. He has the knack of romance when he wants to employ it: a light, allusive manner; a sufficient acquaintance with certain charming historical epochs and the "properties" thereto pertaining—frills, ruffs, rapiers, insinuation; a considerable expertness in the ways of the "world"; gay colors, swift moods, the note of tender elegy. He has also the knack of satire, which he employs more frequently than romance. With what a rapid, joyous, accurate eye he has surveyed the processes of culture in "the Midland town"! How quickly he catches the first gesture of affectation and how deftly he sets it forth, entertained and entertaining! From the chuckling exordium of *The Magnificent Ambersons* it is but a step to *The Age of Innocence* and *Main Street*. Little reflective as he has allowed himself to be, he has by shrewd observation alone succeeded in writing not a few chapters which have texture, substance, "thickness." He has movement, he has energy, he has invention, he has good temper, he has the leisure to write as well as he can if he wishes to. And, unlike those dozens of living American writers who once each wrote one good book and then lapsed into dull oblivion or duller repetition, he has traveled a long way from the methods of his greener days.

Why then does he continue to trifle with his threadbare adolescents, as if he were afraid to write candidly about his coevals? Why does he drift with the sentimental tide and make propaganda for provincial complacency? He must know better. He can do better.

POSTSCRIPT.—He has done better. Almost as if to prove a somewhat somber critic in the wrong and to show that newer novelists have no monopoly of the new style of seriousness, Mr. Tarkington has in *Alice Adams* held himself veracious to the end and has produced a genuinely significant book. Alice is, indeed, less strictly a tragic figure than she appears to be. Desire, in any of the deeper senses, she shows no signs of feeling; what she loves in Russell is but incidentally himself and actually his assured position and his assured prosperity. So considered, her machinations to enchant and hold him have a comic aspect; one touch more of exaggeration and she would pass over to join those sorry ladies of the world of farce who take a larger visible hand in wooing than human customs happen to approve. But Mr. Tarkington withholds that one touch more of exaggeration. He understands that Alice's instinct to win a husband is an instinct as powerful as any that she has and is all that she has been taught by her society to have. In his handling she becomes important; her struggle, without the aid of guardian dowager or beguiling dot, becomes increasingly pathetic as the narrative advances; and her eventual failure, though signalized merely by her resolution to desert the inhospitable circles of privilege for the wider universe of work, carries with it the sting of tragedy.

Mr. Tarkington might have gone further than he has behind the bourgeois assumptions which his story takes for granted, but he has probably been wiser not to. Sticking to familiar territory, he writes with the confident touch of a man unconfused by speculation. His style is still swift, still easy, still flexible, still accurate in its conformity to the vernacular. He attempts no sentimental detours and permits himself no popular superfluities. He has retained all his tried qualities of observation and dexterity while admitting to his work the element of a sterner conscience than it has heretofore betrayed. With the honesty of his conclusion goes the mingling of mirth and sadness in *Alice Adams* as another trait of its superiority. The manners of the young which have always seemed so amusing to Mr. Tarkington and which he has kept on watching and laughing at as his principal material, now practically for the first time have evoked from him a considerate sense of the pathos of youth. It strengthens the pathos of Alice's fate that the comedy holds out so well; it enlarges the comedy of it that its pathos is so essential to the action. Even the most comic things have their tears.

Source: Carl Van Doren, "Contemporary American Novelists: Booth Tarkington," in *Contemporary American Novelists 1900–1920*, The Macmillan Company, 1922, pp. 84–94.

SOURCES

Baldwin, Charles C., "Booth Tarkington," in *The Men Who Make Our Novels*, revised ed., Dodd, Mead, and Company, 1924, pp. 474–86.

Brooks, Van Wyck, "Looking Backward," in his *The Confident Years: 1885–1915*, Dutton, 1952, pp. 334–35.

Collins, Joseph, "The New Mr. Tarkington," in *The Bookman*, Vol. LXV, No. 1, March 1927, p. 17.

Dirks, Tim, "AMC Filmsite: 100 Greatest Films." http://www.filmsite.org/momentsindx.html (accessed November 3, 2009).

Review of *The Magnificent Ambersons, Punch*, March 5, 1919, p. 192.

Van Doren, Carl, "Contemporary American Novelists: Booth Tarkington," in his *Contemporary American Novelists*, The Macmillan Company, 1922, pp. 84–94.

Woodress, James, *Booth Tarkington: Gentleman from Indiana*, J. B. Lippincott Company, 1955, pp. 196–97, 251.

FURTHER READING

Duany, Andres, Elizabeth Plater-Zyberk, and Jeff Speck, *Suburban Nation: The Rise of Sprawl and the Decline of the American Dream,* North Point Press, 2001.

This book, written by three city planners, offers a scathing critique of the unheeded sprawl that surrounds many American cities, brought about largely by poor foresight and the proliferation of automobiles.

Flink, James J., *The Automobile Age,* The MIT Press, 1990.

This comprehensive history of the American automobile focuses not just on the mechanical innovations of early inventors but also on the social changes that this transformational machine brought in its wake.

Price, Nelson, *Indianapolis Then and Now,* Thunder Bay Press, 2004.

This pictorial history of Tarkington's hometown shows how it has evolved over the decades. Included are pictures of Woodruff Place, the suburb upon which Tarkington based the neighborhood of the Ambersons.

Tarkington, Booth, *The World Does Move,* Greenwood Press Reprint, 1976.

Part history, part personal reflection, this collection of essays and stories explores the impact of early twentieth-century technological innovations on the people of the time.

The Natural

1984

The Natural is a 1984 baseball film based on the well-received 1952 novel of the same name by Bernard Malamud. The film was directed by Barry Levinson, a screenwriter-turned-director who had previously only helmed one film, *Diner* (1982). The cast consists of a number of highly regarded actors, including Robert Redford, Glenn Close, Robert Duvall, Kim Basinger, Barbara Hershey, Wilford Brimley, Richard Farnsworth, and Darren McGavin. The newest version of the film currently available on DVD is known as the Director's Cut and differs in some ways from the theatrical version. Levinson asserts in a video introduction to the film that a crushing post-production schedule kept him from finishing the film the way he wanted, and that the Director's Cut is "much closer to the intention that we had in mind."

Professional critics have not been kind to the film, with the most frequently mentioned complaint being that the ending differs substantially from the original novel. However, the film has remained popular with audiences in general and is routinely selected by fans, sports journalists, and athletes as one of the greatest baseball movies ever made; Roy Hobbs has even become a legendary character in the mythology of the sport, with several talented rookies earning favorable comparisons to Hobbs in the press over the years. *The Natural* received four Academy Award nominations, including Best Supporting Actress, Best Cinematography, and Best Musical Score. Even

Bernard Malamud himself recognized that the movie, though different from his book, tapped into a special part of the public consciousness in a way that his literary works had not been able to penetrate. In the DVD feature "Let's Play Ball: Filming the Show," Malamud's daughter Janna Malamud Smith states that the novelist, after seeing the film, told his wife, "Now I'm an American writer."

PLOT SUMMARY

Coming Home and Remembering Youth

The film adaptation of *The Natural* begins with a shot of a young farm boy playing catch in a field. This is Roy Hobbs, the main character of the film. Glimpses of his youth are intercut with scenes of an adult Roy, thirty-five years old, returning to his childhood home. The beginning of the novel, however, does not provide any flashbacks related to Hobbs's childhood—it simply begins with Hobbs on the train to Chicago for his major league tryout. He remembers key moments from his early life: his father dies while chopping wood as young Roy watches, unable to help; lightning splits a tree in the front yard, which Roy then cuts down and uses to make his own baseball bat, which he names "Wonderboy" and emblazons with a lightning bolt. The adult Roy reclaims the bat, stored in a trombone case, when he revisits the house.

The film then flashes back to Roy at nineteen, receiving word that he has been invited to try out for the Chicago Cubs as a major-league pitcher. He spends his last night at home with Iris, his girlfriend, and vows to marry her and bring her to Chicago once he gets signed to the team. Aboard the train to Chicago, Roy meets "the Whammer," a cocky professional ball player referred to by sports reporter Max Mercy as "the best there ever was, best there is now, best there ever will be." Neither the Whammer nor Max is at all impressed by Roy, and they continue playing cards. Max reads from the newspaper that an Olympic athlete and a football star have both recently been shot by an unknown assailant; in both cases, a silver bullet was used.

When the train stops at Iola for a water break, the passengers step out and visit the local carnival. The Whammer wows the local crowd with his hitting ability, and when he ridicules Roy, the two agree to a challenge: Roy has

FILM TECHNIQUE

- Cross-cutting is an editing technique in which two or more scenes are interwoven, with the action shown onscreen cutting back and forth between the scenes. Sometimes this is done to indicate that the action in both scenes occurs simultaneously, but in different locations; this is referred to as inter-cutting. In *The Natural*, Levinson makes use of cross-cutting to introduce actions that take place in the same or similar physical spaces, but years apart. This occurs most notably at the beginning of the film, when Hobbs visits his childhood home and the audience is shown several vignettes from when Hobbs was a boy. After each vignette, Hobbs continues his journey around the property and up to his old room, where he picks up Wonderboy.

- This type of "flashback" cross-cutting is also seen when Hobbs journeys by train to New York after collecting Wonderboy; here he recalls his first train trip, when he travels to Chicago to try out for the major leagues. Levinson uses this technique again later in the film, when Hobbs enters a hotel room and mistakes a housekeeper for Harriet Bird, who is long dead. This type of cross-cutting can be very effective at transitioning between flashback and present action, and provides a great deal of back story in a short amount of screen time.

- To transition between the cross-cut scenes, Levinson makes frequent use of sound bridges; in other words, dialogue and sound effects from one scene carry over into the following scene, or sound effects from the next scene begin before the visual actually changes. Another transition technique used less often by Levinson is the dissolve, in which one scene fades into the next. This is usually done to indicate a passage of time between the two scenes.

three pitches to strike the Whammer out. Roy succeeds and gains the attention of another passenger on the train, a woman named Harriet

Bird. The woman flirts with Roy, and when they reach Chicago, she calls him and invites him to her hotel room. When he arrives, he finds her dressed in black and wearing a veil. She pulls out a gun and shoots him in the abdomen, then kills herself by jumping out the window. The events aboard the train and in Chicago are very similar in the book and the film, though Hobbs pursues Harriet more aggressively in the book.

Roy's Comeback with the Knights

Sixteen years later, Roy shows up at Knights Field in New York. He has been signed to a contract by the scout for the New York Knights, a "last-place, dead-to-the-neck-up ball club" according to their coach and co-owner, Pop Fisher. Despite their dismal standing, Fisher scoffs at the idea of letting a middle-aged rookie with no professional experience play for his team. Fisher first claims that Roy's contract is not valid, but he knows that his hands are tied. He agrees to let Roy suit up and show the team his skills.

The other members of the team, especially right-fielder Bump Bailey—who is dating Fisher's niece, Memo Paris, and functions as the team leader due to his hitting ability—Roy is a joke. Before Roy even has a chance to practice, Fisher changes his mind and sends him to the bench. Fisher's second-in-command, Red Blow, explains the situation to Roy: Fisher lost control of the team when he had to sell a percentage of his share to the Judge, a figure who appears to want Fisher out of the picture. To facilitate this, the Judge—now with a majority interest in the team—has made deliberately poor trades and brought in bad players to keep the team in last place and drive Fisher out. However, if Fisher can manage to win the pennant, he will be able to buy back his shares and once again be in control of the team. According to Red, they need someone to "turn the ball club around like magic."

After a string of painful defeats, Fisher finally relents and lets Hobbs participate in batting practice. Hobbs knocks every pitch into the stands. The next game, when Bailey flubs a catch in the outfield, Fisher pulls him out of the game and lets Hobbs bat in his place. Hobbs, using his bat Wonderboy, hits the ball so hard he knocks the outer skin from it, leaving the core trailing thread as it sails to the outfield. The feat catches the attention of the media and the public, and after Max Mercy—who does not recognize Hobbs from sixteen years earlier—writes a column in which he suggests Wonderboy might be altered to allow for a more powerful swing, the league commissioner examines the bat and confirms that it is legal for play. The team's batboy, Bobby Savoy, asks Hobbs if he could ever make his own bat like that, and Hobbs offers to help him do it. In Chicago, Hobbs's former fiancée Iris reads eagerly about his exploits.

Memo Begins Dating Roy, Knights Start Losing

Fisher, no longer willing to put up with Bailey's poor attitude and mistakes, tells him that he has one more chance to improve, or else he will be replaced by Hobbs. In the next game, Bailey does improve, but he crashes through an outfield wall while pursuing a fly ball and dies. Hobbs becomes the new right-fielder for the Knights and leads them on a winning streak. The other members of the team even begin wearing lightning bolt patches on their uniforms with the hope of duplicating Hobbs's power with Wonderboy.

After his huge success, the Judge summons Hobbs and offers him a more lucrative contract. Hobbs makes it clear that he will do nothing to deliberately lose, sensing that this is what the Judge is asking him to do. Later, Mercy finally remembers where he has seen Hobbs before—the time he struck out the Whammer—and offers Hobbs five thousand dollars for an exclusive story about his past. Hobbs declines. Mercy also sets up a meeting between Hobbs and Gus Sands, a wealthy bookie with a glass eye who Memo Paris now appears to be dating. Sands bets Hobbs one hundred dollars that he can guess how much money, within a dollar, Roy has in his pocket. Sands appears to guess correctly, but Hobbs then produces two silver dollars as part of a magic trick that charms Memo, and the men agree to call it even.

Iris Reconnects with Roy

Hobbs begins seeing Memo, who insists that Sands is just a friend. As his relationship with Paris develops, his athletic performance falters. With the Knights on a losing streak, the team heads to Chicago for a game against the Cubs. Iris decides to attend the game with the hope of seeing Hobbs, whose performance in the early innings is lackluster. In the ninth inning, with Hobbs at bat and two strikes against him, Iris stands up in the stands and Roy is able to catch a glimpse of her lit by the golden sun, her pale hair lit almost like a halo. Levinson clearly meant to highlight Iris as an angelic, good woman, in marked contrast to Memo. On the next pitch, Hobbs knocks the ball so hard it shatters the clock at the back of the stadium. His losing streak is over.

Hobbs's relationship with Iris in the film is significantly different from what it is in the novel. In the novel, Iris is not Hobbs's childhood sweetheart; in fact, he does not meet her until almost two-thirds of the way through the book. Iris is not only a mother but also a grandmother, though she is still slightly younger than Hobbs. Levinson simplifies her character significantly, apparently to set up a simple contrast between "nice" Iris and "bad" Memo.

This film version of Iris has a note delivered to Hobbs, and the two reconnect for the first time in sixteen years. Hobbs tells her what happened with Harriet and the years that followed; Iris tells Hobbs that she has a son, and that the father lives in New York. Iris reveals that her son does not have contact with his father but adds, "But I've been thinking that he needs his father now ... he's at that age." Hobbs does not get to meet her son, because he must continue on the road with the team. His winning streak continues, even without Iris around, which complicates the plans of the Judge and Sands; Bailey had been easy for them to bribe into losing, but Hobbs appears unable to be bought.

When the team returns home, their winning streak has put them back in the running for the pennant. Memo, working with the Judge and Sands, tries to distract Hobbs, but the Knights' streak continues. With only one win needed before securing the National League championship, Memo throws a party for the team at her fancy apartment. Sands approaches Hobbs and tells him point-blank that he has bet a great deal of money against the Knights, and he subtly offers to reward him handsomely if he is willing to throw the game. Hobbs rejects his offer; Sands expresses his disappointment to Memo, who then approaches Hobbs and feeds him a dessert from a plate she is holding. Soon after, Hobbs becomes violently ill. In the novel, Hobbs is not poisoned by Memo at the party before the playoff game; instead, he gorges himself on six hamburgers—after already eating heaping plates' worth of food at a buffet—and makes himself sick. The decision to make Memo, not Roy, responsible for his illness—and by poisoning, no less—further

reinforces the contrast Levinson is trying to draw between the "bad" Memo and "good" Iris.

Roy Refuses to Lose

When Hobbs regains consciousness, he finds himself in a maternity hospital—the closest hospital available. The doctor informs him that his stomach has been seriously damaged due to a silver bullet lodged there, which occurred when Harriet Bird shot him sixteen years before. The doctor discourages him from playing baseball again, though the Knights—despite having lost three games in a row to Pittsburgh while Hobbs was recuperating—still have one more chance to secure the championship pennant. In the novel, when the doctor speaks with Hobbs after he wakes up in the hospital, the doctor encourages him to give up baseball for the sake of his health, but he does tell him that he is well enough to play in the final playoff game. Memo visits Hobbs in the hospital and begs him to give up the sport, telling him that Sands will give them a large amount of money and they can start fresh, just the two of them. Hobbs does not give her an answer.

Worried that Hobbs is going to play, the Judge visits him and gives him twenty thousand dollars to lose the game. The Judge also produces crime scene photos from when Hobbs was shot by Bird—tracked down by Max Mercy—and suggests that he will have Mercy release the story and soil Hobbs's reputation if Hobbs does not cooperate. When Hobbs tells him that the team would win even without him, the Judge confirms that he is also paying off another key player to throw the game.

Iris visits Hobbs at the hospital and tells him that she will be at the game the following day. She renews his conviction to play to win. He leaves the hospital and visits the Judge, where he also finds Sands and Memo. He gives the Judge back his twenty thousand dollars, and tells them that he is going to play his hardest. The Judge threatens to release the story of Hobbs's past, but Hobbs does not care. Memo grabs a gun from the Judge's desk, but cannot bring herself to shoot Hobbs. Here, the film differs significantly from the novel. In the novel, Hobbs accepts the Judge's offer of a payoff in exchange for losing the playoff game, but changes his mind about it in the middle of the game.

Winning the Big Game

The night of the final game against Pittsburgh, Iris is in the stands with her son, a blond teenage boy who looks a lot like Hobbs. During the game, Hobbs notices that Fowler, the pitcher, is the other player the Judge is bribing to lose. Hobbs visits Fowler on the mound and tries to convince him not to do it. Fowler tells him, "I'll start pitching when you start hitting." From then on, however, his pitching improves. For Hobbs's first two at-bats, he strikes out. Iris writes a note and has it delivered to Hobbs in the dugout; the note appears to inform Hobbs that Iris's son is also his son, from the night they spent before he left for Chicago sixteen years before, and that his son is in the stands watching him play. In the novel, Iris and Hobbs share a single night together, after which she writes him a letter telling him that she is pregnant. He neglects to read the letter, however, and does not find out until the final playoff game—when he accidentally hits and injures Iris with a fly ball into the stands. This injury is absent from the film.

In the bottom of the ninth inning with two outs, the Knights are down by two runs. One batter hits a double and another scores a single when the first baseman drops the ball, putting two Knights on base. This brings Hobbs to bat. He passes on the first two pitches, which are balls. The Pittsburgh coach then replaces the team's starting pitcher with a rookie, a Nebraska farm boy with great promise, like Hobbs once had. Hobbs swings at the first pitch and foul tips it through the press box window above home plate. Hobbs swings and misses at the next pitch; with two strikes, he then smashes the ball hard into the stands, but it veers outside the foul line. When he walks back toward the plate, he notices that Wonderboy has split in two. He asks the batboy, Bobby, to pick a new bat for him. Bobby brings him the Savoy Special—the bat Hobbs helped him make from scratch, just like Wonderboy. On the final pitch, Hobbs knocks the ball clear above the stands and into a bank of stadium lights, shattering them and creating a shower of sparks as he rounds the bases and wins the game for the Knights. Levinson makes Hobbs's triumph look almost miraculous, with the sparks flying like shooting stars or fireworks. The big game in the novel ends quite differently. In the novel, it is only during his last at-bat that Hobbs realizes he has made a mistake in accepting the Judge's money, and tries in earnest to hit well and win. However, he still strikes out, and

even though he returns the money to the Judge—beating up both Gus and the Judge—Hobbs ends his career under the suspicion that he was bought off.

At the end of the film, Hobbs is seen back at Iris's family farm, playing catch with his son as Iris watches.

The main difference between the film and novel is that Hobbs as a character is considerably less heroic in the novel, and he is often even described as an antihero. In the film, he is purely heroic. Much of what happens in the novel can be seen as being brought on by Hobbs's own character flaws, such as the overeating that drives him into the hospital during the playoffs and leaves his team losing three games without him. Also in the novel, Hobbs reveals himself to be deeply concerned about money, always looking for a way to increase his wealth, both because he feels that he deserves it and because he thinks it will convince Memo to be with him. In addition, Hobbs's poor choices with regard to women—which seem to be driven largely by his superficiality—ruin his career in baseball not once but twice. He rejects Iris simply because he is disgusted by the thought that she is a grandmother, yet he pursues Memo even after he has been warned by others that she will bring him trouble. Hobbs never grows in any meaningful way, and despite his natural talents, his other failings keep him from achieving his true potential. As Hobbs himself puts it near the end of the novel, "I never did learn anything out of my past life, now I have to suffer again."

CHARACTERS

Bartholomew Bailey
See Bump Bailey

Bump Bailey

Bump Bailey (last name spelled Baily in the novel) is the right fielder and star hitter of the New York Knights when Hobbs joins the team. Bailey is also dating Memo Paris, and is considered the team's leader due to his hitting ability. However, his attitude on the field is characterized by laziness and selfishness, and Fisher threatens to replace him with Hobbs if he does not improve. Bailey does indeed improve, but while trying to catch a deep fly ball during one game, he crashes head-first into the outfield wall and dies. This unfortunate incident leaves a permanent opening on the team for Hobbs. Bump is portrayed in the film by Michael Madsen. The film version of the character is very similar to the one in the novel, though Bailey plays more practical jokes in the book.

Harriet Bird

Harriet Bird is the mysterious woman who rides the train to Chicago along with Hobbs and the Whammer when Hobbs is on his way to try out for the major leagues. During the trip, the Whammer is clearly interested in Bird, who seems to reciprocate. When the train stops in Iola and Hobbs strikes out the Whammer, Bird's interest shifts to the young pitcher. Bird speaks to Hobbs about the mythic qualities of sports, but is disappointed to hear that Hobbs has not thought beyond his goal of just being the best player ever. After they arrive in Chicago, Bird invites Hobbs to her hotel room, and when he arrives, she shoots him. Then she jumps out the window to her death. Harriet Bird is played in the film by Barbara Hershey. The film version of the character is substantially similar to the literary version; however, while Bird commits suicide in the film immediately after shooting Hobbs, the fate of the woman in the novel is unknown.

Red Blow

Red Blow is the assistant coach for the New York Knights, second in command to Pop Fisher. When Hobbs first joins the Knights, it is Red who explains the team's sorry state to Hobbs, as well as Fisher's troubles in dealing with the Judge. In the film, Red is played by Richard Farnsworth.

Pop Fisher

Pop Fisher is a former baseball player turned coach, and co-owner of the New York Knights. When Fisher got into financial trouble the year before Hobbs joined the team, he allowed the Judge to buy a controlling interest in the team. If Fisher is able to win the division championship this season, he will be able to buy out the Judge and regain control of his team; if not, the Judge keeps control. In the novel, Fisher is described as "an old geezer of sixty-five with watery blue eyes, a thin red neck and a bitter mouth, who looked like a lost banana in the overgrown baseball suit he wore." The novel also describes Fisher as having a recurring problem with athlete's foot on his hands, which necessitates wearing bandages.

Other than this, however, the character is relatively unchanged in the film adaptation, which stars Wilford Brimley as Fisher.

Iris Gaines

Iris Gaines (last name Lemon in the novel) is Hobbs's childhood sweetheart before he leaves home to try out for the major leagues in Chicago. On the night before he departs, he tells her he wants to marry her, and that he will return for her. Sixteen years later, Iris finally encounters Hobbs again when she attends a game while the Knights are playing in Chicago, where she lives. She stands up while Hobbs is batting and catches his eye; this helps him end his hitting slump. Iris continues to function as a voice of reason and encouragement for Hobbs, and eventually she reveals to him that he is the father of her teenage son—conceived on their last night before he departed to Chicago. At the end of the film, it is suggested that Iris, Hobbs, and their son return to Iris's childhood home to live as a family. Iris is played by Glenn Close, who received an Academy Award nomination for her work in the film. The younger Iris who appears in flashback is played by Rachel Hall.

Although the personality of Iris is similar in the novel, the character differs in a few important details. Hobbs does not know Iris before he sees her in the stands; she is simply a black-haired woman in a red dress, the opposite of his first view of Memo Paris as a redhead wearing black. Aside from the physical differences between the two Irises, in the novel she tells Hobbs that she is a grandmother, having had a daughter at a young age who also got pregnant while young. Hobbs avoids her after discovering this, and only sees her again when he accidentally injures her with a fly ball during the final playoff game. It is then that he discovers she is pregnant with his child.

Ed Hobbs

Ed Hobbs is Roy's father, who appears in flashback sequences teaching his son how to play baseball. Ed dies of a heart attack while chopping wood in front of the family home as young Roy looks on. Ed Hobbs is played by Alan Fudge in the film; he does not appear directly as a character in the original novel.

Roy Hobbs

Roy Hobbs is the main character of *The Natural*, a man who possesses abilities as a baseball player that border on the supernatural. At the age of nineteen, he leaves home and his sweetheart Iris to travel to Chicago, where he plans to try out for the major leagues. Along the way, he takes part in a challenge against the Whammer, the most successful hitter in the American League, and manages to strike him out in three pitches. This attracts the attention of Harriet Bird, a psychotic woman who shoots Hobbs in the stomach before he has a chance to try out for the majors.

Sixteen years later, at the age of thirty-five, Hobbs finally returns to the game. He is signed to play for the New York Knights, a low-ranked professional ball club coached by Pop Fisher. Although the scout that signs Hobbs notes that he is a powerful hitter, the only reason Hobbs is signed to the team is because the Judge—co-owner of the team—is trying to drive out Fisher by hiring poor performers and washouts that will keep the team at the bottom of the rankings. Despite everyone's expectations, Hobbs succeeds wildly. The Judge and bookie Gus Sands, who both stand to lose large amounts of money due to Hobbs's success, try to bribe and even blackmail Hobbs into losing. However, Hobbs declines.

When Hobbs becomes distracted by a relationship with Memo Paris, seemingly orchestrated by Sands and the Judge, his performance as a player suffers. Only when he encounters Iris again does he improve and lead the team to the championship. During the final playoff game, an injured Hobbs learns that he and Iris have a son together, conceived sixteen years before. Wanting to serve as a role model for his son—just as his own father did for him—Hobbs scores the game-winning home run. Hobbs is portrayed in the film by Robert Redford; the younger Hobbs who appears in flashback with his father is portrayed by Paul Sullivan Jr.

The literary version of Hobbs is substantially different from the film character. In the novel, Hobbs is described as "a tall, husky, dark-bearded fellow with old eyes but not bad features." His face is "strong-boned, if a trifle meaty, and his mouth seemed pleasant enough though its expression was grim." The older Hobbs is depicted as a bitter, money-conscious, lustful man who believes he is entitled to the chance at greatness stolen from him years before by Harriet Bird. Redford, on the other hand, is famously handsome and blond, and appears in the film version as a heroic figure. Probably the most significant difference between the novel and the film is that in the novel, Hobbs accepts the Judge's bribe to lose the final playoff game. Near the end of the game, Hobbs changes his mind and decides to play to win. However, he still strikes out, losing the playoffs and losing his reputation amid rumors that he deliberately threw the game.

Ted Hobbs

Ted Hobbs is Roy and Iris's son, though Roy is not aware of this until he receives a note from Iris during the final playoff game. At the end of the film, Ted is shown playing catch with Roy back on Iris's family's farm. Ted is approximately fifteen years old, and is portrayed by Robert Rich III. The character of Ted Hobbs does not exist in the original novel.

The Judge

The Judge is a shadowy figure who has a controlling interest in the New York Knights. He gained control as part of a loan agreement with Pop Fisher, who was in financial trouble at the time. According to the agreement, if Fisher can lead the team to the league championships, the Judge will relinquish control of the team entirely. In the meantime, however, the Judge makes life difficult for Fisher and also aims to make a league championship impossible by making bad trades, hiring poor players, and keeping team morale low. After Hobbs shows his abilities during a game, the Judge offers to increase his pay; however, Hobbs senses that the extra money would come with strings attached, so he declines. In the film, the Judge is played by Robert Prosky in a role that resembles the literary character in every important detail. His name, as listed in the novel, is Goodwill Banner. In the DVD feature "When Lightning Strikes: Creating *The Natural*," co-screenwriter Phil Dusenberry notes that the character of the Judge is modeled on Branch Rickey, one-time general manager of the Brooklyn Dodgers.

Max Mercy

Max Mercy is a sports columnist who first meets Hobbs when the young player is on his way to Chicago to try out for the major leagues. Mercy, a friend of the legendary hitter known as the Whammer, offers to serve as umpire in the challenge between the Whammer and Hobbs during their train stop in Iola. Although he draws a cartoon commemorating the legendary strikeout,

Mercy does not recognize Hobbs sixteen years later when he joins the New York Knights. When Hobbs knocks the cover off a baseball during his first major league at-bat, Mercy writes a column accusing him of using an illegal bat. Mercy also spends a great deal of time trying to figure out Hobbs's past, and ultimately uncovers the truth about Harriet Bird and the shooting. He passes this information on to the Judge, who attempts to use it to blackmail Hobbs. Mercy is also the one who introduces Hobbs to bookie Gus Sands. Mercy is portrayed in the film by Robert Duvall.

Memo Paris

Memo Paris is Pop Fisher's niece and Bump Bailey's girlfriend. After Bump dies, she begins a relationship with Hobbs; however, it soon becomes clear that her true intent is to help Gus Sands and the Judge keep Hobbs from winning. At a party during the league playoffs, Memo feeds Hobbs a poisoned dessert that sends him into the hospital for several days, leaving his team to lose three games in a row without him. While he is still in the hospital, she begs him to take the Judge's bribe and let the team lose the final playoff game. When Hobbs returns the bribe, Memo pulls a gun on him, but cannot bring herself to shoot him.

Memo Paris is played in the film by Kim Basinger, who was nominated for a Golden Globe as Best Supporting Actress for her work. The differences between the character in the film and the character in the book are rather significant. In the book, Memo is a redhead and appears to be truly in love with Bump Bailey, mourning him intensely after his death. She does not seduce Hobbs as part of a conspiracy to keep Hobbs and the team from winning, as she does in the film, though she does have an ongoing relationship with Gus Sands and tries to convince Hobbs to throw the game.

Gus Sands

Gus Sands is a successful bookie who works in conjunction with the Judge and Memo Paris to sabotage the New York Knights' league championship. He is about fifty years old and has a glass eye. At a party during the league playoffs, Sands approaches Hobbs and subtly offers him money to lose the championship. Hobbs rejects him, and Sands gets Memo to feed Hobbs a poisoned dessert. In the end, Sands loses a great deal of money by betting against Hobbs and the

Knights. Gus Sands is portrayed by Darren McGavin, though the actor is not listed in the film's credits.

Bobby Savoy

Bobby Savoy is the batboy for the New York Knights. After Hobbs joins the team, he serves as Bobby's mentor, helping the boy to create his own bat—the Savoy Special—just like Hobbs carved Wonderboy. After Wonderboy splits in two during the final playoff game, Hobbs asks Bobby to pick a winning bat for him. Bobby brings him the Savoy Special, which Hobbs uses to hit the game-winning home run. Bobby Savoy is a character invented entirely for the film; in the novel, a nameless batboy is mentioned briefly, but Hobbs does not appear to have any relationship with him.

Sam Simpson

Sam Simpson is the scout who discovers Hobbs and brings him to Chicago to try out for the major leagues. It is Simpson who, after being dismissed by the Whammer and Mercy as an "old-timer," bets that Hobbs can strike out the Whammer with three pitches. He also serves as the catcher during the challenge. Simpson is portrayed in the film by John Finnegan. While his brief appearance in the film is similar to that found in the book, Malamud's original character dies while en route to Chicago—presumably from being struck by one of Hobbs's pitches during his challenge against the Whammer—leaving Hobbs alone when he first arrives in the city.

The Whammer

The Whammer is a professional baseball player known for his ability to hit home runs. When Hobbs takes the train to Chicago to try out for the major leagues, he meets the Whammer, who dismisses Hobbs as a bush-league nobody and busies himself flirting with Harriet Bird. Later, when the train stops, Hobbs's scout Sam Simpson bets the Whammer that Hobbs can strike him out in just three pitches. The Whammer accepts the challenge and is stunned when Hobbs succeeds in striking him out. The strikeout presumably saves his life, since it leads Harriet to select Hobbs as her target instead of the Whammer. In the film, the Whammer is played by Joe Don Baker, referred to by sportscaster Bob Costas as "the most convincing celluloid Babe Ruth I've ever seen"—a reference to Malamud's clear inspiration for the original character. The Whammer's brief appearance in the novel is almost identical to his appearance in the film, though he is described as having blond hair, and his full name is revealed to be Walter Wambold.

THEMES

Hubris

One of the main themes found in both the novel and film versions of *The Natural* is hubris. Hubris is another word for pride or arrogance so extreme that it brings a person to feel untouchable by bad fortune or fate. In ancient Greek myth, characters such as Agamemnon were often punished by the gods for displays of hubris. In Agamemnon's case, he claimed that his skills at hunting were equal to those of the goddess Artemis. Artemis punished him by taking away the winds and keeping his soldiers from sailing on to Troy to take part in the Trojan War.

In the film version of *The Natural*, Hobbs is depicted as being arrogant in his young adulthood. He tells Harriet Bird that he will be "the best there ever was" in baseball, yet he does not acknowledge any greater purpose that his talents might be used for. It is in fact this hubris that leads Harriet to shoot Hobbs. There are other notable examples of characters ruled by hubris in the film, such as the Whammer. A legendary pro baller famous for his hitting ability, the Whammer jokingly challenges Hobbs to a test of skills. He does not think the young pitcher could possibly stand a chance against him. This hubris leads to the Whammer being struck out on just three pitches from Hobbs. This is similar to the "punishment of the gods" administered in many Greek myths—though the Whammer unknowingly benefits from this, since it causes Harriet to focus on Hobbs instead of himself.

Two other characters who fall victim to their own hubris are the Judge and Gus Sands. The Judge believes that he is untouchable in his position as majority owner of the Knights, while Sands believes that he can always slant the odds in his favor, making talented players such as Hobbs irrelevant to the game. In the end, the Judge is presumably forced to relinquish control of the team to Pop Fisher, and Sands loses a great deal of money. No character exhibiting great hubris goes unpunished in the film.

Atonement and Second Chances

Another central theme in the film version of *The Natural* is atonement for past actions. When Hobbs returns to baseball after sixteen years away, he is a changed man; he has gained humility and wisdom. Though he clearly still makes mistakes, such as becoming involved with Memo, he is able to recognize his weaknesses and still keep perspective on what is truly important. When Hobbs reunites with Iris, he tells her of his near-indiscretion with Harriet Bird, atoning for his past mistake. When Hobbs finally discovers that Iris's son is his, he takes responsibility for becoming the boy's father. Iris sums up her own personal philosophy to Hobbs, which also functions as one of the film's main messages, when she visits him in the hospital: "I believe we have two lives ... the life we learn with, and the life we live with after that."

In the novel, this theme is also present, though with a far different resolution. When he joins the Knights, Hobbs is aware that he has been given a second chance to achieve his dreams as a professional baseball player. However, he has not changed for the better; instead, he has become bitter and feels that he is entitled to the fame and wealth which were denied to him so many years before. Because of this, he fails. As Hobbs himself puts it, reflecting on Iris's philosophy of two lives, "I never did learn anything out of my past life, now I have to suffer again."

Fathers and Sons

Another recurring theme in *The Natural* is the relationship between a father and a son. As a child, Hobbs is shown learning how to play baseball from his father. After his father dies, Hobbs carries with him his father's dream that he should become "the best there ever was" in baseball. Later, when Hobbs joins the Knights, Pop Fisher ultimately becomes a father-like figure to him, and Hobbs dedicates himself to helping Fisher win the league pennant and regain ownership of his team. Hobbs also becomes a father figure himself. This happens first with the team's bat boy Bobby Savoy, who he helps make a custom bat from a piece of lumber. Then, Hobbs becomes the long-overdue father for his own son, who Iris has raised without Hobbs's knowledge for fifteen years. Hobbs emphasizes the importance of such relationships when he says to Iris, "A father makes all the difference." In the final playoff game, Hobbs strikes out twice before he finds out that he is a father and

READ. WATCH. WRITE.

- The most significant difference between the novel and film versions of *The Natural* is the ending. Compare the two endings in a short essay, and answer the following questions: why do you think the ending to the film was changed from the book? Do you think the film would have been received differently by audiences and critics had the ending not been changed? If so, how?

- When Hobbs appears in the Knights' dugout with a contract in hand, Pop Fisher refuses to believe that his scout would offer a deal to a rookie in his mid-thirties. Though Hobbs proves himself worthy, it has become accepted wisdom that younger players are more likely to have long, successful careers than those starting later. Do you think this should be considered ageism? Why or why not? Do sports differ from more common jobs involving physical labor, in which employees might be less likely to be judged based on age? Pick a major-league sports team and determine the average player age and the average age at which the players entered the major leagues. Write a short report detailing your findings.

- The book and the film share several key plot moments, and some of the dialogue in the film is pulled almost verbatim from character conversations in the book. However, many of these scenes—though superficially similar—can have substantially different meanings due to other changes in the story. For example, in both works, Hobbs finds out during the big playoff game that he and Iris have created a child together; in the book, however, this revelation is given a much more tragic feel than in the film. Find a scene that appears similar in both the book and the film, and compare the two in terms of tone, character, and plot details. How are the scenes similar? How

are they different? In each case, how do these differences affect the overall work? Give a report to your class in which you present your findings.

- Hobbs carves his own bat from a tree struck by lightning near his home when he is young. When he later uses it during his first game with the Knights, there is some controversy about whether or not the bat fits league specifications. Using your library, the Internet, or other available resources, find out the current requirements for a bat that is to be used in a major-league baseball game. Why do you think these specifications are part of the official game rules? How might a bat that does not fit these specifications help to improve a batter's performance? Write a short report detailing your findings, and provide an example of a major-league player who used a non-regulation bat.

- In the film, set in 1939, Hobbs signs a contract to play for the New York Knights as a rookie for five hundred dollars. According to mlb.com, the average salary for a major league baseball player in 2007 was over 2.8 million dollars. Some have argued that economic factors have transformed baseball into a business more than a sport, with ticket prices skyrocketing and stadiums offering gourmet cuisine instead of just hot dogs and peanuts; some players have even turned to performance-enhancing drugs as a way to make themselves more profitable. Others argue that the enduring qualities of the sport remain and have in turn led to its enormous success. What do you think? Write a persuasive essay arguing for or against baseball as big business. Be sure to use real-world examples and data to support your arguments.

(© Photos 12 | Alamy)

that his son is watching from the stands. It is only then that he is able to make contact with the ball and win the game.

STYLE

The Look and Sound of Days Gone By

The Natural is set in 1939, and the filmmakers take great care in evoking the era for modern audiences. Aside from period costumes (including baseball uniforms sporting a special patch that was only worn during the 1939 season), authentic automobiles, and vintage locations, Levinson also incorporated other stylistic elements that hearken back to an earlier time. For example, during Hobbs's winning and losing streaks, Levinson uses a gimmick popular in films from the 1930s and 1940s: the image of a newspaper overlaying the on-screen action that reveals a news headline intended to summarize the action or propel the story forward. He also uses simulated newsreel footage, filmed in black and white, to depict the controversy over Hobbs's homemade bat as well as Bump Bailey's funeral.

The score for the film, composed by Randy Newman, is also reminiscent of a past era. Many reviewers have noted that the music is similar in style to that of Aaron Copland, a composer often credited with developing a distinctly American style of orchestral music in works such as *Fanfare for the Common Man* (1942) and *Appalachian Spring* (1944). In his review for *Time*, Richard Schickel refers to the music as "imitation Copland," though many others have seen the similarity in a more positive light. Indeed, for many, the score has come to serve as a vintage theme for the sport of baseball in all its forms, appearing frequently on televised sports shows and in sports-related video games.

Using Light to Set the Scene

One of the most notable visual characteristics of *The Natural* is the cinematography by Caleb Deschanel. Many scenes in the film are cast in golden light, reminiscent of the natural lighting seen on late summer afternoons and often associated with childhood. As Glenn Close notes in "Let's Play Ball: Filming the Show," this type of lighting only occurs naturally during the "magic hour," a very short period of time in the late afternoon. It also reinforces the idea that the film takes place in summer, during the baseball season. This technique is used to great effect during Hobbs's challenge against the Whammer, as well as in the opening and closing shots of Hobbs and his son that book-end the film. However, the effect is seen most dramatically when Hobbs first sees Iris again in the stands during a game in Chicago. She rises in the stands and becomes backlit, the translucent brim of her hat glowing like a halo. This emphasizes the filmmakers' use of light to indicate goodness and purity.

By contrast, shadow is used to indicate evil and corruption. This is most notable in the scenes involving the Judge. When Hobbs first enters the Judge's office, the two even discuss the Judge's preference for the dark. Hobbs, in an attempt to rile him, turns on his office lights as he leaves. Throughout the film, Hobbs only encounters the Judge or the corrupt bookie Gus Sands—the two main villains—during nighttime or in darkened rooms.

CULTURAL CONTEXT

The Natural is set in 1939, with the United States still slowly crawling its way out of the Great Depression but not yet embroiled in World War II. The film paints this period largely as a time of innocence, the corruption of Gus Sands and the Judge notwithstanding. In the novel, however, Malamud includes several details that offer a grittier portrait of American life at this time. For example, in Malamud's novel, fans are enemies as often as they are supporters, bringing rotten fruit and vegetables to throw at players who do not measure up during the game. The fans also attack each other, with Malamud listing several instances of violence before and during games. Perhaps it is also a reflection of the time period that Hobbs—like several other characters—is acutely aware of money in the novel. During the height of the Great Depression in the 1930s, one in every four able-bodied Americans could not find a job.

Many real-life incidents and details were woven into the fabric of *The Natural*, both in book and movie form. One of the main inspirations for the story came from the tragic real-life shooting of Eddie Waitkus, a first baseman who was shot in the chest in a Chicago hotel by an obsessed fan in 1949. Like Hobbs, Waitkus survived; unlike Hobbs, he was able to resume his professional career the following season despite his serious injury. Another key inspiration for the tale came from "Shoeless Joe" Jackson and the 1919 Chicago Black Sox scandal, in which several players for the Chicago White Sox were bribed in order to lose the World Series to the Cincinnati Reds. While leaving the courthouse during his trial, a young boy is rumored to have pleaded with Jackson, "Say it ain't so, Joe!" This encounter is duplicated at the end of the novel version of *The Natural*, when a young boy approaches Hobbs and says, "Say it ain't true, Roy." Aside from being a powerful hitter like Hobbs, Jackson was also a left-fielder, just as Hobbs was in the original novel. It is also generally accepted that the Whammer, who Hobbs strikes out at a trackside carnival on his way to try out for the major leagues, is clearly inspired by hitting legend Babe Ruth.

Another real-life incident that inspired a scene in the film was the fly-ball shattering of the Ebbets Field scoreboard clock by Braves player Bama Rowell in 1946; Hobbs makes a similar hit after he sees Iris in the stands and thus ends his slump. The film version of Hobbs appears to be more directly based on Ted Williams than Malamud's version, with Hobbs wearing Williams's uniform number—nine—and with Robert Redford even modeling his swing on that

(© Photos 12 | Alamy)

of Williams. Indeed, Ted Williams was famous for one remark above all others, as reported by Mike Meserole on ESPN.com: "All I want out of life . . . is that when I walk down the street folks will say, 'There goes the greatest hitter that ever lived.'" Hobbs makes the same declaration, almost verbatim, more than once in the film.

CRITICAL OVERVIEW

When the film adaptation of *The Natural* was released theatrically in 1984, critics were less than enthralled. Since then, audiences seem to remain loosely divided into two camps. In the first camp are those familiar with the novel, many of whom think the film simplifies and weakens the novel's plot for the sake of mass entertainment. In his review for the *New York Times*, for example, Vincent Canby calls the film a "big, handsome, ultimately vapid screen adaptation." Canby outlines the harmful changes made by the director and writers: "They supply explanations that the novel resolutely avoided, reshape characters for dramatic convenience and, strangest of all, they transform something dark and open-ended—truly fabulous—into something eccentrically sentimental." He is especially critical of the changes to the ending, stating, "The brooding moral fable becomes a fairy tale." Still, Canby concedes that the "baseball sequences are beautifully staged—up to a point," and that the film is "entertaining in short stretches." Dave Kehr, in a review for *Chicago Reader*, states that the film "preserves the Arthurian imagery of Bernard Malamud's baseball novel while stripping away all its darkness and irony," calling the end result "sappy." Kehr lays the blame squarely on Levinson's shoulders: "I've just about had it with directors who use the mythic mode as an alibi for unshaded characterizations, simple-minded plotting, and swells of artificial emotionality." Roger Ebert, in his review for the *Chicago Sun-Times*, does not specifically compare the book to the film, but finds the same problems noted by other critics. Ebert asks, "Why did a perfectly good story, filled with interesting people, have to be made into one man's ascension to the godlike, especially when no effort is made to give that ascension meaning?" Ebert also singles out the ham-handed depiction of professional baseball, with players often making ridiculous errors, and calls the last shot of the film "cheap and phony." John Simon of the *National Review* calls the film "not Malamud's novel, but a sorry illustration of its theme."

The second camp consists largely of those unfamiliar with the novel, who see the film as the ultimate statement about baseball's mythic place in American culture. Scott Weinberg, in his review for *Apollo Movie Guide Online*, states, "While cynics (or non-baseball fans) may dismiss much of this movie as overly sentimental or even corny, this is a film that speaks volumes to those who love the game." Columnists for ESPN.com's Page 2 section selected the film as number six on their list of the top twenty sports movies of all time. Editor Kevin Jackson writes, "I've seen it a hundred times, yet I still marvel at how Levinson turned the game into an art form." Columnist Ralph Wiley calls it "authentic in the nostalgia that's in every adult heart," while Bill Simmons describes it as, "From beginning to end, the best-done, best-acted sports movie of all time." And despite the lukewarm response from critics in 1984, the film received four Academy Award nominations, including nods for cinematographer Caleb Deschanel, supporting actress Glenn Close, and composer Randy Newman. The film has also become a part of modern baseball culture, with rookies often being compared by commentators to the fictional Roy Hobbs and with stadiums and broadcasters making frequent use of Randy Newman's powerful and familiar orchestral theme.

> AFTER ROY BECOMES THE DE FACTO LEADER OF THE TEAM, THE REST OF THE PLAYERS ALL BEGIN WEARING LIGHTNING BOLT PATCHES SIMILAR TO THE DESIGN ON WONDERBOY. IN ESSENCE, THIS BECOMES THEIR COAT OF ARMS, JUST LIKE KNIGHTS OF OLD."

CRITICISM

Greg Wilson

Wilson is an author, literary critic, and mythologist. In this essay, he examines the different elements of classical myth that appear in The Natural.

When *The Natural* was released in 1984, it took a critical drubbing for altering the novel's tale so dramatically and for stretching the limits of realism in a sports film. In actuality, it is somewhat remarkable how much of the original book remains intact within the film, since the end products feel so different. One way in which the film captures the essence of the book is in its use of mythological elements from several different sources. In particular, the film draws upon ancient Greek tales, Christian mythology, and Arthurian legend in an effort to lend a resonant, timeless quality to the narrative.

Some of the most obvious references in the film relate to ancient Greek myth. When Roy Hobbs talks with Harriet Bird on the train to Chicago, she asks him pointblank, "Have you ever read Homer?" This is a reference to the ancient Greek poet who documented much of what the modern world knows of that culture's belief systems in his *Odyssey* and *Iliad*. Bird offers a direct comparison between modern baseball players and the heroes of ancient myth. This connection is also shown in the film's handling of the theme of hubris, or arrogance about one's place in the universe—a common subject in the myths of ancient Greece. It is suggested that Hobbs's hubris—shown when he proclaims he will be the best there ever was, with no goal or understanding of his talents beyond that—leads directly to his shooting by Harriet.

WHAT DO I SEE NEXT?

- *Field of Dreams* (1989) is considered by many to be among the greatest baseball films ever made. Written and directed by Phil Alden Robinson and based on *Shoeless Joe* (1982), a novel by W. P. Kinsella, the film stars Kevin Costner as a farmer who hears a supernatural voice that convinces him to build a baseball diamond in his cornfield. Once the diamond is completed, the ghosts of former baseball players appear and relive their glory days on the field. The film was nominated for four Academy Awards.

- *Eight Men Out* (1988), written and directed by John Sayles, recounts the true story of the 1919 Chicago Black Sox scandal. Like Roy Hobbs, eight players for the Chicago White Sox were offered money in exchange for losing the World Series to the Cincinnati Reds. They were all later banned from the sport for life. The film stars David Strathairn, John Cusack, and D. B. Sweeney, among others.

- *For Love of the Game* (1999), directed by Sam Raimi, stars Kevin Costner as an aging pitcher reflecting on his life during what may be the most important game of his career.

- *The Rookie* (2002), directed by John Lee Hancock, is based on a true story with similarities to *The Natural*. Jim Morris, played in the film by Dennis Quaid, is a former minor league baseball player whose injuries ended his career just as it began. After becoming a science teacher and baseball coach for a west Texas high school, Morris agrees to attend tryouts for a major league team as part of a promise he made to his students. He tries out for the major leagues at the age of thirty-five, and after impressing the scouts with his 98 mile-per-hour fastball, he becomes a pitcher for the Tampa Bay Devil Rays.

- Like *The Natural*, Michael Ritchie's *Downhill Racer* (1969) is a sports film starring Robert Redford as a gifted athlete. Redford plays David Chappellet, a young, cocky downhill skier who joins the United States Olympic men's ski team and clashes with his teammates and coach, portrayed by Gene Hackman.

- Though not a sports film, *O Brother, Where Art Thou?* (2000), like *The Natural*, is a tale greatly inspired by classical mythology and set in 1930s America. Created by the Coen brothers, this film stars George Clooney in a thoroughly Southern re-telling of Homer's epic poem *The Odyssey*.

Another clear reference to Greek myth is the character of Iris. In Greek mythology, Iris was the goddess of the rainbow who carried messages from the gods to the humans. She is often depicted as having golden wings. In the film, Iris Gaines is also associated with the color gold: she has blonde hair (unlike in the novel), and when Hobbs first sees her after many years apart, she is dramatically backlit by the golden glow of the sun. Also like the mythological character, Iris is a messenger; twice she sends important written messages to Hobbs, once while he is in the dugout and once immediately after a game.

There is some suggestion that Hobbs is a character similar to the Greek character Odysseus, who spent twenty years away during and after the Trojan War, striving against all obstacles to return home. This is similar to Hobbs's missing sixteen years, the time between being shot by Harriet and returning "home" to baseball and ultimately Iris. This comparison to Odysseus is also illustrated in the matchup with the Whammer; the character of the Whammer is similar to Polyphemus, the one-eyed giant Odysseus battles during his journeys. In addition to his size, Polyphemus also resembles the Whammer in his choice of "weapon": a large wooden club, not unlike a baseball bat. In both cases, the giant is defeated with his own weapon; the Whammer is struck out, and Polyphemus is blinded when Odysseus stabs him in the eye with his own sharpened club. One could also argue that the contest between Hobbs and the Whammer is similar to the battle between David and Goliath as found in the Bible. In that tale, Goliath is a giant warrior who is defeated by a young man destined to become the king of Israel—just as Hobbs seems destined to become the new legend of the sport.

The film contains other Biblical references as well. When Olsen, a player for the Knights, improves his batting after wearing a lightning bolt patch on his sleeve similar to the design on Hobbs's bat, another player comments that "it's like Samson with his hair." This is a reference to the Biblical tale of Samson, an Israelite who possesses superhuman strength bestowed upon him by God; Samson retains this strength only as long as his hair remains uncut. Also, the character of the Judge may be seen as the embodiment of the demon called Mammon, which represents the worship of money and material things above all else.

Another Biblical reference is the creation of Hobbs's bat Wonderboy from a tree struck by lightning; in the Bible, lightning is generally a sign of divine manifestation, where God is sending a message to a specific person. The burning bush seen by Moses as a manifestation of God parallels the burning tree split by lightning in the film and explains the supernatural strength of Wonderboy. This same lightning appears later in the film prior to Hobbs's great feats on the field, suggesting that his abilities are divinely bestowed.

In addition to these Biblical examples, one scene in particular echoes the betrayal of Jesus before his crucifixion. During the playoff party, when Hobbs rejects Gus Sands's offer of bribery, Hobbs is then given a poisoned dessert by Memo Paris. After she places the dessert in his mouth, she kisses Hobbs on the cheek. This echoes Judas Iscariot's betrayal of Jesus to the soldiers of Caiaphas; Judas identified Jesus to the soldiers by kissing him on the cheek, so the soldiers could arrest him. The kiss itself is seen as an act of betrayal.

The other major mythological influence on the film is the collected legends of King Arthur and the Knights of the Round Table. After defeating the Whammer, Harriet Bird compares Hobbs to Sir Lancelot, King Arthur's most favored knight. This parallel is also apparent in the name of the team for which Hobbs plays: the New York Knights. Hobbs's first name, Roy, is even derived from the French word for "king." After Roy becomes the de facto leader of the team, the rest of the players all begin wearing lightning bolt patches similar to the design on Wonderboy. In essence, this becomes their coat of arms, just like knights of old. Wonderboy itself invites comparison to King Arthur's own weapon, the sword Excalibur. Like Excalibur, Wonderboy seems to possess its own magical powers; also in both tales, the hero is ultimately separated from his weapon, though the parallel events occur under very different circumstances.

Another similarity between *The Natural* and Arthurian myth is pointed out by Janna Malamud Smith, in the DVD extra "Knights in Shining Armor: The Mythology of *The Natural*." Smith notes that the entire story is structured like the quest for the Holy Grail, with the Grail being represented by the league championship pennant. In the Arthurian legends surrounding the Grail, the cup is sought by the knight Percival as a way to heal a wounded king, sometimes referred to as the Fisher King. It is no coincidence that the coach of the New York Knights is named Pop Fisher, after this character. (The comparison is carried even further in the novel, where Fisher truly is wounded—he is afflicted with athlete's foot on his hands—and the condition only goes away when Hobbs leads the team to victory.)

Other mythic elements appear, such as the character of Gus Sands, the one-eyed bookie who claims he can see the future. This might be seen to echo the ancient Greek myth of Tiresias, a man who becomes the pawn in an argument between the goddess Hera and her husband Zeus. When asked to settle an argument between the two, Tiresias sides with Zeus, and Hera renders him blind. Unable to undo what Hera has done, Zeus instead gives Tiresias the ability to see the future as a replacement for his sight. The similarity to Gus Sands is clear, but the character of the blind seer is common throughout many cultural belief systems, and perhaps a better mythic parallel is found in Norse mythology. Odin, the leader of the Norse gods, willingly gives up one of his eyes at Mimir's well in exchange for wisdom and the ability to see the future.

The film also makes great use of the recurring mythic association between evil as darkness and goodness as light. This is most obviously reflected in simple costuming choices, such as putting Harriet Bird in all black and Iris Gaines in white. The evil Judge even talks to Hobbs about how he once feared the dark but has come to embrace it, and now he keeps the lights turned off in his office. On the flip side, when Iris—goddess of the rainbow and messenger for the Greek gods—makes her appearance to Hobbs in the stadium during his losing streak, she literally becomes bathed in golden light, her hat even appearing like the halo of an angel. This is the perfect synthesis of Christian and ancient Greek myth in a modern context.

One criticism of the film is that it simply does not portray baseball in any realistic way: when the players are good, like Hobbs, they are impossibly good, and when they are bad, they are comically bad. However, all the mythic references should provide a clue as to the film's true purpose: it is meant to be a new kind of myth for the modern age, reshaping the reality of baseball into something that exists above and beyond the real world, just as myths of the past have done. It is telling, perhaps, that those who criticize the film for its lack of realism are generally not involved in professional sports. For professional baseball players and sports columnists, the film is quite obviously not meant to portray reality but to convey the timeless essence of the sport—and a good many of them agree that it succeeds in a way few other films have succeeded.

Source: Greg Wilson, Critical Essay on *The Natural*, *Novels for Students 34*, Gale, Cengage Learning, 2010.

Vincent Canby

In this review, Canby echoes the sentiments of many reviewers when he contends that the "brooding moral fable" of the novel is transformed into a "fairy tale."

When it was published in 1952, *The Natural*, Bernard Malamud's first novel, was received with rather grudging admiration. Now, more than 30 years and many celebrated works later, *The Natural*, the story of the rise and fall of a legendary baseball player, is still seen as something of a Malamud aberration. Though it remains one of his most popular novels, it's not easily associated with works like *The Fixer* and *Dubin's Lives*, in which the writer explores aspects of the Jewish experience, past as well as present.

Yet *The Natural* really isn't all that different. Though Roy Hobbs, its almost incredibly innocent hero, is as American as a figure in a Norman Rockwell magazine cover, the tale is full of those concerns for myth and morality that separate Mr. Malamud's narratives from those of all lesser writers.

The story of Roy Hobbs's romantic quest to become "the best there is"—the player against whom all subsequent players will forever be measured to their disadvantage—is as magical, funny and sad as anything Mr. Malamud has ever written. It seems realistic, but it is also fantastic and mysterious. Though Roy Hobbs is the quintessential small-town American boy of the 1920's, he has not only the strengths but also the flaws of the great heroes who survive outside their time.

These things need to be said in connection with the big, handsome, ultimately vapid screen adaptation of *The Natural* that opens today at the Sutton, National and other theaters. When a literary work of such particular and long-lived appeal is turned into a movie, one must assume that the adapters wanted not only to preserve but, possibly, also to illuminate it.

Instead, Roger Towne and Phil Dusenberry, who wrote the screenplay, and Barry Levinson, the director, seem to have taken it upon themselves to straighten out Mr. Malamud's fable, to correct the flaws he overlooked. They supply explanations that the novel resolutely avoided, reshape characters for dramatic convenience and, strangest of all, they transform something dark and open-ended—truly fabulous—into something eccentrically sentimental.

All of this might be justified if the film then succeeded on its own as something else. However, this "Natural" may well baffle people who come upon the remains of its story for the first time and wonder what Mr. Malamud was up to.

When we first see Roy Hobbs (Robert Redford), the year is 1924, and he's on his way from his farm home in the West to Chicago to try out for the Cubs. Enroute, the train makes a whistle stop at a small prairie town, where, at the local carnival, the scout accompanying Roy makes a crazy bet with two fellow passengers, Max Mercy (Robert Duvall), a famous sports columnist, and baseball's then reigning king, the Whammer, who, as played by Joe Don Baker, is the spitting image of Babe Ruth.

The $100 bet is that Roy can strike out the Whammer in three pitches, which is exactly what Roy does, thus promising to change the face of baseball exactly as he has set out to do. Unfortunately, he has also attracted the interest of a pretty young 1920's siren named Harriet Bird (Barbara Hershey). Later that night in the club car, Harriet flirts with Roy and talks to him about Sir Lancelot and Homer. She persists in asking him what he's looking for, but all that poor Roy can say is that he wants to be the best. Roy has never heard of the Holy Grail.

Their first night in Chicago, Harriet invites Roy to her hotel room where, dressed in something sheer and indiscreet, as well as a black hat with a widow's veil, she shoots him in the stomach with a silver bullet. Since this takes place early in the film, I'm not giving away important plot developments. Everything that happens afterward is in some way related to the near fatal-encounter in that Chicago hotel room in 1924.

The film then skips forward 15 years when Roy shows up at the dugout of the last-place New York Knights to become the oldest rookie in the major leagues. The movie, like the book, never tries to explain what Roy has been doing in those 15 years, nor why he has at long last resumed his baseball career.

Instead it concentrates on Roy's miraculous rise to glory, which promises to save the Knights from the greedy clutches of their owner. Very much a part of this are Roy's love affairs, one with Iris Gaines (Glenn Close), the virtuous sweetheart he left at home and who suddenly turns up in the ball park in Chicago to break Roy's losing streak, and Memo Paris (Kim Basinger), the beautiful, wanton niece of the club's manager, Pop Fisher (Wilford Brimley).

Up to this point, the film pretty much follows the outlines of the novel. However, when Roy is once again tempted as he was in Chicago 15 years before, the movie takes it upon itself to save Roy from any further transgressions, possibly because *The Natural* is, after all, a big-budget commercial entertainment of the kind that is supposed to warm the heart, not shiver the timbers. The brooding moral fable becomes a fairy tale.

If the source material were not so fine and idiosyncratic, it would not be worth worrying about the film's peculiar failures. However, given all that it might have been, one wants it to be better.

The baseball sequences are beautifully staged—up to a point: the movie always tells us when Roy and his homemade bat, Wonderboy, are going to hit a homer because that homer ball always comes at him in slow motion. Caleb Deschanel's glowy, idyllic camera work also overstates moods to such an extent that it seems to be an end in itself, rather than a means to an end. In much the same way, Randy Newman's sound track score at times seems to be telling the story two bars ahead of the action on the screen.

The supporting performances are good, especially those of Miss Basinger; Mr. Duvall; Mr. Brimley; Richard Farnsworth, as the Knights' coach; Robert Prosky, as the Knight's scheming owner; and Michael Madsen in the small role of Bump Bailey, the star of the Knights until the appearance of Roy Hobbs. Darren McGavin makes an interesting if unbilled appearance as the big-time bookie who is behind the scheme to wreck Roy's career. Miss Close and Miss Hershey are little more than functions of the plot.

Mr. Redford's performance is difficult to analyze. At times his almost legendary presence as a major movie star perfectly fits the character of Roy, who is as much of a legend as the actor. At other times, his diffidence appears to be that of a movie star who is afraid someone's going to ask for his autograph. Though he looks terrific, especially on the field in action, the performance is chilly. It's so studied that there's very little spontaneous emotion for the audience to react to.

Mr. Levinson, who both wrote and directed *Diner*, the small, exquisitely realized comedy about growing up aimless in Baltimore, here seems to be at the service of other people's decisions. Though entertaining in short stretches, *The Natural* has no recognizable character of its own.

Source: Vincent Canby, "Redford and Duvall in Malamud's 'Natural,'" in *New York Times*, May 11, 1984.

John Simon

In this review, Simon criticizes the film version of The Natural *as a poor, melodramatic oversimplification of Malamud's novel.*

Why do people want to make movies out of novels that are not so famous as to ring the bell at the box office, yet well enough known to make their being turned inside out offensive to some? That is what was done to Bernard Malamud's *The Natural* (1952), a novel about the failure of American innocence, about the way natural talents and resources are corrupted, destroyed, and discarded. This has (so to speak) naturally been turned into a fable of success, of the ultimate triumph of semi-doltish purity. Roy Hobbs (Robert Redford), a great young pitcher, leaves his farm and childhood sweetheart (Glenn Close) to become, with the Chicago Cubs, the greatest player ever. The Chicago train stops at a country fair where this unknown, with three pitches, strikes out The Whammer, the hitherto unchallenged King of Swat. Whereupon a psychotic young woman (Barbara Hershey) invites him by phone to her nocturnal hotel room and shoots him in the gut with a silver bullet. It is not clear whether she is a pathological hater of excellence, the emissary of dark powers, or a misguided fan of Der Freischutz.

Already Malamud's conceit is undercut. A Roy Hobbs who is as pure as the driven snow—or, better yet, as Robert Redford—would not keep such an obviously erotic assignation. It is true that Redford plays it like a veterinarian making a house call for a cranky millionaire's sick pet, but even so it makes no sense. Either the man is really randy in which case he should convey that and give the scene some meaning; or he goes in a state of Prince Myshkin-like innocence, in which case he is worse than a natural—an idiot. Redford is not a bad actor when he lets himself go, but in this movie he does so only on the baseball diamond and treats all other venues as mere zircon: He becomes wary, even worried, like a catcher without a mask. Or perhaps a mask without a catcher.

After a hiatus of 15 years—which the movie eventually tries to explain, though it were better left unexplained—Roy comes back as a 36-year-old rookie for the New York Knights, who have taken to the cellar of the league like inveterate cave-dwellers. He now has to tangle with a web of evil from the owner of the club (Robert Prosky) and his tools: a corrupt bookie (Darren McGavin), his blonde mistress sicked on Roy (Kim Basinger), and a vile sports columnist (Robert Duvall) who dimly remembers Roy from before and wants to expose him. This is not unlike the hatred-of-genius theme that informs the book and movie versions of *The Fountainhead*, but not nearly so inadvertently

funny. Roy also has to conquer the denseness of the team's manager (Wilford Brimley), who keeps him benched, and won't let the sympathetic coach (Richard Farnsworth) change his mind. At this point the film, which started out with mythic overtones, goes megalomythomaniacal. In the beginning, Roy carved his bat from a lightning-struck tree; now the epic and quasi-supernatural elements start to proliferate like giant bunny rabbits. Good and evil work their antithetical wonders, but I shall cite only the most crudely obvious one. When our hero keeps striking out because of his liaison with the bad Miss Basinger, Glenn Close stands up behind the dugout. In a white dress and hat, she is shot with enough backlighting to keep a host of angels in spare haloes, and spreads a benediction that yields instant miracles. Barry Levinson, who here milks directorial effects brazenly—just as Caleb Deschanel does photographic ones—goes into slow motion at the drop of a bat, but that's the least of his tricks. The entire film seems to be forged from fool's gold, sparkling, radiating, deliquescing before our eyes.

Just as Roy seems to be dying from the effort to redeem himself at the end, the screen goes black, whereupon we are transported to a scene similar to one at the beginning. Now Redford, Miss Close (divorced from another man), and their boy (reunited with his true father) are tossing a baseball to one another in a sequence that looks like Norman Rockwell translated into heaven. The holy family's hair is as golden as the surrounding wheat, and there is enough saccharin in Miss Close's smile to sweeten all the decafs of the world. Add to this Randy Newman's "serious" music and you have, not Malamud's novel, but a sorry illustration of its theme. At the sight of so much affluent bliss, there's not a dry palm in the house.

Source: John Simon, "The Natural," in *National Review*, Vol. 36, July 13, 1984, pp. 51–52.

SOURCES

Canby, Vincent, "Film: Redford and Duvall in Levinson's 'Natural,'" in the *New York Times*, May 11, 1984, at http://movies.nytimes.com/movie/review?_r = 4&res = 980CE3DD1E38F932A25756C0 (accessed June 27, 2009).

Costas, Bob, Interview in "Clubhouse Conversations," in *The Natural: The Director's Cut* DVD, supplemental material, Sony Home Pictures Entertainment, 2007.

Ebert, Roger, Review of *The Natural*, in the *Chicago Sun-Times*, at http://rogerebert.suntimes.com/apps/pbcs.dll/article?AID=/19840101/REVIEWS/401010363/1023 (accessed June 27, 2009).

Hample, Zack, *Watching Baseball Smarter: A Professional Fan's Guide for Beginners, Semi-Experts, and Deeply Serious Geeks*, Vintage, 2007.

Kehr, Dave, Review of *The Natural*, in *Chicago Reader*, at http://events.chicagoreader.com/chicago/the-natural/Film?oid=1074127 (accessed June 27, 2009).

Levinson, Barry, *Sixty-Six: A Novel*, Broadway, 2003.

Malamud, Bernard, *The Natural*, Farrar, Straus & Giroux, 2003.

Malamud Smith, Janna, Interview in "Knights in Shining Armor: The Mythology of *The Natural*," in *The Natural: The Director's Cut* DVD, supplemental material, Sony Home Pictures Entertainment, 2007.

———, Interview in "Let's Play Ball: Filming the Show," in *The Natural: The Director's Cut* DVD, supplemental material, Sony Home Pictures Entertainment, 2007.

Meserole, Mike, "'There goes the greatest hitter who ever lived,'" ESPN.com, July 8, 2002, at http://espn.go.com/classic/obit/williams_ted_obit.html (accessed June 27, 2009).

"No. 6: The Natural," in Page 2's Top 20 Sports Movies of All-Time at ESPN.com, at http://espn.go.com/page2/movies/s/top20/no6.html (accessed June 27, 2009).

Schickel, Richard, "Swinging for the Fences," in *Time*, May 14, 1984, at http://www.time.com/time/magazine/article/0,9171,955295,00.html (accessed June 27, 2009).

Simon, John, Review of *The Natural*. *National Review*, July 13, 1984, pp. 51–52.

"Unit 4: Editing," The Florida State University College of Communication Film Studies Web site. at http://comm2.fsu.edu/programs/comm/film/editing.htm (accessed June 27, 2009).

Ward, Geoffrey C., and Ken Burns, *Baseball: An Illustrated History*, Knopf, 1996.

Weinberg, Scott, Apollo Movie Guide's Review of *The Natural*, at http://apolloguide.com/mov_fullrev.asp?CID=3137&Specific=2415 (accessed June 27, 2009).

FURTHER READING

Cahir, Linda Costanzo, *Literature into Film: Theory and Practical Approaches*, McFarland & Company, 2006.
Cahir presents a detailed discussion, with an emphasis on film theory, of the relationship between original works of literature and their film adaptations.

Internet Movie Database (IMDb), entry on Robert Redford. http://www.imdb.com/name/nm0000602.
IMDb provides comprehensive information on the projects of people involved in the film industry. Redford's entry contains a complete list of films in which he acted, directed, or produced, along with links to further information on each film.

Levinson, Barry, ed. David Thompson, *Levinson on Levinson*, Faber & Faber, 1993.
In interviews with David Thompson, Levison traces his career from his beginnings as a comedy writer. He discusses his films and filmmaking practices in detail.

Schoenecke, Michael K., et. al., *All-Stars and Movie Stars: Sports in Film and History*, University Press of Kentucky, 2008.
This is a scholarly collection of essays on the cultural impact and context of the representation of sports in film. It includes extensive discussion of *The Natural*.

Nothing But the Truth: A Documentary Novel

Nothing But the Truth: A Documentary Novel, published by Orchard Books in 1991, is a highly regarded book written by prolific children's author Avi. Named a Newbery Honor Book by the American Library Association in 1992, this novel reflects Avi's ability to create a complex, thought-provoking narrative that makes a compelling statement about American culture. *Nothing But the Truth* is considered one of Avi's best coming-of-age books.

In the novel, Avi explores issues of power, control, honesty, hypocrisy, patriotism, and the complicated nature of the truth. The narrative focuses on ninth grader Philip Malloy, an intelligent but underachieving student and aspiring track star, and his antagonistic relationship with his English teacher, Miss Narwin. Philip hums along to the "Star-Spangled Banner" each morning, even though students are required to be silent while it is played. Miss Narwin considers Philip's actions disruptive and has him suspended from school. His suspension turns into a media circus focused on patriotism. School administrators force both teacher and student out of the school at novel's end.

Nothing But the Truth is based on a true story. Avi presents the complicated nature of "truth" by writing the novel as a series of documents such as memos, diary entries, and letters as well as transcripts of conversations. He allows readers to draw their own conclusions about

AVI

1991

Avi (AP Images)

who is in the right. As Loudoun County Public Library system spokeswoman Beth Wiseman told Charity Corkey of the *Washington Post*, "What's thought to be the truth can be presented in many different ways. At times, it's the combination of many pieces that is the truth."

AUTHOR BIOGRAPHY

Avi was born Edward Irving Wortis on December 23, 1937, in New York City, the son of Dr. Joseph and Helen Wortis. His father worked as a psychiatrist while his mother was a social worker; both were also authors. Avi was raised in Boston among an extended family that included painters and writers. His family also supported radical political causes, and political debates among family members were common in his childhood. Avi became an avid reader but suffered from a learning disability called dysgraphia that made it hard to write. School was difficult for him, but Avi persevered and found a mentor in high school who helped teach him the basics of writing.

Avi graduated from the University of Wisconsin with a B.A. in 1959 and M.A. in 1962. Returning to New York City, he earned a master's degree in library science from Columbia University in 1964 and began working in the New York Public Library while continuing to develop his interest in writing. In 1970, Avi took a post at Trenton State College and began publishing books for children and young adults. He worked as a humanities librarian and assistant professor at the college through 1986.

Avi's first published works were two picture books, *Things That Sometimes Happen* (1970) and *Snail Tale: The Adventures of a Rather Small Snail* (1972). Over the next three decades, Avi focused primarily on novels for young adult readers though he continued to publish books for younger children as well. A number of his young adult books were adventure tales, including *Emily Upham's Revenge; or, How Deadwood Dick Saved the Banker's Niece: A Massachusetts Adventure*, published in 1978, and *The History of Helpless Harry: To Which Is Added a Variety of Amusing and Entertaining Adventures*, published in 1980.

Avi sometimes tackled controversial issues when he started to write historical novels for young adults beginning in the late 1980s, and these books are among his most critically acclaimed. *The True Confessions of Charlotte Doyle*, published in 1990, was a Newbery Honor Book and won the Golden Kite Award from the Society of Children's Authors. The highly regarded 1991 novel *Nothing But the Truth: A Documentary Novel*, took on public school students' right to freedom of speech and challenged the meaning of patriotism. Other significant historical novels included *Finding Providence: The Story of Roger Williams*, published in 1997, and *Don't You Know There's a War On?*, published in 2001. Avi won a Newbery Award for *Crispin: At the Edge of the World*, published in 2006.

Avi continues to write full-time and regularly travels around the country, appearing in schools to talk about his books. As of 2009, Avi lives and works from his home in Colorado.

PLOT SUMMARY

Prologue

The prologue of *Nothing But the Truth* consists of a memo from the Harrison School District. It outlines the procedure for morning announcements

MEDIA ADAPTATIONS

- *Nothing But the Truth: A Documentary Novel* was adapted for the stage by Ronn Smith in 1997 and performed in numerous schools.

over the public address (PA) system, including the playing of the national anthem. The memo specifically states that listeners must "stand at respectful, silent attention."

1—Tuesday, March 13

Ninth-grade high school student Philip Malloy describes his day at school. He is excited because Coach Jamison encouraged him to try out for the track team, and he found out that a girl named Allison Doresett likes him. However, Philip is in conflict with his English teacher, Miss Narwin, whom he regards as "uptight" and "sour." For her part, Miss Narwin has been teaching for twenty-five years and understands that students are hard to reach. She is frustrated by Philip because she believes that he is smart but does not regard literature as important. Miss Narwin does not retire because she would not know what to do without teaching.

2—Thursday, March 15

During morning announcements, Philip is focused on studying for an exam instead of standing during the national anthem and gets caught by his homeroom teacher, Mr. Lunser. Philip is extremely worried about passing his winter term exams, but he happily contemplates his interest in Allison and looks forward to running track.

3—Friday, March 16

For spring term, which starts in a few days, Philip is assigned to Miss Narwin's homeroom. Right before exams for winter term begin, Philip admits to Allison that he has not read Jack London's *Call of the Wild,* which will be covered on the exam. Allison is not impressed as she liked the book.

4—Monday, March 19

Philip does not try hard on his English exam. Miss Narwin gives him a C- and warns him that he might fail the class.

5—Tuesday, March 20

Miss Narwin applies for a grant to attend a summer program on new ways to teach high school literature, hoping to "find new works and new ways to entice the young people of today."

6—Wednesday, March 21

In a memo, Dr. Albert Seymour of the Harrison School District urges teachers to lobby for voter approval of a critical school budget.

7—Friday, March 23

Philip receives his winter term grades. His D in English upsets him, but he is still trying to impress Allison and preparing to try out for track.

8—Monday, March 26

Both Miss Narwin and Philip suffer setbacks. Miss Narwin learns that her application for the grant has been denied by the principal because of budget constraints. Coach Jamison informs Philip that he cannot try out for the track team because of his low English grade. The coach urges him to talk to Miss Narwin and ask for extra work to bring the grade up. In English class, Philip daydreams instead of paying attention to Miss Narwin.

9—Tuesday, March 27

Philip's parents discuss his grades. His mother is concerned that Philip will fail English, while his father is less concerned. Mr. Malloy says he will talk to Philip. When he does, Philip blames Miss Narwin for his grades. He tells his father, "She has it in for me." When Mr. Malloy asks about the track team, Philip lies and says he has decided not to try out. His father is angry because he bought Philip new running shoes for the season. Later, when his parents talk again, his father says he accepts what Philip says about his grades but is still upset that his son will not be trying out for track. But Mr. Malloy decides not to mention it to Philip.

Miss Narvin admits in a letter to her sister that she feels hurt and angry that her grant application was rejected when another, less deserving teacher has received funds.

10—Wednesday, March 28

Spring term begins. On the way to the school bus, Philip tells his friend Ken Barchet that he is going to try to get transferred out of Miss Narwin's homeroom and English class. In homeroom, he hums the national anthem. Miss Narwin tells him to quit, but Philip says that Mr. Lunser did not mind his humming.

Later, Miss Narwin talks to Mr. Benison, a science teacher, about the new homeroom assignments. She complains about Philip and his humming during the national anthem. In the lunchroom, another student, Todd Becker, asks Philip why he is not trying out for the track team. Philip shrugs him off and complains about his English teacher.

Tension between Miss Narwin and Philip continues in English class. Philip does not give a good answer to Miss Narwin's question about Shakespeare's *Julius Caesar*. On the school bus home, Allison tries to talk to Philip about Miss Narwin and not being on the track team, but Philip is hostile. After school, Miss Narwin asks Mr. Lunser about Philip's singing during the national anthem. Mr. Lunser denies allowing him to sing.

At dinner, Philip is quiet. His father pressures him about the track team. Philip tells his parents about the national anthem and humming. His mother thinks that Miss Narwin's response is not fair. His mother tells his father, "He needs your support on something that isn't track. That's him." Later that night, Philip is still upset by school but his father talks to him about the humming incident and offers his support. Mr. Malloy encourages him to stand up for his rights.

11—Thursday, March 29

In homeroom, Philip hums again during the national anthem and does not stop when Miss Narwin asks him to. Miss Narwin sends him to the principal's office. Dr. Joseph Palleni, an assistant principal, asks Philip the nature of the problem. Philip says he likes to hum along and "it's sort of a . . . patriotic thing with me." Philip also tells him that Miss Narwin "always has it in for me." Dr. Palleni tells him that it is a school rule to be silent during the national anthem. Philip asks for a new homeroom and English teacher, but Dr. Palleni dismisses his concerns.

Other people struggle as well. At work, Ben Malloy is castigated by his boss, Mr. Dexter, for a botched job and forced to take responsibility for it. Mr. Malloy is warned not to screw up again. The school principal, Dr. Gertrude Doane, tells Miss Narwin that she does not need to attend the summer program because she is already "a master teacher." Miss Narwin later tells her sister that she appreciates the support of Dr. Doane.

In the evening, Ben Malloy tells his wife Susan about the incident with his boss and laments not standing up to him. At dinner, Philip tells his parents about being sent to the principal's office. His father believes that Philip should stick up for himself. Philip appreciates his parents' support.

12—Friday, March 30

The next day in homeroom, Philip once again hums to the "Star-Spangled Banner." Miss Narwin tells him to stop immediately, but Philip retorts, "I have the right to do it." Philip is once more sent to Dr. Palleni's office. The assistant principal reminds Philip that he cannot sing to the national anthem and refuses to remove Philip from Miss Narwin's homeroom. Dr. Palleni tries to make a deal with Philip. If Philip will stop humming the anthem and apologize, there will be no consequences. If Philip refuses, he will be suspended for two days. Philip refuses to change his mind.

Dr. Palleni has a quick chat with Miss Narwin about the situation. She believes that Philip will be better in a different homeroom and says, "Suspension might be counterproductive." While Miss Narwin believes Philip is "a nice boy," she also tells Palleni that she thinks Philip is "lazy."

Returning to his office, Dr. Palleni once more asks Philip to apologize to Miss Narwin. Philip refuses a second time and is suspended for two days; he calls his mother to come and get him. His mother must leave work to pick him up. Before she arrives, Philip is offered a third chance to apologize, which he turns down.

Susan Malloy tells Palleni that she believes that singing during the national anthem is okay. Palleni points out that Philip is being punished for breaking a rule, not for singing the anthem. Mrs. Malloy expresses how upset she is on the ride home, but Philip points out that his father said he should stand up for himself.

Later, Miss Narwin tells Dr. Palleni that she still wants Philip in her English class. In a letter to her sister, she says that she believes something is wrong in Philip's home life and feels bad about the situation. Philip tells Allison why he was suspended and agrees with her observation that he got under Miss Narwin's skin.

Philip tells the entire story at dinner that evening. Mr. Malloy supports Philip's actions. He talks with Ted Griffen, a neighbor running for the school board, who then asks Philip to speak to Jennifer Stewart, a reporter who is covering the election. Philip does so; meanwhile, Griffen begins to use the story in his campaign speeches.

13—Saturday, March 31

To complete her article, Stewart calls Dr. Seymour, the school superintendent; Dr. Doane, the principal; Dr. Palleni; and Miss Narwin. Stewart is told by Seymour that there is no rule against singing the national anthem, and Dr. Doane also says that singing would not be a problem. Dr. Palleni has no comment, while Miss Narwin says, "The boy was creating a disturbance." Miss Narwin mentions that the school rules prohibit singing, but she has nothing else to say. Dr. Doane calls Dr. Palleni, who tells her that Philip was acting out in class. They plan to avoid the reporter. At home, Philip thinks about asking Miss Narwin for extra credit work to help him raise his grade to make him eligible for the track team.

14—Sunday, April 1

Stewart's article appears in the *Manchester Record*, and it essentially supports Philip. Dr. Seymour calls Dr. Doane about the story. Dr. Doane admits that Philip was punished for creating a disturbance in Miss Narwin's class. Dr. Seymour decides to take charge of the situation.

Philip's parents, who continue to be supportive, show him the article. Miss Narwin tells her sister that the story is slanted and that she is upset that people will believe the worst of her. Griffen continues to use Philip's suspension in his campaign appearances.

15—Monday, April 2

Stewart's article is picked up by national news outlets. Philip's story becomes a favored subject on talk shows, with most hosts siding with Philip. The school board chairman, Mrs. Gloria Harland, and Dr. Seymour talk about the situation and the chairman's concern about its effect on passing the budget. Dr. Seymour says he will make inquiries.

Dr. Seymour again asks Dr. Doane to write a report about the incident and reminds him that the school district's budget is at stake. Another reporter, Robert Duval, calls from St. Louis and wants information. Dr. Doane promises to call him back after he sorts the situation out.

Dr. Doane, Dr. Palleni, and Miss Narwin meet. Miss Narwin tells them her version of the events. She claims that Philip was singing loudly, and she has no idea why he acts this way. Dr. Palleni again blames it on the home. Miss Narwin believes that Philip should not have been suspended over the matter, but Dr. Palleni says that they cannot bend the rules, and Philip had two infractions in one week.

Dr. Palleni writes up a memo that outlines the events. He claims that Philip "caused a disturbance in his homeroom class ... by singing the national anthem in a loud, raucous, *disrespectful* manner." Dr. Doane looks into the matter by talking to other students. Ken says he could not hear Philip sing, while Cynthia says he was not really that loud but a bit rude. Allison tells Dr. Doane that Phil was trying to get Miss Narwin in trouble. Dr. Doane's report echoes Dr. Palleni's memo, which is sent to Mrs. Harland.

Telegrams are sent to the school supporting Philip. At home, Philip's parents are proud that he stood up for himself and remain on his side. Miss Narwin is upset, and her sister wonders if the story is true. It has appeared in her newspaper in Florida. Miss Narwin calls Dr. Doane and learns that there are letters and telegrams at school that are, for the most part, castigating her. Dr. Doane offers her the day off but Miss Narwin does not want to back down. For his part, Philip worries about going back to school the next day.

16—Tuesday, April 3

Letters sent to Miss Narwin at the school accuse her of being unpatriotic. Dr. Seymour and Dr. Doane meet. Dr. Seymour is inclined to shift the blame to Miss Narwin. He requests to see her file.

Philip expresses nervousness about going back to school. On the way to the bus, he tells Ken the real reason why he did not try out for the track team and that he will ask Miss Narwin for extra work. Philip believes that she will be open to giving the work to him.

Meeting with Dr. Doane, Miss Narwin states that she feels unsupported. Dr. Doane tells her, "You have to accept the idea that it's all a misunderstanding." Miss Narwin learns that Philip has been moved to Mr. Keegan's English class, a decision she disagrees with. At school, Allison accuses Philip of humming simply to annoy Miss Narwin. He tries to tell her that it is not true, but Allison will not listen.

The school district issues a memo that states that "there is *no* rule that prohibits a student from singing along" with the national anthem. Philip's new homeroom teacher, Mr. Lunser, teases Philip about singing the national anthem. Philip does not hum along. Philip's peers also tease him throughout the day. He continues to receive letters of support from around the nation, however.

That same morning, Dr. Doane talks to Duval, the St. Louis reporter. Duval has read the superintendent's statement and believes it does not tell Miss Narwin's side of the story nor does it support her. He wants to meet with Miss Narwin, and Dr. Doane gives him her phone number. Dr. Seymour and Griffen meet. Dr. Seymour only cares about the school budget getting passed and tells Griffen that the media confused facts about the school. He blames Miss Narwin for the incident. Dr. Seymour uses Miss Narwin's grant application against her.

Miss Narwin finds that most of her colleagues at the school do not support her, either. Philip goes to her classroom and tries to speak to her about his grade. He learns that he has been reassigned to Mr. Keegan's class; Miss Narwin will not talk to him any further and asks him to leave. Philip then talks to Coach Jamison. The coach supports Miss Narwin and tells Philip he should have been a team player. He also tells Philip to forget about the track team this year but to try again next year.

Dr. Doane and Miss Narwin meet. Dr. Seymour has given her the money to attend the summer program, but he also wants her to take the rest of the term off with pay. Dr. Doane tells her that the pressure is making Dr. Seymour worry about the budget getting passed. Miss Narwin is upset by the situation and later tells her sister that she is unsure what to do. When the reporter from St. Louis calls her and expresses concern that her side of the story is not being presented, she tells him to come to New Hampshire and she will meet with him.

At the Malloy home, Philip's mother tells his father that their son came home upset and is in his room. When Mr. Malloy goes to his son's room, Philip refuses to talk to him. He also will not come down to dinner. In his diary, Philip explains that he is upset because he believes that everyone supports Miss Narwin and because he will not be allowed on the track team.

During a campaign stop, Griffen gives a speech in which he makes Miss Narwin the scapegoat for the entire incident. He states that the school administrators bear no blame and that voters should support the school budget.

17—Wednesday, April 4
Before school the next morning, Miss Narwin calls Dr. Doane and informs her that she is too exhausted to come in. Philip does not want to go to school and tells his parents that he wants to go to another school because he is hated by the other kids. Philip's parents send him to school, but when Ken jokes about a petition being formed to get Philip to say he is wrong, Philip becomes upset and goes back home. He calls his mother at work and tells her where he is. His mother calls his father and tells him that she is going to contact a private school, Washington Academy. Later in the afternoon, Miss Narwin meets with Duval. She tells him her side of the story, including the intense pressure she feels to resign.

18—Friday, April 6
In the Harrison school board election and budget vote, the budget is defeated and Griffen is elected. Miss Narwin calls Duval to inquire about the story. The article was written and filed by him but was never printed because of breaking international news. She goes to Florida to spend time with her sister and think about her options.

19—Monday, April 9
Philip has been enrolled in the Washington Academy. The school does not have a track program. In his first class, he is asked to lead the class in singing the national anthem. He starts crying because he does not know the words.

CHARACTERS

Ken Barchet
Ken Barchet is a student at Harrison High School and a casual friend of Philip Malloy. He lives in Philip's neighborhood and works out with him in the park. Ken supports Philip's version of the events for the most part.

Jake Barlow

Jake Barlow is a talk show host who believes that Philip Malloy was treated poorly by Miss Narwin and that not being allowed to sing along to the national anthem is unpatriotic.

Janet Barsky

Janet Barsky is a friend of Allison Doresett.

Todd Becker

Todd Becker is a student at Harrison High School. He is a member of the track team and once asks Philip Malloy why he did not try out for the team as he is needed on it.

Jacob Benison

Jacob Benison is a science teacher at Harrison High School. He generally shares Miss Narwin's assessment of Philip Malloy as an intelligent student who tends to be lazy.

George Brookover

George Brookover is the principal of Washington Academy, the private school to which Philip Malloy transfers after the events surrounding his suspension become overwhelming. Mr. Brookover informs Philip that the school does not have a track program.

Mr. Dexter

Mr. Dexter is Mr. Malloy's boss at work. On Thursday, March 29, Mr. Dexter sternly talks to Malloy about his work.

Dr. Gertrude Doane

Dr. Gertrude Doane is the principal of Harrison High School who comes into conflict with Miss Narwin. Miss Narwin becomes upset when Dr. Doane, a former pupil, turns down her application for grant money to attend a summer teaching program. When the tensions between Philip Malloy and Miss Narwin reach a crisis, Dr. Doane initially supports the teacher. However, under pressure from Dr. Seymour, Dr. Doane withdraws her support. She removes Philip from Miss Narwin's English class. Dr. Doane also insists that Miss Narwin take time off with pay to get away from the media attention surrounding Philip's suspension, although she promises that the school will fund her summer class. Miss Narwin is upset by what she perceives as Dr. Doane's betrayal.

Allison Doresett

Allison Doresett is Philip Malloy's classmate at Harrison High School. In the beginning of the novel, Allison and Philip are romantically interested in each other. However, Allison's interest in Philip wanes when he becomes more withdrawn because of his problems at school. In the end, Allison supports Miss Narwin over Philip about the humming incident because she believes that Philip is motivated by his dislike for the teacher rather than any patriotic feeling.

Robert Duval

Robert Duval is a reporter with the *St. Louis Post-Dispatch*. After reading the story about Philip's suspension on the newswire, he investigates the incident further. He believes that Miss Narwin is not getting a fair shake in the media, and he flies to New Hampshire to meet with her. Though he writes and files a story, it is not published because of a pressing piece of international news.

Cynthia Gambia

Cynthia Gambia is another student in Miss Narwin's homeroom in spring term. When Dr. Doane questions her about what happened with Philip Malloy, Cynthia says that "he *was* being sort of rude." She is unclear on whether Philip hummed or sang, and how loud he really was.

Sarah Gloss

Sarah Gloss is a student at Harrison High School. She tells Philip that Allison Doresett likes him and also gives him a copy of a novel, *The Outsiders*.

Ted Griffen

The Malloys' neighbor Ted Griffen is running for the school board. A political opportunist, Griffen calls a local reporter about Philip's suspension and then uses the incident during his political campaign. Griffen ultimately wins the seat on the school board.

Steve Hallick

An outstanding runner for a school in Pittsburgh, Steve Hallick is admired by Philip Malloy for his speed and strength.

Mrs. Gloria Harland

Mrs. Harland serves as chairman of the Harrison School District board. Like Dr. Seymour, Mrs. Harland is very concerned about the budget getting passed. She becomes worried when Philip Malloy's suspension becomes a media sensation.

Kimberly Howard

Kimberly Howard is a music teacher at Harrison High School. Miss Narwin resents her for getting a grant to attend a class on band music.

Coach Jamison

Coach Jamison coaches the Harrison High School track team. He wants Philip to be on his team and offers advice on how to be a team player to achieve that goal. When Philip earns a D in English, Jamison tells him to ask Miss Narwin for extra work to restore his eligibility to be on the team. Philip, however, ignores his coach's advice. Although Jamison wants Philip on the team, he supports Miss Narwin in the suspension conflict that ensues.

Mr. Keegan

Mr. Keegan is an English teacher at Harrison High School. Philip is transferred into his class after his suspension makes the national news and the school administrators respond by withdrawing their support from Miss Narwin.

Liz

Liz calls the Jake Barlow talk show to criticize Miss Narwin.

Mr. Bernard Lunser

Mr. Lunser is a teacher at Harrison High School who tries to relate to his students with humor. He is Philip Malloy's homeroom teacher in winter term and again after Philip's suspension.

Mr. Ben Malloy

Ben Malloy is Philip's father. He was once a high school track star but did not get to compete much in college because of a family illness. Malloy now works at a job he dislikes and lives somewhat vicariously through his son's track ambitions. His wife, Susan, reminds Malloy to make an effort to support his son in areas other than his athletic ambitions; in fact, Malloy unconditionally backs Philip in the controversy over humming the national anthem.

Philip Malloy

Philip Malloy is the novel's protagonist. He is a ninth grader at Harrison High School and a budding track star. However, his plans to join the track team are derailed when he earns a D in English in the winter term. Philip does not take his English class with Miss Narwin seriously, does not do the required work, and ends up with a grade too low to try out for the track team. He hides this fact from everyone for much of the novel.

When Philip is transferred to Miss Narwin's homeroom in spring term, their conflict comes to a head. He hums to the national anthem during announcements, claiming he had done so when Mr. Lunser was his homeroom teacher. Miss Narwin finds it annoying and disruptive. She gives him one warning before twice sending him to the assistant principal's office for his defiance. The incident turns into a major event when Philip refuses to apologize and Dr. Palleni suspends him from school for two days.

Philip tells his story to a reporter and it becomes national news, with Miss Narwin portrayed as unpatriotic and Philip as a champion of free speech. While Philip is aware of the support, he really only wants to join the track team. His late efforts to improve his grade in English fail. He ultimately transfers to Washington Academy, which has no track program.

Mrs. Susan Malloy

Susan Malloy is Philip's mother. She works at the telephone company. She is concerned about Philip's grades and well-being, and works to get her husband, Ben, to support their son as well. Like her husband, Susan Malloy backs her son in his conflict with Miss Narwin.

Miss Margaret Narwin

Miss Narwin has devoted her life to teaching and has been an English teacher at Harrison High School for twenty-five years. She is aware that she sometimes has difficulty reaching students like Philip Malloy, and she applies for a grant to attend an intensive summer program to get new ideas and improve her teaching skills. Miss Narwin's request is turned down at first for budgetary reasons.

Miss Narwin soon faces bigger problems. Philip does not pay attention in English class and earns a C- on his winter term exam and a D overall for the term. Philip is contemptuous and annoyed, especially once his English grade prevents him from trying out for the track team. The tension between student and teacher comes to a climax at the beginning of spring term when Philip is assigned to Miss Narwin's homeroom.

He hums the national anthem, a practice she finds disruptive. When he defiantly refuses to stop, she sends him to the assistant principal's office.

Dr. Palleni suspends Philip for two days for his behavior despite the fact that Miss Narwin does not want him suspended. The subsequent newspaper article casts Miss Narwin as unpatriotic, and she is vilified by the community and soon by the school's administrators too. Miss Narwin is pressured to resign to ensure the school budget will pass. She goes to Florida to stay with her sister and consider her options for the future.

Peg Narwin
See Miss Margaret Narwin

Dr. Joseph Palleni
Dr. Joseph Palleni is an assistant principal at Harrison High School. After Miss Narwin becomes exasperated and sends Philip to the principal's office, Dr. Palleni disciplines Philip for breaking school rules requiring students to maintain a respectful silence during the playing of the national anthem. Dr. Palleni first asks Philip to apologize for humming, but he refuses. Dr. Palleni then suspends Philip for two days, even though Miss Narwin herself does not want him suspended. After the situation becomes a media event, Dr. Palleni writes a report about the incident that generally favors Miss Narwin over Philip.

Roger
Roger is a caller to the Jake Barlow Talk Show. Unlike most callers, he believes the story in the newspapers unfairly favors Philip's version of events over Miss Narwin's.

Miss Rooney
Miss Rooney is Philip Malloy's new homeroom teacher at Washington Academy. She invites him to lead the class in the singing of the national anthem, causing him to cry because, as he says, "I don't know the words."

Roger Sanchez
Roger Sanchez is a student at Harrison High School who is in Miss Narwin's English class with Philip Malloy.

Dr. Albert Seymour
Dr. Albert Seymour is the superintendent of the Harrison School District. Miss Narwin notes that he "is a *very* political person. But then, all he wants is to keep *his* job." He is worried that the school district's budget will not be passed by voters, since a previous vote had failed to do so. When the situation with Philip Malloy comes to his attention, he initially supports Miss Narwin. However, as soon as he feels public pressure, Dr. Seymour distances himself and the school district from the teacher in part because he thinks it will help get the budget passed. The budget still fails at the polls.

Steve
Steve is a caller to the Jake Barlow talk show who supports Philip and thinks Miss Narwin should be fired.

Jennifer Stewart
Jennifer Stewart is a reporter covering the educational beat for the newspaper, the *Manchester Record*. Her well-researched story about the national anthem incident favors Philip's version of events. When her story is picked up by the wire services, the incident makes headlines nationwide.

Anita Wigham
Anita Wigham is Margaret Narwin's sister. Anita lives in Florida; Miss Narwin writes her there. When Miss Narwin is forced to resign, she goes to stay with her sister.

THEMES

Power and Control
Two of the primary themes explored in *Nothing But the Truth* are the concepts of power and control. Many of the relationships in the book feature significant power struggles. For example, Miss Narwin needs to have control over her English classroom and the students therein. To maintain order in the classroom, she must exert power. As an adolescent, Philip Malloy wants to gain and exert some power over himself and his life.

To that end, Philip has been disrupting Miss Narwin's carefully crafted sense of power, displaying a lack of interest in what she teaches and not doing the required reading or studying. After

TOPICS FOR FURTHER STUDY

- Avi has said that *Nothing But the Truth: A Documentary Novel* was influenced by Living Newspapers, programs produced by the Federal Theatre Project in the 1930s. Using the Internet, research Living Newspapers, what topics they covered, and how they were presented to audiences. Create a presentation in which you share your findings as well as examples of the influence of the programs on Avi's novel.

- Read Sandra Cisneros's short story, "Eleven," which can be found in her short story collection, *Woman Hollering Creek and Other Stories* (1992). This short story focuses on an eleven-year-old girl named Rachel who is trying to reveal the truth about a situation in which others are focusing on mistaken assumptions. In an essay, compare and contrast Rachel and Philip. How are their actions the same? What else do they have in common? How do they differ?

- In a small group, discuss the role of the media in the events of *Nothing But the Truth*. This book was written in 1991, before the Internet, cell phones, and texting became commonplace. In your discussion, debate how you would update the story to include the effects of today's technology and media influence. Do you think the ending would be any different?

- Read *Call of the Wild* (1903), the novel by Jack London that Philip refuses to read for Miss Narwin's English class. In an essay, describe how you feel about the book. Do you think it relates to the themes of *Nothing But the Truth*? How would you answer Miss Narwin's English exam question about the book? Do you think the book is too old to be relevant to student readers today?

- With two or three other students, read *The Outsiders* (1967), the novel by S. E. Hinton that Philip reads in *Nothing But the Truth*. Discuss why you think Philip likes the novel. Can you relate to the novel as well? Do you think if Miss Narwin had included this novel in her English class that Philip would have made more of an effort in class?

---

he joins her homeroom, the power struggle between them reaches an apex when he begins to hum along to the national anthem. Miss Narwin sees his action as disruptive; she is only following the school's directive that students must maintain a "respectful, silent attention" during the national anthem.

This action sets off a chain reaction that further highlights power dynamics. Dr. Palleni generally follows the rules—a means of control in the school—and suspends the unrepentant Philip. Miss Narwin, knowing that power must be wielded carefully, does not want Philip suspended, though she does not want him to further disrupt her class. Philip believes he is unnecessarily being controlled—after all, he is only humming to the national anthem—by a teacher who does not like him. Encouraged by his father—who cannot exert any power or control over his boss and a tense work situation—Philip stands up for himself.

Philip's story becomes a media sensation after school board candidate Ted Griffen brings it to the attention of a local education reporter. Griffen uses Philip's story in his own quest to gain the power of a school board seat. Most outsiders support Philip over Miss Narwin, while the administration initially takes Miss Narwin's side. However, the continued media pressure compels Dr. Seymour and Dr. Doane to distance themselves from Miss Narwin. They want to control the situation so voters will approve a much-needed school budget. In the end, Miss Narwin is forced out in the power struggle, and Philip feels he can no longer attend Harrison High. The budget is defeated and only Griffen gets what he wants.

Honesty vs. Hypocrisy

Another idea explored in the novel is honesty versus hypocrisy. Both Philip Malloy and Miss Narwin are generally sincere in their understanding and explanation of the events that lead to Philip being suspended. Philip, a ninth grader, is an unmotivated student and does not particularly get along with Miss Narwin. Miss Narwin, in turn, sees that Philip is intelligent but does not try in her class. Both stick to their version of the story as they remember it and understand it when Philip is suspended.

However, many of Harrison High School's administrators are not nearly as principled. After the suspension becomes a national media sensation, the administrators act hypocritically. Initially, Dr. Palleni and Dr. Doane support Miss Narwin and her version of events. The school memo, written by Dr. Palleni, which opens *Nothing But the Truth*, clearly states that students are to be silent during the anthem. Philip later claims that Mr. Lunser let him hum to the national anthem, though this action is not depicted in the text of the novel.

Miss Narwin and Dr. Palleni initially favor a strict interpretation of the rules, which justifies Philip's suspension. Whether Philip is actually being disruptive in the classroom is arguable. However, the administrators eventually act hypocritically after Philip's suspension as media pressure mounts over the "anti-patriotic" incident. On April 3, the school district issues an "Official Statement" which states, "There is *No* rule that prohibits a student from singing along if he/she so desires. The Harrison School District is pleased to *encourage* appropriate displays of patriotism." Administrators shift the blame to Miss Narwin, because they are concerned primarily with preserving their own interests.

Patriotism

A secondary theme in *Nothing But the Truth* is the idea of patriotism. Whether Philip is being patriotic or, rather, challenging Miss Narwin by humming along to the national anthem on two occasions and singing on a third in her homeroom is unclear. Outsiders to the school, however, believe the incident hinges on patriotism—it seems unpatriotic not to be allowed to sing or hum along to the national anthem of a country that values personal freedom. As the story receives national attention, letters and telegrams pour into the school from those who view Philip as a patriot and Miss Narwin as unpatriotic.

In the media circus, whether the school itself is patriotic or not comes up for public debate. Under public pressure, administrators back away from their own rule, which calls for "respectful, silent attention" during the anthem. Only Miss Narwin and Robert Duval, the reporter from the *St. Louis Post-Dispatch*, clearly see that patriotism is not really the primary issue in this controversy.

STYLE

Documentary Novel

Avi calls *Nothing But the Truth* a "documentary novel." A documentary novel is similar to an epistolary novel. An epistolary novel is a novel written as a series of letters. Much of *Nothing But the Truth* consists of letters, telegrams, diary entries from Philip, memos from the school district, and the newspaper article written by Jennifer Stewart. The novel also includes transcripts of conversations between characters and the transcript of a talk show, which add to its documentary feel. This quality is also enhanced by the lack of a character narrator and emphasis on what each character does or says.

Narrator

Nothing But the Truth lacks a narrator that can be identified in the story. A narrator is the teller of the tale at hand. Often, narrators are characters in the book. In the case of *Nothing But the Truth*, the author, Avi, is the narrator. It is he who has created each of the documents and conversations found in the novel.

New Hampshire Setting

The setting of *Nothing But the Truth* plays a subtle but important role in the narrative. The setting is the time, place, and culture in which the story takes place. The novel was written in the early 1990s and reflects American life in that time period. Avi set *Nothing But the Truth* in a community in New Hampshire called Harrison. As Avi has Jake Barlow point out on his talk show, "All their auto plates read 'Live Free or Die.'" This statement is the state's motto and

A high-school classroom *(Image copyright Ferenc Szelepcsenyi, 2009. Used under license from Shutterstock.com)*

reflects Philip's attitude toward life until the pressure compels him to leave Harrison High School at the end of the novel.

HISTORICAL CONTEXT

Children and Education in the early 1990s

During the 1990s in the United States, children's issues received more attention than in previous decades. Recognizing the problems plaguing at-risk children and their families, schools and educators began to advocate taking on more active roles in helping children. Many teachers came to support what were known as "full-service schools." These schools would provide a high-quality education including individualized instruction, team teaching, cooperative learning, alternatives to tracking, effective disciplinary techniques, and encouragement of parent involvement. Schools would partner with community agencies to provide other needed services, such as health and dental screening and services, mental health services, counseling, recreation,

welfare services, mentoring, recreation and sports, parent education, crisis intervention, and so on. Those who advocated this philosophy believed that schools and teachers took on the role of surrogate parents who were responsible for the physical and emotional well-being of their students through early adolescence. In the novel, this type of educational philosophy plays out in the way the school handles Philip, such as Miss Narwin's interest in Philip and his well-being as a student and the way Coach Jamison tries to guide Philip as he interacts with his teachers.

Workplace Issues and the Recession

By the early 1990s, Americans were spending more hours on their jobs than citizens of most other countries. Many employees in this time period worked hard at their jobs for fear of losing them. There was a recession in the United States and other parts of the world from 1990 to 1991, as the economy continued to transition from industrial to technological and knowledge-based enterprises. The Internet revolution was dawning and bringing widespread changes not only in the American economy but society at

COMPARE
&
CONTRAST

- **Early 1990s**: Newspapers and magazines are regarded as an important source of news and information for Americans.

  Today: Because of the spread of the Internet and personal computers, newspapers and other print media have found it hard to retain an audience and attract advertisers. Some newspapers in cities across the United States are closing or ending their print runs to focus on online journalism. Many magazines are folding or slimming down due to the lack of ad pages.

- **Early 1990s**: The United States is dealing with a mild to moderate economic recession.

  Today: The United States is suffering from the biggest economic downturn since the Great Depression in the 1930s. Some observers have called the economic crisis the "Great Recession."

- **Early 1990s**: Popular talk show radio hosts like Rush Limbaugh become a public force, offering their opinions on the day's issues and ensuring their perspective enters the public debate.

  Today: Alhough the Internet has made talk shows less relevant, popular talk show radio hosts like Limbaugh continue to wield an extraordinary amount of power.

---

large. But in this time period, there was much uncertainty about the direction of the economy and what the future held for many in the workplace. Thus, adult characters in the novel like Philip's father and Miss Narwin are concerned about job loss because of the economic pressures of the time.

War and Patriotism

In 1991, the United States joined troops from other nations to fight what was known as Operation Desert Storm, or the Gulf War. Iraq, led by dictator Saddam Hussein, invaded Kuwait in August 1990 to challenge American interests in the Persian Gulf. Because President George H. W. Bush believed that letting this action go unchecked would embolden Hussein, he mobilized American forces and demanded Iraq's withdrawal from Kuwait. Bush then gained the support of the United Nations' Security Council, which started an organization of coalition forces. This military force stepped in to defend Kuwait in early 1991. Kuwait was freed, but Hussein remained in power in Iraq. Because of the war and mobilization of American troops, patriotism and expressions of love for the United States by its citizens reached a new high. However, there were

also many protests in the United States against the war as Americans used their right of free speech to show a critical type of patriotism. This novel explores these tensions in American society, primarily through the response from across the United States to the situation with Philip and the "Star-Spangled Banner." While the reasons behind Philip's suspension are distorted in the media, the Americans who read the story are responding to the patriotism of the era.

CRITICAL OVERVIEW

Since it was published in 1991, critics have embraced *Nothing But the Truth* as a multifaceted novel that reflects many concerns in American society. A contributor to *Kirkus Reviews* calls the novel, "Wryly satirical: nothing but the deplorable truth about our increasingly inarticulate, media-driven society." The reviewer for *Publishers Weekly* concludes, "With frankness and remarkable insight, [Avi] conveys the flaws of the systems while creating a story that is both entertaining and profound."

American flag in a classroom (Image copyright Cameron Cross, 2009. Used under license from Shutterstock.com)

Other reviewers especially appreciate the difficult nature of the novel. In *Booklist*, Stephanie Zvirin comments, "It challenges us to re-examine our ethical standards and to set aside kindergarten concepts of truth and falsity in determining the conduct of our lives." She concludes, "The deceptively simple story also stands up as riveting entertainment."

The novel's characterizations also are praised by critics. Elizabeth S. Watson of *Horn Book Magazine* comments, "The construction is nearly flawless; the characters seem painfully human and typically ordinary. Philip's inability to communicate with anyone is bleakly real."

Some critics praise Avi's use of the documents and transcripts to tell his story in *Nothing But the Truth*. Writing in the *School Library Journal*, Ellen Fader notes, "Each document provides another perspective on the conflict and illuminates the many themes that beg to be discussed—most notably the irony of lives destroyed by the misuse of power and the failure of people to communicate."

> "WHILE A SUSPENSION OVER VOCALLY ACCOMPANYING THE NATIONAL ANTHEM SEEMS ABSURD, THE TRUTH IS MUCH MORE COMPLICATED THAN THAT, AND VERY FEW CHARACTERS IN THE NOVEL CARE TO SEE THE COMPLEXITY OF THE SITUATION."

CRITICISM

A. Petruso

Petruso has a B.A. in history from the University of Michigan and an M.A. in screenwriting from the University of Texas at Austin. In this essay, she looks at the details of the situation presented in Nothing But the Truth: A Documentary Novel *and discerns some of the truths laid out in the novel, especially those concerning Miss Narwin.*

As the title of Avi's acclaimed young adult novel *Nothing But the Truth: A Documentary Novel* points out, truth is an important element of this narrative. The author chose a documentary style to present a more objective viewpoint that can help readers clearly see certain truths. The facts about what happened between ninth grader Philip Malloy and Miss Narwin, his English teacher and later homeroom teacher as well, are sometimes only relatively clear. By examining what has been presented in the novel about the situation and its aftermath, it will become clear that the truth is quite relative and is often in the eye of the beholder. One certainty is that Miss Narwin is not allowed to have her truth considered in a public forum like Philip's truth has been—Robert Duval's more objective article was never published.

Avi makes clear from the beginning of *Nothing But the Truth* that the Harrison School District has a rule against singing or humming along with the national anthem. The memo that opens the book clearly states that students must "stand at respectful, silent attention for the playing of our national anthem." The author also ensures that readers understand how antagonistic Philip and Miss Narwin's relationship is even before he becomes her student in homeroom. In his first

WHAT DO I READ NEXT?

- *The Fighting Ground*, published in 1984, is a young adult novel by Avi. The story focuses on thirteen-year-old Jonathan who lives on a farm near Trenton, New Jersey, during the Revolutionary War. In one day, he joins the Patriots and finds himself caught up in the battle. He grows by experiencing the true horrors of war.

- *Sometimes I Think I Hear My Name*, published in 1982, is another young adult novel by Avi. The novel follows the life of thirteen-year-old Conrad, who has lived with his aunt and uncle in St. Louis since his parents divorced. When his guardians take him on a trip, Conrad finds his parents, learns that they have little interest in him, and comes to appreciate what he has at home.

- *Julius Caesar*, written c. 1599, is a play written by William Shakespeare. Miss Narwin's English class in *Nothing But the Truth* is reading the play aloud. The play focuses on the assassination of the Roman dictator and its aftermath.

- *Strider*, published in 1992, is a young adult novel by Beverly Cleary. Cleary writes the novel as a series of diary entries. The story focuses on Leigh Potts, a high school student whose parents have been divorced for several years. Leigh adopts a dog named Strider with a friend, becomes interested in running. and soon joins the school's track team.

- "Madam and the Rent Man," published in 1949 in the collection *One-Way Ticket*, is a poem by Langston Hughes. The poem explores the differing perspectives of two people on the same situation.

- *Those Damned Rebels: The American Revolution as Seen Through British Eyes* (2000), by Michael Pearson, pulls together diary entries, letters, and official reports by British soldiers and government officials on the American Revolution as interpreted by the British who witnessed it. The book presents a very different perspective on the American patriots than the one learned by American school children.

journal entry, Philip writes about her: "What can you do with an English teacher who's so uptight that she must have been put together with super glue. Try to make a joke—lighten things up a bit—she goes all flinty-faced." For her part, Miss Narwin is frustrated by Philip, as she writes in her first letter to her sister Anita. Miss Narwin states, "Philip . . . is only a middling student, and it's a shame. A nice-looking boy. A boy I like. Intelligent. With real potential. Perhaps that's why he irritates me so."

In his first journal entry, Philip expresses his frustration over what Miss Narwin has the class reading. Philip writes, "Can't believe how stupid and *boring* Jack London is! . . . Ma says she had to read it when *she* was in school. There has to be better stuff to read for ninth grade somewhere."

While Miss Narwin writes to her sister that "I remain steadfast in my belief that my life was meant to be the *bringing of fine literature to young minds*," she also understands that she needs to be open to reaching high school students after twenty-five years. To that end, on March 20, Miss Narwin asks the school district to give her a grant to go to a summer program called "New Approaches to the Teaching of Literature for Today's Students." The class costs two thousand dollars and her application implies that she would pay for it herself, but the cost is too high for someone on a teacher's salary. It also requires a recommendation from and approval of a school administrator. Such a summer class would help her better teach and reach all students, not just Philip, and shows that she is open to new ideas.

While students like Allison Doresett appreciate Miss Narwin's teaching style, Philip remains unimpressed as he heads into winter term exams. His March 15 journal entry states, "I won't waste time on English. . . . Besides, it's just a matter of opinion, anyway!!! If I could only get Narwin to crack a smile." Philip is only concerned with gaining Miss Narwin's approval—not learning what she has to teach. On his English exam, Philip gives a ridiculous answer to the question about the Jack London novel and earns a generous C- from his teacher. Because Miss Narwin gives him a D for his term grade, he is unable to try out for the track team.

Running track is Philip's obsession and primary goal in high school. However, he does not tell anyone—even his parents—the truth about why he cannot try out for the team until the end of the novel. Only Coach Jamison knows, and he asks Philip to meet with him about the matter on March 26. The coach urges him to talk to Miss Narwin about the situation and ask for extra work to bring up the grade. Philip does not decide to talk to Miss Narwin about bringing up his grade until the situation over his suspension has become a media sensation. The gravity of what Philip has set in motion and the effect it has on Miss Narwin is completely lost on him. By the time he tries to talk to her about extra work, it is much too late.

In that meeting, one nugget of truth that Coach Jamison emphasizes to Philip is "sometimes you have to go along to get along. . . . Go with the flow." He is not telling Philip not to be himself, but he wants the boy to stop seeing Miss Narwin as an enemy and begin working with her as a student should. In the same conversation, the coach also reminds Philip that "A rule is a rule. It isn't always easy." None of this advice gets through to Philip. Avi implies that if Philip had taken his coach's advice and paid more attention in class, perhaps the situation would not have played out the same way in the end. But Philip cannot see the world from Miss Narwin's perspective, though as a longtime respected educator, Miss Narwin at least understands her and Philip's limitations in this area.

Miss Narwin tries to engage Philip as a student in a way that is ineffective, and she comes to understand that fact. It is unclear if any teaching method Miss Narwin used would have been effective for Philip as he has decided he does not want to learn in her class, and only he can

change that, not the teacher. Philip will read books—he finds much to like in a copy of *The Outsiders* that a classmate lends him—but resists any attempt Miss Narwin makes to reach him. The teacher's quest to better reach students like Philip is stymied by the cash-strapped school district. Her request for funding for the summer program is turned down, though a music teacher receives money to take a marching band music course. This act outrages Miss Narwin as she takes her job and students to heart.

The stand-off between Miss Narwin and Philip comes to a head when he joins her homeroom on March 28 and hums along to the national anthem. When Miss Narwin tells him to stop, Philip claims, "Mr. Lunser doesn't mind." However, looking back to the one depiction of Philip in Mr. Lunser's homeroom in the first pages of *Nothing But the Truth*, Philip does not sing or hum but studies during morning announcements. When Miss Narwin asks Mr. Lunser if Philip sang to the national anthem in his classroom, Mr. Lunser denies it. And in a conversation that Philip has with Todd Becker later in the day, it is again unclear if Philip has ever accompanied the national anthem with any sort of vocalization before. Though Philip tells his parents later that night that he occasionally sings to the national anthem, Avi makes it unclear if Philip ever really did hum or sing along to the national anthem before joining Miss Narwin's homeroom. This uncertainty implies that Philip was looking to be disruptive before ever entering her homeroom. The last line of the book makes Philip's intent clear. At his new school, when asked to lead a rendition of the national anthem, he tells his teacher that he does not know the words.

As mentioned earlier, Harrison High School has a rule against making any noise during the national anthem. Miss Narwin enforces this rule as do the other teachers. When Philip turns the humming into a power struggle between him and Miss Narwin by humming along once again, then singing once, despite being told not to do so, he is sent to Dr. Palleni's office. The truth is that Philip—encouraged by his father to stand up for himself—broke the rules and created a disruption in Miss Narwin's class. Another truth is that Miss Narwin has not found a way to reach Philip yet, leading her to react defensively to his behavior. A final truth is that Dr. Palleni enforces the school's rules about not making noise during the national anthem and not disrupting the classroom with actions that the teacher determines are detrimental to her authority.

When Philip and his father take the story to school board candidate Ted Griffen, Griffen has them tell the story to a reporter, Jennifer Stewart, from a local paper. While Stewart does talk to everyone involved, the administrators from Harrison High School and the Harrison school district are uninformed at best and at worst only interested in whatever truth will get the much-needed school budget passed. As Miss Narwin observes before any of this drama comes to pass, superintendent Dr. Seymour "is a *very* political person. But then, all he wants is to keep *his* job." The school district acts in support of Miss Narwin at first, issuing a report on April 2 that states Philip broke the rules and disrupted the class. The rule about being silent is quoted, but the truth about Philip is distorted as the administrators all write that he sang "the national anthem in a loud, raucous, *disrespectful* fashion."

This report exaggerates what Philip did and ignores the fact that Miss Narwin did not support the suspension of Philip in the first place. She tells Dr. Palleni on March 30, "Suspension might be counterproductive." In the same conversation, Miss Narwin states that she likes Philip and says, "I wish I could reach him. I just don't seem to." Later that day, Miss Narwin sees Dr. Palleni and again says of Philip, "I don't want to give up on him yet." In a letter to her sister, also written on March 30, Miss Narwin states she wants to "have a heart-to-heart talk" with Philip when he comes back to school. While a suspension over vocally accompanying the national anthem seems absurd, the truth is much more complicated than that, and very few characters in the novel care to see the complexity of the situation.

Over the next few days, the administrators distort the truth about the situation to reduce public outcry and ensure their budget gets passed. While Philip is initially blamed for his poor behavior and attitude, Miss Narwin's place as a respected teacher is thrown aside as questions about the school district's patriotism and values are put into play by the media. On the night of April 2, Miss Narwin is told to take the next day off by the school's principal, Dr. Doane, because of the pressure. The next morning, Dr. Doane tells Miss Narwin the school district will no longer support her. The principal says to the teacher, "Peg, you have to accept the idea that it's all a misunderstanding." With this statement, Avi makes it clear that the truth about the situation no longer matters. What Miss Narwin did or did not do does not matter. Even Philip's real actions do not matter. What concerns Dr. Seymour and the other administrators is ensuring the school district is seen in a positive light in order to please voters, the media, and those people who heard a version of the story and felt they had to comment.

This point is driven home on April 3 when the school district issues a memo which states, "There is *no* rule that prohibits a student from singing along if he/she so desires. The Harrison School District is pleased to *encourage* appropriate displays of patriotism." The rule is changed to reflect a more public-pleasing truth. Later that day, Dr. Seymour uses Miss Narwin's own words against her when talking to Ted Griffen. Quoting from her grant application, Dr. Seymour makes Miss Narwin seem out of date and more of a problem for the school district than a student like Philip. Her skills as a teacher are not respected but vilified. Because of the controversy, neither Philip nor Miss Narwin goes to Harrison High School again. Two lives are tragically altered forever because of poor choices all around. Avi does not fully blame either Philip or Miss Narwin, but he does imply that administrators will do anything to save their jobs. In *Nothing But the Truth*, the truth does not set anyone free because it is not respected and gets lost in personal politics and a media frenzy.

Source: A. Petruso, Critical Essay on *Nothing But the Truth: A Documentary Novel*, in *Novels for Students*, Gale, Cengage Learning, 2010.

Susan P. Bloom

In the following excerpt, Bloom and Mercier offer a critical interpretation of Nothing But the Truth.

Nothing But the Truth extends this discussion. Flipping the mask of comedy to that of tragedy, this "documentary novel" interrogates the nature of heroism as it "prods and provokes readers to question facts, behavior, and motivations." Avi presents information from a variety of sources: newspapers and radio, school administration policies, political speeches, conversations between families and friends, even diaries,

> THIS SHIFT ANTICIPATES TWO STRANDS OF TRUTH THAT DEFINE THE NOVEL: THE AUTHORITATIVE TRUTH THAT BINDS A SOCIETY VERSUS THE PERSONAL TRUTH OF AN INDIVIDUAL."

letters, and memoranda. Avi reports that "Living Newspapers," a type of theater in the 1930s that used dialogue and document readings, inspired the structure of this novel. Because no single narrator tells the story, no single character's viewpoint directs it. Reviews of the novel found this "construction ... nearly flawless" and essential to the book's thematic intention. Avi considers that

> What is unusual about this book ... is that there is no *visible* narration... The story is revealed through an accumulation of documents... These fragments are set out in chronological order but each document is independent of the other. It is the reader—and *only* the reader—who has all this information before him or her. It is the reader and only the reader who connects the documents—who draws the dots, so to speak—so that a picture is created. ("Seeing," 7)

Absence of visible narration does not mean complete lack of narration. In fact, Avi structures the book with absolute authorial control, a command that entices readers to believe that "the author's voice ... *appears* to have been banished from every page" ("Seeing," 7). However, these characters, events, and documents stem from Avi's imagination. *Nothing But the Truth* operates solely within Avi's fictional world. Even though subtitled as a documentary novel, all material presented stems from the author's imagination. Unlike film documentaries that collect facts, all information in this novel is created by Avi; "because the book takes enormous pains to deny the author's hand, it should alert [the reader] that [the author's] hand is *everywhere*" ("Seeing," 7). Like the director of a film documentary, Avi orders the presentation; he chooses where to allow gaps; he assembles the fictional material and presents it as fact.

What point of view does Avi's invisible narration promote? A combined point of view; "at least two people are required to experience literature completely: the writer *and* the reader" ("Seeing," 3). Although this pairing seems essential to any work of fiction, *Nothing But the Truth* makes explicit the interaction between the fiction (writer) and the reader. This novel demands that readers formulate a narrative bias of their own. Moreover, Avi's ordered presentation of the documents "[keeps] his audience unsettled" as it forces them to continually redefine their perspectives, their alliances, and their allegiances when given new information.

The novel begins with an introduction of theme, rather than of character. Two questions precede page one: "Do you swear to tell the truth, the whole truth, and nothing but the truth? Does anyone say no?" Not only does the first question repeat the title of the book, but also it invokes the legal system. The second question immediately causes readers to wonder why no one says "no." "If someone said they would not tell the truth in court, we *would* believe them" ("Seeing," 7). Yet, risking being found in contempt of court, everyone says "yes" without thought, even without option. "In short, we are all required to lie even as we swear to tell the truth" ("Seeing," 7). These two questions plunge readers immediately into the thematic depths of the novel: Truth is elusive; the truthteller, unreliable; and the system, corrupt.

Bearing the school district's letterhead, page one outlines the fill-in-the-blank guidelines for all school morning announcement. This is the only document presented out of chronological order and without reference to a specific date. As a document, the memo serves as a template for morning announcements; as a storytelling device, it identifies the pattern that, once broken, launches the plot. This form-memo appears once in the novel, yet knowledge of the order of events it prescribes becomes key to interpreting the story, as various settings and characters deviate from this norm. For example, the script outlined by the memo can be detected in the first part of chapter 2, set in Bernard Lunser's homeroom class. The departures from the script are more important, however. The teacher cracks jokes and makes fun of the announcements, the school, and the students. His attitude conveys nothing but a coy disrespect for the speaker, the school principal, Dr. Gertrude Doane, and for the process itself. Lunser does not sing the national anthem, he talks through it. The chapter introduces Philip Malloy, whom Lunser mocks for studying quietly during the anthem. Despite the fact that the memo calls for silence, the chapter calls that morning in Lunser's homeroom a "discussion" (*Truth*, 6).

The second homeroom discussion occurs in Margaret Narwin's class. She attempts to sort out the chaos caused by reassigning students to new homerooms. Despite the initial confusion, Narwin quiets the class to listen to the morning program. In contrast to Lunser, she attends to the morning announcements quietly as asked. Therefore, readers, like Narwin, instantly note Philip's digression from the expected procedure. Philip does not cease humming when first asked to by Narwin; when asked a third time, he states that he is "just humming" (*Truth*, 35), and by the fourth request the student and teacher are pitted against one another. The scene depicts the teacher performing her duties and the student continuing to act in ways that other teachers have considered appropriate. Neither party does anything wrong, except the lines of authority that can prevent genuine communications have been drawn. The next chapter shows the same setting on the following day. This time only Narwin's voice is heard. Philip does not answer her questions and she becomes more directive. She concludes the scene by exercising her authority to send Philip to the assistant principal's office for reprimand.

By the third day, the exchange has escalated to an altercation. She recognizes his voice and asks him explicitly to stop singing. This teacher tries to educate, not just teach (as the school motto proclaims) when she tells Philip the reason this behavior must stop: "Your actions are thoroughly disrespectful" (*Truth*, 59). Philip shows adolescent courage as he claims his right to sing; more disturbing, however, is Philip's audacity when he retorts, "It's you who's being disrespectful!" (*Truth*, 60) Whereas the first comment challenges Narwin's authority, the second attacks her personally. This shift anticipates two strands of truth that define the novel: the authoritative truth that binds a society versus the personal truth of an individual.

Avi furnishes the novel with material revealing a personal side to Philip and to Narwin. Readers learn about Philip through his diary, his conversations with his parents, and with his friends; they learn about Narwin through letters to her sister, conversations with her sister and

others, and memos sent to her by Dr. Doane, her principal. Yet even these cannot be trusted to evidence a truthful side to a character. Philip's diaries bespeak his passion for track, yet some conversations with his father betray that passion. Philip writes in early diary entries with spirit, enthusiasm, and confidence. He expresses typical adolescent concerns (and assumptions) about male-female relationships, about school, and about family. His diary entries midway through the novel reveal doubt about his actions with Narwin and stretch to affirm his "rightness." His later entries describe his nervousness about returning to school after his expulsion for disobedience to Narwin; they also divulge his idea of approaching Narwin and disclose a weak optimism about setting right the terribly wrong course of events. His final entry abandons all hope and reveals only a defeated, self-consumed boy.

Putting the diary in the tight chronology with which Avi structures the book also places it within the context of plot events. At the beginning of the novel, Philip is merely another kid at school, although his diary celebrates his uniqueness, his "Malloy Magic" (*Truth*, 3). Ironically, the novel's ending finds Philip a patriotic hero whereas his diary illustrates his fall. What accounts for the change in Philip? He shares with his parents information about what has happened in school, but he also keeps information from them. Philip alternately wants to be like his father, the track star, and revolts against emulating him. He cannot face telling his parents that his poor grade in English removes him from the track team nor does he tell them that the cause of his grade is his poor performance in English. By extension, Philip does not tell the whole truth when he is suspended from school. Rather than honestly describe his relationship with Narwin, the English teacher who has failed him and, therefore, prevented him from participating in track, Philip simply asserts that the teacher has it out for him.

Even though Philip's partial facts preclude his parents from knowing him truly, they also result from Philip's not knowing his parents well. His father struggles at work, and, although eager for his father's support, Philip wants his father only to think well of him. His mother also works to maintain the family. She resents being called from work to pick him up after his suspension. The family gets so caught up in superficialities and details, truths that seem minor in context of the entire novel, that they cannot listen thoroughly.

> 7:12 P.M.
> Discussion between Philip Malloy and His Parents During Dinner
> Mr. Malloy: Okay, Phil. Now, I want to hear the whole thing. Start to finish. Just understand, right from the start, we're on your side. We don't intend to just take it. But I have to know what happened. Go on now.
> Philip Malloy: Same as before.
> Mr. Malloy: Same as *what* before?
> Mrs. Malloy: He's trying to tell you dear.
> Philip Malloy: See, they play "The Star-Spangled Banner" at the beginning of school . . .
> Mr. Malloy: I understand. When I was a kid we pledged allegiance. Go on.
> Philip Malloy: A tape.
> Mr. Malloy: Okay.
> Philip Malloy: When—before—when I was in Mr. Lunser's class, he was like, almost asking me to sing out loud.
> Mrs. Malloy: I always thought Phillip had a good voice.
> Mr. Malloy: That's not exactly relevant! Go on.
> Philip Malloy: But this teacher—
> Mr. Malloy: Mrs. Narwin.
> Philip Malloy: It's Miss.
> Mr. Malloy: Figures.
> Mrs. Malloy: That has nothing to do with it, Ben!
> Mr. Malloy: Go on.
> Philip Malloy: She won't let me. Threw me out of class.
> Mrs. Malloy: The principal said it was a rule.
> Mr. Philip Malloy: Ma, he's the *assistant* principal.
> Mr. Malloy: But why does that mean suspension?
> Philip Malloy: She threw me out twice this week.
> Mr. Malloy: It seems arbitrary. Outrageous.
> Mrs. Malloy: Stupid rules. (*Truth*, 79–80)

This conversation shows ways in which these characters listen past each other. They focus on small details, such as whether the teacher is Mrs. or Miss. They allow their assumptions to constitute their listening rather than hearing out a speaker at greater length.

When Philip finally tells his father that he merely wants to get out of the teacher's class, his father is already so swept up by the political ramifications—and potential for personal power—of this issue that Philip's truth gets lost.

At the same time, these parents clearly care about their child. Although it may simply be easier to believe Philip than to question him and to understand him, they come strongly to Philip's defense. They, like Philip, cannot accept his responsibility for a misunderstanding with Narwin; instead, they defend him so completely that they further distort the truth. Ted Griffen explodes Philip's small act of disobedience in his homeroom into a self-serving political issue in the name of personal rights, patriotism, the lack of morals taught in school, and, ultimately, the school budget. The larger the issue becomes and the more attention it receives, the more incomplete and misconstrued the truth becomes; the more public it becomes, the more it gets lost. Yet, the more unrecognizable the truth becomes, the more Philip begins to recognize the truth of his experience and his complicity in distorting it. By novel's end, the inability to communicate in a full, honest way results in Philip's tragic recognition of his loss and solidifies his isolation.

Even as the chronology and presentation of events force Philip and Narwin into opposition, Avi also compels readers to consider ways in which the situation makes the student and teacher alike. Early in the novel, Narwin applies for school funding to take a workshop in new methods of teaching English. While denying Narwin the money, Dr. Doane nevertheless compliments her on her success and value as a teacher. After removing Philip from her class for the second time, Narwin writes to her sister:

> So you see, Anita, it was gratifying to hear Gertrude [Doane] talk this way to me, exactly the kind of support teachers need. Certainly it's what I need at this time. I can't tell you how much. It bucks me up . . . I'm lucky. (*Truth*, 58)

Immediately following this letter, Avi includes an entry from Philip's diary:

> Lots of kids bad-mouth their parents, say they never stick up for them or understand them. Or pay any attention to them. Stuff like that. My parents are different.
>
> I'm lucky. (*Truth*, 58)

The back-to-back presentation of the letter and diary alerts readers to their shared sentiment and especially their shared language. Narwin and Philip consider themselves supported by authority figures; both feel lucky.

Yet, these excerpts accelerate the novel's irony. Dr. Doane flatters Narwin as she denies the teacher money for further education. Similarly, the earlier discussion demonstrates the misfortunes of miscommunication between Philip and his parents rather than the fortuity expressed in this diary entry.

In fact, as the situation at school escalates, the polarization of these two characters increases, and the misinformation generated by their supporters (namely, Narwin's school administrators and Philip's parents) becomes further distorted by the unwanted assistance of outsiders. Once the media representatives enter the picture, Narwin and Philip become more alike as they are pressed continually into their adversarial positions. Similarly, as the story expands beyond the realm of school and home and enters the larger spheres reached by wire services, less factual information is provided. Narwin and Philip lose distinction as individuals; various strains of the media typecast them in terms of what they appear to represent; the situation ceases to be about a teacher-student misunderstanding as it takes on the issues of censorship and free expression. The resulting sensationalism smothers facts, and, eventually, what happened between Narwin and Philip is of no interest. The favorable letters that Philip receives suffocate and isolate him because he knows that his actions carry no such nobility. Narwin receives only letters of reprimand, accusation, and castigation—none of which are based on knowledge of her or of the situation. Support of Narwin is quickly silenced, or—like Robert Duval, who wants to rewrite the original newspaper report about the event from Narwin's perspective—never voiced at all. As Narwin and Philip trust those with whom they feel lucky, they not only lose control over any possible interpersonal resolution but also become victims—not of each other but of an entire culture of misinformation and miscommunication.

At the point of their greatest polarization, Avi tenders Narwin and Philip as most alike. This time, Narwin speaks, rather than writes, to her sister, whereas Philip speaks to, rather than writes about, his father.

> 6:45 P.M.
> Phone Conversation between Margaret Narwin and Her Sister, Anita Wigham
> Anita Wigham: Peg, I am shocked!

> Miss Narwin: Well, you can imagine how I felt. The dishonesty of it! And from Gertrude of all people. I still find it impossible to believe.
> Anita Wigham: But what are you going to do?
> Miss Narwin: Anita, I don't know. I truly don't know.

> 6:50 P.M.
> Conversation between Philip Malloy and His Father
> Mr Malloy: Philip, I want you to open the door so we can talk.
> Philip Malloy: I don't want to talk.
> Mr. Malloy: What happened in school?
> Philip Malloy: Nothing. (*Truth*, 164–65)

Both characters admit, perhaps even recognize, their own powerlessness. As these two conversations clearly demonstrate, the security and the confidence they had in others as well as their own self-confidence have eroded. Subsequent events echo their abdication of all self-direction as Narwin and Philip retreat further and further. They pull into themselves and away from any opportunities for miscommunication as they reject communication altogether.

The novel moves from mostly written communication into primarily spoken exchanges. Narwin, the English teacher who advocates, practices, and explores the potency of words ironically no longer writes; almost as ironic is Philip's ignorance of the words of the national anthem. Not only does the written word appear more permanent than does the spoken, but it also proves more untrustworthy. Written communication burdens the word with the demand that it relate tone and attitude; it lacks the speaker's body language and intonation as partial bearers of message; in some ways, it must work harder to combine form and content. However, that does not mean that Avi suggests that the written word is more reliable than the spoken. Because of human nature, all forms of communication risk misunderstanding: Speakers and audiences each use their own codes, their own content and context. But messages can go astray, speakers and listeners may talk at cross-purposes, and content may contradict context. Although *Nothing But the Truth* "encourages readers to go beyond their natural self-absorption to posit the existence of other perspectives" (Rovenger, 21), it does not negotiate those variant perspectives for the reader. In fact, readers must remember that the novel, too, stands as simply one form of communication. To identify, to extract a truth from it may well be to misunderstand it. Avi's invisible narration fictionalizes his caution to the reader to "never fully trust the author, never fully trust my characters, never fully trust my story, no, not even my words" ("Seeing," 3). Words are untrustworthy, imperfect vehicles of communication. The readers may follow the author's direction, but they must generate their own meaning, their own elusive, even illusive, truth. It is no wonder that a book that trusts its young adult audience to resolve in individual ways such intricate, even enigmatic, issues not only earned recognition as a Newbery Honor Book but also continues to secure a substantial readership.

Source: Susan P. Bloom and Cathryn M. Mercier, "Nothing But the Truth," in *Presenting Avi*, Twayne, 1997, pp. 79–88.

Alleen Pace Nilsen

In the following essay, Nilsen and Donelson give a generally positive assessment of the novel.

Avi's name has graced so many excellent YA books in the last few years that it's hardly a surprise to discover yet another fine Avi book. But it's surprising that his books differ so much in subject matter. Last year's *The True Confessions of Charlotte Doyle* was a remarkable adventure of a thirteen-year-old girl caught up in a story of the sea and murder. *Romeo and Juliet—Together (and Alive!) at Last* was funny. *A Place Called Ugly* told of the environment and roots. *Devil's Race* was scary. Avi's books have only one thing in common, something common to many other YA authors—the need to survive no matter what.

And we have a survivor of sorts and a victim of sorts in *Nothing But the Truth*. Miss Narwin wants ninth-grader Philip Malloy to care about literature, and Philip wants Miss Narwin to leave him alone and to pass him so he'll be eligible to go out for track. Neither gets what either one wants, and worse yet, he's transferred out of the homeroom of the chief-teacher-clown of the school into Miss Narwin's home room. There what was already miserable for both becomes far worse. Students at Harrison High School are expected to "stand at respectful, silent attention for the playing of our national anthem," but Philip, who's been a smart-ass in Narwin's English classes, decides to hum along with the music during the national anthem.

Narwin quietly asks him not to hum, he persists, she sends him to the assistant principal, and he (over her objection) boots Philip out of school for two days. The word leaks out that a Harrison High student has been disciplined because he was patriotic and wanted to sing along. Patriotic groups and individuals and newspapers across America defend Philip—one paper headlines the story, "Suspended for Patriotism"—and attack the unpatriotic and cruel English teacher. A local talk show host engages in a brief dialogue with a caller.

> Steve (caller): Look—about that kid.
> Jake Barlow (host): The one kicked out of school for singing "The Star-Spangled Banner?"
> Steve: Yeah. Hey, you know, that gripes me. Really does. Things may be different. But, come off it!
> Jake Barlow: Right! What are schools for, anyway?
> Steve: People might call me a—a—
> Jake Barlow: Jerk?
> Steve: Yeah, maybe. But like they used to say, America, love it or leave it. And that school—
> Jake Barlow: It was a teacher.
> Steve: Yeah, teacher. She shouldn't be allowed to teach. That's my opinion.
> Jake Barlow: Right, I'm with you there, Steve. I mean, there are the three R's—reading, 'riting, and 'rithmetic—and the three P's—prayer, patriotism, and parents.

We wonder what kids will think of this book if they read it. Presumably they would sympathize with Philip even though other kids in the book weren't all that sympathetic. Teachers are likely to sympathize with Miss Narwin though she didn't seem to us to be a model of professionalism or talent. The administrators protect themselves at all times and squirm out of the tight spots. School board members come across even worse. So do newspaper reporters. In other words, this is an honest and realistic book— more like real life than most of us want to encounter in a book.

It's subtitled "A Documentary Novel" because it's told through documents—memos, stenographic records of conversations, letters, newspaper stories, and the like. Such pseudo-objectivity doesn't make the reader any more comfortable. Nor does the concluding line in the book, which is an O'Henry-type kicker.

Source: Alleen Pace Nilsen and Ken Donelson, "Review of *Nothing but the Truth: A Documentary Novel*," in *English Journal*, Vol. 81, No. 7, November 1992, pp. 91–92.

SOURCES

Avi, *Nothing But the Truth: A Documentary Novel*, Orchard Books, 1991.

Corkey, Charity, "Award-Winning Novel Chosen for Countywide Reading Program," in *Washington Post*, September 25, 2008, p. LZ03.

Fader, Ellen, Review of *Nothing But the Truth*, in *School Library Journal*, Vol. 37, No. 9, September 1991, p. 277.

Review of *Nothing But the Truth*, in *Kirkus Reviews*, Vol. 59, October 1, 1991, p. 1284.

Review of *Nothing But the Truth*, in *Publishers Weekly*, Vol. 238, No. 40, September 6, 1991, p. 105.

Watson, Elizabeth S., Review of *Nothing But the Truth*, in *The Horn Book Magazine*, Vol. 68, No. 1, January–February 1992, p. 78.

Zvirin, Stephanie, Review of *Nothing But the Truth*, in *Booklist*, Vol. 88, No. 2, September 15, 1991, p. 136.

FURTHER READING

Hunt, Jonathan, "Script Novels; Are They a Flash in the Literary Pan or an Emerging Genre?," in *School Library Journal*, March 1, 2006, p. 52.

This essay discusses the phenomenon of script novels, including *Nothing But the Truth*, and lists some of the best examples of the genre.

Markham, Lois, *Avi*, Learning Works, 1996.

This biography of Avi covers his childhood, how he overcame dysgraphia, his creative process, and some of the recurrent themes of his books.

Scales, Pat, "Freedom for All?," in *School Library Journal*, December 1, 2007, p. 54.

This essay looks at First Amendment and free speech issues and how they can be discussed in the classroom. The author discusses a number of books for younger readers which touch on these issues, including *Nothing But the Truth*.

Tait, Leia, *My Favorite Writer: Avi*, Weigl Publishers, 2007.

This juvenile biography of Avi discusses his life and his most popular books. It also offers tips for creative writing.

Patternmaster

OCTAVIA E. BUTLER
1976

The debut novel from acclaimed African American science fiction author Octavia E. Butler, *Patternmaster*, published in 1976, was the first in what became a series of five novels dubbed the Patternmaster series. The series as a whole covers a period from pre-colonial Africa to the world after a holocaust. *Patternmaster* is set late in the chronology of the series and explores a future society in which Patternists dominate. Patternists are people with powerful mental and telepathic abilities who are joined through a network called the Pattern and controlled by the Patternmaster. Patternists are served by mutes (that is, humans who lack these abilities) and Clayarks (humans who have come into contact with an alien disease, which has mutated them into a cat or griffin-like hybrid).

In *Patternmaster*, Butler focuses on the lives and struggles of two brothers, Teray and Coransee, who are powerful enough to succeed their father, the current, ailing Patternmaster. Throughout the novel, Butler examines ideas such as community, communication, power, and responsibility while telling the brothers' story. She also touches on feminist issues in her female characters, especially through the powerful healer, Amber, who becomes Teray's closest ally and mentor.

Critics have responded positively to *Patternmaster*, though it came to be seen by some critics as one of the weaker novels in the series because it resembled mainstream science fiction more than Butler's other works.

Octavia Butler *(WireImage)*

AUTHOR BIOGRAPHY

Octavia E. Butler was born on June 22, 1947, in Pasadena, California, the daughter of Laurice and Octavia M. (Guy) Butler. Her father worked as a shoe shiner until his death when Butler was still an infant. Raised by her mother, who took jobs as a maid to help support her daughter, as well as her grandmother, Butler was an introverted, solitary child who enjoyed reading from an early age. She read through the entire children's section at the Pasadena Library before she turned fourteen—at which age she was allowed to enter the adult section. Looking for something new to read, Butler discovered science fiction magazines and became fascinated by the genre.

Even before that, when Butler was twelve years old, she had seen the science fiction film *Devil Girl from Mars* and believed she could write something better. She began working on what would eventually become the Patternmaster series. By the age of thirteen, Butler was submitting short stories to magazines. After

completing high school, Butler entered Pasadena City College where she continued to write. She won a short story contest during her first semester. She put her writing career on hold while she earned her A.A. and continued her education at California State University at Los Angeles and the University of California at Los Angeles.

In 1969, Butler's writing career moved forward when she took a class with acclaimed science fiction writer Harlan Ellison through the Open Door Program at the Screen Writers Guild. Ellison advised her to enroll in the six-week Clarion Science Fiction Workshop, held in Pennsylvania to help aspiring science fiction writers. Butler found she fit in among the writers and quickly sold two stories, one of which never made it to print.

While struggling to sell her writing, over the next five years Butler worked as a dishwasher, a floor sweeper, and on an assembly line in order to support herself. She continued to write each morning before work. Shortly before Christmas 1974, she was laid off from her job as a telephone solicitor and decided to use her free time to focus on writing a novel instead of stories. Butler made the project seem more manageable by looking at each chapter as a short story. Using this method, she completed *Patternmaster* (1976) within a few months. Butler added four more titles to what became the Patternmaster series over the next few years.

While publishing Patternmaster novels, Butler received much acclaim for a stand-alone science fiction novel entitled *Kindred* (1979). This best-seller focused on a contemporary African American woman who time travels back to the American South during slavery. In the late 1980s, Butler published the novels in her Xenogenesis series, which focused on life on Earth after a nuclear war in which aliens want to help save surviving humans by interbreeding.

Although Butler sometimes struggled with writer's block, she continued to publish challenging fiction in the 1990s and early 2000s, and was honored with a MacArthur Foundation "genius" grant in 1995. Five years later, she won the PEN Center West Lifetime Achievement Award. After suffering from a myriad of health problems near the end of her life, Butler fell at her home in Washington state and died on February 25, 2006, at the age of fifty-eight.

PLOT SUMMARY

Prologue

As *Patternmaster* opens, Rayal, the Patternmaster, and his lead wife/sister Jansee, are in bed. The Patternist territory has been calm for a year as no major Clayark attacks have occurred. The Clayark are infected, mutated humans with human heads and catlike bodies. The couple has two sons, aged two and twelve, who are being educated at a school far away.

Jansee is concerned about her sons' well-being, and as a Patternist, can connect with them telepathically. However, she wants to send a mute to check on her sons. Mutes are descendants of modern-day humans who lack the telepathic skills of Patternists and now live in servitude to them. Rayal chides his lead wife's unusual interest in the boys, and the couple gets into an argument.

During the sometimes tense discussion, Butler reveals that Rayal killed all his siblings save Jansee in order to become Patternmaster and lead the telepathic race through the powerful network of mental connections between the Patternists known as the Pattern. The strong Jansee only survived the massacre because she chose to submit to him and become his lead wife. By the time the conversation ends, Jansee is upset by Rayal's sometimes cold indifference.

The year of peace is shattered as the Clayarks attack using a huge gun before any sentries detect their presence. The first shot kills Jansee and the second severely injures Rayal, who must use his powers to save his own life instead of deflecting or killing Clayarks. The enemy attacks his House (a unit of social organization in Patternist society, each headed by a powerful Patternist) and those who lived therein.

Chapter One

Years later, Rayal's younger son, Teray, leaves the Redhill School with his wife, Iray. Unlike his wife, Teray has little regret about departing from school because he is quite powerful in his Patternist abilities. Having reached adulthood four years ago, he was waiting for the right position to be offered to him.

As Teray and Iray leave, they are met by Joachim, a Housemaster who has taken on Teray as an apprentice, and Jer, an outsider. (Both outsiders and apprentices are Patternists. However, apprentices are being trained to become the head of a House, while outsiders work for House heads in what is essentially servitude. Outsiders can hold some power in the House over mutes and within their ranks.) Teray and his outsider, Jer, inform Teray that Coransee, the most powerful Patternist heading a House, was recently raided by Clayarks. Joachim also tells him they are going to visit Coransee on the way to Joachim's House. Though Joachim wants to keep Teray away from Coransee as much as possible, Coransee takes an interest in Teray and immediately tries to break through his mental shield to read his thoughts.

Coransee continues to question and challenge Teray, then abruptly changes course to offer Joachim an extremely talented artist, an outsider named Laro. Making a crafty deal with Joachim, Coransee negotiates a trade giving Laro to Joachim for Teray—who is revealed to be Coransee's brother—even though apprentices cannot legally be traded as they are not property.

Leaving Joachim and Coransee, Teray finds Iray, who is outraged at the situation. If the exchange happens, Teray will probably not be an apprentice but an outsider. Outsiders cannot be married or have children and do not control where they live.

At dinner, Teray and Iray learn that the deal has gone through and he will be an outsider in Coransee's House. Joachim promises to try and fix the situation. However, his ability to help them is limited because he has been implanted with certain controls by Coransee.

Chapter Two

After Joachim leaves, Coransee appears at Teray and Iray's door. Coransee and Teray fight telepathically. Coransee dominates, attacking Teray's heart and nearly killing him. Teray regains consciousness in a guest room having been healed by a healer. Iray is by his side and informs him that Coransee told her that because of Teray's power, Coransee might make him an apprentice.

Early the next morning, Teray meets with Coransee as requested. Coransee informs him that they are full brothers, and asks Teray if he wants to control the Pattern. Teray is his only threat to replace the slowly dying Rayal as Patternmaster. Teray tells him he will not contest Coransee for the Pattern when Rayal dies or is replaced because he only wants his freedom and a chance to establish his own House.

Coransee offers Teray a deal whereby Teray would become an apprentice and inherit Coransee's House when Coransee became Patternmaster, but only if Teray agrees to allow Coransee to implant controls in him. Teray refuses. Coransee makes him an outsider in charge of the mutes who look after the House and its grounds.

Teray replaces Jackman as muteherd. Because of Teray's power and inexperience, Jackman reluctantly allows him to absorb all his memories related to managing the mutes and allows himself to be mentally linked to Teray. Teray appreciates that he actually cares about the mutes.

Chapter Three

Teray seeks out Iray and informs her of the situation. She is no longer his wife, and Teray urges her to please Coransee and become part of his household. She soon becomes one of his favorites. Teray feels pain when he sees Iray and Coransee together. Teray also feels frustration because he is not learning anything. Mutes fear him and believe he might abuse them, although he has no such impulses.

Teray heals a mute who works as a cook and has badly burned his foot. He begins to take more of an interest in mutes. A badly injured mute woman named Suliana collapses outside of his door. Teray calls in the resident healer, Amber, to heal the mute woman's injuries.

After Amber informs him that Suliana has been beaten this way a number of times, Teray looks into Jackman's memories to learn why. She is the private property of an outsider named Jason, who beats her because she looks like his former wife who was traded away by Coransee. Amber rebukes Teray for not taking better care of the mutes and learning about such situations.

Teray also learns about Amber, an independent Patternist (not permanently tied to any House) who has worked at Coransee's House for several years as a healer but can leave at any time. Teray reluctantly opens up to Amber to learn the extent of mute abuse in the house and is dismayed by the knowledge. Amber tells him that Coransee knows about the abuse but will not do anything unless Amber agrees to give up her independence and stay.

As they talk, Teray realizes that Amber is easy to communicate with because she is next to him in the Pattern. After Amber leaves, Teray deals with Jason by beating him mercilessly using his strength and speed as a Patternist. Returning to his room and Suliana, Teray tells

her that she does not have to go back to Jason and allows her to stay with him. Over the next few weeks, Teray also plans to run away, probably to Forsyth and Rayal to plead his case and perhaps gain some training.

Chapter Four

Teray studies learning stones on the grounds of Coransee's House and continues to prepare himself to run away by educating himself about relevant terrains. Because he does not pay attention to his personal security, a Clayark comes too near to him. Teray observes him for a moment, then confronts the stunned creature.

While displaying his ability to hurt, if not kill, the Clayark, Teray asks him why his people attack the Patternists and mutes. The Clayark recognizes him as a son of Rayal. Although Teray should kill him, he allows the Clayark to live and leave.

Joachim, a journeyman named Michael, and others visit Coransee's House. (A journeyman is a Patternist who had been an apprentice but never took over a House of his or her own. Instead, journeymen remained powerful officials and servants in a household.) Teray learns from Amber that Joachim has brought Michael to investigate two charges against Coransee in an attempt to help Teray escape the House. Coransee is charged with illegally forcing Teray to join his House while still a student, as well as with competing for the Pattern ahead of time. Coransee uses his skills to turn the table on Joachim, who could be charged himself as apprentices are not allowed to be traded without the Housemaster losing his House.

Joachim avoids charges himself and Coransee suffers no consequences. Teray appreciates the efforts of Joachim and Michael, but is forced to remain where he is. After they leave, Amber shares a message for Teray from Michael, who has offered Teray sanctuary at Forsyth if he can get there alone. Based on the offer, Teray and Amber make plans to leave together as there is more safety in numbers. Teray and Amber then spend the night together.

Chapter Five

The next morning, Teray finds Iray and tells her of his plan to escape. He asks her to come with him, but she is now committed to Coransee and will not leave. Iray tells him to leave soon so that she cannot accidentally betray him to Coransee.

Later that day, Teray and Amber leave on two horses. They travel south to southwest via a coastal route. The pair chose this route, a longer one than necessary, to avoid Patternist caravans and Clayarks who want to attack them. Teray and Amber know there will still be Clayarks, but hope they will be in smaller numbers.

Teray and Amber link together as a safety measure, an easy task considering their closeness in the Pattern. As they travel, Teray learns more about Amber and her past. She tells him the story behind her killing of a Headmaster and relationship with a woman Housemaster named Kai.

The pair run into a small group of Clayarks. Using their combined mental strength, Teray kills the Clayarks by rupturing a large artery near its heart. After the battle, Amber begins to teach Teray a better, quicker way to kill the Clayarks than he learned in school.

Chapter Six

Amber's method involves killing Clayarks in a manner similar to the way Patternists kill each other—overstimulating their brains and disrupting their neural activities. Teray uses that method effectively when Clayarks approach them that night. After this success, Amber asks Teray if he has been fully trained as a healer, but Teray believes what he had been told about having no talent in the craft.

The journey continues to be difficult, and it only becomes worse on the tenth day when they encounter seventeen Patternists. These Patternists are led by Lady Darah, an elderly Housemaster, whom Amber knows from her past. They attempt to capture Teray and Amber and bring them back to Coransee.

Amber takes the lead fighting the Patternists, first by killing some of their horses and throwing them off guard. Teray and Amber ride away without chase.

Teray and Amber continue their travels with anxiety. They feel safer when they exit Darah's sector. The next day, Teray asks Amber about Darah. Amber had worked as Darah's healer a few years before.

Teray asks Amber to be his lead wife when he has his own House. Amber turns him down because she wants a House of her own. As they talk Amber senses more Clayarks nearby. They argue about how to handle the situation. Teray realizes that he and Amber are being pursued, and perhaps driven, by the Clayarks. After

finding shelter, Teray begins to kill the Clayarks. In the melee that follows, Teray's horse is shot and injured. As Amber tends to the horses, Teray realizes that Coransee is near.

Coransee and his party of ten has found them. Amber and Teray argue over how to handle the situation, but Teray eventually gives in and links with Amber to fight off Coransee. Coransee promises not to kill Teray but wants to take him to Forsyth to be judged by Rayal. Coransee only does this after Teray agrees to be captured by Coransee and remain his outsider instead of seeking sanctuary in Forsyth.

Chapter Seven

On the way to Forsyth, Teray and Amber remain linked. They mistakenly believe others were watching for Clayarks. As Teray moves forward to talk to Coransee about Amber, she is shot by a Clayark sniper. Amber, though badly hurt, heals herself.

Teray learns from Cornasee that Coransee is not linked to the others but only that the others are linked in pairs, a situation that makes detection of the Clayarks difficult. Teray then tries to bargain with Coransee for Amber, but Amber, now healed, says she will remain an independent as she has been.

Coransee compels Amber to link to him. Amber remains linked to Teray during this process as well so he can share his strength with her. Amber believes that Coransee will harm Teray.

After more travel, the party rests at night against a rocky ledge. Teray tells Coransee about the Clayark he talked to on the grounds of his House. Coransee is upset that Teray did not kill him, then tells Teray to send Amber to him for the night. Teray hits Coransee but then goes to the camp area to relay the message to Amber. She believes that Coransee is taking Teray to Forsyth to kill him. Amber also informs Teray that she is pregnant by him. Believing that Coransee wants to kill the baby as well, she still goes to Coransee as requested.

Chapter Eight

The next morning, Amber returns to Teray and links with him again. Amber must spend the next night with Coransee as well. She also informs Teray that Coransee cannot link with his ten companions or use their strength because he is close to being the Patternmaster. Teray and Amber plan an attack on Coransee to take advantage of this weakness.

The group is stalked by Clayarks as they travel that day. A Clayark sniper hits Coransee in the shoulder. Teray almost attacks Coransee in this weak state but the wound is not deep enough. Teray and Amber are allowed to go look at the sniper, who Teray has killed. The sniper has a different kind of weapon, more powerful than the usual Clayark gun. Amber destroys the weapon.

When Teray and Amber return, Coransee forces them to break their link. Teray then begins to devise a strategy to deal with his situation. He eventually decides to talk to Rayal through the Pattern, although he is technically misusing it.

At night, Amber sneaks a few moments with Teray until Rain, a Patternist woman traveling with the group, tells her that Coransee wants her to return to him. Rain offers herself to Teray, who refuses her and sends her away. Instead, he connects to the Pattern and reaches Rayal. Rayal refuses to help Teray or Amber, telling Teray that he failed the test. Teray decides he must fight Coransee.

Chapter Nine

The next day, Clayarks bother the Patternist group as soon as they leave camp. When three Clayarks get too close to them, Coransee sees them first and wounds, but does not kill, them. The farther they travel, the more skittish the Patternists' horses become.

As the group nears Forsyth, they enter the ruins of what was once a major city where many mutes lived. Clayarks now live in the remaining buildings. When the Patternists enter the city, horses are shot and killed. Amber is shot in the left hand. Teray discovers that Clayarks are using underground holes as a means of stalking and shooting them at close range.

Finding refuge in the shell of one of the buildings, Amber shows Teray that she has detached her hand and is in the process of regenerating another one. Amber also tells him that she believes he is a latent healer. Because of this skill, he can easily learn certain new skills and is more talented than his brother.

Coransee approaches, and he and Teray telepathically fight. Coransee is stronger and initially has the upper hand. He thinks he is winning and lets down his defenses. Teray takes advantage of that moment to kill Coransee, rupturing a large blood vessel in his chest.

Teray is injured in the battle and Amber heals him. Although the other members of the group have started digging Coransee's grave, Teray directs Amber to have Coransee's body burned to avoid letting the Clayarks eat it. Amber then allows Teray to take charge of Coransee's House. The pair also link again.

As Teray prepares to lead the other Patternists to the Pattermaster's House, he instructs them all to link to him. Although they are reluctant, Teray tells them that it will increase their safety; he must force some of them, including Rain, to link. Teray uses their combined strength, as well as Amber's, to kill thousands of Clayarks around them.

After the massacre, Teray finds Rayal suddenly with him in the Pattern. Rayal instructs him to keep the links to the others but to carefully release their strength. Rayal informs Teray that he has been waiting for him for years and that Coransee was never really his true heir. Rayal has planned for Teray to succeed him because of his skills as a healer—that is, the way a healer can kill. The tired Rayal urges Teray to get to Forsyth soon so he can take over the Pattern.

CHARACTERS

Amber

An extremely powerful Patternist healer, Amber is an independent—that is, she does not belong to any House and is free to travel between them and use her ability to heal. Amber has been at Coransee's House for several years, somewhat against her will as Coransee has tried to learn certain skills from her. Although her relationship with Teray is antagonistic at first, she is very close to him in the Pattern. Amber becomes involved with Teray and they escape Coransee together. During the journey, Amber becomes pregnant with Teray's child but has no interest in becoming Teray's wife if and when he does have his own House. She wants her own House, if anything. Amber aids Teray on his journey to Forsyth, although she must at one point spend nights with Coransee after he catches up to them. It is Amber who recognizes that Teray has abilities that Coransee lacks and teaches him skills that will become important when Teray becomes the Patternmaster.

The Clayark

While Clayarks are found throughout *Patternmaster*, "The Clayark" refers to the one to whom

Teray talks in chapter four. Teray asks this male Clayark why Clayarks raid Patternist lands and do what they do. The Clayark has limited language abilities but answers, "Enemies. Land. Food." The Clayark recognizes Teray as a son of Rayal, and Teray lets him leave with his life.

Coransee

The most powerful Patternist leading a House under the Patternmaster, Coransee is the son of the Patternmaster, Rayal, and his lead wife/sister, Jansee. He is also the elder brother of Teray, a strong young Patternist who has latent healing skills that Coransee lacks. Coransee believes that he is the heir to Rayal and will soon be controlling the Pattern. Unlike Joachim, Coransee does not link with the Patternists in his community on a regular basis for security and connected strength. Instead, Coransee values strength itself and relies primarily on his own strength and power to control and, if necessary, kill others, including Clayarks. Coransee regards Teray as a threat and uses illicit means to get Teray in his House. Coransee uses techniques like implanting controls to ensure potential threats are neutralized, as Joachim had been long before. Coransee wants to do the same to Teray, who would rather be an outsider than cede to his brother. After Teray and Amber escape his House, Coransee pursues them with ten loyal Patternists. After he catches the pair, he continues on to Forsyth with them; however, the brothers duel and Teray kills him. At the end of the novel, it is revealed that Rayal never regarded Coransee as his true heir.

Lady Darah

A Patternist, Lady Darah is the elderly Housemaster. She tracks down Teray and Amber after they leave the House of Coransee and tries to capture the pair for Coransee. The superior strength of Teray and Amber, especially when linked, causes her to back down and let them leave.

Goran

A male Patternist, Goran is a young outsider who travels in the group with Coransee that tracks down Teray and Amber.

Iray

Iray is Teray's young wife when they leave school. She is loyal and loving to her husband as they journey with Joachim. However, after Teray is traded to the House of Coransee and becomes an outsider instead of an apprentice, Iray can no longer be his wife. She soon becomes a favorite of Coransee and chooses not to leave with Teray when he and Amber make their escape.

Isaac

A male Patternist, Isaac travels in the group with Coransee that tracks down Teray and Amber.

Jackman

An outsider in Coransee's House, Jackman serves as a muteherd before being promoted. Teray then replaces him as a muteherd. Teray subsequently learns that while Jackman cared about the mutes, he did little to protect mutes like Suliana from abuse because he lacked the strength and courage to bring the matter to Coransee's attention.

Jansee

Jansee is the sister and lead wife of Rayal, the Patternmaster, and a Patternist herself. Unlike most Patternist women, she is quite attached to and concerned about her sons, Coransee and Teray. Jansee dies in the unexpected Clayark attack described in the prologue.

Jason

An outsider who was forced to join the House of Coransee, Jason severely abuses a mute named Suliana who became his property after his wife, whom Suliana resembles, was traded away by Coransee. Once he becomes a muteherd, Teray takes the strong but slow Jason to task and beats him thoroughly.

Jer

Jer is an outsider in Joachim's House. Though Jer is a young, strong Patternist, Joachim selected Teray to be his apprentice over Jer. Jer travels with Joachim to pick up Teray and Iray from the school and accompanies them on the stop at Coransee's House.

Joachim

Joachim is the head of a Patternist House and takes on Teray as an apprentice early in the novel. He selects Teray as an apprentice because of his strength and closeness to him in the Pattern, since Joachim uses a linked community to protect his House. However, Joachim loses Teray to the more powerful Coransee in an unfair trade. Joachim was once an outsider in

Coransee's House and allowed Coransee's controls to be implanted in him years ago in exchange for his freedom and the chance to become the master of his own House. Joachim tries to save Teray from Coransee by bringing charges against him. Although Michael finds the charges without merit and Teray actually must save Joachim from a charge of his own, Joachim's action indirectly leads to Teray's escape.

Kai

A Patternist, Kai was the female master of a House and was once romantically involved with Amber.

Laro

Laro is the sensitive, talented Patternist artist for whom Joachim trades Teray at Coransee's House in the first chapter of the novel. Although he was "a man of little mental strength," Laro has the unusual ability to pick up latent images from anyone, including mutes and Clayarks. He also is close to Joachim in the Pattern.

Leal

Leal was Amber's schoolmaster who dealt poorly with her gifts.

Lias

Lias is female Patternist who travels with Coransee to track down Teray and Amber.

Michael

A Patternist, Michael begins as an apprentice in Rayal's household and is mentioned in the prologue by Rayal as a potential father for Jansee's future children. Years later, Michael is a journeyman in the Patternmaster's House. It is he who goes to Coransee's House with Joachim to look into charges against Coransee related to bringing and holding Teray in his household. Michael cannot charge Coransee, but, through Amber, makes an offer of sanctuary for Teray if he can make it to Forsyth on his own.

Rain

A female Patternist, Rain travels in the group with Coransee that tracks down Teray and Amber. After Rain tells Amber that Coransee wants her during one stop on the journey, Rain offers herself to Teray who refuses her. Later, after Coransee's death, Rain resents Teray's new positon of leadership and tries to fight his decision to link them all.

Rayal

As the longtime Patternmaster, Rayal controls the Pattern and is the leader of the Patternists. He is the father of many children, including Coransee and Teray by his sister Jansee, who was his lead wife during her lifetime. During the Clayark attack described in the prologue in which Jansee loses her life, Rayal was severely injured in his head and shoulders. These injuries, along with age, eventually affect his ability to manage, if not control, the Pattern as well as he should. Coransee assumes he will succeed Rayal, but it is Teray that is truly Rayal's heir. After Teray defeats his elder brother near the end of the novel, Rayal is ready to hand the Pattern over to him and end his life.

Suliana

A mute, Suliana is the private property of an outsider named Jason who was forced to join Coransee's house. Because she resembles the wife Jason lost when Coransee traded her, Suliana receives much physical abuse at his hands. After Teray becomes the muteherd, she appears at his door with severe injuries. Suliana is healed by Amber and becomes physically involved with Teray, who ensures that Jason will leave her alone.

Teray

Teray is the main protagonist in the novel. He is the son of Rayal and Jansee and the younger brother of Coransee. Teray is introduced as a young Patternist who has reached maturity and demonstrated powerful strength. He leaves school with his wife Iray to become an apprentice in the House of Joachim, who does not fear Teray's power. Shortly after beginning their journey to Joachim's, they stop at the House of Coransee, who is the most powerful Patternist after Rayal and Rayal's self-declared heir. There, Coransee compels Joachim to trade Teray for Laro, an artist.

Now a member of the House, Teray learns that Coransee feels threatened by Teray's strength and potential. Coransee will not make him an apprentice unless Teray agrees to allow certain controls to be implanted within him, as Joachim had done long before. Teray refuses and is assigned outsider status and becomes a muteherd. He loses his wife, Iray, to Coransee because of the change in status.

While Teray comes to terms with his abilities and the limitations in the House of Coransee, he develops a relationship with a powerful healer, Amber. Given a chance to leave when Michael makes an offer of sanctuary, Teray and Amber escape Coransee and begin a harrowing journey to Forsyth. Along the way, Teray impregnates Amber. He also develops his latent healing skills and the ability to efficiently kill Clayarks in a way Coransee cannot master.

Coransee catches up with the pair before they reach Forsyth, and Teray becomes essentially his brother's prisoner as they journey on to Forsyth for judgment. Near the end of the expedition, Teray and Coransee battle, and Teray uses his skills to kill his brother. Linked to Rayal on the Pattern, Rayal acknowledges Teray as his true heir.

THEMES

Class Division and Society

Throughout *Patternmaster*, Butler describes a future in which classes are clearly defined and ordered. At the top of this society are the Patternists, led by the Patternmaster. Below the man or woman serving as Patternmaster are the Housemasters, powerful Patternist men and women who control Houses (small communities). Within the Houses, apprentices are Housemasters in training and as such have more power and freedom than other members of the household. Outsiders usually do not become Housemasters, but are essentially servants, sometimes slaves, within the Houses. They do not receive as much training as apprentices. The Patternmaster's House also includes journeymen like Michael who wield some power as officials, but their power is limited. Independents like Amber function outside of this structure and have freedom to work in any House they like.

Other groups remain outside the Patternist society altogether. Mutes have no power or status; they serve as workers and caregivers for the Patternists. Patternists and mutes do have one thing in common. They both fear Clayarks, the horribly mutated humans who have the head of a person but the body of a catlike animal. Clayark society is focused on ensuring they have enough food and land to support their ever-increasing numbers. To that end, they attack Patternists and their mutes in their never-ending quest to harass, if not cripple, their enemies.

TOPICS FOR FURTHER STUDY

- Watch the science fiction film *Devil Girl from Mars* (1954). Butler saw this film as a child and believed she could write a better science fiction story than the one depicted on screen. Indirectly, this film helped launched her writing career. In an essay, outline why you think *Devil Girl from Mars* inspired Butler to write her own science fiction stories. Are there any similarities between *Patternmaster* and *Devil Girl from Mars*? How do they differ?

- One of Butler's earliest mentors was highly respected science fiction author Harlan Ellison. Create a PowerPoint presentation about Ellison and his effect on the history of science fiction. Include information about his relationship with Butler and offer suggestions about which of his books to read as well. Do not rely exclusively on the Internet in your research; use your school or public library as well.

- In *Patternmaster*, Butler writes, "What was it the Clayarks called themselves? Sphinxes. Creatures out of ancient mythology, lion-bodied, human-headed." Use the Internet to research sphinxes in mythology, then consider how Butler's description of Clayarks relates to sphinxes. Write a paper with your conclusions and include your own original illustration of what you think a Clayark might look like.

- Research a classic pair of rival brothers from history or literature such as Cain and Abel. Write an essay comparing and contrasting the relationship of your chosen brothers with that of Coransee and Teray in *The Patternmaster*.

By creating this ordered society in *Patternmaster*, even with its unpredictable elements like Clayarks, Butler has a framework to explore other ideas such as power, responsibility, communication, and community.

Power and Responsibility

One of the major themes in *Patternmaster* is power and responsibility. Butler clearly delineates who has power in the novel. Patternists have more power in society than mutes, and within the Patternist society, some groups have more power than others. The Patternmaster holds the most power as he controls the Pattern.

This Patternist power manifests itself in various ways in the novel. The Patternmaster, Rayal, though weaker than he has been in the past, still controls the Pattern and who will succeed him. He allows the power struggle between his two sons, Coransee and Teray, to play out, believing that Teray will ultimately triumph as his heir. Coransee has used his strength in the Pattern to become the most powerful Housemaster and self-declared heir to Rayal.

While Coransee embraces the idea of power, he is relatively unconcerned with the responsibility that comes with it. Coransee tries to maintain his power no matter what the cost to anyone else. In contrast, Amber, a powerful healer and independent among the Patternists, values a balance between the two. As a healer, she sees the consequences of struggles for power. For example, in Coransee's household, outsiders were allowed to abuse mutes when Jackman was the muteherder: Amber often cared for them. Jackman lacked the power to get Jason to stop or Coransee to care. Coransee ignored Amber's pleas to end the abuse, blackmailing her by saying he would only intervene if she agreed to give up her independent status and join his House.

However, when Teray becomes muteherder, he understands that with his new power in the household—however small—comes responsibility. Unlike Jackman, he deals with Jason after Suliana is nearly beaten to death. Teray balances his power with responsibility to others. For example, when he and Amber are on the run, they link for increased safety. They each act to protect the other, and each is conscious about the other's needs. Teray's strength coupled with his sense of responsibility make him worthy of becoming the powerful Patternmaster himself.

Communication and Community versus the Individual

At the core of *Patternmaster* are the related ideas of communication and the power of a community over an individual. The primary reason the Patternists have power over mutes is their mental abilities. They can communicate with each other using telepathy. The Pattern links the Patternists together, some closer than others. Some Patternists are stronger in their telepathic abilities, and this ability, or lack thereof, often determines the place of a Patternist in society. Healers like Amber and latent healers like Teray have enhanced communication skills because of their strong empathy and ability to heal.

Butler explores the strength of community over individual when, throughout the novel, she shows that Patternists are the safest when they are mentally linked together. She contrasts Joachim and Coransee in this way, for example. Joachim values Patternists who are close to him and the others in his community in the Pattern. They stay linked at all times, providing strength and security against the Clayarks. Coransee does not value closeness in the Pattern and does not link with anyone in his community unless he wants to control them. His group is subject to almost constant Clayark attacks as they travel to Forsyth.

Although Coransee's individualism makes him quite powerful, it ultimately results in his loss in his quest to become the Patternmaster. The more empathetic, community-oriented Teray fully understands that the Patternmaster must lead a community, and, after a spirited battle with his brother, triumphs and becomes his father's clear heir.

STYLE

Science Fiction

Patternmaster is a science fiction novel. This type of fiction focuses on what the past or future could be like based on an author's imagination of the impact of science or technology on a society. Science fiction is often a speculation on the idea of "what if?" The genre usually blends science fact and fiction. *Patternmaster* is classic science fiction, depicting a society in the future in which people have abilities not found today.

Prologue

The prologue is the introductory section of a work of fiction or nonfiction that establishes the core of the story at hand and provides information about what is to come. *Patternmaster* opens with a prologue that establishes that Rayal is Patternmaster and that Teray and Coransee are is sons. The prologue also shows how family conflicts are resolved among Patternists and demonstrates the power of their enemies, the Clayarks.

Horseback riding on the beach *(Image copyright Bruno Medley, 2009. Used under license from Shutterstock.com)*

The Hero's Journey

The protagonist is the hero or heroine of a literary work who serves as the focus for a story's themes and action. A classic, archetypal hero in literature undertakes a journey of self-discovery and self-development. In *Patternmaster*, Teray embarks on a literal journey to Forsyth. Along the way he learns much about himself, including that he has healing talents and that he is strong enough to defeat—rather than run away from—his enemies. In the end, having proved himself worthy, Teray achieves the ultimate reward, taking over from his father as Patternmaster.

Antagonist

In a literary work, the antagonist is a character who works against or stands in opposition to the protagonist. Coransee is the antagonist in *Patternmaster*. While strong and the self-declared heir to Rayal, Coransee is rightly threatened by his more talented younger brother. Coransee works to control Teray, but in the end, loses his life to him.

HISTORICAL CONTEXT

A Struggling Country

In the mid-1970s, the United States was struggling on several fronts. After an economic boom in the 1960s, the economy of the 1970s slowed and three recessions occurred during the 1970s. The mid-decade recession was caused in part by the oil crisis that began in December 1973. The Organization of the Petroleum Exporting Countries (OPEC), which essentially controlled oil supplies out of the Middle East, engineered a huge spike in the price of oil by curtailing supplies, causing economic turmoil in the United States and other oil-dependent countries. Monetary instability and the decline of the dollar in this time period also deeply affected the economy of the United States, as did rampant inflation.

Americans also grew more distrustful of government in the wake of the Watergate scandal that brought down the Nixon administration. After burglars were arrested breaking into the Democratic National Committee headquarters at the Watergate Hotel during the 1972

COMPARE
&
CONTRAST

- **1970s**: Economic upheaval and widespread cultural changes compel many Americans to return to traditional values and fundamentalist Christian teachings.

  Today: An economic downturn and continued cultural changes give continued life to the conservative movement in the United States. More Americans also embrace religious faith and spirituality as they look for answers and support amidst uncertainty.

- **1970s**: Many Americans are restless and question traditional authority. Public protests and various means of self-expression are common.

  Today: The questioning of authority and finding means of self-expression are an accepted part of American society. Such rebellion has become marketable. Protests, sometimes on the individual level, are now

an established form of self-expression across the political spectrum.

- **1970s**: The high price of oil hurts the American economy and causes the country to look for other sources of oil and implement conservation measures.

  Today: The high price of oil and gas continues to hurt the American economy. Alternative fuel sources continue to be explored.

- **1970s**: On average, women earn only 57 percent of what men earn because of a combination of lack of access to higher paid occupations and lower pay for the same work.

  Today: Women have greater access to higher earning occupations. However, they still earn just 80 percent of what men earn.

---

presidental election campaign, sources slowly revealed that the incumbent Republican administration had been behind the break-in and was attempting to cover up its role in the illegal activities. President Richard Nixon resigned in August 1974 and was replaced by his vice president, Gerald Ford. Soon after taking office, Ford pardoned Nixon—an action which proved controversial and unpopular among Americans. Other scandals during the decade undermined Americans' faith in their government, including a Rockefeller Commission report in June 1975 that outlined many misdeeds by the Central Intelligence Agency.

As more Americans put less trust in big government, there was also less support for changes in social policy. For example, although school busing and racial quota programs were intended to give all Americans equal access to education, some Americans did not support these efforts, and the conservative turn was reflected in Supreme Court decisions such as

Regents of the University of California v. Bakke (1978), which banned quota systems while allowing affirmative action programs to stand.

Feminism, Lesbianism, and the Status of Women

The women's liberation movement became arguably the most important social movement of the 1970s. Because of gains of the activists from the 1960s, many women had new freedoms in the 1970s. Women's liberation groups, including the National Organization for Women (NOW), continued to push boundaries in many ways, demanding a less restrictive society and access to positions of power in business and academe generally reserved for men. Conservatives expressed their belief that challenges to traditional gender roles undermined American society. Undeterred by such attitudes, some women activists fought for an Equal Rights Amendment (ERA) to be added to the U.S. Constitution. The amendment would guarantee women equal

Ocean waves hitting a rocky beach (*Image copyright Kavram, 2009. Used under license from Shutterstock.com*)

rights under the law. While the ERA passed Congress and was approved by thirty-five states, the proposed amendment fell short of ratification by three states.

The 1970s also saw the emergence of lesbian activism. These feminists took on homophobic and heterosexist attitudes in the women's movement itself, forcing, for example, NOW to put lesbian civil rights on its agenda in the early 1970s. Lesbian activists also fought sexism in the gay rights movement. Many lesbian feminists believed in and practiced separatism. Such feminists lived in their own communities and spent their earnings and time with other lesbian feminists, believing that lesbianism was "feminism in practice."

Some lesbian feminists of color such as Audre Lorde, Barbara Smith, and Cherri Moraga believed that feminism and lesbian feminism were both racist and classist. In 1977, the Combahee River Collective published a "Black Feminist Statement," which stated that its members would fight against racism, sexism, heterosexism, and oppression by social class. The statement also took on the idea of separatism. The collective's members did not deny their solidarity with straight feminists, African American men who professed progressive ideals, and others.

CRITICAL OVERVIEW

When *Patternmaster* was published in 1976, critics responded generally positively to one of the first science fiction works written by a female African American. The reviewer for *Publishers Weekly* notes, "The author carefully spells out the ground rules of her unique world, and the ensuing story of love, chase and combat is consistently attention-holding." Similarly, a contributor to *Kirkus Reviews* calls the novel "fine, old-fashioned [science fiction]," and concludes that it represents "escape fiction in the best Patterned tradition."

Some critics came to see *Patternmaster* as one of the weaker novels in the Patternmaster series, in part because of the author's relative inexperience. Among them is T. G. Wagner of

SFReviews.net, who comments that the novel is "an accessible adventure story," but finds problems with the novel's themes. Wagner notes, "Butler has yet to get a handle on how best to deliver the subtextual social commentary that would give the series its depth." In a 1992 *Fantasy & Science Fiction* review, Orson Scott Card dismisses *Patternmaster* as "more magic romance than hard science fiction." However, Card also praises Butler, noting, "We can see Butler's keen sense of truth at work, making characters more real than they ever needed to be for this sort of tale. More important, we already can see her touching on the issues of freedom and slavery, power and responsibility that have made all her writings such vibrant studies of the ethics of power and submission."

CRITICISM

A. Petruso

Petruso has a B.A. in history from the University of Michigan and an M.A. in screenwriting from the University of Texas at Austin. In this essay, she looks at how female characters in Patternmaster *represent various types of women.*

Many of the science fiction novels by feminist African American author Octavia E. Butler are widely praised for the depiction of female characters. A number of her protagonists are African American or mixed race, and they often take on nontraditional roles. Butler's women characters are usually powerful and capable, if not self-sustaining. In some ways, Butler's fiction, including *Patternmaster*, reflects the varied status of women in the 1970s as well as the greater feminist movement of that decade. While the women in *Patternmaster* are secondary to the main story of the emergence of Teray and the struggle with his older, more dominant brother, Coransee, the women are nonetheless interesting and important. Butler uses them to send a message about women reflecting changes in women's roles and place in society in her time.

There are three primary women characters in *Patternmaster*—Jansee, Iray, and Amber, as well as a few secondary ones—Suliana, Darah, mute women, and unseen Patternist women mentioned by Amber. The primary female characters are each very different in their life and outlook, while each of the secondary women

> AMBER CAN TAKE CARE OF HERSELF, WHICH PUTS HER IN STARK CONTRAST TO BOTH JANSEE AND IRAY AND MAKES HER THE EPITOME OF A FEMINIST CHARACTER AND A MODERN WOMAN IN BUTLER'S ENGROSSING NOVEL."

characters echo an aspect of one of the three primary characters.

In the prologue to *Patternmaster*, Jansee makes her only appearance. The lead wife and sister to the Patternmaster Rayal, Jansee is the mother of Teray and Coransee. While Amber is nurturing in her healing and Iray supports Teray while they are married, Jansee is the only character in the novel who is a mother.

Most Patternist women do not raise their children and seem to have little connection to them, but Jansee is different. Rayal teases her, saying, "You're really too much the mute-mother to have more children. You care too much what happens to them." Mute women—humans without the telepathic and mental energy skills of Patternists—are the ones who raise and take care of Patternist children (and adults, for that matter, as the scenes in Coransee's House indicate). When Iray leaves school with her husband Teray, it is a mute woman who "radiated such a mixture of sadness and excitement."

Though Jansee is deeply attached to her sons and their fate, she has had to compromise herself to get to this place. To become Patternmaster, Rayal had to kill his two brothers and one of his sisters. Though he has many wives, Jansee is his primary wife as well as his sister. Undeniably strong in the Pattern—even Rayal called Jansee "my strongest sister" and Teray called his parents "the two strongest Patternists of their generation"—Jansee did not fight him for control of it but saved herself by becoming Rayal's ally and agreeing to become his lead wife. Rayal compliments this decision as "wise" in the prologue.

Realizing that Rayal really did see her as a threat, Jansee says she made this choice for what some would consider a stereotypical female

WHAT DO I READ NEXT?

- *Kindred*, published in 1979, is a stand-alone novel by Butler. It focuses on an African American woman named Dana living in California in 1976, who is transported back to the antebellum South. She finds herself on the plantation of the man who is her ancestor and faces difficult choices about what actions to take.

- *Dustland*, written by African American author Virginia Hamilton and published in 1980, is the second novel in the "Justice" trilogy of science fiction novels for young readers. Like the other novels in the series, *Dustland* focuses on four children—including three siblings—who move beyond their physical bodies to help save humanity with their abilities.

- *Wild Seed*, published in 1980, is another novel in the Patternist series by Butler. This book explains how the Patternists originated—they sprung from Doro and Ayanwu, the patriarch and matriarch respectively. Doro is a four-thousand-year-old Nubian who has survived through time by moving from one body to another.

- *Mind of My Mind*, published in 1977, is another novel in the Patternist series by Butler. This novel is set in the late twentieth century in the Los Angeles suburb of Forsyth. In this time period, the Patternists are the minority (but growing in number) while mutes continue to run society. Doro appears in this novel as well, checking on the tragic Rina, with whom he has a daughter named Mary. Finding Rina unable to care for the talented Mary herself, Doro arranges for her to be cared for by Emma, one of his consorts, who agrees to raise her and help her realize her potential.

- *Survivor*, published in 1978, is another novel in the Patternist series by Butler. This book focuses on a young black woman from Earth named Alanna, who is adopted by a family of white missionaries and taken to another planet to escape the plague and disease that causes people to turn into Clayarks. Issues of race follow Alanna to the alien planet.

- *Graceling*, published in 2008, is a young adult novel by Kristin Cashore. This book focuses on a girl named Katas who can kill men with her bare hands. She faces challenges because of her abilities and must confront rulers with evil intent.

- *The Host*, published in 2008, is a young adult novel by Stephanie Meyer. This science fiction thriller focuses on a time when most people on worlds such as Earth have been taken over by a type of well-intentioned parasite. One girl, Melanie, fights being taken over by these alien souls.

- *The Second Sex*, published in 1949, is a foundational work of feminist philosophy. It was written by Simone de Beauvoir, an important figure in the French philosophical movement known as existentialism. De Beauvoir theorizes that the idea of womanhood is only defined in relation to manhood, putting women in a subordinate position.

---

reason. She says, "I hate killing. We have to kill Clayarks just to survive. I can do that. But we don't have to kill each other." The power she could have had means little to Jansee, and she only fears Clayarks, not her husband.

The scene with Jansee and Rayal takes place at the end of a time of extended peace, just before Clayarks manage a surprise attack on the Patternmaster's House, killing Jansee and severely injuring Rayal. By having Jansee killed so early in the novel, Butler demonstrates that motherhood and its related values are not important to the Patternists. This idea reverberates throughout the text. Neither Coransee or Teray knew their mother yet it is clear that the brothers draw their abilities from both mother and father, despite their lack of contact in childhood.

Iray is the next primary woman character to appear in *Patternmaster*. Like Jansee, Iray is sensitive to and strong within the Pattern, though not nearly as strong or gifted as her husband. Butler explains, Iray was "not strong enough to establish a House of her own, but strong enough to make a secure place for herself in any existing House she chose."

Unlike Jansee, Iray becomes Teray's wife of her own free will. Joachim had been her second (a position not unlike mentor) when she made the transition into adulthood. Butler writes that Teray notes with a hint of jealousy, "She would probably have gone into his House as one of his wives if she had not met Teray." Iray is also easily impressed by celebrity, as when she learns that she and Teray will be stopping at the home of the mighty Coransee with Joachim and his group.

During this stop, Iray's world is altered forever. She is supportive of Teray and understands her place as his wife, but Joachim is forced by Coransee to make what is essentially an illegal trade. Joachim gains a talented artist, Laro, who is close to him in the Pattern, but Coransee gains Teray, a powerful Patternist who is revealed to be his full brother and perceived rival for control of the Pattern.

Unlike Joachim, Coransee will not make Teray an apprentice unless Teray agrees to allow certain controls to be implanted in him. Teray will not make the deal—much to Iray's consternation—and becomes an outsider in Coransee's House. As an outsider, Teray cannot have a Patternist wife. He loses Iray to Coransee, a situation which upsets her. However, she does not fight her fate.

As is custom when a male outsider joins a House, Iray reluctantly but willingly becomes a wife of Coransee and soon is one of his favorites. Showing that she is loyal to whomever she is attached, Iray refuses to go with Teray and Amber when they escape Coransee's House later in the novel. On the whole, Iray does not have Jansee's maternal instincts but does match her loyalty, not out of fear, but because Butler draws her to be that kind of a woman. Iray is not independent and does not think outside of the Patternist box.

Yet Iray does understand why Teray could never accept Coransee's controls. When Teray asks her to come with him as he escapes to sanctuary in Forsyth, Iray is uncomfortable in his presence but states her awareness of his situation. Iray says, "I understand what you did. That's why I never blamed you, never tried to make you change your mind. I knew you'd rather be dead than controlled. You did what you had to do."

The secondary mute character, Suliana, is depicted in a fashion similar to Iray. Suliana is the property of Jason, an outsider in Coransee's household. She endures regular beatings at the hands of Jason. After she is again nearly beaten to death, she shows up at Teray's door. Teray stops the violence, and Suliana moves in with her savior, Teray. She then serves him sexually and otherwise.

While such female characters as Iray and Suliana are relatively weak and unable or unwilling to challenge the status quo, powerful women like Amber abound in *Patternmaster*. In chapter one, Butler mentions that, to gain his House, Coransee "had to kill a powerful woman who had held it for over two decades." Amber also discusses women like Kai, who headed her own House and with whom Amber was once in love. Kai was strong enough to be Amber's second, but Leal, her Schoolmaster, rejected the choice in favor of someone much weaker. During the journey of Amber and Teray, they encounter a powerful aged female Housemaster named Darah. While the pair are able to leave her presence unscathed, they respect her as a Housemaster who has held on to her House years longer than most.

The woman with the most power in *Patternmaster* is Amber. Unlike Jansee and Iray, she does not depend on a man for status. She is an independent and can live in whatever House will have her without restrictions. Amber is also strong in the Pattern and an extremely gifted healer. While healing arts can be considered a strong female quality, Butler imbues them with more as Patternist healers are also considered effective killers, able to easily destroy important body parts of Patternists and not give them time enough to heal.

From the first moment she appears in *Patternmaster*, Amber is not afraid to challenge Teray. Amber is extremely close to Teray in the Pattern and soon initiates a romantic relationship with him. While Amber does fear the stronger Coransee—who has tried to get her to stay in

Blue sky *(Image copyright Adisa, 2009. Used under license from Shutterstockcom)*

his House as one of his wives during her two years' tenure—she is not afraid to leave his House with Teray and risk his wrath.

Amber could have left Coransee's on her own. However, linking with Teray makes them both stronger and they take advantage of their enhanced strength as they make their way to Teray's promised sanctuary in Forsyth. During the journey, Amber's mental strength helps both her and Teray survive Clayark attacks as well as encounters with Patternists who are searching for them. Amber is also able to teach Teray a more effective way to kill Clayarks. Because she can teach him this method, Amber recognizes that Teray is a latent healer who has more potential to learn then he initially realizes.

In addition to being able to teach a strong man to be a more effective killer and healer, Amber also rejects traditional female choices. She is bisexual, telling Teray at one point, "When I meet a woman who attracts me, I prefer women. And when I meet a man who attracts me, I prefer men." Teray wants to make Amber

his lead wife, but she will have none of it, even though she is pregnant with his child. Amber wants to lead her own House and even offers to make him her lead husband. She does not need Teray to survive, especially after Teray kills Coransee. Amber can take care of herself, which puts her in stark contrast to both Jansee and Iray and makes her the epitome of a feminist character and a modern woman in Butler's engrossing novel.

Source: A. Petruso, Critical Essay on *Patternmaster*, in *Novels for Students 34*, Gale, Cengage Learning, 2010.

Marilyn Mehaffy

In the interview that follows, Butler discusses issues of identity and physicality in her novels.

Octavia Butler: OB
Marilyn Mehaffy: MM
AnaLouise Keating: ALK

MM: As you know, the critical focus of our interview project is the use of bodies as a formal narrative convention in American literary texts, that is, how bodies—usually human [laughter]—are inscribed and constructed to serve narrative

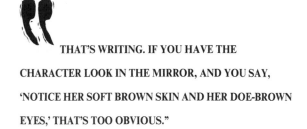

THAT'S WRITING. IF YOU HAVE THE
CHARACTER LOOK IN THE MIRROR, AND YOU SAY,
'NOTICE HER SOFT BROWN SKIN AND HER DOE-BROWN
EYES,' THAT'S TOO OBVIOUS."

purposes. For instance, how do—or do?—literary bodies mirror stereotypes and biases from other popular culture texts like advertising, or television and film, or political discourse? We're interested in how particular texts race bodies in certain ways; and how specific sets of value and aesthetics become attached to particular categories of ethnicity as a result. And, as well, how do literary constructions, in turn, interact with or impact popular perceptions? We're studying writers who devise different approaches to familiar categories of subjective identity—gender and ethnic identity and sexual identity; and how those re-imagined bodies might affect readers and, therefore, popular perceptions about subjective categories like race and gender and sexuality. Here's where you come in because your books, it seems to us, are all about re-creating bodies in different ways.

OB: Well, this sounds interesting. But what you seem most interested in is appearance. I began writing back when I was twelve, and I'd already been reading science fiction. Later, when I realized that people actually publish this stuff, I realized that I had been writing about people for years and I'd never seen any of them. I have the kind of imagination that hears. I think of it as radio imagination. I like radio a lot better than I do television; and, really, I have to go back and try to imagine what characters might look like because when I began writing at age twelve, I couldn't. What I had to do was go back and sort of paint the characters in. What would I like them to look like? I had a character in *Patternmaster*, a very early character. This is somebody that I ran across when I was twelve even though he had a different name. He had lived in my head for over a year when I finally thought, "I gotta know what he looks like." But everything I imagined, or tried to sketch in, was a disappointment because somehow without this kind of—not

bodilessness, because, actually, it was very sexy—he was not what I imagined.

MM: And your books are very sexy, by the way! I always think that—that they're a real turn-on—but I never hear anybody talking about their sexiness.

OB: I hope so because one of the signs—I put signs on my walls as a reminder while I'm writing-is "sexiness," not only sexiness in the sense of people having sex, but sexiness in the sense of wanting to reach readers where they live and wanting to invite them to enjoy themselves.

MM: Maybe this is a good time to ask you my vision question since it's related to your talking about how you don't see characters first. A physical function of the Oankali and the Oankalihuman constructs [in the Xenogenesis Trilogy] that intrigues me is their ability to see without eyes, by means of sensory tentacles or patches rather than human optics. Are you commenting on the prevalence in modern times of optical vision as the privileged mode of seeing and knowing others and their bodies?

OB: You're probably putting more into it than I actually did, but this is something that is left over from my days of being down in the basement in the corner with J.B. Rhine and company. There were books about strange people, books about people who had unusual abilities or deficiencies. Every now and then there would be something about someone who had photosensitive tissue in some strange place. If they couldn't actually read with it, they could at least detect light and dark, or vague images, that kind of thing. I thought, "This would be good," because I wanted these characters to look alien. I go from not paying any attention to how my characters should look to recognizing that it's very important how they look, especially if they're not supposed to be human. I need to help my reader visualize them even though what my reader sees won't be what I had in mind. My characters have their photosensitive tissue elsewhere, and they have a type of vision that's at least as efficient as the human eye. It's just not where you would expect it to be.

ALK: Since we're talking about characters' bodies and how you see them, I think this question goes to that issue. One of the things I'm fascinated to find in your work is the way that you mark bodies by their colors rather than by characters' ethnicity. And you only mention color when it's contextually important to the story. For instance, in *Kindred* readers don't realize that Dana is "black" until page 24, and that Kevin is "white" until page 54. This is something that completely astonishes my students.

OB: That's writing. If you have the character look in the mirror, and you say, "Notice her soft brown skin and her doe-brown eyes," that's too obvious.

ALK: I think you're underselling yourself. "Race" is one of the areas I study, and, over and over, I see other writers mark ethnicity in extremely obvious ways. Generally, they state characters' ethnicity in the opening pages, and you don't do that. Was the delayed description of color in Kindred deliberate?

OB: Yes, that delay was deliberate because of the kind of book I was writing. If I had given the characters' race away earlier, that aspect would have had less impact and possibly the reader wouldn't react, but, instead, maybe discard that information and then start wondering what the problems were later on. But what if I hit the reader with it in a very dramatic way? In that case, ethnicity, based in history, based in antebellum slavery, as a component of Kevin's and Dana's relationship, would have a lot more power and a lot more saying power.

ALK: Even in Survivor, *it's not until Alana thinks back to her parents and provides readers with a visual description that we learn her mother was black and her father Asian. It just kind of comes through as a description, and not until page 27. You do the same thing in* Dawn *and the same thing in* Parable of the Sower—*when ethnicity fits the context, we learn about it within that particular context. You don't appear to use ethnicity to influence or predetermine readers' perceptions of a character.*

OB: Which is also something in my life. I had a friend when I was in junior high and high school who was of mixed background, and I never knew that until somebody else mentioned it. It turns out her parents lived next door to one of my relatives, and one day I learned that her mother is Japanese and her father is black. Afterward I thought about it, and I thought, "Well, gee, I've been thinking all this time that she was Latina." It didn't change anything about the way I thought about her except that I was intensely curious about her life. How is her life different because she's from this unusual situation?—unusual at the time. But in my life a lot of times there have been situations where either I didn't know or I found out late or something like that, and it's been a lot

> THE PASSIONATE, ABIDING IMPORTANCE OF THE NURTURING OF NEW LIFE, WHICH CLEARLY INFORMS THE *XENOGENESIS* PASSAGE I HAVE QUOTED, EQUALLY DEEPLY INFORMS THE ENTIRE TRILOGY, AS IN EVERY BOOK OF HERS I HAVE READ."

more interesting. I don't know what it would have been like if I had known immediately. Probably I would have just put it away and forgotten about it, but, again, the punch.

ALK: When you were talking earlier about the "bodiless" character in Patternmaster, *were you referring to Teray? I don't think you ever really do identify him physically.*

OB: Well, he was my first boyfriend [laughter]; and he had this wonderful bodiless body, where he could be marvelously sexy and good looking without my actually ever defining what that meant. So I guess I carried that forward into the fiction. It had not occurred to me that I hadn't described him, but you're right. I was in such a habit of not describing him and when I tried, it didn't work at all.

ALK: His personality comes through perfectly.

OB: He's very young and he's still learning to be a man . . .

Source: Marilyn Mehaffy and AnaLouise Keatin, "'Radio Imagination': Octavia Butler on the Poetics of Narrative," in *MELUS*, Vol. 26, No. 1, Spring 2001, pp. 45–77.

Burton Raffel

In the following excerpt, Raffel reviews Patternmaster *and several other novels by Butler.*

Just as you cannot always tell a book by its cover, so too you cannot always know a novel by its apparent or even by its declared genre. Is *Crime and Punishment* merely a detective (or mystery) novel? *Huck Finn* simply (as Mark Twain once said of it) "another boy's book," *War and Peace* merely historical, *The Trial* only a *Mittel Europa* Perry Mason drama? Is *Middlemarch* (as its title page proclaims) nothing more than "a study of provincial life"?

A book's transcendence of straightforward genre distinctions can be in part thematic, but is mostly a matter of execution: far more importantly than its intention, what a novel *does* with its chosen materials stands directly at the heart of its achievement, as it also defines its very nature. Whatever his own artistic imbalances, no one knew this better than Henry James: "There are bad novels and good novels, as there are bad pictures and good pictures, but that is the only distinction in which I see any meaning ... It goes without saying that you will not write a good novel unless you possess the sense of reality; but it will be difficult to give you a recipe for calling that sense into being. Humanity is immense, and reality has a myriad forms ... and when the mind is imaginative ... it takes to itself the faintest hints of life, it converts the very pulses of the air into revelations." In this 1884 essay, "The Art of Fiction," James therefore lays down one standard: "The only obligation to which in advance we may hold a novel, without incurring the accusation of being arbitrary, is that it be interesting." Or, as the equally but on the face of it oppositely dedicated D. H. Lawrence put it, in a pair of essays published in 1925, "The novel is the highest example of subtle inter-relatedness that man has discovered. Everything is true in its own time, place, circumstance, and untrue outside of its own place, time, circumstance. If you try to nail anything down, in the novel, either it kills the novel, or the novel gets up and walks away with the nail ... The novel is a perfect medium for revealing to us the changing rainbow of our living relationships ... the one bright book of life."

Operating as I try to do, more or less according to the standards set out by James and Lawrence, I have just finished reading, seriatim, eight of the ten published novels of Octavia E. Butler, initially drawn on by the utterly unexpected power and subtly complex intelligence of her extraordinary trilogy, *Xenogenesis*, but sustained and even compelled by the rich dramatic textures, the profound psychological insights, the strong, challenging ideational matrices of virtually all her books. And in my seventh decade of reading fiction, there are not many novelists, neither those so bubbly light as Wodehouse nor even so broadly and diversely rewarding as Dickens or Balzac, Proust or Thomas Mann, who could have held me so long or so closely. Every one of these eight novels (and I stopped at eight only because I could not easily find her

second and third books, some fifteen years out of print) was published under the explicit rubric of "science fiction," but four completely transcend the genre and only one is, though neither weak nor bad, less than absolutely first-rate. Perhaps just as significantly, I do not think any of these eight books could have been written by a man, as they most emphatically were not, nor, with the single exception of her first book, *Patternmaster* (1976), are likely to have been written, as they most emphatically were, by anyone but an African-American. Butler's work, in short, is both fascinating and highly unusual, representing—not only in my mind, but to the growing number of critics and scholars being drawn to it—a richly rewarding and relatively rare fusion of sensibility, perception, and a driven, insightful intelligence.

That this is serious literature I have no doubt. But I must stress from the start that Butler is not, like some science fiction practitioners, overtly (and is never, like more than a few, overbearingly) "literary." Her prose is crystalline, at its best, sensuous, sensitive, exact, but not in the least directed at calling attention to itself. The moving final paragraph of the *Xenogenesis* trilogy—the title signifying "the fancied projection of an organism altogether and permanently unlike the parent"—is thus a model or quietly passionate writing:

> I chose a spot near the river. There I prepared the seed to go into the ground. I gave it a thick, nutritious coating, then brought it out of my body through my right sensory hand. I planted it deep in the rich soil of the riverbank. Seconds after I had expelled it, I felt it begin the tiny positioning movements of independent life.

Carefully, expertly crafted, deeply satisfying as it is to the reader of more than seven hundred preceding pages, and tautly, firmly resolving as it does the major plotline question, this is nevertheless determinedly functional, essentially unobtrusive prose—unlike, say, the highly literary writing of Samuel R. Delany (the only other black s.f. writer of major status): "It was foggy that morning, and the sun across the water moiled the mists like a brass ladle. I lurched to the top of the rocks, looked down through the tall grasses into the frothing inlet where she lay, and blinked." Delany makes it work; as Henry James noted, the very good are very good. But more typically, "literary" s.f. prose reads like the early work of a writer who has since learned better, Walter Jon Williams, whose *Ambassador* of *Progress* opens, with a self-conscious flourish, "In a storm of rain, its brightness a steadier glow among lightning flashes, the shuttle dropped into the high pasture, scattering alarmed cattle who ran in a clatter of bells for the sheltering trees." One can go a good deal farther down the literary ladder; this is for my purposes quite far enough. Plainly, Octavia Butler does not thus tongue a golden-mouthed trumpet, summoning the word-drunk flocks to drink from her overflowing flagons of sweet-scented nectar.

The passionate, abiding importance of the nurturing of new life, which clearly informs the *Xenogenesis* passage I have quoted, equally deeply informs the entire trilogy, as in every book of hers I have read. It seems to me feminist writing at its very best, writing which, like the poetry of Sheryl St. Germain I have discussed in these pages (see *TLR*, Fall 1993), proudly and utterly comfortably accepts itself as female. That strong, self-assured stance toward the fact of femaleness has been in Butler's work from the very first. The protagonist of *Patternmaster* is, unlike the central figures in her other work, male. But he is quickly made to realize that the major female figure in the book, the woman "healer" with whom he binds himself, though clearly female and just as clearly both attractive and attracted to him, is "harder than she felt." Soon thereafter, he learns that her sexual interests are not limited to men. And some pages still further, when another female character makes the mistake of assuming that the healer is "his" woman, she is quickly, forcefully corrected. "I'm my own woman, Lady Darah. Now as before." (The two women have had prior contact, professional rather than sexual.) Finally, the protagonist asks the healer, bluntly, "Which do you prefer," men or women? She replies, "I'll tell you ... But you won't like it ... When I meet a woman who attracts me, I prefer women ... And when I meet a man who attracts me, I prefer men." The protagonist then effectively closes the discussion by announcing: "If that's the way you are, I don't mind." Nor does he, even though, when he asks her to marry him, she refuses, once again for reasons of independence. "As my lead wife," he argues, "you'd have authority, freedom," but she swiftly responds, "How interested would you be in becoming my lead husband?"

For all its excellences, however, *Patternmaster* is a smaller, less complex, less far-reaching fiction; in many ways it suggests the sweep and depth of *Xenogenesis* without quite achieving the trilogy's impact ...

> AMBER HAS THE CHANCE TO MARRY THE GREAT PATTERNMASTER; INSTEAD, SHE PREFERS HER INDEPENDENCE."

Source: Burton Raffel, "Genre to the Rear, Race and Gender to the Fore: The Novels of Octavia E. Butler," in *Literary Review*, Vol. 38, No. 3, Spring 1995, pp. 454–61.

Ruth Salvaggio

In the excerpt that follows, Salvaggio looks at Amber as a powerful female protaganist in Patternmaster.

A traditional complaint about science fiction is that it is a male genre, dominated by male authors who create male heroes who control distinctly masculine worlds. In the last decade, however, a number of women writers have been changing that typical scenario. Their feminine and feminist perspectives give us a different kind of science fiction, perhaps best described by Pamela Sargent's term "Women of Wonder." In a sense, Octavia Butler's science fiction is a part of that new scenario, featuring strong female protagonists who shape the course of social events. Yet in another sense, what Butler has to offer is something very different. Her heroines are black women who inhabit racially mixed societies. Inevitably, the situations these women confront involve the dynamic interplay of race and sex in futuristic worlds. How a feminist science-fiction character responds to a male-dominated world is one thing; how Butler's black heroines respond to racist and sexist worlds is quite another.

Butler's concern with racism and sexism is a conscious part of her vision. As she herself explains, a particularly "insidious problem" with science fiction is that it "has always been nearly all white, just as until recently, it's been nearly all male." Confronting this "problem" head-on, Butler places her heroines in worlds filled with racial and sexual obstacles, forcing her characters to survive and eventually overcome these societal barriers to their independence. Sometimes her black heroines are paired with white men who challenge their abilities; sometimes they are paired with powerful black men who threaten their very autonomy and existence. And, always, the society in which they live constantly reminds them of barriers to their independence. Tracing the plight of each heroine is like following different variations on a single theme, the yearning for independence and autonomy. That Butler's women, despite all odds, achieve that autonomy makes her science fiction a fresh and different contribution to the genre, and makes Butler herself an exciting new voice in the traditional domains of science fiction, feminism, and black literature.

This article is intended to introduce Octavia Butler through her science-fiction heroines—beginning with the defiant Amber in *Patternmaster* (1976), then moving to the confused but powerful Mary in *Mind of My Mind* (1977) and the compromising Alanna in *Survivor* (1978.) The heroine I leave until last is one we encounter as the old woman Emma, hovering in the background of *Mind of My Mind.* She later appears as Anyanwu in Butler's most recent science-fiction novel, *Wild Seed* (1980). In Anyanwu we discover the inspiring force for all of Butler's heroines. And in *Wild Seed* we discover dimensions of Butler's fictive world—not the typical feminist utopia, but a flawed world in which racially and sexually oppressed individuals negotiate their way through a variety of personal and societal barriers.

Germain Greer's term "obstacle race" seems particularly appropriate when discussing Butler and her fiction, largely because the women discussed in both situations confront peculiarly social obstacles. Just as women artists, according to Greer, should be seen "as members of a group having much in common, tormented by the same conflicts of motivation and the same practical difficulties, the obstacles both external and surmountable, internal and insurmountable of the race for achievement," so Butler's heroines share in this social and personal struggle for assertion and understanding.

Their particular struggle, however, is accentuated by the extraordinary mental facilities they possess: Each of Butler's four science-fiction novels is built around a society of telepaths linked to each other through a mental "pattern." Thus when Anyanwu, the African woman in *Wild Seed*, is transported on a slave ship to colonial America, she senses the horror of slavery well before she actually witnesses its real-life horrors. Or when Mary, in *Mind of My Mind*, ultimately confronts her oppressive father, she

kills him through the machinations of a gruesome mental war game. The violence that accompanies such racial and sexual conflict rarely centers on women in the way that it does in Butler's novels. Here we have females who must take the kind of action normally reserved for white, male protagonists. White males, curiously, play an important role in Butler's fiction—sometimes as enemies, sometimes as foils to the women. We might begin with a discussion of them in Butler's first novel, *Patternmaster.* There they dominate the plot until, as one female science-fiction writer describes in a different context, "a woman appeared." Let us begin, then, with the traditional science-fiction plot, and the sudden intrusion of a woman.

It should not be surprising that *Patternmaster*, Butler's first novel, revolves around that typical science-fiction plot: It employs two of the most traditional mythic structures—the inheritance of sons and the journey motif. Rayal, the Patternmaster, is dying; his two sons, Coransee and Teray, vie for control of the Pattern. This rivalry of sons for possession of the father's empire follows the outlines of an archetypal literary construct: Coransee, the stronger and more obvious heir, is defeated by the young and inconspicuous Teray, who ultimately proves himself—despite all outward appearances—to be the righteous heir. Ostensibly, then, *Patternmaster* is a novel which presents us with a "goodson" hero. We are glad when the honest Teray defeats his sinister sibling; we are glad that this decent young man has overcome the corruption and power lust of the older brother.

But all this is not really what *Patternmaster* is about. Before the adventures of our hero begin to unfold, our heroine appears—Amber. The circumstances of her appearance are just as curious as she is. Teray, captive in his brother's household, calls for a "healer" to treat a woman who has been beaten by a man. Enter Amber—a Patternist with extraordinary mental abilities to mend the human body. Immediately, her strong-minded, judgmental character emerges, and before long she and Teray, both captives in Coransee's household, plot to escape.

The story of their escape, their quest for freedom, now begins to change the typical "quest" motif that defines so much science fiction. For one thing, Teray soon realizes that he cannot physically survive their journey without Amber's healing powers—she may, in fact, be more physically powerful than Teray himself. For another, the fascinating relationship between hero and heroine overthrows all of our expectations about conventional romantic and/or sexual love. Because Teray is white and Amber black, their relationship continually reminds us of racial distinctions. And because Amber is a woman who refuses to act out traditional female roles (she will not be any man's wife, she is sexually androgynous, she is stronger and more independent than most men), their relationship continually highlights sexual and feminist issues.

Racism and sexism, then, are matters fundamental to an understanding of both plot and character. Coransee's household, for instance, is hierarchically structured so that those who possess power necessarily abuse those who are powerless: "Housemasters" control "Outsiders" who control "Mutes." In this futuristic mental society in which people have the ability to comprehend each other's thoughts, mental understanding gives way to mind control and ultimately mental oppression. The great "Pattern" itself—holding forth the promise of a mentally-unified culture which might use its combined intellectual powers for human advancement—instead has become the prize for Machiavellian power seekers. No wonder Butler continually uses the term "slavery" to describe the "mental leashes" which keep this society in its state of oppression.

Though Teray, the good son destined to inherit the Pattern, is the figure in whom we must place our trust and hope, it is Amber who most dramatically personifies independence, autonomy, and liberation. Forced, as a captive in Coransee's household, to be one of his "women," she nonetheless boasts, "'But I'm not one of his wives . . . I'm an independent'" (ch. 3). Asked by Teray, whom she truly does come to love, to be his wife, she refuses, "'Because I want the same thing you want. My House. Mine'" (ch. 6). Discussing with Teray her former sexual relationship with another woman, she explains, "'When I meet a woman who attracts me, I prefer women . . . And when I meet a man who attracts me, I prefer men'" (ch. 6). This is clearly not your typical romance heroine. This is certainly not your typical science-fiction heroine. Ironically, *Patternmaster* makes Amber out to be the perfect prize for two rival brothers. Instead, this "golden brown woman with hair that was a cap of small, tight black curls" (ch. 3) turns out to be a model of independence and autonomy.

All ends well in *Patternmaster*. Teray and Amber, with their combined powers, defeat Coransee. And Teray, as the good son, will inherit the Pattern. But it is Amber who somehow stands out as having transcended this political war of wits. In a final exchange between Amber and Teray, she reminds him of how easily she can tip the scales of power. Teray's response is filled with respect, but tinged with fear: "Not for the first time, he realized what a really dangerous woman she could be. If he could not make her his wife, he would be wise to make her at least an ally" (ch. 9) . . .

Marriage is often a feminist issue in Butler's novels. Amber in *Patternmaster* refuses marriage; Mary in *Mind of My Mind* is forced to marry. Alanna's marriage to a non-human creature ironically turns out to be the most successful and respectable of all these marriage situations. Her joining with the Tehkohn leader at once liberates her from the enslaving Christianity of her missionary parents and the enslavement of the meklah drug. Moreover, it offers her the promise of establishing a home with people she has come to respect and love. Perhaps the most bitter irony of the novel is that the Christian earthlings, who call their new home "Canaan," cannot accept the marriage of their daughter into a tribe that will offer them their only hope of peaceful existence . . .

Butler's heroines, as I have been trying to show, can tell us much about her science fiction precisely because they are the very core of that fiction. These novels are about survival and power, about black women who must face tremendous societal constraints. We might very well expect them to be rebellious. We might expect them to reverse the typical male science-fiction stereotype and replace male tyranny with female tyranny. This does not happen. Though Butler's heroines are dangerous and powerful women, their goal is not power. They are heroines not because they conquer the world, but because they conquer the very notion of tyranny.

They are, as well, portraits of a different kind of feminism. Amber has the chance to marry the great Patternmaster; instead, she prefers her independence. Mary can easily become an awesome tyrant; instead, she matures into a caring mother. And Alanna, who possesses no extraordinary Patternist powers, learns to survive through accommodation rather than conflict. That very willingness to accommodate and compromise is what allows Anyanwu to endure over a century of oppressive patriarchy. At the end of each novel, we somehow get the impression that the victory of these women, though far from attained, is somehow pending. White men control the war, while black women fight a very different battle.

Source: Ruth Salvaggio, "Octavia Butler and the Black Science-Fiction Heroine," in *Black American Literture Forum*, Vol. 18, No. 2, Summer 1987, pp. 78–81.

SOURCES

Butler, Octavia E., *Patternmaster*, Doubleday, 1976.

Card, Orson Scott, Review of *Patternmaster* and *Survivor*, in *Fantasy & Science Fiction*, January 1992, pp. 52–54.

"Income," *United States Census Bureau*.http://www.census.gov/hhes/www/income/income.html (access November 1, 2009).

Review of *Patternmaster*, in *Kirkus Reviews*, Vol. XLIV, No. 10, May 15, 1976, p. 612.

Review of *Patternmaster*, in *Publishers Weekly*, Vol. 209, No. 24, June 14, 1976, p. 104.

Wagner, T. M., Review of *Patternmaster*, in *Sci Fi Reviews.net*, http://www.sfreviews.net/patternmaster.html (accessed July 25, 2009).

FURTHER READING

Butler, Octavia E., "A Few Rules for Predicting the Future," in *Essence*, Vol. 31, No. 1, May 2000, p. 165.

In this essay, Butler shares her perspective on how she writes about the future while living in the present.

Gregg, Sandra, "Writing Out of the Box," in *Black Issues Book Review*, Vol. 2, No. 5, September 2000, p. 50.

This interview with Butler and Walter Mosley offers biographical information on both authors as well as insights about their work and experiences gained while being African American authors writing in unexpected genres.

Hampton, Gregory Jerome, and Wanda M. Brooks, "Octavia Butler and Virginia: Hamilton: Black Women Writers and Science Fiction," in *English Journal*, Vol. 92, No. 6, July 2003, pp. 70–74.

This critical essay discusses how both Butler and Hamilton explore themes of alienation, marginalization, and African American identity in their science fiction.

Sturgis, Amy H., "The Parables of Octavia Butler: A Science-Fiction Writer's Rich Libertarian Legacy," in *Reason*, Vol. 38, No. 2, June 2006, p. 72.

This obituary is a tribute to Butler and her power as a writer. Sturgis touches on what she considers Butler's most enduring themes as well.

Young, Earni, "Return of Kindred Spirits: An Anniversary for Octavia E. Butler is a Time for Reflection and Rejoicing for Fans of Speculative Fiction," in *Black Issues Book Review*, Vol. 6, No. 1, January–February 2004, p. 30.

This essay offers biographical information, a discussion of Butler's later works, and a reflection on her novel *Kindred*.

Pelle the Conqueror

MARTIN ANDERSEN NEXØ

1906–1910

Pelle the Conqueror is a novel in four volumes by Danish author Martin Andersen Nexø. Volume 1, *Boyhood*, was published in 1906; Volume 2, *Apprenticeship,* appeared in 1907, followed by Volume 3, *The Great Struggle*, in 1909 and Volume 4, *Daybreak*, in 1910. An English translation by Jessie Muir and Bernard Miall was published between 1913 and 1916. This translation was reprinted in one volume by Mondial in 1990, and it remains in print.

Pelle the Conqueror tells the story of Pelle Karlsson, who immigrates with his father from Sweden to the Danish island of Bornholm in 1877. Pelle is then eight years old, and the novel follows his life into adolescence and adulthood. When he is eighteen he goes to Copenhagen on the Danish mainland and eventually becomes a leader in the labor movement at a time when living and working conditions for the working classes in the heavily industrialized city are extremely poor.

Much of the novel draws on Nexø's own experiences. He was born in Kristianshavn, the Copenhagen slum where his fictional hero Pelle lives when he first moves to Copenhagen. As a boy, Nexø lived on the island of Bornholm, and like Pelle, he was apprenticed to a shoemaker.

Pelle the Conqueror is not very well known in the English-speaking world, but it tells a stirring tale. Not only is it a coming-of-age story about a likeable and capable young man, it also

Martin Andersen Nexø (© *RIA Novosti* / *Alamy*)

shows in vivid detail the rise of the labor movement and of socialist ways of thinking that played such a large role in Danish as well as many other European societies during the course of the twentieth century.

AUTHOR BIOGRAPHY

Martin Andersen (he added Nexø to his name in 1894) was born in Kristianshavn, a poor area of Copenhagen, Denmark, on June 26, 1869, to Hans and Mathilde Jorgen. His father was a stonemason. In 1877 the family moved to Nexø, a coastal town on the island of Bornholm. When he was fifteen, Nexø was apprenticed to a shoemaker for six years. He attended high schools on Bornholm and in Jutland, on the mainland, obtained a teaching certificate, and began to teach at a school in Odense in 1893. However, he became ill with tuberculosis and traveled to Italy and Spain to recover his health. In 1898 he married Margarete Thomsen, and in

the same year published his first book, *Shadows*, a collection of short stories. In 1901, he quit teaching in Copenhagen to become a full-time writer. Five years later he published the first volume of *Pelle the Conqueror*; the fourth and final volume appeared in 1910. This proved to be his most popular and well-known work.

Always politically minded, Nexø joined the Danish Social Democratic Party in 1910. By 1918, however, he had become disillusioned with the Social Democrats and resigned from the party. Later he would join the Danish Communist Party. His next novel, *Ditte, Humanity's Child* (1917–21), was about the failure of the Social Democrats to do anything for the very poor.

In the early 1920s Nexø traveled to the Soviet Union, and from 1923 to 1930 he lived in Germany. His first marriage had ended in divorce in 1913; a second marriage ended in 1924, and in the following year, 1925, Nexø married his third wife, Johanna May.

During World War II Denmark was occupied by Germany. Nexø was arrested for being a member of the Communist Party and spent three months in prison. In 1943 he escaped to Sweden, returning to Denmark after World War II ended in 1945. Between 1945 and 1948 he published the first two volumes of *Morten the Red*, another long novel featuring a working-class hero.

In 1951, Nexø settled in Dresden, East Germany, where he died on June 5, 1954. The third volume of *Morten the Red* was published posthumously in 1957.

PLOT SUMMARY

Volume 1: Boyhood, Chapters I–VIII

Pelle the Conqueror begins in May 1877 in Bornholm, a Danish island. Lasse Karlsson, a widower in his fifties, arrives from Sweden with his eight-year-old son Pelle. They are looking for work as farm laborers, but the search is hard. Eventually Lasse gets hired as a herdsman at Stone Farm. Owned by Kongstrup, this is the biggest farm on the island. Many people work and lodge there in a state of poverty and dependency; it is an oppressive place. Lasse and Pelle live in a makeshift room at the end of the cow stable. They are ordered around by the men in authority at the farm and they have to endure it.

MEDIA ADAPTATIONS

- A 20th Century Fox film of the first volume of *Pelle the Conqueror* was made in 1988, directed by Billie August and starring Pelle Hvenegaard and Max von Sydow. It won an Oscar for Best Foreign Language film and was released on DVD in 2004.

In an early incident, some of the farmworkers whip and humiliate Pelle before he is rescued by Karna, a milkmaid. The older boys and men play practical jokes on Pelle and sneer at him for being Swedish.

Despite the sometimes harsh treatment, Pelle usually enjoys himself; he plays, runs errands, and learns how to look after the cattle. He makes friends with Rud, a boy his own age, and they play together every day; Pelle eagerly learns about the world around him.

Lasse and Pelle visit Kalle, Lasse's brother, who owns his own land, and whom Lasse has not seen for many years. Kalle has a Danish wife and twelve children, with another on the way.

When Lasse and Pelle talk about their future, Lasse is discouraged. They have little money and no freedom; they are virtually slaves on the farm.

Volume 1: Boyhood, Chapters IX–XVI

Pelle learns to stand up for himself, knowing his father cannot always protect him. He begins to learn the value of money and wants to become rich. But his friend Rud persuades him to give him his half-krone piece in exchange for allowing Pelle to whip him with nettles.

Pelle attends school and spends the first two weeks learning the letters of the alphabet. The schoolmaster, Fris, does not like the children and often beats them. Pelle latches on to the youngsters who spend their time at the seashore, even though he cannot swim and gets teased for not knowing as much as they do. Pelle has a few adventures, jumping into the ice-filled water in the winter, just to prove himself, and rescuing Lasse when his father is attacked by a bull.

Kongstrup's wife is kind to Pelle, and he learns from her that she hates her husband. Pelle also observes the conflicts between the bailiff, who is a bully, and the farmhands, especially Erik, who is impulsive and violent. One day the bailiff strikes Erik, but Erik stops him by threatening to take him to the magistrate. Later that Saturday evening, Gustav and Anders fight over a girl, Bodil. Anders stabs Gustav, but Gustav recovers from the wound.

One late autumn there is a break in the routine: the men from Stone Farm go to one of the fishing villages in their horses and carts to collect large quantities of herring, their basic food, as a big catch has come in. The women clean and pickle the fish. The quarrel between the bailiff and Erik comes to a head, and the bailiff knocks Erik senseless by hitting him on the head with a tree branch.

Lasse wants to remarry and takes up with Madam Olsen, a woman who lives near the fishing village. Her husband is missing at sea, presumed drowned. Meanwhile, Bodil elopes with a boy from the farm, and when she returns she is dismissed, while the boy is thrashed by the farmer. Beatings are common at the farm.

Volume 1: Boyhood, Chapters XVII–XXIV

Pelle and the other schoolchildren watch as a ship goes aground on a reef near the fishing village where the school is. A young fisherman, Niels Koller, takes a rowboat out to rescue the sailors. He is drowned, but his companion, Karl Nilen, succeeds in rescuing the men.

On Midsummer Eve, people from all over the island go on an outing to the highest part of the island to celebrate, taking plenty of food and drink with them. Although some fights break out, Pelle and Lasse have their most enjoyable day since they arrived on Bornholm.

However, back at Stone Farm, all is not well. Exasperated beyond endurance by her husband's unfaithfulness, one night Kongstrup's wife takes violent revenge, castrating him. He seems to forgive her, and they live more quietly and affectionately together.

One day, Madam Olsen's husband returns, to everyone's surprise, and Lasse is ashamed of having courted a married woman.

The schoolmaster Fris dies suddenly at his desk, and this ends Pelle's schooling. For a while he goes back to helping his father on the farm. He almost gets thrown out of his confirmation class for beating up the parson's son who insulted Lasse, but Kongstrup's wife intervenes with the parson and Pelle, now fourteen years old, is confirmed. He leaves Lasse and the farm and goes to the island's only town to seek employment.

Volume 2: Apprenticeship, Chapters I–IX

In the town, Pelle is apprenticed to Jeppe Kofod, an old master shoemaker. He learns the trade with several other apprentices, working hard in cramped and stuffy conditions. After a while he is homesick and goes back to Stone Farm to visit Lasse, but he is told that Lasse has gone away. He and Karna are trying to buy a farm or a house.

Pelle enjoys being in the town, but he is often mocked for being a farmer's boy, and he does not like the trade he is learning, which he thinks will earn him no respect. He roams around the town learning all he can between running errands. The street urchins pick on him but he is rescued by Nilen, his former schoolmate. He is no better off financially in the town than he was on the farm. He lives in the apprentices' garret and has few clothes to wear, and they are full of holes. For a while he keeps company with three young sisters, including Manna, who live nearby.

Pelle learns that Lasse and Karna have bought some land, and he visits them. The soil is poor and Lasse is going to have to work very hard to make a living. But he is confident of doing so.

Pelle is lonely and gets sick. But he does make friends with Morten, the son of a strong stone-cutter known as the "Great Power." He also gets closer to Jens, another apprentice, who is Morten's brother. They take him to their home, where their mother is worried because her husband has been gone for several days. He is being sought by the authorities for assaulting Monsen, the wealthy shipbuilder. While Pelle is there, the Great Power returns drunk.

Volume 2: Apprenticeship, Chapters X–XVIII

Pelle listens to all the conversations in the workshop as the local tradesmen gather and gossip. He is still eagerly learning about the world. In the town, many people are close to destitute, and in the workshop the men talk of changing times.

They scornfully mention the new movement of Social Democrats, which they think stands for revolution.

A troupe of actors arrives, and Pelle takes Lasse, who is visiting him, to the theater. The old man does not understand that the play is merely a fiction; upset by what he sees, he makes a scene and walks out.

When spring comes, Pelle is restless. He wants to do something great. He is enthralled by the stories told by Garibaldi, a well-traveled shoemaker who comes to the workshop and tells everyone how the world is.

Pelle wonders why so many people in the town, including himself, remain poor. He thinks he has to hit back against the well-off boys or they will ridicule him. One day he is attacked by three grammar school boys and he kicks one of them hard. This gets him into trouble with the authorities, and he is flogged in the town hall, a deeply humiliating experience. He feels he has been branded and is an outcast from society, but he soon gets back into the favor of the town boys by going swimming with them.

One of the Great Power's children is drowned; this is the first time Pelle has encountered death and he wonders why it happened. He feels called to do something in life, but he does not know what it is.

Business declines at the workshop. Old Jeppe scoffs at the idea that on the mainland, shoes are made in factories. He believes shoe-making must be done by individual craftsmen.

Volume 2: Apprenticeship, Chapters XIX–XXVII

The men in the workshop are alarmed because the pastry cook has hired a new journeyman who is a Social Democrat. At the harbor, the Great Power has become aggressive and is threatening to blow people up with dynamite. The authorities threaten to shoot him, but he is led away by his mother.

That winter is a troubled one. Lasse's fortunes decline, and he seeks a bank loan to try to stay afloat. Jeppe's son, young Master Andres, becomes seriously ill. Then there is a huge snowstorm that cuts everyone off from one another, followed by a famine.

Master Andres dies, and old Jeppe sells the business. Pelle, now eighteen, has one year of his six-year apprenticeship to go, but he refuses to continue, feeling he has already wasted five years. He rents an attic and at first idles his time away, sinking further into poverty and helped only by the kindness of Marie Nielsen, a young widow. He takes work as a laborer at the harbor and mixes with the very poor. Seeking something better, he joins up with Sort, a traveling shoemaker. As they travel around the island, they meet Lasse, who has lost all his land to creditors; his companion, Karna, has died of overwork. Sort generously takes Lasse into his home, while Pelle departs for Copenhagen, determined to make a lot of money.

Volume 3: The Great Struggle, Chapters I–XII

In Copenhagen Pelle quickly discovers that the workers are more active and aggressive in pursuit of their rights than they were on the island. He gets some work from the court shoemaker and others, joins the shoemakers' trade union, and takes lodgings initially with three orphans (Marie, Peter, and Karl) in a run-down area of the city in a building known as the Ark. His goal is to become independent so he can deal directly with his customers and keep all the profits himself. For a while he pays some attention to a young woman, Hanne Johnsen, who lives with her mother in the Ark, but the relationship does not develop and he later regrets that he got caught up with her. Pelle also becomes involved in the growing socialist movement and recruits others to the organization. He feels he is destined to be a pioneer in some way that he does not yet understand. Idealistic, he wants to improve the lot of the poor. After he makes a speech at a public meeting, he meets Otto Stolpe, a veteran union organizer, and Stolpe's daughter, Ellen. Pelle starts to court Ellen.

Pelle is fired from his work with Meyer, the court shoemaker, because of his involvement with the labor movement. Encouraged by Stolpe, Pelle helps to organize an embargo by his union against Meyer. The aim is to shut him out of the labor market by depriving him of workers. But the union is not yet strong enough and the embargo fails. However, Pelle is undaunted by defeat.

Volume 3: The Great Struggle, Chapters XIII–XXIV

Lasse arrives, Pelle having sent for him. Although he is seventy years old, he manages to find some work as a stonebreaker at the lime works. Pelle marries Ellen and they rent a two-room dwelling. For a while Pelle loses interest in union activities.

He prefers to spend his free time at home with his wife and the young son, Lasse, who soon arrives.

However, economic times are hard, and the trade union movement continues to grow. Peter, one of the three orphans who live in the Ark, loses several fingers in an industrial accident. With Pelle's help, he manages to return to work. Shocked by the vulnerability of workers such as Peter, Pelle once more takes charge as president of the shoemakers' union. He leaps back into organizing for the labor movement, his main task being to get employers to stick to the wage agreements they have made, since many employers deliberately keep wages low. But he has a setback when he is fired by Master Beck, from whom he had been receiving a lot of work, because of his union activities.

Undeterred, Pelle again takes on his old enemy, Meyer. This time he is more successful. Meyer is hated so much by the workers that they refuse to work for him. Meyer tries to co-opt Pelle by offering him a well-paid job, but Pelle refuses. After a struggle lasting a year, Meyer's business fails, and Pelle's reputation in the labor movement soars. He quickly achieves his ambition of creating a federation of trade unions that will be able to exert their power as one body across the entire nation.

It is a hard, cold winter for the poor. Unemployment is high. Four hundred laborers, including Pelle, go on strike when the working day is lengthened. Pelle inspires them with a speech, but there is little the men can do when the contractor brings in strikebreakers to take their places.

Volume 3: The Great Struggle, Chapters XXV–XXXVII

In midwinter, Ellen gives birth to a daughter, and Pelle takes a badly paid job as a factory laborer. An engineer happens to notice a drawing Pelle did of some machinery, and he offers Pelle a salaried job in the drawing office. His fortunes are rising. However, tensions between workers and employers have been rising for years. In the spring a strike breaks out where Pelle works, and it soon spreads to other industries. At first it does not involve him, as he works in the office, but when he is asked to do the job of a striking worker he refuses and joins the strike. A great industrial struggle begins; the workers endure hunger and idleness as the employers, especially the iron industry, bring in strikebreakers, many of them from abroad, to keep their factories going. Pelle has much work to do, organizing the nearly forty thousand striking workers. The men acknowledge him as their leader and he tries to inspire them with hopes of victory.

Lasse is reduced to scavenging and begging in order to survive, and Pelle grows distant from his wife. Pelle takes employment at the iron foundry but only so he can convince the strikebreakers there to walk out, which he does successfully. Pelle is hailed by the workers as a hero. But then he discovers that Ellen, desperate to provide for her family, has resorted to prostitution. Pelle leaves her. Still focused on the labor struggle, he persuades the city's sanitation workers to join the strike. This proves to be a key factor, and soon the strike is over, the employers having capitulated. In the meantime, however, Lasse has died. Then the Ark is destroyed in a fire. Pelle saves a child from the burning building, barely escaping alive. The next day Pelle marches at the front of a huge parade of triumphant workers, but within days he is arrested on trumped-up charges of counterfeiting currency, based on a design he once made in an idle moment of a ten-kroner note on a piece of wood.

Volume 4: Daybreak, Chapters I–VIII

Pelle is released from prison after six years. At first during his imprisonment he railed against his fate, but later he calmed down and did a lot of reading and reflection. He has retained his optimism, and he has also forgiven Ellen, knowing she acted only in the best interests of her family. In Copenhagen, he finds conditions for the workers have improved considerably. An election is taking place, and the labor movement expects to win some seats in the parliament. He tracks Ellen down and they are reconciled.

Pelle finds it hard to find work; machinery has taken the place of the individual craftsman in his occupation. The family survives financially for a while by taking in lodgers. Pelle studies socialism in the library, reading the works of Karl Marx. But debts pile up and the family's furniture is repossessed.

Volume 2: Daybreak, Chapters IX–XVI

Meanwhile, Pelle has made friends with an old, wealthy librarian, Brun, who introduces him to the works of Charles Darwin and the idea of the "survival of the fittest"—an idea he rejects. With the help of a loan from Brun, Pelle eventually establishes a cooperative shoemaking workshop in which profits are shared among the workers, although Pelle still reserves for himself the leadership role.

He moves his family out to a house in the country, and they find happiness there. The happiness darkens when Johanna, the companion of Pelle's friend, the author Morten, stays at their house, becomes progressively sicker, and dies. Pelle is once again in demand as a speaker at trade union meetings, where he explains the idea of the cooperative system. He argues with Peter Dreyer, one of his employees, who is anarchistic and favors a more aggressive approach to solving the problem of the relationship between capital and labor.

Volume 4: Daybreak, Chapters XVII–XXIII

Brun and Pelle have the idea of building houses for their workers, to be owned by the cooperative company. They decide to build thirty houses in the country, near Pelle's house, to create a new workers' community, with much room for expansion. They envision free schools and comfortable homes for the elderly. Construction begins in the winter. Pelle is happy and filled with optimistic visions of the future, but not everything is smooth. Always in conflict with the police, Peter Dreyer, before he is due to address a meeting of the unemployed, shoots a policeman who tries to arrest him and then kills himself. Pelle addresses the meeting himself, persuading the men to disperse peacefully and avoid further conflict with the police.

In the final chapter, set in spring, Morten, who has had difficulty finding the right subject for his work, tells Pelle that he plans to write about Pelle's life in a book that will be called *Pelle the Conqueror*.

CHARACTERS

Albinus

Albinus is Pelle's cousin, the son of Kalle, and Alfred's twin brother. He moves to the town and is employed by a tradesman. He likes to perform acrobatic feats and eventually joins a circus.

Alfred

Alfred is Albinus's twin. He leaves the countryside for the town and becomes apprenticed to a painter.

Anders

Anders is a young man who works at Stone Farm. He is involved in a fight with Gustav over the girl, Bodil.

Master Andres

Master Andres is the twenty-nine-year-old shoe-maker who is in charge of the daily running of the workshop where Pelle is apprenticed. He is the son of Jeppe Kofod. Andres is a good-humored, easygoing man who treats Pelle with kindness, and Pelle repays him with loyalty. There is an understanding between them. Andres is a great reader and seems to know about the world, although he never travels. He has a crippled leg and is also sick. He dies young of a lung disease after Pelle has been an apprentice for five years.

Anker

Old Jeppe's first cousin, Anker is considered mad by everyone. He makes a living by selling sand.

Karl Anker

Karl is the youngest of the three orphans who live in the Ark and befriend Pelle. Later he becomes a successful businessman.

Anna

Anna is the daughter of Kalle Karlsson and is Pelle's cousin. She marries Due but it is her fate to be murdered by her husband.

The Bailiff

The bailiff is one of the authority figures at Stone Farm. He is in continual conflict with the men, and is always ready for a fight. When he is attacked by Erik Erikson, he leaves the farm-hand permanently damaged.

Master Beck

Master Beck is a well-established shoemaker who employs Pelle in Copenhagen. He dismisses him later for being involved in union activities.

Bjerregrav

Bjerregrav is the tailor in the town where Pelle is apprenticed. He is an old man who walks with the aid of crutches. He is always questioning everything, wondering why things are the way they are. He dies toward the end of Pelle's apprenticeship.

Bodil

Bodil is a pretty young girl who works at Stone Farm. She takes up with Gustav but then elopes with another young man. When she returns she is dismissed from service by Kongstrup.

Henry Bodker

Henry Bodker is a boy who attends the same school as Pelle. The two boys become friends.

Brun

Brun is a wealthy old librarian and philosopher. He meets Pelle after Pelle has been released from prison and is rebuilding his life. Brun, a bachelor whose best companions are books, befriends and encourages the younger man. He uses much of his inherited wealth to help the poor, and he is instrumental in developing with Pelle the ideal workers' community.

Peter Dreyer

Peter Dreyer is an apprentice of the shoemaker Jeppe. Pelle meets up with him later in Copenhagen and persuades him to join the labor movement. Many years later, Pelle employs him in the cooperative, and Peter is a good worker. He is more extreme in his views than Pelle, however, and is impatient for radical social change. He prints an anarchist newspaper and is harassed by the police. When Peter is about to address a meeting of the unemployed, a policeman tries to arrest him, but Peter kills the policeman and then shoots himself.

Due

Due becomes Kalle's son-in-law when he marries Kalle's daughter, Anna. He finds work as a coachman, and he, Anna, and their children seem reasonably happy. Pelle is therefore shocked to learn later that Due strangles Anna because she has been unfaithful and also kills the children. He gives himself up and is hanged.

Emil

Emil is the oldest apprentice of the shoemaker Jeppe. He becomes a journeyman and goes to Copenhagen, but soon returns disillusioned to Bornholm and finds work as a laborer at the harbor.

Erik Erikson

Erik Erikson is a strong, aggressive young man who works at Stone Farm. He has been arrested for abusing his wife, and for fighting. Lasse thinks he is a troublemaker. Erik and the bailiff are enemies, and Erik seeks a confrontation with him. But he comes out of it the loser. The bailiff hits him on the head with a tree branch, knocking him senseless and permanently damaging his brain. He becomes docile and half-witted.

Ferdinand

Ferdinand is the eighteen-year-old son of Madam Frandsen. As a child he stood up for his mother against his drunken father. He is resourceful and looks after his mother in whatever way he can, which may include committing robberies. He is sought by the police and is eventually arrested and imprisoned.

Madam Frandsen

Madam Frandsen is the lonely, widowed mother of Ferdinand.

Fris

Fris is the village schoolmaster in Bornholm. He dislikes the children and uses his cane on them, but after they leave the school he thinks more fondly of them. He does not teach the children much reading and writing but he does like leading them in hymn-singing. Fris dies suddenly at his desk, bringing Pelle's schooling to an end.

Garibaldi

Garibaldi is a thin, tall, adventurous shoemaker who has traveled the world. When he returns for a few days to Jeppe's workshop, he keeps all the men, including the young Pelle, enthralled with his tales of what he has seen on his travels.

Gustav

Gustav is a seventeen-year-old worker at Stone Farm. He likes Bodil but she prefers a tailor's apprentice in the village. He also picks a fight with Anders over Bodil.

Mason Hansen

Mason Hansen has been a member of the labor movement since the earliest days, but he becomes a strikebreaker so he can support his family. He is harassed by the strikers and eventually commits suicide.

Johanna

Johanna is Hanne's daughter. Hardship causes her to become a child prostitute, from which she is rescued by Morten, who takes her in and cares for her until her death from tuberculosis.

Hanne Johnsen

Hanne Johnsen is Madam Johnsen's daughter. She is beautiful and others refer to her as the princess. She dreams of a Prince Charming who will rescue her from a life of poverty. She flirts with Pelle but they do not become seriously involved. Later she gives birth to an illegitimate child. Hanne dies strangely: she has a fever but goes to a dance and dances herself to death.

Madam Johnsen

Madam Johnsen is Hanne's mother. She lives in the Ark and endures a life of hard work and poverty. Her husband drowned himself in the sewer. Her one desire is to see her homeland, Jutland, before she dies, but she is too poor to afford the train fare and dies unfulfilled.

Jens Jorgensen

Jens Jorgensen is a son of the "Great Power." He is the second-youngest apprentice at Jeppe's workshop. When he becomes a journeyman, he does not have the nerve to go to Copenhagen, like many others do. Instead, he remains in the town on Bornholm, renting a room and repairing the shoes of the poor.

Morten Jorgensen

Morten Jorgensen is a son of the "Great Power." He and Pelle become close friends when Pelle is an apprentice. They meet again in Copenhagen where Morten is working as a pastry cook. Morten is a quiet man who reads a lot and later becomes a writer. He and Pelle have many discussions about the labor movement, and usually disagree about important points. But they remain friends and are reunited after Pelle returns from prison. Morten has taken into his home Johanna, a former child prostitute, and is devastated when she dies of tuberculosis.

Peter Jorgensen

Peter Jorgenson is a stonecutter and architect who is known as the "Great Power" because of his enormous strength. He is the father of Jens and Morten. Jorgensen is an unpredictable man, given to sudden outbursts of violence, as when he assaults Monsen, the shipowner. He is also talented and creative. A self-taught architect, he won a contract to construct a bridge, but he made enemies because of his arrogance. Now he is hated and feared by almost everyone. He had ideas for how to proceed in a project at the harbor, but his plans were stolen by those in charge. He ends up as an embittered laborer.

Kalle Karlsson

Kalle Karlsson is Lasse's brother. He owns some land on Bornholm and lives with his wife, mother-in-law, and thirteen children. They live on modest means but they are happy. Kalle is a good-natured man who is content with what he has.

Kalle's Mother-in-Law

Kalle's mother-in-law is an old, blind, but content woman. She even regains her sight when Pelle is a boy, and she spends much time recalling events from her happy life. She dies with no regrets.

Lasse Karlsson

Lasse Karlsson is a Swede who arrives on the Danish island of Bornholm with his eight-year-old son Pelle in order to find work. Lasse's wife has just died, and he arrives on Bornholm with little more than the clothes on his back. He is in his fifties and has a stooped appearance, as if he has been bent by too much hard work. Lasse is fiercely devoted to Pelle and looks after him as best he can. He never beats him. He frequently brags to his son about how he will wreak vengeance on anyone who crosses either of them, but in practice he is a meek man who knows he is in no position to assert himself. Lasse is disappointed by the continual poverty he must endure, and eventually manages to strike out on his own, buying some land with his companion Karna. But the soil is poor and the work is hard, and Lasse is eventually forced to give the land up because he cannot satisfy his creditors. When he is seventy he joins Pelle in Copenhagen and is able to find work even at his advanced age. But when times become hard he is forced into scavenging for food and living in a cellar in a granary.

Maria Karlsson

Maria Karlsson is Kalle Karlsson's wife. She is a cheerful, hard-working Danish woman.

Pelle Karlsson

Pelle Karlsson is the son of Lasse Karlsson. He is eight years old when his father first brings him to the island of Bornholm. Pelle is a lively, curious boy who makes himself useful around the farm. He is subject to teasing and bullying by the older people there, but this does not affect him for long. He is basically an optimistic, resilient boy who does not get embittered by his poverty or his status as an outsider, a Swede, growing up on a Danish island. His father believes Pelle is born lucky, and Pelle himself believes that eventually he will find something great to do. When he is fourteen he leaves the farm for the town and is apprenticed to a shoemaker. As the youngest apprentice, he is again subject to some bullying, but he learns his trade well. At the age of eighteen he departs for Copenhagen on the mainland, and soon becomes involved in the labor movement. He becomes passionately committed to the cause of the working man and finds he has a gift for organization. Others look to him as a leader. He marries Ellen Stolpe and they start a family, but when times get hard and Ellen resorts to prostitution to bring in money, Pelle leaves her. Soon after his triumph in leading a successful strike, he is imprisoned for six years on trumped-up charges. When he is released he is more reflective, less impulsive, and more mature. He is reconciled with his wife and returns to the labor movement with his visionary idea for the formation of workers' cooperatives. Having triumphed over adversity, he is a happy man.

Karna

Karna is a dairymaid at Stone Farm. She is a big woman of about forty. She becomes Lasse's companion, although they never actually marry. They do buy some land with money Karna has saved, and they live together, but the land is hard to cultivate, and Karna eventually dies of overwork.

Jeppe Kofod

Jeppe Kofod is the master shoemaker who owns the workshop at which Pelle is apprenticed. He is from the old school and likes to keep the apprentices in line with strict discipline. He is often referred to as the "old master."

Jorgen Kofod

Jorgen Kofod is the baker in the town on Bornholm. He is the brother of old Jeppe, and he likes to discuss current events with the men in the shoemakers' workshop.

Peter Kofod

Peter Kofod is a poor orphan who attends the village school. He is known as "Howling Peter" because he is always crying. He twice tries to hang himself. He later becomes a sailor and meets up again with Pelle in Copenhagen. He has learned how to take care of himself and is good in a fight.

Niels Koller

Niels Koller is a young man who tries to rescue some sailors from a ship that has hit a reef. He is drowned in the attempt.

Kongstrup

Kongstrup is the owner of Stone Farm. He came to Bornholm from Copenhagen about twenty years before Lasse and Pelle came, and when he first acquired the farm he had many ideas for how to improve it, and he treated his workers well. But things changed and now the place has an oppressive atmosphere. The farmworkers are kept poor and dependent. Kongstrup himself is amiable and rather easygoing, but his flaw is that he cannot stop seducing women and fathering children by them, much to his wife's distress. Eventually she can accept his behavior no more and attacks him in the night, castrating him. After that he becomes more docile and affectionate with her.

Kongstrup's wife

Kongstrup's wife is an unhappy woman, devastated by her husband's infidelity. She can often be heard crying, and she drinks in secret. She tells Pelle she wants to kill her husband, although she also regards him as the most handsome man in the world.

Manna

Manna is the oldest of three young sisters who live nextdoor to the shoemakers' workshop when Pelle is apprenticed there. Manna is a tomboy and she and Pelle become friends. She is jealous when Pelle makes friends with Morten, but when she gets older she forgets all about Pelle, causing him some disappointment.

Marie

Marie is one of the three orphans who befriend Pelle in the Ark in Copenhagen. She later dies in childbirth.

Karl Meyer

Karl Meyer is the court shoemaker in Copenhagen. Originally from Germany, he is an arrogant, unscrupulous man who succeeds at the expense of others. Pelle takes him on in an industrial dispute and ruins his business.

Monsen

Monsen is a shipowner and is the wealthiest man on Bornholm.

Marie Nielsen

Marie Nielsen is a kind widow and former dancer who befriends Pelle when he is at a low ebb after having left his apprenticeship.

Nikas

Nikas is the journeyman at old Jeppe's workshop. Something of a bully, he is referred to as little Nikas, and he is in a position of authority over Pelle.

Karl Nilen

Nilen is one of the boys at the village school. He is a strong, aggressive boy who is always fighting, and Pelle admires him. Later he moves to the town and becomes a baker's boy.

Long Ole

Long Ole is a farmhand at Stone Farm who loses three fingers in an accident involving a threshing machine. Unable to work, he is taken in by Johanna Pihl.

Madam Olsen

Madam Olsen lives near Stone Farm. Lasse is all set to marry her, thinking she is a widow, but her husband, believed lost at sea, returns unexpectedly.

Per Olsen

Per Olsen is a farmhand who is accused by a girl of fathering her child. He goes to court and swears her story is untrue. Not everyone believes him, but he becomes the head man at Stone Farm and is well liked.

Peter

Peter is one of the three orphans who befriend Pelle in the Ark. Later, he loses first his right hand and then his left hand in industrial accidents. He becomes a messenger and also studies anarchist literature.

Johanna Pihl

Johanna Pihl was seduced by Kongstrup when she was a dairymaid at Stone Farm. Her son Rud is Kongstrup's son. She is referred to as the sow, because of her weight.

Rud Pihl

Rud Pihl is Pelle's playmate when they are both young boys.

Pipman

Pipman is an old shoemaker in Copenhagen from whom Pelle gets work when he first moves there.

Sort

Sort is a traveling shoemaker and also a preacher. Pelle and he travel around the country for a while after Pelle quits his apprenticeship.

Sort is fond of Pelle and is sorry to lose him when Pelle leaves for Copenhagen.

Ellen Stolpe

Ellen Stolpe is the daughter of Otto Stolpe. She is tall and dark, Pelle is immediately attracted to her, and they marry after a short romance. Ellen is not interested in Pelle's work in the labor movement but only in their family life and the improvement of their home. The couple is happy at first, but after Pelle returns to his labor activism, he neglects his family, and Ellen, desperate to provide for them, is forced to turn to prostitution. When Pelle finds out, he leaves her, but the two are reconciled after Pelle is released from prison. Ellen works hard to ensure their home life is happy.

Otto Stolpe

Otto Stolpe is an old and respected organizer in the labor movement. He becomes Pelle's father-in-law when Pelle marries Ellen, Stolpe's daughter.

THEMES

Coming of Age

The novel shows how Pelle grows from boy to man and discovers his purpose in life. As a child he relies on the protection of his father, Lasse, and there is a strong bond between the two. Pelle's boundaries are those of the farm on which he lives and its immediate environment. At first he is at the mercy of others, and he finds they can be cruel. It is not an advantage to be a Swedish boy on a Danish island. But Pelle is blessed with a natural strength, resilience, and optimism. He appears to carry no scars from his harsh boyhood. His first major leap into adulthood comes when he is fourteen years old and he leaves the farm to seek employment in the town. As an apprentice, he is once more in a subordinate position and has to endure the discipline meted out by others in the workshop. He also learns that being a cobbler is not a very high station in life and others do not regard it with respect. He notes the other apprentices are not successful, and feels as if he has wasted five years. For a while he sinks into apathy, working at the harbor as a laborer, without purpose or goal. However, despite these setbacks and although his early years are all spent in poverty, Pelle "always retained an obstinate feeling of his own worth, which no one could take away from him."

TOPICS FOR FURTHER STUDY

- Write an essay in which you discuss Pelle's relationship with Ellen. Why is he attracted to her in the first place? Why does he grow apart from her, and why does he return to her when he is released from prison? How would you characterize their relationship at the end of the novel?

- In Chapter VIII of Volume 3, *The Great Struggle,* Morten reads to Pelle a poem he has written about the struggles of the poor. None of the words of the poem appear in the text. Write the poem you think Morten, a passionate defender of the poor, might have written, and read it to your class.

- Make a drawing or painting of Pelle addressing a crowd. Try to capture Pelle's charisma, the power he has over his audience, and the feeling in the crowd that he is their leader.

- Research some of the heroes of the American labor movement and give a class presentation, with the use of PowerPoint, about two or three such figures. Describe the contributions they made and why they might be considered heroes. Names you might want to research include César Estrada Chávez, Eugene Victor Debbs, Joe Hill, Peter J. McGuire, Mother Jones, and Lucy Randolph Mason. You can find information about Chávez in *Farmworker's Friend: The Story of Cesar Chavez* by David R. Collins (1996).

It is this quality that stands Pelle in good stead when he goes to Copenhagen at the age of eighteen. It is during these Copenhagen years that he discovers his true calling in life. He has always been concerned with the welfare of others, and the plight of the poor moves him to tears. He also discovers he has the ability to organize people, and he emerges as a leader. He is a charismatic speaker, passionate and eloquent in his calls for the workers to organize themselves, and others look up to him. Murmurs of excitement go around the crowd when he enters a hall for a meeting.

While in Copenhagen, Pelle is instrumental in winning a great victory for organized labor, yet he also knows failure and neglect. However, he turns these setbacks to advantage. Imprisoned for six years on false charges, he reads widely and reflects. He emerges not embittered but wiser and steadier, and still optimistic about the role he can play in improving the pay and conditions of the working class. He decides to stand apart from the mainstream labor movement, and he follows his own instincts about the way of the future. He is a visionary.

In his personal life, too, Pelle is successful. He has a good capacity for friendship, especially among the poor folk, and others like him. His relationships with women eventually work out well, although they are troubled at first. He has his first sexual experience with Manna while he is still an apprentice; she later ignores him. Later, in Copenhagen, he flirts with Hanne but will not get drawn into a deep relationship with her. Eventually he finds love with Ellen and marries her, although for many years their relationship is a troubled one. He neglects her for his union work, just as he also neglects Lasse for a while. Pelle is not perfect, but he has the capacity to learn from his experience. He and Ellen go through many upheavals, separations, and disappointments before they finally learn how to love in a mature and consistent way, forgiving each other for their weaknesses and failures.

The Fight for Social Justice

As Pelle grows up, he experiences several different kinds of social and labor organization. At Stone Farm, a feudal system prevails. The workers are entirely dependent on the owner of the farm, and he keeps them living at an almost subsistence level. They have no rights and are subject to arbitrary discipline and dismissal. They do not organize collectively. Nexø shows how weak the men in this situation are in the story of Erik Erikson. Erik is a very strong man physically, and he rebels against his dependent situation by attacking the bailiff. But the bailiff repays force with even more force, and Erik ends up brain-damaged and docile. A shadow of his former self, he follows the bailiff around like an idiot. Erik's fate shows the futility of individual action in this feudal system. The employer holds all the power. Another example of how the feudal system oppresses people is when Lasse finally

strikes out on his own. All the best land is already in the hands of the large farm owners, and Lasse and Karna have to make do with some acres of poor, unproductive land and endure a life of backbreaking labor and poverty.

When Pelle moves to the town he becomes part of a declining guild system. Shoemakers and tailors are craftsmen who work directly with their hands to create their product. But the days of the individual artisan are numbered, and on the mainland shoes are now being made in factories. When Pelle moves to Copenhagen he finds a city that is highly industrialized. The population has swelled as people migrate to the city from rural areas. But there are no labor laws to regulate the new industries. Pay is low, hours are long, working conditions are dangerous, and living conditions terrible. This exploitation of the working man results in a widespread brutalization of life, as shown in the many individual portraits of lives blasted by drunkenness and violence. People suffer early deaths because of the unsanitary conditions in which they are forced to live; children raise themselves as orphans, and some (like Morten's Johanna) get pushed into prostitution.

In Copenhagen, Pelle finds that a journeyman cobbler who takes pride in his craft has little power and can easily be exploited by the bigger employers. He begins to realize that only through collective bargaining can the workers claim their rights to fair pay and decent working conditions. He plunges into an activist role in the labor movement, accepting the premise that in a capitalist economy the workers have nothing to sell but their labor. This is at once their weakness and their strength. If they elect to withdraw their labor, they have a powerful weapon with which to force employers to accede to their demands for fair treatment. Much of Volume 3 is taken up with this ruthless struggle between employers and workers. Early strikes do not succeed but eventually, when all the workers join together across industries, they are successful. In what amounts to a general strike in which vital services in society are about to break down, the employers capitulate. Over the next few years, working conditions in factories improve and workers' rights are recognized. Social Democrats and representatives of the labor movement win seats in the Danish parliament. However, unemployment is still on the rise and conditions for the very poor have not improved.

Max von Sydow as Lassefar and Pelle Hvenegaard as Pelle the 1988 film version of Pelle the Conqueror *(© Photos 12 | Alamy)*

The Utopian Ideal

After he is released from prison, Pelle acts on his vision of the future ideal workers' community. He has long thought about establishing cooperative enterprises in which all profits from the business would be shared equally. When he meets the wealthy Brun he sees an opportunity to put this vision into action. He establishes his own workshop in which he and the other workers make high-quality, hand-sewn boots and shoes. He also develops his plan for creating ideal communities for workers. In addition to the workshops themselves, these communities would include housing specially built in settings close to nature, not in overpopulated, unhealthy cities. Pelle rejects the more radical ideas of Peter Dreyer and the anarchists who are prepared for violent confrontation with the employers and civilian authorities. He regards his vision as the way of the future for workers throughout the world: "a world-wide, peaceful revolution which was to subvert all existing values....His system of profit-sharing must be the starting-point for a world-fight between Labor and Capital!"

STYLE

Folktale and Myth

The basic structure of the novel resembles a folktale or myth about the all-conquering hero. The hero is born into poor or humble circumstances, but he overcomes adversity through his perseverance, strength, and creativity. He battles the dragon, demon, or other evil being and succeeds in leading and liberating his people. He also gets to marry the princess. That Nexø had such a scheme in mind is clear from the comments made by Pelle's friend Morten at the end of the novel, when he announces that he intends to write his "great work" about "a prince who finds the treasure and wins the princess." This suggests that Pelle, although born poor, is a natural prince who has now found his true status. (The princess, of course, is his wife, Ellen.) Indeed, even as a boy Pelle feels he is destined for something special; despite his disappointments, he seems blessed with good fortune, as if the gods favor him. As a boy his hair forms a "cow's lick" over his forehead, which according to folklore means he will be lucky. After he has grown to maturity he enters upon his great adventure, and the people acknowledge him as their leader. Pelle is "idolized" in the Ark, where he lives, and "his comrades looked up to him; if there was anything important in hand their eyes involuntarily turned to him."

The dragon Pelle takes on and kills is the industrial system that exploits and destroys the workers; this is the "evil power" that is stifling the hope of the people. It is personified in the figure of Meyer, the court shoemaker, and it is as if Pelle and Meyer engage in single combat, like the good and evil figures in a myth. Pelle is presented as a "righteous avenger," and Meyer is the "colossus" who must be brought down. When this happens the people rejoice; even before the great victory they have been commenting about Pelle, "The devil couldn't stand up against him."

Pelle therefore is at once prince and savior. There is also an element of religious myth involved. Pelle agrees wholeheartedly with one of the labor leaders who refers to his people as wandering in the wilderness, just as the Israelites wandered in the wilderness until they were led by Moses to the Promised Land. Now, the man says, the workers, the poor people of the world, stand at the brink of the Promised Land. The religious element is reinforced by references to the New Testament that suggest Pelle's role as savior. He believes the labor movement is fulfilling Christ's promise to the poor. He calls it "the great Gospel of the Poor," and he feels he is a servant of this great work. When he first joins the trade union he feels it is like a baptism (just as Christ was literally baptized by John the Baptist), which suggests a kind of religious dimension to his thinking, although he is not an overtly religious man. He does, however, believe he is leading his people into a new era, which is symbolized both by the title of the last volume, *Daybreak*, and the name he and Ellen give to their house in the country, Dawn.

Symbolic Events

Many of the events in the novel have a symbolic as well as literal meaning. This means that such events signify some deeper truth that the author wishes to convey. For example, he frequently uses the deaths of characters to make a point about the direction in which society is developing. This can be seen in the deaths of Kalle's

mother-in-law in *Boyhood*, of Master Andres in *Apprenticeship*, and of Peter Dreyer in *Daybreak*. Kalle's mother-in-law represents the old, vanishing way of life in which people lived close to the land, in harmony with nature and each other. When she dies it suggests that those days are gone forever—although Pelle will try to re-create them to suit new social and economic times. The death of Master Andres suggests the dying out of the individual craftsman before the tide of industrialization. The old guild system is breaking down. The death of the anarchist Dreyer suggests that the violent confrontation with the authorities—a struggle he represents— is not the way of the future; it is the nonviolent visionary Pelle and the scholarly thinker and writer Morten who survive to greet the new age.

There is also a symbolic element in the episode in which the Ark burns down. This dilapidated building symbolizes all that is wrong with the social and economic system that forces so many into poverty and degradation. Significantly, the Ark burns down immediately after the labor movement wins its massive struggle with the employers. This shows that a new time is coming, and the bad things that characterize the old system are being destroyed. Significant too is that Pelle braves the flames and rescues an infant. The infant symbolically represents the new birth that Pelle is helping to bring about for the whole society.

HISTORICAL CONTEXT

The Labor Movement in Nineteenth-Century Denmark

The Great Struggle, the third volume of *Pelle the Conqueror*, focuses on the progress of the labor movement in Copenhagen and Denmark as a whole during the 1890s. By that time the labor movement had been an organized force for over twenty years. It took a major step forward in 1871, when the socialist Louis Pio (1841–1894) created an organization that combined trade unions with a new political party that later became the Social Democratic Party. The new organization immediately came into conflict with the government, and three of its leaders, including Pio, were arrested and charged with treason. In 1877, the authorities paid for the three leaders to emigrate to the United States. They settled in Kansas and tried to set up a socialist colony, but the experiment was short-lived.

COMPARE
&
CONTRAST

- **Late nineteenth century:** As the capital city of Denmark, Copenhagen grows rapidly in population. By the turn of the century, 400,000 people live there.

  Today: The population of Greater Copenhagen and its regions is 1,800,000. The British magazine *Monocle* ranks Copenhagen as the finest city in the world for quality of life for its residents.

- **Late nineteenth century:** The Social Democratic Party is formed in Denmark and begins to challenge the existing conservative power structure through parliamentary means. The party wins seats in the Folketing (People's Assembly).

  Today: Denmark has a center-left government. In national elections in 2007, the largest four parties in the 179-seat Folketing were the Liberal Party (46 seats), Social Democrats (45), Danish People's Party (25), and Socialist People's Party (23). In 2009, the prime minister is Lars Løkke Rasmussen, the leader of the Liberal Party.

- **Late nineteenth century:** As Denmark rapidly becomes industrialized, labor unions are formed to fight for shorter working hours, higher wages, and more job security.

  Today: Labor unions play a large role in Danish society. About 75 percent of employees are members of a union, and employers and unions consider themselves partners, not adversaries. Union representatives even sit on company boards.

In the 1880s, the Danish labor movement grew stronger, and in 1884 the first Social Democrats were elected to the *Folketing* (People's Assembly). In *Pelle the Conqueror*, these are the socialist politicians who are so despised and feared among the traditional workers at Jeppe's workshop on the island of Bornholm, and who dislike the influx of new ideas.

By 1890, a national worker's organization had been established, and throughout the decade organized labor sought to assert itself against the power of the employers. In the spring of 1899, there was a massive labor dispute in Denmark, with many strikes. This was the dispute at the heart of *The Great Struggle*. Many at the time feared the conflict was so serious it would lead to a national economic crisis. But the dispute was settled after almost five months. (In the novel, the dispute lasts for a year.) Under what was known as the September Agreement, trade unions were granted the right to represent their workers. This is the victory Pelle celebrates in the novel, although historians argue the victory was largely symbolic and did not effect major change. But the long strike did convince the workers that they were able to organize and stand up to their employers.

The Social Democrats continued to increase their political representation. In 1898, the party won 12 of 114 seats in the *Folketing,* and this increased to 14 in 1901.

Realism

Although Pelle the Conqueror employs elements of folktale and myth, it belongs for the most part to the nineteenth-century literary movement known as realism. According to M. H. Abrams, writing in *A Glossary of Literary Terms,* "The realist sets out to write a fiction which will give the illusion that it reflects life as it seems to the common reader." *Pelle the Conqueror*, for example, gives a detailed, realistic portrait of life on Stone Farm, in old Jeppe's workshop, and in strike-torn Copenhagen. The setting, characters, dialogue, and unfolding of the plot all follow the principles of realism. Realist writers focused on ordinary or average people in everyday situations; the focus was not on the aristocracy or the

Pelle the Conqueror

Houses in Bornholm (© WoodyStock / Alamy)

powerful but on middle-class and sometimes working-class characters. Thus *Pelle the Conqueror* examines the lives of the poor; it accurately reports what life was like for the disadvantaged people in Danish society at the time.

As a literary movement, realism is associated with the novels of Honoré de Balzac, Gustave Flaubert, George Eliot, and William Dean Howells, among many others.

CRITICAL OVERVIEW

When *Pelle the Conqueror* was first published in English, Danish scholar Otto Jespersen wrote that he expected to see the book win a favorable reception beyond the shores of Denmark. He writes of the author, "His sympathy is of the widest, and he makes us see tragedies behind the little comedies, and comedies behind the little tragedies, of the seemingly sordid lives of the working people whom he loves." (His comments are reprinted as a Note in Mondial's one-volume edition of the novel.) Jespersen was correct in his

assessment, and reviews in the United States were positive. The reviewer for the *Nation,* reviewing the final volume, notes that in its totality, the novel is "the story of a manhood struggling with all sorts of obstacles, often thrown down and trampled upon, yet making its way steadily and with unquenchable confidence, towards a mastery of life." The reviewer concludes:

> Such a work of imagination as this, with its deep humor, its deep humanity, brings home to us, as nothing else can, the artificial nature of those boundaries which language and custom set between one race and another. It is a book for the world; one cannot lay it down without a sense of quickened emotion and enlarged vision.

After the film version of Volume 1 of the novel garnered some attention in 1988, that volume was reprinted to equally generous reviews. For example, in the *New York Times Book Review,* Constance Decker Kennedy argues that the author's "robust sense of life, his convincing evocation of childhood, his moral vision—and, above all, his brave young hero—make this novel generous and grand." Writing in 1991 after the reprinting of the second volume, the reviewer for

Publishers Weekly notes the darker aspects of the novel: "Pelle is caught in the archaic artisan system, which is more effective at exploiting its young workers than training them."

CRITICISM

Bryan Aubrey

Aubrey holds a Ph.D. in English. In this essay he discusses how in Pelle the Conqueror *the characters Morten Jorgensen and Peter Dreyer act as foils to Pelle.*

When the film based on the first volume of *Pelle the Conqueror* was released in 1988, it created new interest in the novel among English-speaking readers. The novel as a whole, however, is still not very well known in the United States, and no moviemaker has yet adapted the remaining three volumes for film. Were such a project ever to be attempted, it would of course have to be selective, since not all of this vast and complex novel could be conveyed on screen. Perhaps such a film might focus on the lives of just three characters out of the more than seventy that appear in the novel. These three characters might be Pelle Karlsson, Morten Jorgensen, and Peter Dreyer. Nexø not only features these characters in Volumes 2, 3, and 4, he also uses Morten and Peter as foils for Pelle. In literature, a foil is a character who sets off another character by contrast.

These three characters start out with a lot in common. They are about the same age, and they meet when they are in their mid-teens. They all come from poor families and do not receive much formal education. Without any social advantages, they all at different times find their way to Copenhagen, seeking to make their way in the world. All three are serious young men who think deeply about social issues such as how to secure justice, including better pay and working conditions, for the working classes. But they reach very different conclusions about how to proceed.

Pelle meets Peter Dreyer first. Like Pelle, Peter is apprenticed as a shoemaker to old Jeppe in the town on Bornholm. The town is Rønne, although it is not named in the novel. Peter is slightly older than Pelle, and in *Apprenticeship* he does not appear as an important character. He is presented as "the rogue," a mischievous, aggressive boy who has the nerve to talk back to old Jeppe. When he finishes his apprenticeship, he

> PELLE . . . HAS A RARE GIFT, THAT OF THE ORATOR WHO IS ABLE TO TAP INTO THE COLLECTIVE CONSCIOUSNESS OF HIS AUDIENCE, TELLING THEM WHAT THEY LONG TO HEAR, ARTICULATING IT BETTER THAN THEY EVER COULD, AND INSPIRING THEM TO BELIEVE GREAT ACCOMPLISHMENTS ARE POSSIBLE."

is more than happy to take the steamer to Copenhagen to try to find work. But Pelle hears that he meets with little success and becomes a postman, making some extra money by practicing his shoemaking craft at night.

When he is an apprentice, Pelle also meets Morten, and they immediately become close friends. Morten is the son of the "Great Power," and knows a thing or two about growing up in poverty with a father who drinks and is reviled by almost everyone. Morten possesses a "gentle capable mind," and likes to tell Pelle about the books he has been reading. Pelle professes contempt for books, saying he wants to discover the world directly. He and Morten lose touch when Pelle walks out on his apprenticeship and sinks into apathy for a while.

The two young men meet again by chance in the sprawling, recently industrialized Copenhagen soon after Pelle arrives. They are both trying to make it on their own. Morten has taken a job as a pastry cook. He has become radicalized and tells Pelle the working people have been cheated of what is rightfully theirs and must organize themselves so they can get it back. He has been studying, quite unlike Pelle, who at this point is not one to spend his time reading books. It is Morten who gives Pelle his first introduction to socialist thinking. He thinks a working man should be as well paid as a doctor, since the workers are the ones who produce everything.

Pelle is still naïve about such matters, but when he sees the miseries wrought by poverty he too realizes the need for organization. He and Morten attend meetings together, and Morten begins to respect him. Morten tells Pelle that working people are as valuable as the counts and barons of the world, urging him to have

WHAT DO I READ NEXT?

- *Ditte Everywoman* is another long novel by Nexø (the title is sometimes translated as *Ditte, Humanity's Child*). It is a three-volume work consisting of *Girl Alive, Daughter of Man,* and *Toward the Stars,* and was first published between 1917 and 1921. The novel was reprinted by Mondial in 2007. It follows the life of Ditte, a girl who was born into poverty in early twentieth-century Denmark. Ditte spends her early years as a servant on a farm before moving to Copenhagen and trying to make her way in the world as a working woman with a family to support.

- Widely considered the masterpiece of French writer Émile Zola, *Germinal* (1885) is a novel about a strike by coal miners in France in the 1860s. The main character is Étienne Lantier, a young man unable to find work who travels to northern France to take a difficult and dangerous job as a coal miner. He soon learns about the appalling conditions under which the miners work, and he ends up leading a strike that creates a life-or-death situation for the miners and their families. Like *Pelle the Conqueror,* the novel shows the ruthlessness of the conflict between employers and workers in nineteenth-century Europe. *Germinal* is available in a 2004 Penguin Classics edition.

- *Coming of Age Around the World: A Multicultural Anthology,* edited by Faith Adiele and Mary Frosch (2007), is a collection of twenty-four stories by international authors about young people as they grow up and seek to understand themselves and their place in the world. Introductions to the stories provide historical and cultural context. The writers include Patrick Chamoiseau, Alexandra Fuller, Oonya Kempadoo, Rohinton Mistry, Chang-rae Lee, Colum McCann, Ben Okri, Marjane Satrapi, and Hanan al-Shaykh.

- *A Separate Peace* (2003) by John Knowles is a coming-of-age tale for young adult readers, set in a New England prep school just prior to World War II. Two boys form a complex friendship that eventually leads to violence and a confession. The novel has received excellent reviews for the way it captures the feelings of the teenagers involved.

- *Oliver Twist,* a novel by Charles Dickens first published in 1838, tells the story of a young orphan boy growing up in poverty. Oliver spends his early years in a workhouse and then journeys to London, where he is given accommodations by the notorious criminal Fagin and his young gang of pickpockets. The innocent Oliver thinks they make wallets and handkerchiefs. Like the picture presented of Copenhagen in *Pelle the Conqueror, Oliver Twist* shows the brutal effects of industrialism in nineteenth-century London. A modern edition was published by Tor Classics in 1998.

- *North and South,* by Elizabeth Gaskell, is known as an example of the "industrial novel." First published in England in 1855, it tells the story of Margaret Hale, a young woman who moves with her parents from an untroubled environment in the south of England to the northern manufacturing city of Milton (the fictional town based on Manchester), where she is exposed to the suffering and injustice that have accompanied industrialism. Together with Margaret's romantic involvement with a factory owner, this causes her to reexamine her beliefs about social class. A modern edition of the novel was published by Wordsworth Editions in 1998.

more respect for his own class. Morten's role here is to get Pelle to see things in a different light than he has done before, and Pelle takes due note of it.

After Pelle has married and is involved only in his own private world with Ellen, he happens to meet Morten in the street, and Morten lectures him about the plight of the homeless and the poor. He is indignant about it. This awakens Pelle once more to the reality of poverty and troubles his conscience. But he and Morten do not agree about what to do about the situation. At this point, their dialogue dramatizes the different voices in the labor movement at the time. Morten wants and expects a revolution. The workers will never be given their rights; they must seize them. "Revolution is the voice of God," he says, and he speaks with a passion that disturbs Pelle. Pelle tells Morten it is better for the workers to be patient and get organized; everything will come to them with time. His is the voice of moderation and of reason.

Meanwhile, Pelle has run into Peter Dreyer as well. Like Morten, Peter has been deeply affected by his exposure to the ruthlessness of the city and the plight of the workers. He has become hardened, but while Morten is full of socialist ideas, Peter is merely disillusioned; he believes in nothing. "There's nothing worth believing in," he tells Pelle. Pelle manages to persuade him at least to join the labor movement, but Peter does so without enthusiasm.

Here, then, are those three young men in Copenhagen in the 1890s as each reacts to the social and economic problems they encounter there: Pelle the organizer, the optimist, tinged with idealism; Morten the thinker, the supporter of revolution; and Peter the hostile, cynical one. Of these three, it is of course Pelle who in *The Great Struggle* rises to prominence and makes a name for himself in the labor movement. Unlike Morten, he is not driven by anger, and he senses in the most practical of terms what is possible for the workers to accomplish. He is also a born leader, again unlike Morten. Morten, for all his fiery talk to Pelle, is not primarily a man of action. He is not much interested in organization, either of the union or of a political party; he works more behind the scenes, trying to help with individual cases of need or injustice, and in doing so he shows himself to be a man of compassion. Pelle, on the other hand, has a rare gift, that of the orator who is able to tap into the collective consciousness of his audience, telling them what they long to hear, articulating it better than they ever could, and inspiring them to believe great accomplishments are possible.

Pelle, Morten, and Peter meet up again in Volume 4, *Daybreak*, after Pelle has been released from six years' imprisonment. Morten has acquired a reputation as a writer of books that advocate working-class causes. Pelle visits him and they try to put behind them the differences that had cooled their relationship toward the end of the long labor dispute, when Morten repeatedly forced Pelle to examine his own actions and motivations and warned him about how things might go wrong. Morten is still expecting a revolution; he is unimpressed by the gains the working classes have so far made, which he says are largely illusory. He also realizes that in spite of his books, he is not having much influence on the causes he espouses. He explains this discrepancy by claiming his ideas are "too far in advance of the great body of them [the working classes], and have no actual connection." But he also holds out the hope that he is destined "to reach the heights before you others, and if I do I'll try to light a beacon up there for you!" Morten correctly perceives part of the essential difference between him and Pelle: Pelle is a leader who can connect with the workers and get them to believe in themselves. But Morten is wrong when he paints himself as a visionary to whom others must catch up. In fact, it is Pelle, with his ideas about cooperative businesses, who is the visionary thinker that Morten, for all his learning, fails to become.

As Pelle repairs his relationship with Morten, he also reestablishes contact with Peter Dreyer. Up to this point in the novel Peter has been somewhat of a peripheral figure, but he now assumes a more prominent role. Set against Pelle, who is at once visionary and pragmatic, and the thinker and intellectual Morten, Peter has become an agitator who nurses a deep grudge against the existing system. He despises existing laws, which he says "are only a mask for brute force." He now produces an anarchist newspaper, and he is monitored by the police. He has been imprisoned several times. Peter claims his "inoffensive little paper" merely encourages people to think for themselves, and he also argues that the poor are to blame for their exploitation because they passively and without protest continue to produce all the for full wages, they receive together a trifling wage. The unfolding of the boy's intelligence in the environment of the farm, while he herds cattle in the meadows in summer and cares for them in the stables in winter, and as he tries to establish himself among his playmates on the farm and in the little religious school, is remarkable record of imaginative realism. After his confirmation he is considered ready to shift for himself and goes to the neighboring seaport town, where he is apprenticed in the shoemaker's trade.

The second volume [*Apprenticehip*] continues the story of the boy's development as an apprentice in the hard school of the city. The curiosity about the life around him which characterized his farm experiences here has a larger field for exploration; and there is little about the town and its inhabitants that he does not have an opportunity to learn while he serves his apprenticeship. The difficulties of orientation are much greater; but in the attempt to find himself in his surroundings his character gains in strength and stability. At length his curiosity about that life beyond the narrow town horizon, which sends him strange intimations from time to time, attracts him away from Nexö to the capital before his apprenticeship is fully served.

The third volume, called *The Great Struggle*, is concerned with the period of young manhood in Copenhagen. There he finds himself at the very heart of a problem that had come to him in mysterious hints and perplexing suggestions on the farm and in the town. He sets himself to solve this in the same way in which he had learned to face and overcome the smaller problems of his adjustment to his simpler youthful environment. His method is to throw himself with great energy into the labor movement, of which he becomes eventually the leader. This is not a volume on labor unionism; it is still the life of a strong and magnetic personality. The bitter conflicts between his loyalty to a cause and the needs of his own life—his loves, wife, and family—give the account an intimately personal impression. At the height of his success as a labor leader, just when he has won a great general strike, he is sent to prison on a false charge of forgery.

The last volume recounts his attempts, after his release from prison, to rehabilitate himself and to reëstablish his family life, broken up even before his imprisonment through his devotion to the labor cause. Henceforth his interest in the labor problem takes the form of attempting to

organize a coöperative shoemaking industry in the capital. This enterprise involves him in endless struggles with the manufacturers' association, but he gradually succeeds and extends his coöperative principle into other activities. His personal fortunes are improved and his family happily reunited and established on a country estate known as Daybreak. *Daybreak* is the title of the last volume. Different from the realistic novels of the day, this ends with a note of optimism.

Although the novel is thus primarily an account of Pelle's personal life, this is deftly interwoven into a report of conditions that have a wide economic and historical significance. Certain well-known problems are here shown as they are viewed from their centre. *Boyhood* presents the centralizing tendency in competitive agriculture, with its accompanying maladjustments. The better farms of the island are being acquired by the wealthy farmers while the barren plots are being left for the poor. A miserable existence must be eked out by occasional labor in the stone quarries. The independent peasantry is being transformed into a proletariat. The young men and women stream away from the dismal prospect on the land to a deceptively hopeful future in the towns, and their places are in turn occupied by immigrants. Pelle migrates with them to the town.

There he observes the same centralizing tendency in the trades. These are coming under the control of the masters, who succeed by exploiting the toil of their apprentices. The masters themselves are being forced to the wall by the competition of machine-made goods from the larger industrial centres. The apprentices, when their service is finished, finding no work at their trades, drift, like the peasants, into the ranks of the proletariat. The problem of increasing unemployment and acute poverty, recurring each winter, begins to attract an uneasy curiosity. Since the prospects in a trade are after all no better than they were in the country, Pelle gives up his service and is caught up in the drift toward Copenhagen, still seeking the promised land.

The capital is the centre toward which all the blind forces of life converge. Here all the evils of town and country are aggravated. There are crowded tenements, hideous slums, sweated labor, monopoly, usury, drunkenness, disease, desperate poverty, and all that familiar category. A new phenomenon is labor grown rebellious and refusing to work when conditions become intolerable. Out of luxuries enjoyed by the rich: "Capital literally sleeps with its head in our lap, and abuses us in its sleep; and yet we don't cut its throat!"

Peter is as angry as Morten used to be, and Pelle, who has mellowed in prison, has little sympathy with his extreme views or his anger, but he does respect his former fellow-apprentice as a worker, and he offers Peter a position in the cooperative. Peter turns out to be a loyal and reliable worker, although he does not lose his anger at social conditions in the cooperative, and he regards it as just another form of capitalism that does nothing for those in real need. Peter's tragic demise, in which he kills himself after shooting a policeman who was about to arrest him, dramatically shows the contrast between him and Pelle. Peter was about to address a meeting of the unemployed, and a demonstration was planned. But Pelle gets the men to disperse peacefully rather than risk a violent confrontation with the police who are waiting in force down a side street. In the end it is the sunny and practical optimism of Pelle that triumphs rather than the bookish lectures of Morten or the nihilism of Peter. Pelle's secret, not shared by either of his friends, is his belief in the essential goodness of humanity:

> It was his experience that every one in reality was good: the evil in them could nearly always be traced back to something definite, while the goodness often existed in spite of everything. It would triumph altogether when the conditions became secure for everybody.

Source: Bryan Aubrey, Critical Essay on *Pelle the Conqueror* in *Novels for Students,* Gale, Cengage Learning, 2010.

Joel M. Johanson

In the following excerpt, Johanson praises the universality of the work and the characterization of Pelle.

Pelle the Conqueror, a four-volume novel by Martin Andersen Nexö, appeared a few, years before the outbreak of the war. Its author was probably quite unknown to American readers until the translation of his novel was completed. Then his work began to be favorably compared with Rolland's *Jean-Christophe*, which had caused such a stir a short time before, and its author to be considered in the first rank among contemporary novelists. The deluge of ephemeral and partisan literature loosed by the war soon eclipsed his name. But now that the

> THE DANISH NOVEL IS THE TRUE EPIC OF LABOR. IT IS SIMPLE, FOR IT IS THE STORY OF THE SIMPLE TOLD BY THEMSELVES. IT IS UNIFIED, FOR IT IS THE STORY OF THE MULTITUDINOUS OBSCURE, CONVENIENTLY KNOWN AS THAT SINGLE ENTITY, THE MASSES."

reconstruction time has come his work will no doubt regain its former interest. This is the more likely because it represents in living terms the collapse of the competitive system of industry and the groping for some substitute, which ends in a steady drift toward the coöperative. In Denmark, it will be remembered, the Cöperative organization had progressed farther than anywhere else in Europe before the war. During the war the movement advanced rapidly everywhere in Europe, and now it has reached the United States, not only in the form of propaganda but in the practical programme of such a party as the Non-Partisan League in the western states. A review of the Danish work, which presents the antecedent chaos, the tentative beginnings, the successful organization, and the prospective triumph of coöperation, is therefore peculiarly opportune.

Pelle the Conqueror is not doctrinaire. The idea of coöperation is not its hero. It is the vivid transcript of a Swedish immigrant boy's life in Denmark. Doctrine and opinion may be made out of this boy's experiences just as practical wisdom is formed out of the experiences of life.

The four volumes of the novel deal with four phases of its hero's development: boyhood, apprenticeship, the struggles of maturity, and the victory.

The first volume [*Boyhood*] is one of those realistic studies of boyhood in which modern realistic literature abounds. Pelle and his aged father come from Sweden to the Danish island of Bornholm in the Baltic and seek employment as farm-workers. They are domiciled on Stone Farm, which is owned by the Kongstrups, reputed to be the island's severest taskmasters. Since the father is too old and the son too young this attitude grow unionism and its accompaniments: strikes, lockouts, mediations, parleyings, protocols, mutual hatred, and suspicion. The sanguine immigrant from Sweden has come, after many chances, to this end. It seems that another emigration is his only hope. But he concludes that emigration would bring him merely a repetition of his Danish experiences; it would be another course from pillar to post. Therefore, if the land of promise is not to be found abroad, it must be made at home. So he becomes an active member in the labor agitation, finally leads it, and brings it to preliminary success. Thus labor wins the right to organize and respect for its organization. Pelle's imprisonment at this juncture is an omen little understood by triumphant unionism. Between the conditions revealed in Denmark and those in any other industrial country there is little real difference; they are everywhere the same. All the phenomena of sociological investigation are recorded as the incidents of the central figure's life.

The fourth volume presents a phase of the problem that is relatively new in America. It suggests that unionism, now recognized and respectable, has not obtained the results it struggled for. There is as much poverty and unemployment as before. It further suggests that the new aspect of the movement, the parliamentary and political, will yield no more acceptable results. Then it points a way of escape through the organization of coöperative industries to be owned by the laborers themselves. Pelle leads this new movement, both by the object lesson of his own coöperative equal-sharing shoe factory, and by active propaganda. The new principle progresses against all the obstacles that competitive industry can contrive for it until it controls certain trades, highly organized from the soil to the consumer. The capital for the first venture comes from outside his class, an expedient that Pelle is reluctant to accept. He becomes reconciled to it by the reflection that labor must constructively employ in its proposed new order all those instrumentalities that the two groups, capital and labor, had hitherto used against each other. Thus he goes about making his promised land at home.

In this review it is seen that the hero of the novel, the completely realized character, reveals through his life the fortunes of the laboring class. This class Disraeli once dignified by the name of nation. When he looked out upon the civil discord and strife of England he spoke of his

country as being divided into two nations. More and more since his time does it become apparent how well he understood the situation; every industrial country is divided into two nations contending with each other for power and position. Pelle represents the consciousness of one of these nations in Denmark, and similarly in the entire western world where the same conditions exist. The novel is intimately personal in its realism, but it is not that isolated and exceptional experience that is recorded in so many modern investigations into the individual soul. It acquires an epic sweep and significance because of the universal nature of this one individual. The background upon which the pattern of his life is traced has been made completely familiar to us by countless social researches in the last generation. In the respect that the hero rises to be a leader in the most significant of modern movements the epic quality is heightened and maintained. The book is therefore similar to the great national epics, in which the personal fortunes of the hero are indeed, as in *Pelle the Conqueror*, of primary interest, but acquire a greater significance by their intimate union with their people's destinies. The heroes of the *Iliad* and the *Odyssey* are the builders of the Greek states. Beowulf's magnificent combats establish a people in security. Æneas founds Rome. The hero must be an autonomous individual as well as representative of national or universal destiny.

If the hero is made a symbol, or is governed by purposes beyond his control, or serves some abstract idea, so that the spontaneous expression of his personality is thereby limited, the epic loses one of its distinguishing qualities. The Æneid is therefore an inferior epic, since its hero is felt to be rather the high destiny of imperial Rome than a self-governing personality. Like the Æneid in this respect are those interesting works, *The Adventures of Gargantua* and *Pantagruel* and *Don Quixote*, which are, of course, not epics, although they present widesweeping views of life. They are the works of reflective and skeptical men, the summaries of discredited cultures, presented in a burlesque and farcical imitation of that epic manner which would have been appropriate before the cultural unity of the time they satirize had been destroyed. To continue a swift historical sketch, the romances of roguery return simply to the realities of contemporary life among the commons, with however light a purpose. Upon these realities, more seriously considered, the enduring works must eventually be built. In the history of *Tom Jones* there are realism, unity, and characterization seriously directed. But Tom Jones remains an interesting type of one kind of Englishman; he does not represent the fate or fortunes of England. In such a work, on the other hand, as Hugo's *Les misérables*, which, it may be observed in passing, is an obvious inspiration for the Danish novelist, there is found a wider significance in the life of the hero without his reduction to a symbol. The epic impression is impaired, however, by Hugo's characteristic lyrical gift, and his attempted realizations are not sufficiently objective.

To come quickly to the present (if that distant time before the war may be called the present) *Jean-Christophe*, the well-known novel by Romain Rolland, summarizes the civilization of Europe just turned into the new century, as reflected in the life of a master-musician. It is not a national novel; it is frankly cosmopolitan. But cosmopolitanism has unfortunately not yet arrived as a reality in the world, although Erasmus could avow himself a cosmopolitan with some show of truth, since he represented a universal power and spoke in an international language. Art was once said indeed to be limited by no national barriers; and musicians may have been the true internationals before the war. But now that notion has vanished. In any event it is difficult to think of an artist, intent upon self-realization in pure artistic expression, as representing the simple realities of the workaday world. During the war the author of *Jean-Christophe* issued from his Swiss retreat a pamphlet explaining his attitude as Above the Conflict. This attitude during the past crisis will explain why there is a lack of vital consistency between the life of Jean and the author's interpolated reflections on European civilization as seen from a high intellectual eminence. The novel is in the tradition of *Wilhelm Meister*, whose cosmopolitan author considered the cultural development of his hero with Olympian detachment in the midst of troublous times.

The Danish novel is the true epic of labor. It is simple, for it is the story of the simple told by themselves. It is unified, for it is the story of the multitudinous obscure, conveniently known as that single entity, the masses. It is universal, for ye have always the poor with you. It marks the clear emergence of the laborer as self-sufficient hero, and the final articulate realization of his dignity. There have been many side-references to the life of the humble, many bird's-eye views of the ancient lowly, but hitherto probably no work that views life from the laborer's centre, interprets it by his philosophy, and attempts to construct the world upon his principles.

The wisest have always been known to seek counsel; and in these times even statesmen, caught in the whirl of events, acknowledge the need of guidance. Institutions are in a plastic condition and may be rationally moulded, or passively allowed to fix again into their former dangerously rigid shapes. If they are to be rationally moulded, there must be a more general understanding of labor; its miseries, its blind struggles, its almost infinite patience, its slow coming to self-consciousness, and its growing determination that competition must yield to something kindlier. The poor hath hope, and iniquity stoppeth her mouth. He who would understand labor could scarcely do better than to study the life of Pelle.

Source: Joel M. Johanson, "Pelle the Conqueror: An Epic of Labor," in *Sewanee Review*, Vol. XXVII, No. 2, Spring 1919, pp. 218–26.

Nation

In the following review of the fourth volume of Pelle, *the critic assesses the value of the entire work, praising it for its humor, humanity, and universal appeal.*

Now that the fourth and last volume of *Pelle* is before him, the English reader may well feel moved to reread the earlier volumes, which have appeared at considerable intervals, in order to test or to refresh his impression of the work as a whole. The very fact that each of these volumes taken by itself showed uncommon stability and definition—was, in a sense, a complete story—may have tended to obscure its place in the tetralogy. *Jean-Christophe*, with which Pelle challenges comparison in several respects, is only intelligible in the light of its conclusion; its division into parts, whether the ten parts of the original or the four parts of the English version, is arbitrary. The work as a whole has no recognizable form or comeliness. *Pelle,* on the other hand, not only hangs together as a whole, but represents a series of distinct phases in the career which we are following. As with *Jean-Christophe*, it is a career of experiment, of search for the meaning of life—and a successful search. Rolland chose a genius, an artist, for his protagonist: Nexö has chosen one to whom life is a thing distinct from art and infinitely more important.

To this final volume is appended a note about the author by Professor Jespersen of the University of Copenhagen. It seems that Nexö was very little known in Denmark when the first part of *Pelle the Conqueror* appeared, some ten years ago. He was a teacher in Copenhagen who had done a little travelling and a little writing—chiefly some short stories which a few people had recognized as exceptional. Copenhagen was the place of his birth (1869); its circumstances were of the humblest. The knowledge of slum life shown in his pictures of the Ark and its mean and filthy surroundings was evidently gained at first hand. So was his knowledge of rustic squalor, since most of his boyhood, like Pelle's, appears to have passed upon the island of Bornholm in the Baltic. His very name is taken from the town of Nexö on that island, where, like Pelle again, he became a shoemaker's apprentice and made his first ardent and awkward experiments in the direction of happiness. There was other work for his hands, chiefly as a bricklayer, before he won the schooling which prepared for his work as a teacher. It was all a preparation for his work as a writer. The story of Pelle is the story of a manhood struggling with all sorts of obstacles, often thrown down and trampled upon, yet making its way steadily and with unquenchable confidence, towards a mastery of life. The test of character, after all, is not that we should be always sure where we are going, but that we should never doubt ourselves to be on our way. When Pelle first sets out townwards and fortunewards, leaving poor Father Lasse on his dunghill, his high-heartedness belongs to youth and health merely—or might have so belonged. And he is in real peril of losing it, as he faces the rough world of the town and passes from boyhood along the dangerous bridge of adolescence. There are times when even the safeguard of his egotism fails him. The world is all a muddle. The poor are the helpless victims of the rich, for example, and he is merely one of the poor; therefore he may as well drown his pain in the gutter. But even at his lowest spiritual ebb there remains the seed of something fine and valiant in him; and more than once there is a woman to remind him of it, and to spur him back to himself.

By degrees, it will be recalled, his husk of youthful selfishness is stripped away, and zeal for the service of his kind takes its place: for his kind in a narrow sense, perhaps his fellow-workers as against those who employ and profit by them. He becomes the champion and leader of the workpeople in a long struggle. It culminates in a phase of violence which results in defeat at the hands of authority and Pelle's imprisonment for a term of years. Meanwhile, as the result of his devotion to the cause, his family have nearly starved, and he discovers that his wife has sold herself to feed them and him. So the third part ended, on a note of apparent defeat and despair. The fourth, which is now before us, opens on the day when Pelle is released from prison and goes forth to face the world again. He has served a sort of martyrdom, and has some vague expectation of being received with enthusiasm by the people whom he has led. He finds that the cause has made progress, that the work-people are in better case than formerly, but that he himself is half-forgotten. Moreover, his own point of view has changed, and when the chance comes to assert himself once more as a leader he finds little to say, and nothing at all in the old militant vein. His wife at least has welcomed him, he has forgiven her, and we are to see their imperfect mating become as nearly perfect as the difference in their natures permits. But for a long time he remains unaroused to further efforts at leadership. There is hard going at home. He takes to his old trade of cobbler and so manages a bare living. Meanwhile he is not unhappy, his spirit broods and bides its time; his old confidence remains somewhere in the background of his consciousness. Presently, through the perfecting of his friendship with a member of the class which he has despised, the fresh impulse to action comes. Once more, but this time no longer in single-handed self-sufficiency or in a spirit of conflict, he takes up the burden of the workers and modestly initiates, in the character of employer, a system of coöperation which is to prove the basis of a new and happier social order. There is less of the panoramic in the concluding part of the narrative than in its predecessors. But this is natural, since Pelle has to lay the foundation of his broader usefulness in the establishment of just relations with the intimate few. We see him here learning to be a husband and a father and a friend, and by this very process confirming his manhood and fitting himself for wider service. Every member of the little surrounding group which contributes to his growth is painted with extraordinary vividness and thoroughness: his wife Ellen first of all; then Brun, the old librarian and born aristocrat whose pure love of humanity finally wins Pelle from his pride; Johanna, the desolate and yet not altogether hopeless child-victim of social wrong; Morten the writer, who is to find in Pelle and what he stands for a solider inspiration than in all the books upon Brun's shelves. Such a work of imagination as this, with its deep humor, its deep humanity, brings home to us, as nothing else can, the artificial nature of those boundaries which language and custom set between one race and another. It is a book for the world; one cannot lay it down without a sense of quickened emotion and enlarged vision.

Source: "A Career of Experiment," in *Nation*, Vol. CIV, No. 2696, March 1, 1917, pp. 241–42.

New York Times Book Review

In the following review, the author offers a positive evaluation of Pelle.

Is the very long novel—the novel in several volumes becoming once more the fashion? It is only a short while ago that the last portion of *Jean Christophe* was published; Compton Mackenzie's new book is avowedly but the opening part of his hero's story, and now in *Pelle the Conqueror* we have a novel in four volumes, of which this one, containing the account of Pelle's boyhood, is the first. According to the introduction by Prof. Otto Jespersen, much of the story is autobiographical, and we can well believe that this is true, for it reads, not like fiction, but like an exceptionally vivid record of actual events; events commonplace enough as commonplace as life itself. When we first meet Pelle and his father Lasse they have but just arrived at the island of Bornholm in the Baltic, whither they have come from their native Sweden, seeking employment. Or, to be accurate, Lasse is seeking employment, for Pelle is only a very little boy, much excited over this, his first journey. Lasse is at last hired by the bailiff of Stone Farm, where he takes care of the cattle, Pelle being expected to pay for his board by running errands and later acting as herd boy. The book tells of their daily life during the years at Stone Farm and ends when Pelle, having been confirmed by the parson and equipped with the Prophets, the Judges, the Apostles, the Ten Commandments, and one hundred and twenty hymns, leaves the farm to seek his fortune in the town which he has never seen.

It is all related with the utmost simplicity. Pelle is a real boy, full of energy and fun, ready to play or fight and loving to tease the schoolmaster, but tender-hearted and devotedly attached to his father. All the happenings upon the big farm—the constant toil, the quarrels, and the love making, sickness, and holiday joys, birth, and death—we see through the child's eyes. They are a rough and primitive people among whom his lot is cast, but not so brutal as those of whom we have read in other novels. Many of them are kindly, and there is a quite unconscious readiness for self-sacrifice in Kalle and his wife and the old grandmother, who, despite privation and grief, had found life very good. Living close to the soil, superstitious, humble before the master and mistress, who seemed to them creatures belonging almost to another world, grumbling sometimes, but usually content with little, they represent an old order whose first faint stirrings of change appear in the boy Pelle and in his father's desire that he shall learn to read and write, for then, Lasse thinks, he may become anything, even a clerk or a schoolmaster.

Lasse is perhaps a more appealing because a more pathetic character than Pelle, the son of his old age. His bravado, whose futility he knows so well, his pitiful attempts at self-assertion, which end in nothing; his desire to keep his role of Providence to the boy who believes in him utterly, his frustrated endeavors to clutch at the manhood he feels is fast slipping from him, the trick Fate plays him at the end, when peace and comfort seem almost within his grasp, above all his devotion to his only child, make of him a memorable figure. He does nothing spectacular. During the thrilling scene of the shipwreck he, like the reader, is a mere looker-on, yet one remembers him after the hero of that dramatic episode is forgotten. Lasse is a Père Goriot, who reaps love instead of ingratitude.

However, it is the boy Pelle about whom the whole revolves—Pelle, who was often cold, frequently overworked, and occasionally abused, yet found time for play, and could feel on looking back upon it that he had had a happy childhood. That childhood is here presented neither in rosy nor in very dark colors; there is neither the false sentiment which gushes over the delights of penury, nor that other, equally false, which makes no allowance for habit or temperament, but a genuine realism which shows the mingling of pleasure and sorrow, the joys of play and the brook during Summer, the hardships of the long, dark Northern Winter. And we feel and see it all—the barns and outhouses, the broad fields, with sand dunes beyond, and beyond them again the sea. And the homely folk, dairy maids and laborers, the headman upon whom there fell so terrible a calamity, the young fisherman, who expiated his sin with his life we know them every one. There is no straining after effect; it is all natural, seemingly spontaneous.

So far as one may judge who is unable to read it in the original Danish, the book seems well written and the translation excellent. Certainly, the construction is good, and though the plot is simplicity itself, the narrative never drags. The character-analysis, moreover, is done with a line here, a few words there—and the individual stands before us, a live human being. Pelle himself is of course portrayed more at length than are any of the others; his ideas the half-pathetic, half-comic and often wholly grotesque ideas of a child his feelings toward those around him, his unconscious centering of all his little world about himself, the gradual barely perceptible change of his attitude toward his father, from one of utter dependence to one almost protective, are alike skillfully and naturally drawn. We leave the book anxious to know what sort of a man this boy will make, and certain that he will become one worth hearing about. Martin Andersen Nexø is not destined long to remain, so far as the American reading public is concerned, an unknown author. All those who care for good work should and doubtless will hasten to make his acquaintance.

Source: "Review of *Pelle the Conqueror*," in *New York Times Book Review*, December 7, 1913, p. 720.

SOURCES

Abrams, M. H., *A Glossary of Literary Terms,* 4th ed., Holt, Rinehart and Winston, 1981, p. 153.

Bjørn, Claus, and Gylendal Leksikon, "The Labour Movement," *Denmark DK: The Official Website of Denmark,* https://www.denmark.dk/en/menu/About-Denmark/History/The-Period-1720-1900/18641901TheModernBreakthrough/TheLabourMovement/ (accessed November 3, 2009).

"Brief History About Copenhagen," *Copenhagen Portal—A Much Different Tourist Site and Cultural Guide,* http://www.copenhagen.dk/CPH-History.htm (accessed August 17, 2009).

"A Career of Experiment," in *The Nation,* Vol. CIV, No. 2696, March 1, 1917, pp. 241–42.

Intelligence Agency, *The World Factbook: Denmark,* https://www.cia.gov/library/publications/the-world-factbook/geos/da.html (accessed November 3, 2009).

Fuller, Thomas, "Workers and Bosses: Friends or Foes?" *New York Times,* January 11, 2005, http://www.nytimes.com/2005/01/10/world/10iht-unions2.html (accessed November 3, 2009).

Ingwersen, Faith, and Niels Ingwersen, *Quests for a Promised Land: The Works of Martin Andersen Nexø,* Greenwood Press, 1984.

Jespersen, Otto, "Note," in *Pelle the Conqueror,* translated from the Danish by Jesse Muir and Bernard Miall, Mondial, 2006.

Kennedy, Constance Decker, Review of *Pelle the Conqueror,* in *New York Times Book Review,* Vol. 94, September 3, 1989, p. 14.

Nexø, Martin Andersen, *Pelle the Conqueror,* translated from the Danish by Jesse Muir and Bernard Miall, Mondial, 2006.

Review of *Pelle the Conqueror,* in *Publishers Weekly,* Vol. 238, No. 26, June 14, 1991, p. 52.

FURTHER READING

Jespersen, Knud, J. V., *A History of Denmark,* Palgrave, 2004.

This is a concise introduction to the history of Denmark from 1500 to the present. Particularly useful for the reader of *Pelle the Conqueror* are the sections in Chapter 4 on social democracy and the development from class warfare to a national consensus.

Nexø, Martin Andersen, *Under the Open Sky: My Early Years,* Vanguard Press, 1938.

This account of Nexø's early life in Copenhagen and on the island of Bornholm is valuable because it shows the extent to which the early part of *Pelle the Conqueror* is based on Nexø's own life.

Slochower, Harry, *Mythopoesis: Myth Patterns in the Literary Classics,* Wayne State University Press, 1970, pp. 284–89.

This is an examination of the universal mythic elements in the novel, with Pelle's development seen as the epic journey of Everyman.

———, *Three Ways of Modern Man,* International Publishers, 1937, pp. 105–44.

Slochower analyzes Nexø's use of mythic patterns and symbols and also points out some of the character flaws in Pelle.

Three Junes

JULIA GLASS
2002

Three Junes, published in 2002 to critical acclaim, was Julia Glass's debut novel. A triptych, or work of art in three parts, *Three Junes* unfolds over three different summers, during the years 1989, 1995, and 1999. Set in Greece, Scotland, Greenwich Village, and Long Island, the novel tells the intersecting stories of Scottish widower Paul McLeod, his son Fenno, who owns a bookstore in Manhattan, and a young widowed artist, Fern Olitsky. Thematically, the novel has universal appeal in its portrayal of grief, fate, hope, and family connection. It earned Glass a National Book Award.

After *Three Junes*, Glass published *The Whole World Over* in 2006, a novel that featured several characters from *Three Junes*. A recurring theme in her novels, beginning with *Three Junes* is memory, particularly the ways in which people struggle to heal emotional scars from the past that prevent them from fully living in the present. As the three protagonists of *Three Junes* learn how to experience intimacy after the death of a loved one, Glass shows the truth in the old adage that "time heals all wounds."

AUTHOR BIOGRAPHY

Julia Glass was born in 1956. She did not pursue a writing career until completing her education at Yale University, where she graduated with a

Julia Glass (*AP Images*)

degree in art. After Yale, she earned a fellowship to study figurative painting in Paris, but upon returning to the United States and settling in New York City, she took a job as a copy editor at *Cosmopolitan* magazine. During that time, she began to pen occasional magazine columns and short stories. One of her earliest short stories, never published, anticipates Paul's conflict in *Three Junes*. A semiautobiographical piece called "Souvenirs," the story was inspired by a student trip she took to Greece and someone she had met: an older man, recently widowed.

In the early 1990s, Glass suffered several personal tragedies; her marriage ended in divorce, she was diagnosed with breast cancer, and her younger sister committed suicide. Glass used writing to work through her pain and turned back to the story of the widower she had met in Greece. She expanded the short story to novella length, changed the point of view, and renamed the piece, "Collies." The short story won the Pirate's Alley Faulkner Society Medal in 1999 and served as the cornerstone for *Three Junes*. In 2000, Glass became a New York Foundation for the Arts fellow.

From 2004 to 2005, Glass served as a fellow at the Radcliffe Institute for Advanced Study. Her second book, *The Whole World Over: A Novel* (2006), follows pastry chef Greenie Duquette, who, with son in tow, leaves her husband behind to take a position as the personal chef to the governor of New Mexico. Fenno, a character from *Three Junes* also appears in this novel. *The Whole World Over: A Novel* takes place against the tragic backdrop of September 11, 2001, and like Glass's first novel, it is grounded in family life. The book was well received by reviewers.

In 2008, Glass published *I See You Everywhere*, about two sisters who examine and learn how to deal with their tumultuous, competitive relationship. Echoing the themes of family conflict, grief, and mourning found in *Three Junes*, *I See You Everywhere* is told through two alternating points of view.

Glass's work has been honored with three Nelson Algren Awards and the Tobias Wolff Award.

PLOT SUMMARY

Collies 1989: Chapter 1
Three Junes opens with Paul McLeod on a tour of Greece. Paul becomes captivated by a young American artist named Fern, on holiday with her college friend Anna. Fern reminds him slightly of his late wife Maureen, but she also appeals to him in her own awkward way. Paul flashes back to meeting Maureen after World War II. She told him her dream of raising a kennel of collies. Once they married, after his father's death, they sold his family home and used the proceeds to buy a house outside Edinburgh which they called Tealing. Maureen raised dogs, as was her dream, alongside their three sons. Paul ran the newspaper his father owned.

Collies 1989: Chapter 2
Paul thinks back to when Maureen got sick and their sons came home to visit her. Their eldest son Fenno brought his friend Mal as a guest, and Paul wondered if the thin and frail Mal was ill as well. Paul tried to connect with Fenno but knew there was too much distance between them, figuratively and literally, as Fenno lived in New York City. Paul questioned his son's sexuality, believing that he and Mal were lovers.

In the present, Paul admits to Jack, the tour guide, that he prefers "the idea of everything planned. No surprises." Paul remembers the week before Maureen died, when a plane exploded over Lockerbie, Scotland. As a newspaperman, he went to the crash site and pocketed a tube of lipstick from the wreckage.

Paul feels himself loosening up in Greece and grows closer to Fern. Paul thinks back to a time when Maureen was healthy, and Colin Swift, an Englishman who owned a large neighboring estate, dropped by to discuss the new kennel. Colin asked Maureen if she had some pups he could train along with his hounds.

In Greece, Paul bonds with another tourist, Marjorie Guernsey-Jones, and they briefly discuss what it is like to lose a loved one.

Paul ruminates on the past, again thinking of Colin Swift. He and Maureen watched him "on the hunt," and while Maureen admired his skill with his horse and hounds, Colin's abilities annoyed Paul. Back in the present, Paul spends time with Jack and Fern. Paul and the other tourists are on a boat to another island. The sea is rough. Paul wonders if Fern's parents worry about her. Later, Paul catches Fern "kissing Jack like a prodigal lover she thought she had lost for all time." Paul thinks again about his relationship with Maureen and remembers learning about Colin's death. He suspects Maureen had been in love with Colin.

Collies 1989: Chapter 3

Paul remembers Maureen's funeral when Fenno asked him if Paul was selling the family house. Fenno told Paul he could sell the house but not the collies. He suggested that David take two and Fenno take the one named Rodgie.

Paul spends time with Marjorie, with her talking and him listening. He wonders what it would be like to be unpredictable like Jack. He imagines what it would be like to retire or travel, maybe tell Fenno to be responsible for the house. He encounters Marjorie again and is inspired by the way she changed her life's direction when her horse farm burned down. He recalls the moment when he found the lipstick from the Lockerbie site in his pocket, two days after Maureen's funeral. In the present, Fern gives Jack a gift to give to Paul: her sketches of an olive tree and of a mother and child.

Upright 1995: Chapter 4

Fenno McLeod flies to Scotland for his father's funeral. Paul McLeod had a heart attack in a house on Naxos, a small island in Greece. Fenno recalls his mother's death, when he and his brothers were by her bedside. In the present, when he arrives at the family home, he finds his brother Dennis cooking for the family. The house smells delicious and takes on a new identity, like something from "a dream, where everything yet nothing is the way it should be, where the best of what you have and what you wish for are briefly, tantalizingly united." He reminisces with Dennis and feels content to be home under the circumstances.

Fenno thinks about the inheritance he and his brothers received from his grandfather, who was a publishing magnate. David had attended veterinary school and was working for a dull practice. He used the money to begin his own work back in Scotland. Dennis had moved from job to job, but his share prompted him to relocate to Paris and become a pastry chef. Fenno did not use the money right away. Instead, he lingered through graduate school at Columbia University. He became friends with Ralph Quayle, a professor of English, and upon Quayle's suggestion and encouragement, Fenno thought about starting his own business.

Fenno begins to rediscover his family. He recalls how he first met David's wife Lil, when they were both undergraduates at Cambridge. Despite his homosexuality, he was captivated by her and admired her performance in a solo modern dance.

Upright 1995: Chapter 5

Fenno remembers the moment in 1986, just after the United States had bombed Libya, when he and Ralph found Armand, the baker who lived near Fenno, dead in his garden. He also remembers the night he discussed with Ralph the idea of opening a bookstore. One night when he was planning the details of his bird-themed bookstore, he heard loud opera music across the street, the smashing of plates, and someone yelling, "Basta!" After the scene quieted, he went to find a folio of bird prints given to him as a child by his mother. Two mornings later, he discovered pieces of plates in the garbage across the street, plates similar to those his mother once owned and rarely used.

Fenno spends time with Dennis and feels both useful and comfortable in the kitchen. In his room at night, Fenno overhears his sisters-in-law, Veronique and Lil, talking about children. Veronique is trying to convince Lil that she will one day have a child, but Lil is frustrated by her unsuccessful fertility treatments. Before going to sleep, Fenno thinks about his selfish desire not to spread his father's ashes in Greece. He also flashes back to the opening of his bookstore called Plume. Shortly after the opening, he met Mal, a music critic who evaluated the music section of the shop and gave Fenno his card. He learned that Mal was the owner of the smashed china, the neighbor he had heard screaming and playing loud opera music in the middle of the night.

Upright 1995: Chapter 6

Fenno awakens to his two nieces peering at him, wanting to play. Later, he goes downstairs and finds the family preparing for the funeral. In looking for vases, Fenno comes across two medals Paul earned in the war. He and his family question if they belonged to Paul, since their mother never bragged about his war experiences. Fenno remembers a time when Mal visited the bookshop with his parrot, Felicity. Felicity took to Fenno quickly, and Mal asked Fenno if he would take her as a boarder. Mal could no longer keep her since his doctors had diagnosed him as "immuno-compromised," due to his AIDS-related condition.

Upright 1995: Chapter 7

Fenno wakes up to find Veronique in the garden, and she enlists his help in gathering flowers. She tells him the family would like him to visit more. Fenno flashes back to when he met Tony Best, a photographer, on one of his morning walks.

Fenno attends his father's funeral and rides home with Lil. He longs for her attention, feeling as captivated with her as when they were in college. He wants to talk with her more, but they arrive home too soon. He toasts to his father's ashes, which are in a box in the front hall. He spends some time alone in his father's library and arrives at the luncheon late. He slips into a seat next to Marjorie Guernsey-Jones from Devon, who tells him that she knew Paul mostly through their correspondence, though they met on tour in Greece, and that Fenno was his favorite. Marjorie gives him a packet of

letters, then decides she cannot part with them. They exchange addresses.

Fenno thinks about his relationship with Mal. They began to share details about their families and spent more time together. During that time, Fenno was developing a physical relationship with Tony.

Upright 1995: Chapter 8

When Fenno awakens, he is faced with an envelope addressed to him that he found in an upstairs desk the previous night. He does not read it, but rather goes in search of his family's company. No one is home. After a small breakfast, he opens the envelope to find a composition book, his birth certificate, a letter, a drawing, and a tube of lipstick. He is confused by the lipstick, flips through his mother's book, looks at the drawing—of an olive tree on one side and a mother and child on the other—and reads the letter from his father, dated July 4, 1989.

Fenno remembers how, at the start of his relationship with Tony, he did not learn much about the man. Around the same time, he would visit Mal two or three times a week. Ralph asked if they were lovers, and Fenno said no. Fenno shopped for and ate dinners with Mal, but still did not learn much about Mal's childhood. They talked about dying and death, and Fenno asked Mal if he would like to accompany him to Scotland since his mother was dying.

In the present, Veronique commands Fenno to go to the store with her. When they stop at a garden on the edge of town, they discuss Lil's fertility. Veronique says Lil and David want him to help them have a child by donating sperm to be used to impregnate Lil. Veronique reveals that David cannot get Lil pregnant. She gives him a letter from Lil. He does not know how to react at first, but ultimately tells Veronique that he must get away. He leaves the family home behind as he drives off.

Upright 1995: Chapter 9

Fenno remembers leaving Tony a note before he left for Scotland and his mother's funeral. He resolved to make Tony more a part of his life when he came back to New York. When he went to Mal's apartment to have dinner a few days before they left on their trip, he met Mal's mother Lucinda.

In the present, Fenno drives through the countryside and thinks about Lil's request. He goes to Arran, where he and Mal spent some time during Mal's visit. He finally reads Lil's letter. She does not want him to feel pressured and will accept whatever decision he makes.

Fenno comes home to Dennis, who asks where Fenno put Paul's ashes, which are apparently missing. Fenno grows angry at the notion that his family thinks he hid them, despite the fact that he does not want his father's ashes spread in Greece. Dennis reveals that David used to spy on their mother and saw her with Colin Swift's foreman, suspecting that they had been intimate with each other. Fenno reminisces about being close to his mother, helping her in the kennel and at dog trials. He realizes that he once had parental instincts, but they never flourished.

Upright 1995: Chapter 10
Fenno recalls going to the house where he met Tony and finding a woman there who told him that Tony had gone home. Fenno realized that Tony did not live in the house but was a house-sitter. He felt hurt and betrayed. He spent some time with Ralph, who was a bit standoffish because Fenno had not been as attentive to their friendship for a long while. He connects a memory of a reading at the bookstore in New York to the memory of his mother's funeral. Tony showed up at the reading, and Fenno remained cool to him. Fenno confronted him with the fib, but Tony insisted that he had not meant to mislead Fenno. They reunited as a couple, and Tony confessed that he enjoyed house-sitting because his apartment was small. Fenno admired his photography and bought four of his prints.

In Scotland, Fenno sits in front of the horse clinic where David and Lil work. He goes inside the barn to talk to Lil. Fenno asks her what role he would play in the baby's life if he helped them. She asks him what role he would want to play, and he does not know.

Upright 1995: Chapter 11
Fenno remembers a time when Tony took the trouble to inform him that he was leaving for Paris. Although Tony was traveling the next day, Fenno saw his considerate behavior as a positive sign. Fenno spent more time with Mal during Tony's absence. In the present, Fenno and his family try to figure out what happened to their father's ashes. They think the ashes somehow

ended up in the trash after the funeral luncheon. Fenno and David search through bags of garbage to see if they can locate the box.

Upright 1995: Chapter 12
Fenno thinks back to the time he bought a plane ticket to Paris to visit Tony during his photography exhibition. Fenno lied to Mal and Ralph, telling them he had to travel to Scotland because his brother had been in a traffic accident. The evening of the show, Fenno accidentally fell asleep and went to the exhibit later than he planned. He saw himself in many of the photos and became enraged at the way Tony had invaded his privacy. When Fenno returned to New York, he was happy to be reunited with Felicity, who greeted him with true affection. Fenno checked his phone messages and found out that Mal was at St. Anthony's hospital.

In the present, Fenno spends time with his family before going back to New York. Before he donates his sperm for Lil, he tries to boost her self-esteem, which has taken a beating from all her efforts to conceive a child. He also goes to say good-bye to Thea, Laurie, and Christine, who are sleeping. Climbing up to the attic room his mother called "the foxhole," he recalls playing with his brothers. He had been the leader of the pack, envisioning some possible future "family venture, Fenno McLeod & Brothers," a venture that never took shape. Fenno is happy to see the girls' new memories filling the "foxhole" and discovers that they had been using the box containing his father's ashes as a tea party table.

Fenno thinks back to the day Mal was released from the hospital. He learned from Lucinda that Mal had been hospitalized after collapsing in the early hours of the morning after they had dined together. The doctors suspected Mal had contracted salmonella from the raw meat he had eaten.

Upright 1995: Chapter 13
Fenno flashes back to the weeks leading up to Mal's death. Fenno helped Mal commit suicide by taking an overdose of medication. After finding Mal dead, Fenno tried to clear Mal's apartment of any incriminating evidence (such as the pill bottles). Fenno found a box of photographs marked with the name "Christopher" and realized he had stumbled upon mementoes from a relationship the teenaged Mal once had with a cellist, a relationship that had produced a son,

Christopher. After Mal's death, Fenno spent more time with Ralph. Tony came back to town, but Fenno kept his distance.

In the present, Laurie discovers that Fenno found out she took the ashes. She reveals that she did not want her grandfather to be thrown into the ocean. She admits that she misses Paul, who promised to take her to a castle. Fenno enjoys spending a few last moments with his family before leaving, though he is anxious to get home. He realizes he is "learning to live."

Boys 1999: Chapter 14

This chapter starts Fern's point of view. She is with Tony in a large cottage on the water in Amagansett, which happens to be owned by Ralph Quayle. Tony is house-sitting, as usual. Fern and Tony have been friends for more than a decade, but he remains somewhat of a mystery. Fern is pregnant and does not want to face the father of her child just yet. Stavros, the father, is in Greece helping his mother take care of her mother, who is dying. Fern does not know how he will react to the fact that she is pregnant.

Fern works as a book designer, where she has risen to a senior position, yet she wonders if she should move on to a more lucrative "corporate office." Fern thinks back to when she went to Europe on a fellowship. She met Tony during this time and they had a romantic relationship. After suspecting him of being interested in men she broke off the relationship and traveled across Italy and Greece for a month. Tony and Fern later became friends and both found themselves living in New York. She became an artist, living in Brooklyn, but only sold a few paintings. At thirty, and working as a waitress, she married Jonah, an art historian. Jonah later died in a freakish accident, for which Jonah's mother held Fern responsible.

Back in the present, Fern decides to tell her parents about her pregnancy.

Boys 1999: Chapter 15

When Fern wakes up she sees Tony watching a group of young men playing tennis. Tony tells Fern they will have a dinner guest: Fenno, who Tony describes as a friend of the professor who owns the house.

Fern remembers the day Jonah died. There was tension between them, and, although he was late for dinner, which was unusual for him, she was too angry at him to worry. When Stavros

and two policemen came to the door later in the evening, Stavros told her that the superintendent of the apartment building had found Jonah lying in the courtyard behind the building. Apparently, Jonah had fallen from their apartment and died. Fern found Stavros's presence comforting.

In the present, Fern cannot sleep and thinks of her baby. When Fern wakes in the morning, she meets Fenno, who entered the house without knocking but apologizes for scaring her. He is dirty from digging a hole in the back corner of the yard and explains that he is a friend of Ralph's. Fern is curious about the man and his van, which does not seem to be the type of vehicle he would drive. Fenno tells her the van belongs to his friend's mother, Lucinda. He also says he is there to bury his dog. An over-eager young man named Richard, a lover of Tony's, also shows up, as does Fenno's brother Dennis, who had been swimming in the sea.

Boys 1999: Chapter 16

Fern thinks about her role in her family. She was the "perfect daughter," deemed as such by her parents to the irritation and envy of her siblings, Heather, Forest, and Garland. Fern teaches Dennis how to properly shuck corn. Dennis, a chef, is having fun letting others do the cooking. Fern deduces that Fenno and Tony were once lovers by the way they interact. They all spend an enjoyable summer afternoon. Fenno reveals that he volunteers at a center for pregnant girls, and they produce a small newspaper. Fern also realizes that she has visited his bookshop in Greenwich Village, after Tony mentions the name. They all discuss mothers and mothering. Fern remembers meeting Stavros two months after Jonah's death, and how he helped her handle a potentially uncomfortable meeting with her former mother-in-law.

In the present, Fenno offers Fern a sip of wine and they discuss children, her baby, and his nieces and nephews. When they go into another room to share the pie Fern made with Richard, Tony, and Dennis, the group discusses AIDS, and the conversation gets somber.

Boys 1999: Chapter 17

Fern thinks about Jonah's death and knows it was not suicide. However, Jonah's mother believes it was and blames Fern for driving her son to kill himself. The police could not find any evidence to prove anything either way.

Fern and Fenno look outside for the missing Dennis, finding him on the tennis court apparently intoxicated. Fenno and Fern share a parental moment in looking after Dennis.

Fern remembers making dinner for Stavros the night after he helped her with Jonah's mother. They discussed her future plans, and when she wondered how she would be able to stay in the apartment after everything that happened, Stavros suggested staying where she was, just rearranging things for herself. Later that month, Fern ended up meeting some of Stavros's family for Thanksgiving in Queens, and, over the next year, she and Stavros got to know each other. A year after they began dating, she became pregnant.

In the present, Fern cannot sleep and goes downstairs for a drink, where she finds Fenno. Fenno asks where her husband is while she is at the shore. Fern tells him her husband is dead but rushes to explain about Stavros. Fenno asks if she will marry him but Fern does not know. Fenno tells Fern that he gave his sperm to his brother David and his wife Lil to help them have a child. They have twins now, Fenno explains.

In the morning, Fern encounters Tony and Fenno in the kitchen. The neighbor woman has invited them for brunch at her home. Fenno says he has to return to the city, and Fern asks if she might hitch a ride. They drive into the city with Dennis, who falls asleep in the back of the bus. Fern enjoys Fenno's company and realizes she might have fallen in love with him in another time and place. She falls asleep in the van and dreams of a dinner with Richard, Fenno, Dennis, Tony, and her own brothers. She awakens to a traffic jam and asks Fenno if she can use his phone. She checks her answering machine at home. Stavros has left a few messages—he is in town and wants to see her. Fern longs to see him. Fern calls Stavros, who is not home, and leaves a message, telling him she is on her way. She thinks about where he might be and plans to hunt him down. Fenno invites her to dinner one night soon with Stavros—if she likes. She imagines her son someday holding his father's hand as they stroll through a village in Greece and realizes she will probably find Stavros in Washington Square playing chess with his father. The novel ends with Fenno and Fern gazing at each other with contentment and a sense of peace.

CHARACTERS

Armand
Armand is Fenno's neighbor, a baker who dies of complications from AIDS.

Tony Best
Tony is a mysterious, charismatic photographer and house-sitter with whom Fenno begins a sexual relationship. Tony also had a sexual relationship with Fern Olitsky, whom he met in Paris. Fern breaks up with him when she discovers his interest in young men. She remains friends with him, and through him, meets Fenno.

Malachy Burns
Nicknamed "Mal," the flamboyant Malachy Burns gives his neighbor Fenno his parrot, Felicity, marking the start of a deep, close friendship. Mal also travels to Scotland with Fenno and is the catalyst for Fenno's realization that he is not fully embracing life. Mal lives luxuriously and appreciates high culture, like opera. He contracts AIDS and eventually commits suicide.

Marjorie Guernsey-Jones
A forceful schoolmistress from Devon, Marjorie meets Paul on the tour in Greece and meets his son Fenno at the meal in Scotland to honor Paul's death.

David McLeod
Twin to his brother Dennis, David is an equine surgeon living in the family home with his wife Lillian. David is the more serious twin, "devoid of wit," as Fenno says. Fenno also considers David his least favorite brother.

Dennis McLeod
Twin to his brother David, Dennis is a chef, husband to his French wife Veronique and father to daughters Laurie, Christine, and Thea. Dennis is Fenno's favorite twin and is nurturing and affectionate.

Fenno McLeod
The eldest son of Paul and Maureen McLeod, Fenno is a bookstore owner in Greenwich Village. He was inspired to open the bird-watching-themed shop after graduate school following a conversation with his literature professor, Ralph Quayle. He is aloof, observant, cautious. He does not like to get too emotionally attached to people. Fenno is one of three protagonists in the novel.

Lillian McLeod

Lillian is married to David McLeod and asks her brother-in-law Fenno to help her and David have a child.

Maureen McLeod

Maureen is Paul's late wife, who trained collies. She was aggressive, focused, intense. She treated Paul like an afterthought, perhaps not as valuable as her dogs. They met in a bar where she was waitressing. Maureen died from lung cancer.

Paul McLeod

Father to Fenno, Dennis, and David, newspaperman McLeod mourns his wife Maureen at the start of the novel. He travels to Greece, where he becomes smitten with a young woman—Fern—who has eyes for the tour guide. Paul decides to reside in Greece in order to start a brand-new life. Like Fenno, Paul is cautious and holds back from emotionally connecting with people.

Veronique McLeod

Mother to Laurie, Christine, and Thea, Veronique is a French flower designer who serves as a go-between when Lillian wants to ask Fenno to help her get pregnant.

Fern Olitsky

A book designer and widow whom Paul meets on his trip to Greece, Fern connects with Fenno at the end of the novel through their mutual friend Tony. After painful relationships with her husband Jonah and Tony, Fern must trust herself and her feelings before she can give her heart to Stavros, with whom she expects a child.

Ralph Quayle

Ralph Quayle is a professor of English who befriends Fenno and gives him the space and capital to open his bookstore in Greenwich Village.

Stavros

An eldest son, Stavros is the father of Fern's child. His father owns the building where Fern rented an apartment. To Fern, he represents stability, passion, and a future. He tells her stories of his Greek family history and of his homeland. He is the one who tells her that her husband accidentally fell from their apartment window.

Colin Swift

Colin Swift is a larger-than-life Englishman who comes to Maureen McLeod for advice on how to raise champion dogs. He is killed in a car accident.

THEMES

Death

Death serves as the core theme of *Three Junes*. The novel begins after the death of Paul's wife Maureen. Paul has traveled to Greece on a tour in order to grieve in his own space and time. Glass creates the narrative by interspersing flashes of the past with "present" action. Paul recalls when he met Maureen, the early days of their marriage, and other moments throughout their life as their family grew. Paul also remembers when Maureen became ill with lung cancer. Death, to Paul, seems rooted in memory and reflection, as well as in the present. Simple moments in the present draw him back into the past, as do the people he meets. From time to time, he cannot help but compare Fern, the young American artist, to Maureen, and the passive role that he used to play in his relationship with Maureen affects his hesitant relationship with Fern. Maureen's death makes Paul evaluate his life with her; it also inspires him to think about what he wants from his future life. Paul's death definitively anchors the second part of the novel, narrated by Fenno. Paul's children gather at the family home, Tealing, to prepare for the funeral. Paul's death inspires Fenno to look inward, to examine himself and who he has become. The contrast of Paul's death, which occurred in Greece, to Maureen's death, which happened at home with her family, pushes Fenno to evaluate the relationships he had with his parents and other members of his family. The death of his parents also prompts Fenno to reflect on the death of his close friend Mal, whom he once brought to Scotland for a visit. Neither Paul nor Fenno can seem to live in the moment; all too often they are caught in thoughts of the past in order to hold on to someone they have lost.

Memory

Memory plays a key role in *Three Junes*, as it goes hand in hand with mourning. Early in the novel, a conversation between Fern and Paul

TOPICS FOR FURTHER STUDY

- The settings of *Three Junes* serve as a structural device for the novel, as well as an aid in character and conflict development. In an essay, discuss how each setting—Greek islands, Scottish hamlet, West Village of New York City, and Long Island town—reflects a certain character and his or her emotional journey. How does each setting help build the plot of the novel?

- In *Three Junes*, Glass gives Fenno a first-person narrative. With a small group of your classmates, discuss the effect of that choice. How does this type of narration make his characterization different from the others in the novel? Be prepared to share your findings with the rest of the class.

- *Three Junes* is built on connections between the characters. In an essay, discuss at least three of the complex relationships and the way in which those overlapping connections serve in the personal development each character involved. What does the reader learn about the characters from these relationships? What does the character learn about himself or herself?

- One could say that *Three Junes* as a triptych reflects Glass's background as a painter.

Write an essay discussing how the division of this novel into three parts demonstrates her artistic leanings. Specifically, what does Glass gain by purposefully structuring the novel in three distinct parts that overlap? Look at images of triptychs online to inspire and support your ideas.

- With a small group of your classmates, discuss the way death is portrayed in the novel. How do different characters handle death? How does Glass seem to view death? Do your views on death align more with one character over another?

- *Three Junes* has been compared to Virginia Woolf's multi-perspective novel *Mrs. Dalloway* (1925), which inspired Michael Cunningham's multi-perspective novel *The Hours* (2000). Read either *Mrs. Dalloway* or *The Hours* and write an essay comparing it to *Three Junes*. Do the books share common themes? How are the themes expressed? Do the books reach similar conclusions about life, death, and love? Is there, in any sense, a central focal point around which the action in the novels revolves—an event, a person?

introduces the idea of a person's memory as untrustworthy or inauthentic. However, the only way Paul and Fenno can cope with the present is to search deep within themselves and examine the past. Paul escapes to Greece after Maureen's death and immediately begins seeing her in various women he encounters. Paul also tries to associate the tour guide Jack with his son Fenno, but cannot see much similarity. In trying to deal with his parents' deaths, Fenno retreats into memories of his days in New York during the 1980s. Fenno thinks about his mother and his childhood, as well as the birth and progression of certain friendships. Paul and Fenno look to these

memories to discover meaning in their lives and a better understanding of who they are. In the third part of the novel, Fern tries to deal with the memory of her husband Jonah, whose unexpected death came during a lonely marriage. She turns to the events before and after Jonah to come to terms with her feelings and to mourn the person she was when she was with him. Her memories intersect with Paul's as she thinks back on her trip to Greece, and with Fenno's as Fern's connection to Fenno's friend Tony is revealed. Paul, Fenno, and Fern use memories to take stock of who they are without the person they lost and to envision who they want to be.

The village of Oia in Santorini, Greece (*Image copyright Gregory Guivarch, 2009. Used under license from Shutterstock.com*)

Renewal

Although death, mourning, and grief serve as the thematic foundation for *Three Junes*, the story also emphasizes the idea of renewal, particularly during and after a period of personal tragedy and heartache. Paul travels to Greece to renew his spirit and discover new pleasures in an exotic setting. However, Paul cannot completely renew himself, especially in the wake of his wife's death; he has too many memories. Ultimately, he moves to the Greek isles to live out the rest of his life, in hopes that he can change his usual habits and "preoccupations," like fixating on the wrinkles in his own shirt.

Lil and David's desire for a child lends the possibility of hope and renewal to a family absorbed in the pain of loss. Lil and David ask Fenno to supply the sperm with which to fertilize her eggs. Although their longing to involve him in their creation of a new life makes him uncomfortable and a bit resentful at first, Fenno decides to help. He gradually comes to see the possible child as symbolic of life and as a sign that his family, his memories, and he himself, will live on. Another sign of renewal and hope for Fenno arrives when his niece Laurie takes the box of his father's ashes because she does not want them thrown in the sea. Fenno realizes that he has the same feelings—he cannot let go of his father or the memories. But in easing Laurie's mind, he eases his own, particularly as he thinks back to spreading the ashes of his friend Mal over a lake, in accordance with his final wishes. Fenno recognizes that he can move on. In the death of his friend Mal, he finds a way to move forward, and at the end of Fenno's narrative, he learns how to live.

Fern finds renewal of her life through her relationship with Fenno. For Fern, renewal comes in the form of security, as becomes clear at the end of the novel. Like Fenno, she reviews her past in order to discover who she is in the present, but fears moving forward. With Fenno, she "feels as if she's just waking up."

STYLE

Triptych

The structure of *Three Junes* resembles a triptych, an altarpiece or other work of art made up of a main central panel and two panels attached on either side. The subjects of the two "wings" can stand alone but also support or add meaning to the center panel. The novel's present action takes place in three separate years and is told through three points of view. The individual narratives of Paul and Fern, who meet on a tour of the Greek islands, supplement and enhance the narrative of Paul's son Fenno, told in first-person point of view and positioned second in the organization of the novel.

Point of View

Glass uses two different types of point of view to tell the story of *Three Junes*. The first section, "Collies," and the last section, "Boys," are told in third-person limited or subjective point of view, in which the author uses pronouns such as "he," "she," and so on, to chronicle the actions and thoughts of the character in focus. The perspective is of a single character, and the reader is privy only to the thoughts of that character. In the second section, "Upright," Glass allows Fenno to tell his own story in first-person point of view, using the pronouns "I" and "me."

Flashback

Glass uses flashbacks to piece together the stories of Paul, Fenno, and Fern. A flashback interrupts the narrative chronology to "flash back" to an incident that happened before the main time frame of action. In the first section of the novel, Paul's Greek holiday triggers him to think back to his life in Scotland and his memories of his late wife Maureen. In young Fern and in other women, he is reminded of his early relationship with his wife and of how their relationship unfolded over the years. The flashbacks in the novel are not in chronological order, but jump from time to time, from one event to another.

HISTORICAL CONTEXT

Terrorism

Three Junes takes place in three separate years: 1989, 1995, and 1999, and the characters often refer to events that took place throughout the 1980s and 1990s. For example, a week before Maureen died, Paul visited the crash site in Lockerbie, Scotland, of Pan Am flight 103, which exploded on its way from Heathrow Airport in London to New York's John F. Kennedy Airport. He pocketed a tube of lipstick from the wreckage, an object that has personal resonance and reappears in the novel when, after his death, he bequeaths the lipstick to his son Fenno. The Lockerbie tragedy took place on December 21, 1988, the result of a terrorist plot by Abdel Basset Ali al-Megrahi, a Libyan man, who was convicted in Scotland in 2001 and sentenced to life imprisonment. Al-Megrahi was released in 2009 for "compassionate" reasons (he was terminally ill) and sent back to Libya.

During Fenno's narrative, he mentions the bombing of Libya by the United States on April 15, 1986. After rising tensions with Libya, which the United States had linked to terrorist activities, the United States ordered an air strike to deter Libya from further support of terrorism. The air strike killed one hundred people. The explosion of Pan Am 103 over Lockerbie, Scotland, was seen by many as a retaliation for this air strike.

The AIDS Epidemic

The novel also makes reference to Ronald Reagan's presidency (1981–1989) and its "AIDS legacy." Although AIDS was first identified in the early 1980s, Reagan did not address the AIDS issue publicly until the Third International AIDS Conference held in Washington, D.C., in 1987. Craig Rimmerman, writing on the treatment of AIDS during the administrations of Ronald Reagan and Bill Clinton, says, "The Reagan administration treated AIDS as a series of state and local problems rather than as a national problem," which "helped to fragment the limited governmental response early in the AIDS epidemic." Furthermore, the conservative political climate of the Reagan White House may have hindered any positive step toward the public understanding of and response to AIDS. Because many of the early victims of AIDS were homosexual men, religious leaders such as the Reverend Jerry Falwell, a Reagan supporter, declared that "AIDS is the wrath of God upon homosexuals." In 2003, Michael Cover, former associate director for public affairs at Whitman-Walker Clinic, an AIDS health-care organization in Washington, claimed, "In the history of the AIDS epidemic, President Reagan's legacy is one of silence. It is the silence of tens of thousands who died alone and unacknowledged, stigmatized by our government under his administration."

The Parthenon at the Acropolis of Athens in Athens, Greece, one of the most famous archeological sites in the world (Image copyright Bryan Busovicki, 2009. Used under license from Shutterstock.com)

In 1989, Republican George H. W. Bush became the 41st president of the United States. During this year, scientists made important discoveries about the AIDS virus: it could be transmitted through sexual intercourse or blood transfusions; by intravenous drug users; and from pregnant women to their unborn children. Despite these conclusions, the disease was still primarily considered to be a "gay" disease, concentrated within the homosexual community. Scientists began to work on various treatments and vaccines but did not devise effective treatments until the mid-1990s. In 1989, 1.4 million Americans had contracted AIDS.

CRITICAL OVERVIEW

Winner of the National Book Award, *Three Junes* garnered praise from both literary critics and readers. A few reviewers found flaws with the novel, including Edward Hower who critiqued the book for *The World and I*. Hower remarked that the story had "a lack of dramatic tension. All the characters are sensitive, nice people, and they are always nice to each other.... Never do conflicts arise in the story, and it contains no real suspense." However, Hower also comments that "the book's great strength lies in its two skillfully developed characters, Fenno and Mal, and in the author's ability to set scenes evocatively." Other reviewers complimented Glass on her deft characterization and her richly textured and thematically resonant plot. *Los Angeles Times Book Review* contributor Mark Rozzo comments that the novel "goes after the big issues without a trace of fustiness and gives us a memorable hero." Similarly, Walter Wadas of the *Lambda Book Report* calls the *Three Junes* "a subtly textured, emotionally rich tale, written in language equally affecting. Julia Glass has in Fenno McLeod created a major character, a gay male protagonist, with a complete melodrama of a life. And that's very satisfying to read." *New York Times Book Review* contributor Katherine Wolff reaches an equally positive conclusion. She comments that

WHAT DO I READ NEXT?

- Glass's second novel, *The Whole World Over* (2006), tells the story of pastry chef Greenie Duquette, who accepts a position as the personal chef to the governor of New Mexico, taking her son and leaving her husband behind.

- *I See You Everywhere* (2008), Glass's third novel, deals with two sisters who work through their jealousy and a history of family competition. The novel contains thematic shades of *Three Junes*, as its conflict rises from grief, death, and family struggles.

- *The True and Outstanding Adventures of the Hunt Sisters* (2005), by Elisabeth Robinson, is her debut novel. It features a film producer, Olivia Hunt, who through letters to friends and family, chronicles the ups and downs of her life. The story unfolds as she travels back and forth to visit her younger sister Madeline, who has been diagnosed with leukemia.

- *The Alphabet Sisters* (2005), the American debut by Australian author Monica McInerney, tells the story of three estranged sisters whose grandmother coerces them into returning to Clare Valley, Australia, for her eightieth birthday.

- *Sister of My Heart* (2000) is a novel by Chitra Banerjee Divakaruni. Divakaruni chronicles the lives of two cousins born on the same day. They love each other as sisters, but after both enter into arranged marriages, they discover a secret that forever alters their relationship.

- *Vital Signs: Essential AIDS Fiction* (2007), edited by Richard Canning, is an anthology of AIDS fiction written in the 1980s and 1990s, during a period when AIDS was almost always fatal. The anthology includes Edmund White's classic novella *An Oracle*, symbolically set in the Greek islands.

- *What Looks Like Crazy on an Ordinary Day* (1998), by Pearl Cleage, was an Oprah Book Club pick. The female protagonist, Ava Johnson, has a wonderful life and owns a successful hair salon, until she discovers she is HIV-positive. She returns to her home town where she finds love, community, and a new sense of purpose.

"masterfully, *Three Junes* shows how love follows a circuitous path, how its messengers come to wear disguises. Julia Glass has written a generous book about family expectations—but also about happiness, luck, and, as she puts its, the 'grandiosity of genes.'"

CRITICISM

Michelle S. Lee

Lee is an assistant professor at Daytona State College and has taught courses in composition, rhetoric, film adaptation, and literature. In this essay, she discusses how the three narratives of Three Junes *are thematically united in the emotional longings and development of the novel's three protagonists.*

The triptych-like structure of *Three Junes* hinges on three different points of view and three intersecting narratives. Each of the three main characters—Paul, his son Fenno, and Fern, a woman they both meet at different points in their lives—experience similar emotional journeys, journeys that reflect each other on a thematic level. All three protagonists long for intimacy and personal connection in their lives. All three protagonists also engage in intense relationships that eventually reveal what they lack in their lives and motivate them to pursue what they truly desire. Furthermore, Paul,

> ❝ LIKE PAUL RESIDING OUTSIDE MAUREEN'S
> LIFE, FENNO STANDS AT THE PERIPHERY OF MAL'S
> LIFE, SIMPLY WATCHING.❞

Fenno, and Fern each discove a promising future once they acknowledge their desires.

Although the relationships that each of the three protagonists engage in are very different—Paul's long-term marriage to Maureen, Fenno's friendship with Mal, and Fern's affair with Tony and her young marriage to Jonah—none of these relationships offer the intimacy that Paul, Fenno, and Fern subconsciously crave. In Paul's case, he raised three children with Maureen and made a home in the Scottish countryside. Yet throughout their marriage, Paul was always waiting for Maureen's time and attention. In fact, "Paul had always assumed that at the end, whenever it might be, he and Maureen would have great stretches of time together, alone. They would talk about everything." That fantasy is never fulfilled because of Maureen's untimely death; however, even if Maureen had lived, Paul's dream of connecting with her probably would not have happened. Paul spends their entire marriage watching her pour all her energies into raising and disciplining her dogs. He feels as though he resides on the periphery of her life and is rarely allowed inside. Paul wished to be the object of her intense focus and "wondered sometimes if this was a standard against which his own attention might be secretly held—and found wanting." At the end of his life, Paul finds solace in Greece, where he decides to live. He stops waiting for his life to start and turns his attentions to new friends who enjoy his company. To acknowledge this new-found happiness, his younger sons believe they should spread his ashes in Greece after he dies.

Fenno, Paul's eldest son, also seeks intimacy, yet is too afraid at first to claim it. His relationship with Mal represents this conflict between wanting to have a personal connection with someone and being frightened of getting too close. Mal inserts himself into Fenno's life and forges a bond that Fenno cannot break. Though they do not have a romantic relationship, Fenno

and Mal develop a friendship based on trust, commitment, and loyalty. When he contracts AIDS, Mal foists his bird, Felicity, on Fenno to care for. At first, Fenno resists the request, but keeping the pet turns out to be a gift that will change Fenno's life. Like Paul residing outside Maureen's life, Fenno stands at the periphery of Mal's life, simply watching. Before they even meet, Fenno spies Mal through his apartment window, passionately smashing plates as operatic music plays. He sees Mal host vibrant parties to which he is not invited. Fenno feels left out, even slighted, but does not attempt to change the situation. But when Felicity enters his home, the bird exposes Fenno to feelings he does not expect. He comes to love the bird, "loved [her] at times to the point of doubting [his] sanity." He "loved her weighty presence on [his] shoulder when [he] reshelved books." Fenno gradually views Felicity not as a bird but rather a "soul mate."

Yet Fenno's relationship with Mal remains somewhat distant, even after Fenno becomes his caretaker of sorts. Fenno is terrified of growing close to this man who is dying and does not know what to say or do. He spends his time just listening to his friend, avoiding any discussion about the man's declining health. Fenno's uncertainty and hesitation actually enables him to help Mal die with dignity, as Mal knows Fenno will not become too emotional and refuse to carry out his plan. Later, after Mal's death, in remembering how he cared for Mal and Felicity, Fenno realizes that he does not want to be on the edge of people's lives. When his brother David and sister-in-law Lil ask him to donate his sperm so they might finally have a child, at first Fenno is hesitant, but he soon realizes that he wants that unique connection to someone, just as he wants to develop more meaningful relationships with his family and friends.

Fern, like Paul and Fenno, secretly longed to connect on a deeper level in her early relationships, particularly with her lover Tony and her husband Jonah. She was attracted to the charismatic Tony, so much so that she ignored his erratic, peculiar behavior and "let her misery bloom in passive silence . . . because of the way he loved her." For example, he would often leave her bed just after she fell asleep and sneak out of the apartment. Fern soon suspected Tony was having illicit affairs with young men, but she chose to turn a blind eye to the possibility because in his love "she felt almost holy." Not until she encountered him on the street, whispering in a boy's ear, did she face the fact that she had felt completely consumed by him, yet he had never really committed himself to her. As a result, when she meets Jonah, she is attracted to "what she perceived to be his serene decisiveness, his fidelity of focus." Jonah is predictable and safe. She can count on Jonah for his habits, and as an art historian, he complements her artistic pursuits. He seems perfect.

But Jonah, like Tony, does not give Fern what she needs from a relationship. After a year of marriage, Jonah is no longer interested in intimacy, and Fern finds herself pouring herself into books, paying special attention to their graphic design. As she did with Tony, she confronts Jonah, letting him know how lonely she feels in their marriage and how she wants it to work. He denies their problems, suggesting that all she needs is "patience." Fern explodes at his refusal to work on their relationship and his dismissal of her feelings. That night, she finds out that Jonah fell from their apartment window and was killed instantly.

The emotional distance she experienced with Tony and Jonah affects her future relationship with Stavros, her landlord's son. Though Stavros is kind, steadfast, and passionate, she holds back from getting fully involved with him, even after she finds herself pregnant with his child. Fern is afraid of one more relationship ending before it even begins. But in imagining her child and thinking of how much family and personal history means to Stavros, Fern realizes that she must let go of her fears from the past and trust Stavros if she wants the life she has always desired.

Paul, Fenno, and Fern ultimately discover hopeful and rewarding futures as a result of their disappointing pasts. Paul misses Maureen at first but discovers that her absence is "not entirely unwelcome." Fenno starts volunteering with Mal's mother Lucinda at the home for young unwed mothers and finds a passion in helping these women. At the same time, he opens his heart to the prospect of becoming an "uncle," though the children will be biologically his. Fern, at the end of the novel, cannot wait to be loved fully by Stavros and her child. Each of these three protagonists learns to overcome the pain caused by the distance in their relationships and to allow themselves to trust again. They take risks in changing who they are to who they

Olive Trees in a Mountain Landscape by Vincent van Gogh (Francis G. Mayer / Corbis)

would rather be. Julia Glass uses this internal conflict to thematically unite the three narratives that drive the novel. The emotional through-line enables all three characters and their stories to overlap and intertwine, making it possible for each separate point of view to relate to and reflect the others.

Source: Michelle S. Lee, Critical Essay on *Three Junes*, in *Novels for Students*, Gale, Cengage Learning, 2010.

Julia Glass

In this essay, Glass discusses writing and those writers who have influenced her work.

Nearing the end of my book tour for *Three Junes*, I'm surprised to find that my favorite part of the "events" is not reading aloud from the book itself but answering questions about my life as a writer (which suddenly feels a lot less dull), the lives of my characters (whom I'll talk about as interminably as I will about my children; all I'm missing are snapshots), and my

> *THREE JUNES*, AS I SEE IT, IS A NOVEL ABOUT HOW WE LIVE BEYOND HEARTBREAK, SHAME, AND REGRET OVER OPPORTUNITIES LOST BECAUSE OF THE EMOTIONAL BARRIERS WE RAISE; HOW WE MANAGE NOT TO GIVE UP ON LOVE; HOW MYSTERIOUS, INTANGIBLE GIFTS COME OUR WAY THROUGH THE PEOPLE AROUND US, BOTH PEOPLE WE LOVE AND PEOPLE WE HARDLY KNOW."

"methods" (best summed up as seat–of–the–pants). Certain questions come up repeatedly: How long did it take you to write this book? Are the characters based on people you know? Did you write from an outline? Others catch me off–guard: Are you writing a sequel? Where did you get those *shoes*? But there's one question I'd been told to expect yet so far haven't been asked: What writers influence your writing?

Perhaps my questioners know, as I have learned, that influence is (somewhat sadly) a matter of serendipity—and of largely unrequited craving. It's a lot like true love: It tends to come, if and when it comes, from somewhere you'd never have predicted. But that doesn't mean you can't pine, now and then, for the might-have-been. Beyond Shakespeare and Pope and other Unattainables, what writers do I *wish* might ravish me with influence—their ways with words, with morality and humor and pathos, seeping like sap through the neurons in my brain, the keys of my computer, deep down into my prose? At times, such longing feels like another, more youthful kind of angst: those writers like the boys in leather jackets who rarely if ever looked my way.

But oh, I have my list. At its head resides George Eliot—though perhaps she's more like a patron saint or muse, a benevolent Unattainable. Behind her, depending on my current struggles, the wish list tends to vary but almost always includes Andre Dubus the Elder (for the way he writes about love), Alice Munro (for the way she writes about the mysteries and epic repercussions of chance), Jim Harrison (for the gloriously flawed people he creates and the glorious predicaments they land themselves in), Iris Murdoch (for the devilish, earth-shaking choices she makes her characters face), Ralph Lombreglia and John Dufresne (for being both so exquisitely, painfully funny, so full of heart, inciting laughter on a sensual par with good sex). Charles Baxter, Rachel Ingalls, Richard Russo, John Casey... I'm greedy once I get going. Alas, influence is something for which you can only pray.

But inspiration, that's a kinder, gentler matter—and if I turn a less covetous eye on my list, I could say it's a list of writers who inspire me: amplify my senses of the physical world, my joy in language, my faith in the power of make–believe. The only impediment to reading their books is the urge—the almost literal itch—they sometimes give me to heave them aside like burning coals and get to work on mine.

I have heard writers claim that while they're working on a new book, they won't read anything contemporary, won't read anything they haven't read before, or simply won't read at all. They're too impressionable, they claim. I find such restrictions as absurd as protesting that you can't eat out if you're the household cook or can't give birth if you're an obstetrician. And when, after all, is a writer *not* working? In my head at least, the business of spinning stories has no closing time. Twists in my characters' lives, glimpses of their secrets, obstacles to their dreams... all arrive unbidden when I'm getting cash at the ATM, walking my son to camp, singing a hymn at a wedding. A significant character in *Three Junes* was conceived in a traffic jam, after prolonged exposure to this bumper sticker: LIFE. WHAT A BEAUTIFUL CHOICE. The point is, I'm never *not* working.

The books I read, if they intrude on my writing, do so as weather will pass through and touch a landscape—affecting it, yes, but only now and then leaving a permanent mark. This kind of inspiration struck, perfectly timed, when I was about two-thirds of the way through writing *Three Junes*. I'd bought—simply because I picked it up in a bookstore and found it appealing—Peter Cameron's third novel, *Andorra*, which I consumed with the appetite of a pie-eating contestant. Its narrator is a genteel but enigmatically haunted man who makes of himself a literal exile—only to find, of course, that's there no escape (from what, he will not fully confess, even to himself). The great pleasure of discovering a "midcareer" writer is having more to read at once, so I went right out and bought a collection of Cameron's stories and his previous novel, *The Weekend*, a book that would prove fortuitous to the completion of mine.

Three Junes, as I see it, is a novel about how we live beyond heartbreak, shame, and regret over opportunities lost because of the emotional barriers we raise; how we manage not to give up on love; how mysterious, intangible gifts come our way through the people around us, both people we love and people we hardly know. In each of the novel's three parts, a different character has suffered through a recent death, though the ways they live with their losses are as different as the characters themselves: a wealthy Scottish widower in his sixties, his gay expatriate son, and a young American woman whose life intersects with both of theirs on either side of a decade. Nearly all the book's characters are "privileged" people: well educated, well housed, bolstered by family, worries about money rarely urgent. And the settings, too, are mostly places of privilege: a fine old house in Scotland, an island in Greece, a cottage with a view of the ocean on Long Island. Periodically, writing about such characters, I have a crisis of faith: Who *cares* about the pain of such people, of people in such beautiful surroundings? Does it even, in this world of so much unbearable sorrow, "rate" as pain? Come to think of it, how trivial are *my* sorrows, and just how sheltered am I?

I was floundering at such a place when I picked up *The Weekend*. I was also facing down the true challenge of writing a novel: ending it. I knew who the characters were in the final third of the book, I knew the present action would take place over a weekend at that house on Long Island, I knew the alliances as they would stand at the end and that the end would be hopeful, but I did not know quite how the characters would get there. In *The Weekend*, I was surprised (and a little unnerved) to encounter a cast of characters from the very same world, even (as in *Three Junes*) a man still mourning the loss of another man to AIDS and a mother preoccupied with the fate of a small child. More remarkably, the novel ended, as I knew mine would, with the main character's return to New York City. I might have been depressed at the similarities, but I was energized (as well as

deeply moved by the novel itself)—and I became curious about what it was that had moved the modest "actions" of this story so powerfully forward in feeling. Where was the engine of change in these characters' lives? For Cameron's characters, like mine, do not face the consequences of war or famine or hurricanes or murder (bad manners might be their worst crime). They face the consequences of their memories, their emotions, their loyalties and betrayals, their words to the people around them.

I felt as if I had traveled abroad and run into next-door neighbors I'd never met at home or as if my characters, drifting about in my head, had discovered a gang of soul mates—souls who seemed not frivolous but tragically weighted. I was heartened by this kinship, even though Cameron's writing has a conciseness I could only envy. (Two thirds through, I was wrestling with 300–some pages and counting; *The Weekend*, like a prayer book, is paradoxically quite small.) And now I confess to an act of theft.

I looked at the superficial features our stories had in common: a weekend at a summer house; characters in mourning and characters fretful (as parents, as lovers, as siblings) for the future. What I saw in *The Weekend* was how everything that *happens* is created by a collision of the various characters' longings and fears and that accelerating this collision is the unplanned intrusion on a group of intimates by other people who are incompatible or somehow estranged. In the haphazard chemistry of their mingling emotions, seemingly ordinary interactions drive these characters together and apart in ways that crack open their hearts. Perhaps it's a variation on the old "stranger comes to town" plot device, but never mind; this is what I was striving for. What I stole was, simply, the arrival of unexpected guests, including a virtual stranger. I played here with a number of characters, two of whom I ultimately banished. Thinking about parties I had been to in the past, I came to the intuitive conclusion that gatherings of five are especially precarious.

In a strange way, Peter Cameron's novels and stories (whose settings are as rich as their characters) also revealed to me two things about my book that I had not seen quite so clearly before. I saw that I had chosen some of my settings not because I knew them well (some I hardly knew at all) but, unconsciously, because of the way they complemented the predicaments of my characters: For instance, that I chose Greece as the place to which a man flees when he wants to get a view of his past, and Scotland (land of clans and tartans) as the stage for a drama of family allegiance and deceit, suddenly took on added depth—which I was able to work with as I revised *Three Junes*. I saw as well, without apology, that it is about people who appear to the outside world as if they have everything—and while it's true that they have almost everything, that *almost* is a narrow but treacherous chasm mined with tragedy of an intimate kind. Such people, conscious of the good fortune they do have, often conceal their inner mourning in ways that only deepen the sorrow.

Last May, as I waited for *Three Junes* to become a real book, I was pleased to discover that Peter Cameron's latest novel, *The City of Your Final Destination*, was also landing on bookstore shelves. Reading it—savoring it—was an especially rich experience. Just like his previous novels, it is a page-turner whose suspense is almost purely emotional. A book about letting go—of defenses, secrets, ambitions, and other internal barriers—it is moving, exquisitely written, and ends perfectly, the only way it can.

At my readings, people who've read *Three Junes* often tell me they miss its characters and want to know what's become of them since the novel's end. Two people have surprised me now by asking if I'm plotting a sequel. The answer, for now, is no. But if I never bring them back from literary limbo, perhaps there's a heaven of sorts for characters readers still wonder about—and if there is, I know where mine are now: at a beautiful weekend house, by the sea or in the mountains, all in love but continuing to struggle . . . and sharing that heaven are the characters laid to rest by Peter Cameron.

Source: Julia Glass, "A Matter of Inspiration: When Characters from One Book Find Soul Mates in Another," in Powells.com, "From the Author," 2009

Dana Braga

This article is a features piece on Glass and Three Junes.

Sitting in traffic jams does wonders for novelist Julia Glass.

The Massachusetts native, who won the 2002 National Book Award for "*Three Junes*," her first novel, came up with the character Lucinda while stuck in a traffic snarl. She also came up with the idea for her second novel sitting in another backup.

"Traffic jams are amazing," Glass said. "It's valuable time to be alone with yourself and get into your thoughts, like in the shower, running errands, I like that time. I come up with a lot of ideas this way. This is why I don't ever want to get a cell phone," she said.

Glass, whose friends and family call her "Julie," is traveling to Massachusetts this weekend to begin a book tour promoting the paperback release of "*Three Junes*." It is a story that follows the lives of a Scottish family and their friends and lovers in Scotland, Greece, and Manhattan over two generations. The plot unfolds in flashbacks and flash-forwards, told by three separate narrators during the month of June, 1989, 1995 and 1999.

Glass has been an inspiration to aspiring writers since winning the National Book Award. Hers was not a conventional literary path. At age 46, she finished writing "*Three Junes*" on the kitchen table of her cramped Greenwich Village apartment in between editing corporate brochures and mothering her two young sons, ages 7 and 2.

"My wildest dream was to win one of those first novel prizes, not the National Book Award," she says excitedly. After winning, she received phone calls from friends and peers, one even congratulating her on winning the Pulitzer Prize.

"I didn't dream of achieving these heights. Once I found out I was a finalist I remember walking around wishing it could be protracted. I was certain I couldn't win it."

Then, of course, she did win it.

"Every day I just laugh that this has happened." She's under a lot of pressure now to make the next book just as good. But she takes all the commotion in stride.

"There is a cliche that the second novel is the sophomore slump," Glass said with a laugh. Her second book is under way. It is a story about marriage and fidelity and the consequences of trying to pursue happiness, not just for ourselves, but for those we love. The main character is a pastry chef named Greenie Duquette who is offered an unusual opportunity that uproots her family.

"She's innately happy and has a strong sense of direction, unlike my usual characters who are conflicted and tormented," Glass said.

Glass's parents still live in the Lincoln home the family moved to in 1965 when she was 9. She has lived in New York since 1980 but still thinks of Lincoln as home.

"I'm excited to come home. I still keep thinking I'll end up there," she said.

Glass, the oldest of two girls, worked in the Lincoln Public Library from fourth grade through high school. She loved books, but she was more drawn to art. At Yale in 1974, she was an art major. She thought about being an English major, but "I couldn't read a book a week. I'm a slow reader. I loved the visual arts and felt very challenged. I worked 10 years as a painter."

She graduated summa cum laude in 1978 and then spent a year in Paris on a painting fellowship. Like other contemporary authors, she moved to New York in 1980, and began work as a freelance writer and copy editor.

She lived in the West Village and got married. She eventually got a job as an editor at *Cosmopolitan*. She painted and read (George Eliot is her favorite).

In 1991 her marriage ended, in 1992 she was diagnosed with breast cancer and her sister committed suicide. Eventually her canvas became her computer that she filled with her stories and words, a process that she says was very "self-indulgent" and "healing." She wrote in "mental isolation" for many years, drawing on the hardships she coped with in her personal life.

"A good day of writing feels more ephemeral to me than a good day of painting. When I was a painter you're always creating a physical body of work. When you write it is in your computer or on paper in a drawer. It doesn't feel as real. With a painting you can look at what you've done and say, 'there, I've made something.'"

Busy at work on the book tour, writing her next novel and raising her two sons with her "mate," photographer Dennis Cowley, Glass is in a "wonderful" place now. Fun is playing with the children in the sandbox and the last movie she saw was "Spirited Away." She also will write a collection of short stories.

Source: Dana Braga, "Beginner's Luck?: First-time Author Julia Glass Never Expected National Book Award," in *The Patriot Ledger*, April 26, 2003, p. 49.

> **I THINK THAT A LOT OF WRITING FICTION COMES OUT OF THE LONGING TO LEAD OTHER LIVES, TO HAVE OTHER PROFESSIONS, TO BE IN DIFFERENT PLACES, TO JUST KNOW MUCH MORE."**

Ronald Kovach

In this excerpt, Kovach interviews Glass about Three Junes.

In an interview in Milwaukee, I chatted with Glass, 47, about *Three Junes*, her disregard for writing conventions, and her seat–of–the–pants methodology. She is a personable woman full of wit and intellectual vitality.

Your novel has an unhurried pace, almost like a 19th–century novel. It's quiet, it's not full of action, its suspense is largely emotional. Did you think this was a rather risky book in today's publishing climate?

I didn't think about anything except that I was kind of leading this daydreamy life of compulsively putting this story down. You know, there are pros and cons to not having gone through an MFA program or really studied creative writing at all [and one is that] you're enough out of the loop that you're too naive to know what everybody else is writing, except in so far as you're a reader, too. Having small children, I get so little reading done compared to what I used to do that I'm also not so in touch with a lot of contemporary fiction.

If you're a fiction writer, you can't choose what kind of fiction you're going to write; it comes from your word gut. It comes from your heart. I will say, when I was reading over what I was writing, I was thinking, "This is so old-fashioned." And that was about the only judgment I would pass sometimes.

It was also odd to be writing from a British character's point of view because we all have those stodgy associations with a British voice, so that Fenno's voice would sometimes seem very New York and kind of hip to me, and other times just hopelessly pompous.

But I didn't think about how the book would play in the marketplace.

Fenno just kept speaking to you, didn't he?

Yes. I was possessed by that character. Some writer I really admired said something like, "The biggest mistake that fledgling writers make is writing in the first person ... It's a deadly trap, only in the hands of the most accomplished and experienced of novelists does the first person work."

I have to say that one thing I really love about being given the platform I have at the moment is to give the lie to a lot of the so–called rules of writing fiction. You know, I just think you can be hamstrung by all the things you read about the things you must and should do.

I felt like, "Oh, my God, I have to get this into the third person," and I would try and it was like trying to steer a cafeteria tray down a luge course; I could not change the nature [of the material].

Speaking of "rules" for writers, you said once in reference to the adage "Write what you know," "Write what you want to know."

You do have to start with what you know, but if you stay with what you know, you're going to be writing in a tunnel. I say, write what you know but also write what you want to know, and pretend you know a lot more than you really do, and do your research later. That's my method.

I think that a lot of writing fiction comes out of the longing to lead other lives, to have other professions, to be in different places, to just know much more. You know how they say, when you want to be an actor, "You can only become an actor if that's all you want to be"? Well, I've kind of decided the opposite is true of being a fiction writer: that you can only be a really good fiction writer if there are too many things you want to be. Because you have to have this desire to be inside of so many other people.

So you live other lives, you imagine yourself into other situations; some fiction writers imagine themselves into other historical times. But you have to have that hunger to go beyond your own cosmos. There obviously must be exceptions—there are writers who, I suppose, excel in very introspective or very domestic fiction. But I think [it's wrong] to feel constrained by the idea that, "Oh, well, I can't write from a gay man's point of view because I don't know what it's like to be a gay man," or "I can't write from a war veteran's point of view because I don't know what it's like to be a war veteran."

And nowadays there's also the ugly aspect of political correctness. It's like, "How dare you write about a more oppressed kind of person than yourself?" Or someone who's undergone a kind of suffering that you have not experienced. And I don't think writers in previous eras ever had to deal with this issue.

It is totally possible to imagine yourself into a life and a soul and situation or a time of history that you will never experience firsthand.

Any other well-worn writing advice you care to differ with?

The one "rule" that kind of drives me nuts is that you have to write every day to be a good writer. It is not true. Now, you do have to write every day if you want to be a prolific writer.

Peter Cameron—he's somebody I really love—said in an interview last year that the lion's share of the writing is thinking. You do have to persevere, and you do have to put in the time, but the time may not be put in in a routine way at a typewriter. The putting down of the fictional dramas that go on in your head is really, timewise, a minority of the amount of writing.

Now, of course, the trick is to replay the things that are going on in your head, these narratives. I have a theory that the cell phone is doing away with people's ability to be in their own company—you walk down the streets of New York and everybody's having a conversation. That is when I have the most fruitful interior life. A very fruitful time for me in terms of stories of my characters unfolding is when I'm walking down the street, whether I'm shopping or going to pick up my kids.

I'm not saying you shouldn't aim to write every day, but you don't have to, you really don't have to at all.

This is a fairly sprawling novel. You're in several different countries, you have a number of interesting major and minor characters and many scene shifts and flashbacks, yet the control you sustain is impressive. With all the potential distractions in your life, how did you manage this?

A lot of making the plot run smoothly is revision. Every time I sit down to write, I start by sort of going back to what I wrote before and revising, and then move into the future. So that, in fact, probably two thirds of every time I sit down to write, it's [to work] on what I've already written.

At one point, for continuity, I had to create a time line separately in the computer.

Many of our readers are concerned with juggling family responsibilities and finding time to develop as a writer.

If you can stay up late or get up early, that's great. My best working time is afternoon. In my case, I think the way that I did it was to sacrifice, was to say, "OK, I'm 40 years old, I'm living in a one–bedroom apartment with a kid, and I am going to sacrifice." I had an adequate income, along with my partner, to support the family, but he wasn't making any more money than I was. It's not like he was supporting me. Realistically, I think that if you're in a relationship where you can ask the partner to shoulder the weight, that's the best way. I didn't do that.

All our friends were getting bigger apartments, getting country houses, going on these vacations. I just wasn't even considering those things. I mean, I'm proud I was able to do it, to just say I could be spending more hours being a journalist, I could be aiming to be a higher level of journalist, but I'm not going to do that, because my aim is going to be a fiction writer. So I'm going to make some compromises, and those compromises are going to mean that I'm making less money, I'm living in a smaller space; God only knows whether it'll pay off.

I mean, now it's sort of wonderful, to think back that often when I'd be infused with this guilt and panic—"My God, how am I ever going to put my kid through college? What if I never publish this novel?"—it's very gratifying (and it doesn't turn out that way for everyone) to feel like I made those sacrifices, and it paid off for me. The best thing about succeeding as a fiction writer—and by succeeding, I mean finding readers who love your book—is that you just feel like, "Oh, my God, I really was meant to do this, I really can do this."

You've spoken of the series of painful experiences that all happened to you within about one year: the "triple whammy" of a divorce; then being diagnosed with breast cancer (later followed by surgery and other treatment); then, 12 days after your diagnosis, your sister's suicide. How did those experiences shape you as a writer?

Let's just say, they didn't turn me into a fiction writer. I was already writing fiction when I sort of hit this spinout in my life.

Certainly, some of the fiction I had been writing before then seems like child's play to me.

I didn't do a lot of writing after my sister's death, and I was going through the treatment for my cancer. [At some point] I went back to this story ["Souvenirs," the precursor of "Collies"] in which Fern was kind of the main character and had this affair with this tour guide and Paul McLeod was this very minor character, and I looked at this story and I thought that he, this widower war veteran, is the most interesting character. I think it's that I just felt so much empathy for him. I felt like I was kind battle-weary. I wasn't a war veteran, I hadn't lost my lifetime spouse, but I had been through the wars.

A lot of the questions that I was grappling with in writing *Three Junes* came out of those losses. I had lost my only sibling, whom I loved dearly, and who was a very colorful, successful person, and I think that's also why I wrote so much about siblings [the McLeod brothers]. I wrote about brothers, not sisters, but I think I was writing a very parallel narrative to mine.

A cancer scare is also a loss—it's a loss of confidence in your health and your body.

So yes, there's no doubt that those events influenced the scope of this narrative.

Aside from not taking the "rules" of writing too seriously, do you have any other general advice for developing writers?

I found that what was very fruitful for me when I was writing short stories—and I think this helped get me under my agent's nose—was to submit to all those competitions sponsored by [literary] quarterlies. I entered tons of those. And I won a few and got runners–up in a few, and then I had kind of a little resume, and that helped get me taken seriously. Those things are very encouraging, and in some cases, you get to meet other writers who are the judges, or you get feedback on your work.

I'm a great believer in revise, revise, revise. That's the foundation of writing. Just as the lion's share of creating the novel is thinking, the lion's share of writing is revising.

Source: Ronald Kovach, "Late Bloomer: In Winning a National Book Award for Her First Novel, Julia Glass Beat the Odds—and Broke the 'Rules,'," in *The Writer*, Vol. 116, No. 11, November 2003, pp. 23–27.

SOURCES

Engelmann, Rebecca, Keren Gelfand, and Amalia Gio-karis, "AIDS Epidemic: 1989," in *The Web Chronology Project*, March 8, 2000, at http://www.thenagain.info/WebChron/World/Aids.html (accessed June 16, 2009).

Hower, Edward, "Bonds of Love and Loss—A Sensitive Portrayal of Family Relationships Set During Three Fateful Summers," in *World and I*, Vol. 18, No. 4, April 2003, p. 239.

Rozzo, Mark, Review of *Three Junes*, in the *Los Angeles Times Book Review*, May 26, 2002, p. 14.

Wadas, Walter, Review of *Three Junes*, in *Lambda Book Report*, September 2002, p. 21.

White, Alan. "Reagan's AIDS Legacy: Silence Equals Death." *San Francisco Chronicle*, June 8, 2004, B9.

Wolff, Katherine, Review of *Three Junes*, in the *New York Times Book Review*, June 16, 2002, p. 16.

FURTHER READING

Dearth, Kim, *Your Border Collie's Life: Your Complete Guide to Raising Your Pet from Puppy to Companion*, SUNY Press, 2003.

> For those interested in raising collies, this book provides advice on selecting a puppy, bringing it home, grooming, training, and other necessities in caring for a healthy dog.

Fitzgerald, Helen, *The Grieving Teen: A Guide for Teenagers and Their Friends*, Fireside, 2000.

> This book addresses the needs of teenagers coping with the death of a loved one and offers strategies to help them work through their pain and grief.

Hamby, Zachary, *Mythology for Teens: Classic Myths for Today's World*; Prufrock Press, 2009.

> This book puts a contemporary spin on learning classical mythology by relating ancient stories to modern culture, art, and literature.

Huegel, Kelly, *GLBTQ: The Survival Guide for Queer and Questioning Teens*, Free Spirit Publishing, 2003.

> Written in a direct tone aimed at young people, the book addresses questions about developing sexuality and covers issues such as "coming out," dating, religion, and life at school, work, and home.

Hutchison, Colin, *Scottish Highlands and Islands Handbook, 4th: Travel Guide to Scotland Highlands and Islands*, Footprint, 2009.

> A guidebook to the region written by a native Scotsman, this guide provides everything a person needs to know for a rich, exciting, and historically informative trip to Scotland.

Levithan, David, *Full Spectrum: A New Generation of Writing about Gay, Lesbian, Bisexual, Transgender, Questioning, and Other Identities*, Knopf, 2006.

> This anthology includes forty "real-life" stories of sexual identity, specifically targeting youth ages thirteen to twenty-three.

Schuurman, Donna, *Never the Same: Coming to Terms with the Death of a Parent*, St. Martin's, 2004.

> This guide offers advice about how to deal with losing a parent at an early age.

Winick, Judd, *Pedro and Me : Friendship, Loss, and What I Learned*, Demco Media, 2002.

> Winick, cast member of MTV's *The Real World 3: San Francisco*, tells the story of his friendship with Real World housemate and friend Pedro Zamora, an AIDS activist and educator who died of the disease in 1994—a friendship that led to personal enlightenment about AIDS awareness.

Glossary of Literary Terms

A

Abstract: As an adjective applied to writing or literary works, abstract refers to words or phrases that name things not knowable through the five senses.

Aestheticism: A literary and artistic movement of the nineteenth century. Followers of the movement believed that art should not be mixed with social, political, or moral teaching. The statement "art for art's sake" is a good summary of aestheticism. The movement had its roots in France, but it gained widespread importance in England in the last half of the nineteenth century, where it helped change the Victorian practice of including moral lessons in literature.

Allegory: A narrative technique in which characters representing things or abstract ideas are used to convey a message or teach a lesson. Allegory is typically used to teach moral, ethical, or religious lessons but is sometimes used for satiric or political purposes.

Allusion: A reference to a familiar literary or historical person or event, used to make an idea more easily understood.

Analogy: A comparison of two things made to explain something unfamiliar through its similarities to something familiar, or to prove one point based on the acceptedness

of another. Similes and metaphors are types of analogies.

Antagonist: The major character in a narrative or drama who works against the hero or protagonist.

Anthropomorphism: The presentation of animals or objects in human shape or with human characteristics. The term is derived from the Greek word for "human form."

Anti-hero: A central character in a work of literature who lacks traditional heroic qualities such as courage, physical prowess, and fortitude. Anti-heroes typically distrust conventional values and are unable to commit themselves to any ideals. They generally feel helpless in a world over which they have no control. Anti-heroes usually accept, and often celebrate, their positions as social outcasts.

Apprenticeship Novel: See *Bildungsroman*

Archetype: The word archetype is commonly used to describe an original pattern or model from which all other things of the same kind are made. This term was introduced to literary criticism from the psychology of Carl Jung. It expresses Jung's theory that behind every person's "unconscious," or repressed memories of the past, lies the "collective unconscious" of the human race: memories of the countless typical experiences of our ancestors. These memories are said to prompt illogical associations that trigger powerful emotions in the reader. Often, the emotional process is primitive, even primordial. Archetypes are the literary images that grow out of the "collective unconscious." They appear in literature as incidents and plots that repeat basic patterns of life. They may also appear as stereotyped characters.

Avant-garde: French term meaning "vanguard." It is used in literary criticism to describe new writing that rejects traditional approaches to literature in favor of innovations in style or content.

B

Beat Movement: A period featuring a group of American poets and novelists of the 1950s and 1960s—including Jack Kerouac, Allen Ginsberg, Gregory Corso, William S. Burroughs, and Lawrence Ferlinghetti—who rejected established social and literary values. Using such techniques as stream of consciousness writing and jazz-influenced free verse and focusing on unusual or abnormal states of mind—generated by religious ecstasy or the use of drugs—the Beat writers aimed to create works that were unconventional in both form and subject matter.

Bildungsroman: A German word meaning "novel of development." The *bildungsroman* is a study of the maturation of a youthful character, typically brought about through a series of social or sexual encounters that lead to self-awareness. *Bildungsroman* is used interchangeably with *erziehungsroman,* a novel of initiation and education. When a *bildungsroman* is concerned with the development of an artist (as in James Joyce's *A Portrait of the Artist as a Young Man*), it is often termed a *kunstlerroman.*

Black Aesthetic Movement: A period of artistic and literary development among African Americans in the 1960s and early 1970s. This was the first major African-American artistic movement since the Harlem Renaissance and was closely paralleled by the civil rights and black power movements. The black aesthetic writers attempted to produce works of art that would be meaningful to the black masses. Key figures in black aesthetics included one of its founders, poet and playwright Amiri Baraka, formerly known as LeRoi Jones; poet

and essayist Haki R. Madhubuti, formerly Don L. Lee; poet and playwright Sonia Sanchez; and dramatist Ed Bullins.

Black Humor: Writing that places grotesque elements side by side with humorous ones in an attempt to shock the reader, forcing him or her to laugh at the horrifying reality of a disordered world.

Burlesque: Any literary work that uses exaggeration to make its subject appear ridiculous, either by treating a trivial subject with profound seriousness or by treating a dignified subject frivolously. The word "burlesque" may also be used as an adjective, as in "burlesque show," to mean "striptease act."

C

Character: Broadly speaking, a person in a literary work. The actions of characters are what constitute the plot of a story, novel, or poem. There are numerous types of characters, ranging from simple, stereotypical figures to intricate, multifaceted ones. In the techniques of anthropomorphism and personification, animals—and even places or things—can assume aspects of character. "Characterization" is the process by which an author creates vivid, believable characters in a work of art. This may be done in a variety of ways, including (1) direct description of the character by the narrator; (2) the direct presentation of the speech, thoughts, or actions of the character; and (3) the responses of other characters to the character. The term "character" also refers to a form originated by the ancient Greek writer Theophrastus that later became popular in the seventeenth and eighteenth centuries. It is a short essay or sketch of a person who prominently displays a specific attribute or quality, such as miserliness or ambition.

Climax: The turning point in a narrative, the moment when the conflict is at its most intense. Typically, the structure of stories, novels, and plays is one of rising action, in which tension builds to the climax, followed by falling action, in which tension lessens as the story moves to its conclusion.

Colloquialism: A word, phrase, or form of pronunciation that is acceptable in casual conversation but not in formal, written communication. It is considered more acceptable than slang.

Coming of Age Novel: See *Bildungsroman*

Concrete: Concrete is the opposite of abstract, and refers to a thing that actually exists or a description that allows the reader to experience an object or concept with the senses.

Connotation: The impression that a word gives beyond its defined meaning. Connotations may be universally understood or may be significant only to a certain group.

Convention: Any widely accepted literary device, style, or form.

D

Denotation: The definition of a word, apart from the impressions or feelings it creates (connotations) in the reader.

Denouement: A French word meaning "the unknotting." In literary criticism, it denotes the resolution of conflict in fiction or drama. The *denouement* follows the climax and provides an outcome to the primary plot situation as well as an explanation of secondary plot complications. The *denouement* often involves a character's recognition of his or her state of mind or moral condition.

Description: Descriptive writing is intended to allow a reader to picture the scene or setting in which the action of a story takes place. The form this description takes often evokes an intended emotional response—a dark, spooky graveyard will evoke fear, and a peaceful, sunny meadow will evoke calmness.

Dialogue: In its widest sense, dialogue is simply conversation between people in a literary work; in its most restricted sense, it refers specifically to the speech of characters in a drama. As a specific literary genre, a "dialogue" is a composition in which characters debate an issue or idea.

Diction: The selection and arrangement of words in a literary work. Either or both may vary depending on the desired effect. There are four general types of diction: "formal," used in scholarly or lofty writing; "informal," used in relaxed but educated conversation; "colloquial," used in everyday speech; and "slang," containing newly coined words and other terms not accepted in formal usage.

Didactic: A term used to describe works of literature that aim to teach some moral, religious, political, or practical lesson. Although didactic elements are often found in artistically pleasing works, the term "didactic" usually refers to literature in which the message is more important than the form. The term may also be used to criticize a work that the critic finds "overly didactic," that is, heavy-handed in its delivery of a lesson.

Doppelganger: A literary technique by which a character is duplicated (usually in the form of an alter ego, though sometimes as a ghostly counterpart) or divided into two distinct, usually opposite personalities. The use of this character device is widespread in nineteenth- and twentieth-century literature, and indicates a growing awareness among authors that the "self" is really a composite of many "selves."

Double Entendre: A corruption of a French phrase meaning "double meaning." The term is used to indicate a word or phrase that is deliberately ambiguous, especially when one of the meanings is risqué or improper.

Dramatic Irony: Occurs when the audience of a play or the reader of a work of literature knows something that a character in the work itself does not know. The irony is in the contrast between the intended meaning of the statements or actions of a character and the additional information understood by the audience.

Dystopia: An imaginary place in a work of fiction where the characters lead dehumanized, fearful lives.

E

Edwardian: Describes cultural conventions identified with the period of the reign of Edward VII of England (1901-1910). Writers of the Edwardian Age typically displayed a strong reaction against the propriety and conservatism of the Victorian Age. Their work often exhibits distrust of authority in religion, politics, and art and expresses strong doubts about the soundness of conventional values.

Empathy: A sense of shared experience, including emotional and physical feelings, with someone or something other than oneself. Empathy is often used to describe the response of a reader to a literary character.

Enlightenment, The: An eighteenth-century philosophical movement. It began in France but had a wide impact throughout Europe and

America. Thinkers of the Enlightenment valued reason and believed that both the individual and society could achieve a state of perfection. Corresponding to this essentially humanist vision was a resistance to religious authority.

Epigram: A saying that makes the speaker's point quickly and concisely. Often used to preface a novel.

Epilogue: A concluding statement or section of a literary work. In dramas, particularly those of the seventeenth and eighteenth centuries, the epilogue is a closing speech, often in verse, delivered by an actor at the end of a play and spoken directly to the audience.

Epiphany: A sudden revelation of truth inspired by a seemingly trivial incident.

Episode: An incident that forms part of a story and is significantly related to it. Episodes may be either self-contained narratives or events that depend on a larger context for their sense and importance.

Epistolary Novel: A novel in the form of letters. The form was particularly popular in the eighteenth century.

Epithet: A word or phrase, often disparaging or abusive, that expresses a character trait of someone or something.

Existentialism: A predominantly twentieth-century philosophy concerned with the nature and perception of human existence. There are two major strains of existentialist thought: atheistic and Christian. Followers of atheistic existentialism believe that the individual is alone in a godless universe and that the basic human condition is one of suffering and loneliness. Nevertheless, because there are no fixed values, individuals can create their own characters—indeed, they can shape themselves—through the exercise of free will. The atheistic strain culminates in and is popularly associated with the works of Jean-Paul Sartre. The Christian existentialists, on the other hand, believe that only in God may people find freedom from life's anguish. The two strains hold certain beliefs in common: that existence cannot be fully understood or described through empirical effort; that anguish is a universal element of life; that individuals must bear responsibility for their actions; and that there is no common

standard of behavior or perception for religious and ethical matters.

Expatriates: See *Expatriatism*

Expatriatism: The practice of leaving one's country to live for an extended period in another country.

Exposition: Writing intended to explain the nature of an idea, thing, or theme. Expository writing is often combined with description, narration, or argument. In dramatic writing, the exposition is the introductory material which presents the characters, setting, and tone of the play.

Expressionism: An indistinct literary term, originally used to describe an early twentieth-century school of German painting. The term applies to almost any mode of unconventional, highly subjective writing that distorts reality in some way.

F

Fable: A prose or verse narrative intended to convey a moral. Animals or inanimate objects with human characteristics often serve as characters in fables.

Falling Action: See *Denouement*

Fantasy: A literary form related to mythology and folklore. Fantasy literature is typically set in non-existent realms and features supernatural beings.

Farce: A type of comedy characterized by broad humor, outlandish incidents, and often vulgar subject matter.

Femme fatale: A French phrase with the literal translation "fatal woman." A *femme fatale* is a sensuous, alluring woman who often leads men into danger or trouble.

Fiction: Any story that is the product of imagination rather than a documentation of fact. characters and events in such narratives may be based in real life but their ultimate form and configuration is a creation of the author.

Figurative Language: A technique in writing in which the author temporarily interrupts the order, construction, or meaning of the writing for a particular effect. This interruption takes the form of one or more figures of speech such as hyperbole, irony, or simile. Figurative language is the opposite of literal language, in which every word is truthful, accurate, and free of exaggeration or embellishment.

Figures of Speech: Writing that differs from customary conventions for construction, meaning, order, or significance for the purpose of a special meaning or effect. There are two major types of figures of speech: rhetorical figures, which do not make changes in the meaning of the words, and tropes, which do.

Fin de siecle: A French term meaning "end of the century." The term is used to denote the last decade of the nineteenth century, a transition period when writers and other artists abandoned old conventions and looked for new techniques and objectives.

First Person: See *Point of View*

Flashback: A device used in literature to present action that occurred before the beginning of the story. Flashbacks are often introduced as the dreams or recollections of one or more characters.

Foil: A character in a work of literature whose physical or psychological qualities contrast strongly with, and therefore highlight, the corresponding qualities of another character.

Folklore: Traditions and myths preserved in a culture or group of people. Typically, these are passed on by word of mouth in various forms—such as legends, songs, and proverbs—or preserved in customs and ceremonies. This term was first used by W. J. Thoms in 1846.

Folktale: A story originating in oral tradition. Folktales fall into a variety of categories, including legends, ghost stories, fairy tales, fables, and anecdotes based on historical figures and events.

Foreshadowing: A device used in literature to create expectation or to set up an explanation of later developments.

Form: The pattern or construction of a work which identifies its genre and distinguishes it from other genres.

G

Genre: A category of literary work. In critical theory, genre may refer to both the content of a given work—tragedy, comedy, pastoral—and to its form, such as poetry, novel, or drama.

Gilded Age: A period in American history during the 1870s characterized by political corruption and materialism. A number of important novels of social and political criticism were written during this time.

Gothicism: In literary criticism, works characterized by a taste for the medieval or morbidly attractive. A gothic novel prominently features elements of horror, the supernatural, gloom, and violence: clanking chains, terror, charnel houses, ghosts, medieval castles, and mysteriously slamming doors. The term "gothic novel" is also applied to novels that lack elements of the traditional Gothic setting but that create a similar atmosphere of terror or dread.

Grotesque: In literary criticism, the subject matter of a work or a style of expression characterized by exaggeration, deformity, freakishness, and disorder. The grotesque often includes an element of comic absurdity.

H

Harlem Renaissance: The Harlem Renaissance of the 1920s is generally considered the first significant movement of black writers and artists in the United States. During this period, new and established black writers published more fiction and poetry than ever before, the first influential black literary journals were established, and black authors and artists received their first widespread recognition and serious critical appraisal. Among the major writers associated with this period are Claude McKay, Jean Toomer, Countee Cullen, Langston Hughes, Arna Bontemps, Nella Larsen, and Zora Neale Hurston.

Hero/Heroine: The principal sympathetic character (male or female) in a literary work. Heroes and heroines typically exhibit admirable traits: idealism, courage, and integrity, for example.

Holocaust Literature: Literature influenced by or written about the Holocaust of World War II. Such literature includes true stories of survival in concentration camps, escape, and life after the war, as well as fictional works and poetry.

Humanism: A philosophy that places faith in the dignity of humankind and rejects the medieval perception of the individual as a weak, fallen creature. "Humanists" typically believe in the perfectibility of human nature and view reason and education as the means to that end.

Hyperbole: In literary criticism, deliberate exaggeration used to achieve an effect.

I

Idiom: A word construction or verbal expression closely associated with a given language.

Image: A concrete representation of an object or sensory experience. Typically, such a representation helps evoke the feelings associated with the object or experience itself. Images are either "literal" or "figurative." Literal images are especially concrete and involve little or no extension of the obvious meaning of the words used to express them. Figurative images do not follow the literal meaning of the words exactly. Images in literature are usually visual, but the term "image" can also refer to the representation of any sensory experience.

Imagery: The array of images in a literary work. Also, figurative language.

In medias res: A Latin term meaning "in the middle of things." It refers to the technique of beginning a story at its midpoint and then using various flashback devices to reveal previous action.

Interior Monologue: A narrative technique in which characters' thoughts are revealed in a way that appears to be uncontrolled by the author. The interior monologue typically aims to reveal the inner self of a character. It portrays emotional experiences as they occur at both a conscious and unconscious level. images are often used to represent sensations or emotions.

Irony: In literary criticism, the effect of language in which the intended meaning is the opposite of what is stated.

J

Jargon: Language that is used or understood only by a select group of people. Jargon may refer to terminology used in a certain profession, such as computer jargon, or it may refer to any nonsensical language that is not understood by most people.

L

Leitmotiv: See *Motif*

Literal Language: An author uses literal language when he or she writes without exaggerating or embellishing the subject matter and without any tools of figurative language.

Lost Generation: A term first used by Gertrude Stein to describe the post-World War I generation of American writers: men and women haunted by a sense of betrayal and emptiness brought about by the destructiveness of the war.

M

Mannerism: Exaggerated, artificial adherence to a literary manner or style. Also, a popular style of the visual arts of late sixteenth-century Europe that was marked by elongation of the human form and by intentional spatial distortion. Literary works that are self-consciously high-toned and artistic are often said to be "mannered."

Metaphor: A figure of speech that expresses an idea through the image of another object. Metaphors suggest the essence of the first object by identifying it with certain qualities of the second object.

Modernism: Modern literary practices. Also, the principles of a literary school that lasted from roughly the beginning of the twentieth century until the end of World War II. Modernism is defined by its rejection of the literary conventions of the nineteenth century and by its opposition to conventional morality, taste, traditions, and economic values.

Mood: The prevailing emotions of a work or of the author in his or her creation of the work. The mood of a work is not always what might be expected based on its subject matter.

Motif: A theme, character type, image, metaphor, or other verbal element that recurs throughout a single work of literature or occurs in a number of different works over a period of time.

Myth: An anonymous tale emerging from the traditional beliefs of a culture or social unit. Myths use supernatural explanations for natural phenomena. They may also explain cosmic issues like creation and death. Collections of myths, known as mythologies, are common to all cultures and nations, but the best-known myths belong to the Norse, Roman, and Greek mythologies.

N

Narration: The telling of a series of events, real or invented. A narration may be either a simple narrative, in which the events are recounted chronologically, or a narrative with a plot, in which the account is given in a style reflecting the author's artistic concept of the story. Narration is sometimes used as a synonym for "storyline."

Narrative: A verse or prose accounting of an event or sequence of events, real or invented. The term is also used as an adjective in the sense "method of narration." For example, in literary criticism, the expression "narrative technique" usually refers to the way the author structures and presents his or her story.

Narrator: The teller of a story. The narrator may be the author or a character in the story through whom the author speaks.

Naturalism: A literary movement of the late nineteenth and early twentieth centuries. The movement's major theorist, French novelist Emile Zola, envisioned a type of fiction that would examine human life with the objectivity of scientific inquiry. The Naturalists typically viewed human beings as either the products of "biological determinism," ruled by hereditary instincts and engaged in an endless struggle for survival, or as the products of "socioeconomic determinism," ruled by social and economic forces beyond their control. In their works, the Naturalists generally ignored the highest levels of society and focused on degradation: poverty, alcoholism, prostitution, insanity, and disease.

Noble Savage: The idea that primitive man is noble and good but becomes evil and corrupted as he becomes civilized. The concept of the noble savage originated in the Renaissance period but is more closely identified with such later writers as Jean-Jacques Rousseau and Aphra Behn.

Novel: A long fictional narrative written in prose, which developed from the novella and other early forms of narrative. A novel is usually organized under a plot or theme with a focus on character development and action.

Novel of Ideas: A novel in which the examination of intellectual issues and concepts takes precedence over characterization or a traditional storyline.

Novel of Manners: A novel that examines the customs and mores of a cultural group.

Novella: An Italian term meaning "story." This term has been especially used to describe fourteenth-century Italian tales, but it also refers to modern short novels.

O

Objective Correlative: An outward set of objects, a situation, or a chain of events corresponding to an inward experience and evoking this experience in the reader. The term frequently appears in modern criticism in discussions of authors' intended effects on the emotional responses of readers.

Objectivity: A quality in writing characterized by the absence of the author's opinion or feeling about the subject matter. Objectivity is an important factor in criticism.

Oedipus Complex: A son's amorous obsession with his mother. The phrase is derived from the story of the ancient Theban hero Oedipus, who unknowingly killed his father and married his mother.

Omniscience: See *Point of View*

Onomatopoeia: The use of words whose sounds express or suggest their meaning. In its simplest sense, onomatopoeia may be represented by words that mimic the sounds they denote such as "hiss" or "meow." At a more subtle level, the pattern and rhythm of sounds and rhymes of a line or poem may be onomatopoeic.

Oxymoron: A phrase combining two contradictory terms. Oxymorons may be intentional or unintentional.

P

Parable: A story intended to teach a moral lesson or answer an ethical question.

Paradox: A statement that appears illogical or contradictory at first, but may actually point to an underlying truth.

Parallelism: A method of comparison of two ideas in which each is developed in the same grammatical structure.

Parody: In literary criticism, this term refers to an imitation of a serious literary work or the signature style of a particular author in a ridiculous manner. A typical parody adopts the style of the original and applies it to an inappropriate subject for humorous effect. Parody is a form of satire and could be considered the literary equivalent of a caricature or cartoon.

Pastoral: A term derived from the Latin word "pastor," meaning shepherd. A pastoral is a literary composition on a rural theme. The conventions of the pastoral were originated by the third-century Greek poet Theocritus, who wrote about the experiences, love affairs, and pastimes of Sicilian shepherds. In a pastoral, characters and language of a courtly nature are often placed in a simple setting. The term pastoral is also used to classify dramas, elegies, and lyrics that exhibit the use of country settings and shepherd characters.

Pen Name: See *Pseudonym*

Persona: A Latin term meaning "mask." *Personae* are the characters in a fictional work of literature. The *persona* generally functions as a mask through which the author tells a story in a voice other than his or her own. A *persona* is usually either a character in a story who acts as a narrator or an "implied author," a voice created by the author to act as the narrator for himself or herself.

Personification: A figure of speech that gives human qualities to abstract ideas, animals, and inanimate objects.

Picaresque Novel: Episodic fiction depicting the adventures of a roguish central character ("picaro" is Spanish for "rogue"). The picaresque hero is commonly a low-born but clever individual who wanders into and out of various affairs of love, danger, and farcical intrigue. These involvements may take place at all social levels and typically present a humorous and wide-ranging satire of a given society.

Plagiarism: Claiming another person's written material as one's own. Plagiarism can take the form of direct, word-for-word copying or the theft of the substance or idea of the work.

Plot: In literary criticism, this term refers to the pattern of events in a narrative or drama. In its simplest sense, the plot guides the author in composing the work and helps the reader follow the work. Typically, plots exhibit causality and unity and have a beginning, a middle, and an end. Sometimes, however, a plot may consist of a series of disconnected events, in which case it is known as an "episodic plot."

Poetic Justice: An outcome in a literary work, not necessarily a poem, in which the good are rewarded and the evil are punished, especially in ways that particularly fit their virtues or crimes.

Poetic License: Distortions of fact and literary convention made by a writer—not always a poet—for the sake of the effect gained. Poetic license is closely related to the concept of "artistic freedom."

Poetics: This term has two closely related meanings. It denotes (1) an aesthetic theory in literary criticism about the essence of poetry or (2) rules prescribing the proper methods, content, style, or diction of poetry. The term poetics may also refer to theories about literature in general, not just poetry.

Point of View: The narrative perspective from which a literary work is presented to the reader. There are four traditional points of view. The "third person omniscient" gives the reader a "godlike" perspective, unrestricted by time or place, from which to see actions and look into the minds of characters. This allows the author to comment openly on characters and events in the work. The "third person" point of view presents the events of the story from outside of any single character's perception, much like the omniscient point of view, but the reader must understand the action as it takes place and without any special insight into characters' minds or motivations. The "first person" or "personal" point of view relates events as they are perceived by a single character. The main character "tells" the story and may offer opinions about the action and characters which differ from those of the author. Much less common than omniscient, third person, and first person is the "second person" point of view, wherein the author tells the story as if it is happening to the reader.

Polemic: A work in which the author takes a stand on a controversial subject, such as abortion or religion. Such works are often extremely argumentative or provocative.

Pornography: Writing intended to provoke feelings of lust in the reader. Such works are often condemned by critics and teachers, but those which can be shown to have literary value are viewed less harshly.

Post-Aesthetic Movement: An artistic response made by African Americans to the black aesthetic movement of the 1960s and early '70s. Writers since that time have adopted a somewhat different tone in their work, with less emphasis placed on the disparity between black and white in the United States. In the words of post-aesthetic authors such as Toni Morrison, John Edgar Wideman, and Kristin Hunter, African Americans are portrayed as looking inward for answers to their own questions, rather than always looking to the outside world.

Postmodernism: Writing from the 1960s forward characterized by experimentation and continuing to apply some of the fundamentals of modernism, which included existentialism and alienation. Postmodernists have gone a step further in the rejection of tradition begun with the modernists by also rejecting traditional forms, preferring the anti-novel over the novel and the anti-hero over the hero.

Primitivism: The belief that primitive peoples were nobler and less flawed than civilized peoples because they had not been subjected to the tainting influence of society.

Prologue: An introductory section of a literary work. It often contains information establishing the situation of the characters or presents information about the setting, time period, or action. In drama, the prologue is spoken by a chorus or by one of the principal characters.

Prose: A literary medium that attempts to mirror the language of everyday speech. It is distinguished from poetry by its use of unmetered, unrhymed language consisting of logically related sentences. Prose is usually grouped into paragraphs that form a cohesive whole such as an essay or a novel.

Prosopopoeia: See *Personification*

Protagonist: The central character of a story who serves as a focus for its themes and incidents and as the principal rationale for its development. The protagonist is sometimes referred to in discussions of modern literature as the hero or anti-hero.

Protest Fiction: Protest fiction has as its primary purpose the protesting of some social injustice, such as racism or discrimination.

Proverb: A brief, sage saying that expresses a truth about life in a striking manner.

Pseudonym: A name assumed by a writer, most often intended to prevent his or her identification as the author of a work. Two or more authors may work together under one pseudonym, or an author may use a different name for each genre he or she publishes in. Some publishing companies maintain "house pseudonyms," under which any number of authors may write installations in a series. Some authors also choose a pseudonym over their real names the way an actor may use a stage name.

Pun: A play on words that have similar sounds but different meanings.

R

Realism: A nineteenth-century European literary movement that sought to portray familiar characters, situations, and settings in a realistic manner. This was done primarily by using an objective narrative point of view and through the buildup of accurate detail. The standard for success of any realistic work depends on how faithfully it transfers common experience into fictional forms. The realistic method may be altered or extended, as in stream of consciousness writing, to record highly subjective experience.

Repartee: Conversation featuring snappy retorts and witticisms.

Resolution: The portion of a story following the climax, in which the conflict is resolved.

Rhetoric: In literary criticism, this term denotes the art of ethical persuasion. In its strictest sense, rhetoric adheres to various principles developed since classical times for arranging facts and ideas in a clear, persuasive, appealing manner. The term is also used to refer to effective prose in general and theories of or methods for composing effective prose.

Rhetorical Question: A question intended to provoke thought, but not an expressed answer, in the reader. It is most commonly used in oratory and other persuasive genres.

Rising Action: The part of a drama where the plot becomes increasingly complicated. Rising action leads up to the climax, or turning point, of a drama.

Roman à clef: A French phrase meaning "novel with a key." It refers to a narrative in which real persons are portrayed under fictitious names.

Romance: A broad term, usually denoting a narrative with exotic, exaggerated, often idealized characters, scenes, and themes.

Romanticism: This term has two widely accepted meanings. In historical criticism, it refers to a European intellectual and artistic movement of the late eighteenth and early nineteenth centuries that sought greater freedom of personal expression than that allowed by the strict rules of literary form and logic of the eighteenth-century neoclassicists. The Romantics preferred emotional and imaginative expression to rational analysis. They considered the individual to be at the center of all experience and so placed him or her at the center of their art. The Romantics believed that the creative imagination reveals nobler truths—unique feelings and attitudes—than those that could be discovered by logic or by scientific examination. Both the natural world and the state of childhood were important sources for revelations of "eternal truths." "Romanticism" is also used as a general term to refer to a type of sensibility found in all periods of literary history and usually considered to be in opposition to the principles of classicism. In this sense, Romanticism signifies any work or philosophy in which the exotic or dreamlike figure strongly, or that is devoted to individualistic expression, self-analysis, or a pursuit of a higher realm of knowledge than can be discovered by human reason.

Romantics: See *Romanticism*

S

Satire: A work that uses ridicule, humor, and wit to criticize and provoke change in human nature and institutions. There are two major types of satire: "formal" or "direct" satire speaks directly to the reader or to a character in the work; "indirect" satire relies upon the ridiculous behavior of its characters to make its point. Formal satire is further divided into two manners: the "Horatian," which ridicules gently, and the "Juvenalian," which derides its subjects harshly and bitterly.

Science Fiction: A type of narrative about or based upon real or imagined scientific theories and technology. Science fiction is often peopled with alien creatures and set on other planets or in different dimensions.

Second Person: See *Point of View*

Setting: The time, place, and culture in which the action of a narrative takes place. The elements of setting may include geographic location, characters' physical and mental environments, prevailing cultural attitudes, or the historical time in which the action takes place.

Simile: A comparison, usually using "like" or "as," of two essentially dissimilar things, as in "coffee as cold as ice" or "He sounded like a broken record."

Slang: A type of informal verbal communication that is generally unacceptable for formal writing. Slang words and phrases are often colorful exaggerations used to emphasize the speaker's point; they may also be shortened versions of an often-used word or phrase.

Slave Narrative: Autobiographical accounts of American slave life as told by escaped slaves. These works first appeared during the abolition movement of the 1830s through the 1850s.

Socialist Realism: The Socialist Realism school of literary theory was proposed by Maxim Gorky and established as a dogma by the first Soviet Congress of Writers. It demanded adherence to a communist worldview in works of literature. Its doctrines required an objective viewpoint comprehensible to the working classes and themes of social struggle featuring strong proletarian heroes.

Stereotype: A stereotype was originally the name for a duplication made during the printing process; this led to its modern definition as a person or thing that is (or is assumed to be) the same as all others of its type.

Stream of Consciousness: A narrative technique for rendering the inward experience of a character. This technique is designed to give the impression of an ever-changing series of thoughts, emotions, images, and memories in the spontaneous and seemingly illogical order that they occur in life.

Structure: The form taken by a piece of literature. The structure may be made obvious for ease of understanding, as in nonfiction works, or may obscured for artistic purposes, as in some poetry or seemingly "unstructured" prose.

Sturm und Drang: A German term meaning "storm and stress." It refers to a German literary movement of the 1770s and 1780s that reacted against the order and rationalism of the enlightenment, focusing instead on the intense experience of extraordinary individuals.

Style: A writer's distinctive manner of arranging words to suit his or her ideas and purpose in writing. The unique imprint of the author's personality upon his or her writing, style is the product of an author's way of arranging ideas and his or her use of diction, different sentence structures, rhythm, figures of speech, rhetorical principles, and other elements of composition.

Subjectivity: Writing that expresses the author's personal feelings about his subject, and which may or may not include factual information about the subject.

Subplot: A secondary story in a narrative. A subplot may serve as a motivating or complicating force for the main plot of the work, or it may provide emphasis for, or relief from, the main plot.

Surrealism: A term introduced to criticism by Guillaume Apollinaire and later adopted by Andre Breton. It refers to a French literary and artistic movement founded in the 1920s. The Surrealists sought to express unconscious thoughts and feelings in their works. The best-known technique used for achieving this aim was automatic writing—transcriptions of spontaneous outpourings from the unconscious. The Surrealists proposed to unify the contrary levels of conscious and unconscious, dream and reality, objectivity and subjectivity into a new level of "super-realism."

Suspense: A literary device in which the author maintains the audience's attention through the buildup of events, the outcome of which will soon be revealed.

Symbol: Something that suggests or stands for something else without losing its original identity. In literature, symbols combine their literal meaning with the suggestion of an abstract concept. Literary symbols are of two types: those that carry complex associations of meaning no matter what their contexts, and those that derive their suggestive meaning from their functions in specific literary works.

Symbolism: This term has two widely accepted meanings. In historical criticism, it denotes an early modernist literary movement initiated in France during the nineteenth century that reacted against the prevailing standards of realism. Writers in this movement aimed to evoke, indirectly and symbolically, an order of being beyond the material world of the five senses. Poetic expression of personal emotion figured strongly in the movement, typically by means of a private set of symbols uniquely identifiable with the individual poet. The principal aim of the Symbolists was to express in words the highly complex feelings that grew out of everyday contact with the world. In a broader sense, the term "symbolism" refers to the use of one object to represent another.

T

Tall Tale: A humorous tale told in a straightforward, credible tone but relating absolutely impossible events or feats of the characters. Such tales were commonly told of frontier adventures during the settlement of the west in the United States.

Theme: The main point of a work of literature. The term is used interchangeably with thesis.

Thesis: A thesis is both an essay and the point argued in the essay. Thesis novels and thesis plays share the quality of containing a thesis which is supported through the action of the story.

Third Person: See *Point of View*

Tone: The author's attitude toward his or her audience may be deduced from the tone of the work. A formal tone may create distance or convey politeness, while an informal tone may encourage a friendly, intimate, or intrusive feeling in the reader. The author's attitude toward his or her subject matter may also be deduced from the tone of the words he or she uses in discussing it.

Transcendentalism: An American philosophical and religious movement, based in New England from around 1835 until the Civil War. Transcendentalism was a form of American romanticism that had its roots abroad in the works of Thomas Carlyle, Samuel Coleridge, and Johann Wolfgang von Goethe. The Transcendentalists stressed the importance of intuition and subjective experience in communication with God. They rejected religious dogma and texts in favor of mysticism and scientific naturalism. They pursued truths that lie beyond the "colorless" realms perceived by reason and the senses and were active social reformers in public education, women's rights, and the abolition of slavery.

U

Urban Realism: A branch of realist writing that attempts to accurately reflect the often harsh facts of modern urban existence.

Utopia: A fictional perfect place, such as "paradise" or "heaven."

V

Verisimilitude: Literally, the appearance of truth. In literary criticism, the term refers to aspects of a work of literature that seem true to the reader.

Victorian: Refers broadly to the reign of Queen Victoria of England (1837-1901) and to anything with qualities typical of that era. For example, the qualities of smug narrow-mindedness, bourgeois materialism, faith in social progress, and priggish morality are often considered Victorian. This stereotype is contradicted by such dramatic intellectual developments as the theories of Charles Darwin, Karl Marx, and Sigmund Freud (which stirred strong debates in England) and the critical attitudes of serious Victorian writers like Charles Dickens and George Eliot. In literature, the Victorian Period was the great age of the English novel, and the latter part of the era saw the rise of movements such as decadence and symbolism.

W

Weltanschauung: A German term referring to a person's worldview or philosophy.

Weltschmerz: A German term meaning "world pain." It describes a sense of anguish about the nature of existence, usually associated with a melancholy, pessimistic attitude.

Z

Zeitgeist: A German term meaning "spirit of the time." It refers to the moral and intellectual trends of a given era.

Cumulative Author/Title Index

Cumulative Nationality/Ethnicity Index

Subject/Theme Index

Sexuality
  The Magnificent Ambersons, 209
  Three Junes, 309
Shame
  A Handful of Dust, 148
  Three Junes, 324
Sibling relations
  East of Eden, 102
  Three Junes, 328
Sin and redemption
  East of Eden, 109
Social class
  Adam Bede, 4, 6
  The Castle, 67–69
  The Great Train Robbery, 135–136
  A Handful of Dust, 150
  Patternmaster, 266
Social criticism
  A Handful of Dust, 148
Social justice. *See* Social reform
Social reform
  Pelle the Conqueror, 293
Sophistication
  Davita's Harp, 81
Sorrow
  Adam Bede, 27
  Three Junes, 324
Spanish history
  Davita's Harp, 81, 84, 90
Sports
  The Natural, 216, 228, 231
Strength
  The Natural, 230
Struggle
  Pelle the Conqueror, 302
Suburban life
  The Magnificent Ambersons, 204–205
Suicide
  The Natural, 221
  Three Junes, 312, 313–314
Supernatural
  The Magnificent Ambersons, 207
  The Natural, 221, 230
Surrealism
  The Castle, 69–70
Symbolism
  Arrowsmith, 43–44
  The Castle, 72, 73
  Pelle the Conqueror, 295
Sympathy
  The Castle, 77

T

Teacher-student relationships
  Nothing But the Truth: A Documentary Novel, 235, 238–239, 242, 243–244
Temptation
  Arrowsmith, 30, 35, 38, 43
Terrorism
  Three Junes, 318
Tone
  A Handful of Dust, 168
Tradition
  A Handful of Dust, 148, 166
Tragedies (Drama)
  A Handful of Dust, 158
Tragedy (Calamities)
  Adam Bede, 1
  Three Junes, 317
Transformation
  The Magnificent Ambersons, 208, 211
Translation
  The Castle, 58–59
  Journey to the Center of the Earth, 170, 182
  Pelle the Conqueror, 282
Triumph
  The Natural, 220
Trust (Psychology)
  The Castle, 77
Truth
  Nothing But the Truth: A Documentary Novel, 235–236, 248–251, 252

U

Unfaithfulness. *See* Adultery
Upper class
  The Great Train Robbery, 135–136
  A Handful of Dust, 160
Urban life
  The Magnificent Ambersons, 205
Utopianism
  Pelle the Conqueror, 294

V

Values (Philosophy)
  A Handful of Dust, 168

Vice
  A Handful of Dust, 168
Victorian period literature, 1832–1901
  Adam Bede, 19
Victorian values
  The Great Train Robbery, 126, 138–139
  Journey to the Center of the Earth, 180
Vision
  Pelle the Conqueror, 294

W

Wars
  Nothing But the Truth: A Documentary Novel, 247
Wealth
  The Magnificent Ambersons, 193, 194, 201–202
Wilderness
  Arrowsmith, 38
Women in literature
  Adam Bede, 16–19
  Patternmaster, 271–274
Women's rights
  Davita's Harp, 87
  Patternmaster, 269–270
Work
  The Magnificent Ambersons, 203
  Nothing But the Truth: A Documentary Novel, 246–247
Workers
  Davita's Harp, 83
  Pelle the Conqueror, 286, 293
World War I, 1914–1918
  The Castle, 70
  East of Eden, 106, 110–111
World War II, 1939–1945
  East of Eden, 112–114

Y

Youth
  The Magnificent Ambersons, 211
  The Natural, 217